The Guide to UK Company Giving 1999

John Smyth and Dave Casson

Additional assistance:
Barbara Weber

Contributions from:
Dr Henry Drucker, Oxford Philanthropic
Jerry Marston, The Littlewoods Organisation PLC
Michael Tuffrey, Corporate Citizenship Company
Hugh Venables, ActionAid

DIRECTORY OF SOCIAL CHANGE

THE GUIDE TO UK COMPANY GIVING
1999 edition
John Smyth and Dave Casson
Copyright © 1999 Directory of Social Change

Published by
Directory of Social Change
24 Stephenson Way
London NW1 2DP
Tel: 0171-209 5151; fax: 0171-209 5049
e-mail: info@d-s-c.demon.co.uk
from whom further copies and a full publications list are available.

Directory of Social Change is a Registered Charity no. 800517

No part of this book may be stored in a retrieval system or reproduced in any form whatsoever without prior permission in writing from the publisher. This book is sold subject to the condition that it shall not, by way of trade or otherwise, be lent, resold, hired out or otherwise circulated without the publisher's prior permission in any form of binding or cover other than that in which it is published, and without a similar condition including this condition being imposed on the subsequent purchaser.

The views expressed in this guide are those of the individual contributors and do not necessarily reflect those of the Directory of Social Change. Whilst every care is taken to provide accurate information, neither the publishers, nor the contributors undertake any liability for any error or omission.

Printed & bound by Page Bros., Norwich

A catalogue record for this book is available from the British Library.

ISBN 1 900360 51 9

Other Directory of Social Change departments:

London
Courses and conferences 0171-209 4949
Charityfair 0171-209 1015
Charity Centre 0171-209 0902
Research 0171-209 4422

Liverpool
Federation House, Hope Street, Liverpool L1 9BW
Courses and conferences 0151-708 0117
Research 0151-708 0136
e-mail: liverpool@d-s-c.demon.co.uk

We are grateful to the following companies for their support in the production of this guide:

Allied Dunbar Assurance plc
Boots Company plc
Express Dairies plc
IMI plc
The Post Office

Contents

Introduction	5
Contributions	
Corporate community involvement in the UK *by Dr Henry Drucker*	9
Giving by another name *by Jerry Marston*	13
Getting the measure of community involvement *by Michael Tuffrey*	15
Keeping good company *by Hugh Venables*	19
Charity stays at home *by John Smyth*	23
Facts & figures	27
Applying to companies	31
Geographical index	35
Company activity index	40
Alphabetical listing of companies	45
Member organisations	
PerCent Club	365
Professional Firms Group	367
BitC	369
Arts & Business (ABSA)	373
Omitted companies	375
Useful contacts	377
Index	379

Introduction

This second edition of *The Guide to UK Company Giving* arrives at a time not only when we are approaching a new millennium, but also when there is a growing belief that society is undergoing a fundamental change. Part of this change revolves around the emergence of a new political economy which, through the so-called 'third way', seeks to fuse the social revolution of the 1960s with the economic revolution of the 1980s. In attempting to find a better balance between individual rights and social justice, and the realities of market economics, there clearly exists a role for companies as full members of New Labour's 'active community'.

To what extent this is acknowledged by companies in the UK is indicated to some degree by the research conducted for this guide. With information on over 500 companies which together give nearly £400 million in community support, including over £240 million in charitable donations, the guide includes details of 52 companies which each gave over £1 million in donations to charities last year. We trust that you will find the results of our research both informative and useful, increasing your chances of success through careful targeting of applications to companies.

What's new?

The bulk of this guide is taken up with details of the individual companies, especially information about their policies regarding support for the community and where their charitable donations went. This year, however, we have also included a number of articles written by individuals with either direct involvement or an informed interest in the relationship between the corporate and voluntary sectors. We hope these prove stimulating.

Company information

The basic criterion for a company to be included in the guide is that it gave £40,000 or more in cash to charities in the latest financial year. A few companies gave less than this, but have been included either because they give substantial support in other ways or because in previous years they have given more and there is no obvious reason for the recent decrease.

Where possible, we have quoted the declared charitable donations figure stated in the company annual report.

A number of companies (125) have also supplied a total community contributions figure. This includes the charitable donations figure, plus other support such as arts sponsorship, the value of gifts in kind and the value of secondments and employee volunteering.

Geographical and activity indices

Most companies state that a link must exist for any appeal to be considered – the most obvious of these being geographical, business activity or employee involvement. To help you prepare a preliminary list of companies to consider (not to immediately write to!), we have included an index to head office location (page 35) and an index to business activity (page 40). Whilst the head office index is necessarily biased towards London – over 200 companies are based there, though many have other locations throughout the UK – it provides a useful starting point.

More comprehensive search facilities are on the CD-ROM version of this guide, which also lists directors, brands, subsidiaries and main locations.

Company listings

Whilst the guide probably accounts for 80–90% of total giving by companies, there are other companies which, by virtue of membership of one or more specific organisations, have declared an interest in supporting the community. We have therefore listed all current members of the PerCent Club, Arts & Business (formerly ABSA – Association for Business Sponsorship of the Arts), and Business in the Community, even though the companies do not necessarily have an entry in this guide.

We have also included details of the Professional Firms Group (PFG) – an increasing and potentially very useful source of support for charities. The PFG is made up of a group of professional practices (including surveyors, architects, accountants and solicitors) each of which has offered to provide their professional services free of charge to voluntary and community groups in their locality.

Unfortunately, as we were unable to obtain an updated list of PFG members, we have had to provide regional office contacts only. A brief explanation of each of these organisations is given at the start of the relevant section.

Introduction

Sector comparisons

As ever, the level of giving by companies in this guide varies greatly (from £40,000 to £30 million). Perhaps because of this, we tend to equate 'big giver' with 'most generous', but this may not actually be the case. Whilst very large companies are applauded for giving £5 million in donations, smaller companies giving £100,000 may actually be giving a far greater proportion of their profits to charity.

To give an example: though British Nuclear Fuels and Cooper Gay (Holdings) appear towards opposite ends of the donations scale (£5.5 million compared to £110,000), when this is expressed as a percentage of pre-tax profits their positions are reversed, with 2.76% and 27.6% respectively. Although the usefulness of comparisons made in this way is a matter for dispute (profits can go down as well as up), the *Facts and figures* section includes a comparative table covering eight industry sectors which makes interesting reading.

Measuring corporate support

One of the enduring dilemmas in compiling this and past guides has been the necessity to accept in good faith the figures given to us by the companies for their charitable donations and community contributions, knowing that these will have been arrived at in various ways. Were we comparing like with like?

Gifts in kind, for example, may be valued at cost or retail price, with the latter providing a more generous impression (something acknowledged by Boots as not quite ethically correct, hence their decision to revalue their in-kind support at cost price). Similarly, some companies include the cost of administering their charitable budget, while others do not. Even comparing direct charitable donations is not always as straightforward as it may seem. Some companies include donations given through a charitable trust, which was perhaps set up with an initial sum from the company, but now generates some of its income from investments. But more on this later.

The work of the London Benchmarking Group (LBG) has been helpful in this respect. The LBG is a group of leading companies who are attempting to standardise the way in which companies report on their community involvement. The Group originally had six members: BP, Diageo, IBM, Marks & Spencer, NatWest Group and Whitbread, who were joined by a further 12 in 1997: American Express, BT, Camelot, Centrica, Levi Strauss, Nationwide Building Society, News International, Railtrack, Rio Tinto, SmithKline Beecham, Unilever and United Utilities. The entry for Diageo in this guide gives an illustration of how the LBG model works out in practice. It was also used by Eastern Group in calculating their total contributions for the year.

A detailed account of the aims and practices of the LBG is given in this guide in the article entitled *Getting the measure of community involvement*. It is also worth noting that the 1998 PerCent Club Annual Report includes, for the first time, company community contribution figures calculated against a measurement template broadly similar to, though less complex than, that drawn up by the LBG.

Hopefully, the result of this push to standardise the way in which total community contributions are calculated by companies will enable us to present a more accurate picture of their support in future editions. What has become clear, even at this early stage, is that we are likely to see the level of non-cash support continue to rise steeply (up from £315 million in 1996/97, to £399 million in 1997/98) as more companies calculate a value for this. Unfortunately, it will be quite a few years before we can tell whether this has been an increase in real terms.

Trends in corporate support

Like fashion, trends in company giving can be difficult to predict accurately. Whilst many companies' level of donations remains fairly constant year on year, others fluctuate significantly, and for no apparent reason. In general terms, however, we can confidently say that each year, with a few exceptions, the top 25 companies by charitable donation and community contribution will remain the same. Similarly, as the general economic upturn has increased business confidence, so charitable donations and community contributions as a percentage of pre-tax profit have risen (up from 0.22% to 0.24%, and 0.33% to 0.40% respectively). There is every reason to believe this will continue next year.

As mentioned in previous years the larger companies in particular are becoming more proactive in their support, and this trend continues. Cynically, this could be viewed as a neat way of avoiding the need to deal with the large number of appeals many companies receive each week. More kindly, it may well be evidence of their oft-stated desire to have a positive, practical and sustained input into their local communities. If so, then the stability such long-term support can provide to charitable and community projects is to be welcomed.

We noted earlier that difficulties can arise where companies are making donations through a charitable trust, i.e. can money given by a charitable trust be included in a company's charitable donations? This depends on the trust's source of income. At one end of the scale are the trusts which are funded by the company each year – perhaps through a deed of covenant – and pay out all or most of this money in grants. The total amount given by the trust in this case is part of the company's giving as it has no separate assets or endowment. This is the case, for example, with the Coutts Charitable Trust.

At the other end of the scale are trusts which were originally set up by the company, but which now receive no income from the company (which makes its donations through some other channel). Though the trust may remain closely linked, we would not include its grants in the donations figure for the company. For this reason we have omitted the entry for J Barbour & Co, as money distributed by the Barbour Trust and previously attributed (mistakenly by us) to the company, comes from the dividend on shares held by the trust in the company.

Introduction

Perhaps because it is a tax-effective means of giving, we are seeing an increasing number of company trusts being established (nearly 70 are covered in this guide). In general, companies giving through such trusts have more clearly defined policies, with a tendency to support employee-led or local appeals. Of the newer ones, we will look forward to seeing detailed accounts for the foundations set up by the Nationwide Building Society and Northern Rock plc, both of which promise to be large benefactors.

With future demutualisations possible, it is interesting to note that both the Yorkshire and Coventry Building Societies have sought to distance themselves from the perceived negative aspects of such a move by requesting that beneficiaries hand over any windfalls, which will then presumably be put to charitable use. One final occurrence in this area, which we sincerely hope does not become a trend, is explained in the article opposite, reproduced with the kind permission of *Private Eye* Magazine.

Warning

Companies continue to receive many unsolicited appeals for support. The purpose of this guide is to enable companies to publish clear policies so that charities can make appropriate applications to relevant companies. For further information see *Applying to companies*. Before approaching any company included in this guide, the entry should be read carefully. As we have stated previously, unless there is a clear link with a company, or your project is clearly within its defined areas for support, you should not be applying.

Acknowledgements

We would like to thank all the companies who have helped to compile this guide. Each was sent a questionnaire compiled jointly with Charities Aid Foundation, for use in their corporate research. Although drafts of all entries were sent to companies and corrections noted and incorporated, the text, and any mistakes within it, remain ours rather than theirs.

We would also like to thank the contributors for their articles and the staff of the Charity Commission in Liverpool for their cooperation.

And finally ...

If you have any comments about the guide, positive or negative, please get in touch with us at the Research Department of the Directory of Social Change (Northern Office), Federation House, Hope Street, Liverpool L1 9BW (0151-708 0136; fax: 0151-708 0139; e-mail: liverpool@d-s-c.demon.co.uk

---

TAPPING THE TAXPAYER

IRRITATED by the number of people who can't pay their water bills, and nervous about cutting them off, the water companies have come up with an ingenious plan to get help from an unusual source: the taxpayer.

The plan works like this. Set up an independent charitable trust whose main aim is to help poor people pay their water bills. Make a donation to the charity. Get the charity to "recoup" a third of the donation from the Inland Revenue. Hey presto! Most of the donation (and the tax rebate) comes back to the water companies in water bills which might not otherwise have been paid.

The pioneer of this scheme among the big water companies is Anglian Water, which in 1996 set up the Anglian Water Trust Fund. Susan Jordan, director of the fund, assures the *Eye* that she and all the trustees and staff of the fund are "entirely independent" of Anglian Water.

The only part of the fund which is not independent is the money, all of which comes from Anglian Water.

Each year Anglian Water shells out £1.5m to the fund, which duly claims from the Inland Revenue the £500,000 which the water company would have paid in tax on the money. Of the £3.5m spent by the trust fund since it was set up, £2m has gone back to Anglian Water in paid water bills. Susan Jordan explains that water bills are a priority because "water is fundamental to life". She stresses the complete independence of her trust and the fact that some of the money goes to help the poor in other ways.

The Anglian Water scheme has excited other water companies. The biggest of them, Severn Trent, has set up a very similar trust fund. So has Yorkshire Water. What company after all could resist the opportunity to turn a bad debt into a charity and get the Inland Revenue to help pay the bills?

Corporate community involvement in the UK

Dr H M Drucker[1]

Some of the largest, best known, wealthiest and most powerful institutions in our world are companies. This is not new. The power of the joint stock company, as it was known, was well appreciated in the last century. However, our century and, most especially the last decades of this century, have seen an important increase in the relative power of privately owned corporations. 'Globalisation' – the process by which a small number of major corporations learn how to overwhelm when they are not circumventing the power of public authorities is an important part of this process. In the UK we have seen the relative power of the private corporation grow too, because of the waning of the power of those groups which might once have countervailed it: trade unions, the co-operative movement, opposition political parties and local government.

At the same time, and not perhaps coincidentally, the gap between the many poor and few rich within each country, and between the poor countries and the rich ones, grows. It is important to look at the challenges that these trends pose for the charitable sector, and what the response should be. Companies are becoming ever more powerful and pervasive. In many countries, including Britain, large chunks of what was once the public sector are passing into private hands. There are few areas of life immune from the attention of the corporate marketeers. In Oxford, for example, companies can sponsor safety messages on fire engines.

It is helpful to look back to what happened in the 1980s. That decade saw the privatisation of swathes of what had until then been seen in this country and across most of the world as natural public monopolies – gas, telephones and electricity. Privatisation led to the creation of very large, well-capitalised companies making huge, and occasionally publicly vilified, profits.

The newly privatised companies saw that one route to respectability was for them to become major philanthropic players and this, in turn, led to some large-scale corporate philanthropic programmes. A recent example is Camelot, which put £5 million into their new Foundation in 1996; this represented 6.45% of their pre-tax profit. The cynical might see the spur of the threat of losing their licence in this action. I see not the mote in the eye.

There is a real danger that the generosity seen from many recently privatised firms may be short-lived. Globalisation is not necessarily a very helpful trend. As firms are swallowed up by French and American corporations the importance to them of being seen to be good corporate citizens in the UK may well diminish. This is not a problem for tomorrow. Many FTSE 100 companies already do much of their business abroad. Zeneca, Amvesco, Rio Tinto, Siebe, SmithKline Beecham, Charter, GlaxoWellcome, Vendome, BBA, BA, Diageo, Shell, Wassall and Cookson all generate 90% or more of their revenue abroad.

Companies that operate globally can subscribe to the importance of community involvement. Indeed, BP states that this is part of its 'leading edge business strategy', but we cannot assume that they will. Neither can we assume that they will contribute equitably to all the communities in which they operate.

When the business environment is turbulent, charitable giving may suffer. British Gas was a large corporate philanthropist. However, during dismemberment it suspended its charitable giving. It recently established the BG Foundation which 'will be seeking to make a real and positive difference to community activities'. We shall see. The 'fat cat companies' are being taken over – often by overseas enterprises. It remains to be seen how generous or community minded their new owners will be.

It would be cheering to think that American companies coming to Britain would always give as generously as they do at home. Unfortunately, this should not be assumed. In the course of our work we have come across a US company more than 100 years old which, in its home territory, is seen as a staid corporate citizen with many worthy programmes. When this company came to the UK in the early 1990s, its reputation, in short order, became that of a cowboy organisation with few concerns for the environment or the citizenry and minimal interest in its philanthropic programme except as an adjunct of its marketing division.

The UK corporate world is changing in another way. We have recently seen a wave of demutualisation among building societies and life insurance companies. To be sure, many of them were not noticeably philanthropic when they were owned by their policy holders. Even so they always could give, and most gave something. Their demutualisation is, of course, a particular threat to those counties and cities which benefited from housing a headquarters which may now move to London, if not abroad. Bristol & West is now part of Irish Bank. C&G is a subsidiary of Lloyds. There has also been a threat to the mutual status of the Co-operative Bank.

The way demutualisation has been carried out is a tragedy for the poor. Most of the societies which are being 'given' to their present policy holders were set up to assist the poor in their localities. It would have been more respectful to the founders of their societies if other societies had followed the example of Northern Rock and dedicated a proportion of the wealth which is now going to policy holders to the endowment of a new Trust.

What is to be done?

A society that is totally dominated by organisations which – very properly – pursue a single end, their own profit, is an impoverished society. A society in which this increase in corporate power is accompanied by a reduction in the ability of the state to meet the needs of the poor – partly created by a reduction in corporation tax – needs assistance badly.

The corporate sector needs to be challenged about its achievements. The Royal Society for the encouragement of Arts, Manufactures and Commerce (RSA) sponsored an inquiry into the 'Responsible Company', which leading UK companies have endorsed. Their Report, published in 1995, urged companies to take their responsibilities to all their 'stakeholders' (not just share holders) seriously. This would mean attending to the needs of their employees, their customers and the communities in which they operate. The rhetoric is smooth. Where is the action?

The truth is that much of the established corporate sector in the UK has become complacent about its philanthropic role. In 1985 the Prince of Wales set up the organisation Business in the Community (BitC). Its mission is 'to inspire business to increase the quality and extent of their contribution to social and economic regeneration by making corporate social responsibility an essential part of business excellence'. BitC embraces a myriad of worthwhile activities – for example there is a programme to encourage firms of lawyers and accountants to give time to voluntary projects, and another to challenge companies to encourage their employees to support local community projects.

One of the earliest and most high profile projects for BitC is the PerCent Club. This now comprises a group of some 300 leading national and international companies operating in the UK. To become a member, a company should contribute at least 0.5% of pre-tax (UK) profits or one PerCent of dividends to the community. Improvements are afoot, as the PerCent Club has announced that its minimum level for membership will increase to the full 1% as of 1 January 2001. This is to be commended, but there are still many problems.

1. Neither the PerCent Club nor anyone else monitors what is counted by the corporate members as part of their contribution. 'Social reporting', whereby an external audit is conducted into the extent to which a company fulfils its declared philanthropic commitments, has only very recently been adopted, and by very few companies. However, some companies still count some rather extraordinary things. The 1993 Annual Report of the PerCent Club contains a picture of a delightful cottage known as the Pink House. This is the Dow Chemical Responsible Care Centre in Kings Lynn, Norfolk. The Centre 'contains information about Dow, its people and products'. It also contains a library of environmental materials. In other words, its first function is corporate Public Relations – yet it is counted as a 'community contribution'.

2. The total given by the major corporations in no way reflects their power or wealth as a group. Barings Asset Management calculated that the total given by all quoted British companies in 1995 was £262 million[2]. This figure was eclipsed by the expenditure of one large trust – the Church Commissioners. Or, as the *Guardian* report on the Barings document of 25 April 1997 notes:

The relatively obscure Masonic Trust for Girls and Boys spent £10.2 million in 1995, equivalent to 10 times the giving of Southern Electric in the year to March 1996. The Bedford Charity, hardly a household name, spends £24 million a year, easily outstripping the £18.7 million donated by the energy giant BP.

3. The PerCent Club makes no attempt to encourage companies to give in cash. Gifts in kind can be counted. Thus it is possible for BT to 'give' unsold space in their *Yellow Pages* free to charities and count this as a community contribution. It is not altogether surprising then that in 1996 £12.1 million of the £14.8 million given by BT comprised donations in kind. The total roughly scraped the minimum 0.5% commitment level; however, BT insists that it is trying to build a partnership with its charitable recipients. In the words of its Internet site: 'The programme is not about one-way handouts but about active participation and collaboration'. When I studied political theory a 'partnership' was one of a number of possible relationships between equals. However, things are potentially looking up as BT recently submitted itself to a 'social report'. The results are yet to be known.

4. Perhaps all this is not surprising. The most recent annual report I had for the PerCent Club was for 1994. Enquiry revealed that there was no annual report for 1995. This is because these reports are really published in order to be given to members at the annual PerCent Dinner. There was no dinner in 1996, hence no annual report for 1995. The 1997 report was not distributed because too few companies provided a total community contributions figure. You can draw your own conclusions from that.

There are, of course, some generous and imaginative corporate donors. Allied Dunbar and Shell UK are among my favourites. So too, for quite different reasons is the Co-operative Bank.

What should we be pressing companies in general to do in the face of these criticisms?

1. Despite the membership increase announcement, BitC needs to be challenged to set higher targets.

An immediately useful first step would be for the PerCent Club to form a higher level club for companies that make more substantial contributions. This could act as a spur to some laggards. BitC also needs to be pressed to be somewhat more rigorous in what is counted.

2. We need to stress the value of contributions in cash – not just in kind. It is cash which charities need and can often use most effectively. The BT example cited above shows that things can get out of hand.

There is another Prince of Wales initiative that might contribute to a worsening situation. In November 1996 the Prince launched 'Gifts in Kind UK'. This organisation is a branch of an American enterprise.

Companies give Gifts in Kind merchandise they cannot sell. Gifts in Kind passes these on to its member charities.

The charities pay a fee to gain membership. In principle the fee is to cover the expenses associated with that charity.

There have been serious complaints about the US branch that the charity is in the hands of its corporate donors and not working in the interests of its charity members. Many charities have been complaining that the 'goods' they get from Gifts in Kind are not so good. In America Gifts in Kind seems to be doing well out of the $3 million annual membership fees from its charity members. In the UK this has not happened (yet)[3]. Instead, Gifts in Kind UK has to appeal to foundations and trusts (in competition with 'real' charities) for operating funds. Who is this really helping?

3. We need to stress the need for greater rigour in defining companies' philanthropic contribution and better monitoring of what they give. Here, at least, some progress can be reported. In 1994, prior to the introduction of 'social reporting', the Corporate Community Involvement Officers of six large companies – National Westminster Bank, IBM, Whitbread, Grand Metropolitan, BP and Marks & Spencer – joined forces. Calling themselves 'The London Benchmarking Group', their purpose was 'to meet the need for accurate and comparable information about how companies define, fund and manage their community involvement activities'. In March 1997 they published their report *Companies in Communities, Getting the Measure.* Part of this categorises 'the activities of a company in society'.

At the base of a triangle are the companies' core business tasks.

On the next level are commercial initiatives which directly promote their corporate and brand identities or business policies in partnership with charities. An example would be Flora margarine's sponsorship of the London Marathon. Such 'cause-related marketing' is avidly encouraged by BitC.

On the next level is community investment. This is a policy of sustained involvement in resolving a few social issues carefully chosen by a company to protect its long-term corporate interests and enhance its reputation. An example would be Allied Dunbar's donation of £1.1 million over 5 years to help with the development of support to carers in Yorkshire.

At the apex is charity – gifts of cash and other forms of assistance in response to appeals or at the companies' initiative.

The Group has created a template which 'summarises the complete potential range of a company's contributions to the community'. These contributions encompass assistance in cash, in time and in kind. It is becoming apparent that these benchmarks will be applied throughout the corporate world as a basis for accounting for community contributions. This will, at least, provide a basis for comparison.

The work by the London Benchmarking Group is undoubtedly a step forward. Nevertheless I remain uncomfortable about its thrust. The Group do, it is true, express their interest in the results of companies' philanthropic investment. Nonetheless, they remain largely concerned that companies report and claim credit for all that they do, not just for the charitable giving.

Thus they are more concerned with changing public perceptions than with changing reality.

Ways forward

Therefore we also need to recognise that an intelligent corporate giving policy is not just a matter of giving – though that is fundamental. The Centre for Corporate Community Relations at Boston College (Massachusetts) has argued that companies should adhere to Four Standards of Excellence in their Corporate Community Programmes.

Standard 1 – The company should have a social vision statement that explains the company's relationship to the community. This should be incorporated in its business mission. Senior management should demonstrate their personal commitment to it.

Standard 2 – Key staff in the company should have designated responsibility for managing community relations.

Standard 3 – Key internal stakeholders should be involved in the development and implementation of these programmes.

Standard 4 – The Community Programmes should reflect company and community concerns.

There is sense in each of these standards. I am particularly struck by the statement that corporate community involvement should be led by the company leadership. The British company which seems to me to most clearly embody this is Co-operative Bank. I salute the Bank for its campaign against land-mines, and for the way this policy is carried through the entire company's work.

Companies are much more enthusiastic about commercial initiatives and community investment than they are about straight charitable giving. When I was Director of *Campaign for Oxford* we were always seeking to obtain gifts from companies' budgets for research, or staff recruitment and development, or marketing and promotion. These budgets are far larger than companies' charitable budgets. Interestingly, the London Benchmarking Group categorises gifts to universities under the heading of commercial initiatives because they are designed to promote and protect commercial interests. So even this category is widely defined.

The definition of community investment as sustained involvement in resolving a few social issues is particularly important. Companies should be able to offer consistent, reliable long-term partnerships. Companies may have educational budgets from which literacy and numeracy programmes could be supported; or promotional budgets which trusts could help to channel towards worthwhile local projects. Some local foundations have succeeded in convincing a small number of companies that they should let the foundations administer the company's charitable and community involvement budgets. This is a process which should be encouraged.

As one of the local foundations' greatest strengths is their strong localised roots, these organisations should be seeking to become one of the prime vehicles through which large companies channel their contributions to local areas. The 'globalisation' of the corporate world works, initially, in the other direction. However, it also creates a need for effective intermediaries for local charities to deal

Corporate community involvement in the UK

with companies that cannot possibly know what is important in each of the localities in which they operate.

The rhetoric about companies as corporate citizens has an important implication – companies have a responsibility to give back to those areas from which they take. This certainly holds for overseas companies operating in the UK, and there are companies which have taken that message to heart. Some of the most generous donors to *Campaign for Oxford* were inward investors. I think of Citibank, Nissan and Bristol Myers Squibb.

I have emphasised the changes and the challenges created by the globalisation of the corporate world. Perhaps we are too passive in the face of this trend. When major companies move plants from Britain to countries whose workers will accept a much lower wage, they leave behind them a pool of poverty and unemployment which may last for decades. Companies such as these, and the former mutual societies which are 'demutualising' should be pressed to make a significant contribution in their area to respect the intentions of the early generations who made the mutual societies great.

I have emphasised the particular challenges that arise from the 'globalisation' of the corporate world. There is, perversely, an opposite trend that can also open opportunities. Some UK companies say that they will only give in the vicinity of their headquarters. Boots, the chemists, is one example. Boots told us that it has decided to make substantial donations only within 30 miles of its Nottingham headquarters. It is noticeable that Boots does not, however, confine its profit-making activities to the same 30 mile limit. Many companies which impose these limits do so because they fear the deluge of appeals they would need to consider if they did not. They wish to invest in activities in which they can have some assurance of quality and possibly involvement.

I have focused on what we can do to encourage corporate community responsibility. In 1998, MORI surveyed attitudes to Corporate Community Involvement[4]. They found that nearly 60% of top executives thought industry and commerce paid sufficient attention to their social responsibilities. Yet only 9% of the general public thought so and only 4% of Labour MPs concurred. This is something companies must attend to.

Perspective

This must, however, be kept in perspective. The corporate sector, for all its wealth and power, is, as yet, a small player in the charitable world. At Oxford Philanthropic we produced our own estimates of the amount given in the UK. We calculated that in 1995 the figure was £10.562 billion. That was roughly 1.49% of GDP. Companies gave approximately £470 million or 4% of this, far less than their power, wealth, prestige and visibility suggest is appropriate.

Behind all this are some important lessons: our donors' world changes. We need to change with it. Companies must be pressed to give more generously – and to claim less credit for the small sums they do give – but we need to keep our eye on the larger ball.

I will conclude by quoting from *Giving USA 1996*. Under the heading 'Giving in the United States by Japanese Business', *Giving USA* says:

'The Japan External Trade Organisation (JETRO) surveyed 2,716 Japanese-affiliated companies about their philanthropic activities in the United States. 47%, or 1,269 responded and 80% of the respondents reported they engaged in corporate philanthropy. 91% of companies that supported non-profits did so by making cash contributions.

'Company representatives emphasised that they view philanthropy as a responsibility that should not fluctuate with profits. Moreover, few companies reported monitoring the benefit to the company that accrued from its charitable activities. Companies believed that the impact of corporate philanthropy should be felt by the beneficiaries, not the contributor. This is an admirable attitude that should be adopted in Britain. As one respondent stated, "We live on this earth together and have to help each other. We can do more as a company than we can do individually."'

---

1 This article is a modified and updated version of a talk given by Dr Drucker to the ACTAF Good Foundations Conference, 14–16 May 1997.

2 We think this is a considerable underestimate.

3 *Chronicle of Philanthropy* 20 March 1997, p1.

4 Results published in *'A Financial Times Guide: Business in the Community'*, December 1998. Statistics quoted from p26.

Dr Henry Drucker is Managing Director of Oxford Philanthropic Ltd.

Giving by another name

Jerry Marston

It's become fashionable to categorise company support to the community under three broad headings: gifts of cash, gifts of time and gifts in kind. Recent surveys have indicated that gifts in kind could account for up to 30% of the support companies actually provide, and that percentage is increasing. It's probably true that many charities do not appreciate the actual value of company support given in this way, or the potential it has to generate further support.

The most obvious categories are products, and unwanted or surplus equipment. While much of this giving is clearly going on all the time, it has yet to reach anything like its full potential. One reason for this is that many companies baulk at the prospects of spending time and energy identifying appropriate outlets or beneficiaries. The odd donation to a local school or hospital is quite straightforward, but trying to do it on any larger a scale can be problematic. First, the company has to find the charities which need its goods. Then it has to ensure that they are bona fide organisations which will make proper use of them and not allow them to end up on market stalls or in car boot sales. The problems can easily outweigh the perceived benefits. Yet the benefits can be considerable if the initiative is properly managed, in terms of goodwill generated for the company and its brands, and if used as an adjunct to the cash and people support they may also be giving.

Donations of this kind have been made significantly easier for both giver and receiver with the arrival of Gifts In Kind UK, and I make no apology for giving them a big plug. Gifts In Kind UK was set up to make it easier for companies to donate goods and obtain the benefits without incurring the management costs. Set up at the end of 1996 on the American model, Gifts In Kind America, which has been channelling surplus to voluntary organisations in the United States for the past 15 years, Gifts In Kind UK went operational in early 1997.

Two years later, Gifts In Kind UK has a 10,000 sq. ft. warehouse in Accrington full of items, every one of which is headed for a good cause somewhere in the UK. 230 companies have donated their goods, ranging from office equipment and stationery, household furniture, carpets and flooring, household goods of all kinds, cleaning products, toiletries, books, software and educational games, toys, sports goods and clothing.

Their network of charities – over 900 as at the end of 1998 – extends through England, Scotland, Wales and Northern Ireland, and while all the voluntary organisations are based in the UK many of them operate in other parts of the world, engaged in emergency relief and community development in poor countries. Charities in the network pay an annual registration fee based on income, and receive a list of the goods that are currently available. They request items from the list, paying an administration fee which includes delivery, and a £1 nominal sales price is added which ensures that companies do not have to pay VAT on the value of goods they donate.

The system is very simple. All a company has to do is fax a donation form to Gifts In Kind UK saying what they have available, and a collection is then arranged. When everything is distributed the company receives a report from Gifts In Kind UK listing all the charities who have benefited and what work they do in the community. So the company has a clear picture of the impact of its generosity.

The tax situation on gifts in kind is not as favourable in this country as it is in the US, where companies get a 'double dip' in tax terms, which acts as a major incentive to giving. But the tax position here can at least be neutralised. If goods have a notional value and would therefore on the face of it be liable to tax, they can be given through a charitable trust. And, as mentioned before, because of the way Gifts In Kind UK structures its relationship with charities, there is no liability to VAT.

Chief Executive Robin Boles estimates that since they began, 18,000 cubic metres of potential landfill have been saved – goods often end up being dumped because the company can find no outlet for them and they are costing money by taking up valuable storage space. While their figures are very impressive, their organisation very sound (Littlewoods are a satisfied customer!) and worth considering registering with, it would nevertheless be fair to say that Gifts in Kind UK's share of the market will always be a minority one, for two reasons.

Firstly, it is the smaller companies, who massively outnumber the major plcs and are the hunting ground for the majority of charities, who are more susceptible to supporting community in this way rather than through making a cash donation, or lending precious staff and they will, with a few exceptions, continue to be most effectively accessed by direct approach at a local level.

Giving by another name

Secondly, donations of surplus product or equipment are by no means the only way that companies can give in-kind support. The list below is compiled from my experience of being a poacher and gamekeeper in my past and current employment, and so represents only a sample of the possibilities for in-kind support:

- donating coach/airline/train/ferry tickets
- advertising space on the company website/notice board/in-house magazine
- use of surplus warehousing space/storage/sports facilities
- donating hotel accommodation
- use of telephones for helpline/appeal responses
- access to premises to sell your wares, or give lunchtime briefings on your work and services
- free or low-cost use of spare office space
- spare places on in-house training courses
- use of training/meeting rooms, video conferencing, editing facilities
- use of spare transport capacity
- the design and printing of your leaflet/poster/annual report
- donation of surplus food/beverages
- getting a relevant question or two into the annual employee survey
- information insert into a relevant product, e.g. breast cancer screening advice leaflet with undergarments
- access to information on customer demography/attitudes/preferences
- use of vacant sites for recreation projects/safe off-the-road activities/murals
- free loan of plant, equipment, scaffolding, marquees, portaloos, etc.
- donation of topsoil, rubble, tarmac, etc.
- free advertising space on temporarily unused sites
- raffle prizes – everything from hot air balloon rides, to surplus promotional items like umbrellas, to tickets at corporate hospitality events
- including your charity leaflet/appeal in a regular business or customer mailshot
- free servicing of your vehicle(s)
- getting your message on the franking machine.

There will be many more, and together they offer a host of opportunities for both achieving some of your mainstream activities, and establishing the beginnings of a working relationship with a company, that would probably be much harder to achieve through a straight request for cash or employee involvement. They can often be a conduit to these other forms of support, because they provide a low-cost and safe option for the company, who can, in many instances, use the experience to draw conclusions about your organisation and the potential for further support.

A few prompts by way of conclusion:

- do your research – just as you would for any other request for support
- be flexible – take the rough with smooth, it's likely to be worth it in the end
- think laterally – gifts in kind can often effectively replace or reduce your cash requirement
- think long term – see the added value as relationship building and awareness raising
- be bold – you will often have the more inventive and radical idea, don't be afraid to test it out!
- treat gifts in kind like any other requests – say what you want, why it is important to you, what it will help you achieve, and how you will acknowledge it
- say thank you and keep the company informed.

… and remember, the company most likely to support you, is also the most likely to give you a gift in kind.

Gifts In Kind UK
PO Box 140
4 St Dunstan's Hill
London EC3R 5HB
Tel: 0171-204 5003; Fax: 0171-204 5551

Jerry Marston is Head of Public Affairs at Littlewoods plc. He was previously Managing Director of Comic Relief, and spent eight years as Community Affairs Manager at Allied Dunbar Assurance plc.

Getting the measure of community involvement

Michael Tuffrey

Faced with considerable confusion over what companies really contribute to the community, the London Benchmarking Group has devised a practical business tool that helps companies manage, measure and report their support for charities and involvement in wider social issues. This article describes how it works, in the context of historic and current trends in corporate citizenship.

Companies are an integral part of their local communities and of wider society. Their foremost contribution is in providing goods and services which customers want to buy, and thereby creating jobs and paying taxes. Traditionally they have also made an additional voluntary contribution; whether it was the model villages of the early industrialists or the public endowments of Victorian philanthropists, there has always been a mixture of motivations between altruism and self-interest.

Evolution of corporate community involvement

Today, corporate community involvement has become increasingly complex, with three clear phases of development identified by commentators such as David Grayson of Business in the Community. Now, in our view, a fourth phase is on the horizon.

Phase 1

Reactive corporate philanthropy, in which the company makes a wide range of charitable donations, typically small in amount and often at the personal instigation of senior directors. Business benefit is largely incidental.

Phase 2

Strategic contributions, in which donations are managed effectively and focused on a limited number of chosen topics of relevance to the business. The number tends to be fewer but the amounts larger. The topics are chosen with a view to longer-term business benefit, usually by enhancing external corporate reputation and sustaining the local 'licence to operate'.

Phase 3

Mainstream involvement, in which community involvement is linked to more immediate operational business concerns. In addition to external reputation, and this is where it differs from phase 2, attention is focused internally, to enhance staff morale and competence, to attract customer loyalty and to build stable relationships with suppliers. Involvement is also broadened from money to encompass in-kind resources, such as staff time and expertise, donated products and access to company facilities.

Phase 4

Corporate accountability, in which the company has a full, open and long-term engagement with all those having an interest in the business, both geographic communities and communities of interest – providers of capital, current and potential staff, customers, suppliers, local and central government and agencies, and current and future generations especially on environmental matters. Clear about their values and mission, companies measure and report not just policies but also practices, with independent verification ('social auditing') and dialogue in setting objectives.

Very few companies indeed have yet reached the fourth phase of development, but whatever the development phase, all those wishing to be active in the community suffer from similar problems of lack of common definitions, inconsistent approaches, poor data on the cost of contributions and all too rare evaluation of what is being achieved.

London Benchmarking Group

In response to these needs, six leading UK-based companies came together in 1995 to examine how they manage and measure their community involvement programmes, seeking to learn from each other and explore common definitions and performance measures. After two years' work, the group of companies (BP, Diageo, IBM, Marks & Spencer, NatWest Group and Whitbread) agreed to publish their findings in a report, *Companies in Communities: getting the measure*[1] authored by David Logan.

Then in 1997, the original six were joined by another 12 (American Express, BT, Camelot, Centrica, Levi Strauss, Nationwide Building Society, News International, Railtrack, Rio Tinto, SmithKline Beecham, Unilever and United Utilities). Representing a broad spread of industry sectors, they are funding a new initiative to refine further the measurement techniques and to promote the approach widely in the UK and abroad, supported by The Corporate Citizenship Company and the Charities Aid Foundation.

The key achievement of the benchmarking group has been to establish a common definition for community involvement, for the valuation of inputs and the measuring of outputs. The challenge now is to extend the number of companies adopting this approach to recording, measuring and reporting the community programmes.

For the not-for-profit sector, the London Benchmarking Group model yields more data on what companies are doing, how they can make a contribution and, crucially,

Getting the measure of community involvement

why the companies are investing resources. These developments ought to form the basis for better communication and collaboration across the sectors – a key goal of the follow-on project which is why CAF has joined with funding.

Current reporting practice

Currently, companies registered in the United Kingdom must by law disclose in their annual reports the totals of UK charitable and political contributions unless together they amount to not more than £200 (Section 234 of Companies Act 1985). Most major companies add at least a brief description of their community involvement activities but only a small minority calculate a larger figure for their total community contribution. This includes financial contributions to community causes which are charitable but not constituted charities, along with in-kind contributions of paid staff time and gifts of facilities, products or equipment.

Such data as companies do make available, by law or voluntarily, are presented to fundraisers and others interested through the annual Directory of Social Change *The Guide to UK Company Giving* and, in lesser detail, in CAF's *Dimensions of the Voluntary Sector*. Neither is yet able to offer a comprehensive picture of companies' community involvement, so estimates of total community giving by UK companies are certainly understatements. The current problems in measuring and reporting corporate community involvement can be summarised as follows:

- too few companies produce a figure valuing their total community contribution
- those that do, do not use a consistent methodology
- where a figure for contribution is available, too often it is only a total – we do not know how much is devoted to improving educational standards or protecting the environment or supporting small enterprises; how much is cash and how much in kind, especially staff time and skills
- published figures only measure the input cost, not the outputs achieved, still less the ultimate impact on the company and the community beneficiaries
- often data only cover the United Kingdom, not the global spread of operations
- figures are not verified independently
- few standards are available to judge good practice and best examples
- impact on society is narrowly defined as community contribution (what about taxes paid for public services, employment of staff, environmental factors, working with local suppliers to foster the local economy rather than simply buying from today's cheapest source, providing 'uneconomic' services as required under regulation such as BT's remote rural pay phones?)
- people in the community, often through pressure groups, increasingly want a real say in what the company does – to enter into dialogue and be engaged – not simply be given a limited picture of what is going on.

This list presents a formidable and challenging agenda for action by companies, which the benchmarking initiative is helping to address. The not-for-profit sector has a part to play too, mainly in encouraging companies to improve their reporting, in suggesting adoption of the London Benchmarking Group approach, and in helping to evaluate the social impacts of community projects as a guide to the most efficient use of scarce resources.

Basic model

The starting point of the London Benchmarking Group model is the range of motivations for community involvement, covering:

- a sense of moral and social responsibility, also responding to expectations from society for community involvement
- a belief that companies have a long-term interest in fostering a healthy community, sometimes known as enlightened self-interest
- the knowledge that community interventions involving employees, customers and suppliers can have direct benefits, through increased profitability, stronger company image, reduced costs, better employee morale and improved customer loyalty.

These three concurrent and complimentary motivations for CCI (Corporate Community Involvement) provide the basis for a new approach to reporting the totality of a company's community involvement, based on three headings:

- charitable gifts, corresponding to moral and social responsibility
- community investment, corresponding to long term corporate benefits
- commercial initiatives, corresponding to bottom line commercial benefits.

Under these headings, the London Benchmarking Group has created a new template to report in detail individual community activities, including those beyond traditional charitable giving, and to draw together the totality in a common form. It provides clear definitions for each type of activity, specifying how the costs incurred (inputs) are to be valued. It also acknowledges that the costs of managing community relations must be included.

Costing the community contribution

In more detail, under charitable gifts come contributions which respond to local or national appeals to support good causes. This will include occasional donations to charities and social sponsorships not part of a marketing strategy. Also included are gifts by the company to match staff fundraising or encourage volunteering.

Under community investment come the costs of sustained involvement in issues important to the company. An example is a grant by a retailer, concerned about vandalism and shoplifting, to a community group trying to reduce school truancy and prevent crime.

The third category is commercial initiatives as partnerships to promote and protect commercial interests, and includes sponsorships, cause-related marketing and community assignments for staff training.

In addition, the programme management costs should be included, covering the salaries, benefits and overheads of staff fully or partly engaged in managing community relations.

Finally, there is a range of community interventions and activities associated with basic business activity and policy – examples include choices over the location of new manufacturing plants, the approach taken to closures, decisions over diversity in hiring of staff, training and other employment policies, and so forth. These are reported separately as business basics and not evaluated as part of the LBG model.

Outputs – and impacts

This detailed model allows a more comprehensive valuation of the 'input' cost but it also goes further, to cover what the programme actually achieves. Outputs, or at least examples of them, are plotted on a matrix against input costs. Such outputs are defined in terms of:

- leverage of cash and resources from other sources drawn in by the programme
- the community benefit, such as the number of people in society who benefit
- the business benefit which accrues.

Examples of leverage are the cash generated from a marketing campaign on behalf of a charity and government funds attracted to a local community by the company contribution. An indicator of community benefit is the number of young people gaining jobs from a company-supported training scheme. Business benefits would include enhanced reputation from a donation and increased sales during a cause-related marketing promotion.

One area of frequent confusion is the difference between the cost to the company of, for example, in-kind donations of goods and the 'opportunity cost' (notional sales income foregone) if the charity had had to purchase the goods on the open market. Some companies use the latter (larger) figure as their contribution, but in the view of the London Benchmarking Group this is incorrect: only the actual cost of manufacturing the goods counts as the input figure; an amount for the worth to the charity, based on a sales price, can be used as an output measure of benefit to the community. Indeed, under the charity SORP rules, this is the figure normally used in the beneficiary's accounts.

Then comparing input costs and outputs achieved between companies allows a judgement to be made about the effectiveness of community involvement programmes. In this way, the LBG model becomes a dynamic management tool. Whitbread, for example, spends a relatively small amount at corporate centre (less than £50,000 out of a total programme of around £3 million) on supporting pub fundraising which generates around £2 million locally. Such fundraising is not the company's contribution, of course, and is treated as leverage in the model, revealing how a small investment can still generate considerable community benefit.

Finally, including programme management costs, as the LBG model does, allows a judgement about efficiency. Charities are often asked about their spending overheads as a proportion of direct programme expenditure, and companies need to be similarly vigilant.

Beyond outputs are impacts; inevitably these are harder to evaluate because of the difficulty in isolating the causes and the longer timescales. Typically inputs are measured over one year, outputs over one to two years and impacts up to ten.

Reporting

One of the primary benefits of better recording of information is internal to the company, from improved management control. But given the growing interest in companies' impact in society, firms are starting to use the framework to improve external reporting. The LBG format encourages consistency between companies which facilitates benchmarking.

Up until now, the main comparison was the cost of total community contribution against pre-tax profits, with 0.5% being the norm for the minimum acceptable. This 'standard' comes from the PerCent Club, an informal grouping of UK companies launched in 1986. This brings moral suasion to bear based on two measures – the contribution as a percentage of pre-tax profit, where the minimum is defined as 0.5% rising to 1.0% by the year 2000, and the percentage of dividends, where the minimum is currently 1%.

However, this measure suffers from several weaknesses:

- because of profit fluctuations, only an average over the business cycle is truly meaningful, not a one-year figure
- the scale of voluntary effort by staff and by customers, facilitated by the company, is not captured in a single figure for the company's own contribution
- a figure for the whole company can hide wide national variations within international groups.

The broader approach adopted by the LBG methodology overcomes these problems. It goes beyond narrowly-defined charity or philanthropy to include the good citizenship aspects of the whole business. It also allows companies to be known for what they accomplish in the community, not just what they give.

Applying the model

When companies first apply the model, they often have to make judgements about when an activity counts towards the community contribution and when it is really part of business basics. The utilities, in particular, need to distinguish between 'community' expenditure required by the industry regulators and genuine voluntary contributions, often in the area of special needs customers. United Utilities, for example, has a broad programme of support for 'extra needs' customers, provided by the business, but goes beyond regulatory requirements with further activity through the community programme.

In general, companies which have already applied the LBG model have found that the reported totals of the cost of their contributions go up, even though the volume of activity has not increased. There are four main reasons for this:

- management costs are included, often for the first time
- improved monitoring and measuring provides more information on current activities
- the community element of commercial initiatives, such as cause-related marketing, is brought into the total, previously overlooked
- the full scope of the programme internationally is covered, beyond the requirement to report UK donations.

Thus SmithKline Beecham, for example, calculated a worldwide total of £21.6 million in 1997 when the LBG methodology was applied, compared to £7.4 million

Getting the measure of community involvement

previously; likewise, BT's more complete assessment rose from £15.6 million to £27.6 million in the same year – the discipline of applying the model revealed activity previously unknown at corporate centre. In contrast, when NatWest applied the approach, the total did not vary significantly, as good systems were already in place. This emphasises the key point that an increased figure reflects better monitoring and measuring, not necessarily more activity.

So why ultimately does it matter? A common basis for monitoring, measuring and reporting helps community affairs managers to make the case for expanding and diversifying their activities. Better data allows better management, benefiting business and wider society. The not-for-profit sector, too, will profit, through a greater understanding of what companies can do, how and why. Well-managed and evaluated community programmes are not just more effective, they are sustainable even when resources in the business are under pressure. It is in everyone's interest to get the measure of the community involvement.

---

1 For copies of the full LBG report, price £50, contact the Corporate Responsibility Group on 0171-222 2121.

Companies interested in using this model can contact The Corporate Citizenship Company on 0171-945 6130 for help and advice.

Mike Tuffrey is editor of Community Affairs Briefing, the bi-monthly journal of corporate citizenship, and is a founding director of the consultancy, The Corporate Citizenship Company, which specialises in research and evaluation about community involvement for corporate clients.

Keeping good company
– a company-centred approach to partnership

Hugh Venables

There is a new agenda for engagement between the private sector and not-for-profit organisations in the development sector. The power of international business to affect the lives of poor people in developing countries is growing with the opening up of the global economy. Private investment flows have been expanding through the 1990s, while official aid flows have declined. Official aid flows now account for less than a quarter of total financial resource flows. It is all part of a general worldwide retreat from the idea of 'government as provider' to government as 'enabler and rule-setter'.

So most development non-governmental organisations (NGOs) now accept that their mission to banish or reduce poverty has to take account of the private sector. How they are doing this varies, and the approach depends partly on what NGOs think is the impact of business on poverty.

Few people would disagree that business *can* have negative effects on society. Many NGOs would say that the globalisation of capitalism may generate unprecedented wealth for some, but it also impoverishes others. Are these malign effects unintentional and indirect, as some believe? Or does multinational business success actually depend on making the poor poorer in order to make the wealthy wealthier, as others suggest? The latter perception has been sharpened by the analysis of writers like David Korten, whose devastating critique of global capitalism in *When Multinationals Rule the World* has inspired those exploring human-centred alternatives to free market economics.

NGOs respond in two ways to these perceptions of the impact of business on the poor. They *campaign* against the most malign effects, for example over shortcomings in human rights, labour standards or the environment. And they *engage* with companies, seeking to improve their practices, for example through helping them develop and implement codes of conduct.

The engagement approach can be taken further. Clare Short, Secretary of State for International Development, speaking at Worldaware's annual awards ceremony in 1998, suggested that the development community will fail if it does not enlist the resources, skills and reach of business. She said it is unrealistic to write off the business sector as irrelevant or antipathetic to development.

For those who think Ms Short has a point the challenge is to find ways of engaging with business which:

- make business decision makers more sensitive to the needs of poor people
- access private resources which can promote development
- can lead to strategic partnerships for development.

It was in this spirit that ActionAid's Marketing Department decided two years ago to redesign its strategy for cultivating business interest in supporting development. We began by speaking to business to find out their attitudes to development and how they viewed development agencies like ActionAid.

A series of interviews with leading UK companies established that development NGOs have skills and experience that can be relevant to business needs. NGOs do not have to be the supplicants in the relationship. Take HIV/AIDS in Africa. The community-based strategies for responding to the pandemic, pioneered by ActionAid and others, could be a lifeline to companies struggling to cope. Or ActionAid's adult literacy and numeracy programme, REFLECT, which is relevant to workplaces where staff literacy and numeracy levels matter. Our micro-business and micro-credit programmes are the building blocks of community economic development, creating the entrepreneurs and markets of the future.

Some companies felt that they had things to learn from NGOs' participatory style, and about motivating people to work in remote locations. An insurance firm suggested an exchange between its risk assessment experts and NGO staff concerned with predicting and responding to complex emergencies such as conflict.

These unexpected insights into how an NGO's strengths might be viewed by the corporate sector set us thinking about how to play them back to companies. We decided to adapt the already well-established model of corporate social responsibility developed by David Logan for the London Benchmarking Group of companies. How would a company's responsibilities to society look from a development NGO's perspective? And, where these responsibilities coincide with the NGO's mission, are there appropriate ways for the NGO to assist a company to fulfil them?

The company in society

David Logan's model of the company in society identifies four kinds of community interaction:

- charity
- social investment
- commercial initiatives and
- the business basics.

Keeping good company

Charity is giving cash and other forms of support, often in response to an appeal. For many companies a charitable gift is the simplest way of contributing to society. They are not looking to derive a benefit to themselves, other than knowing that they are supporting a well chosen and deserving cause. For example, the palm-top computer maker Psion supports ActionAid's education work in Uganda and Mozambique. Psion likes its staff to feel involved in the projects it supports, and it likes its customers to know about them too, featuring them in *Psion User*, a customer magazine.

Matched giving and payroll giving are standard instruments in business charity, and they are both used by ActionAid's corporate donors to facilitate and make more tax efficient their charitable donations. Child sponsorship – which is ActionAid's prime source of funding – also appeals to a number of companies. They find it generates goodwill and helps motivate staff.

Social investment

The second kind of community interaction is called *social investment* (sometimes *community investment*). It suggests a company enhancing society or improving the environment by using skills and experience, often in partnership with the public and non-profit sectors, to create sustainable, healthy communities. Many people in the development community believe that society has much to gain from imaginative collaboration between charities and business.

In India, for example, ActionAid India's *Partners in Change* project was set up four years ago to promote partnerships between socially responsible companies and disadvantaged communities. The idea is to make it easy for companies to get involved in social development. So *Partners in Change* helps companies plan their social investment to ensure it is effective and meets local needs, introduces them to NGOs with whom they might work and provides monitoring and evaluation of the company's social projects. The bottom line is channelling business resources towards development, and in the process sensitising companies to the needs of the poor.

There are no short cuts, and progress can be slow, but *Partners in Change* has now brokered twenty corporate partnerships. A recent one involves the US management consultancy A T Kearney and Deepalaya, an NGO working with Delhi's slum children.

Deepalaya has been going for twenty years. It works in some 40 slums, reaching out to 20,000 children and their families. Two schools, over 300 educational centres and many skills training, health care and community programmes mark the organisation's progress. But Deepalaya's rapid growth had posed some typical organisational challenges, which the staff knew they were not equipped to overcome on their own.

At this time A T Kearney was establishing an office in Delhi and was looking to establish a social programme in the city. One of the firm's strengths is human resource (HR) development. *Partners in Change* spotted the opportunity for a partnership. A meeting between the consultants and the NGO produced enthusiasm on both sides: for the consultants, it was their first visit to a slum and their first chance to work with an NGO. *Partners in Change* ran an orientation session for the AT Kearney team, introducing them to NGO culture and practice.

In October 1997 A T Kearney began to design a *pro bono* human resources renewal study for Deepalaya. Consultants would visit the NGO and its project sites on Saturdays. The NGO environment and its objectives were new to them, and their recommendations had to take account of the constraints under which NGO managers operate. Adapting familiar management principles to the not-for-profit context was a challenge, and the team did some research into best practice on NGO governance. The recommendations were finally presented and Deepalaya has set about implementing them.

The consultancy's support continues. As Anita Balchandani, a business analyst at A T Kearney remarked, 'although there were four of us handling it, everyone pitched in, especially at the brain storming sessions. As opposed to writing out a cheque, this enabled the greatest degree of participation as more people got involved'.

Partners in Change recently commissioned an impact assessment, funded by the Ford Foundation, to find out what effects the Indian corporate partnerships were having on the partners. For the Kearney-Deepalaya partnership it found that the consultancy firm gained new skills and an HR product which they could sell to other organisations. A T Kearney's involvement with the NGO also stimulated internal reflection about the firm's own organisational development. For Deepalaya, the partnership produced a set of HR initiatives which would allow Deepalaya to build more productive staff teams and manage its growth better.

Sometimes, social investment can be quite spontaneous. Alan Warren, Regional Business Manager of Janssen Cilag Ltd, a healthcare products company, was looking for a team-building exercise for his staff. 'ActionAid came up with an ideal project giving strong support throughout. A truck full of vital equipment reached schools and hospitals in The Gambia and my team strengthened skills necessary for their own work.'

Commercial initiatives

The third tier of a company's social interaction is *commercial initiatives*, meaning activities in support of the business, directly supporting its brands in partnership with charities. Many charities are now pioneering imaginative commercial initiatives with companies. ActionAid has a strong appeal to category ABC1s and schools, and it also has a 130,000 strong supporter base in Europe. These attributes help make for good partnerships in cause-related marketing initiatives.

The ActionAid–Bank of Scotland Mastercard has brought in over half a million pounds since its launch. The Bank's Affinity Cards manager, Stephen Currie, says 'ActionAid's supporter base has proved one of the most responsive of all charities for us. Over a six-year relationship we have been highly impressed with the charity's professionalism and creativity'.

Dell Computers were launching a new product, and the company needed to stimulate its re-sellers. The strategy was to promise £5 to a school in Mozambique for every completed enquiry call. 'The promotion we ran with ActionAid was hugely successful' the company says. 'Enquiries were beyond expectations, the support for ActionAid's work being a real incentive.'

The most successful commercial initiative so far for ActionAid has been an on-pack promotion for Proctor and Gamble Dash soap powder. It raised over a million pounds for health centres and water projects in Ethiopia. For the company, 'the joint promotion with ActionAid in Italy was a very effective branding exercise for our product Dash. With a well-designed promotion we were able to defend our leading market position'.

Business basics

The final element of the company in society, according to the London Benchmarking Group model, is called *Business Basics*. This refers to the core activities of the company in providing the goods and services society wants in an ethical and cost-efficient manner and with due regard to the interests of shareholders. It is the least explored area for collaboration between business and NGOs, but it is the one with the greatest potential.

Many business leaders agree that a successful company is one that is responsive to the needs of all its stakeholders. With their long record of sensitivity to the needs of poor communities, and their participative approach to economic development, development agencies are well placed to help companies relate to some key stakeholders and issues.

Companies are increasingly being called upon by consumers and other stakeholders to demonstrate that their core activities are carried out ethically. A recent response to this need is the Ethical Trading Initiative (ETI). ETI is an alliance of companies, trade union organisations and NGOs, together with the UK Department for International Development, set up to help make substantial improvements to the lives of working people around the world. It encourages companies to implement codes of conduct of internationally agreed minimum standards on labour conditions and human rights in the workplace. ETI is also evolving a common approach to monitoring and verifying compliance with these codes.

As well as participating in ETI, ActionAid is working directly with suppliers to the worldwide garments trade, in Bangladesh. The garments sector in Bangladesh is the country's biggest export earner and a major employer in urban areas. The focus of this work is to demonstrate that good health, safety and employment practices are good for business. This is now a mainstream idea in the West but it is still a novelty in Bangladesh.

In Africa we have been making available to companies our expertise in community-based approaches to HIV/AIDS. For obvious reasons, the disease has a disastrous impact on business operations, and the special competence of NGOs has been welcomed. The report of Booker Tate's 1997 medical conference noted: 'NGOs can be regarded as sources of professional advice and expertise in areas in which business is likely to be deficient in time and resources. They should be regarded as professional consultants with the capacity to contribute to the employee health and community development needs of business in Africa and elsewhere'.

As Nigel Twose, of the World Bank's corporate citizenship programme *Business Partners for Development*, says, 'Development agencies, particularly those like ActionAid with practical experience of presenting the case for social development to companies and facilitating their involvement with marginalised communities, are now being seen as a key part of the solution to global poverty'.

Our impact assessment of NGO-business partnerships in India shows that successful collaborations take a lot of patience to set up and require unusual commitment and adaptability on both sides. So it is worth asking if there are any guidelines for business-charity partnerships. Here are some suggestions.

From the company's point of view, look for a charity which:
- takes the company's own needs seriously
- can integrate these needs with its own objectives
- presents a coherent approach to its charitable cause, in a way that involves the company.

In turn, a charity should be looking for a company which is open to more imaginative engagements. These are the ones that will add most value in the long term – both in terms of influencing the company culture and of contributing to improvements in the lives of poor people. As the ground continues to shift under the for-profit/ not-for-profit relationship, these imaginative engagements will become templates for the future.

'The traditional notion of philanthropy is not adequate' says the mission statement of Timberland, the footwear company. 'It is not smart or wise to approach social problems with the financial leftovers of companies.' Not everyone will agree with such an indictment of corporate giving. Yet it is clear that if NGOs want to involve companies in development in ways that make the most of private sector strengths, they have to find ways of engaging companies beyond the fundraising relationship. ActionAid's experience to date suggests that there are many avenues to explore.

Note: ActionAid works in more than 30 countries in Africa, Asia, Latin America and the Caribbean, helping to reduce poverty and improve quality of life for people living in the world's poorest communities.

For copies of the ActionAid brochure *Keeping Good Company* please call the Corporate Development Department on 0171-561 7561.

Hugh Venables works with the International Firms Initiative Department at ActionAid.

Charity stays at home
John Smyth

'No more Mr Slice Guy', announced the headline of a recent *Guardian* article containing a somewhat cynical account of how two American fast-food millionaires had recently given away vast portions of their wealth to charity. According to the article, they had joined 'a long but not always distinguished line of gilded do-gooders' unwilling to forgo the quid pro quo.

Billionaire Tom Monaghan, founder of Domino's Pizza chain, sold 90% of his holding for $1 billion (£590 million), with most of the proceeds going to his foundation to support the building of Roman Catholic schools across America. Meanwhile Joan Kroc, widow of the man responsible for putting double 'Golden Arches' on major high streets around the world, recently donated $80 million to the Salvation Army, the largest gift in its 118-year history, together with a 12-acre plot of land for a community centre in San Diego, California.

Add to these the names of Ted Turner (ex-owner of CNN), who donated $1 billion to the United Nations and Bill Gates (need I say more), who donated $200 million to a library foundation, and we have philanthropy on a scale which is seen as predominantly American in character and driven by ulterior motives such as gaining a plenary indulgence (Tom is an ardent penitent, apparently), taking advantage of tax breaks ('Sign here, Ted'), or boosting the company image/stock value (need I say more!).

Britain, too, has its major individual donors such as Sainsbury, Hamlyn and Clore, and some confusion exists about the precise distinction between corporate and personal philanthropy, with several instances where company support has closely mirrored the personal concerns of the Chief Executive. It is of course sometimes necessary to examine the motives behind individual or company donations, as it is useful to question the reasons given for asking for support. But we should beware the jaundiced view which suggests that givers cannot be classed as genuine until they have suffered Dickensian ruin similar to that of Mrs Jellby's family in *Bleak House*.

However, the idea that charity begins at home and, for the most part, remains there, is an interesting one to explore. If the US is leading a renewed push towards individual donations, to what extent is it in the vanguard of corporate giving? By looking at four US companies: Domino's Pizza, Wendy's International (burger chain), the Sara Lee Corporation (bakery products and Douwe Egberts coffee, amongst many other goods), and Ben & Jerry's Ice Cream, we will see to what extent corporate philanthropy exports itself along with product to the United Kingdom. Ronald McDonald was excluded from our analysis since the company's policy is comparatively well established in the UK and information on it published in this guide.

Domino's Pizza Inc

Founded in 1960, Domino's is a recognised world leader in pizza delivery, with over 6,000 stores spread throughout more than 60 nations worldwide.

In 1998, Domino's Pizza Inc began a long-term relationship with Easter Seals, a charity founded in 1919 to serve children with disabilities, by making an initial corporate donation of $40,000. This was followed by a personal donation from the company President, Tom Monaghan, of $50,000 for a capital campaign to build a new service facility. This year alone (1999), Domino's Pizza has contributed over $200,000 in money and service materials to Easter Seals.

In addition to the above, Domino's recognises that franchisees live locally and have both a professional and personal investment in their community. Through sponsorship of America Delivers TM, an ongoing national programme, it commends the work of otherwise unsung heroes who have had a positive impact in their community.

Domino's Pizza Group Ltd

In the UK, a charitable budget exists at both national and local store level, with the national budget reserved for national charities. There is no preference for particular causes, so all applications are considered on their merit. As for the size of these budgets, no indication was given as to whether they were deep pan or thin and crispy. I was, however, advised that employee fundraising activities are matched by the company and that there are no plans to set up a foundation in the UK.

Contact: *Chris Moore, Marketing Director, Domino's Pizza Group Ltd, Lasborough Road, Kingston, MILTON KEYNES MK10 0AB (01908-580 000).*

Wendy's International, Inc

Wendy's are pretty big on burgers (over 630 restaurants worldwide) and, it seems, on supporting children. Wendy's founder, Dave Thomas, established the Dave Thomas Foundation for Adoption over five years ago with the aim of making the adoption process easier and more affordable, while creating awareness and educating the public. Today, it acts as a voice for over 100,000 children in the public child welfare system who are waiting for homes

Charity stays at home

and families. Various events are organised to raise money for the charity including one (Wendy's Three-Tour Golf Challenge) which alone raised $925,000 in 1997.

Another part of the group, the Tim Horton chain, which operates across Canada and parts of the US, runs four adventure camps for 'monetarily underprivileged' children from communities with Tim Horton outlets. Approximately 2,000 children ranging in age from 9 to 12, attend the 10-day residential camps with all costs (food, transport and lodging) being covered by the Tim Horton Children's Foundation. A further 3,000 local children are also bused in for day-camp programmes.

In addition, Wendy's actively supports minority and female-owned businesses and environmentally responsible companies, through purchasing their goods and services (this increased by 15% in 1997). Franchisees are also encouraged to organise events and programmes in support of their local communities.

Wendy's International (UK)

Certainly not a 'Whopper' in the UK (around 19 outlets at present), Wendy's proved not to be very 'filling' as far as information regarding their community support (or lack of it?) was concerned. Despite writing, repeated telephone calls and voice-mail messages, I was unable to obtain any details at all.

Contact: *Sarah Kelly, Marketing Director, Wendy's International, 4th Floor, Congress House, Lyon Road, HARROW HA1 2EN (0181-861 8400).*

The Sara Lee Corporation

A leading corporate citizen in America, Sara Lee gives at least 2% of their US pre-tax income annually through cash and product donations to not-for-profit organisations. This has amounted to nearly $220 million (worldwide) in the last 10 years, $32 million of which was given in 1998. Many of the Corporation's philanthropic activities are overseen by the Sara Lee Foundation (established in 1981) which spent around $9 million in 1998.

To ensure their giving is effective and makes a difference, they concentrate on four specific areas: women, culture, hunger, and people in need.

Women – around 20% of the Foundation's donations are earmarked for programmes that help women realise their full potential, professionally and personally. Through the annual Front Runner Awards, $50,000 is given to a not-for-profit organisation nominated by the leading woman (front runner) in each of four categories: the arts, business, government and the humanities.

Culture – art is a top priority, receiving at least 40% of the Foundation's cash grant funds. A wide range of work is supported from exhibitions to cutting-edge projects, and especially organisations that make art more meaningful and accessible.

Hunger – more than 25 organisations working to eradicate hunger are supported. A long-standing relationship exists with Second Harvest, the largest charitable hunger relief organisation in the United States. Through its network of food banks more than 40,000 food pantries, soup kitchens, homeless shelters and other not-for-profit agencies are supplied. 99.7% of all donations received go directly to hunger assistance.

People in Need – action against poverty is taken by funding organisations that deal with education, job placement, housing, drug prevention and other programmes.

Sara Lee also believes its employees should help channel donations and so a significant proportion of its annual giving is decentralised through them. Employee fundraising activities are matched by the Foundation and amounted to about $1.3 million in 1998. Individual company divisions also contribute volunteer time and make product donations.

An excellent website exists at www.saralee.com with links to the work of the Foundation. Anyone wanting more detailed information on any of the above, or with an interest in seeing how a good website should behave, are recommended to pay a visit.

Sara Lee Household & Bodycare UK Ltd

Support in the UK tends to be focused on schools, hospitals and charities local to company sites, although national charities are occasionally helped. Cash and/or product donations may be made. The company also supports employees' fundraising activities.

There are no plans to establish a UK foundation, either now, or in the future. Decisions at present lie with the contact given below.

Contact: *Alan Brown, Personnel Director, Sara Lee Household & Bodycare UK Ltd, 225 Bath Road, SLOUGH SL1 4AU (01753-523 971).*

Ben & Jerry's Homemade Inc

Founded in 1978 in a renovated petrol station in Burlington, Vermont by childhood friends Ben Cohen and Jerry Greenfield, Ben & Jerry's gives away 7.5% of its pre-tax earnings from the sale of ice cream products to good causes. This is done in three ways: through the Ben & Jerry's Foundation; via Community Action Teams at five Vermont sites; and through corporate grants made by the Director of Social Mission Development.

The Ben & Jerry's Foundation was established in 1985 through a donation of stock in Ben & Jerry's Homemade Inc. These funds are used as an endowment. The Foundation considers proposals that address issues affecting: (i) children and families; (ii) disenfranchised groups; (iii) the environment. Projects that will lead to societal, institutional or environmental change, help ameliorate an unjust or destructive situation by empowering constituents, and address the root causes of social or environmental problems are favoured. Grants are only given to programmes concerned with social change, not social service i.e. those that address communities, systems and institutions, rather than aiding and assisting individuals.

In 1996, the Foundation's Grant-making Committee (composed entirely of employees and representatives from each Community Action Team) gave away $323,000 in 64 grants. Grants ranged from $250 to $15,000 and averaged $7,500.

Ben & Jerry's website at www.benjerry.com is another excellent example of how useful a source of information and advice these sites can and should be. Again there is a direct link to the work of the Foundation which provides clear guidelines on: areas of interest, restrictions, types of grants, how to apply, and deadlines. It also gives tips on writing a successful grant application and, just as importantly, for those who don't meet the criteria, other potential funding sources.

In keeping with its concern for the environment, the large volume of applications received each quarter are separated and recycled, having been appropriately dealt with first!

Ben & Jerry's Homemade Ltd

The company has recently set up a trial project in the UK where they have purchased an old American school bus to travel around the country raising money on behalf of Childline. About £40,000 has been invested by Ben & Jerry's, who expect to raise £250,000. If this proves successful, a further three or four buses will be purchased, each designated to raise money on behalf of a specific charity.

Ice cream products may also be given for charitable purposes, especially where less usual causes are concerned. The company hopes to set up a UK foundation in the year 2000.

Contact: *Ian Hills, Product Brand Manager, Ben & Jerry's Ice Cream, 3a The Deans, Bridge Road, BAGSHOT GU19 5AT (01276-473366).*

It appears from the above that there is no automatic link between business practice and corporate responsibility. While sales systems and business methods transfer, charitable activity does not. Nowhere, for example, do the UK divisions of these companies exhibit the same transparency regarding their charitable support policy as their parent companies do, and they certainly have some way to go before they are as openly committed to supporting their local communities. As a result, accusations will continue to be levelled that corporate responsibility is an afterthought arising out of surplus money, rather than an integrated part of the business whole.

John Smyth is a Researcher at the Directory of Social Change.

Facts & figures

How much do companies give?

Given that there is a statutory obligation for companies to declare their charitable donations where the total exceeds £200 in any one year (Section 19 of the 1967 Companies Act as amended by Statutory Instruments No. 1055 1980 refers), getting a figure is relatively easy – you just need a copy of the annual report or to check the company website. The figure for community contributions, however, is more difficult to obtain and less precisely arrived at as its calculation varies from company to company, if it is calculated at all.

Total cash donations made by the companies in this guide amount to £242 million, with a further £157 million declared as being given in other forms of support. This gives a total community contributions figure of £399 million (i.e. cash donations plus other community contributions) which, whilst markedly higher than figures for previous years, is almost certainly still a long way short of what is actually given. Just under one-quarter of the companies in the guide declared a separate figure for contributions other than cash donations, which is up on last year's figure.

Community contributions

Total amount given

Of the £399 million given in total by all the companies in the guide, 98% was given by the top 400, and 45% by the top 25. The latter are listed in Table 1 opposite. The minimum figure required to gain entry to this illustrious group has increased slightly to £2.9 million, confirming that last year's substantial increase to £2.8 million was not a short-term rise.

Six of the top 25 do not declare a separate figure for non-cash contributions, but are in the table on the strength of their cash donations alone.

Changes in giving

Table 3 overleaf gives figures for the top 400 contributors for the last eight years, and shows that contributions continue to rise impressively (up by 24%). In part, this is due to the greater number of companies declaring a figure for this guide. This is likely to be an increasing trend as the PerCent Club and London Benchmarking Group continue to define and encourage more companies to take into account non-cash support.

Several companies are new to the top 25, including British Airways and Severn Trent.

Contributions as a percentage of profit

Compared to last year, contributions as a percentage of pre-tax profit have risen from 0.33% to 0.40%. Although lower than the peak of 1993/94, and a long way short of the 1% guideline recently proposed for the millennium by the PerCent Club, the sustained increase is encouraging after the lean years of the mid-nineties.

Table 1

Top 25 by community contribution

1	Lloyds TSB Group plc	£30.0 million
2	British Telecommunications plc	£15.6 million
3	NatWest Group	£14.3 million
4	Barclays PLC	£13.5 million
5	Marks & Spencer plc	£10.1 million
6	Diageo plc	£8.3 million
7	British Petroleum Company plc	£7.5 million
8	GlaxoWellcome plc	£7.0 million
9	British Airways plc	£6.8 million
10	ZENECA Group PLC	£5.7 million
11	British Nuclear Fuels plc	£5.5 million
12	Scottish & Newcastle plc	£5.0 million
13	Unilever	£5.0 million
14	Boots Company PLC	£4.9 million
15	Shell UK Limited	£4.9 million
16	Severn Trent Plc	£4.3 million
17	Bank of Scotland	£4.0 million
18	Camelot Group plc	£3.9 million
19	Cadbury Schweppes plc	£3.8 million
20	Allied Dunbar Assurance plc	£3.4 million
21	Halifax plc	£3.1 million
22	Ecclesiastical Insurance Group plc	£3.0 million
23	Reuters Holdings PLC	£3.0 million
24	United Utilities PLC	£3.0 million
25	Tesco plc	£2.9 million

Note: 1997/98 UK community contribution figures were unavailable for Allied Dunbar, British Nuclear Fuels, Diageo, Ecclesiastical Insurance, Reuters and ZENECA. However, their level of charitable donations alone merit inclusion.

Facts and figures

Charitable donations

Total amount given
Of the £242 million given in cash by the companies in the guide, over 97% (£236 million) was given by the top 400, an increase of £37 million on 1996/97, and 43% by the top 25. These are listed in Table 2 opposite.

Changes in giving
Lloyds TSB, as anticipated in the last edition, increased their cash donations to over £20 million – a figure which is expected to rise again to around £30 million in the year 2000. Even at current levels the quoted figure of £21.5 million is over two-and-a-half times that of the next largest giver (Diageo), so it will be interesting to see whether or not this gap remains constant over the next 12–18 months.

Diageo, born out of a merger between Guinness and Grand Metropolitan (both previously large givers in their own right), may not compare favourably with Lloyds TSB in this respect – but, then, who does? Nevertheless, the merger has not been seen as an opportunity to cut back on their charitable support. Rather, they have increased it beyond the previous combined figure for the two companies and it is to be hoped this continues.

Notable additions to the top 25 include Nationwide Building Society and Northern Rock plc, both of whom have established foundations.

Donations as a percentage of profit
As can be seen from Table 3 below, the level of donations expressed as a percentage of pre-tax profit, shows a slight increase after having stayed remarkably similar for the previous three years. Whether this will continue to rise towards the level of the early nineties remains to be seen, given the significant jump in overall contributions caused by increasing (increased declaration of) non-cash support.

The potential for company giving

Based on the 125 companies in the guide which gave a separate figure for both cash donations and non-cash contributions, it is possible to estimate the overall potential level of support. Assuming that most of the other companies give non-cash support at similar levels (roughly twice the value of cash donations), the total value of community support by the companies in this guide could be as high as £500 million.

Taking the above extrapolation to extremes, if all the companies in the guide joined the PerCent Club (under one-third are actually members) at the level of commitment of 1% of pre-tax profits, this guide would have covered contributions of over £1,000 million!

Table 2
Top 25 by charitable donation

1	Lloyds TSB Group plc	£21.5 million
2	Diageo plc	£8.3 million
3	GlaxoWellcome plc	£6.0 million
4	Marks and Spencer plc	£6.0 million
5	ZENECA Group PLC	£5.7 million
6	British Nuclear Fuels plc	£5.5 million
7	Barclays PLC	£4.4 million
8	Unilever	£4.0 million
9	Camelot Group plc	£3.5 million
10	British Petroleum Company plc	£3.4 million
11	Allied Dunbar Assurance plc	£3.4 million
12	Ecclesiastical Insurance Group plc	£3.0 million
13	Reuters Holdings PLC	£3.0 million
14	Imperial Chemical Industries plc	£2.8 million
15	Nationwide Building Society	£2.8 million
16	British Telecommunications plc	£2.7 million
17	Boots Company PLC	£2.7 million
18	NatWest Group	£2.4 million
19	J Sainsbury plc	£2.4 million
20	Royal Bank of Scotland Group plc	£2.3 million
21	EMI Group plc	£2.1 million
22	The Post Office	£2.0 million
23	Halifax plc	£2.0 million
24	Northern Rock plc	£2.0 million
25	Centrica plc	£1.7 million

Note: *These figures are for statutorily declared charitable donations only. As stated above, this greatly understates community contributions, particularly for the largest companies.*

Table 3

Charitable donations – Top 400

	1990/91	1991/92	1992/93	1993/94	1994/95	1995/96	1996/97	1997/98
Total	£133m	£157m	£151m	£157m	£158m	£182m	£199m	£236m
% Pre-tax profit	0.25%	0.30%	0.28%	0.28%	0.21%	0.21%	0.22%	0.24%

Community contributions – Top 400

	1990/91	1991/92	1992/93	1993/94	1994/95	1995/96	1996/97	1997/98
Total	£225m	£255m	£248m	£264m	£269m	£252m	£315m	£392m
% Pre-tax profit	0.42%	0.49%	0.46%	0.47%	0.36%	0.29%	0.33%	0.40%

Facts and figures

Sector comparisons

It is very difficult to compare accurately the level of giving by different companies. This is not just because of the different types of support given, but also because worldwide profit and/or community contribution figures are often declared, whilst the figure for charitable donations is usually a UK one.

In comparing companies within eight different sectors (see Table 4 opposite), we decided it would only be meaningful if we used like contribution figures. Therefore, the figure for contributions as a percentage of pre-tax profit (%) is calculated on the UK donations figure if no separate contributions figure was declared, or where only a worldwide figure was given.

In purely monetary terms, contributions from the Banking sector put it at the forefront in the generosity stakes, helped to no small degree by the exceptionally high giving of Lloyds TSB, which is more than double that of NatWest, the next largest giver. However, as a percentage of pre-tax profits these two companies' positions are reversed, with NatWest laying claim to being the only true PerCent Club member among the banks.

The Oil & Gas/Fuel sector is another generous giver: British Nuclear Fuels contributions have more than doubled to account for 2.76% of their pre-tax profits. This year we also include BG plc and Centrica plc, from whom full year figures were not previously available following the demerger of British Gas.

Last year we commented upon the generally poor showing of the national companies within Utilities, and this year is no exception. Again only National Grid has made substantial contributions, which begs the question of what happened to PowerGen, National Power, and British Energy, who between them declared pre-tax profits of over £1,200 million. Our fears concerning continued regional support appear to have been unfounded, although interestingly, four out of the five utilities listed are there on the basis of their non-cash support.

Finally, although comparisons between companies are fraught with danger as we have already stated, and those between sectors perhaps even more so, looking at pound signs alone does not necessarily tell the full story. Averaging out the figures for contributions as a percentage of pre-tax profits within each sector, we find the most generous sectors to be Oil & Gas/Fuel – 0.86%, closely followed by Life Assurance/Insurance (excepting the figure for Ecclesiastical) – 0.85%, followed by Banking – 0.69%. Some way behind these, unfortunately, lie Media and Pharmaceuticals at 0.49% each, with the beleaguered Supermarkets on the bottom shelf with 0.30%.

Key to Table 4 (opposite):

- ◆ worldwide contributions figure only declared (see entry)
- ▲ no separate contributions figure declared

Business sector	Donations	Contributions	%
Banking			
Bank of Scotland	£1,200,000	£4,000,000	0.54
Barclays plc	£4,400,000	£13,500,000	0.79
Halifax plc	£2,000,000	£3,050,000	0.18
Lloyds TSB Group plc	£21,450,000	£30,000,000	0.95
NatWest Group	£2,400,000	£14,300,000	1.41
Royal Bank of Scotland	£2,280,000	£2,500,000	0.25
Brewers/Distillers			
Allied Domecq PLC◆	£770,000	£770,000	0.17
Diageo plc▲	£8,300,000	£8,300,000	0.43
Scottish & Newcastle plc	£550,000	£5,000,000	1.18
Seagram Distillers PLC	£170,000	£200,000	0.37
Vaux Group plc	£170,000	£200,000	0.57
Whitbread PLC	£840,000	£2,200,000	0.58
Life Assurance/Insurance			
Allied Dunbar Assurance▲	£3,370,000	£3,370,000	1.66
AXA Sun Life Assurance▲	£670,000	£670,000	0.23
Ecclesiastical Insurance▲	£3,040,000	£3,040,000	12.16
J & H Marsh & McLennan	£150,000	£500,000	1.65
Prudential Corporation▲	£1,400,000	£1,400,000	0.12
Royal & Sun Alliance Ins.	£1,200,000	£2,400,000	0.60
Media			
British Sky Broadcasting	£320,000	£710,000	0.26
Carlton Commns. plc▲	£1,100,000	£1,100,000	0.35
Daily Mail & Gen. Trust▲	£720,000	£720,000	0.50
News International	£1,000,000	£1,500,000	0.36
Pearson plc▲	£1,270,000	£1,270,000	0.98
Reuters Holdings PLC▲	£3,000,000	£3,000,000	0.48
Oil & Gas/Fuel			
BG plc	£1,500,000	£2,700,000	0.22
British Nuclear Fuels▲	£5,500,000	£5,500,000	2.76
British Petroleum Co.	£3,400,000	£7,500,000	0.27
Centrica plc▲	£1,750,000	£1,750,000	(loss)
Esso UK plc	£1,500,000	£2,720,000	0.49
Shell UK Limited	£1,140,000	£4,860,000	0.57
Pharmaceuticals			
Boots Company PLC	£2,680,000	£4,900,000	1.13
GlaxoWellcome plc	£6,000,000	£7,000,000	0.26
Reckitt & Colman plc	£326,000	£550,000	0.18
SmithKline Beecham plc◆	£1,600,000	£1,600,000	0.10
Warner Lambert UK Ltd▲	£80,000	£80,000	0.73
ZENECA Group PLC▲	£5,700,000	£5,700,000	0.53
Supermarkets			
ASDA Group plc	£100,000	£1,800,000	0.44
Morrison Supermarkets	£135,000	£470,000	0.31
Safeway plc	£75,000	£360,000	0.11
Sainsbury plc▲	£2,400,000	£2,400,000	0.28
Somerfield Stores plc▲	£550,000	£550,000	(loss)
Tesco plc	£1,260,000	£2,890,000	0.35
Utilities			
Eastern Group plc	£110,000	£1,510,000	0.58
Midlands Electricity plc▲	£470,000	£470,000	0.28
National Grid Group plc	£360,000	£1,000,000	0.17
Northern Electric plc	£220,000	£1,000,000	0.91
Severn Trent Plc	£270,000	£4,290,000	1.15
United Utilities PLC	£580,000	£3,000,000	0.64

VOLUNTARY ACTION CAMDEN
INSTRUMENT HOUSE
207/215 KINGS CROSS ROAD
LONDON WC1X 9DB
REG. CHARITY NO 802186

Applying to companies

This section gives basic information for putting together applications to companies.

To make an effective appeal to industry you must have a basic understanding of why firms give. This enables you to put forward good reasons why they should support your work. Some companies in this guide receive up to 100 applications each week. You need to make a good case for yours to be successful. A company will not be particularly impressed with a general plea to 'put something back into the community'. They want something more substantial. You should be able to demonstrate a clear link with the company, be it geographical, product, employee contact, or some other connection.

Why companies give

The main reason for company giving is often said to be enlightened self-interest, rather than pure altruism and they see their giving as 'community involvement' or 'community investment'. The following are some of the reasons why companies give.

- To **create goodwill.** Companies like to be seen as good citizens and good neighbours, so they support local charities. They also like to create goodwill amongst employees.
- To **be associated with certain causes** that relate to their business. Mining companies often like to support environmental projects, pharmaceutical companies health projects, banks economic development projects and so on.
- Because **they are asked** and **it is expected of them.** They receive appeals, and they know that other companies also receive appeals and give their support. They will often support trade charities such as a benevolent fund or an industry research organisation; beyond that they will probably pitch their level of giving more or less at that of their rivals.
- Because **the Chairperson or other senior managers have a personal interest in that cause,** this is particularly the case for smaller companies. Even where a company has well-established criteria for giving, if you can get a friend of the Managing Director to ask on your behalf, you are more likely to get a donation, even when your cause does not exactly fit those criteria.

Generally it is worth emphasising the sheer chaos of company giving. Few companies have any real policy for their charitable giving. Mostly they cover a wide range of good causes or attempt to deal with each appeal on its merits.

However, some companies do have clear policies. **Where policies are printed please respect them**; dealing with a mass of clearly inappropriate applications is the single biggest headache in corporate giving and has caused some to consider winding up their charitable support programmes altogether.

What companies give

There are a variety of ways in which companies can support charities:

- cash donations
- sponsorship of an event or activity
- sponsorship of promotional and educational materials
- sponsorship of an award scheme
- joint promotions, where the company contributes a donation to the charity in return for each product sold in order to encourage sales
- making company facilities available
- secondment of a member of staff, where a member of the company's staff helps on an agreed basis whilst remaining employed (and paid) by the company.
- contributing a senior member of staff to the charity's Management Board
- providing expertise and advice
- encouraging employees to volunteer
- organising a fundraising campaign amongst employees
- advertising in charity brochures and publications.

Key factors in approaching companies

Research

Research is very important, not just into companies, but also into personal contacts. When planning an appeal, an important first step is to find which of the people associated with your charity have influence or know people who have. If you can find a link between one of your supporters and a particular company – use it.

- One of your trustees/members may be on the board of directors or have contacts there – it will prove useful for them to write or sign the appeal letter.
- One of your volunteers or supporters may be an employee of the company.
- Your clients/users (or their parents) may work for the company.

Alternatively, you might be able to tie your appeal in to a known personal interest of a director.

Applying to companies

Getting in touch

Generally an appeal through a personal contact will work the best. But if you haven't got a contact and can see no way of developing one, then you will have to come up with another link.

As a first step you might contact the company to find out the following:

- who is responsible for dealing with charitable appeals
- their name and job title
- what information they can send regarding their company
- any procedure or timetable for submitting applications
- whether they might be interested in coming to see your organisation at work.

Visits are useful when discussing bigger donations with the larger companies, but are difficult to arrange for anything small.

Almost certainly your appeal will be in the form of a letter. Make this as personal as you can. Circular letters tend to end up in the bin. Make the letter short and to the point.

Be specific in your approach

Rather than sending out a circular mailing to 100 or 1,000 companies, you will be more successful if you select a few companies you believe will be particularly interested in your project, and target your application to them and their policy. (Many companies will not consider circular appeals as a point of policy.)

Find a good reason why you believe the company should support you and include this prominently in your letter. You may be able to relate what you are doing as a charity to companies which have some relevance to your work: for example, a children's charity can appeal to companies making children's products; a housing charity to construction companies, building societies, etc. Any relationship, however tenuous, creates a point of contact on which you can build a good case for obtaining the company's support. If there is no relationship, should you be approaching that company at all?

There may be occasions where a charity will not want to accept money from a company in a related industry. A health education charity may not want to accept money from a tobacco or brewery company or from the confectionery industry, or similarly an environmental group may not wish to accept a donation from a nuclear power company. These may feel that as a result of doing so they would be seen to be compromised. Similarly, a local charity might not want money from a company who has made people in the area redundant. Each charity has to judge where it draws the line.

Be clear about why you need the money

You must be clear about the objectives of the work you are raising money for, particularly its time-scale and how it relates to your overall programme of work. Try to think in project terms rather than seeking money to cover basic administration costs. This can be difficult, because most people spend most of their money on administration in one form or another, so you need to conjure up projects out of your current activities to present to potential donors. You can build a percentage of administration costs into the costs of a project. If you relate what you are doing to a specific time-scale, this again makes what you are applying for appear more of a project than a contribution to your year-on-year core costs.

Be persistent

Do not underestimate the persistence factor. If you do not receive a donation in the first year, do not assume that the company will never support you. Go back a second and even a third time.

If you are going back, mention the fact that you have applied to them previously, perhaps saying that you are now presenting them with something different which may be (you hope) of more interest to them.

If they give you reasons for refusing support, use them to help you put in more appropriate applications in the future. If they said that they do not give to your particular type of activity then you know that it is absolutely no use your going back. If they said their funds were fully committed, you can try to find out when would be a better time to apply (although it might only have been a convenient excuse because they did not want to give to you).

Note the response to your appeal and use any information you can glean to improve your chances the next time. People respect persistence, so it really is important to go back again and again.

How to find out which firms to approach

The firms to approach must depend on what sort of organisation you are. If you are a national organisation then an appeal to the country's leading companies is appropriate. Local groups should approach local firms and local branches of national companies which have a presence in their area. All organisations can approach companies in allied fields: for example, theatres can appeal to fabric companies.

You will find the names and other details of companies in a whole series of useful directories (the top 536 companies are listed in this book).

Sources of information:

The Times 1,000

The Kompass Register of British Industry and Commerce (available in regional sections)

Guide to Key British Enterprises

Stock Exchange Official Year Book

Jordan's Top Privately Owned Companies (2 volumes)

To find key contacts in companies:

The Directory of Directors and *Who's Who* are useful for finding out more about company directors.

Corporate Register – updated quarterly – a guide to decision makers in UK Stockmarket companies.

For local companies in addition to this guide:

The appropriate regional section of *Kompass*

The local Chamber of Commerce

Confederation of British Industry regional contacts.

Whichever directories you are using make sure they are up-to-date copies. Company personnel and/or donations policies change regularly.

If you want gifts in kind, you should find likely suppliers of what you need. Trade associations will often provide a list of its member companies. Another idea is trade exhibition catalogues which give details of all exhibitors.

One big problem is the ownership of seemingly independent companies. Many companies are in fact a part of a much larger concern. In recent years there has been a substantial number of mergers and take-overs, plus the buying and selling of business between corporations. A useful source of information is the directory *Who Owns Whom,* which has a subsidiary index listing most subsidiaries of companies included in the guide. You can also use company annual reports, which (for most companies) can be obtained on request. These reports provide good background information on the company, and occasionally information on the company's corporate support programme. Some private (and occasionally public) companies will not send out annual reports except to shareholders; in such cases you can go to Companies House to get hold of a copy. The main offices are situated in Cardiff, Edinburgh, Belfast and London, with satellite offices in Birmingham, Glasgow, Leeds and Manchester.

Finally there are national and local newspapers which can provide useful information and ideas about who to approach. Informal sources of information may include the local business school, rotary, round table, Chamber of Commerce, Business Breakfast Clubs, as well as clients of your auditor, banker, legal advisor or suppliers.

The types of companies that give

Foreign owned multinational companies

Many of the large multinationals have global giving programmes. Some have an international structure for managing their giving with budgets set for each country and a common policy for the sorts of activity they are interested in supporting. Others may give each country a small budget to spend on charitable projects of its choice. With others, community involvement policy remains a purely local matter for company management in the country concerned.

Leading national companies

Most of the companies in this guide fall into this category. Many support large national charities, of which many have departments set up to raise money from companies. Some make grants through regional offices and most will give preference to charities local to their main operating sites.

Larger local companies

In any city or region there will be large companies who are important to the local economy. These companies will often feel a responsibility to do something to support voluntary action and community initiatives in those areas, and value the good publicity that this will provide. It is a good idea to form some kind of relationship with larger companies in your area.

There are also companies that have a regional remit, such as water, electricity and television companies. The support of these companies is usually confined within these regional boundaries.

Smaller local companies

Almost everyone is targeting the large companies, because good information is available on these for fundraisers and there is little available information on smaller local companies. Many of these are privately owned and the approach will often be through the managing director or senior partner. Most of these companies will have no policies about what to give to and may prefer to give in kind, for example a prize for a raffle or a fundraising event. It might be easier to approach these companies for this sort of support in the first instance; and later on, once they have given something, to persuade them to make a cash donation.

Constructing an appeal letter

Important points to consider

- *Think up a project or aspect of your work that the business sector might like to support.* Generally, do not appeal for administration costs or a contribution to an endowment fund (although there will be cases where this approach will succeed). Recognise that companies are likely to be interested in some ideas and not others. For example, a drugs charity would be more likely to get money for education than rehabilitation. An appreciation of the kind of projects that companies like to support will be very helpful to you.

- *Your letter should be as short as possible. Try to get it all on one side of A4.* You can always supply other information as attachments. Company people are busy. You can help them by making your appeal letter short and to the point. It should be written clearly and concisely and be free from jargon. Someone not acquainted with what you are doing should be able to read and understand it and be persuaded to act on it. Give your letter in draft to someone outside your charity to read and comment on before finalising it and sending it out.

- *You should state why you need the money and exactly how it will be spent.* The letter itself should be straightforward. It should include the following information (not necessarily in this order): what the organisation does and some background on how it was set up; whom the organisation serves; why the organisation needs funds; how the donation would be spent if it were to be forthcoming; and why you think the company might be interested in supporting you.

- *You should attempt to communicate the urgency of your appeal.* Fundraising is an intensively competitive business; there is a limited amount of money to give away, and you have to ensure that some of it comes your way. If it appears that although you would like the money now it would not matter terribly much if you got it next year, this will put people off. But don't give the impression you are fundraising at the last minute. Show them you are professional and you have carefully planned your fundraising appeal. You should also try to show that your charity is well-run, efficient and cost-effective in how it operates.

- *You should mention why you think the company should support your cause.* This could range from rather generalised notions of corporate responsibility and the creation of goodwill in the local community to much more specific advantages such as preventing children painting graffiti on their factory walls or the good publicity companies will get from supporting your cause. If the firm's generosity is to be made public, for

Applying to companies

example through advertising or any publicity arising from the gift, then emphasise the goodwill which will accrue to the company. Most companies would say that they do not require any public acknowledgement for the contributions they make, but most will appreciate and welcome this.

- *Ask for something specific.* It is all too easy to make a good case and then to mumble something about needing money. Many companies, having been persuaded to give, are not sure how much to give. You can ask them to give a donation of a specific amount (matched to what you believe their ability to contribute to be), or to contribute the cost of a particular item. You can suggest a figure by mentioning what other companies are giving. You can mention a total and say how many donations you will need to achieve this. Don't be unreasonable in your expectations. Just because a company is large and rich, it doesn't mean that it makes big grants.

- *If you can demonstrate some form of 'leverage' this will be an added attraction.* Company donations on the whole are quite modest, but companies like to feel they are having a substantial impact with the money they spend. If you can show that a small amount of money will enable a much larger project to go ahead, or will release further funds say on a matching basis from another source, this will definitely be an advantage.

- *Having written a very short appeal letter, you can append some background support literature.* This should not be a fifty-page treatise outlining your latest policies, but like your letter it should be crisp and to the point, a record of your achievements, your latest annual report, press cuttings or even a specially produced brochure to accompany your appeal.

- *Make sure that the letter is addressed to the correct person at the correct address.* It pays to do this background research. Keep all the information on file as it will make your job much easier next time.

- *If you are successful, remember to say thank you; this is an elementary courtesy which is too often forgotten.* If the company gives you any substantial amount of money, then you should probably try to keep them in touch with the achievements related to their donation (such as a brief progress report or copies of your annual report or latest publications).

- *If you do not succeed, go back again next year* (unless they say that it is not their policy to support your type of organisation or to give to charity at all). Persistence can pay. If you have received a donation, go back again next year. The company has demonstrated that it is interested in what you are doing and in supporting you. It may well do it again next year, especially if you had thanked them for the donation and kept them in touch with how the 'project' developed.

Some basic don'ts when applying to companies

✗ Don't write indiscriminate 'Dear Sir/Madam' circular letters to any company you come across.

✗ Don't use any guide you may have access to as a simple mailing list.

✗ Don't write to a company which specifically says it does not support your kind of work.

✗ Don't write to a company unless **at least one** of the following applies:

- The company has a declared policy indicating a specific interest in your group's area of work.
- The company operates in the same locality as your group and a clear product link exists between your needs and their supplies.
- You have a strong personal link with a senior company officer, or a member of their staff is actively involved in your work.
- There is some good reason to write to that particular company. The fact that the company makes a profit and your group needs money is not a sufficiently strong link.

How companies reply to you

Many companies will not even reply to your appeal. A few may acknowledge receipt of your letter, and occasionally you will get thanked for your request and be told that it is being considered and you will only hear the outcome if you are successful. Up to half of the companies you approach will write back depending on the spread of the companies you approach. Larger companies have a system for dealing with charity mail, and most will see it as good PR to give a reply. Smaller companies which are not giving much charitable support will not have the time or the resources to do anything but scan the mail and throw most of it in the bin.

What sort of reply should you expect? If you do an extensive appeal, you will inevitably get a lot of refusals. These will normally be in the form of a pre-printed or word-processed letter or a postcard. Occasionally you will get an individually typed letter of reply. If they say yes, you will get a cheque or a Charities Aid Foundation or Charities Trust voucher. But more often they will say no.

There may be various reasons given or phrases used by a company for refusing your request. The company may not mean what it says. Funds may still be available for those appeals the company wishes to support; the company may be able to give support and just not want to; or it may not want to now or in the future. You should try to read between the lines. Companies in trying to be polite may in fact be misleading you if you take what they say at face value.

The application letter – checklist

- Is it only one side of A4?
- Does it state what your link is with the company?
- Does it stress the benefits to the company?
- Is it clear why you need the money?
- Is it clear what you are asking for?
- Is it addressed to the correct contact?
- Is it attractive to the company?
- Is it endorsed?

Geographical index of head offices

This geographical index is based purely on the head office address given at the start of each company entry. While it is generally the case that companies give some preference to charities local to their operating sites including the head office, this is not always so. Once this index has been used to produce a preliminary list of potential companies to approach, the individual entries for each company should be read carefully to determine whether or not your particular project falls within the company's criteria.

Bedfordshire
Bedford
  NFC plc
Luton
  Huntleigh Technology plc
  Sapalux Ltd
  Vauxhall Motors Ltd

Berkshire
Bracknell
  3M UK Holdings plc
  BMW GB Ltd
  Hewlett-Packard Ltd
  Ocean Group plc
  Panasonic UK Ltd
  Powell Duffryn plc
  Racal Electronics plc
Maidenhead
  Southern Electric plc
Newbury
  Bayer plc
  Vodafone Group plc
Reading
  BG plc
  English China Clays plc
  Foster Wheeler Ltd
  Honda Motor Europe Ltd
  Rockwell International Ltd
  Thorn UK
Slough
  BPB plc
  Centrica plc
  Citroen UK Ltd
  Fiat Auto (UK) Ltd
  ICL plc
  Mars UK Ltd
  Slough Estates plc
Theale
  Danka plc
Windsor
  Household International UK Ltd
  Morgan Crucible Company plc
  Reckitt & Colman plc
  Reed Executive plc
  Siebe plc

Yattendon
  Yattendon Investment Trust plc

Bristol
  BCH Group plc
  Bristol & West plc
  Clerical Medical Investment Group
  Imperial Tobacco Group plc
  Orange plc
  Somerfield Stores plc
  South Western Electricity plc
  Spandex plc
  Wessex Water plc

Buckinghamshire
Amersham
  Field Group plc
Aylesbury
  Rothmans International Tobacco UK
Beaconsfield
  McBride plc
Bourne End
  Lex Service PLC
Gerrards Cross
  British Alcan Aluminium plc
High Wycombe
  Mayflower Corporation plc
  Monsanto plc
Little Chalfont
  Nycomed Amersham plc
Milton Keynes
  Abbey National plc
  Argos plc
  Mobil Holdings Ltd
Stoke Poges
  The Albert Fisher Group plc

Cambridgeshire
Huntingdon
  Anglian Water plc
Peterborough
  British Sugar plc
  EMAP plc
  Pearl Assurance plc
  Perkins Foods

Cheshire
Cheadle Hulme
  BASF plc
Chester
  Manweb plc
  Trinity International Holdings plc
Hartford
  AMEC plc
Knutsford
  Marlowe Holdings Ltd
Macclesfield
  Ciba Speciality Chemicals PLC
Warrington
  British Nuclear Fuels plc
  The Greenalls Group plc
  North West Water Ltd
  United Utilities PLC
Wilmslow
  Norcros plc
  United Assurance Group plc

Cumbria
Barrow-in-Furness
  Marconi Marine
Carlisle
  Stobart Investments Ltd
Kendal
  AXA Provincial Insurance plc

Derbyshire
Burnaston
  Toyota Motor Manufacturing (UK)
Derby
  Hazlewood Foods plc
  Thorntons plc
  Williams plc
Ilkeston
  Charnos plc

Devon
Exeter
  Pennon Group plc

Geographical index

Dorset
Bournemouth
Liverpool Victoria Friendly Society
Wimborne
Cobham plc

Durham
Darlington
Cummins Engine Co Ltd
Durham
Northumbrian Water Group plc
Peterlee
Claremont Garment Holdings plc

East Sussex
Hove
SEEBOARD plc
Portslade
Palmer & Harvey McLane Ltd

East Yorkshire
Driffield
Dewhirst Group plc
Hull
Northern Foods plc

Essex
Brentwood
Ford Motor Company Ltd
Chelmsford
Essex & Suffolk Water plc
Colchester
Royal London Mutual Insurance
Harlow
Yule Catto & Co plc
Harrow
Wickes plc
Loughton
Clinton Cards Plc

Gloucestershire
Cheltenham
Kraft Jacobs Suchard Ltd
Spirax Sarco Engineering plc
Gloucester
Ecclesiastical Insurance Group plc
Wotton-under-Edge
Renishaw plc

Greater Manchester
Eccles
Makro Self-Service Wholesalers Ltd
Manchester
Airtours plc
British Vita plc
BTP plc
Co-operative Bank plc
Co-operative Insurance Society Ltd
Guardian Media Group plc
Kellogg's
Manchester Airport plc
Oldham
Seton Scholl Healthcare plc
Stockport
Cussons International Ltd

Hampshire
Basingstoke
Arjo Wiggins Appleton plc
De La Rue plc
Eli Lilly & Company Ltd
Eastleigh
Warner Lambert UK Ltd
Farnborough
British Aerospace plc
Portsmouth
Pall Europe Ltd
Southampton
Exxon Chemical Ltd
Vosper Thornycroft Holdings plc
Winchester
National Express Group plc

Hereford & Worcester
Hereford
H P Bulmer Holdings plc
Wyevale Garden Centres plc

Hertfordshire
Cheshunt
Tesco plc
Hemel Hempstead
Dixons Group plc
FI Group plc
Kodak Ltd
Hoddesdon
Merck Sharp & Dohme Holdings
Kings Langley
Astra Pharmaceuticals Ltd
Stevenage
Medical Insurance Agency Ltd
Watford
Camelot Group plc
Ladbroke Group PLC
Welwyn Garden City
Roche Products Ltd

Kent
Bexleyheath
Woolwich PLC
Folkestone
Eurotunnel plc
Saga Leisure Ltd
Sandwich
Pfizer Group Ltd
Sevenoaks
Marley plc
Tunbridge Wells
MCL Group Ltd
West Malling
GKN plc
Kimberley Clark Ltd

Lancashire
Barnoldswick
Silentnight Holdings plc
Blackburn
Scapa Group plc
Bolton
Warburtons Ltd

Darwen
Wolstenholme Rink plc
Fleetwood
Lofthouse of Fleetwood Ltd
Ramsbottom
TNT UK Ltd
Rochdale
Co-operative Retail Services Ltd

Leicestershire
Ibstock
Wilson Bowden plc
Leicester
Express Dairies plc
Next plc
Markfield
Aggregate Industries plc

Lincolnsire
Louth
Linpac Group Ltd

London
Abbott Mead Vickers plc
Acatos & Hutcheson plc
Akzo Nobel UK plc
Alliance & Leicester plc
Allied Domecq PLC
Allied London Properties plc
Amerada Hess Ltd
Arthur Andersen
Andersen Consulting
Antofagasta Holdings plc
Arcadia Group plc
Asprey Holdings UK Ltd
Associated British Foods plc
Associated British Ports Holdings
AXA Sun Life Insurance plc
BAA plc
William Baird plc
Bank of England
Barclays PLC
Barlow International PLC
Bass plc
BBA Group plc
Bestway (Holdings) Ltd
BICC plc
Blue Circle Industries PLC
BMP DDB Ltd
Booker plc
British American Tobacco plc
British Land Company plc
British Petroleum Company plc
British Steel plc
British Telecommunications plc
Brixton Estate plc
BTR plc
Bunzl plc
BUPA Ltd
C & A Stores
Cable & Wireless plc
Cadbury Schweppes plc
Cadogan Estates Ltd
Caledonia Group Services Ltd
Camellia plc
Caparo Group Ltd
Carlton Communications plc

Geographical index

Charter plc
Charterhouse plc
Chelsfield plc
Christie's International plc
Compass Group plc
Cookson Group plc
Cooper Gay (Holdings) Ltd
Cordiant Communications Group
Cornhill Insurance plc
Courtaulds Textiles plc
Coutts & Co
Daejan Holdings plc
Daily Mail & General Trust plc
De La Rue plc
Debenhams plc
Delta plc
Deloitte & Touche
Deutsche Morgan Grenfell
Diageo plc
Diamond Trading Company
Dresdner Kleinwort Benson
Economist Newspaper Ltd
Eidos plc
Elementis plc
EMI Group plc
Enterprise Oil plc
Express Newspapers plc
Favermead Ltd
Robert Fleming Holdings Ltd
Flextech plc
General Electric Company plc
Gerrard Group plc
GGT Group plc
Glencore UK Ltd
Granada Group plc
Great Portland Estates plc
GTECH UK Corporation
Guardian Royal Exchange plc
Hambros PLC
Hammerson plc
Hanover Acceptances Ltd
Hanson plc
Heath Group plc
Henderson plc
Hillsdown Holdings plc
House of Fraser PLC
HSBC Holdings plc
Hunting plc
IBM United Kingdom Holdings Ltd
Imperial Chemical Industries plc
Inchcape plc
Independent Insurance Group plc
Interpublic Ltd
Jardine Lloyd Thompson Group
Johnson Matthey plc
Jupiter Asset Management
Kingfisher plc
KPMG
Laird Group plc
Lambert Fenchurch Group plc
Land Securities PLC
Laporte plc
LASMO plc
Lazard Brothers & Co Ltd
Legal & General plc
Levi Strauss (UK) Ltd
John Lewis Partnership plc
Limit plc

Lloyd's of London
Lloyds TSB Group plc
London Electricity plc
London Forfaiting Company PLC
London Stock Exchange
Lowe Group
LucasVarity plc
M & G Group plc
E D & F Man Plc
Marks and Spencer plc
J H Marsh McLennan Ltd
McDonald's Ltd
Medeva plc
MEPC plc
Mercury Asset Management Group
Meyer International plc
MFI Furniture Group plc
Mirror Group plc
Morgan Stanley & Co International
Napier Brown Holdings Ltd
National Magazine Co Ltd
NatWest Group
Neville Russell
Newarthill plc
News International plc
Nortel Ltd
Northern & Shell Group Ltd
Osborne & Little plc
P & O Steam Navigation Company
Pannell Kerr Forster
Pearson plc
Pentland Group plc
Philips Electronics UK Ltd
PIC International Group PLC
The Post Office
PricewaterhouseCoopers
Prudential Corporation plc
Psion plc
Railtrack Group plc
The Rank Group Plc
Reader's Digest Association Ltd
Reuters Holdings PLC
Rexam PLC
Richer Sounds plc
The Rio Tinto plc
Rolls-Royce plc
N M Rothschild & Sons Ltd
Royal Automobile Club Ltd
J Sainsbury plc
St James Place Capital plc
Salomon Smith Barney Europe Ltd
Save & Prosper Group Ltd
Savills plc
Schroders plc
Sears plc
Sedgwick Group plc
Shell UK Limited
Singer & Friedlander Group plc
W H Smith Group plc
David S Smith Holdings plc
Smith & Nephew plc
Smiths Industries plc
Standard Chartered plc
Storehouse plc
J Swire & Sons Ltd
Tate & Lyle plc
Taylor Woodrow plc
TBI plc

Telegraph Group Ltd
Tempus Group plc
Texaco Ltd
Thomson Corporation
3i Group plc
Tioxide Group Ltd
Tomkins plc
Transport Development Group plc
Unigate plc
Unilever
United News & Media plc
Vendôme Luxury Group plc
Vickers plc
Wassall plc
Whitbread plc
Willis Corroon Group plc
Willmott Dixon Ltd
Wogen Group Ltd
Rudolf Wolff & Co Ltd
WPP Group plc
Young & Rubicam Holdings UK plc
ZENECA Group PLC

Merseyside
Ellesmere Port
Van Leer (UK) Holdings Ltd
Liverpool
Littlewoods Organisation PLC
Mersey Docks & Harbour Company
Royal & Sun Alliance Insurance
Stanley Leisure plc
St Helens
Pilkington plc

Middlesex
Brentford
SmithKline Beecham plc
Enfield
Raine's Dairy Foods Ltd
Tibett & Britten Group plc
Greenford
GlaxoWellcome plc
Hayes
H J Heinz Company Ltd
Safeway plc
Hounslow
Bristol-Myers Squibb Holdings Ltd
British Airways plc
Isleworth
British Sky Broadcasting Group plc
Gillette Industries plc
Southall
Serco Group plc
Stanmore
Dhamecha Foods Ltd
Uxbridge
Coats Viyella plc
Coca Cola Great Britain
Tetra Pak Ltd
Unisys Ltd
Xerox (UK) Ltd
West Drayton
Dow Chemical Company Ltd
United Biscuits (UK) Ltd

Geographical index

Norfolk
Norwich
- Bernard Matthews plc
- Norwich Union plc

North Yorkshire
Scarborough
- McCain Foods (GB) Ltd

York
- Nestlé UK Ltd
- Persimmon plc
- Shepherd Building Group Ltd

Northamptonshire
Kettering
- Weetabix Ltd

Northampton
- Avon Cosmetics Ltd
- Christian Salvesen PLC
- Travis Perkins plc

Wellingborough
- Scott Bader Company Ltd
- R Griggs Group Ltd

Worksop
- Wilkinson Hardware Stores Ltd

Nottinghamshire
Nottingham
- Boots Company PLC
- East Midlands Electricity plc

Oxfordshire
Abingdon
- RM plc
- TI Group plc

Didcot
- AEA Technology plc

Eynsham
- Oxford Instruments plc

Henley-on-Thames
- Hallmark Cards (Holdings) Ltd
- Perpetual plc

Oxford
- Electrocomponents plc
- Oakhill Group Ltd
- UGC Ltd Unipart Group of Cos

Shropshire
Telford
- EDS International Ltd

South Yorkshire
Barnsley
- S R Gent plc

Edlington
- Polypipe plc

Harworth
- RJB Mining plc

Staffordshire
Leek
- Britannia Building Society

Rocester
- J C Bamford Excavators Ltd

Stoke-on-Trent
- Michelin Tyre plc
- Waterford Wedgwood UK plc

Suffolk
Ipswich
- Eastern Group plc

Surrey
Addlestone
- Toshiba Information Systems (UK)

Camberley
- Johnson Wax Ltd

Cobham
- Berkeley Group plc
- Cargill plc

Croydon
- Allders plc
- Mott Macdonald Group Ltd

Dorking
- Biwater Ltd
- Friends' Provident Life Office

Guildford
- Colgate-Palmolive Ltd
- Hays plc
- Sanofi Winthrop Ltd

Kenley
- Gardner Merchant Services Group

Kingston-upon-Thames
- Bentalls plc

Leatherhead
- Esso UK plc

Richmond
- Compaq Computer Ltd

Surbiton
- Samsung Electronics UK Ltd

Sutton
- Securicor plc

Thorpe
- RMC Group plc

Wallington
- Canon (UK) Ltd

Walton-on-Thames
- Air Products plc

Weybridge
- Caradon plc
- Gallaher Group Plc
- Sony United Kingdom Ltd
- TI Group plc

Windlesham
- BOC Group plc

Tyne & Wear
Gosforth
- Northern Rock plc
- Procter & Gamble Ltd

Newcastle upon Tyne
- Bellway plc
- Fenwick Ltd
- The Go Ahead Group PLC
- Greggs plc
- Newcastle Building Society
- Northern Electric plc
- Proctor & Gamble UK

Sunderland
- Arriva plc
- Reg Vardy plc
- Vaux Group plc

Warwickshire
Gallows Hill
- Conoco Ltd

Kenilworth
- CEF Holdings Ltd

Rugby
- Rugby Group plc

West Midlands
Birmingham
- Betterware plc
- Birmingham International Airport
- Britannic Assurance plc
- Glynwed International plc
- IMI plc
- Severn Trent plc
- Specialist Computer Holdings Ltd
- Wagon plc

Coventry
- Jaguar Cars Ltd
- The National Grid Group plc
- Peugeot Motor Company plc
- PowerGen plc

Oldbury
- Albright & Wilson plc

Wolverhampton
- Birmingham Midshires Building Society
- Tarmac plc

West Sussex
East Grinstead
- Rentokil Initial plc

Littlehampton
- Body Shop International PLC

Geographical index

West Yorkshire
Bingley
Bradford & Bingley Building Society
Bradford
Congregational & General Insurance
Ellis & Everard plc
Empire Stores Group plc
Wm Morrison Supermarkets plc
Provident Financial plc
Yorkshire Building Society
Burley-in-Wharfedale
Fine Art Developments plc
Halifax
FKI plc
Halifax plc
Huddersfield
L Batley (Holdings) Ltd
Keighley
Peter Black Holdings plc
Leeds
ASDA Group plc
Evans of Leeds plc
Thistle Hotels plc
Waddington plc
Yorkshire Bank plc
Yorkshire Electricity Group plc
Yorkshire-Tyne Tees Television Ltd
Yorkshire Water plc
Saltaire
Filtronic plc
Wakefield
Kalon Group plc

Wiltshire
Bradford-on-Avon
Avon Rubber plc
Swindon
Allied Dunbar Assurance plc
Burmah Castrol plc
Intel Corporation UK Ltd
National Power PLC
Nationwide Building Society
Raychem UK Ltd
Thames Water plc

Worcestershire
Whittington
Midlands Electricity plc

Ireland
Belfast
Bombardier Aerospace – Short Brothers plc
Viridian Group PLC

Scotland
Aberdeen
Chevron UK Ltd
Elf Petroleum UK PLC
FirstGroup plc
Ramco Energy plc
Total Oil Marine plc
John Wood Group plc
Bellshill
William Grant & Sons Distilleries Ltd
Dundee
Alldays plc
Low & Bonar plc
Edinburgh
Bank of Scotland
British Energy
Kwik-Fit Holdings plc
John Menzies plc
Morrison Construction Group Ltd
The Royal Bank of Scotland Group
Scottish Equitable plc
Scottish & Newcastle plc
Scottish Widows' Fund & Life Assurance Society
Glasgow
Aon UK Ltd
Celtic PLC
Clydesdale Bank PLC
Devro plc
Grampian Holdings plc
Scottish Media Group plc
Scottish Power plc
Weir Group plc
Glenrothes
Tullis Russell Group Ltd
Paisley
Seagram Distillers PLC
Perth
The Highland Distilleries Co plc
Scottish Hydro-Electric plc
Stagecoach Holdings plc
Stirling
Scotia Holdings PLC
Scottish Amicable Life plc

Wales
Aberdare
Celtic Group Holdings Ltd
Cardiff
Hyder plc
Matsushita Electric (UK) Ltd
Deeside
Iceland Group plc
Ewloe
Redrow Group plc
Talacre
BHP Petroleum Ltd

Classification of companies by activity

This section classifies the companies included in the guide according to their main activities. It should enable charities to target companies for specific appeals or services. Companies which fall into two or more categories are listed under each one, except in the more obvious cases, for example building companies and property companies, where the categories have been cross-referenced. Retailers have been split into further separate categories due to the diversity covered.

Accountants
- Arthur Andersen
- Andersen Consulting
- Deloitte & Touche
- KMPG
- Neville Russell
- Pannell Kerr Forster
- PricewaterhouseCoopers

Advertising/marketing
- Abbott Mead Vickers plc
- BMP DDB Ltd
- Cordiant Communications Group
- GGT Group plc
- Interpublic Ltd
- Lowe Group
- Tempus Group plc
- WPP Group plc
- Young & Rubicam Holdings plc

Aerospace
- Bombardier Aerospace – Short Brothers plc
- British Aerospace plc
- Cobham plc
- Hunting plc
- LucasVarity plc
- Smiths Industries plc

Agriculture/farming
- Camellia plc
- E D & F Man plc
- Pfizer Ltd
- PIC International Group plc

Airport operators
- BAA plc
- Birmingham International Airport
- Bombardier Aerospace – Short Brothers plc
- Manchester Airport plc
- TBI plc

Auctioneers
- Christie's International plc

Aviation
- British Airways plc
- J Swire & Sons Ltd

Banks
- Abbey National plc
- Alliance & Leicester plc
- Bank of England
- Bank of Scotland
- Barclays plc
- Bristol & West plc
- Charterhouse plc
- Clydesdale Bank plc
- Co-operative Bank plc
- Coutts & Co
- Deutsche Morgan Grenfell Group
- Dresdner Kleinwort Benson
- Robert Fleming Holdings Ltd
- Halifax plc
- Hambros plc
- Household International UK Ltd
- HSBC Holdings plc
- Lazard Brothers & Co Ltd
- Lloyds TSB Group plc
- NatWest Group plc
- N M Rothschild & Son Ltd
- Royal Bank of Scotland Group plc
- Singer & Friedlander Group plc
- Standard Chartered plc
- Woolwich plc
- Yorkshire Bank plc

Brewers/distillers
- Allied Domecq plc
- Bass plc
- Diageo plc
- William Grant & Sons Ltd
- Highland Distillers plc
- Scottish & Newcastle plc
- Seagram Distillers plc
- Vaux Group plc
- Whitbread plc

Building/construction
(see also Property)
- AMEC plc
- Bellway plc
- Berkeley Group plc
- Caradon plc
- Eurotunnel plc
- Hillsdown Holdings plc
- Morrison Construction Group Ltd
- Newarthill plc
- Persimmon plc
- Redrow plc
- Shepherd Building Group Ltd
- Tarmac plc
- Taylor Woodrow plc
- Willmott Dixon Ltd
- Wilson Bowden plc

Building materials
- Aggregate Industries plc
- Blue Circle Industries plc
- BPB plc
- BTR plc
- Hanson plc
- Marley plc
- Meyer International plc
- Polypipe plc
- Rexam plc
- RMC Group plc
- Rugby Group plc
- Tarmac plc
- Travis Perkins plc
- Wickes plc
- Williams plc
- Yule Catto & Co plc

Building societies
- Birmingham Midshires Building Society
- Bradford & Bingley Building Society
- Britannia Building Society
- Nationwide Building Society
- Newcastle Building Society
- Yorkshire Building Society

Company activity index

Business equipment
Danka UK plc
Xerox (UK) Ltd

Business services
Canon (UK) Ltd
EDS International Ltd
Hays plc
Reed Executive plc
Rentokil Initial plc
Serco Group plc
Thomson Corporation
Tullis Russell Group Ltd
WPP Group plc

Cash & carry
L Batley (Holdings) Ltd
Bestway (Holdings) Ltd
Dhamecha Foods Ltd
Makro Self-Service Wholesalers

Catering services
Gardner Merchant Services Group Ltd

Chemicals & plastics
Air products plc
Akzo Nobel UK plc
Albright & Wilson plc
Scott Bader Company Ltd
BASF plc
Bayer plc
BOC Group plc
British Alcan Aluminium plc
British Vita plc
BTP plc
Burmah Castrol plc
Ciba Specialty Chemicals PLC
Cookson Group plc
Dow Chemical Company Ltd
Elementis plc
Ellis & Everard plc
English China Clays plc
Exxon Chemical Ltd
Glynwed International plc
Imperial Chemical Industries plc
Kodak Ltd
Laporte plc
Pfizer Ltd
3M UK Holdings plc
Tioxide Group Ltd
Yule Catto & Co plc
ZENECA plc

Clothing manufacture
William Baird plc
Peter Black Holdings plc
BTR plc
Charnos plc
Claremont Garment Holdings plc
Coats Viyella plc
Dewhirst Group plc
S R Gent plc
R Griggs Group Ltd
Levi Strauss (UK) Ltd
Pentland Group plc

Commodity traders
Cargill plc
Glencore UK Ltd
Rudolf Wolff & Co Ltd

Computers (see Electrical/computers)

Computer software
Eidos plc
FI Group plc
GTech UK Corporation
RM plc

Confectionery
Cadbury Schweppes plc
Lofthouse of Fleetwood Ltd
Mars UK Ltd
Nestle UK Ltd
Palmer & Harvey Mclane Ltd
Thorntons plc

Construction (see Building/construction)

Defence
British Aerospace plc
Cobham plc
Hunting plc
Marconi Marine
Vickers plc

Distribution
Booker plc
Bunzl plc
Cargill plc
Marlowe Holdings Ltd
John Menzies plc
Napier Brown Holdings Ltd
Unigate plc
Wassall plc

Drinks manufacture
Bass plc
H P Bulmer Holdings plc
Cadbury Schweppes plc
Coca-Cola Great Britain
Nestle UK Ltd
SmithKline Beecham plc

Edible oils
Acatos & Hutcheson plc

Electrical/computers
BTR plc
CEF Holdings Ltd
Cobham plc
Compaq Computer Ltd
Delta plc
Electrocomponents plc
Filtronic plc
General Electric Company plc
Hewlett-Packard Ltd
IBM United Kingdom Holdings Ltd
ICL plc
Intel Corporation Ltd
Matsushita Electric (UK) Ltd
Nortel plc
Panasonic UK Ltd
Philips Electronics UK Ltd
Psion plc
RM plc
Samsung Electronics UK Ltd
Sony United Kingdom Ltd
Spandex plc
Specialist Computer Holdings Ltd
Toshiba Information Systems (UK)
Unisys Ltd

Electricity
British Energy plc
British Nuclear Fuels plc
Eastern Group plc
Hyder plc
London Electricity plc
Manweb plc
Midlands Electricity plc
National Grid Company plc
National Power plc
Northern Electric plc
PowerGen plc
Scottish Hydro-Electric plc
Scottish Power plc
Seeboard plc
South Western Electricity plc
Southern Electric plc
United Utilities PLC
Viridian Group plc
Yorkshire Electricity Group plc

Engineering
AEA Technology plc
AMEC plc
BBA Group plc
BICC plc
Biwater plc
Caparo Group Ltd
Charter plc
Cummins Engine Co Ltd
Delta plc
FKI plc
GKN plc
IMI plc
Laird Group plc
Marconi Marine
Mayflower Corporation plc
Morgan Crucible plc
Powell Duffryn plc
Raychem UK Ltd
Renishaw plc
Rexam plc
Rockwell International plc
Rolls Royce plc
Scapa Group plc
Siebe plc
Smiths Industries plc
Spirax Sarco Engineering plc
TI Group plc
TT Group plc
Vickers plc
Vosper Thornycroft Holdings plc
Wagon plc
Wassall plc
Weir Group plc
John Wood Group plc

Company activity index

Financial companies (see also Banks and Insurance)
Caledonia Group Services Ltd
Camellia plc
Charterhouse plc
Clerical Medical Investment Group Ltd
Gerrard Group plc
Henderson plc
HSBC Holdings plc
Jupiter Asset Management
Liberty International Holdings plc
Liverpool Victoria Friendly Society
Lloyds TSB Group plc
London Forfaiting Company plc
M & G Group plc
E D & F Man Plc
Mercury Asset Management plc
Morgan Stanley & Company International Ltd
NatWest Group
Northern Rock plc
Perpetual plc
Prudential Corporation plc
St James Place Capital plc
Salomon Smith Barney Europe Ltd
Save & Prosper Group Ltd
Schroders plc
3i Group plc
Wilson Bowden plc

Food manufacture
Associated British Foods plc
Diageo plc
Express Dairies plc
Greggs plc
Hanover Acceptances Ltd
Hazlewood Foods plc
H J Heinz Company Ltd
Hillsdown Holdings plc
Kellogg's
Kraft Jacobs Suchard Ltd
McCain Foods (GB) Ltd
Bernard Matthews plc
Monsanto plc
Napier Brown Holdings Ltd
Nestle UK Ltd
Northern Foods plc
Perkins Foods plc
Raine's Dairy Foods Ltd
Unigate plc
Unilever
United Biscuits (Holdings) plc
Warburtons Ltd
Weetabix Ltd

Food services
Alldays plc
Compass Group plc
Albert Fisher Group plc
Christian Salvesen plc

Furniture manufacture
Cadogan Estates Ltd
MFI Furniture Group plc
Silentnight Holdings plc

Gaming
Camelot Group plc
Ladbroke Group plc
Littlewoods Organisation plc

Garden centres
Wyvale Garden Centres plc

Glass
Pilkington plc

Healthcare (see also Chemical, and Pharmaceutical)
Boots Company plc
BUPA Ltd
Pfizer Group Ltd
Proctor & Gamble UK
Seton Scholl Healthcare plc
Smith & Nephew plc
SmithKline Beecham plc

Household/personal care
Avon Cosmetics Ltd
Peter Black Holdings plc
Bristol-Myers Squibb Holdings Ltd
Colgate-Palmolive Ltd
Cussons International Ltd
Dewhirst Group plc
Gillette Industries plc
Johnson Wax Ltd
Kalon Group plc
Kimberley Clark Ltd
McBride plc
Osborne & Little plc
Proctor & Gamble UK
Reckitt & Colman plc
Sapalux Ltd
Unilever
Warner Lambert UK Ltd
Waterford Wedgwood UK plc
Wilkinson Hardware Stores Ltd

Industrial services
Camellia plc
Caparo Group Ltd
Foster Wheeler Ltd
Tomkins plc

Instrumentation
Huntleigh Technology plc
Oxford Instruments plc

Insurance (see also Life assurance)
Aon UK Ltd
AXA Provincial Insurance plc
BUPA Ltd
CGU plc
Co-operative Insurance Society Ltd
Congregational & General Insurance plc
Cooper (Gay) Holdings Ltd
Cornhill Insurance plc
Ecclesiastical Insurance Group plc
Friends' Provident Life Office
Guardian Royal Exchange plc
Heath Group plc
Household International UK Ltd
Independent Insurance Group plc
Jardine Lloyd Thompson Group Services
Lambert Fenchurch Group plc
Legal & General plc
Limit plc
Liverpool Victoria Friendly Society
Lloyd's of London
J & H Marsh & McLennon Ltd
Medical Insurance Agency Ltd
Norwich Union plc
Provident Financial plc
Prudential Corporation plc
Royal Bank of Scotland Group plc
Royal London Mutual Insurance Society Ltd
Royal & Sun Alliance Insurance Group plc
Scottish Equitable plc
Sedgwick Group plc
Willis Corroon plc

Leisure
Airtours plc
Allied Domecq plc
Bass plc
Caledonia Group Services Ltd
Celtic PLC
Chelsfield plc
Granada Group plc
Greenalls Group plc
Ladbroke Group plc
Rank Group plc
Saga Leisure Ltd
Scottish & Newcastle plc
Stanley Leisure plc
Thistle Hotels plc
Vaux Group plc
Whitbread plc

Life assurance
Allied Dunbar Assurance plc
AXA Sun Life Assurance plc
Britannic Assurance plc
Pearl Assurance plc
Scottish Amicable Life plc
Scottish Widows Fund & Life Assurance Society
United Assurance Group plc

Logistics
NFC plc
Christian Salvesen plc
TNT UK Ltd
Transport Development Group plc

Media
British Sky Broadcasting Group plc
Carlton Communications plc
Daily Mail & General Trust plc
Economist Newspaper Ltd
EMAP plc
Express Newspapers plc
Flextech plc
Granada Group plc
Guardian Media Group plc

Company activity index

Mirror Group plc
National Magazine Co Ltd
News International plc
Northern & Shell Group Ltd
Pearson plc
Reader's Digest Association Ltd
Reuters Holdings plc
Scottish Media Group plc
Telegraph Group Ltd
Trinity International Holdings plc
United News & Media plc
Yattendon Investment Trust plc
Yorkshire-Tyne Tees Television Ltd

Metals

British Alcan Aluminium plc
British Steel plc
Glynwed International plc
Johnson Matthey plc
Wogen Group plc

Mining

Antofagasta Holdings plc
Celtic Group Holdings Ltd
Diamond Trading Company
Rio Tinto plc
RJB Mining plc

Miscellaneous

Post Office Group

Motors & accessories manufacture/distribution (including car hire)

Arriva plc
Avon Rubber plc
BCH Group plc
BMW GB Ltd
Citroen UK Ltd
Fiat Auto (UK) Ltd
Ford Motor Company Ltd
Honda Motor Europe Ltd
Inchcape plc
Jaguar Cars Ltd
Kwik-Fit Holdings plc
Lex Service plc
LucasVarity plc
MCL Group Ltd
Michelin Tyre plc
Oakhill Group Ltd
Peugeot Motor Co plc
Royal Automobile Club Ltd
Toyota Motor Manufacturing (UK) Ltd
UGC Unipart Group of Companies
Reg Vardy plc
Vauxhall Motors Ltd

Music

EMI Group plc

Oil & gas/fuel

Amerada Hess Ltd
BG plc
BHP Petroleum Ltd
British Nuclear Fuels plc
British Petroleum Company plc
Burmah Castrol plc
Centrica plc
Chevron (UK) Ltd
Conoco Ltd
Elf Petroleum UK plc
Enterprise Oil plc
Esso UK plc
Hunting plc
Hyder plc
LASMO plc
Mobil Holdings Ltd
Ramco Energy plc
ScottishPower plc
Seeboard plc
Shell UK Ltd
Texaco Ltd
Total Oil Marine plc
United Utilities plc

Pharmaceutical

Astra Pharmaceuticals Ltd
BASF plc
Bayer plc
Boots Company plc
Bristol-Myers Squibb Holdings Ltd
Cussons International Ltd
Glaxo Wellcome plc
Eli Lilly Group Ltd
Medeva plc
Merck Sharp & Dohme Ltd
Monsanto plc
Nycomed Amersham plc
Reckitt & Colman plc
Roche Products Ltd
Sanofi Winthrop Ltd
Scotia Holdings plc
SmithKline Beecham plc
Warner Lambert UK Ltd
ZENECA plc

Plant equipment

J C Bamford Excavators Ltd
Barlow International plc

Print/paper/packaging

Arjo Wiggins Appleton plc
Barlow International plc
Bunzl plc
De La Rue plc
Devro plc
Field Group plc
Linpac Group Ltd
Low & Bonar plc
Norcros plc
Rexam plc
Scapa Group plc
David S Smith (Holdings) plc
Tetra Pak Ltd
Tullis Russell Group Ltd
Van Leer (UK) Holdings Ltd
Waddington plc
Wolstenholme Rink plc

Property

Allied London Properties plc
AMEC plc
Berkeley Group plc
British Land Company plc
Brixton Estate plc
Cadogan Estates Ltd
Caledonia Group Services Ltd
Chelsfield plc
Daejan Holdings plc
Dhameca Foods Ltd
Evans of Leeds plc
Favermead plc
Great Portland Estates plc
Hammerson plc
Hanover Acceptances Ltd
Kingfisher plc
Land Securities plc
MEPC Group plc
Newarthill plc
P & O Steam Navigation Company
Redrow plc
Savills plc
Singer & Friedlander plc
Slough Estates plc
J Swire & Sons Ltd
Taylor & Woodrow plc
TBI plc
Wilson Bowden plc

Quarrying

Aggregate Industries plc

Retailers

Catalogue retail

Argos plc
Avon Cosmetics Ltd
Betterware plc
Empire Stores Group plc
Fine Art Developments plc
Littlewoods Organisation
Next plc
Storehouse plc

Clothing & footwear

Arcadia Group plc
C & A Stores
Grampian Holdings plc
Marks & Spencer plc
Next plc
Sears plc

Department & variety stores

Allders plc
Bentalls plc
Co-operative Retail Services Ltd
Debenhams plc
Fenwick Ltd
House of Fraser plc
Kingfisher plc
John Lewis Partnership plc
Littlewoods Organisation
W H Smith Group plc
Storehouse plc

DIY/furniture

Kingfisher plc
MFI Furniture Group plc
J Sainsbury plc
Wickes plc
Wilkinson Hardware Stores Ltd

Electrical (including rental)

Dixons Group plc
Granada Group plc
Kingfisher plc
Richer Sounds plc
Thorn UK

Off-licence
Allied Domecq plc
Greenalls Group plc
Seagram Distillers plc

Restaurants/fast food
Allied Domecq plc
Compass Group plc
Diageo plc
McDonald's UK
Whitbread plc

Supermarkets
ASDA Group plc
Co-operative Retail Services Ltd
Iceland Group plc
John Lewis Partnership plc
Wm Morrison Supermarkets plc
Safeway plc
J Sainsbury plc
Somerfield Stores plc
Tesco plc

Miscellaneous
Alldays plc *(Convenience stores)*
Asprey Holdings UK Ltd *(Jewellers)*
Body Shop International plc *(Cosmetics)*
Boots Company plc *(Chemist)*
Clinton Cards Plc *(Greeting cards)*
EMI Group plc *(Music, books)*
Fine Art Developments plc *(Stationery)*
Greggs plc *(Bakers)*
Hallmark Cards (Holdings) Ltd *(Greeting cards)*
John Menzies plc *(Toys)*
Richer Sounds plc *(Hi-fi)*
Thorntons plc *(Confectionery)*
Vendome Luxury Group plc *(Luxury products)*

Security services
Securicor plc
Williams plc

Securities/shares
London Stock Exchange

Sugar refiners
British Sugar plc
Tate & Lyle plc

Telecommunications
British Telecommunications plc
Cable & Wireless plc
Nortel Ltd
Orange plc
Racal Electronics plc
ScottishPower plc
Toshiba Information Systems (UK)
Vodafone Group plc

Textiles
Coats Viyella plc
Courtaulds Textiles plc
Dewhirst Group plc
Osborne & Little plc

Tobacco
British American Tobacco plc
Gallaher Group plc
Imperial Tobacco Group plc
Palmer & Harvey McLane Ltd
Rothmans International Tobacco (UK) Ltd

Transport & shipping
Arriva plc
Associated British Ports Holdings plc
FirstGroup plc
Go Ahead Group plc
Grampian Holdings plc
Mersey Docks & Harbour Company
National Express Group plc
Ocean Group plc
P & O Steam Navigation Company
Powell Duffryn plc
Railtrack plc
Securicor plc
Stagecoach Holdings plc
Stobart Investments Ltd
J Swire & Sons Ltd
Tibbett & Britten Group plc
Transport Development Group PLC
Unigate plc

Waste management
Biwater plc
North West Water Ltd
Severn Trent Plc

Water
Anglian Water plc
Essex & Suffolk Water plc
Hyder plc
North West Water Ltd
Northumbrian Water Group plc
Pennon Group plc
Severn Trent plc
Thames Water plc
United Utilities plc
Wessex Water plc
Yorkshire Water plc

Water filtration products
Pall Europe Ltd

Alphabetical listing of companies

This section gives information on over 530 companies from all sectors of industry, mainly gained from annual reports and information supplied by Financial Times Information Ltd, supplemented by our own research. The general layout showing the information on each company is on pages 46–47.

Types of company

A company may be: a public limited company (designated plc), normally a company with shares quoted on the stock exchange; a privately owned company; or a subsidiary company. If it is a subsidiary it may have retained its own identity for charitable donations and we would include an entry in this guide. Other subsidiaries included are British based subsidiaries of an overseas-based company.

Where a company has been recently acquired it may not yet have decided whether it will continue to manage its own donations budget.

Through acquisitions and mergers, companies may now be owned by a holding company, a conglomerate, or a transnational company. We usually only give the name of the holding company. You may have to do your own research to link local companies and plants with the head office that may have ultimately control over their donations. The company annual report, usually available free on request, lists subsidiary and associate (less than 50% owned) companies and reports on the activity of the company during the year. We have included the main subsidiaries of each company within the entry. However, for many companies this is taken from the latest annual report, which can be several months out of date. The *Who Owns Whom* directory also lists subsidiaries of UK companies.

Interpreting financial information

The charitable donations figure given is that published by the company. It usually relates only to cash donations and does not include the value of secondments, gifts in kind, advertising or sponsorship. Furthermore, a company's present level of donations does not necessarily indicate future commitments. Sending an appeal to less generous companies may even persuade them to increase their donations. Certainly if they never receive appeals there will be no outside pressure on them to change their policy, although in general if a company is only giving a little your chances of success are reduced.

Normally a coordinated company donor will budget a certain sum for its charitable donations and stick within this amount. Some allocate all their budget at an annual meeting; others spread donations throughout the year. Some give to causes they wish to support until the budget is used up and then stop; others continue to give even after the budget is spent if an appeal takes their fancy. If they reply to your appeal, many will write and say that their budget is 'fully committed'. Often this is simply a polite way of refusing support.

The year end is important in that if you get your appeal in soon afterwards the company will not have spent its charitable budget for the coming year. However, if a company allocates its budget evenly throughout the year and receives a flood of applications at the start of its new financial year, some which would have been supported later in the year now miss out. There is no fail-safe answer to this problem. However, your chances of success are usually improved by sending the application earlier rather than later in the company's financial year.

How to interpret the donations policy

There are certain standard phrases that appear in the policy of the company entries.

No response to circular appeals

This means that 'Dear Sir/Madam' letters, whether they are hand-signed or use photocopied signatures, are probably not even read, let alone replied to.

Preference for local charities in areas of company presence
Preference for appeals relevant to company business
Preference for charities where a member of staff is involved

These are self-explanatory. Local charities should check whether appeals can be made locally or must be sent to head office. Any link with the company should be highlighted.

Preferred areas of support are …

We asked companies to tick preferred areas of support to indicate the sort of appeals most likely to interest them

Exclusions (No grants for …)

The same list was used as for the preferred areas, with common exclusions being: fundraising events, advertising in charity brochures, appeals from individuals, denominational (religious) appeals, political/campaigning activity and bricks and mortar appeals.

Before applying, potential applicants should always consider whether there is a particular reason why the company might want to support them.

Fictitious Productions PLC

68 Nowhere Street, Anytown AN6 2LM
0151-000 0000; Fax: 0151-100 0000
website: www.fictprod.co.uk

Correspondent: A Grant, Public Relations Manager

Chief officers: *Chair:* T Story ;
Chief Executive: S Yarn

Year end	Turnover	Pre-tax profit
30/09/98	£863,200,000	£210,670,000

Nature of company business
The company is involved in production of fictitious information. Subsidiaries and locations include *Cashflow Industries* (Grimsby), *False Publications* (Liverpool), *Sundry Matters* (Bristol), and *Wage Packet Co* (Perth).

UK employees: 5,409

Charitable donations
1998: £250,000
1997: £210,000
1996: £240,000
1995: £190,000
1994: £125,000
Total community contributions: £650,000
Membership: %club; BitC

Company name: The full name of the company is given with the companies listed in alphabetical order.

Address: Head office to which appeals should be sent unless otherwise stated.

Telephone: Appeals should be submitted in **writing**, but you may wish to ask for details of the appeals procedure, request a copy of the latest annual report, or check the contact for charitable donations.

Contact for appeals: Only the very large corporate donors have specialist staff dealing with appeals. Appeals to many companies will be dealt with by the company secretary or public relations department.

Officers: We give the names of the *Chair; Chief Executive and/or Managing Director*. There is not room to list all members of the main board.

Financial statistics: The *year end, turnover, pre-tax profit* (a figure in brackets denotes a loss) and *employees*. Most relate to 1997/98. The figures give an indication of the scale of the company's giving relative to its size.

Nature of company business: The main area of activity is given, together with subsidiaries and locations (where known). This can be useful if you are looking for a product or geographical link.

Charitable donations: Figures for the last five years are given, together with a figure for total community contributions (which includes the cost of in kind giving, arts sponsorship, secondments etc.), where available.

Community support policy

The company is a member of the PerCent Club and Business in the Community. Community contributions totalled £650,000 in 1998, including in kind giving, cost of secondments and arts sponsorship as well as charitable donations.

Charitable donations: The company prefers to support local organisations in areas of company presence. It focuses its giving on sickness and disability, the arts, heritage, social welfare, education and youth, environment. National grants range from £100 to £10,000. Local grants range from £50 to £500.

Major grant recipients in 1998 included Any Town Disability Network, Perth Parent & Toddler Association and the local wildlife trust.

In kind support: The company donates surplus or used furniture/equipment to local causes.

Employee involvement: A payroll giving scheme is operated by the company. A charity is selected each year to benefit from employee fundraising, with the company making a contribution.

Enterprise: The company supports local enterprise agencies and considers secondment of employees to local economic development initiatives.

The arts: The typical sponsorship range is from £100 to £25,000. It sponsors Liverpool Symphony Orchestra and supported festivals in Grimsby and Perth.

Exclusions

No response to circular appeals. No grants for fundraising events, purely denominational (religious appeals), local appeals not in areas of company presence, large national appeals, overseas projects, political activities or individuals. Non-commercial advertising is not supported. It does not sponsor individuals or travel.

Applications

In writing to the correspondent. Applications are considered by a donations committee.

Community support: We state whether the company is a member of certain organisations and what support is given in addition to cash donations.

Charitable donations: The policy of the company in terms of what it prefers to support and whether there is any geographical preference.

Typical grants range, to indicate what a successful applicant can expect to receive.

Examples of grants, listing where possible the purpose and size of the grants. Large grants are often a good indicator of the company's priorities.

Some companies give gifts in kind, which can be anything from used stock to printing facilities.

Many company employees give time and money to local causes, including fundraising and expertise.

Information on the company's support for educational, enterprise and environmental initiatives, which may include cash donations and/or other forms of support.

Sponsorship and support for the arts is listed separately, stating whether the company is a member of Arts & Business

Exclusions: Listing any areas, subjects or types of grants the company will not consider.

Applications: Including how to apply and when to submit an application. We also state whether there is further information available from the company.

Abbey National plc

Abbey House, 201 Grafton Gate East,
Milton Keynes MK9 1AN
01908-341126; Fax: 01908-341200

Correspondent: K J Taylor, Secretary, Abbey National Charitable Trust

Chief officers: *Chairman:* Lord Tugendhat;
Chief Executive: Ian Harley

Year end	Turnover	Pre-tax profit
31/12/97	n/a	£1,424,000,000

Nature of company business
Principal activity: provision of personal financial services.
Main subsidiaries include: First National Bank; Cater Allen; HMC Group; Wagon Finance; Scottish Mutual Assurance.
Main locations: London; Milton Keynes; Bradford; Glasgow.

UK employees: 25,464

Charitable donations

1997: £565,000
1996: £464,000
1995: £450,000
1994: £450,000
1993: £420,000

Total community contributions: £1,430,000

Membership: *BitC*

Community support policy

In addition to including support in the form of gifts in kind, good cause sponsorship, training schemes and the value of staff time, the total community contributions figure also includes the total of donations made by the trust (which receives some of its income from its own investments), rather than the total made by the company, which is lower.

The Abbey National Charitable Trust

The trust (Charity Commission number 803655) was set up with an initial donation from Abbey National plc of £5 million following the sale of shares unclaimed since the company's flotation. This endowment fund received a further £750,000 from Abbey Housing Association Ltd, increasing the endowment fund to £5.75 million. By 1997, the assets stood at £8 million.

In 1997, the Abbey National Charitable Trust received £565,000 from the company and income from its own investments, giving a total income of £890,000. Total cash donations were £965,000 in 1997, of which £900,000 was given through the trust and the rest through other Abbey National Group companies.

In 1998, the trust supported charities dealing with the problems of homelessness and special housing needs and increased the proportion of donations targeted at charities working in the fields of equal opportunities for people with disabilities and families in crisis. This was achieved mainly through selection of appropriate recipients under the trust's major donation programme, whereby a few larger donations are made every year to organisations selected by the trustees.

Support for disability projects increased to £356,000, for family charity support to £135,000 and for housing and homelessness projects to £234,000. In all, 813 grants were made during the year. Donations do not normally exceed £20,000, and those given in response to unsolicited appeals are usually small (up to £500).

Under the policy to match employee donations, 376 staff donations were matched, totalling £124,000. The Workaid payroll giving scheme is operated.

The larger grants made by the trust were to Family Policy Studies Centre and Prince's Youth Business Trust (£25,000 each), Business in the Community (£21,500), Milton Keynes Community Trust, Almshouse Association and Barnardo's (£20,000 each). There were 60 donations of £5,000 or more.

In 1999, the priorities will be:

- equal opportunities for people with disabilities
- education and training for disadvantaged groups
- employment opportunities for disadvantaged groups.

The trust favours smaller charities, local charities or local appeals from national charities. Donations are normally given direct to charities and not through intermediaries. Consideration will be given to applicants seeking to match funds provisionally granted by the various lottery boards, provided they are for aspects of the proposed project which reflect the priorities of the trust.

Other support

In kind support: Support included equipment or materials free of charge and staff time.

Sponsorship: The company undertakes good cause sponsorship at national level, for example sponsorship of the RADAR People of the Year Awards. The arts are not sponsored.

Enterprise: The company is a member of Business in the Community. It helps youth unemployment through the 'Step up to Work' scheme.

Education: The company is involved in local education/business partnerships. It operates work experience schemes for pupils. It runs local school partnerships called 'Helping Hands'.

Exclusions

No support for fundraising events, advertising in charity brochures, appeals from individuals, local appeals not in areas of company presence, large national appeals, animal welfare charities, the arts, environment, medical research, political appeals, religious appeals, sport or overseas projects.

Applications

Appeals should be addressed to K J Taylor, Secretary, Abbey National Charitable Trust Ltd, at the address above. There is no formal application form. When applying for support, the trust requests that you give information on the activities, objectives and financial needs of your organisation, indicating clearly how they relate to the priorities of the trust. It is also helpful to include a recent newsletter or annual report. If you are successful in obtaining a donation from the trust, you may be contacted by a branch manager from Abbey National to arrange for a local presentation.

Information available: The company reports on its community involvement in its annual report and in the staff newsletter. A brochure is available on the company's community involvement.

Abbott Mead Vickers plc

151 Marylebone Road, London NW1 5QE
0171-616 3500; Fax: 0171-616 3600
Email: amvbbdo@amvbbdo.co.uk

Correspondent: Jeremy Hicks, Finance Director

Chief officers: *Chairman:* Peter Mead;
Chief Executive: Michael Baulk

Year end	Turnover	Pre-tax profit
31/12/97	£431,323,000	£17,282,000

Nature of company business
Advertising agency and marketing services.

Main subsidiaries include: McBain, Noel-Johnson & Co; Clarke Hooper Consulting; Craik Jones Watson Mitchell Voelkel; Momentum Integrated Communications; Frew, Macmaster; Redwood Publishing; Aurelia Public Relations; Freud Communications; Barraclough Hall Woolston Gray; Fishburn Hedges Boys Williams; New PHD; Drum PHD.

UK employees: 1,250

Charitable donations
1997: £99,000
1996: £159,000
1995: £105,000
1994: £136,000
1993: £75,000
Membership: *BitC %Club*

Community support policy

The company is a member of the PerCent Club and Business in the Community.

It prefers to support appeals relevant to company business and supports national (UK) charities rather than local causes. Up to 20 charities are supported each year, with the main beneficiary being the National Advertising Benevolent Society (NABS). Other beneficiaries include the Music Therapy Trust, Cancer Research, Designers and Art Directors Association and Royal Opera House Trust.

The company also offers strategic advice and develops advertising on a not-for-profit basis for a few charities including RSPCA, International Red Cross, Amnesty International, the Empty Homes Agency, Business in the Community and English Heritage.

Applications
In writing to Peter Warren or Adrian Vickers.

Acatos & Hutcheson plc

30 Orchard Place, London E14 0JH
0171-418 1500; Fax: 0171-987 0209

Correspondent: Stephen Filmer, Company Secretary

Chief officer: *Chairman:* I S Hutcheson

Year end	Turnover	Pre-tax profit
29/3/98	£150,901,000	(£2,897,000)

Nature of company business
The main activity of the company is the processing and marketing of oil and fat products.

Main subsidiaries include: Pura Food Products Ltd; Britannia Food Ingredients Ltd; Lean Frankel Ltd; Wallworths Ltd.

UK employees: 842

Charitable donations
1998: £53,540
1997: £20,440
1996: £90,542
1995: £72,883
1994: £26,243
Membership: *%Club*

Community support policy

The company is a member of the PerCent Club and has seen its charitable donations more than double in the last year, although it has not returned to the high of 1996.

The company only supports local charities near to its main operating sites ie. East London, Liverpool and Manchester. Areas of concern are: children/youth, education, elderly people and social welfare.

Two of the main beneficiaries of support are South Canning Town Youth House and Street Project (£18,000) and St Angela's School in Forest Gate (£25,000 towards computer-aided design equipment). Support was also given to Sargent Cancer Care for Children and the Malcolm Sargent Festival Choir.

The company is also involved in arts sponsorship, with a three-year commitment to the Spitalfields Festival and support for Christmas Concerts in Christ Church, Spitalfields, and a lunchtime concert in Cabot Hall, Canary Wharf, given by children from local East End schools.

Exclusions
No support for animal welfare charities, the arts, environment/heritage, political appeals, religious appeals or science/technology.

Applications
In writing to the correspondent.

AEA Technology plc

329 Harwell, Didcot, Oxfordshire OX11 0RA
01235-433542; Fax: 01235-436656
Website: www.aeat.co.uk

Correspondent: Mrs Cathy Wright, Corporate Community Involvement Manager

Chief officers: *Chairman:* Sir Anthony Cleaver; *Chief Executive:* Dr Peter Watson

Year end	Turnover	Pre-tax profit
31/3/98	£308,400,000	£29,000,000

Nature of company business
A broadly-based science and engineering business focused on five areas: technology-based products, specialised science, environmental management, improving the efficiency of industrial plant and risk assessment and safety management.

Main subsidiaries include: ERG Environmental Resource Group; Forensic Alliancen; Code International; DSB Special Batteries.

UK employees: n/a

Charitable donations
1998: £42,086
1997: n/a
1996: £34,415
1995: £15,200

Total community contributions: £160,000 (1996)

Membership: *BitC %Club*

Community support policy

The company supports activities in a small number of key areas. These are the environment, children and youth, the arts, overseas projects and creating awareness and understanding in education of the value of science, engineering and technology. Emphasis is given in these areas to activities which are close to company locations or involve company employees. Grants to local/national organisations range from £1,000 to £4,000.

The three main areas of non-cash support are arts sponsorship, gifts in kind and training schemes.

Exclusions

No support for fundraising events, advertising in charity brochures, appeals from individuals, purely denominational (religious) appeals or local appeals not in areas of company presence.

Applications

In writing to the correspondent. Sponsorship appeals should be addressed to Liz Roberts at the above address.

Aggregate Industries plc

Bardon Hall, Copt Oak Road, Markfield, Leicestershire LE67 9PJ
01530-816600; Fax: 01530-816666
Website: www.aggregateindustries.co.uk

Correspondent: Mrs Mary Ford, Assistant Company Secretary

Chief officers: *Chairman:* M E Warren; *Chief Executive:* P W G Tom

Year end	Turnover	Pre-tax profit
31/12/97	£600,700,000	£45,400,000

Nature of company business
The principal activities are quarrying, coated stone, surfacing, ready-mix concrete, sand and gravel, soil remediation, distribution of bitumen, concrete blocks, builders merchants, waste disposal, and architectural stone and memorials.

Main subsidiaries include: Bardon Aggregates; CAMAS Building Materials.

UK employees: 2,862

Charitable donations
1997: £49,000
1996: £49,000
1995: £18,000

Community support policy

Aggregate Industries plc was formed by the merger of CAMAS and Bardon in 1997. The charitable donations policy is not yet well established and it is therefore difficult to be more than vague. However, the company provided the following information for this guide.

The company has sites all over the UK, particularly in the East and West Midlands, London, the South West, Scotland and northern England. It supports charities local to those sites, especially those involved with environment/heritage or allied to the construction industry, medical research, science/technology, sickness/disability charities and social welfare. The company may also support animal welfare charities, the arts, children/youth, education, elderly people, enterprise/training, fundraising events and overseas projects.

Main beneficiaries in 1997 included The Lighthouse Club, Students Partnership Worldwide, Ilfracombe Lifeboat Station and Leukaemia Research Fund.

In addition to cash donations, the company undertakes good-cause sponsorship.

Exclusions

No support for advertising in charity brochures, political or religious appeals.

Applications

In writing to the correspondent.

Air Products plc

Hersham Place, Molesey Road, Walton-on-Thames, Surrey KT12 4RZ
01932-249200; Fax: 01932-249565

Correspondent: Mrs Prim Kennard, Secretary to the Charities Committee

Chief officer: *Chief Executive:* John Baker

Year end	Turnover	Pre-tax profit
30/9/95	£300,731,000	£12,536,000

Nature of company business
Principal activities: industrial gases and equipment manufacturers.
Main subsidiaries include: Anchor Chemical Group PLC; Anchor Chemical Ltd; Gardner Cryogenics Ltd; On-Sites Engineering Services Ltd.

UK employees: 1,999

Charitable donations
1997: £60,000
1996: £63,000
1995: £52,776
1994: £60,000
1993: £60,000
Membership: *BitC*

Community support policy

The information for this company has not been updated, but it has consistently given about £60,000 a year in charitable donations.

Charitable donations: The company continues to support:

(a) higher education institutions, where there is some relevance to the company's broad areas of interest

(b) organisations in the localities of its operations (Surrey, Crewe, Manchester, Basingstoke, Didcot, Sandwell, Gateshead and north Wales) concerned with health and welfare, local community and arts.

Grants are occasionally given to the local branch of national organisations and range from £250 to £6,000. Grants are more commonly given to local organisations and are for £50 to £5,000.

In kind support: Used equipment is passed on to schools, as are products with the company logo for use as raffle prizes. Discounts on balloon gas are occasionally offered to charities.

Employee involvement: The company gives preference to charities in which a member of staff is involved. It operates a payroll giving scheme for employees. Employees who are active in charitable fundraising frequently have funds matched (50% of the amount raised up to £1,000) by the company, primarily in the health and welfare fields. Staff are encouraged to become volunteers in their own time and to become school governors. Staff are also seconded to voluntary organisations such as Homestart.

Enterprise: The company is a member of Business in the Community and supports local enterprise agencies.

Education: The company provides work experience schemes for pupils and educational materials for schools.

Exclusions

No support is given to circular appeals, fundraising events, third parties, appeals from individuals, purely denominational (religious) appeals, local appeals not in areas of company presence, large national appeals, overseas projects, political parties or organisations, or for advertising in charity brochures.

Applications

In writing to the correspondent. The contributions committee meets every two months and reviews all appeals.

Airtours plc

Parkway Three, Parkway Business Centre, 300 Princess Road, Manchester M14 7QU
0161-232 0066; Fax: 0161-232 6533

Correspondent: Jill Hayward, Personnel Officer

Chief officers: *Chairman:* D Crossland; *Managing Director:* A H Coe

Year end	Turnover	Pre-tax profit
30/9/97	£2,174,300,000	£120,300,000

Nature of company business
The principal activities are within the leisure travel industry.
Main subsidiaries include: Airtours Holidays; Eurosites; Sun Cruises; Going Places; Leisure Travel; Blue Sea Investments.

Charitable donations
1997: £57,000
1996: £30,000
1995: £3,000

Community support policy

The company's donations have increased markedly over the last two years.

It prefers to support charities concerned with children and young people, usually giving most of its support to a couple of well-known UK charities, such as the Variety Club and the Family Holiday Association.

Exclusions

No support for advertising in charity brochures, appeals from individuals or purely denominational (religious) appeals.

Applications

In writing to the correspondent.

Akzo

Akzo Nobel UK plc

50 George Street, London W1A 2BB
0171-612 1000; Fax: 0171-612 1500

Correspondent: D A Stevens, Deputy Company Secretary

Chief officers: *Chairman:* David Lees;
Chief Executive: G A Campbell

Year end	Turnover	Pre-tax profit
31/3/98	£1,957,000,000	£105,000,000

Nature of company business
The group is an industrial materials company involved in polymer technology and surface science. Business areas are: coatings and sealants; polymer products (principally packaging); and fibres and chemicals.

Main subsidiaries include: International Paint Ltd; Technical Absorbents Ltd.

UK employees: 6,500

Charitable donations
1998: £54,113
1997: £187,428
1996: £217,236
1995: £203,433
1994: £219,714

Community support policy

This company was previously listed as Courtaulds plc. The latter company was taken over by Akzo Nobel NV in 1998 and subsequently changed its name. The following policy was obtained from the company for the last edition of this guide and may change with the reorganisation of the business within the Akzo Nobel group.

The company channels its sponsorship and charitable donations to causes which: publicise its products in relevant markets; foster an understanding of the chemical industry (particularly in schools and universities); benefit local communities in which it is a significant employer; or otherwise benefit the company.

The company continues to support the Courtauld Institute of Art, Friends of the Royal Botanic Gardens, Kew, National Museum of Science & Industry, Museum of the Chemical Industry and the Chemical Industries Education Centre at the University of York.

Education: The company supports a number of academic posts at universities in the UK and USA, and was involved in the establishment of the China Europe International Business School in Shanghai. Relationships with local communities are conducted at business unit level. They are designed to encourage an understanding of the company and its activities, and to ensure that local concerns are understood by the business unit and properly reflected in its conduct. The company states: 'Involvement in local education is given particular emphasis'.

Charitable donations: Support, preferably for registered charities, is restricted to charities that have a link with the company in some way. Grants range from £50 to £5,000. Local factories and offices have small amounts to give away. The company has also given stock or equipment free of charge or with a discount.

Exclusions
No support for advertising in charity brochures, appeals from individuals, animal welfare, social welfare, sport, purely denominational appeals, political appeals or local appeals not in areas of company presence.

Applications
In writing to the correspondent. Applications are considered continuously by the Appeals Committee. Sponsorship proposals should be addressed to Miss C Felton, Manager Media Relations.

Albright & Wilson plc

PO Box 3, 210–222 Hagley Road West, Oldbury, Warley, West Midlands B68 0NN
0121-429 4942; Fax: 0121-420 5151
Website: www.albright-wilson.com

Correspondent: J Stratton, Public Affairs Manager

Chief officers: *Chairman:* Sir Christopher Benson;
Chief Executive: P F Rocheleau

Year end	Turnover	Pre-tax profit
31/12/97	£702,000,000	£32,000,000

Nature of company business
A chemical manufacturing company which focuses on speciality and intermediate chemicals for a wide group of end users, including the detergent, toiletries, water treatment, food, electronics, pharmaceutical and other process industries.

UK employees: 2,000

Charitable donations
1997: £149,000
1996: £103,000
1995: £91,000

Community support policy

The main area of non-cash support is good-cause sponsorship. The company operates a payroll giving scheme.

The company does support national charities, although most support is given in areas of company presence (Avonmouth, Oldbury, Warley, Widnes and Whitehaven), including assisting local community groups, local universities and schools, the arts, enterprise/training, environment/heritage and science/technology initiatives. The company may advertise in charity brochures.

Strong links have been forged with Understanding Industry, Catalyst Museum, Forward Birmingham Lifeboat Campaign, and arts support continued with National Art Collections Fund and City of Birmingham Symphony Orchestra. Other beneficiaries in 1997 included SDIA and the University of Oxford. Many are regular beneficiaries.

Exclusions
No support for political or religious appeals.

Applications
In writing to the correspondent.

Alldays plc

Strathtay House, Dundee Technology Park, Dundee DD2 1TP
01382-592000

Correspondent: M F McGregor, Deputy Company Secretary

Chief officers: *Chairman:* James Watson;
Chief Executive: Colin Glass

Year end	Turnover	Pre-tax profit
2/11/97	£637,500,000	£21,477,000

Nature of company business
Distribution of foodstuffs.

Main subsidiaries include: Alldays Stores Ltd; Ensign Holdings Ltd; Trademarket Ltd; Riverside Rentals Ltd.

UK employees: 6,676

Charitable donations
1997: £105,000
1996: £90,000
1995: £70,000
1994: £35,016
1993: £29,154

Community support policy

This company has recently changed its name from Watson & Philip to Alldays.

Grants are given through the Alldays Charitable Trust, formerly the Watson & Philip Charitable Trust, which was founded in 1978 and is registered in Scotland (SC004653). The group now sets aside 0.5% of its pre-tax profits for charity, resulting in some £105,000 being available for distribution in 1997.

In 1997, the trust nominated Childline as its charity of the year and in particular was the principal sponsor of a new venture called 'Childline in Partnership with Schools' (CHIPS). The trust will contribute a substantial sum to the project and match £ for £ monies raised by employees. During 1997/98, the total raised was £110,000.

Other major grant beneficiaries during 1997 included Childline Scotland, Aberlour Childcare Trust, Edinburgh Festival Theatre (educational), Home-Start (UK), and IGD Provision.

Employees are encouraged to put something back into the community by fundraising for local causes or, if preferred, local efforts for larger charities. A sum of £20,000 has been set aside to match on a £ for £ basis money raised by staff for worthwhile causes.

Since the summer of 1997, employees have been kept informed of the group's charitable support and fundraising activities through the publication of a trust newsletter.

Exclusions
The company does not welcome unsolicited applications. No support for the arts, political appeals, religious appeals or sport.

Applications
In writing to the correspondent.

Allders plc

Centre Tower, The Whitgift Centre, Croydon, Surrey CR9 1WE
0181-929 5500; Fax: 0181-929 5505
Website: www.allders.co.uk

Correspondent: Larry Thomson, Marketing Director

Chief officers: *Chairman:* John Pattisson;
Chief Executive: Harvey Lipsith

Year end	Turnover	Pre-tax profit
30/9/97	£490,878,000	£23,052,000

Nature of company business
The main activity is that of a department store operator.

UK employees: 5,118

Charitable donations
1997: £186,700
1996: £8,320
1995: £8,000

Community support policy

The level of charitable giving has increased dramatically in the last year from under £10,000 to over £180,000. The company has stated in the past that it has no set policy. Local stores have their own budgets and tend to donate products to local charities.

The latest annual report states: 'As a Group, we endeavour to combine our efforts to raise awareness of our brand with our charitable activities in the wider community'. In the run-up to Christmas 1996, it raised £175,000 in a national promotion that involved all stores and departments.

Applications
In writing to the correspondent.

Alliance & Leicester plc

Principal Office, 49 Park Lane, London W1Y 4EQ
0171-629 6661

Correspondent: Diane Henderson or Amanda Evans, Personal Assistants

Chief officer: *Chief Executive:* P R White

Year end	Turnover	Pre-tax profit
31/12/97	n/a	£394,600,000

Nature of company business
Principal activity: supplier of financial services.
Main subsidiaries include: Girobank.

UK employees: 9,735

Allied Domecq

Charitable donations
1997: £400,000
1996: £917,641
1995: £258,666
1994: £283,000
1993: £299,222

Total community contributions: £580,517

Membership: *BitC*

Community support policy

Total community contributions in 1997 were £580,000 including £400,000 in cash donations, with other support in the form of gifts in kind, management secondments, and matching donations by staff.

The correspondent has stated that the charities committee selects charities to support and, as such, is unable to encourage other appeals. Unsolicited applications will not be acknowledged.

Charitable donations are targeted at organisations with the object of promoting the welfare of the family (particularly the needs of children and relieving the problems of unemployment) and the security of the home and crime prevention. In 1997, two of the main grants given were to Citizen's Advice Bureaux and Business in the Community.

Sponsorship: Sponsorship is always seen as a marketing activity, not as patronage or a charitable donation, and therefore must have some direct relevance to the company's business plan. Ideally it should give a return to the company equal to that which is produced by conventional advertising.

Exclusions

No support for circular appeals, fundraising events, advertising in charity brochures, appeals from individuals, purely denominational (religious) appeals, local appeals not in areas of company presence or overseas projects.

Applications

In writing to the correspondent however, please note the comments above regarding unsolicited applications. Sponsorship proposals to T Pile, Director of Marketing.

Allied Domecq PLC

24 Portland Place, London W1N 4BB
0171-323 9000; Fax: 0171-323 1742

Correspondent: Clive Burns, Secretary, Charitable Trust

Chief officers: *Chairman:* Sir Christopher Hogg; *Chief Executive:* A J Hales

Year end	Turnover	Pre-tax profit
31/8/98	£4,308,000,000	£455,000,000

Nature of company business
Principal activities: marketing, selling and production of spirits and wine, the operation of public houses and off-licences, and franchising.

Main subsidiaries include: Allied Distillers Ltd; James Burrough Ltd; The Victoria Wine Co Ltd; Britannia Soft Drinks Ltd; Cantrell & Cochrane Group Ltd.

Main brands include: Ballantine's; Teacher's; Laphroaig; Beefeater; Courvoiser; Kahula; Tia Maria; Maker's Mark; Lambs Navy Rum; Victoria Wine; Haddows; Big Steak; Wacky Warehouse; Firkin; Mr Q's; Porterhouse; Scruffy Murphy's; Baskin-Robbins; Dunkin' Donuts.

Charitable donations
1997: £748,000
1996: £865,000
1995: £650,000
1994: £743,000
1993: £770,000

Total community contributions: £3,500,000 worldwide

Community support policy

In 1997/98, the group committed over £3.5 million worldwide to community activities including direct donations to charities, donations in kind, secondments and sponsorships. Charitable donations in the UK of £773,000 included £675,000 to the Allied Domecq Trust, which itself gave some £620,000 to a wide range of charitable causes.

The company states: 'We receive an enormous number of appeals ... and cannot respond to most of them ... We have recently decided to concentrate our charitable donation strategy on certain projects in the fields of the arts, education and the environment'.

The arts

'We not only provide financial support for the arts, but strive to develop constructive partnerships with the organisations which we sponsor while gaining wider recognition and commercial advantages for Allied Domecq.

'Much of our effort is targeted particularly at the theatre and we have been principal sponsor of the Royal Shakespeare Company since 1994. This support has developed and our brands now back individual productions in the UK and overseas touring programmes. At grassroots level we support pub theatre, through The Bush, The Gate and The Kings Head theatres, all of which are in our own outlets, and through promotion of the Allied Domecq Drama Awards with prizes for new playwrights and for new translations of existing works.'

Education

'We sponsor the Prince of Wales's Shakespeare School – an annual programme which teaches drama to secondary school teachers in the UK. We fund a Chair in Water Management at Bristol University. In each of these projects we have been able to combine help for education with one of our other objectives.'

Environment

'Allied Domecq pursues a policy which aims to minimise any damaging impacts of our activities on the environment. We are members of VALPAK, a legal compliance scheme which aims to minimise and recycle packaging waste. We sponsor the University of Cambridge's Environment Committee and help fund an annual lecture programme.'

Other support

Other charitable causes are supported, but these should have a special connection to the company or its employees. The company's support is supplemented by a whole range of activities undertaken by employees worldwide who give their time as well as financial support to a variety of projects. The company gives financial support to employees' volunteering/charitable activities.

The company supports a payroll giving scheme and matches employee giving and fundraising.

Exclusions

While donations may be given in other areas, the main areas of support are the arts, education and environment.

Applications

Appeals to head office should be addressed to the correspondent. The group supports a large number of organisations, and charities are therefore advised to consider carefully the nature of their appeal – priorities are identified as the arts, education and the environment. It may be more beneficial to apply to one of the subsidiary companies, especially if there is a local connection. If you do apply, send any promotional material with your application.

Sponsorship proposals should be addressed to Michael Crofts, Corporate Communications Manager, although most sponsorship is undertaken at a local level by subsidiary companies.

Allied Dunbar Assurance plc

Allied Dunbar Centre, Swindon SN1 1EL
01793-511227; Fax: 01793-506982
Email: comm.aff@dial.pipex.com

Correspondent: John Bickell, Community Affairs Director

Chief officers: *Chairman:* Sandy Leitch; *Chief Executive:* Phil Hodkinson

Year end	Turnover	Pre-tax profit
31/12/97	n/a	£203,000,000

Nature of company business
Allied Dunbar is a member of the Zurich Financial Services (UKISA) Group. It is the UK's largest unit-linked life assurance and pensions company with its head office based in Swindon (it is one of the town's major employers). It also operates a large UK network of self-employed sales people.

UK employees: 3,078

Charitable donations
1997: £2,300,000
1996: £2,452,000
1995: £2,000,000
1994: £2,300,000
1993: £1,900,000
Membership: *BitC %Club*

Community support policy

Allied Dunbar continues to be a leader in the field of corporate responsibility. Its own support is routed through the Zurich Financial Services (UKISA) Community Trust while staff fund and manage the Allied Dunbar Staff Charity Fund and the self-employed Sales Force funds and manages its own Allied Dunbar Foundation.

The company is a member of the Corporate Responsibility Group and Association of Charitable Foundations as well as Business in the Community and the PerCent Club.

In celebration of the company's 25th anniversary in 1996/97, the Charitable Trust and Foundation jointly committed £2 million to build Britain's first national cross-disability training, coaching and dance centre for ASPIRE. The centre is based at the Royal National Orthopaedic Hospital at Stanmore and was opened officially in September 1998.

Zurich Financial Services (UKISA) Community Trust

The trust receives 1.25% of the company's pre-tax profits (of which 0.25% is passed to the Allied Dunbar Foundation – see below). It operates on the following principles:

- focusing on a limited geographical area of the community and on a limited number of issues
- seeking 'the multiplier effect' from funding
- developing partnerships with people rather than just giving grants to organisations
- giving larger amounts to fewer organisations over longer periods.

In 1997, the trust (including associate funds) had an income of £3.3 million including £2.6 million from deeds of covenant, of which £2.3 million came from the company.

The current major programmes are:

Dementia: £2 million has been committed to this programme of which over £1 million has already been allocated. The programme provides support to improve awareness and develop services for the 672,000 people throughout the UK with dementia.

Domestic Violence: £2 million was committed over five years from 1994, primarily working with women's aid organisations in England and Northern Ireland to improve support for women experiencing domestic violence.

India: This is an open-ended programme with a current annual budget of £150,000. The focus of the programme is on capacity building of a small number of partner NGOs in Southern India. The programme combines grants with staff development assignments of four weeks' duration.

Active Citizenship: A small research programme (£250,000) over three years to 1998 working with the Citizen

Allied Dunbar

Organising Foundation to support the training and development of community leaders.

Grants made by the trust in 1997 totalled £3.4 million with the 60 largest listed in the trust's accounts. The largest went to Aspire, London Connection, Citizen Organising Foundation, Alzheimer Scotland and Alzheimer's Disease Society.

Allied Dunbar Staff Charity Fund

This fund receives income from staff by deeds of covenant and fundraising, and manages Swindon area grant giving on behalf of the Charitable Trust. All income raised by staff is matched by the Charitable Trust.

Most grants are awarded to charities within a 30 mile radius of Swindon (excluding other major towns). There are three policy areas managed entirely by committees of staff volunteers:

- *Independent living:* will support projects which enable people of all ages with special needs, learning difficulties, mental/physical illness or disability, to live more independent and rewarding lives.
- *Children and young people:* will support people up to the age of 18 on issues of concern to them and their families.
- *Crisis support:* is seeking to fund projects which help and support people in the local community who are facing a crisis in their lives.

In addition, the fund has an overseas policy with a budget of about £30,000 which supports practical initiatives in developing countries through grants to UK-based development charities.

Volunteering programme

The company's employee volunteering programme encourages Swindon staff to engage in a wide range of volunteering activities from one-off events to long-term commitments. Support includes:

- Providing and co-ordinating opportunities for staff to become involved. One such opportunity is the annual 'Challenge' under which teams take on specific one-off tasks put to them by local organisations.
- Supporting staff in projects of their own choice. For example, under the 'Time Out' scheme the company matches time off when staff volunteer for such initiatives as working on a summer camp for socially disadvantaged children, or training to become a Relate counsellor.
- Matching the use of professional skills to the needs of local voluntary organisations under the ALPHA (Allied Professional Help and Advice) scheme. This provides help in areas such as accountancy, marketing or training in computer systems. In any year, around 40 projects are undertaken providing 600 hours of professional experience.

Allied Dunbar Foundation

The foundation is the fundraising and grant-making arm of the Allied Dunbar Sales Force, and was the first charitable fund supported entirely by self-employed sales people. Income is through deeds of covenant, fundraising by local branches and central events, and the foundation receives a covenant of 0.25% of company profits. The foundation's total income was £811,000 in 1994.

The foundation structures its grant giving policies through biennial themes and these have included 'Hearts...and Minds!', 'Action for Youth' and 'On The Road'. Under the latter, over £1 million has been given to 73 projects throughout the UK and in developing countries. Applications to the foundation must be made through members of the Allied Dunbar Sales Force or Branch staff. Applications are not accepted direct from charities.

Exclusions

No response to circular appeals. No grants for fundraising events, animal welfare charities, the arts, enterprise/training, environment/heritage, medical research, political or religious appeals, science/technology, sport, advertising, sponsorship or in response to appeals from individuals.

Applications

The Community Affairs Department based at Swindon is responsible for the management of all the major funds and the volunteering programme. Several publications are available from the Department, including a general Community Involvement Report.

Note: The Zurich Financial Services (UKISA) Group (which comprises Allied Dunbar, Eagle Star, Zurich's UK businesses and Threadneedle Asset Management) is currently developing community involvement across all companies based on the experience in Allied Dunbar. To facilitate this, the Trust was renamed the Zurich Financial Services (UKISA) Community Trust on 8 September 1998.

Allied London Properties plc

Allied House, 26 Manchester Square, London W1A 2HU
0171-486 6080; Fax: 0171-486 5428

Correspondent: J H Nixon, Company Secretary

Chief officers: *Chairman:* H T Stanton; *Managing Director:* M J Ingall

Year end	Turnover	Pre-tax profit
30/6/97	£50,948,000	£12,025,000

Nature of company business
Principal activity: property investors.

Main subsidiaries include: Gough Cooper Properties Ltd; Pellam Homes Ltd; Hamiltonhill Estates Ltd.

UK employees: 90

Charitable donations

1998: £47,000
1997: £72,000
1996: £41,000
1995: £61,000
1994: £62,000

Community support policy

Although, previously a member of the PerCent Club and Business in the Community, the company appears to be no longer a member of either. Total charitable donations rose in 1996/97 by about 75% to over £70,000, but have since decreased to £47,000.

Charitable donations: Support is given to a wide range of charitable organisations, especially in the fields of education, health and community affairs. Recent support has been given to Industry in Education, Prince's Youth Business Trust, Action on Addiction, Wellbeing, British Red Cross, Variety Club and NSPCC.

Grants to national organisations range from £100 to £10,000. Grants to local organisations from £50 to £500.

Exclusions

No support for appeals from individuals or overseas projects.

Applications

The company does not wish to receive unsolicited requests.

AMEC plc

Sandiway House, Hartford, Northwich, Cheshire CW8 2YA
01606-883885; Fax: 01606-883996
Website: www.amec.co.uk

Correspondent: C L Fidler, AMEC Charitable Trust Trustees

Chief officers: *Chairman:* Sydney Gillibrand;
Chief Executive: Peter Mason

Year end	Turnover	Pre-tax profit
31/12/97	£2,774,300,000	£68,400,000

Nature of company business
Principal activities: building and civil engineering, mechanical and electrical engineering, property development and housing.

Main subsidiaries include: Fairclough Homes; Matthew Hall; Denco; CV Buchan; Watson Steel.

Main locations: Surbiton; Swinton; Leicester; Ipswich; Adlington; Colnbrook; Darlington; Renfrew; Hereford; Wallsend on the Tyne; Aberdeen; Durham; Glasgow; Leicester; London; Perth; Bolton.

UK employees: 23,694

Charitable donations

1997: £88,000
1996: £190,000
1995: £139,000
1994: £71,000
1993: £127,000
Membership: ABSA BitC %Club

Community support policy

The company is a member of the PerCent Club, with worldwide charitable donations in 1997 being £190,000 including £88,000 in the UK.

Charitable donations: The parent company prefers to support national charities. Support to local charities and causes is given through subsidiary companies. Grants to national organisations range from £500 to £2,500 and to local from £50 to £250.

There is a small trust associated with the company (the AMEC Charitable Trust), which in 1994 gave £5,000 in grants. It has 'general charitable purposes' and receives donations in the form of gifts, lump sums and covenants from AMEC plc and subsidiary companies. The trustees of the charitable trust are also directors of the company.

In addition to the company's donations, employees raise funds for a number of charities, often local causes.

Education: AMEC sponsors students at selected universities throughout their academic careers before taking up permanent positions in group companies. It is also funding the first Chair in Engineering Project Management at the University of Manchester Institute of Science and Technology (UMIST). One subsidiary has begun a schools/industry link on north Tyneside.

The arts: The company is a member of ABSA, and has supported the English National Opera.

Exclusions

Non-charitable grants cannot be considered.

Applications

In writing to the correspondent.

Amerada Hess Limited

33 Grosvenor Place, London SW1X 7HY
0171-823 2626; Fax: 0171-887 2199
Website: www.hess.com

Correspondent: Charles Naylor, Head of Corporate Affairs

Chief officers: *Chairman:* W S H Laidlaw;
Managing Director: F R Gugen

Year end	Turnover	Pre-tax profit
31/12/97	£829,607,000	£123,226,000

Nature of company business
Principal activity: exploration for, and production of, oil and natural gas from the UK Continental Shelf. The ultimate holding company is the Amerada Hess Corporation based in the USA.

Main subsidiaries include: Western Gas Limited.

Main locations: Aberdeen; London.

UK employees: 623

Charitable donations

1997: £77,000
1996: £71,000
1995: £53,000
1994: £60,000
1993: £61,000

Community support policy

Charitable donations: The company prefers to support appeals relevant to company business and local charities in areas of company presence with head office (London) supporting mainly charities working in London, and the Aberdeen office dealing with appeals relevant to that region.

Andersen

Preferred areas of support are environment/heritage, medical research, science/technology and sickness/disability charities. Grants can be up to £10,000. Support tends to be given to specific projects and employee involvement is encouraged. The company matches employee giving to charities.

The following information is taken from the company's annual report for 1997. The company aims to support causes where its contribution can make a substantial difference, and have a real local impact.

In particular the company continued to support the Restoration of Appearance and Function Trust (RAFT). Grounds for Learning, which helps Scottish schools turn their grounds into environmentally friendly 'open air classrooms' has received a further years support.

A sponsorship agreement between Amerada Hess Gas Limited and Age Concern means that vulnerable older people at risk in cold weather will be informed on how best to keep warm and minimise their fuel bills.

The arts: Amerada Hess continues to support the Virtuosi Society in Scotland by awarding bursaries to help young artists and musicians going on to further education with the cost of materials, instruments and tuition.

Art in the Park was a major sponsorship as part of the Silver Jubilee of Aberdeen International Youth Festival. Four artists worked together to create pieces of art for the Winter Gardens in Duthie Park, Aberdeen that were accompanied by work by local children.

Exclusions

No support is given for advertising in charity brochures, animal welfare charities, appeals from individuals, purely denominational (religious) appeals, local appeals not in areas of company presence, overseas projects or political events.

Applications

Appeals from national charities should be addressed in writing to the correspondent. The Aberdeen office (Scott House, Hareness Road, Altens, Aberdeen AB12 3LE, 01224-243000) deals with appeals relevant to that region.

Arthur Andersen

1 Surrey Street, London WC2R 2PS
0171-438 3000; Fax: 0171-831 1133

Correspondent: Charles Bremner, Partnership Secretary

Chief officers: n/a

Year end	Turnover	Pre-tax profit
31/8/97	n/a	n/a

Nature of company business
Chartered accountants.

UK employees: n/a

Charitable donations
1997: £666,588
Membership: *ABSA BitC %Club*

Community support policy

The firm is a member of the PerCent Club and Business in the Community. It supports a number of enterprise organisations as well as the arts, hospices, education, community action and disabled groups' charities. The firm also operates the CAF payroll giving scheme. Charitable donations are made through the Arthur Andersen Foundation.

The Arthur Andersen Foundation

(Charity Commission number 284024)

In March 1996, the former Arthur Andersen & Co. Foundation in the UK split into two, which brought about the formation of The Andersen Consulting Foundation on 1 September 1996. The assets of the original foundation were divided between The Arthur Andersen Foundation (as this foundation is now known) and The Andersen Consulting Foundation, reflecting office and partner balances at the time. The foundation supports registered or exempt charities working for educational, medical, community, cultural and charitable causes. The trustees are J N Woolf (Chairman), D J Ashton, M Beverley, R J Simmons and N P Thompsell.

In 1996/97, the income from partners of Arthur Andersen was £666,588. In addition, a one-off payment of £423,773 was received from The Andersen Foundation (United States). The total income for the year was £1,142,005, with a balance at the year end of almost £1 million.

Donations, totalling £874,800 were broken down as follows:

Category	Offices £	%	Partners £	%	Total £	%
Education	109,000	30	85,800	17	194,800	22
Health	53,700	15	140,600	28	194,300	22
Community	124,300	34	113,500	22	237,800	27
Arts	63,900	17	29,800	6	93,700	11
Other	17,200	4	137,000	18	154,200	18

Previously, the comprehensive annual report produced by the foundation broke down the grants further, by office and category, and showed the pattern of giving over the last five years. No such detail was included in the report for 1996/97, neither was a grants list included.

Exclusions

No support for advertising in charity brochures, individuals, fundraising events, medical research, overseas projects, political appeals, religious appeals, science/technology and sport.

Applications

In writing to the correspondent. Sponsorship proposals should be addressed to Colin Bayley, Director of Marketing Services.

Andersen Consulting

2 Arundel Street, London WC2R 3LT
0171-438 5000; Fax: 0171-831 1133

Correspondent: Stephen Walker, Partnership Secretary

Chief officers: n/a

Year end	Turnover	Pre-tax profit
31/8/97	n/a	n/a

Nature of company business
Chartered accountants.

UK employees: n/a

Charitable donations

1997: £589,273
Membership: *BitC %Club*

Community support policy

The firm is a member of the PerCent Club and Business in the Community. It supports enterprise organisations, the arts, hospices, education, community action and disabled groups' charities. The company also operates the CAF payroll giving scheme. Charitable donations are made through the Andersen Consulting Foundation.

The Andersen Consulting Foundation

(Charity Commission number 1057696)

In March 1996, the former Arthur Andersen & Co. Foundation in the UK split into two, which brought about the formation of The Andersen Consulting Foundation on 1 September 1996. The assets of the original foundation were divided between The Arthur Andersen Foundation (see separate entry for Arthur Andersen) and The Andersen Consulting Foundation, reflecting office and partner balances at the time.

The foundation supports registered or exempt charities working for educational, medical, community, cultural and charitable causes, ie. similar causes to the Arthur Andersen Foundation. The trustees are D Mowat (Chairman), A Middleton, D Milner, N Sloane, D Thomlinson and N P Thompsell.

In 1996/97, the income from partners of Andersen Consulting was £589,273. In addition, a one-off payment of £324,630 was received from The Andersen Foundation (United States). The total income for the year was £969,348, with a balance at the year end of just over £1 million.

Donations, totalling £578,945 were broken down as follows:

Category	Offices £	%	Partners £	%	Total £	%
Education	115,965	29	8,005	4	123,971	21
Health	79,281	20	34,129	19	113,410	20
Community	76,111	19	129,194	71	205,305	36
Arts	28,253	7	4,688	3	32,940	6
Other	97,520	25	5,800	3	103,320	8

No further information on the grants made was included in the foundation's accounts.

Exclusions

No support for advertising in charity brochures, individuals, fundraising events, medical research, overseas projects, political appeals, religious appeals, science/technology and sport.

Applications

In writing to the correspondent.

Anglian Water plc

Anglian House, Ambury Road, Huntingdon, Cambridgeshire PE18 6NZ
01480-323000; Fax: 01480-443115
Website: www.anglianwater.co.uk

Correspondent: Mrs Glynis Hammond, Sponsorship Manager

Chief officers: *Chairman:* Robin Gourlay;
Chief Executive: Chris Mellor

Year end	Turnover	Pre-tax profit
31/3/98	£850,000,000	£274,000,000

Nature of company business
Water supply and sewage treatment and disposal.

Main subsidiaries include: Hartlepool Water PLC; Rutland Insurance Ltd; Powermarque Ltd; Geodesys Ltd; Alpheus Environmental Ltd.

UK employees: 5,131

Charitable donations

1998: £104,603
1997: £106,377
1996: £125,675
1995: £26,720
1994: £55,000

Total community contributions: £400,000

Membership: *BitC*

Community support policy

The company is a member of Business in the Community and supports a wide range of causes/charities in the Anglian Water area. Areas of support include the arts, children/youth, education, elderly people, enterprise/training, science/technology, fundraising events, overseas projects, sickness/disability charities and social welfare. WaterAid is the only overseas charity supported.

In 1997/98, main beneficiaries included Wildlife Trusts, RSPB, Citizen's Advice Bureaux, NSPCC and WaterAid.

In 1996/97, in addition to its charitable donations the company also contributed £100,000 to the Learn to Swim Campaign, supporting local swimming pools to encourage children to learn to swim.

The main areas of non-cash support are arts and good cause sponsorship. The company's arts sponsorship in 1997/98 included partnerships with City of London Sinfonia, Music for Youth and local schools to enable local audiences to enjoy performances rarely available in the region.

Antofagasta

The company matches employee fundraising and operates a payroll giving scheme and volunteering scheme. The employee charity of the year in 1998 was the NSPCC.

In common with similar companies, several environmental initiatives are undertaken in the region. Two of note are the development of a new nature reserve at Bowthorpe and Earlham Marshes near Norwich and the launch of a five-year programme to reintroduce ospreys to Rutland Water. The company also runs Caring for the Environment Awards to encourage environmental projects in the region. £40,000 was awarded in the last year. Projects supported include native woodland creation in Cambridgeshire, where local schools and communities planted trees, and the building of a viewing platform in Northamptonshire to see rare butterflies.

The Anglian Water Trust Fund

This trust was set up at the end of March 1996 with a donation of £1.5 million from the company. It received further donations in 1997 and 1998, but although funded by the company it operates independently. The trust has two programmes of grant-making:

- organisations can apply to improve, increase or install money advice services throughout the region
- individuals who are customers of Anglian Water plc and are experiencing hardship can apply for help with water and sewerage debts. Also, assistance is available for general welfare needs including other priority debts and essential items of clothing or household equipment.

Further details on this trust can be found in *A Guide to Local Trusts in the South of England*.

Exclusions

No support for advertising in charity brochures, appeals from individuals, political appeals or sport, unless at educational level, animal welfare charities, medical research or religious appeals.

Applications

In writing to the correspondent.

Antofagasta Holdings plc

Park House, 16 Finsbury Circus, London EC2M 7AH
0171-374 8091; Fax: 0171-628 3773

Correspondent: Philip Adeane, Managing Director

Chief officers: *Chairman:* A A Luksic;
Managing Director: P J Adeane

Year end	Turnover	Pre-tax profit
31/12/97	£152,800,000	£36,000,000

Nature of company business
The principal activities are mining, the transport of freight by rail and road, banking, telecommunications, manufacture of non-ferrous products, water distribution, forestry and natural resources. These activities are mainly based in Chile.

UK employees: 3

Charitable donations
1997: £53,458
1996: £51,698
1995: £29,433
1994: £31,963

Community support policy
The company has no set policy regarding its charitable donations.

Applications
In writing to the correspondent.

Aon UK Ltd

145 St Vincent Street, Glasgow G2 5NX
0141-248 5070

Correspondent: Elma Stewart, Associate Director

Chief officers: *Chairman:* Anthony Howland Jackson;
Chief Executive: Ron W Forrest

Year end	Turnover	Pre-tax profit
31/12/95	£201,324,000	£25,991,000

Nature of company business
Insurance.

Main subsidiaries include: Bain Hogg International; Nicholson Jenner Leslie; Alexander Howden.

UK employees: n/a

Charitable donations
1995: £106,000
1994: £115,000

Community support policy
The figures given above refer to Bain Hogg Group plc, which was acquired by Aon UK Ltd in October 1996. The donations figure is probably at about the same level as in previous years.

The company supports a wide range of causes with a preference for national charities and local charities in areas where the company conducts business. The company matches employee fundraising.

Exclusions
No support for appeals from individuals or political appeals.

Applications
In writing to the correspondent.

Arcadia Group plc

Colegrave House, 70 Berners Street, London W1P 3AE
0171-636 8040; Fax: 0171-927 7806

Correspondent: Jane Rome, Charities Controller

Chief officers: *Chairman:* Adam Broadbent; *Chief Executive:* J L Hoerner

Year end	Turnover	Pre-tax profit
31/8/98	£1,451,300,000	£81,100,000

Nature of company business
Fashion retailer, retailing through national chains of large stores and small shops. It concentrates its retailing in broad categories, aimed separately at men, women, children and home. The company is also involved in property development.
Main subsidiaries include: Burton Retail; Dorothy Perkins; Evans; Principles Retail; Top Man/Top Shop.
Main brands include: Hawkshead; Top Man; Dorothy Perkins; Top Shop; Evans; Principles; Racing Green; Wade Smith.

UK employees: n/a

Charitable donations
1998: £220,000
1997: £922,000
1996: £233,854
1995: £200,526
1994: £159,613
Membership: *BitC %Club*

Community support policy

Arcadia (formerly Burton Group) is a founder member of the PerCent Club. Its main areas of support in addition to cash donations are arts and good cause sponsorship and gifts in kind. The aim has been to construct a programme which maximises the company's contribution to the community in a way which doesn't conflict with, but rather helps, its other corporate obligations.

The group established Burton Aid in 1996. This charity donates stock to charities supporting people in the UK who are homeless or underprivileged. It has worked nationally with the Salvation Army and locally in two towns where the group's stores work with local charities.

Charitable donations: Following the exceptional £922,000 given in 1997, the company's level of donations has decreased to its apparently more normal level of about £200,000.

The company believes that its resources can be used to best effect by supporting a limited number of main charities, thus making a real and worthwhile contribution. Preference is given to children and youth, social welfare and trade charities including Cottage Homes. In the field of health care the company gives substantial support to SANE, the schizophrenia charity which it helped to set up. Since 1995, the group has supported the Crimestoppers Trust by covering production costs of the trust's quarterly magazine. The company is also keen to support projects in which its employees are involved, matching funds raised by staff in many parts of the country, and meeting the costs of the Give As You Earn scheme.

Enterprise: The company has concentrated its main efforts on the broad area of the promotion of enterprise and economic regeneration. Its flagship enterprise initiative is Design Works in Gateshead. A large warehouse was converted into work-units to encourage young designers in the North East to set up in business. The centre provides work-space for over 100 designers, as well as advisory services, marketing, training and exhibition facilities. The company is a member of Business in the Community.

Exclusions
No support is given to circular appeals, appeals from individuals, purely denominational (religious) appeals, political appeals, large national appeals or for advertising in charity brochures.

Applications
In writing to the correspondent. All grant decisions are made at head office.

Advice to applicants: The company stresses that it will continue to focus its attention on one or two major areas aiming to use its resources as effectively as possible and maximise the benefits to both the community and the group. This means that relatively few charities actually receive money from the company and potential applicants should think very carefully about the nature of their appeal before contacting the company to be certain of a reply. Applicants should include a sae with their request.

Argos plc

489–499 Avebury Boulevard, Saxon Gate West, Central Milton Keynes MK9 2NW
01908-690333

Correspondent: Hazel Richardson, Charities Co-ordinator

Chief officers: *Chairman:* Lord Wolfson; *Chief Executive:* T Duddy

Year end	Turnover	Pre-tax profit
27/12/97	£1,820,000,000	£128,400,000

Nature of company business
Catalogue retailer.

UK employees: n/a

Charitable donations
1997: £204,000
1996: £180,000
1995: £111,938
1994: £92,334
1993: £82,190

Community support policy

The company's level of donations has increased steadily over the last five years. It supports charities which aid those suffering from disabilities or debilitating diseases; research into disease; care of the elderly; hospitals and hospices; and children's charities. It receives about 500 letters a month from fundraising groups and provides a mix of goods, Argos vouchers and cheques to support a variety of localised fundraising activities.

Arjo

The company also supports one particular charity each year (chosen by staff) by donating a percentage of the purchase price of selected products in its catalogue. At the time of going to print, the 1998 charity CLIC (Cancer and Leukaemia in Children) had already received a cheque for £50,000 for the first half year. The nominated charity for 1999 is the Cystic Fibrosis Trust.

In addition, a matched giving scheme is operated to support individual staff fundraising activities, providing they fit with the policy statement. Selected projects where Argos is a major employer are also supported.

Exclusions

No support for circular appeals, advertising in charity brochures, animal charities, education, environment/heritage, political appeals, religious appeals, science/technology, sport or overseas projects. No sponsorship is undertaken.

Applications

In writing to the correspondent.

Arjo Wiggins Appleton plc

Gateway House, Basing View, Basingstoke, Hampshire RG21 4EE
01256-723000; Fax: 01256-723723

Correspondent: Christopher Biggs, UK Communications Manager

Chief officer: *Chairman:* Ken Minton

Year end	Turnover	Pre-tax profit
31/12/97	£3,266,600,000	£216,100,000

Nature of company business
The manufacture of selected premium paper grades and the distribution of printing and writing papers.

Main locations: Hampshire.

UK employees: n/a

Charitable donations

1997: £39,000
1996: £41,000
1995: £100,000
1994: £151,000
1993: £110,000

Community support policy

The company has seen a decline in its level of charitable giving over the last three years and is now barely eligible to qualify for an entry in this Guide. However, the company's pre-tax profits have shown a 200% increase over this period.

It prefers to support charities in areas where it operates ie. Hampshire, particularly in the fields of education, environment and training. If there is a local or employee link, consideration may be given to charities in other fields, namely the arts, children/youth, elderly people, fundraising events, medical research, science/technology, sickness/disability charities and social welfare. The main beneficiaries in 1997 included the Paper Federation of GB, Basingstoke Common Purpose – Business Sponsorship Initiative – Basingstoke, The Mayor's Charity Appeal – Basingstoke and Chincham Tigers – Basingstoke.

In addition to charitable donations, the company's main area of non-cash support is gifts in kind. Employee fundraising is also matched by the company.

Exclusions

No support for advertising in charity brochures; animal welfare; appeals from individuals; political appeals; religious appeals; overseas project and sport.

Applications

'The company's Donations Committee determines the recipients of donations independent of applications.'

Arriva plc

Admiral Way, Doxford International Business Park, Sunderland SR3 3XP
0191-520 4000

Correspondent: Robert Blower, Director of Corporate Communications

Chief officers: *Chairman:* Sir James McKinnon; *Chief Executive:* G W Hodgson

Year end	Turnover	Pre-tax profit
31/12/97	£1,421,000,000	£101,000,000

Nature of company business
The company changed its name from Cowie Group plc to Arriva plc in November 1997.

The principal activities of the group comprise: finance (contract hire, fleet management, leasing); bus operators (London and provincial bus services, coach commuter services, private hire); motor (sale, service and repair of motor vehicles, supply of parts, self-drive hire); bus and coach distribution (distribution, rental and finance).

Main subsidiaries include: Clydeside Buses Ltd; County Bus & Coach Co Ltd; Crosville Wales Ltd; Derby City Transport Ltd; Eden Bus Services Ltd; Grey Green Ltd; Kentish Bus & Coach Co Ltd; LDT Ltd; Leaside Bus Co Ltd; London & Country Ltd; Londonlinks Buses Ltd; Maidstone & District Motor Services Ltd; Midland Fox Ltd; North East Bus Ltd; Northumbria Motor Services Ltd; North Western Road Car Co Ltd; South London Transport Co Ltd; Stevensons of Uttoxeter Ltd; Tees and District Transport Co Ltd; Teesside Motor Services Ltd; The Bee Line Buzz Co Ltd; United Automobile Services Ltd; West Riding Automobile Co Ltd; Yorkshire Woollen District Transport Co Ltd.

UK employees: 19,280

Charitable donations

1997: £59,277
1996: £47,000
1995: £52,000
1994: £22,000
1993: £33,674
Membership: BitC

Community support policy

The company supports a number of projects helping disadvantaged people in the communities where it has a major presence which, if the list of subsidiaries given above is accurate, is most of the UK.

Exclusions

No grants for sport, arts, science research or heritage appeals.

Applications

In writing to the correspondent.

ASDA Group plc

ASDA House, Southbank, Great Wilson Street,
Leeds LS11 5AD
0113-243 5435; Fax: 0113-241 8666

Correspondent: Christine Watts, Director of Corporate Affairs

Chief officers: *Chairman:* A Norman;
Chief Executive: A Leighton

Year end	Turnover	Pre-tax profit
2/5/98	£7,619,000,000	£405,000,000

Nature of company business
Principal activities: retailing of fresh food and clothing through 220 ASDA superstores.
Main subsidiaries include: Gazeley Properties Ltd; McLagan Investments Ltd; The Burwood House Group PLC; Gazeley Holdings Ltd.

UK employees: 78,450

Charitable donations

1998: £100,000
1997: £100,000
1996: £100,000
1995: £100,000
1994: £200,000

Total community contributions: £1,800,000

Membership: *BitC   %Club*

Community support policy

The company is a member of the PerCent Club and Business in the Community. Community contributions in 1997/98 totalled £1.8 million, of which cash donations comprised only £100,000. The main area of non-cash support is through a new 'community days' initiative where each store has 10 days a year for active involvement. Contributions are also made through gifts in kind and joint promotions. The Give As You Earn payroll giving scheme is operated.

Charitable donations: Donations are given through the ASDA Foundation which operates primarily in support of causes recommended and supported by its store colleagues and customers. It is intended to provide support for causes that create involvement and participation by colleagues. 'ASDA's 223 stores and 80,000 colleagues are committed to serving the communities in which they operate. Colleagues participate in a wide range of community activities both in a fundraising capacity for charities and through supporting local groups and schools with practical help and in-kind support.'

The company focuses on these value areas: women's health issues, children and education, people with disabilities and local good causes.

In 1997/98, the company adopted the charity Breast Cancer Support, raising over £500,000 during a four-week period.

The ASDA Foundation

Full accounts are on file at the Charity Commission for the foundation. The giving by the charitable foundation should increase markedly over the next year following the statement in its 1996/97 report: 'Profit generated by the chain as a result of the midweek National Lottery will be donated to the Foundation'. This was estimated to be about £250,000 in 1997/98. The foundation also receives donations from Asda Stores Ltd on a quarterly basis, the first of which was £60,000 in April 1997. The following information refers to the previous year.

In 1996/97, the trust had an income of £64,000 and gave grants totalling £146,000. Charitable status is a prerequisite for support, with a preference for local organisations in areas of company presence, those connected with company business, and those concerned with children, youth and families. Grants normally range between £500 and £1,000. The grants made in 1996/97 were categorised as follows.

Children	£49,000	34%
Community projects	£21,000	14%
Victims of crime	£5,000	4%
Education	£9,000	6%
Alleviation of hardship	£4,000	3%
Medical	£27,000	18%
Miscellaneous	£9,000	6%
Special needs	£18,000	12%
Trade benevolent funds	£3,000	2%
Women	£1,000	1%

The largest grants (£10,000) went to Cash for Kids, Children First and Scout Services Ltd. There were seven grants of £5,000 to Addenbrooke's Charities, Barnardo's, Intake High School, Parents At Work, Shaw Trust, Victim Support and Wider Share Ownership Educational Trust. A further 35 grants were for £1,000 or more including those to Bolton Hospice, Childline, Foundation for the Study of Infant Deaths, Groundwork Leeds, Marie Curie Cancer Care, Wine and Spirit Trade Benevolent Society and Worshipful Company of Butchers.

Both national and local charities are supported with examples of smaller grants to local organisations including Anglia Veteran's Pilgrimages, Bournemouth Mencap Society, Leeds Junior Chamber of Commerce, Opera North, Rosettes Majorette Troupe and Woodslee Primary School.

Asprey

Exclusions
No response to circular appeals. No support for advertising in charity brochures, appeals from individuals, purely denominational (religious) appeals, local appeals not in areas of company presence, large national appeals, political appeals or overseas projects.

Applications
Very few donations are made centrally. The first contact should be made with the local store.

Asprey Holdings UK Ltd

167 New Bond Street, London W1Y 0AR
0171-493 6767; Fax: 0171-331 2657

Correspondent: Wendy Kiener, Group Human Resources Director

Chief officer: *Chairman:* HRH Prince Abdul Hakeem

Year end	Turnover	Pre-tax profit
31/3/96	£58,139,000	(£4,505,000)

Nature of company business
The principal activities are as goldsmiths, silversmiths, jewellers, watch retailers and retailers of luxury goods.

Main subsidiaries include: Asprey Plc; Mappin & Webb Ltd; Garrard & Co Ltd; Nayler Brothers Silversmiths Ltd; Nathan & Co Ltd; E A Barker Ltd; T M Sutton Ltd; Hamilton & Inches Ltd; Watches of Switzerland Ltd; J W Benson Ltd; Tomasz Starweski Ltd.

UK employees: 1,262

Charitable donations
1996: £129,183

Community support policy

The figure stated in the latest annual report for Asprey plc (1994/95) was just over £21,000. However, the jewellers has recently joined Save the Children's corporate membership scheme which commits it to raising £300,000 for the charity over three years.

The figure given above (£129,000), was the latest and in fact only figure available from Extel Financial for the company Amedeo Crown. This company trades under the names listed above.

We have no information as to the types of causes the other retail outlets support.

Applications
In writing to the correspondent.

Associated British Foods plc

Weston Centre, Bowater House, 68 Knightsbridge, London SW1X 7LQ
0171-589 6363; Fax: 0171-584 8560

Correspondent: Fiona M Foster, Administrator, Garfield Weston Foundation

Chief officer: *Chairman:* Garry H Weston

Year end	Turnover	Pre-tax profit
13/9/97	£5,203,000,000	£850,000,000

Nature of company business
The activities of the group primarily concern the processing and manufacture of food. The ultimate holding company is Wittington Investments Ltd and the immediate holding company is George Weston Holdings Ltd.

Main subsidiaries include: AB Ingredients Ltd; ABN Ltd; ABR Foods Ltd; AB Technology Ltd; Allied Bakeries Ltd; Allied Foods Ltd; Allied Grain Ltd; Allied Mills Ltd; Burtons Gold Medal Biscuits Ltd; Fishers Agricultural Holdings Ltd; Germains Ltd; Jacksons of Piccadilly Ltd; Jordans Ltd; Lax & Shaw Ltd; Mauri Products Ltd; Namosa Ltd; Primark Stores Ltd; Provincial Merchants Ltd; R Twinings & Co Ltd; The Ryvita Co Ltd; Trident Feeds Westmill Foods Ltd; Weston Research Laboratories Ltd.

Main brands include: The Bakers Oven; The Harvest Bakery; HiBran; Mighty White; Kingsmill; Speedibake; Sunblest; Vitbe; Silver Spoon; Nelsons of Aintree; Rowallan Creamery; Silbury Frozen Foods; Twinings; Jacksons of Piccadilly; Burton's Gold Medal Biscuits; Ryvita; Crazy Prices.

UK employees: 40,371

Charitable donations
1997: £400,000
1996: £400,000
1995: £400,000
1994: £300,000
1993: £300,000

Community support policy

At head office there are no particular preferred areas of charitable activity for which support is given. Charitable status is normally a requirement.

We have no further information on the £400,000 declared in the company's annual report as its charitable donations in 1997, other than that subsidiaries control a large part of the group's donations programme, and policies are therefore determined largely at local level.

The Garfield Weston Foundation is also administered from the address given above. However, this trust does not receive the money (ie. £400,000) stated as the company's charitable donations; it receives its income from its almost 80% holding of Wittington Investments Ltd which is the ultimate holding company of Associated British Foods plc. This trust is one of the largest UK grant-making trusts, and further information can be found in *A Guide to the Major Trusts Volume 1*.

Exclusions
No sponsorship is undertaken.

Applications
We were not able to establish whether or not there was anyone at the head office who dealt with charitable donations made by directly by the company, and can only assume that most donations are made by subsidiary companies.

Associated British Ports Holdings PLC

150 Holborn, London EC1N 2LR
0171-430 1177; Fax: 0171-430 1384
Email: pr@abports.co.uk
Website: www.abports.co.uk

Correspondent: Miss L Wright, Assistant Corporate Communications Manager

Chief officers: *Chairman:* Sir Keith Stuart; *Managing Director:* Andrew Smith

Year end	Turnover	Pre-tax profit
31/12/97	£287,000,000	£99,000,000

Nature of company business
Principal activities: the provision of port and other transport services; property development and investment. Its 23 ports handle 25% of the UK overseas trade by volume at the following locations: Ayr, Barrow, Barry, Cardiff, Colchester, Fleetwood, Garston, Goole, Grimsby, Hull, Immingham, Ipswich, King's Lynn, Lowestoft, Newport, Plymouth, Port Talbot, Silloth, Southampton, Swansea, Teignmouth, Troon and Whitby. Property interests are handled by the subsidiary Grosvenor Waterside Group which develops land at port sites.

Main subsidiaries: Colchester Dock Transit Co Ltd; Humber Pilotage (CHA) Ltd; Ipswich Port Ltd; Masthead Services Ltd; Red Funnel Crewing Services Ltd; Slaters Transport Ltd; Southampton Free Trade Zone Ltd; Southampton, Isle of Wight and South of England Royal Mail Steam Packet PLC (Red Funnel); The Teignmouth Quay Company (Holdings); Vectis Transport Ltd; Whitby Port Services Ltd; Ocean Village Holdings PLC; Exxtor Group Shipping Services Ltd; Grosvenor Waterside Group PLC.

UK employees: 2,300

Charitable donations
1997: £81,356
1996: £76,118
1995: £83,349
1994: £79,000
1993: £75,000

Community support policy

Charitable donations: In general, donations are made to three broad categories:

(a) charities related to the ports industry or maritime charities

(b) charities which have been of direct assistance to employees and their families

(c) major national medical research charities.

Within these categories, support is given to a range of charitable activity, including children and youth, enterprise and training, medical work and the arts. Most support is given in the area of South Wales, Humber, East Anglia, Cumbria, Southampton and the South West. Preference is given for supporting charities in which a member of staff is involved and a payroll giving scheme is operated.

Main beneficiaries in 1997 included King George's Fund for Sailors, Corporate Action Trust, St John Ambulance, The Development Trust, Cancer Relief Macmillan Fund, Imperial Cancer Research Fund and Royal National Mission to Deep Sea Fishermen.

Donations are made centrally to the above with grants ranging from £1,000 to £3,000. At a local level, port managers have small budgets with which to make donations to charities working in the region of ABP ports. Grants to local organisations range from £100 to £1,000.

Enterprise: Enterprise agencies operating in the locality of ABP-owned ports are supported through annual donations.

The arts: The company sponsors one large project annually, usually with an opera or ballet company. Support is also given to local festivals in areas where the company's ports are located.

Exclusions
No support for circular appeals, appeals from individuals, purely denominational (religious) appeals, political appeals, local appeals not in areas of company presence, animal welfare charities, environment/heritage, education, elderly people, fundraising events, sickness/disability charities, science and technology, sport or overseas projects. Advertising in charity brochures is rare, as the company prefers to make a direct donation.

Applications
In writing to the correspondent. Applications are sorted and likely candidates referred to the chairman. Arts sponsorship proposals to Mrs M Collins, Corporate Communications Manager.

Astra Pharmaceuticals Ltd

Home Park, Kings Langley, Hertfordshire WD4 8DH
01923-266191

Correspondent: Elizabeth Parsons, Grants Administrator

Chief officers: n/a

Year end	Turnover	Pre-tax profit
31/12/97	n/a	n/a

Nature of company business
Manufacture of pharmaceuticals.

UK employees: n/a

Charitable donations
1997: £900,000
1996: n/a
1995: n/a
1994: £900,000

Avon

Community support policy

The company set up the Astra Foundation in 1992 (Charity Commission number 1014774). It supports medical education and research in the UK. In 1997 (the only accounts on file at the Charity Commission since those for 1994), the trust had an income of £916,000, of which £900,000 was grants received from the company. £841,000 was given in grants and the balance rose to £366,000.

The objects of the trusts are:

- to advance public education in medical science
- to undertake or promote research into the causes and cure of any disease or illness and publish the useful results of any such research
- such charitable purposes or for the benefit of such charitable institutions as the trustees shall from time to time decide.

Unfortunately, no grants list was included with the accounts on file at the Charity Commission either for 1997 or 1994. This situation may change, as may the general donations policy, following the recent merger with Zeneca plc. At the time of going to press, however, no details were available.

Applications

In writing to the correspondent.

Avon Cosmetics Ltd

Nunn Mills Road, Northampton NN1 5PA
01604-232425; Fax: 01604-232444

Correspondent: Vicky Smith, Corporate Public Relations Officer

Chief officer: *President:* Mrs Sandy Mountford

Year end	Turnover	Pre-tax profit
31/12/97	£245,721,000	£28,356,000

Nature of company business
A direct seller of beauty and related products including cosmetics, fragrances, toiletries, fashion jewellery and accessories, gifts and toys. In the UK, Avon sells direct through the activities of 150,000 independent sales representatives.

UK employees: 2,051

Charitable donations

1997: £47,921
1996: £72,571
1995: £82,899
1994: £44,599
1993: £81,733
Membership: *BitC %Club*

Community support policy

Avon Cosmetics Ltd is a member of the PerCent Club and Business in the Community.

In 1992, Avon established its Crusade Against Breast Cancer, organising activities to support sales of fundraising merchandise. More than £5.7 million has been raised and shared between Breakthrough Breast Cancer and Macmillan Cancer Relief. In 1998, Avon sponsored Breakthrough's Fashion Targets Breast Cancer campaign which raised £1 million.

With this major commitment to raise awareness and funds for the fight against breast cancer, other activities are limited to supporting local causes, particularly those concentrating on support for initiatives of particular relevance to women.

Applications

In writing to the correspondent.

Avon Rubber plc

Manvers House, Kingston Road, Bradford-on-Avon, Wiltshire BA15 1AA
01225-861100; Fax: 01225-861199

Correspondent: D Bedford, Group Financial Controller

Chief officers: *Chairman:* Christopher P King; *Chief Executive:* Steve Willcox

Year end	Turnover	Pre-tax profit
3/10/98	£267,085,000	£23,905,000

Nature of company business
Principal activities: manufacture of components for the automotive industries; manufacture of other polymer-based products.
Main subsidiaries include: CQC PLC; Nova Insurance Ltd; Cow Polymers Ltd; Hi-Fi Rubber PLC.

UK employees: 5,534

Charitable donations

1998: £69,000
1997: £100,000
1996: £114,000
1995: £52,000
1994: £87,000

Community support policy

The company supports local charities in areas of operation via the Wiltshire Community Foundation. The headquarters of the company is at Bradford-on-Avon, with other sites at Trowbridge and Chippenham.

Support is given to education, medical research and religious appeals, as well as through advertising in charity brochures and support for fundraising events.

Exclusions

No support for animal welfare charities, circular appeals, appeals from individuals, local appeals not in areas of company presence, large national appeals or overseas projects.

Applications

All applications are dealt with by the Wiltshire Community Foundation, details of which can be found in *A Guide to Local Trusts in the South of England*.

AXA Provincial Insurance plc

Stramongate, Kendal, Cumbria LA9 4BE
01539-723415; Fax: 01539-732819

Correspondent: Harry Lowe, Charity Co-ordinator

Chief officers: *Chairman:* G M Wood;
Chief Executive: A Homer

Year end	Turnover	Pre-tax profit
31/12/97	n/a	£61,100,000

Nature of company business
Principal activity: general insurance.
Main subsidiaries include: Venture Preference Ltd; Provincial Training Ltd; Best Legal Protection Ltd; ACE Helpline Ltd; Insurance Management International Ltd; UAP Provincial Insurance Co Ltd (Kenya).
Main brands include: AXA; AXA Direct.

UK employees: 2,091

Charitable donations

1997: £83,804
1996: £82,409
1995: £82,563
1994: £84,237
1993: £110,378
Total community contributions: £150,000

Community support policy

Total community contributions in 1997 were £150,000, just over half of which was given in charitable donations. The main areas of non-cash support are gifts in kind and training schemes.

The company has a preference for projects in areas where it has a presence, especially north west England, and projects involving a member of staff. Preferred areas of support: the arts; children/youth; education; elderly people; environment/heritage; medical research; overseas projects (Kenya only); religious appeals (south Lakeland only); science/technology; sickness/disability charities; social welfare. Typical grants are in the range £250 to £2,500. Main beneficiaries in 1997/98 included: Cancer Relief Macmillan; St John's Hospice – Lancashire; Cumbria Association of Youth Clubs; Cumbria High Sheriff Crimebeat Trust; Brathay Hall Trust and Community Action Trust.

Main donations are made through the Charities Aid Foundation, while local donations (in Cumbria) are channelled through the Provincial Trust for Kendal. This trust makes donations of between £100 and £1,000 to various organisations and individuals in Cumbria. In 1997/98, the trust made grants totalling £9,576.

The Give As You Earn payroll giving scheme was introduced in 1990. Staff are also allowed time off for activities of community benefit and encouraged to become volunteers in their own time.

The company's subsidiary in East Africa supports charities in its areas of operation.

Exclusions

No support for appeals from non-charities, advertising in charity brochures, animal welfare charities, fundraising events, circular appeals, appeals from individuals, political appeals, religious appeals, enterprise/training, sport or large national appeals. The group does not second to charities or enterprise agencies and undertakes no major arts sponsorship, although it does undertake a limited amount of sponsorship of local concerts and charities.

Applications

Applications should be addressed to the correspondent. Appeals and requests for arts sponsorship should be sent to the Marketing Department.

Local charities seeking financial support from the Provincial Trust for Kendal should submit an appeal to the Hon. Secretary, giving full details of the project.

AXA Sun Life Assurance plc

107 Cheapside, London EC2V 6DU
0171-606 7788; Fax: 0171-796 2216
Website: www.sunlife.co.uk

Correspondent: Brian Symonds, Charitable Appeals Executive

Chief officers: *Chairman:* Lord Douro;
Managing Director: A L Owen

Year end	Turnover	Pre-tax profit
31/12/97	n/a	£290,000,000

Nature of company business
The group engages in ordinary long-term insurance business, namely, life assurance, annuities, pension and permanent health insurance business through subsidiary companies. It also engages in unit trust and investment, and property management.
Main subsidiaries include: AXA Insurance Co Ltd; Prospero Direct Ltd; AXA Equity & Law Assurance Society PLC; Suntrust Ltd; AXA Equity & Law Investments Managers Ltd; AXA Equity & Law Unit Trust Managers Ltd.

UK employees: n/a

Charitable donations

1997: £667,000
1996: n/a
1995: £400,000
1994: £350,000
1993: £350,000
Membership: *BitC %Club*

Community support policy

Sun Life is a member of the PerCent Club. The company establishes a list of priority charities at the beginning of each year and gives a few large donations, rather than lots of small ones. Preference is given to children/youth (if needy or infirm), elderly (if needy or infirm), enterprise/training, medical research, sickness/disability and social welfare, although good appeals from other categories will be considered. There is also a preference for appeals from organisations which are national or active in London, Bristol or Coventry (main staff locations). Grants to national organisations range from £5,000 to £15,000 (predominantly for capital items); grants to local organisations from £50 upwards. In 1997, 47 donations of at least £5,000 were made, along with 70 smaller donations to local charities.

The company has an award-winning Community Partnership Programme which encourages many activities, including employee volunteering and the matching of funds raised by members of staff. Over 100 charities received grants in 1998 because of active employee involvement (in addition to mainstream grant-making).

Donations are made in the following areas:

(a) hospitals and medical research

(b) social services, including projects for unemployed and disadvantaged people in the inner cities, drug and alcohol abuse, homelessness and elderly people

(c) miscellaneous, including arts, cathedrals and churches, young people and overseas aid.

Beneficiaries included the Mental Health Foundation, Royal Hospital for Neuro-Disability, Prince's Youth Business Trust, Greater Bristol Foundation, Macmillan Nurse Appeal and Guinness Trust.

Employee involvement: The society encourages activity of community benefit including encouraging staff to become school governors. A payroll giving scheme was re-launched in 1995. Short-term secondments are made through the Action Resource Centre.

Enterprise: The society is a member of Business in the Community and supports enterprise agencies. Donations are made to enterprise projects.

Education: The society is involved in the Bristol area Compact scheme to enhance business-education partnerships. It also provides work experience schemes for pupils and educational materials for schools.

Exclusions

No support for appeals from non-charities, campaigning work by charities, appeals from individuals, small purely local appeals not in an area of company presence, advertising in charity brochures, circular appeals, fundraising events, purely denominational (religious) appeals, animal welfare charities, education, political appeals or science/technology.

Applications

In writing to the correspondent, at PO Box 1810, Bristol BS99 5SN. All grant decisions are made centrally by a donations committee which meets in the spring and autumn each year. Small local appeals, for up to £100, are considered by the Charitable Appeals Executive within one month of receipt.

Information available: The society reports on its community involvement in its annual report and in staff newsletters.

BAA plc

130 Wilton Road, London SW1V 1LQ
0171-834 9449; Fax: 0171-932 6699

Correspondent: Rachel Rowson, Company Secretary

Chief officers: *Chairman:* Lawrence Urquhart; *Chief Executive:* Sir John Egan

Year end	Turnover	Pre-tax profit
31/3/98	£1,679,000,000	£480,000,000

Nature of company business
BAA plc owns and operates seven UK airports: Heathrow, Gatwick, Stansted, Aberdeen, Edinburgh, Glasgow and Southampton. Each airport is run by a separate operating company. Revenue comprises airport and other traffic charges (30.2%) retail revenue (52.2%) and revenue from other activities including advertising (2.9%).

Main subsidiaries include: Heathrow Airport Ltd; Gatwick Airport Ltd; Stansted Airport Ltd; Glasgow Airport Ltd; Edinburgh Airport Ltd; Aberdeen Airport Ltd; Southampton International Airport Ltd; Lynton plc; World Duty Free Europe Ltd.

Main brands include: BAA; World Duty Free; Heathrow Express.

Main locations: Heathrow; Gatwick; Stansted; Aberdeen; Edinburgh; Glasgow; Southampton.

UK employees: 9,059

Charitable donations

1998: £780,000
1997: £719,000
1996: £646,000
1995: £553,000
1994: £541,000
Membership: *BitC*

Community support policy

The company established its own charity, the BAA 21st Century Communities Trust (Charity Commission number 1058617) during 1996/97. It was set up to channel the company's donations to help the local communities 'face the challenges of the new millennium, particularly in the areas of the three Es – education, economic regeneration and the environment'.

The trust will help local communities in three ways:

- assist projects which are developing educational opportunities including those for the disadvantaged
- help groups nurture the physical environment
- assist those whose work is helping to develop employment opportunities.

Generally, grants to national organisations range from £50 to £20,000 and to local organisations from £50 to £2,500. Most support is given locally in south east England and Scotland. Projects are also recommended by airport staff.

Examples of projects supported since the trust was established include: Slough Foyer Appeal which received £50,000 from Heathrow Airport; Springboard Charitable Trust (which funds decoration and repairs for elderly residents in their own homes) which received £12,000 from Stansted Airport; Horley and Crawley Countryside management project which received support from Gatwick Airport towards the running cost of a Land Rover; Waverley Care Trust which received support from Edinburgh Airport for its education programme supporting relatives and carers of HIV and AIDS sufferers; Dyslexia Institute which received support from Aberdeen Airport to introduce into the region dedicated teachers, trained to help dyslexic people. Support has also been given to the Media Trust and special schools.

The first accounts for the trust were for the nine-month period ending 31 March 1997. The trustees are R L Everitt; Dr A C Barrett; Lord Wright of Richmond, D Wilson and C D Hoare. In that period it received donations of £210,000 principally from BAA plc. Grants totalled £134,000.

The largest grants were £40,000 to Brentford Community Boat Trust, £22,500 for a teacher resource pack and £10,000 to Hazelwick School towards their bid for technical status. Five other organisations received over £5,000: Horley/Crawley Countryside Management (£9,250), Scottish Wildlife Trust (£7,500), Time Out from school (£7,000), Environmental improvement – Montfitchet (£6,600) and Surrey & Sussex Young Enterprise (£6,000).

There were a further 12 grants for £5,000 or less including those to Harlow Symphony Primary Prom, Bishop Stortford Kickstart and Homestart – Runnymede.

The company have a night noise penalty which has been extended throughout the day, the fines are then donated to the local community.

The company operates the Give As You Earn payroll giving scheme, and matches both employee giving and fundraising. Staff are also given company time off to volunteer.

Enterprise: The company is involved with the Renfrew Development Company Ltd in the development and the economic redevelopment of the area around Glasgow Airport, and the West London Leadership Organisation.

Environment: The company supports a number of organisations concerned with conservation including Essex Heritage Trust and the wildlife trusts of Essex, Hampshire, Scotland and Sussex.

Education: Education initiatives supported include Common Purpose 'Your Turn' in Schools, Young Engineers through the Standing Conference on Schools, Science and Technology, and the Scottish Council Foundation. The company is also involved in local education/business partnerships, support of Young Enterprise, Business in the Community's Head Teacher Mentoring Programme and supporting the London Leadership Centre's work in management skills for head teachers.

Exclusions

No support is given to circular appeals, fundraising events, individuals, purely denominational (religious) appeals, local appeals not in areas of company presence, advertising in charity brochures, animal welfare charities, the arts, overseas projects, social welfare or sickness/disability charities.

Applications

Applicants are advised to write to the community relations manager at the airports.

Heathrow Airport Ltd: Hounslow, Middlesex (0181-745 4494)

Gatwick Airport Ltd: Public Affairs, Gatwick, West Sussex RH6 0NP (01293-504192)

Stansted Airport Ltd: Community Relations Manager, Stansted, Essex CM24 8QW (01279-502710)

Scottish Airports Ltd: Head of Public Affairs, St Andrew's Drive, Paisley, Renfrewshire PA3 2ST (0141-848 4293)

Southampton International Airport Ltd: Southampton SO9 1RH (01703-629600).

Scott Bader Company Ltd

Wollaston, Wellingborough, Northants NN29 7RL
01933-663100

Correspondent: Denise Sayer, Commonwealth Secretary

Chief officers: *Chairman:* Derek Muir; *Managing Director:* Ian Henderson

Year end	Turnover	Pre-tax profit
2/1/98	£90,527,000	£3,007,000

Nature of company business
The company manufactures and distributes synthetic resins and chemical intermediates.

UK employees: 395

Charitable donations
1997: £168,000
1996: £225,188
1995: £115,088
1994: £108,526
1993: £167,301

Community support policy

The company was given into common ownership by its founder Ernest Bader in 1951 and is now a leading member of the common ownership movement. Its large philanthropic expenditure reflects the ethos of the company.

The Scott Bader Company is wholly owned by the Scott Bader Commonwealth Ltd, a company limited by guarantee and a registered charity. The Commonwealth's income comes almost exclusively from distributions of profit made to it by Scott Bader Company. As of December 1989 a policy was adopted whereby 5% of pre-tax profits are committed to charitable purposes via the Commonwealth.

In 1997, the company paid £320,814 to the Scott Bader Commonwealth in respect of 1996 profits. The charitable trust gave grants totalling £156,881 during the year.

Projects supported

The Scott Bader Commonwealth confines its giving to purposes accepted in law as charitable. The primary objective is to contribute to the development of a genuinely just and peaceful industrial and social order. It seeks to do this by investing time, money and energy in four main areas of concern:

1. 'Sharing the fruits of our labours with those less fortunate' leads the community to look for projects, activities or charities which respond to the needs of those who are most underprivileged, disadvantaged, poor or excluded.
2. 'To question to what extent violence resides in the demands we make upon the earth's resources' leads the community to look for projects, activities or charities which encourage the careful use and protection of the earth's resources. Those which assist poor rural people to become self-reliant are particularly encouraged.
3. 'To foster a movement towards a new peaceful industrial and social order' leads the Commonwealth to look for peace – building projects, activities or charities through education, conflict resolution, reconciliation or citizen diplomacy.
4. 'Far reaching reconstruction' and a change through 'the principle of common-ownership' leads the Commonwealth to look for projects and community activities which seek to encompass these principles of co-operation and democratic participation.

Preferred areas of support are children and youth; social welfare; medical; overseas aid/development; pump-priming and newer charities.

Criteria

The board are guided by the following criteria in determining whether to recommend a project to members of the community:

- Does the project enable people to help themselves?
- Does the amount of money and assistance given by the Commonwealth make a significance difference?
- Are others involved in the project by way of contributing funds or in other ways?
- Is the project adopted by a member of the Commonwealth who will stay in contact with the project and keep members informed on progress?

In trying to decide rationally where to offer support, board members will look for evidence of:

1. clear, relevant and realistic objectives
2. the competence to achieve them
3. potential for replication of the innovative aspects of a project
4. the effect that a Commonwealth grant is likely to have on other potential funding sources
5. where necessary, a medium/long term funding strategy
6. projects, activities or charities which find difficulty raising funds
7. projects, activities or charities which are innovative, imaginative or pioneering
8. projects which are initiated and/or supported by local people and which will improve the self respect and self reliance of those involved.

The latest accounts on file at the Charity Commission were those for 1997 when the charity giving can be split into three categories: local, national (UK) and international. The local donations, while greater in number, tend to be for smaller amounts. Local charities also benefited from the members' Charity Nomination Scheme, whereby each member can nominate a charity, or charities, of their choice to receive up to £200. A total of £52,300 was given through this scheme.

Drug abuse/education problems were targeted as a specific area for UK donations. No geographical restrictions are placed on the international funds. However, the southern Africa designated funds were donated to people in need in southern African countries which included South Africa, Zimbabwe and Malawi. The grants over £1,000 are listed in the charity accounts under the following headings.

International: Grants totalled £36,600 including those to VSO Tanzania (£4,724), Hope & Homes for Children – Albania (£4,000), Azafady – Madagascar (£3,840), Tigre Trust (£3,600) and Confederation Argentina Apoyo Familiar (£3,000).

UK drug abuse/education: Beneficiaries included CCTL (£5,000), Breez (£1,000), Ermason Youth Centre (£1,000) and Resolv (£1,000). £8,000 was given in this category.

UK general: £37,200 was listed under this heading with larger grants including those to Corby Accommodation Project (£3,000), Service Six (£2,800), Busy Bees Pre-school Playgroup (£2,650) and Hearing Dogs for the Deaf (£2,500).

Southern African Funds totalled £7,800 including Africa Now (Repoz) South Africa (£2,800), Africa Now (Honde Valley) Zimbabwe (£2,000), Selborne Routledge College, Zimbabwe (£2,500) and Ntebe Primary School, Zimbabwe (£500).

Exclusions

No support for 'bricks and mortar' appeals, fundraising events, advertising in charity brochures, appeals from individuals, the arts, purely denominational (religious)/political appeals, environment/heritage, large national appeals, animal charities or overseas volunteers. Sponsorship proposals are not considered.

Applications

In writing to the correspondent. Applications for donations can be made at any time.

There is no application form, but the following points should be taken into account in applying for a grant:

- applications should be no longer than four A4 sides
- supporting material may be sent, but is unlikely to be seen by board members.

The following should be included:

- a short general description of the project and its aims
- a budget broken down under different expenditure headings, indicating what part of the budget is requested from the trust and if the grant is for more than one year
- the names of any other agencies likely to contribute to the cost, and an indication of where money will come from when any funding from the Commonwealth runs out

- information on how the project is to be monitored and, if possible, evaluated and made known to others
- for on-going projects a set of audited accounts.

All applications received are reviewed by the Commonwealth Secretary and, if the criteria are met, the application will be considered at a monthly meeting of the Commonwealth Board of Management. Members in a general meeting have the final decision on grants of over £5,000. General meetings are held in February, May, August and November each year. Only those who work within the Scott Bader Company Ltd are able to become members of The Scott Bader Commonwealth, and to participate in the charitable and philanthropic work of the Commonwealth.

William Baird plc

2 Cavendish Square, London W1M 0BF
0171-612 9600

Correspondent: Mrs P M Alsop, Company Secretary

Chief officers: *Chairman:* T D Parr;
Chief Executive: D R Suddens

Year end	Turnover	Pre-tax profit
31/12/97	£598,358,000	£33,360,000

Nature of company business
Principal activities: the design, manufacture and sale of clothing.
Main subsidiaries include: Alexander of England; Bairdwear; Career Apparel; Centaur; Cloud Nine; Dannimac; Melka Tenson; Planet Fashions; Precis Petites; Van Gils; Windsmoor.

UK employees: 15,579

Charitable donations

1997: £54,300
1996: £50,000
1995: £62,664
1994: £81,743
1993: £61,102

Community support policy

The company will consider any charitable requests, but tends to regard those for the relief of suffering, poverty and illness most favourably.

Exclusions

No support for circular appeals, fundraising events, advertising in charity brochures, appeals from individuals, purely denominational (religious) appeals, local appeals not in areas of company presence or overseas projects.

Applications

In writing to the correspondent. Only written appeals will be considered.

J C Bamford Excavators Ltd

Rocester, Uttoxeter, Staffordshire ST14 5JP
01889-590312

Correspondent: L Mitchell, Administrator, Bamford Charitable Foundation

Chief officer: *Chairman:* A P Bamford

Year end	Turnover	Pre-tax profit
31/12/97	n/a	n/a

Nature of company business
The company manufactures hydraulic earth-movers.

UK employees: n/a

Charitable donations

1997: £137,002
1996: £129,707
1995: £131,480
1994: £120,282
1993: £127,450

Community support policy

The company channels its funds through the Bamford Charitable Foundation (Charity Commission number 279848). Support is given to projects in the areas of community services, health and medicine, education, science and religion. Only appeals originating within 25 miles of the company are considered. Preference is given to projects in which a member of staff is involved.

In 1996/97, the trust had an income of £168,000 and gave £137,000 in charitable donations.

The main grant in 1996/97 was again to Denstone College – Language Centre which has, in recent years, been receiving donations of over £20,000 a year. Other large grants included those to Tommy's Campaign and Elton John's AIDS Foundation (£10,000 each). Other beneficiaries included Queensway House – Staffs (£2,500), St George's Hospice (£1,125), St Katherine House Hospice, a regular beneficiary and Cheadle Crime Prevention Panel (£1,000 each) and Royal British Legion and Stafford Association of Boys Clubs (£500).

Exclusions

No support for advertising in brochures, small purely local appeals not in areas of company presence, larger national appeals, overseas projects or circulars. The company does not welcome proposals for arts sponsorship.

Applications

In writing to the correspondent. A donations committee meets quarterly. Local branches do not have an independent grant making policy and local appeals should be addressed to head office. The company welcomes relevant appeals from charities, but the guidelines above should be carefully considered as appeal mail is becoming too large to handle.

# Bank of England

Threadneedle Street, London EC2R 8AH
0171-601 4444; Fax: 0171-601 4837
Website: www.bankofengland.co.uk

Correspondent: Mrs Linda Barnard, Community Relations Manager

Chief officer: *Governor:* Eddie George

Year end	Turnover	Pre-tax profit
28/2/98	n/a	£121,300,000

Nature of company business
The Bank of England is the central bank of the United Kingdom and aims to maintain a stable and efficient monetary and financial framework in pursuance of a healthy economy.

The bank is based in London and has agencies in Birmingham, Bristol, Leeds, Manchester, Newcastle, Glasgow, Liverpool, Nottingham, Winchester, Wales, East Anglia and the South East and Greater London. It operates a printing works in Loughton, Essex, in addition to its Registrar's Department in Gloucester. Subsidiaries include companies purchased in the course of its function of regulating the financial markets including Minories Finance (formerly Johnson Matthey Bankers following the sale of that company's principal business).

UK employees: 3,383

Charitable donations

1998: £451,000
1997: £324,000
1996: £340,000
1995: £348,000
1994: £328,000

Total community contributions: £1,461,000

Membership: *BitC*

Community support policy

Although not a member of the PerCent Club, the bank meets the criteria of contributing no less than half a per cent of its pre-tax profit to the community. In 1997/98, a total of £1,461,000 (0.8% of pre-tax profit) was given in support of the bank's community programme. This includes the cost of secondments, donations to charities and to academic research, and contributions to other community-related activities.

£357,000 was given to registered charities and £94,000 to other organisations, whilst the cost of secondments and subsidised accommodation totalled £1,010,000.

The bank's policy on charitable giving focuses on initiatives which enable disadvantaged people to access worthwhile employment through training and on supporting the staff's community involvement.

£51,600 was donated to charities and schools in recognition of the funds raised or time given by staff. The bank also matched, on a £ for £ basis, £61,000 donated by staff and pensioners to registered charities under the Give As You Earn scheme; £10,500 of staff fundraising; and donations totalling £16,500 made by staff and pensioners to the Diana, Princess of Wales memorial Fund.

The bank encourages a range of education business partnership activities, particularly in areas close to the bank, such as Tower Hamlets, Hackney and Islington. It offers work experience placements, arranges for staff to act as group facilitators at job-finding workshops, as interviewers at practice interview sessions, as business reading partners and as mentors to headteachers. It also supports training for staff who are school governors.

Exclusions

No response to circular appeals. No support for personal appeals, sponsorship requests, fundraising events, advertising in charity brochures, purely denominational (religious) appeals, local appeals not in areas of company presence, overseas projects, the arts, political appeals, science/technology, sport or animal charities.

Applications

Donations can be made locally at the discretion of the branch agent and subject to a limited budget. Otherwise, appeals should be addressed to the correspondent.

Bank of Scotland

Public Relations Department, PO Box No.5, The Mound, Edinburgh EH1 1YZ
0131-243 7058/7060; Fax: 0131-243 7081

Correspondent: Fiona Dawson, Assistant Manager

Chief officers: *Governor:* Sir Alistair Grant;
Chief Executive: Peter A Burt

Year end	Turnover	Pre-tax profit
28/2/98	n/a	£742,000,000

Nature of company business
Banking, financial and related services in the UK and abroad, provided through branches, offices and subsidiaries.

Main subsidiaries include: Capital Bank; Capital Incentives; Daewoo Direct Finance; Edward Rushton Son & Kenyon; Equity Bank; Forthright Finance; Godfrey Davis (Contract Hire); Kellock; British Linen Bank Group; Bank of Wales; Uberior Investments.

UK employees: c.18,000

Charitable donations

1998: £1,300,000
1997: £800,000
1996: £1,600,000
1995: £760,000
1994: £527,000

Total community contributions: £4,000,000

Membership: *ABSA BitC %Club*

Community support policy

The bank is a member of the PerCent Club and of Scottish Business in the Community. In addition to charitable donations, it supports over 300 events throughout the UK through its diverse and responsible sponsorship programme. During 1997, the group contributed £4.0 million to the community, including donations of £1.3 million to charitable organisations. In addition to good-cause sponsorship, gifts in kind are the main area of non-cash support.

Barclays PLC

Community and Social Affairs, 8th Floor, 54 Lombard Street, London EC3P 3AH
0171-699 2969
Email: corp.comms@barclays.co.uk
Website: www.barclays.co.uk

Correspondent: Mrs Angela Tymkow, Community Manager

Chief officers: *Chairman:* A R F Buxton; *Chief Executive:* Sir Peter Middleton

Year end	Turnover	Pre-tax profit
31/12/97	n/a	£1,716,000,000

Nature of company business
Barclays PLC is a UK-based financial services group and one of the UK's largest companies. It provides retail banking products to a wide range of personal and business customers, as well as investment banking and asset management to a global client base.

UK employees: 60,800

Charitable donations

1997: £4,400,000
1996: £4,400,000
1995: £2,600,000
1994: £1,800,000
1993: £1,000,000

Total community contributions: £13,500,000

Membership: *ABSA BitC %Club*

Community support policy

Barclays is a founder member of the PerCent Club. In 1997, total contributions were £15.1 million, including £13.5 million in the UK and £1.6 million through local offices overseas. Of the total in the UK, £4.4 million was in charitable donations, with the other main areas of support being arts and good-cause sponsorship and secondments.

Charitable donations: A much greater proportion of Barclays support is now channelled through the group's local offices around the country, rather than through its central Community Affairs Department. Supporting staff in their own community activities is also a priority.

Support is only given to registered charities or for clearly charitable purposes. The five main categories supported are:

- local communities
- social needs (including young people, people with disabilities and disadvantaged people)
- education and training
- economic regeneration
- the environment.

Main beneficiaries include John Grooms Association for disabled people, Scout Association, National Disabled Persons Housing Service, YMCA and Opportunities for People with Disabilities.

Local appeals are assessed by Barclays network of regional offices and major sites, each of which has its own

---

Sponsorship is only undertaken on a commercial basis and the bank does NOT sponsor charities. The events cover the arts, agriculture, sport and community-based events, and range from the very small to the very large. The bank also seconds staff to work with particular organisations and operates the Give As You Earn payroll giving scheme.

Charitable donations: Grants to national and local organisations range in size upwards from £250. The main focus is on charitable organisations which provide support for underprivileged people in Scotland, particularly to young people.

Other areas for support include education, elderly people, enterprise/training, science/technology, sickness/disability charities and social welfare.

The arts: The bank is a patron of ABSA. It provides sponsorship for arts events throughout the country. Examples include: Scottish Chamber Orchestra, Edinburgh International Festival and Pitlochry Festival Theatre.

Exclusions

The following are not generally supported: circular appeals, fundraising events, advertising in charity brochures, appeals from individuals, local appeals not in areas of company presence, medical research, overseas projects, purely denominational appeals or political appeals.

Applications

Donations are decided upon by a donations committee which meets as required. Appeals should be addressed to the correspondent. Note that although the bank welcomes appeals, it is receiving too many 'mailshot' appeals without sufficient thought being given as to why the bank might wish to support the particular appeal. Local appeals can be addressed to the local branch manager.

Sponsorship applications should be made to Fiona Dawson, assistant manager at the above address. Please note that the bank does not sponsor charities or fundraising events in aid of charities.

Two subsidiaries, the Bank of Wales plc and Capital Bank PLC, make grants independently of head office. Applications should be addressed to the secretary in each case.

Capital Bank plc: Capital House, City Road, Chester CH99 3AN; *Chairman:* Sir J C Shaw; *Secretary:* R Nixon.

British Linen Bank Ltd: 4 Melville Street, Edinburgh EH3 7NS; *Chairman:* W C C Morrison; *Secretary:* J W Robertson.

Bank of Wales plc: Kingsway, Cardiff CF1 4YB; *Chairman:* Sir Alun Davies; *Secretary:* G Rees.

Kellock Ltd: Abbey Gardens, 4 Abbey Street, Reading; *Chairman:* J R Browning; *Secretary:* B N Short.

donations budget. Overseas support is given through the group's operations in the countries concerned.

Sponsorship: Barclays sponsorship programme focuses on a small number of major national schemes – all of which are long-term commitments. Currently these are: Barclays New Futures (school/community partnership projects), Barclays Stage Partners (supporting high-quality touring drama) and Barclays SiteSavers (transforming neglected land into recreational facilities). Although no other national sponsorship can be considered, local sponsorship opportunities can be directed to its network of regional offices.

Employee involvement: Barclays encourages fundraising by staff through a matching £ for £ scheme, which contributed £1.5 million in 1997. A payroll giving scheme is operated. It also provides resources and financial support for employee volunteering groups.

Secondments: The group introduced its Transitional Secondments Programme in 1996 and currently has in excess of 100 employees seconded to a range of charitable and community organisations.

Economic regeneration: Barclays is a member of Business in the Community and funding for business links and similar small business support organisations is coordinated by Barclays Small Business Services.

Education: The principal focus of the group's support is through the Barclays New Futures, its £5 million five-year community service learning sponsorship operated in collaboration with Community Service Volunteers. The scheme provides cash and resources to secondary schools to enable them to work with their local communities in tackling a wide variety of issues. Barclays is also involved in local education/businesss partnerships and provides work experience schemes for pupils and student sponsorship.

Environment: Barclays SiteSavers is a £1 million, three-year programme which aims to help local communities transform derelict land into new recreational and leisure facilities. These include safe play areas, community parks and adventure playgrounds. The sponsorship is managed by Groundwork and other partners in the scheme are the British Trust for Conservation Volunteers, the Wildlife Trust and Scottish Conservation Projects. Barclays CountryFocus is a £500,000 four-year sponsorship supporting the greater enjoyment of National Trust countryside.

The arts: Barclays is a founder member of ABSA and supports a wide range of regional arts organisations and initiatives through its regional offices. The national programme now concentrates on theatre. Barclays Stage Partners encourages regional theatre partnerships to stage and tour new productions nationwide. The three-year programme is worth £2.5 million, including £1 million from the Arts Council of England. Barclays Theatre Awards recognise excellence in all aspects of theatre and is a three-year sponsorship presented in collaboration with the Theatrical Management Association.

Exclusions

No support for circular appeals, appeals from individuals, medical research, purely denominational (religious) appeals or political appeals, animal welfare charities, the arts, fundraising events, overseas projects, science/technology or intermediate fundraising bodies.

Applications

Appeals to head office should be sent to the correspondent above. Local appeals should be sent to regional offices which have their own budgets.

Economic regeneration proposals should be sent to the appropriate regional office, or in need, to P Kelly, Senior PR Manager, Small Business Services, Westwood Business Park, PO Box 120, Coventry CV4 8JN.

Information available: Barclays publishes information on its community investment affairs in a variety of brochures and leaflets, as well as in its annual report and accounts.

Advice to applicants: Barclays has made the following comments about the appeals it receives.

1. No specific application forms are required. However, it will be necessary to send a copy of the latest annual report and audited accounts (the last two years in the case of an initial approach).
2. The group sometimes receives appeals from several different sources within the same charity, or the same appeal is sent to several different employees within the group. This should be avoided.
3. It dislikes the use of advertising agencies to sell space in magazines, brochures or programmes for charity benefits.
4. It receives too many appeals from the same charities during a 12-month period.

Barlow International PLC

16 Stratford Place, London W1N 9AF
0171-629 6243; Fax: 0171-409 0556

Correspondent: Carolyn Munro, Joint Secretary to the Charities Committee

Chief officer: *Chairman:* R M Mansell-Jones

Year end	Turnover	Pre-tax profit
27/9/97	£781,834,000	£50,571,000

Nature of company business
Barlow International PLC is a wholly owned subsidiary of Barlow Ltd of South Africa. The company is an international group of manufacturing and distribution companies. Activities comprise the distribution and servicing of materials handling equipment, earth-moving equipment and other capital equipment; paper making and converting; and the manufacture of laboratory, optical and scientific equipment.

UK employees: 2,951

Charitable donations
1997: £97,000
1996: £111,000
1995: £40,000
1994: £32,000
1993: £72,000

Community support policy

Support is given to 'traditional charities', particularly those concerned with elderly, young, sick and disabled people, education, the arts, enterprise and training, environment and heritage, medical research, science and technology and social welfare on both a national and local basis. Preference is given to projects in areas where the company has a presence and to appeals where a member of staff is involved. The company broke down its donations in 1996/97 made through its UK corporate office as follows:

Local 22.67%
    The young 50.00%
    The old 6.67%
    The sick and infirm 26.67%
    General 16.66%

National 77.33%
    The young 19.55%
    The old 21.50%
    The sick and infirm 29.63%
    General 29.32%

Grants normally range from £50 to £1,000, with most being for £250 or £500. Examples of typical grants include:

- £1,000 to Age Concern England and Counsel and Care for the Elderly
- £500 to Centrepoint Soho and Meningitis Research Foundation
- £250 to Baby Life Support Systems and Invalids at Home.

The company operates a payroll deduction scheme for employee contributions which it occasionally matches. It also encourages staff to become volunteers in their own time.

The arts: Appeals for donations are considered selectively.

Exclusions

The company does not support appeals from non-charities, and rarely advertises in charity brochures for fundraising events. No support for animal welfare charities, appeals from individuals, fundraising events, overseas projects, political appeals, religious appeals or sport.

Applications

Written applications should be sent to Carolyn Munro or Ruth Pollard, Joint Secretaries to the Charities Committee which meets quarterly to consider appeals.

BASF plc

PO Box 4, Earl Road, Cheadle Hulme, Cheshire SK8 6QG
0161-485 6222

Correspondent: Barry Mansfield, Director of Public Affairs & Employee Communications

Chief officer: *Chairman:* H H Stechl

Year end	Turnover	Pre-tax profit
31/12/96	£904,300,000	n/a

Nature of company business
Chemicals, paints, plastics, pharmaceuticals.

Main subsidiaries include: Cheadle Colour and Chemicals Ltd.

Main locations: Cheadle; Ellesmere Port; Seal Sands; Leicester; Didcot; Wolverhampton; Sinfold; Huyton.

UK employees: 1,346

Charitable donations
1996: £51,613
1995: £80,943
1994: n/a
1993: £63,116
Total community contributions: £126,330
Membership: *ABSA BitC*

Community support policy

The company prefers to support local charities in areas where the company operates (mainly in the North West and the North East) working in: the arts; children/youth; education; elderly people; sickness/disability; and science/technology. Donations range from small payments to several thousand pounds. Local sites manage their own local donations. The company is a member of Business in the Company.

Education: The company has close links with local schools and colleges, especially related to science and the environment. It has also funded primary and secondary school chemistry kits and resource material produced and developed by the Chemical Industry Education Centre.

The arts: The company is a member of ABSA and sponsors the Hallé Concerts Society. Support has also been given to the Palace Theatre, Manchester.

Exclusions

No grants for purely denominational (religious) appeals or local appeals not in areas of company presence.

Applications

In writing to the correspondent.

Bass plc

20 North Audley Street, London W1Y 1WE
0171-409 1919; Fax: 0171-409 8501

Correspondent: Walter J Barratt, Charities Administrator

Chief officer: *Chairman:* Sir Ian Prosser

Year end	Turnover	Pre-tax profit
30/9/98	£4,609,000,000	£834,000,000

Nature of company business
Bass is a leisure group operating in hotels, leisure retailing and branded drinks.

Main subsidiaries include: Holiday Hospitality Corporation; Britvic Soft Drinks Ltd.

Main brands: Inter-Continental; Holiday Inn; Crowne Plaza; All Bar One; Fork & Pitcher; Harvester; Innkeeper's Fayre; O'Neill's; Toby; Carling; Tennent's; Caffrey's; Hooper's Hooch; Tango; Robinsons.

UK employees: 83,461

Charitable donations

1998: £1,200,000
1997: £1,100,000
1996: £1,100,000
1995: £772,000
1994: £843,000
Membership: *BitC*

Community support policy

The main areas of non-cash support are gifts in kind, joint promotions and training schemes. Employees are also allowed company time off to volunteer.

The Policy Guidelines (which are available from the Charitable Donations Committee) state:

1. Bass supports a wide range of charities and in particular seeks to work with charities for mutual benefit. Charities where Bass employees are actively involved are also supported through the Bass Community Award Scheme.
2. The main impetus of funding effort is directed to four broad areas – community, youth and education, environment and the arts.

The company tries to give substantial donations to selected charities, which are supported over several years.

Community
Community care is an important part of the company's charitable giving, embracing such areas as help for the sick, terminally-ill, disabled, homeless, young offenders and numerous other aspects of real need within the community. Many organisations within this category operate most effectively at a local level.

Youth and education
Bass continues to identify itself as a company committed to the development of young people. The company also supports the development of skills of citizenship and social awareness of young people outside places of education. In supporting youth-orientated charities the company looks with special interest at the development of adult youth leaders. Bass supports the furtherance of interest in careers within industry.

Environment
Bass supports projects and programmes of work to protect and/or improve the physical landscape and the urban environment with particular emphasis on areas where the company has a significant presence.

Arts
Bass provides patronage for the visual and performing arts. Development of the talents of young people and encouragement of national initiatives and organisations are prime objectives.

3. A substantial share of the charitable funds are distributed through the operating divisions of the company's retail businesses. Many donations are given in response to appeals initially made to Bass operating companies.
4. Projects requiring capital investment may be considered in exceptional circumstances as part of a wider programme of support.

Included in the above will be projects/organisations involved with elderly people, enterprise/training, science/technology and sport. Grants to local organisations range upwards from £250 and grants to national organisations range from upwards of £1,000.

The five main beneficiaries of grants during 1997/98 were: Millennium Greens, Understanding Industry, Northern Youth Venture Fund, Corporate Action Trust and Nottingham Trent University.

Special consideration to appeals:

- originating in areas where the company has a substantial presence
- with which an employee has a close and active association.

The company operates the CAF payroll giving scheme.

Exclusions
Because resources are limited, the following will not be considered:

- charities not registered nor of legal charitable status
- political parties or organisations with political affiliations
- charities or organisations with religious affiliations
- expeditions and adventure travel groups
- individuals seeking personal sponsorship
- intermediaries acting between charity and donor
- applications from organisations from areas where we have no involvement
- advertising space in souvenir programmes, brochures, lotteries, sponsored events, etc.

Applications
In writing to the correspondent. Local appeals should be addressed to the public relations manager at the appropriate regional office. Established charities should always send up-to-date audited accounts with any appeal. Policy guidelines are available from the correspondent.

L Batley (Holdings) Ltd

Leeds Road, Huddersfield, West Yorkshire HD2 1UP
01484-544211; Fax: 01484-510213

Correspondent: L W McCormick, Managing Director

Chief officer: *Chairman:* L Batley

Year end	Turnover	Pre-tax profit
2/5/98	£525,219,000	£12,269,000

Nature of company business
The main activity of the company is that of a cash and carry wholesalers.

UK employees: 1,519

Charitable donations
1998: £99,451
1997: n/a
1996: £41,915
1995: £57,378

Community support policy
We have no information on the donations policy of the company, other than that in 1997/98, most support was given to Guide Dogs for the Blind.

Applications
In writing to the correspondent.

Bayer plc

Bayer House, Strawberry Hill, Newbury, Berkshire RG14 1JA
01635-563000

Correspondent: Steve Painter, Head of Corporate Communications

Chief officers: *Chairman:* Dr H J Mohr; *Managing Director:* L T Aberg

Year end	Turnover	Pre-tax profit
31/12/96	£453,585,000	£7,425,000

Nature of company business
Marketing of around 2,000 pharmaceutical, chemical and agro-chemical products of Bayer AG.

Main subsidiaries include: Haarman & Reimer Ltd; Microbial Developments Ltd; Florasyth Ltd.

UK employees: n/a

Charitable donations
1996: £147,665
1995: £142,518
1994: £169,020
1993: £69,525

Total community contributions: £450,000 (1995)

Community support policy
The company was 'unable to provide up-to-date information' but has given about £150,000 in charitable donations in recent years. For the previous edition of this guide the company provided the following information: total community contributions in 1995 were £450,000, about a third of which was in the form of cash donations.

The company supports charities that have a business link, a staff link or a geographical link. The company's main sites are Selby, Newbury, Marlow, Bridgend, Bromsgrove and Bury St Edmunds.

The decision as to which causes receive support and to what extent is, with few exceptions, taken by local community trusts and Education Business Partnerships, to whom requests should be made. Preference is given for charities in which a member of staff is involved and for children/youth, education and environment, either to save life or alleviate human suffering, or to expand the public appreciation of cultural experience.

Exclusions
No support for political, religious or animal welfare organisations, events or individuals which would usually expect major funding from statutory sources. No support for advertising in charity brochures, circular appeals or local appeals not in areas of company presence.

Applications
In writing to the correspondent.

BBA Group plc

70 Fleet Street, London EC4Y 1EY
0171-842 4900; Fax: 0171-353 5831
Website: www.bbagroup.com

Correspondent: Sam Vickers, Office Manager

Chief officers: *Chairman:* V E Treves; *Chief Executive:* R Quarta

Year end	Turnover	Pre-tax profit
31/12/97	£1,192,600,000	£156,700,000

Nature of company business
An international group of engineering and transportation businesses which supply products and services to the industrial textile, automotive, aviation and electrical contracting industries.

Main subsidiaries include: Terram Ltd; APPH Ltd; Aviation Component Repair Services Ltd; Trinity Aerospace Engineering Ltd; Ajax Magnathermic Europe Ltd.

UK employees: 1,945

Charitable donations
1997: £42,000
1996: £40,000
1995: £60,000
1994: £88,000
1993: £101,000

Community support policy
The group supports general charitable purposes, preferring the fields of children and youth, education, environment and heritage, and the arts. Grants from headquarters are made to national registered charities. Local organisations should contact their local company.

Grants usually range from £250 to £3,000, and to local organisations from £100 to £1,000.

There is also a small trust associated with the company, the BBA Centenary Trust. It was set up in 1980, and the company covenanted £45,000 a year for seven years.

The objects of the trust are as follows:
1. relief in need of ex-employees
2. advance the education of people who live in Cleckheaton, West Yorkshire
3. general.

The latest year for which information was available was 1995/96, when the trust had assets of £139,000 and an income of £19,000. Grants totalled £46,000 and were mostly given locally (in the Cleckheaton area).

Exclusions
No support is given for advertising in charity brochures.

Applications
In writing to the correspondent. The budget is allocated annually in November/December.

Applications to the trust should be made to: Managing Director, BBA Friction, BBA Group plc, PO Box 18, Hunsworth Lane, Cleckheaton, West Yorkshire BD19 3UJ.

BCH Group plc

Oakwood Park, Lodge Causeway, Fishponds, Bristol BS16 3JA
0117-908 2000; Fax: 0117-908 9000
Website: www.bch.co.uk

Correspondent: Christian Meylan, Marketing Supervisor

Chief officers: *Chairman:* A K Mitchard;
Chief Executive: R M Pepper

Year end	Turnover	Pre-tax profit
31/12/97	£55,812,000	£2,990,000

Nature of company business
The principal activity of the group is the provision of vehicle management services to external customers, including the arrangement of vehicle financing, and the sale of used motor vehicles.

UK employees: 154

Charitable donations
1997: £49,660

Community support policy
The company was floated on the London Stock Exchange in November last year. In 1997, it gave over 1.5% of pre-tax profits in charitable donations. Historically it has tended to support the charity ChildLine.

Applications
In writing to the correspondent.

Bellway plc

Seaton Burn House, Dudley Lane, Seaton Burn, Newcastle upon Tyne NE13 6BE
0191-217 0717; Fax: 0191-236 6230
Website: www.bellway.co.uk

Correspondent: Peter Stoker, Company Secretary

Chief officer: *Chairman:* Howard C Dawe

Year end	Turnover	Pre-tax profit
31/7/98	£444,873,000	£60,723,000

Nature of company business
The company's main activity is housebuilding.

Main subsidiaries include: Litrose Investments Ltd; The Victoria Dock Co Ltd.

Main locations: Chelmsford; Bedworth; Eastcote; Altrincham; Glasgow; Merstham; Tamworth; Wetherby; Chadderton; Uxbridge; Cardiff; Ringwood; Wakefield.

UK employees: 1,530

Charitable donations
1998: £36,690
1997: £52,368
1996: £31,609
1995: £31,707

Community support policy
The company's level of donations fell in the last year, despite a rise in turnover and pre-tax profits.

The company supports a wide range of both local and national charities (the locations of the main offices are listed above). No further information was available on the types of charities supported.

Applications
In writing to the correspondent.

Bentalls plc

Anstee House, Wood Street, Kingston-upon-Thames, Surrey KT1 1TS
0181-546 2002; Fax: 0181-547 3880

Correspondent: The Chairman

Chief officers: *Chairman:* E Bentall; *Chief Executive:* D Elliott

Year end	Turnover	Pre-tax profit
31/1/98	£104,257,000	£11,736,000

Nature of company business
The principal activity is the operation of department stores, the principal being in Kingston-upon-Thames, with branches in Ealing, Worthing, Bracknell, Tonbridge, Lakeside Thurrock and Bristol.

UK employees: 1,167

Charitable donations
1998: £57,872
1997: £53,315
1996: £37,984
1995: £30,038
1994: £26,462
Membership: %Club

Community support policy

The company is a member of the PerCent Club and supports local charities and branches of national charities situated in its areas of operation (see list above). There is a preference for children and youth, social welfare, elderly people, education and medical causes. Fundraising events may be supported. Grants to organisations range from £10 to £1,500.

The company has supported national retail charities such as Cottage Homes and Purley School Trust. It has also sponsored the Kingston and Richmond Young Enterprise Awards evening at Kingston University as well as Kingston and District Sea Cadet Corps and Kingston Grammar School.

Staff are encouraged to be involved in local charities and be school governors.

Exclusions

No support for large national appeals, overseas projects, political appeals, science/technology, appeals from individuals or for advertising in charity brochures.

Applications

In writing to the correspondent.

For amounts under £100, to the stores at Kingston-upon-Thames, Worthing, Ealing, Bracknell, Tonbridge, Lakeside Thurrock and Bristol. For amounts over £100, to Mrs A Adam, Secretary to the Chairman at the address above.

Berkeley Group plc

19 Portsmouth Road, Cobham, Surrey KT11 1JD
01932-868555; Fax: 01932-868667

Correspondent: Rebecca Hurst, Personal Assistant to the Managing Director

Chief officers: *Chairman:* G J Roper;
Managing Director: A W Pidgley

Year end	Turnover	Pre-tax profit
30/4/98	£599,596,000	£100,320,000

Nature of company business
Principal activity: housebuilding and commercial property investment and development.
Main subsidiaries include: Beaufort Western Ltd; Crosby Homes Ltd; The Beaufort Homes Development Group PLC; St Andrew PLC; St David Ltd; St George Ltd; Sandgates Development Ltd; Community Housing Action Ltd; Retirement Homes Ltd; St George's Hill Property Co Ltd; Sitesecure Ltd; Thirlstone Group Ltd.

UK employees: 1,116

Charitable donations
1998: £163,000
1997: £104,000
1996: £60,000
1995: £61,000
1994: £52,000

Community support policy

The company supports a wide range of local and national charities as long as they are based near to offices of operation. Preferred areas of support are: children/youth, elderly people, environment/heritage and sickness/disability charities.

Previous beneficiaries have included: Princess Alice Hospice (Esher, Surrey), St John Ambulance (Surrey), Paishill Park (Cobham, Surrey) and various cancer charities and children's hospitals. The company also advertises in charity brochures.

Exclusions

No support for: animal welfare charities; appeals from individuals; the arts; education; enterprise/training; fundraising events; medical research; overseas projects; political appeals; religious appeals; science/technology; social welfare or sport.

Applications

In writing to the correspondent however, the company has a charity committee which tends to plan its giving in advance.

Bestway (Holdings) Ltd

Abbey Road, Park Royal, London NW10 7BW
0181-453 1234

Correspondent: Don Taylor, The Bestway Foundation

Chief officer: *Chairman:* M A Pervez

Year end	Turnover	Pre-tax profit
30/6/96	£484,473,000	£14,984,000

Nature of company business
The subsidiaries of the holding company are involved in the operation of cash and carry warehouses supplying groceries, tobacco, wines and spirits, beers and other household goods.
Main subsidiaries include: Icecross; Map (UK).
Main locations: Bristol; Croydon; Leicester; Southall (London); Romford.

UK employees: n/a

Charitable donations
1996: £297,500
1995: £260,000
1994: £260,000
1993: £250,000
Membership: %Club

Betterware

Community support policy

The company is a member of the PerCent Club, with the charitable donations rising to almost £300,000 in 1995/96. It donates about 2.5% of its operating profits to the Bestway Foundation (Charity Commission number 297178).

The foundation's objects are to assist disadvantaged individuals by means of bursaries for higher education, health care provision and social work support.

In 1995/96, the foundation had assets of £1.7 million and an income of £469,000 which included £297,500 from the company. It classified its expenditure as follows.

Donations to charitable trusts £135,000
Charity fundraising event expenses £83,000
Other donations ie. to foreign charities and appeals £28,000

The first category included four grants of over £10,000. These were to Age Concern England (£40,000) for its 'Coldwatch' programme, Duke of Edinburgh's Award (£16,000), Bordesley Green Girls School (£15,000) for the completion of a library extension and adult literacy facility and Francis Holland School (£12,500). The other grants ranged from £35 to £10,000 including those to Ilford Islamic Centre, Liverpool School of Tropical Medicine, Pakistan Women's Welfare Association, School of Oriental & African Studies and Wine & Spirit Trades' Benevolent Society.

The third category included £10,000 each to Business & Professional Women's Organisation and the Society for the Welfare of Patients of Urology and Transplants, and £7,000 to Nishtar Medical College.

Applications
In writing to the correspondent, but note the above.

Betterware plc

Stanley House, Park Lane, Castle Vale, Birmingham B35 6LJ
0121-693 1000

Correspondent: Wendy Cohen

Chief officer: *Chairman:* Andrew L Cohen

Year end	Turnover	Pre-tax profit
1/3/97	£60,715,000	£9,287,000

Nature of company business
Catalogue retail of housewares.

UK employees: 350

Charitable donations
1996: £93,000
1995: £140,530
1994: £144,000
1993: £96,000
Membership: %Club

Community support policy

The company is a member of the PerCent Club and 1% of company profits are donated to the Betterware Foundation. However, we have not been able to obtain a more recent figure from the company since that for 1996, when £93,000 was donated.

Preferred areas of support are: advertising in charity brochures; animal welfare charities; appeals from individuals; children/youth; elderly people; environment/heritage; fundraising events; sickness/disability charities; and social welfare. Both national (UK) and local charities are supported, including many small projects nominated by sales people. The company also advertises in charity brochures.

Financial support is provided in respect of employees' volunteering/charitable activities.

Applications
Charitable appeals should be addressed to:
Wendy Cohen, Betterware Foundation, 5 Stanmore Hill, Stanmore, Middlesex HA7 3DP.

BG plc

100 Thames Valley Park Drive, Reading, Berkshire RG6 1PT
0118-935 3222; Fax: 0118-935 3484
Website: www.bgplc.com

Correspondent: Mary Harris, Director, BG Foundation

Chief officers: *Chairman:* R Giordano;
Chief Executive: D Varney

Year end	Turnover	Pre-tax profit
31/12/97	£5,351,000,000	£1,251,000,000

Nature of company business
The company distributes and sells gas to industry and domestic customers. It comprises three main businesses: *Transco*, the developer and operator of Great Britain's gas transportation network; a substantial, mainly gas producing *Exploration and Production* business which operates in UK offshore waters and overseas; and a growing international *Downstream* gas business engaged in the development and supply of gas markets.

Main subsidiaries include: Premier Power Ltd.

UK employees: n/a

Charitable donations
1997: £1,500,000
1996: £2,200,000
1995: £2,500,000
1994: £1,300,000
1993: £2,000,000
Total community contributions: £2,700,000 (1996)
Membership: *ABSA BitC*

Community support policy

The company states: 'We believe it is vital to contribute to the communities in which we operate both at home and abroad. We seek to make a real difference to community activities and we do this for three reasons:

- our mission is to behave in a social and responsible manner wherever we operate
- our sustained commercial success is only possible if our local communities are also thriving
- helping the community also benefits our company reputation.'

The BG Foundation coordinates and implements BG's social responsibility programme. The strategy is to:

- concentrate support in three main areas of activity
- place strong emphasis on being forward-looking so as to anticipate society's issues, and thus pilot innovative practical solutions
- ensure help is given to local community projects at a grassroots level.

The three areas of activity are:

Developing community well-being
'We seek to minimise social deprivation and to re-generate local communities. We support projects that help people turn their community into a safer, more prosperous and better place.'

Improving local environments
'We want to make run down and economically deprived areas more enjoyable places to live. We will fund projects that make a contribution to improving living surroundings – both urban and rural.

'We also encourage energy efficiency and support projects that aim to save energy and help low income groups.'

Life-long learning
'We believe people should be equipped with the right skills for a better future. That means, we look for projects that develop abilities, unlock potential and build confidence in people of all ages.'

Support is given in four different ways:

Flagship and major projects
A number of projects are selected each year, to which significant levels of funding, employee skills and time are donated. These projects receive board level involvement.

One initiative is support for Green Futures, which the foundation funds in partnership with Groundwork. The programme runs in the government's priority areas: Merseyside, East Midlands, South Yorkshire and the North West, and aims to bridge the gap between long-term unemployment and mainstream jobs. It will enable young people to receive paid work and training through delivering environmental services and help them find permanent employment or further training.

Regional involvement
To benefit the community at a grassroots level support is given to a programme of local projects, which also provides employees with opportunities to get involved. An additional Innovation Fund rewards and encourages innovative ideas from the regions.

One example, under the category, Life-long learning, is involvement with a primary school in Reading. In conjunction with Business in the Community, 16 volunteers from BG spend one lunch hour a week reading with children. This has led to other support by BG for the school, such as computer equipment, money for new books and field trips. The company hopes to extend the literacy project to some of its other businesses.

Another initiative in the Reading area has been the development of training courses for young offenders at Reading Prison. In year one of the scheme, the BG Foundation paid for 50 forklift training courses.

Matching employee fundraising
Within the foundation's three areas of activity, employee fundraising for local groups is matched by the foundation up to a limit of £250 per employee per year.

International assistance
The company operates in 17 countries, and each international office is actively involved in helping the differing needs of their local communities. The foundation supports those international projects which come under its three chosen areas of activity (see above).

Examples include:

Philippines – sponsoring the first day-care facility for mentally handicapped Filipino children, in the form of financial support for training special staff and providing transportation for the children.

Egypt – supporting an orphanage in Cairo, including help towards building a baby unit.

Trinidad – supporting FundAid, a local organisation helping generate employment opportunities for young unemployed people and single mothers.

India – helping to promote healthcare programmes and equipping a local hospital with a mobile healthcare van.

Transco Grassroots Scheme
The operating company Transco runs an annual environmental sponsorship scheme. In 1997, it distributed a total of £100,000 in awards to 34 schemes. They varied in value from £395 for a tree nursery in Cornwall to one maximum award of £7,000 for a community nature park in Stirling. This initiative continued in 1998, with a commitment of £120,000 – £40,000 for schools projects and £80,000 for environmental charity/community group projects.

The scheme is competitive, offering money for well-planned conservation and environmental projects in England, Wales and Scotland. It is open to individual secondary and middle schools, conservation charities and community groups. Typical projects eligible for funding range from improving pathways, restoring natural habitats, to creating city farms or environmental facilities for disabled people.

The entry brochure is mailed out to about 7,000 schools and 3,000 voluntary groups and charities. An independent panel of judges includes senior figures from the environmental sector, media and education. The entry period is April to May, with judging in June. Winners are notified in July.

The contact for the scheme is: Transco Grassroots Administration, c/o Kallaways Ltd, 2 Portland Road, London W11 4LA (0171-221 7883).

Exclusions

No support is given to circular appeals, appeals from individuals, purely denominational (religious) appeals, large national appeals, political appeals, bricks and mortar appeals or animal organisations.

Applications

In writing to the correspondent. British Gas Regions deal with requests for assistance to local projects. The unit at headquarters handles all requests which have national implications.

BHP Petroleum Ltd

Point of Ayr Terminal, Station Road, Talacre, Flintshire CH8 9RD
01745-881302; Fax: 01745-886465

Correspondent: Mrs Frances Waltham, External Affairs Officer

Chief officer: *Chief Executive:* John B Prescott

Year end	Turnover	Pre-tax profit
31/5/97	n/a	n/a

Nature of company business
BHP Petroleum Ltd is involved in oil and gas exploration and production. It operates the Liverpool Bay oil and gas field and two gas fields in the North Sea. It is part of the Broken Hill Properties Company Ltd, Australia's largest company.

UK employees: n/a

Charitable donations

1997: £60,000
1996: n/a
1995: £500,000

Community support policy

Donations policy: The company prefers to support local charities in areas of company presence, ie. north west England and north Wales. It concentrates on projects in education, community welfare, medical research, youth, the arts and the environment. Support is also given to elderly people, sport, sickness/disability, science/technology and enterprise/training.

The five main donations were those to: British Advancement of Science Association, Southport District Scout Council, Dee Estuary Strategy – Education Group, Llangollen International Music Eisteddfod and Sefton Borough Council – Leisure Services.

Lennox First Oil Fund

In February 1996, the company set up The Lennox First Oil Fund to celebrate the flow of first oil from its Lennox Field. This fund provides grants of up to £2,000 for projects which provide clear environmental or safety benefits to the Sefton (in Merseyside) community and have strong community involvement. Applicants should either have a proven track record or be able to demonstrate the ability to achieve their stated aims and objectives and should provide information on their management and financial status. BHP expect some appropriate form of recognition for their donation.

If your organisation fits the above criteria, before making an application, contact the correspondent for a copy of the Lennox First Oil Leaflet for further details of the fund. Unlike the company, this fund will not support sporting activities.

Exclusions

No support for national charities, individuals, religious organisations, activities of a hazardous nature, dinners, cultural events, fundraising making bodies or projects which BHP feels fall within responsibilities of local or national government.

Applications

Applications should be made in writing to the Corporate Affairs Manager, BHP Petroleum Ltd, Point of Ayr Terminal, Hollywell, Flintshire CH8 9RD.

BICC plc

Devonshire House, Mayfair Place, London W1X 5FH
0171-629 6622; Fax: 0171-409 0070
Website: www.bicc.com

Correspondent: Stuart Murray, Company Secretary

Chief officers: *Chairman:* Viscount Weir;
Chief Executive: Alan Jones

Year end	Turnover	Pre-tax profit
31/12/97	£4,139,000,000	(£30,000,000)

Nature of company business
The group specialises in cables and construction, principally for the communications and power industries, and is involved in electrical, mechanical and civil engineering.

Main subsidiaries include: Balfour Beatty; BICC Cables.

UK employees: 895

Charitable donations

1997: £100,000
1996: £200,000
1995: £200,000
1994: n/a
1993: £200,000
Membership: *BitC*

Community support policy

There is very little information available about this company's charitable donations despite it consistently having given £200,000 a year (1997 being the exception). It has requested not to be included in the guide, but we maintain our policy of including details of all relevant companies.

Support is only given to charities of direct relevance to the company's operations where the person making the appeal is known to the company.

Employee involvement: Staff are encouraged to become volunteers in their own time.

Enterprise: The company is a member of Business in the Community.

Exclusions

The company prefers to give directly rather than through fundraising events, advertising in charity brochures or sponsorship. No support for fundraising events, circular appeals or individuals.

Applications

An appeals committee meets occasionally. Note that the company states: 'Only applications from people known to the group will be considered. All others will be binned unanswered.'

Birmingham International Airport plc

Birmingham B26 3QJ
0121-767 7311; Fax: 0121-767 7490
Website: www.bhx.co.uk

Correspondent: Marie Barnes, Birmingham Airport Community Trust Fund

Chief officer: *Chairman:* J L Hudson

Year end	Turnover	Pre-tax profit
31/3/97	£62,716,000	£17,754,000

Nature of company business
The principal activity is the operation and management of Birmingham International Airport and the provision of associated facilities and services.

UK employees: 700

Charitable donations
1997: £63,410

Community support policy

The company has recently set up a trust to fund a wide range of community-based projects which will benefit the community and environment around Birmingham Airport. The fund acts independently of the airport management, with representatives of the following bodies making up the trustees: The Airport Consultative Committee, Birmingham City Council, Birmingham International Airport and the Metropolitan Borough of Solihull.

The company will give an annual contribution of £50,000, with further income collected through fines imposed on airlines whose planes break night noise limits. The money from fines has already increased the fund to £160,000.

Grants are only made to local organisations for projects that improve the environment by:

- involvement in heritage conservation
- improving awareness of environmental issues
- encouraging and protecting wildlife
- building community links through sport, recreation and other leisure time activities.

Priority will be given to projects which are based locally, or under local control; projects involving facilities or access to take account of people with special needs and the elderly; and projects where the grant from the trust will be at least supplemented by contributions from other sources. Low priority will be given to local branches of large national organisations and also organisations which receive substantial support from elsewhere.

Geographical area: The trust will support projects in areas which are affected by the airport's operations. Applicants should explain how their area is affected and the benefits of the proposed project.

Size of grants: Grants are usually for up to £3,000. Only in exceptional circumstances will larger grants be considered, and if approved payments may be staged, based on the achievement of agreed milestones.

Types of grants: Both capital and revenue projects are considered. The trust will not commit to recurring expenditure.

Exclusions

No grants to individuals, projects which have already been carried out or paid for, organisations which have statutory responsibilities, hospitals, schools, etc. for example, unless the project is clearly not a statutory responsibility. Grants are not normally given towards the purchase of land or buildings; however, requests for equipment, fixtures and fittings may be supported. Grants will also not normally be recurrent.

Applications

On a form available from the correspondent. When the form is sent, applicants will be advised when the next grant allocation meeting is being held. The trust may want to visit the project. All applications will be acknowledged.

Applications can be submitted at any time, with grants awarded twice a year in April and October. Successful applicants are required to submit a progress report after six months, and again after 12 for longer projects.

Birmingham Midshires Building Society

PO Box 81, Pendeford Business Park, Wobaston Road, Wolverhampton WV9 5HZ
01902-302000
Website: www.birmingham-midshires.co.uk/bmbs/

Correspondent: Debbie Dance, Personal Assistant to the Head of Corporate Relations

Chief officers: *Chairman:* John Leighfield;
Chief Executive: Ian Kerr

Year end	Turnover	Pre-tax profit
31/12/96	£526,700,000	£70,700,000

Nature of company business
Building society.

Main subsidiaries include: Bavarian Mortgages No.2 Ltd; Europe Mortgages Co Ltd; The Tamar Mortgage Corpn Ltd; London Credit Ltd; Peaktons Ltd; Western Trust & Savings Holdings Ltd; BMMS Land Development Ltd; Western Trust & Savings Ltd.

UK employees: n/a

Charitable donations
1997: £78,000
1996: £46,000
1995: £51,237
1994: £35,382
1993: £8,950

Total community contributions: £120,000 (1995)

Community support policy
The following is taken from the society's 1997 Annual Report.

'Birmingham Midshires actively contributes to the well-being of the communities in which it operates and in which our members and customers live. We believe this to be a social responsibility which our people and our customers respect and expect us to fulfil.

'We continue to focus our community involvement on areas that relate to our business, particularly on helping people overcome financial difficulty and assisting with the plight of the homeless.

'We donated and encouraged our people and customers to raise £78,000 for charities in 1997 (£46,000 in 1996). This included £15,000 in support of National Debt Line, a Birmingham-based organisation which provides advice to consumers facing financial problems and support to the Wolverhampton-based Good Shepherd Trust, which helps homeless people in our home town.

'We continued to sponsor highly successful community schemes with regional newspapers in Liverpool, Birmingham and Bristol. Through these we recognise and reward the courage shown by adults and children in situations of adversity and the contribution made by exceptional individuals to the communities in which they live.

'We also encourage our people to be active in their own communities, through voluntary work, school governorships and by raising money for good causes.'

Exclusions
No response to circular appeals. No support for advertising in charity brochures, appeals from individuals, purely denominational (religious) appeals, local appeals not in areas of company presence, large national appeals, overseas projects, building restoration or political purposes.

Applications
In writing to the correspondent, from whom policy guidelines are available.

Biwater PLC

Biwater House, Station Approach, Dorking RH4 1TZ
01306-740740; Fax: 01306-885233

Correspondent: Larry Magor, Finance Director

Chief officers: *Chairman:* A E White; *Chief Executive:* P L Smith; *Managing Director:* D F W White

Year end	Turnover	Pre-tax profit
31/3/98	£209,000,000	£1,200,000

Nature of company business
Principal activities: contracting, including civil engineering, water and waste water treatment; manufacturing.

UK employees: 1,766

Charitable donations
1997: £47,506
1996: £100,000
1995: n/a
1994: £172,000
1993: £259,000

Total community contributions: £70,670

Community support policy
Currently (1998/99) the company is channelling all its support to Epsom Hospital. The only other charities the company supports are very local Dorking charities.

Exclusions
No support is given to individual appeals, purely denominational (religious) appeals or overseas projects. No sponsorship or advertising in charity brochures is undertaken.

Applications
In writing to the correspondent.

Peter Black Holdings plc

Keighley, West Yorkshire BD21 3BB
01535-661131; Fax: 01535-609973

Correspondent: Carol Prior, Charities Co-ordinator

Chief officers: *Chairman:* Gordon L Black; *Chief Executive:* Stephen Lister

Year end	Turnover	Pre-tax profit
30/5/98	£184,775,000	£17,516,000

Nature of company business
The company's main activities are in personal care products, footwear and accessories.

UK employees: 1,538

Charitable donations
1998: £36,212
1997: n/a
1996: n/a
1995: £25,901

Community support policy

The company appears to route its charitable support through the Peter Black Charitable Trust (Charity Commission number 264279). In 1996/97, this trust had an income of £83,000, virtually all in Gift Aid donations received. Grants totalled only £41,000, resulting in an increase in the assets from £43,000 to £60,000.

The largest grants during the year were to the Imperial War Museum (£7,500), Aston Trust and Cookridge Cancer Centre Appeal (both £5,000), Aysgarth School (£2,500), Yorkshire Ballet Seminars and One to One Peace treks (both £2,000). There were three grants of £1,000, given to Ardenlea Marie Curie Centre, Bootham School and Quest Cancer Research.

There were a further 45 grants of £25 upwards given to a range of organisations with a preference for local causes in Yorkshire where the company is based. Beneficiaries included Candlelighters Trust, Grassington Millennium Project, Ilkley Literature Festival, Keighley Police Summer Scheme and Yorkshire Wildlife Trust.

In all, the grants totalled £36,000, with the other £5,000 categorised as given to 'Outward Bound Project' to the Dales Centre and other minibus costs.

Applications

In writing to the correspondent.

Blue Circle Industries PLC

84 Eccleston Square, London SW1V 1PX
0171-828 3456
Website: www.bluecircle.co.uk

Correspondent: Miss Sarah May, Corporate Communications Officer

Chief officers: *Chairman:* Lord Christopher Tugendhat; *Chief Executive:* K Orrell-Jones

Year end	Turnover	Pre-tax profit
31/12/97	£1,938,800,000	£246,300,000

Nature of company business
Blue Circle Industries PLC is the parent company of an international group of companies whose core businesses are the manufacture and sale of heavy building materials and heating and bathroom products.
Main subsidiaries include: Associated International Cement; Crossways 25.
Main locations: Aberthaw, South Glamorgan; Cauldon, Stoke-on-Trent; Cookstown, County Tyrone; Dunbar, East Lothian; Hope, Derbyshire; Ipswich; Northfleet, Kent; Plymouth; Weardale, Bishop Auckland; Westbury, Wiltshire; Warwick; Dartford; Armitage, Staffs.

UK employees: 7,668

Charitable donations
1997: £286,644
1996: £247,486
1995: £156,773
1994: £351,424
1993: £312,479
Membership: *BitC   %Club*

Community support policy

Blue Circle is a member of the PerCent Club. In 1997, £750,507 was given in charitable donations worldwide, of which £286,644 was given in the UK.

Charitable donations: The causes supported in the UK with the proportion of funds they received were as follows (1996 figures in brackets):

Social causes	*15%*	*(18%)*
Education	*18%*	*(43%)*
Medicine	*52%*	*(10%)*
Environment, the arts and sport	*15%*	*(29%)*

The company states that the main criteria for making a donation 'is to provide benefit in an area where a donation will have a significant impact on a local community where the company has a business presence'. 40% of grants were to national organisations and 60% to local. The above areas supported include charities working with children, elderly people, sickness/disability and science/technology. Grants range from £100 to £100,000 and are usually paid in CAF vouchers. Some preference is given to projects in which a member of staff is involved and appeals related to company presence. The company also matches employee fundraising.

'Our policy towards covenant commitments aims to concentrate more substantial funds to three national charities for a three-year period, whilst adhering to the principal guidelines detailed above.'

For 1997 to 1999, support is being given to:

- Construction Industry Trust for Youth
- Cancer Research Campaign/Hospice Movement
- Groundwork Kent Thameside.

In addition, each year a major donation is given to a charity selected from a shortlist, which is chosen to establish a close link with a particular area of the company. In 1997, Methodist Homes for the Aged and Multiple Sclerosis Society were joint charities of the year.

Enterprise: Blue Circle is a member of Business in the Community. The Blue Circle Trust assists ex-employees wishing to set up businesses by providing technical and financial advice.

Education: Many Blue Circle companies have strong links with schools in their area involving careers counselling, factory tours and sponsorship, and including many young people with special needs or disabilities. Leigh City Technology College has received a major donation.

BMP

Environment: Activities have included support for Groundwork Kent Thameside, local community initiatives and a number of county wildlife trusts. More recently, Blue Circle has become a member of the corporate environmental responsibilities group set up by Earthwatch. The group has also undertaken to top-up landfill tax credit payments to benefit a number of local community environmental causes.

The arts: The company undertakes limited sponsorship of opera.

Exclusions

No response to circular appeals. No support for fundraising events, advertising in charity brochures, appeals from individuals, overseas projects, political appeals, religious appeals, animal charities or prisoners' welfare charities.

Applications

In writing to the correspondent. Grant decisions at head office are made by a donations committee. Local appeals should be addressed to the relevant regional office.

Other information: The company says that it welcomes appeals from charities, but due to the large number of requests received only a very small percentage of applicants can be given a favourable response. Applicants should therefore be aware of the company's preferences in its grants policy.

BMP DDB Ltd

12 Bishops Bridge Road, London W2 6AA
0171-298 7000; Fax: 0171-724 8292

Correspondent: Mrs Fiona Shafran, Head of Human Resources

Chief officer: *Chief Executive:* M Birkin

Year end	Turnover	Pre-tax profit
31/12/96	£749,206,000	£8,866,000

Nature of company business
The principal activity of the company is advertising and marketing services.

Main subsidiaries include: Doremus & Co Ltd; First City/BBDO Ltd; BMP DDB Ltd; Griffin Bacal Ltd; Macmillan Davies Hodes Advertising Ltd; Paling Walters Targis Ltd; TBWA Simons Palmer Ltd; Floral Street Holdings Ltd; Omnicom UK Ltd; Prism International Ltd; WWAV Rapp Collins Group Ltd; CPM International Group Ltd; Interbrand Group Ltd; Gavin Anderson Ltd; BMP Countrywide Ltd; Countrywide Communications Ltd; Ketchum Public Relations PLC; Scope Communications Group Ltd; Medi Cine International PLC; Billco Ltd; Interbrand UK Ltd; Premier Magazines Ltd; Specialist Publications Ltd; The Computing Group Ltd; WWAV Rapp Collins Ltd; Countrywide Porter Novelli Ltd; Market Access Ltd; DAS Financial Services Ltd; Omnicom Finance Ltd; Alcone/Europe Ltd; BBDO Europe Ltd; Colour Solutions Ltd; Data Warehouse Ltd; Genesis Digital Creation Ltd; Alcone Marketing Group Ltd; Macmillan Davies Hodes Consultants Ltd; Markforce Associates Ltd; Perception Design Ltd; Porter Novelli Ltd; Scope Ketchum Sponsorship Ltd; Smythe Dorward Lambert Ltd; Solutions in Media Ltd; The Anvil Consultancy Ltd; TISSA Ltd.

UK employees: n/a

Charitable donations
1996: £102,000
1995: £66,000
1994: £56,000
1993: £56,000

Community support policy

BMP DDB Ltd is one of the companies in the Diversified Agencies Services Group under which name the company appeared in the last edition of this Guide. However, charitable support is dealt with by BMP DDB which is a member of the PerCent Club. The 1998 annual report of the latter includes some details of the company's policy, from where much of the following information is taken.

The company supports national and international charities with direct donations, covenants and sponsorship totalling £45,300 in 1997. Organisations supported include Charities Aid Foundation, Design & Art Directors Foundation, Mencap, NABS, Cancer Research, Leukaemia Research, Breathing New Life Awareness and ASBAH. Local organisations to receive support have included the fire brigade, a theatre group and a church. The company also redesigned the prospectus for College Park, a local special needs school.

Education: In 1997, the company joined the Westminster Learning Partnership 'Business Working in Schools' Mentoring Project. The Agency is twinned with the North Westminster Community School. 15 members of staff meet pupils from year 10 on a fortnightly basis, acting as befrienders and encouraging the students to enhance their performance. Through D&AD the creative department is linked with Falmouth College, offering support and advice to students and taking placements throughout the year.

BMP also continues its partnership with Oxford Brookes University.

Applications
See donations policy above.

BMW GB Ltd

Ellesfield Avenue, Bracknell, Berkshire RG12 8TA
01344-426565; Fax: 01344-480203
Website: www.bmw.co.uk

Correspondent: Rosemary Davies, Public Relations Executive

Chief officers: *Chairman:* G Falco;
Managing Director: K Gaskell

Year end	Turnover	Pre-tax profit
31/12/97	n/a	£162,712,000

Nature of company business
The principal activity is the importation, storage and distribution of BMW products in the UK.

Main subsidiaries include: Park Lane Ltd.

UK employees: 323

Charitable donations
1996: £52,397
1995: £41,118
1994: £283,100

Community support policy

Major donations are given to two or three national charities selected by the company, preferably related to the motor industry (BEN is the favoured charity), children or a charity in which a member of staff has a particular interest.

Smaller donations are made to local charities through the Berkshire Community Trust. Grants to national organisations range from £250 to £5,000 and to local organisations from £50 to £1,000.

The company operates the BEN payroll giving scheme.

The company has a separate arts sponsorship programme. Arts organisations sponsored recently include the City of Birmingham Symphony Orchestra, English Chamber Orchestra, English National Orchestra and Royal Academy of Arts.

A separate education programme is designed to respond to student enquiries and provide resource materials for schools rather than giving money to projects/schools.

Exclusions

No response to circular appeals.

Applications

The policy outlined above means that BMW is unable to respond positively to letters requesting support/sponsorship.

BOC Group plc

Chertsey Road, Windlesham, Surrey GU20 6HJ
01276-477222; Fax: 01276-471333

Correspondent: Anne Leggatt, Administrator – Appeals and Donations Committee

Chief officers: *Chairman:* David John;
Chief Executive: Danny Rosenkranz

Year end	Turnover	Pre-tax profit
30/9/98	£3,549,900,000	£247,200,000

Nature of company business
The BOC Group is a major international company operating in more than 50 countries throughout the world. Principal activities: manufacture and supply of industrial gases and related products; vacuum technology; distribution services.
Main subsidiaries include: Edwards Vacuum International Ltd; London Cargo Group Ltd.

UK employees: 11,107

Charitable donations
1997: £612,000
1996: £557,000
1995: £641,000
1994: £367,000
1993: £490,000
Membership: *ABSA BitC %Club*

Community support policy

BOC is a member of the PerCent Club and Business in the Community. The group prefers to maintain a small number of long-term commitments, preferably related to its activities. Some preference is also given to appeals from local organisations in areas where the group has a site. The main categories of support are as follows.

Environment projects funded through the BOC Foundation for the Environment (an independent body), which spent £397,000 on projects in the year. The foundation provides funding for projects which aim to demonstrate in a practical way how pollution can be reduced in the UK. So far it has focused mainly on issues of waste management and water quality. It has a particular interest in projects where partial funding has already been obtained from other sources. Applications should be made in writing to: The Director, The BOC Foundation, 5–8 The Sanctuary, London SW1P 3JS.

The main criteria on which applications will be judged are as follows:

- ideally projects should be capable of completion in 6 to 18 months – though a longer duration can be acceptable
- projects must have clearly defined goals – preferably with a series of milestones against which progress can be measured
- projects should involve research to be carried out in Britain and to be concerned with some aspect of environmental control or pollution abatement
- more than one organisation may be involved as long as responsibility is effectively allocated
- if successful, the results or approach of the project should have the potential for replication.

Employee donations: The company matches £ for £, donations its employees make to charities of their choice. The company operates a Give As You Earn payroll scheme.

Heritage and the arts: The company supports selected heritage projects in the UK, usually focused on helping to preserve one of 'the nation's great architectural treasures'. For example, Salisbury and Winchester cathedrals and Westminster Abbey have been supported. BOC is a member of ABSA. Its on-going sponsorship of the BOC Covent Garden Festival means it cannot consider any arts sponsorship projects at present.

Social welfare and community services are supported by the group's operating subsidiaries. Overseas support is given by BOC subsidiaries in their countries of operation. Typically, national grants in the UK range from £500 to £25,000, although occasional long-term commitments are higher than this. Grants to organisations local to the headquarters range up to £1,000.

Body

Exclusions
No support for appeals from individuals, fundraising events, circular appeals, political or religious organisations. Support for social welfare causes (eg. elderly people, sickness/disability charities) is given through employee matching donations.

Applications
Appeals to head office and local appeals from the Surrey area should be addressed to the correspondent. Otherwise, they should go to the group's regional offices around the UK. Grant decisions at head office are made by a donations committee in combination with specialist staff members in the community affairs department.

Advice to applicants: It is advised that applicants always write rather than telephone. Main complaints: too often the group receives multiple applications from a single charity; the applicants do not appear to read earlier replies from the company.

Body Shop International Plc

Watersmead, Littlehampton, West Sussex BN17 6LS
01903-731500; Fax: 01903-726250
Email: info@bodyshop.co.uk
Website: www.the-body-shop.com

Correspondent: David Newton, Company Giving Co-ordinator

Chief officers: *Chairmen:* Gordon Roddick and Anita Roddick

Year end	Turnover	Pre-tax profit
28/2/98	£293,100,000	£38,000,000

Nature of company business
The Body Shop is a multi-local, values-led, global retailer. The group sell skin and hair care products through its own shops and franchised outlets in 47 markets worldwide.

Main subsidiaries include: Soapworks.

UK employees: 2,852

Charitable donations
1998: £925,771
1997: £751,993
1996: £846,997
1995: £771,861
1994: £881,068

Community support policy
'The company is committed to safeguarding the economic and social well-being of the communities in which it trades, while continuing to advance its social and environmental agenda with a commitment to strengthening its ethical business position. While community support is inherent in the business as a whole, the company does most of its charitable giving through its registered charity, The Body Shop Foundation.'

The Body Shop Foundation
An annual donation is made from the company to the foundation. The total company donations in 1997/98 of £900,000 included £800,000 to the foundation. Other donations are made to the foundation by franchisees, employees and friends of The Body Shop. The foundation also receives donated cosmetics and toiletries, etc. which are passed on to beneficiaries.

Three of the foundation's trustees are board directors of The Body Shop International. The other three comprise members of staff and an international head franchisee. From the latest accounts filed at the Charity Commission (1995/96), the trustees were Anita Roddick, Gordon Roddick, Jilly Forster, Mark Griffiths, Patrick Ballin, Ivan Levy and Barbara Brookway.

The foundation looks to support:
- small innovative groups with an activist agenda and initiatives which create sustainable trade and enable communities in need to develop independence through commercial activity
- human rights, locally, nationally and internationally, with a particular focus on indigenous peoples
- alternatives to animal testing in the cosmetics industry
- protecting endangered species
- environmental improvement.

It prefers to work with new, dynamic organisations and aims to make a difference in areas where other organisations are neither prepared nor sufficiently resourced to go. (For further information see the foundation's excellent and thorough *Effectively Taking Risks* or *Notes on Grant Making Policy*.)

In 1995/96, the foundation had assets of £345,000 and an income of £1 million (about two thirds of which was from Body Shop International). In the accounts, the foundation's spending was broken down as follows: grants £580,500 (£575,000 to 208 organisations and £5,500 to 13 individuals), other direct expenditure £309,000 (Childcare – £136,000, Healthcare – £64,000 and support – £109,000) and indirect expenditure. The Restricted Funds – Local Charity Working Groups, which have been formed in three locations spent £117,500 (Easterhouse – £61,500, Brixton – £23,000 and Littlehampton – £33,000).

Some of the income has been designated to specific funds/causes.

The Endangered Species Fund had £50,000 to help endangered animals around the world (it spent only £10,000 of this).

The Brazilian Healthcare Project spent all its £31,000 on the health of indigenous groups along the Xingu River in Brazil.

The Eastern Europe Relief Drive spent all its £180,000 providing social aid welfare to orphaned children in Romania and Albania.

The foundation lists the 50 largest grants of the 208 given which ranged from £2,000 to £52,000. Seven of these grants were of £20,000 or more to:

Unrepresented Nations & Peoples Organisation (UNPO) for ongoing support costs, including fundraising and computer acquisition for this Hague-based organisation

Academy for Socially Responsible Business Foundation for academic set-up costs of the Academy's office, including salaries, computers and other equipment

Mother Jones, a US-based investigative magazine – part of the Foundation for National Progress for research, publication and dissemination of projects on shrimp aquaculture, women's economic development and sustainable agriculture

Mazunte – to help villagers set up sustainable cosmetics production

Dr Hadwen Trust for Humane Research – the second of three years funding for research into skin sensitisation as an alternative to animal testing in the cosmetics industry

Missing Persons Bureau – the final payment of three years funding towards the costs for a national helpline to aid the finding of missing persons

Women's Environmental Network Trust (WENDI) – the final £20,000 of three-year funding for the salary of the co-ordinator of the information hotline for consumer questions on the environment.

There were 13 grants of around £10,000 to £16,600 which included those to: CSV for production of an awareness raising video; Bioregional Development Group for traditional lavender oil production in South London; Forest Monitor towards research on logging in South East Asia and for legal assistance for communities in the Solomon Islands and Vanuatu; Movement for the Survival of the Ogoni People for support of the then imprisoned Ken Saro-Wiwa; Women's Refuge Project in Brighton; European Communications Centre (a women's movement); John Wheatley College (part of the Easterhouse Community in Glasgow) and some local groups in Sussex.

Large grants were also given to: Parks and Recreation (Glasgow City Council) – 50% towards the costs of a sports coaching project with local primary schools; Body Positive Women's Group towards a weekly support evening for 50 women and 10 children with AIDS; Age Concern – Southwark; WOMANKIND Worldwide – in India; Comic Relief – matched funding for money raised by staff; Centrepoint towards a worker for a mother and baby unit; Catholic Children's Society – Brixton group); National Peace Council towards a children's festival in London; Pathways Sheltered Workshop – to a project making bird boxes and garden furniture and St Barnabas Hospice (Littlehampton group).

Only around 1% of the 600 requests received each month are considered. Grants vary from around £1,000 to £50,000.

Other support

In kind support: Some written-off products are donated for fundraising raffles or for use in hospices and women's refuges when the projects fall within the foundation's stipulated areas of support.

Community shops: The company operates community shops in four cities around the world which provide financial assistance to and staff involvement in, local community projects and organisations.

Employee involvement: Employees of the company and its franchised shops are encouraged to commit themselves to local community projects. All employees at head office, for example, have a half day per month in paid company time to engage in community projects. In Brighton, for instance, employees work at Port Meadows School for severely disabled children and at Gatwick with St Catherine's Hospice day centre. Others work with local organisations on environmental conservation. Several shops are attached to local projects working against domestic violence and drug abuse.

The company also operates a Give As You Earn scheme, enabling employees to donate to the foundation, as well as other registered UK charities.

At head office, there is a Local Charities Group consisting of staff volunteers, which raises funds from written-off stock and makes donations to charitable organisations within the West Sussex area.

Staff fundraising initiatives on behalf of charitable organisations often attract matched funding from the foundation.

Enterprise: Soapworks in Glasgow's Easterhouse district was opened by The Body Shop in 1988 and now employs over 120 local people and produces the majority of soap sold in the company's retail outlets worldwide. A commitment was given to donate 25% of Soapworks cumulative after-tax profits to local community projects.

Education: The company can sometimes provide educational materials for schools and give local slide presentation/talks on such topics as animals in danger.

Campaigns: The Body Shop encourages regular interaction with campaigning organisations and decision-making bodies, particularly relating to human rights and environmental concerns. Recent campaigns have included support for the Ogoni people of Nigeria, whose lands have been devastated as a result of oil drilling, and support for women's organisations against domestic violence.

Exclusions

The foundation does not consider support for advertising in charity brochures, medical research, political or religious appeals, science/technology, sickness/disability, sports or the arts worlds, students or individuals, or capital venture projects.

Applications

All applications for funding or donations in kind should be made in writing to The Body Shop Foundation.

Bombardier Aerospace – Short Brothers plc

Airport Road, Belfast BT3 9DZ
01232-458444; Fax: 01232-457759
Email: kellys@shorts.co.uk
Website: www.bombardier.com

Correspondent: Sylvia Kelly, Corporate Community Involvement Manager

Chief officer: *Chairman:* Sir Roy McNulty

Year end	Turnover	Pre-tax profit
31/1/98	£432,463,000	£43,816,000

Booker

Nature of company business
The principal activities of the company are the design, development, manufacture and sale of aircraft components, defence systems and related products and services.
Main subsidiaries include: Belfast City Airport Ltd; Airwork Ltd; Bombardier UK Ltd.

Charitable donations
1998: £340,760
1997: £343,130
1996: £291,590
1995: £82,462
1994: £20,403
Membership: *BitC %Club*

Community support policy

The company has a charity committee that decides which applications are supported. Preference is given to appeals relevant to company business, service charities, local charities and community organisations in areas of company presence.

The company is a member of Business in the Community and the PerCent Club. Previously, we have had little information on the company's community support policy despite its substantial level of giving and its commitment to the PerCent Club. However, it gave some details in the 1998 annual report of the PerCent Club from which most of the following information was taken.

In 1998/99, donations rose to £438,160. The company's activities include charitable donations, assistance with employee volunteering, financial support for employee payroll giving and employee charitable fundraising, sponsored community projects often with Shorts apprentices undertaking them in work time as part of their training, involvement with key Northern Ireland social and economic organisations such as the Northern Ireland Growth Challenge, as well as education and industry programmes for schools and universities.

Charitable donations are made by the Shorts Foundation, a charitable trust, which receives 1% of the company's income before tax. The foundation supports local Northern Ireland charities which are educational, cross community, social/welfare, or provide economic regeneration. It also matches £ for £ donations to approved charities by the Employees Charity Committee which manages payroll giving.

Recently, the company, either through the foundation or through supporting the activities of employees, has provided donations or practical help to community support bodies, community and hospice care, schools and agencies for disabled children and adults, bodies promoting better cross-community relationships, community regeneration projects and equal opportunities programmes with schools and colleges.

Applications
In writing to the correspondent.

Booker plc

85 Buckingham Gate, London SW1E 6PP
0171-411 5500; Fax: 0171-411 5555
Website: www.booker-plc.com

Correspondent: Ms Sue West, Head of Corporate Affairs

Chief officers: *Chairman:* John Napier; *Chief Executive:* Stuart Rose

Year end	Turnover	Pre-tax profit
27/12/97	£5,265,000,000	£71,400,000

Nature of company business
Booker, its subsidiaries and associates are engaged principally in food distribution and agribusiness.
Main subsidiaries include: Bluecrest Freebooter Ltd; Kilron Seafoods Ltd; Scotprime Seafoods Ltd; Scottish Seafoods Ltd; Fletcher Smith Ltd; Marine Harvest McConnell.
Main brands include: Chef's Larder; Happy Shopper; Family Choice.

UK employees: 24,404

Charitable donations
1997: £130,000
1996: £165,000
1995: £145,000
1994: £79,000
Membership: *ABSA BitC*

Community support policy
In addition to donations the company sponsors the Booker Prize (£20,000) and the Russian Prize (£10,000).

Charitable donations: Booker plc considers appeals from a wide range of charities and keeps a record of all donations made. Operating companies are largely responsible for their own donations. Preference for appeals relevant to company business and charities in which a member of company staff is involved. There may be a preference for children/youth, education, enterprise/training, and the arts. Grants to national organisations range from £100 to £2,500. Grants to local organisations range from £100 to £500.

In 1996, main beneficiaries included British North American Research, Book Aid International, Exeter University Foundation, Bodleian Library Development Appeal and National Life Story Collections.

Employee involvement: The company operates the Give As You Earn payroll deduction scheme, matching employee giving £ for £, and totalling about £30,000 a year.

Education: Since 1990, Booker has sponsored a Chair in Retail Marketing at Durham University Business School.

Arts sponsorship: The company is a member of ABSA. The main sponsorship is the well-established Booker Prize for Fiction, with book recordings for the blind. It has also sponsored the English National Opera, Royal National Theatre, London Mozart Players and supported the Bodleian Library Appeal. Subsidiary companies are responsible for their own sponsorship focusing in areas where they operate.

Exclusions
Generally no support for elderly people, animal welfare charities, medical research or advertising in charity brochures. No grants to individuals.

Applications
In writing to the chairman. All appeals are usually responded to whether a donation is given or not. Donations are on an ad hoc basis.

THE BOOTS COMPANY
Working with the community

The Boots Company PLC

Group Headquarters, 1 Thane Road West,
Nottingham NG2 3AA
0115-950 6111
Website: www.boots-plc.com

Correspondent: Martin Howarth or Meredith Lee, Appeals Development Officer, Boots Charitable Trust

Chief officers: *Chairman:* Sir Michael Angus; *Chief Executive:* Lord Blyth of Rowington; *Managing Directors:* D A R Thompson and S G Russell

Year end	Turnover	Pre-tax profit
31/3/98	£5,021,900,000	£431,900,000

Nature of company business
The Boots Company embraces businesses operating principally in retailing, the manufacture and marketing of health and personal care products throughout the world and the development and management of retail property.

Main subsidiaries include: Boots the Chemists; Boots Opticians; Halfords; Boots Contract Manufacturing; Boots Healthcare International; Boots Properties.

UK employees: n/a

Charitable donations
1998: £2,680,000
1997: £2,126,000
1996: £2,060,000
1995: £2,204,000
1994: £1,831,000
Total community contributions: £4,900,000
Membership: ABSA BitC %Club

Community support policy

In 1997/98, the company's total community contributions were £4.9 million. This included donations for charitable and educational purposes in the UK of £2,680,000. In addition to direct donations the Boots Charitable Trust makes top-up donations to employees' fundraising activities.

The Boots Recycling Project distributed an estimated £2.2 million worth of surplus stock (calculated at cost or written down value rather than retail value as in the previous year) to Nottinghamshire-based charitable groups. Much of this merchandise consisted of store returns, gifts with purchase and consumables approaching their best before dates. Some returned goods are sorted and repaired through a partnership with Nottinghamshire Probation Service.

The company is proactive in developing partnerships and has continued its strategy of building on existing partnerships with voluntary and public sectors. For example, strengthening the partnership with the Nottinghamshire Police through a range of local force initiatives and sponsorship of Operation Respect – a multi-agency strategy to prevent and target youth crime. Continuing partnership with the British Association for Early Childhood Education (Early Education) resulted in two successful conferences during 1997/98 and the development of a travelling exhibition which promotes and explains the vital importance of quality in early education.

Boots continued its programme of support in other areas of education as a key sponsor of both the Boots Science Building at the University of Nottingham (£200,000 a year for five years) and the Nottingham Trent University Boots Library (£62,500 a year for eight years).

200 Boots employees signed up as voluntary tutors with 'Success For All', a major literacy pilot scheme operating in the deprived Meadows area of Nottingham. A donation of £10,000 funded the training of volunteers and provision of materials for the scheme. The scheme is a partnership involving the Meadows family of schools, Boots and other local employers, Business in the Community and the University of Nottingham.

Another major initiative, Boots Books For Babies, with funding totalling £152,000 over three years, has been developed in partnership with Nottinghamshire County Council, Nottingham City Council and Health Visitors in Nottinghamshire. The programme aims to encourage parents to read books with their babies from nine months onwards.

Education liaison
The Education Liaison Unit co-ordinates the Boots group's links with the education sector. It encourages a partnership approach through a wide variety of activities including teacher placements, curriculum projects, work experience, industry days, support for conferences and a range of projects. Funding is regarded as a secondary issue compared to Education Liaison's enabling role of supporting and/or generating initiatives with all sectors of education. Contributions include personnel time for school-based activities, educational materials, gifts of equipment and sometimes donations. Support for specific activities will be considered if the projects:

- develop skills of pupils, staff and others
- involve partnership(s) with The Boots Company
- relate to health, equal opportunities, science/technology, citizenship or careers education and guidance.

BPB

All requests are turned down if
- they do not meet the above criteria
- they are for individual sponsorship
- they are for a school capital project
- they are for specialist college status
- they are purely a sponsorship opportunity.

Charitable donations

Boots Charitable Trust made donations totalling £486,000 in 1997/98. The company budget, managed by the Community Relations Manager is used to finance donations where the company has a special interest and projects qualifying for support are sought on a proactive basis. The company does not, therefore respond to appeals other than through the Boots Charitable Trust.

Charitable Trust

Boots was founded in Nottingham over 100 years ago and still has its headquarters there. Priority is therefore given to charities benefiting Nottinghamshire, although appeals are also considered from organisations in other areas where Boots Company PLC has a major representation and which are supported by a strong recommendation from the local business unit.

The trust's funding priorities are as follows:
- *Healthcare:* this includes blind, deaf, physically disabled, mental health, epilepsy, long stay and terminal care, hospitals (excluding private hospitals), nurses and nursing, alcoholism, drug addiction, and elderly people.
- *Economic development:* appeals which are capable of generating sustainable growth in the local economy, especially those which expand and improve the quality of employment.
- *Education:* educational initiatives that address specific issues, such as health, citizenship (including crime, racism, bullying and truancy), and equal opportunities, in particular approaches with the capacity to influence a wide audience within Nottinghamshire.
- *Family, maternity, and child welfare:* of particular interest are organisations promoting the development of childcare services and those assisting parents to combine work with family responsibilities.

The response to Nottinghamshire-based appeals outside the above priorities will normally be by gift voucher or the donation of merchandise through the Boots Recycling Project.

Overseas Aid – in the UK financial support for overseas aid is channelled through one charity only – the headquarters of Save the Children Fund. (The Boots Company's overseas businesses respond directly to appeals from within the countries in which they are located.)

In 1997/98, major grant recipients included Nottinghamshire Council for Voluntary Service (£20,000), Birkin Avenue Patch Improvement Association (£16,000), Crossroads Nottingham Young Carers Project (£20,000) and Save the Children Fund (£15,000). Main beneficiaries in the previous year were WISH – Women in Special Hospitals (£15,000), Winged Fellowship Trust (£15,000), Age Concern (£10,000), Chase Neighbourhood Centre (£10,000), all based in Nottinghamshire, and Save the Children Fund (£20,000).

Employee involvement: Boots Charitable Trust operates a top-up scheme for employee fundraising. The company also offers a payroll giving facility.

Membership: The company is a member of BitC, ScotBiC, NorBiC, Corporate Responsibility Group and Race for Opportunity. Boots Charitable Trust is a member of the Association of Charitable Foundations.

Exclusions

No support is given to private fundraising groups (fundraising events outside Nottinghamshire are rarely supported), individuals, organisations which are not registered charities or overseas projects.

Applications

Appeals to Boots Charitable Trust should be addressed to the Appeals Development Officer. A preliminary phone call is advisable. Grant decisions are made by the trustees who meet quarterly.

Sponsorship proposals should be addressed to: Sarah Smith, Assistant Community Relations Manager.

Education liason: Mary Brittain, Education Liason Coordinator. Proposals should detail how the criteria will be met and outline a process for monitoring and evaluation. Requests will also be accepted if they support a store manager, school governor or other company personnel who are developing links with the education sector.

Information available: Boots publishes information on its community affairs in its annual report, and in an annual 'Community Review' publication.

Advice to applicants: Over 27,000 requests for help were received in 1997/98. Applicants are advised to ensure that applications meet criteria, that they are brief and accompanied by the latest report, accounts and relevant budgets.

BPB plc

Langley Park House, Uxbridge Road, Slough, Berkshire SL3 6DU
01753-898800; Fax: 01753-898888
Website: www.bpb.com

Correspondent: Clare Carpenter, Assistant Company Secretary

Chief officers: *Chairman:* A G Gormly;
Chief Executive: D C Leonard

Year end	Turnover	Pre-tax profit
31/3/98	£1,300,000,000	£135,000,000

Nature of company business
The principal activities of the company are gypsum products, supplying plasters and plasterboard and with investments in the manufacture of complementary building materials and paperboard products.

Main subsidiaries include: Artex Blue-Hawk Ltd; Berpul Products Ltd; British Gypsum-Isover Ltd; Fiberite Packaging; Merton Chambers Packaging; Abertay.

UK employees: 3,864

Charitable donations
1998: £201,000
1997: £217,000
1996: £58,000
1995: £42,000
1994: £33,000

Community support policy

The substantial increase in the company's 1997 level of giving followed a review of policy by the group's charities committee. Markedly greater help will now be given to a more focused range of charities over the next few years.

It has continued to contribute both finance and building materials to CRASH, the UK construction industry's initiative to provide temporary shelters for homeless people during winter. It also made contributions to the Foyer Federation (supporting the nationwide construction of low-cost accommodation for young people, linked to skills training and job opportunities), Macmillan Cancer Relief (contributing to the training and provision of cancer-care nurses) and the British Heart Foundation.

BPB only gives to registered charities. A very limited number of grants are available to local charities close to group operations.

Exclusions

Generally no support for local appeals not in areas of company presence or overseas aid/development. No sponsorship is undertaken.

Applications

In writing to the correspondent.

Bradford & Bingley Building Society

Crossflatts, Bingley, West Yorkshire BD16 2UA
01274-555555
Website: www.bradford-bingley.co.uk

Correspondent: Barbara Smith, Community Projects Manager

Chief officers: *Chairman:* J Lindsay Mackinlay; *Chief Executive:* Christopher Rodrigues

Year end	Turnover	Pre-tax profit
31/12/97	n/a	£93,900,000

Nature of company business
Building society.

UK employees: 3,500

Charitable donations
1997: £105,000
1996: £58,149
1995: £61,072
1994: £51,833

Total community contributions: £500,000
Membership: *ABSA BitC*

Community support policy

The company prefers to give to national and local charities in areas of company presence, in the fields of social regeneration, sickness/disability, homelessness, children, elderly people and rescue services. The major beneficiary in 1997 was Debate of the Age.

The total community contributions of the company were £500,000 in 1997, which in addition to cash donations of £105,000, included secondments and support for a school reading scheme. The company also matches employee fundraising and giving (through the Give As You Earn scheme).

Exclusions

No support for political appeals, overseas charities, religious appeals or animal charities.

Applications

In writing to the correspondent at: 1–2 Church Place, Piccadilly, London SW1Y 6HU (0171-287 3255).

Bristol & West plc

Bristol & West Building, PO Box 27, Broad Quay, Bristol BS99 7AX
0117-929 2222; Fax: 0117-929 3787

Correspondent: Cheryl Williams, Community Affairs Manager

Chief officer: *Chairman:* Patrick J A Molloy

Year end	Turnover	Pre-tax profit
31/3/98	n/a	£91,200,000

Nature of company business
The company provides a range of financial services. It has recently merged with the Bank of Ireland.

UK employees: 2,300

Charitable donations
1998: £91,282
1997: n/a
1996: £126,583
1995: £92,004
1994: £84,158
Membership: *BitC*

Community support policy

As the Bristol & West Building Society, the company's annual report fully disclosed its charitable donations by providing a full list of grant recipients. Following the merger with the Bank of Ireland, however, this is no longer the case (based on the 1998 Annual Report) and the donations policy of the company may well have changed. We have been unable to obtain confirmation of this, and therefore refer to the then Bristol & West Building Society annual report for 1996 which states that the focus of its corporate community involvement programme is education.

During 1996 it gave £126,583 to charities, with most donations being made through the Bristol & West Charitable Trust (established 1990). Preferred areas of

Bristol-Myers

support: children and youth, education, the arts and enterprise/training. Preference is also given to charities in which a member of staff is involved. Most of the trust's income is in the form of donations and gifts from the company.

There is a strong emphasis, as would be expected, on charities in the South West, especially the former county of Avon. In 1996, the company gave 90 charitable donations to beneficiaries including: Anchor Society, Avon Autistic Foundation, Bath & District Samaritans, Bristol Cancer Help Centre, Bristol Institute for Brain Injured Children, Cotswold Care Hospice, Dolphin Society, Hope UK South West and St Stephen's Church, Bristol. Other grant recipients included Action Aid, African Initiatives, King George's Fund for Sailors, National Art Collections Fund, Relate and Youth for Christ International.

The company operates the Give As You Earn payroll giving scheme and is a member of Business in the Community.

The Bristol & West 1997 Charitable Fund was set up to receive voluntary contributions from members of the Bristol & West Building Society, following its merger and the payment of windfalls totalling £600 million to members. This fund is managed by the Greater Bristol Foundation. The fund will allocate grants according to broad criteria: the improvement of people's quality of life and the environment in which they live. The building society had a national remit and grants will be distributed nationally. This will be coordinated by the Greater Bristol Foundation through the community trust network.

Exclusions
No support is given to appeals from individuals, purely denominational (religious) appeals, overseas projects or for advertising in charity brochures.

Applications
In writing to the correspondent.

Bristol-Myers Squibb Holdings Ltd

BMS House, 141–149 Staines Road, Hounslow, Middlesex TW3 3JA
0181-572 7422; Fax: 0181-577 1756
Website: www.bms.com

Correspondent: Mary O'Kane, Sponsorship Coordinator

Chief officers: *Chairman:* Richard L Gelb; *Managing Director:* Charles S Heimbold

Year end	Turnover	Pre-tax profit
31/12/96	£556,819,000	£55,672,000

Nature of company business
The subsidiaries of the company are involved in the manufacture, marketing and distribution of ethical pharmaceutical products, personal care and household consumer products and appliances, and surgical equipment and appliances.
Main subsidiaries include: Conva Tec Ltd; Zimmer Ltd.

UK employees: n/a

Charitable donations
1996: £69,000
1995: £49,000
1994: £54,800
1993: £68,000

Community support policy
The company only supports local charities in areas of company presence and appeals related to company business. We have had difficulty obtaining information directly from the company. The following information was included on the website of Bristol-Myers Squibb Company, based in the US.

The company funds the Bristol-Myers Foundation which supports 'philanthropic initiatives that help and enhance human life'. It supports a broad range of programmes that address important health matter and social issues around the world. Key initiatives include:

- *Unrestricted Biomedical Research Grants Programme*
Funding for research in the areas: cancer, cardiovascular and metabolic disease, neuroscience, nutrition and orthopaedics.

- *Women's Health Education Programme*
The company have supported projects to educate inner-city women about the importance of preventive care and to promote healthier lifestyles.

- *Maths and Science Education Programme*
This includes the fellowship programme in academic medicine for minority students.

- *Donations of pharmaceutical products* to people in need in developing countries and to victims of natural disasters and civil unrest throughout the world.

- *Contributions to community organisations* in countries and localities where Bristol-Myers Squibb maintains offices, manufacturing facilities and research centres.

Exclusions
No support for denominational (religious) appeals, appeals from individuals or circular appeals.

Applications
In writing to the correspondent.

Britannia Building Society

Britannia House, Leek, Staffordshire ST13 5RG
01538-399399

Correspondent: Louis Mullinger, Deputy General Manager

Chief officers: *Chairman:* Calum MacLeod; *Chief Executive:* John Heaps

Year end	Turnover	Pre-tax profit
31/12/97	n/a	£57,100,000

Nature of company business
Building society.

UK employees: 2,465

Charitable donations

1998: £225,000
1997: £209,023
1996: £198,000
1995: £44,580
1994: £43,046

Community support policy

The Britannia Building Society Foundation (Charity Commission number 1069081) was set up by the society in 1997 and received its first donation of £225,000 from the company in 1998.

The foundation will support projects which address the following issues and those which focus on making a difference in local communities:

- *Homelessness*, which includes helping those in need to preserve their housing position, and remain in their own homes (whether owner-occupied or rented).
- *Educational achievement and aspirations*, with particular focus on increasing levels of educational attainment, from GCSE onwards, and encouraging people to develop skills and qualifications and raise their horizons. Applications should produce either measurable improvements in achievement, or encourage ambitions through participation in voluntary or community activities across the whole range of abilities.
- *Community safety*, with particular interest in applications that will help to build community harmony and encourage positive race relations.
- *Encourage prudent money management* by improving financial literacy and money advice services.

Support is only given to organisations within 25 miles of Leek, where the society is based, in the counties of Staffordshire, Cheshire and Derbyshire. This area covers the city of Stoke on Trent, and the towns of Stafford, Stone, Uttoxeter, Ashbourne, Buxton, Macclesfield, Congleton and Crewe and the rural communities between.

Grants range from £250 to £25,000, with preference for specific items and not for large appeals. Capital projects and running costs will be supported; however, there are limited funds for this type of application. Grants for running costs will normally be restricted to three years, with a maximum of five years. Any non-profit organisation can be supported and applicants need not be registered charities so long as a registered organisation is supporting them and will accept the grant on their behalf.

The main areas of non-cash support are enterprise agencies, gifts in kind and training schemes.

Exclusions

Generally no support for circular appeals, advertising in charity brochures, individuals, purely denominational (religious) appeals, animal welfare organisations, sport, science/technology, local appeals not in areas of company presence or overseas projects. No donations are made for political purposes.

Applications

On a form available from the correspondent. Before making an application a copy of the grants and donations policy should be obtained from the foundation to check eligibility. The trustees meet quarterly.

Britannic Assurance plc

1 Wythall Way, Wythall, Birmingham B47 6WG
01564-828888; Fax: 01564-828822

Correspondent: David Ellis, Marketing Support Manager

Chief officers: *Chairman:* H Cottam; *Chief Executive:* B H Shaw

Year end	Turnover	Pre-tax profit
31/12/97	n/a	£1,355,000,000

Nature of company business
The principal activity is the transaction of life assurance and certain clauses of general insurance business.

UK employees: 3,598

Charitable donations

1997: £58,000
1996: £51,000
1995: £62,000
1994: n/a
1993: £42,878

Community support policy

The company restricts its support to national charities involved in medical research. Grants range from £25 to £1,000. Employees' volunteering/charitable activities are supported through matching employee fundraising and giving, and allowing company time off to volunteer.

Exclusions

No response to circular, telephone or fax appeals. No support for advertising in charity brochures; animal welfare charities; appeals from individuals; the arts; children/youth; education; elderly people; enterprise/training; environment/heritage; fundraising events; overseas projects; political appeals; religious appeals; science/technology; sickness/disability charities; social welfare; or sport.

Applications

In writing to the correspondent.

British Aerospace

British Aerospace plc

Warwick House, PO Box 87, Farnborough Aerospace Centre, Farnborough, Hampshire GU14 6YU
01252-373232
Website: www.bae.co.uk

Correspondent: D S Parkes, Subscriptions & Donations Committee

Chief officers: *Chairman:* Sir Richard Evans; *Chief Executive:* J P Weston

Year end	Turnover	Pre-tax profit
31/12/97	£8,546,000,000	£596,000,000

Nature of company business
The group has two principal activities: Defence – comprising military aircraft, guided weapons, ordnance and electronic systems; Commercial Aerospace – comprising design and production of wings for the Airbus Industrie range of jet airliners, and the manufacture of the RJ series of regional jet airliners.
Main subsidiaries include: Reflectone UK; Royal Ordnance.

UK employees: n/a

Charitable donations

1997: £897,000
1996: £690,000
1995: £625,000
1994: £913,000
1993: £1,349,792

Total community contributions: £1,930,000 (1996)

Membership: ABSA BitC %Club

Community support policy

The company is a member of the PerCent Club. In addition to charitable donations it gave between £500,000 and £1 million in non-cash support in the areas of enterprise agencies, gifts in kind, secondments and training schemes.

Sponsorship: The group sponsors education, sports and arts events for young people and is involved in a wide range of projects to promote better understanding between industry and education, both at national and local level.

Charitable donations: National charities and appeals, and disaster appeals, are considered by the Subscriptions and Donations Committee, not by the individual business units. The committee tends only to support service/ex-service charities, children's/young people's charities and medical research, education, sickness/disability and enterprise/training projects together with appeals local to head office. The company is a keen supporter of local conservation projects. Direct support is preferred, but fundraising events are supported on certain occasions. Grants tend to range from £100 to £20,000. The recent main beneficiaries were the Multiple Sclerosis Society, CSV, Christie's Cancer Hospital, CHICKS and SSAFA. £100,000 of the total figure was given to a single charity (see employee involvement below).

All local charities will be referred to the relevant business unit. Sites each have an independent donations budget, and also give support by providing facilities and transport, and allowing apprentices to do work for charities. Grants to local organisations range from £10 to £10,000.

The company prefers to give directly, but does support advertising in charity brochures and fundraising events on certain occasions.

In kind support: The company has provided equipment and materials, professional services and the use of in-house facilities either free of charge or with a discount.

Employee involvement: In the autumn of 1989 the British Aerospace Challenge was launched. This scheme challenges young employees to invent imaginative ways of raising funds for charities. In 1996, £474,000 was raised by employees for local charities. In response, BAe matched this £ for £ up to a ceiling of £100,000 to its nominated charity for the year – Macmillan Fund for Cancer Relief. The charity is chosen each year by the Subscriptions and Donations Committee, with the Multiple Sclerosis Society selected in 1997/98.

A number of staff give time and energy to support local community programmes involving education and training and the development of local business enterprise initiatives. A payroll deduction scheme is operated in some parts of the business. Staff are also seconded to charities and enterprise projects, through the individual business units rather than head office. The company matches employee fundraising and has a matching scheme for hours spent by employees volunteering (up to an allocated amount).

Enterprise: The company is a member of Business in the Community. It seconds employees to local enterprise agencies and has contributed to the Special Development Fund, which provides aid for local enterprise agencies.

Education: In addition to sponsorship (see above0, the company aims to strengthen its links with a number of schools, technology colleges and universities.

The arts: The company has sponsored the European Community Youth Orchestra, Scottish Festival of Youth Orchestras and Music for Youth. Local events are also sponsored such as Rushmoor Borough Council Arts Festival. Each of its autonomous companies allocate their own sponsorship budgets.

Exclusions

No support for circular appeals, appeals from individuals, purely denominational (religious) appeals, local appeals not in areas of company presence, political appeals or overseas projects.

Applications

In writing to the correspondent. The committee meets quarterly. Sponsorship proposals should be directed to R Ellis, Corporate Communications Department. Local appeals are handled by the regional site managers. Letters should at least be topped and tailed.

Information available: The company has reported on its environmental and community activities in its annual report.

British Airways plc

Waterside, PO Box 365, Harmondsworth, Middlesex UB7 0GB
0181-562 5238; Fax: 0181-738 9847

Correspondent: Jacky Ive, Community Relations

Chief officers: *Chairman:* Sir Colin Marshall; *Chief Executive:* Robert Ayling

Year end	Turnover	Pre-tax profit
31/3/98	£8,642,000,000	£580,000,000

Nature of company business
Principal activities: the operation of international and domestic air services; provision of ancillary airline and travel services.
Main subsidiaries include: Air Miles Travel Promotions Ltd; Go Fly Ltd; Speedbird Insurance Co Ltd; The Plimsoll Line Ltd; Travel Automation Services Ltd.

UK employees: 48,541

Charitable donations
1998: £1,214,000
1997: £1,070,000
1996: £594,000
1995: £582,000
1994: £479,000

Total community contributions: £6,808,172
Membership: *BitC %Club*

Community support policy

The company's community contributions totalled £6.8 million in 1997/98, arrived at using the PerCent Club guidelines, although not taking account of commercial initiatives, as defined in the guidelines of the London Benchmarking Group. The main areas of support are youth development and education, environmental, heritage and tourism projects, which may receive tickets, equipment and manpower as well as funds, or a combination thereof.

Charitable donations: After a very large increase in 1997, with donations totalling over £1 million, there has been a further increase in the following year to over £1.2 million. Support is only given to appeals in areas in which the company operates and which provide the opportunity for substantial staff involvement. Other causes such as the arts or fundraising events may be supported if they fit within the priorities listed above. Causes such as medical research or sickness/disability charities may be supported if there is a staff link.

The company has continued its 'Change for Good' relationship with UNICEF. In the first three years, £4 million was raised for projects in over 40 countries.

In the past, major support has been given to: The National Trust, Prince's Youth Business Trust, Prince of Wales Business Leaders Forum, Royal Geographic Society and UK/South Africa Sports Initiative. Other initiatives range from support for local language colleges to the company's Leadership Challenge programme, aimed at tomorrow's social and business leaders.

Employee involvement: Numerous charities are supported by employee fundraising, including causes run by the staff themselves, such as Operation Happy Child and Dreamflight, for underprivileged and sick children. The company operates an employee volunteering scheme and a payroll giving scheme. Other support for staff involvement includes tickets to assist employees supporting overseas projects, merchandise for raffles and consultancy support to staff charities.

Exclusions
No support for appeals from individuals, political appeals or religious appeals. Advertising in charity brochures is rarely undertaken.

Applications
Appeals should be addressed to: Jacky Ive, British Airways plc, Australasia House (HBBG), Waterside, PO Box 365, Harmondsworth, West Drayton UB7 0GB.

However, please note that the company states that they do not wish to generate a significant number of additional requests as most resources are already allocated to long-term sustainable projects within the established programme.

British Alcan Aluminium plc

Chalfont Park, Gerrards Cross, Buckinghamshire SL9 0QB
01753-233200; Fax: 01753-233299

Correspondent: Barbara Payne, Secretary to the Charitable Trust

Chief officers: *Chairman:* J Bougie; *Managing Director:* G Batt

Year end	Turnover	Pre-tax profit
31/12/97	£565,000,000	£11,900,000

Nature of company business
Production and processing of aluminium and alumina chemicals. The principal UK operations are Alcan Smelting & Power (Fort William, Ashington and Kinlochleven), Alcan Rolled Products (Newport, Falkirk and Glasgow), Alcan Recycling and Alcan Aluminium Can Recycling (Warrington) and Alcan Chemicals (Burntisland and Widnes).
Main subsidiaries include: The Lochaber Power Company.

UK employees: 2,945

Charitable donations
1997: £293,000
1996: £103,000
1995: £51,000
1994: £249,000
1993: £283,000

Community support policy

Charitable donations given by the company have more than doubled in each of the last two years, to the present level of £293,000.

Charitable donations: Priority is given to charities in need of funds rather than very well-supported charities, and to charities close to British Alcan locations. Preferred areas of

British American

support are children and youth, social welfare, medical, environment and heritage, and elderly, homeless and disabled people. Money is channelled through the British Alcan Charitable Trust. Grants to national organisations range from £250 to £500 and to local organisations from £50 to £300. Donations are made direct to charities and not by supporting special events organised in their aid. The company operates a matching scheme for employee fundraising.

Sponsorship: The company undertakes arts and good cause sponsorship on a national and local level. The typical sponsorship range is from £100 to £1,000. Although not a member of ABSA, the company does undertake limited arts sponsorship. For example, it has supported the Alfred Gilbert Exhibition at the Royal Academy, Birmingham Symphony Orchestra and English National Opera.

Education: The company is involved in education/business partnerships. The donations figure includes an initial £87,000 donated to Oxford University's Department of Materials under a five-year programme.

Exclusions

No support for non-charities, advertising in charity brochures, fundraising events, circular appeals, appeals from individuals, purely religious or political appeals, local appeals not in areas of company presence, overseas projects, the arts, environment/heritage, science/technology, sport, large national appeals and animal charities.

Applications

Appeals to head office should be addressed to the correspondent. Grant decisions are made by a donations committee which meets bi-monthly. All divisions/subsidiaries channel appeals to the trust. Arts proposals, commercial sponsorships, etc., should be addressed to M Daniels, Corporate Relations Manager.

British American Tobacco plc

Globe House, 4 Temple Place, London WC2R 2PG
0171-845 1000

Correspondent: Paul Richmond

Chief officers: *Chairman:* M Broughton;
Managing Director: U Herter

Year end	Turnover	Pre-tax profit
n/a	n/a	n/a

Nature of company business
This company is the world's second largest international tobacco company, selling over 240 brands. It was incorporated in 1997, following the demerger of BAT Industries financial services businesses and tobacco businesses. The former merged with Zurich Insurance Company and now operates as Allied Zurich, the main operating company of which, Allied Dunbar, has its own entry in this guide.

Charitable donations

No figures yet available, likely to be in the region of £1 million in the UK

Community support policy

BAT Industries used to give charitable donations totalling in the region of £3.5 million a year, including about £2 million from Allied Dunbar.

British American Tobacco plc, now a totally separate company, is still in the process of developing its own community involvement policy which is not yet available.

Applications

In writing to the correspondent.

The contact for Allied Zurich is Brian Hutchinson, Manager, Community Affairs.

British Energy plc

10 Lochside Place, Edinburgh Park, Edinburgh EH12 9DF
0131-527 2000; Fax: 0131-5272277
Website: www.british-energy.com

Correspondent: Vicki Fuller, Public Relations Assistant

Chief officers: *Chairman:* John Robb;
Chief Executive: Dr Robert Hawley

Year end	Turnover	Pre-tax profit
31/3/98	£1,954,000,000	£276,000,000

Nature of company business
The group's principal activity is the generation and sale of electricity.

Main subsidiaries include: Nuclear Electric Ltd; Scottish Nuclear Ltd; Lochside Insurance Ltd; United Kingdom Nirex Ltd.

UK employees: 5,672

Charitable donations

1998: £217,000
1997: £220,000
Membership: *BitC*

Community support policy

The company focuses its support on safety, the environment, teamwork and the key role to be played by the next generation. In 1997/98, support included funding for a mobile first-aid unit for the St Andrew's Ambulance Association, support for a number of arts projects including Northern Ballet's Edinburgh season and sponsorship of the first international festival of youth rugby.

The company was also a major sponsor of the first Global Environment Conference on the internet – Environment 97 – accessible through the company's website.

The company is a member of Business in the Community.

Exclusions
No support for circular appeals, fundraising events, appeals from individuals, purely denominational (religious) appeals, local appeals not in areas of company presence or overseas projects.

Applications
In writing to the correspondent.

British Land Company plc

10 Cornwall Terrace, Regent's Park, London NW1 4QP
0171-486 4466; Fax: 0171-935 5552

Correspondent: John Ritblat, Chairman

Chief officer: *Chairman:* John Ritblat

Year end	Turnover	Pre-tax profit
31/3/98	n/a	£127,00,000

Nature of company business
Property investment and development, finance and investment.

Main subsidiaries include: Adamant Investment Corporation; Bayeast Property Company; B L Holdings; Real Property & Finance Corporation; 135 Bishopsgate Financing.

UK employees: n/a

Charitable donations
1998: £79,000
1997: £78,000
1996: £49,000
1995: £36,000
1994: £44,000
Membership: *BitC %Club*

Community support policy

'British Land is strongly committed to investing in the future by providing facilities for young people and children through sponsorship of the arts, sport and education and funding and fostering support for improvement of the environment.' The company supports the Civic Trust, Business in the Community and is a member of the PerCent Club.

Charitable donations: Particular support is given to charities involving young people, especially in activity-based projects. Recent beneficiaries include Barnardo's, the British Red Cross and Mencap.

Education: The company has produced a number of educational broadsheets in conjunction with the Design Council, which have been distributed to 15,000 primary and secondary schools throughout the UK. It is also a funding partner of the London Business School.

The arts: British Land recently sponsored the new permanent illustrated catalogue of the National Gallery's collection of works by British Artists by Judy Egerton. Support has also been given to the Bodleian Library, Buildings Books Trust, London Philharmonic Orchestra, English National Opera, Royal Opera House, National Theatre and Regent's Park Open Air Theatre. The company is a founder benefactor of the Royal Opera House Development Appeal and a founding exhibition patron of the Royal Academy of Arts.

Exclusions
No grants for fundraising events, individuals or local appeals not in areas of company presence.

Applications
In writing to the correspondent.

British Nuclear Fuels plc

Risley, H280, Warrington, Cheshire WA3 6AS
01925-832000; Fax: 01925-835619
Website: www.bnfl.com

Correspondent: Robert Jarvis, Head of Corporate Community Involvement

Chief officers: *Chairman:* J R S Guinness;
Chief Executive: J Taylor

Year end	Turnover	Pre-tax profit
31/3/98	£1,341,000,000	£199,000,000

Nature of company business
The principal activities are nuclear fuel services and electricity generation. The group acquired Magnox Electric plc on 30 January 1998.

Locations: Capenhurst (Cheshire), Chapelcross (Annan), Risley (Warrington), Sellafield (Cumbria) and Springfields (Preston), Bradwell Power Station (Essex), Hinkley Point A Power Station (Somerset), Sizewell A Power Station (Suffolk), Berkeley Power Station (Gloucester), Trawsfynydd Power Station (Gwynedd), Dungaress A Power Station (Kent), Oldbury Power Station (Gloucestershire), Wylfa Power Station (Gwynedd), Hunterston A Power Station (Ayrshire).

Main subsidiaries include: Magnox Electric plc; International Nuclear Fuels Ltd; BNFL Inc; F2 Chemicals Ltd; Deva Manufacturing Services Ltd; BNFL Engineering Ltd; BNFL Instruments Ltd.

UK employees: n/a

Charitable donations
1998: £5,500,000
1997: £2,400,000
1996: £2,100,000
1995: £1,800,000
1994: £266,250
Membership: *ABSA BitC %Club*

Community support policy

The company is a member of the PerCent Club and reports on its community involvement in its latest annual report. Its policy is to establish long-term relationships with the local communities around sites, with support covering economic regeneration, education, charitable help and sponsorship particularly in the north west of England and south of Scotland.

The donations figure quoted above, taken from the company's latest annual report, includes £4.3 million to support West Cumbrian economic regeneration initiatives.

British Petroleum

It has given support for 10 years to the West Cumbria Development Fund as well as various development companies, investment and enterprise agencies.

Charitable donations: Preference is given to organisations concerned with community and economic welfare, health issues, sports and renewal activities, enterprise and training, science and technology, environment and heritage, cultural activities and education, especially when targetted at under-privileged people, particularly children/youth and elderly people. Fundraising events may also be supported. Typical national grants range from £100 to £15,000. Local grants range from £25 to £1,000.

The company is currently focusing support on youth-related issues, especially those tackling social problems such as: drugs, youth crime and homelessness. Recent examples include: a grant to install the latest alarm system for building evacuation to a home for blind people in Whitehaven; support to Jibcraft, Barrow, which provides workshop facilities for long-term unemployed people and people with disabilities; funding of two development posts at the Kepplewray Project at Broughton-in-Furness; the establishment of the West Cumbria Charitable Trust, set up to support organisations and groups dealing with urban/rural regeneration, environmental improvements and helping the young and elderly; support for a Life Education Centre in Lancashire promoting drug awareness; support for an Open Arts Project in Runcorn to raise the self-esteem and confidence in young people who have become disaffected through exclusion from school, being in care, or experiencing trouble with the law. Support has also been given to Prince's Trust Volunteers/Merseyside Youth Association, Medlocks Links, WISE, Duke of Edinburgh's Award Scheme and Furness Homeless Support Group.

Employee involvement: Staff are encouraged to become volunteers in their own time. The company runs the Give As You Earn payroll giving scheme and matches employee fundraising.

Enterprise: The company is a member of Business in the Community and is especially concerned with job creation and economic regeneration.

Education: The company has given substantial support to the West Lakes Science & Technology Park near Whitehaven. It is involved in schemes such as Young Enterprise and Understanding Industry and seconds employees to major education initiatives. It provides educational materials for schools and work experience schemes for pupils and teachers. It launched a CD-Rom recently entitled *Kingdom* designed to encourage interest and careers in engineering. Employees are encouraged to become school governors.

Environment: The company is involved in various schemes: The Yottenfews Environmental Project, West Cumbria; The Nature Trail at Springfields, Preston; Pennington Flash, Leigh and Sustainability NW.

The arts: Appeals for arts sponsorship are welcomed. Arts, theatre productions and musicals are all sponsored. Support has been given to the Warrington Male Voice Choir, Royal Exchange Theatre, Opera North and Royal Northern College of Music.

Exclusions

No support for circular appeals, large national appeals (except North West based), small purely local appeals not in areas of company presence, advertising in charity brochures, purely denominational (religious) appeals, animal welfare charities, appeals for individuals, enterprise and training, overseas projects and political appeals.

Applications

In writing either to the correspondent above or to the General Manager of the nearest factory. A donations committee meets monthly.

The British Petroleum Company plc

Britannic House, 1 Finsbury Circus, London EC2M 7BA
0171-496 4000; Fax: 0171-920 8263
Website: www.bpamoco.com

Correspondent: The Manager, BP Community Affairs

Chief officers: *Chairman:* Peter Sutherland;
Chief Executive: E J P Browne

Year end	Turnover	Pre-tax profit
31/12/97	£43,460,000,000	£2,820,000,000

Nature of company business
The British Petroleum Company is the holding company of one of the world's largest petroleum and petrochemical groups. Its main activities are exploration and production of crude oil and natural gas; refining, marketing, supply and transportation; and the manufacturing and marketing of petrochemicals. BP has major operations in Europe, North and South America, Asia, Australasia and parts of Africa.

UK employees: 18,050

Charitable donations

1998: £3,400,000
1997: £3,400,000
1996: £3,400,000
1995: £5,000,000
1994: £5,000,000

Total community contributions: £7,500,000

Membership: *BitC*

Community support policy

BP's community activities in the UK are generally developed in partnership with the local communities where it has operating sites. These are in south east Essex (BP Oil Coryton Refinery), Poole (BP Exploration, Wytch Farm), Hull (BP Chemicals plant), Easington (BP Exploration terminal), Aberdeen (BP Exploration offices), Grangemouth (BP Oil Grangemouth and BP Chemicals plant), Sunbury on Thames (all BP businesses), Port Talbot (Baglan Bay Chemicals plant), Milton Keynes (BP Retail and Commercial offices), Northern Ireland (BP Oil Terminal) and London (International Headquarters).

Appeals which directly support the local communities around these areas are considered by the site itself. As well as local community activities, the company also runs a number of national and international initiatives, including an international conservation awards programme – BP Conservation Awards – and an environmental science programme in schools worldwide (Science Across the World).

Nationally, BP runs the BP Schools Link programme with schools close to its sites, and a Matched Giving Scheme for all UK employees as its main employee involvement activities.

BP also has a long-standing involvement in road safety. BP has one of the longest running programmes for business sponsorship of the arts in the UK, working with organisations including: the Tate Gallery, National Portrait Gallery and the British Museum. The company also has an educational service providing advice, information and resources to schools and can be contacted on 0102-669940.

In 1997, the company gave £19.5 million in community support worldwide. This was categorised as follows:

Community development	42%	£8.19 million
Education	32%	£6.24 million
Arts	10%	£1.95 million
Environment	8%	£1.56 million
Other	8%	£1.56 million

Community support in the UK accounted for 38.5% (£7.5 million) of the worldwide total.

Following the recent merger between BP and Amoco future policy may change. See 'Applications' below for contact details.

Exclusions

There are no pre-defined areas of preference although environment, education and local community development are areas where the company has an interest.

Applications

For more information on any of BP's community activities, organisations should contact: BP Community Affairs on 0181-658 0712 or see the company website at http://www.bpamoco.com. The BP Educational Service can be reached on 01202-669940 for advice, information and resources.

British Sky Broadcasting Group plc

6 Centaurs Business Park, Grant Way, Isleworth, Middlesex TW7 5QD
0171-705 3000; Fax: 0171-805 7600
Website: www.sky.co.uk

Correspondent: Andrea J Sullivan, Director of Corporate Affairs

Chief officers: *Chairman:* Jerome Seydoux; *Chief Executive:* Mark Booth

Year end	Turnover	Pre-tax profit
30/6/98	£1,434,100,000	£270,900,000

Nature of company business
The leading satellite pay television operator, BSkyB launched its digital television services in the UK on 1 October 1998 offering 200 channels including sport, news, first-run films and general entertainment.

Main subsidiaries include: Sky Television Ltd; BSkyB Finance Ltd; Sky Subscribers Services Ltd; Sky In-Home Service Ltd; Sky Ventures Ltd.

Main brands include: Sky; Sky Digital; Sky Sports; Sky News; Sky One; Sky Premier; Sky MovieMax; Sky Cinema.

UK employees: 4,634

Charitable donations
1998: £319,000
1997: £368,000
1996: £224,000
1995: £138,000
Total community contributions: £708,000

Community support policy

In 1997/98, the company's total community contributions were £708,000 including support for local schools and sponsorship of the arts as well as £319,000 in charitable donations.

The company has supported a variety of causes, particularly those aiming to encourage young people in pursuing education, the performing arts, television and sports. One major commitment is a pledge of £12 million to the Millennium Experience which, in part, will support a dedicated, long-term programme focusing on opportunities for young people across the UK.

The company supports both national charities and charities in areas local to main offices in Isleworth, Livingston and Dunfermline. Main beneficiaries in 1997/98 included the National Film and Television School, Cinema and Television Benevolent Fund, Crisis, Media Trust and Chicken Shed Theatre Company.

Applications
In writing to the correspondent.

British Steel

British Steel plc

15 Marylebone Road, London NW1 5JD
0171-314 5500; Fax: 0171-314 5600
Website: www.britishsteel.co.uk

Correspondent: Richard J Reeves, Company Secretary

Chief officers: *Chairman:* Sir Brian Moffat; *Chief Executive:* J Bryant

Year end	Turnover	Pre-tax profit
28/3/98	£7,166,000,000	£315,000,000

Nature of company business
The manufacture, sale and processing of steel. Major manufacturing businesses are located in Port Talbot and Llanwern in South Wales, Scunthorpe and Teesside, Rotherham, Sheffield, Shotton and Ebbw Vale, with distribution outlets throughout the UK and Europe.
Main subsidiaries include: Avesta Sheffield Holdings; CEDG; Cold Drawn Tubes; Industrial Steels (UK); European Electric Steels; European Profiles; Orb Electrical Steels; Precision Metal Forming; Tubular Supply Services.

UK employees: 40,600

Charitable donations
1998: £621,000
1997: £586,000
1996: £504,000
1995: £353,000
1994: £363,000

Total community contributions: £624,000

Membership: *ABSA BitC*

Community support policy

In addition to charitable donations in the UK totalling £621,000, the company also supports community projects by sponsorship, gifts of materials and secondments, and has maintained its support for the arts, environmental projects and educational activities.

The company makes grants centrally, mainly to national appeals. It also has a preference for local charities in areas of company presence, appeals relevant to company business and charities in which a member of staff is involved. It also supports the arts, environmental projects and educational activities. Other areas of support are children/youth, elderly people, enterprise/training, social welfare (if related to the NHS), religious appeals and sport. Grants to national organisations range from £250 to £10,000. Grants to local organisations range from £1,000 to £5,000.

Employee volunteering is encouraged by giving financial support and matching employee fundraising. Some support may be given in Lambeth and Westminster.

Enterprise: British Steel (Industry) Ltd is a member of Business in the Community. It offers services and resources for new industry, including financial incentives. BS Industry, which is self-funded, supports projects in the local business enterprise and job creation field.

Education: The company is involved in local education/business partnerships, provides educational materials for schools and work experience schemes for pupils and teachers. Support is given to City Technology Colleges and in the form of student sponsorships.

Exclusions
No support for purely denominational appeals, small purely local appeals not in areas of company presence, appeals from individuals, fundraising events or circulars.

Applications
Applications (including sponsorship) should be in writing to the correspondent, although local appeals should be made through local offices of British Steel.

British Sugar plc

Oundle Road, Peterborough, Cambridgeshire PE2 9QU
01733-563171; Fax: 01733-563068
Website: www.britishsugar.co.uk

Correspondent: Angela MacDougall, Charity Co-ordinator

Chief officers: *Chairman:* G H Weston; *Chief Executive:* P J Jackson

Year end	Turnover	Pre-tax profit
13/9/97	£829,000,000	£179,000,000

Nature of company business
British Sugar is a wholly-owned subsidiary of Associated British Foods (see separate entry). It operates from locations in East Anglia and the West Midlands (Allscott, Bardney, Bury St Edmunds, Cantley, Ipswich, Kidderminster, Newark, Peterborough, Wissington and York).

UK employees: n/a

Charitable donations
1997: £94,000
1996: £95,000
1995: £100,000
1994: £100,000
1993: £100,000

Community support policy

In addition to charitable donations, the company's community action programme includes support for enterprise agencies (£5,000) and gifts in kind (£3,000).

Charitable donations: Donations are administered through the British Sugar Foundation (Charity Commission number 290966). Support is focused on projects of particular benefit to the communities in which British Sugar operates and in which employees live and work. The following are the policy guidelines:

- The foundation has particular interests in projects in the following areas: health and healthcare; education; environment; enterprise.
- Projects inspired by company employees will receive special attention.
- Charitable projects benefiting the communities in which company employees and their families live will receive special attention.
- The directors of the foundation reserve the right to make final decisions regarding grants to beneficiaries.

However, it is the foundation's aim to accept employee suggestions wherever consistent with policy and available resources.

- The foundation funds local projects where local benefit will accrue; it may not always support local fundraising schemes where national or international charities are the beneficiaries.
- The foundation will make every effort to encourage participation in community fundraising projects among its employees. (It is also an approved charity agency for the payroll giving scheme.) In previous years, half the grant total has been contributed as part of the company's scheme to match employee fundraising.

In 1997/98, the foundation had an income of £94,000, all of which was paid out in grants. Most of the annual income comes from the company with some from employee payroll giving contributions. Unfortunately, no list of grants was included with the accounts.

Locally (ie. East Anglia, East Midlands and other areas where the company have sites) support is also given to social welfare, sport, medical research/disability/sickness and science/technology.

Sponsorship: Sponsorship of local events ranges from £20 to £500.

The company has particular concern for the environment and preserves sites of special scientific interest on three factory sites.

Exclusions
General and national appeals are not normally supported. No support for circular appeals, appeals from individuals, advertising in charity brochures, local appeals not in areas of company presence, overseas projects, purely denominational (religious) appeals, political appeals, the arts or sport.

Applications
In writing to the correspondent. The company produce a useful Policy and Guidelines for Applicants leaflet.

British Telecommunications plc

BT Community Partnership Programme, Room 3054, BT Centre, 81 Newgate Street, London EC1A 7AJ
0171-356 5750
Website: www.bt.com

Correspondent: Stephen Serpell, Head of Community Partnership

Chief officers: *Chairman:* Sir Iain Vallance;
Chief Executive: Sir Peter Bonfield

Year end	Turnover	Pre-tax profit
31/3/98	£15,640,000,000	£3,219,000,000

Nature of company business
British Telecom is the principal supplier of domestic and international telecommunications services and equipment to customers in the UK. It is divided into five operating divisions: Personal Communications (focusing on the needs of the personal consumer from those requiring a single telephone to those such as home workers who require a variety of telecommunications services); Business Communications (responsible for all the needs of business customers around the world); Worldwide Networks (providing telecommunications services and products internationally); Special Businesses (responsible for Yellow Pages, Mobile Communications, Visual & Broadcast Marketing Information Services); and Development & Procurement.

UK employees: 120,200

Charitable donations
1998: £2,700,000
1997: £2,573,100
1996: £2,700,000
1995: £2,231,000
1994: £2,197,518

Total community contributions: £15,600,000

Membership: *BitC %Club*

Community support policy
The company, through its BT Community Partnership Programme, supports a variety of organisations and good causes. The projects supported must:

- be of positive relevance to BT
- bring demonstrable benefit to the community
- offer clearly understood and recorded mutual benefits
- provide opportunities for BT people to be involved
- enhance BT's reputation.

BT supports a wide range of community initiatives, both local and national. It concentrates its support in the areas of health and welfare, education, regeneration, arts and sports, disability, supporting the community activities of BT people, and the environment. Particular emphasis is placed on education and training, the improvement of communication skills, support for people with disabilities, and the involvement of BT people. The main areas of non-cash support are secondments and training schemes. Employee volunteering is encouraged through financial support and BT matches employee giving.

In 1997/98, it gave over £15 million in contributions including financial donations and other support.

The general policy is to give a significant gift for a specific purpose rather than scatter smaller sums, and to give fewer but larger donations. Grants to national organisations range from £250 to £100,000, and to local organisations from £50 to £50,000. The company also has a programme of provision of management support for community and charitable organisations.

Voluntary sector partnerships
BT seeks to improve the quality of life of people in need and at risk, supporting projects which make use of its technology to provide practical help, and which are concerned with enabling individuals to communicate better, either at home, at work or in the wider community.

A number of award schemes have been introduced which focus on specific elements of BT's Community Programme, including interpersonal relationships, technology and mental health and employability.

British Telecommunications

During 1998, a programme has been started that enables charities and voluntary groups to make more effective use of communications technology. In collaboration with the charity Oneworld On Line, training and support is being offered to small charities to help them run their own internet sites.

Other initiatives developed during the year, included work with the Anchor Trust to develop remote health monitoring systems to help older people continue to live independently, and work with RNID to improve deaf people's access to arts venues around the country.

Examples of projects supported during 1996/97 include:

- £135,000 to develop the Winston's Wish child grief support programme on a nationwide basis
- £25,000 to provide bursary awards for Speech and Language Therapists
- £45,000 to the British Stammering Association for its Primary Healthcare Workers Project, which aims to ensure that dysfluent pre-school aged children are referred for therapy as early as possible
- £45,000 to the Royal London Society for the Blind's 'Workbridge' project.

Initiatives specifically concerned with people with disabilities include:

- *BT Countryside for All*, which set out standards and guidelines to make the countryside as accessible as possible to disabled people.
- *BT Swimming and BT Athletics* (organised in partnership with Disability Sport England, the UK Sport Association for the Disabled and the British Paralympic Association) both aim to develop participation in their respective sporting areas from grass roots through to both international and paralympic team events.
- *BT Kielder Challenge*, undertaken with the Fieldfare Trust. This involves teams of able-bodied youngsters in a series of outdoor team-building events.

The company also supports a wide range of projects involving training in the use of new technology aimed to improve the skills and job opportunities for people with physical, sensory and learning disabilities and to enhance the quality of life for severely disabled people. Other projects supported include the signing of theatre performances, awards to encourage disabled people in a range of pursuits, and improving access.

Examples of grants include: £117,000 over three years to the Queen Elizabeth Foundation for the Disabled to fund courses ranging from computer literacy to horticulture; £60,000 to SENSE for caring for deaf-blind people; and £20,000 to the Home Farm Trust to provide training in care for people with mental disabilities.

BT has a special *Age & Disability Unit* whose main objective is to maintain and, where possible, enhance the provision of products and services which meet the needs of disabled and elderly people. Its programme is directed by a committee which includes independent members as well as senior BT managers.

The unit publishes a free annual guide to the products on offer for disabled people, available from BT shops and offices. A network of managers has been established throughout the country to develop and coordinate the special services which disabled customers may need. The price of some specialised telephone equipment for disabled people is being kept down to those of standard products by writing off the development costs. Typetalk, run by the Royal National Institute for the Deaf with funding from BT, enables deaf and speech-impaired people to use the telephone network.

Economic regeneration

This programme is focusing on improving the skillbase of the UK through increasing access to training and qualifications, especially for young people, and job creation through the promotion of enterprise.

Grants included: £180,000 for the Youth Initiative Projects, which are run by young people for young people, through which they can learn and practise enterprise skills; £375,000 for Countrywork, which supports projects encouraging employment opportunities in rural areas; £235,000 for REACHOut, giving parents in Liverpool a second chance to further their education and training while providing a positive example for their children; and £245,000 for a call centre providing training and work experience for unemployed people in Glasgow.

Education

The company is committed to building partnerships between business and education. Its wide-ranging programme invests about £3 million each year through, among other things, award schemes for schools, colleges and universities. It runs national programmes and at local level has full-time education industry liaison managers to develop local links. Partnership activities include:

- the production of a range of curriculum material for primary and secondary schools
- a programme of placements for primary and secondary school teachers in BT
- a series of workshops to provide an industrial dimension to in-service training
- a school link scheme, with local BT units developing links with over 120 secondary schools
- support for link agencies such as Young Enterprise, Understanding Industry and locally-based partnerships.

BT also provides a wide programme of work experience for pupils and runs training activities and support to staff wishing to be school governors.

Links with higher education are also being developed, with activities including: an annual conference to review its relations with UK universities; the production of a newsletter, three times a year, reporting on BT's links with higher education; the annual BT University Development Awards scheme for which universities are invited to apply on a competitive basis.

Environment

Support is given to UK-wide environmental concerns as well as to the physical regeneration of destitute areas, conservation and national heritage.

Examples of sponsorships include BT Environment Week, co-ordinated by the Civic Trust, in which £50,000 was distributed to well over 3,000 projects undertaken by over one million people; BT Environment City, a Royal Society for Nature Conservation initiative to promote a wide range of environmental improvement schemes in towns and cities throughout the UK; and the BT Young Naturalist of the Year Awards aimed at 7 to 11 year olds to encourage them to become more aware and involved in environmental issues. The company also sponsor the BT/WWF Partnership Awards to encourage the development of environmental initiatives which are completed in partnership with other groups in the community.

The company supports a number of projects with local Groundwork Trusts. Grants (totalling £85,000 over two years) are also given to schools in inner city areas to improve their environments through the BT/Learning Through Landscapes Urban Challenge.

Arts

The programme is based on selected countrywide projects rather than major events in central London. This includes sponsorship of major company tours of the UK, usually to locations which otherwise would not normally receive work of the calibre presented – for example, Northern Ballet Theatre, South Bank Centre's National Touring Exhibitions and the BT New Contemporaries Art Exhibition and Tour which features the work of young artists. Support is also given to amateur arts including the BT Biennial for amateur theatre and 'Making More of Music', a programme of over 100 events in support of amateur music organised by the National Federation of Music Societies.

Two major additions to the programme in 1994 were: the BT Orchestral Series involving all major British Symphony Orchestras in a series of concerts between September 1994 and June 1997; and the BT National Connections involving work with the National Theatre and groups of young people throughout the UK in a three-year project including professionally led workshops, regional festivals and a showcase of their work at the National Theatre.

A wide range of local projects such as the Edinburgh Festival, the Belfast Festival and the Welsh International Eisteddfod make up the programme.

Secondment

'The secondment and funding of managers and staff ... is intended to support the main programme areas and provide close involvement in projects alongside any financial contributions.' At present, secondments are focused on:

- job creation and training for disadvantaged groups
- education/industry partnerships
- inner city regeneration
- charities.

The company also funds the 'secondment' of ex-BT staff on the register of Manpower, to community organisations.

Employee involvement

BT people's voluntary involvement in their local communities is keenly encouraged. A number of divisions within the company run their own volunteer support schemes, which feed into the nationwide BT Community Challenge. This competition provides £60,000 'prize money' in the form of donations which are made to the charities of the winners' choice.

BT's commitment to Give As You Earn enables employees to donate up to £1,200 before tax per year to the charity of their choice. Employees' donations during 1996/97 amounted to almost £1.2 million, which was matched by the company on a £ for £ basis.

Exclusions

No response to circular appeals. No support for denominational appeals, political appeals, appeals from individuals or brochure advertising.

Applications

Decisions on major grants are made at head office by the Board Community and Charities Committee which meets quarterly. Smaller grants can be made by staff of the relevant Community Unit at their discretion. Local appeals should be sent to the appropriate BT local office. (Each BT zone has its own community affairs staff operating a programme which reflects the needs of that area.)

Contacts:

Voluntary sector partnerships 0171-356 6678

Education and employment partnerships 0171-356 4079

Arts and marketing partnerships 0171-356 5834.

British Vita PLC

Oldham Road, Middleton, Manchester M24 2DB
0161-643 1133; Fax: 0161-653 5411
Website: www.vita.co.uk/vita

Correspondent: Alan Teague, Company Secretary

Chief officers: *Chairman:* R McGee; *Chief Executive:* J Mercer

Year end	Turnover	Pre-tax profit
31/12/97	£808,400,000	£66,200,000

Nature of company business
The manufacture and processing of polymers, including cellular foams, synthetic fibre fillings, specialised and coated fabrics, polymeric compounds and mouldings, and engineering thermoplastics.

Main subsidiaries include: Ball & Young; Caligen Foam; Jackdaw Polymers; Kay-Metzeler; H E Mowbray & Company; Royalite Plastics; The Rossendale Combining Company; Vitacom; Vitafoam; Vitafibres; Vitamol.

UK employees: 4,282

Charitable donations

1997: £77,964
1996: £54,973
1995: £74,818
1994: £87,521
1993: £70,500

Community support policy

The charitable donations figure given is in fact the sum of a large number of normally modest donations by separate Vita companies. There is therefore a preference for local appeals where these companies operate, those relevant to company business and those in which a member of staff is

Brixton

involved. Priority is given to charities concerned with children and youth, education and enterprise/training.

In kind support: The company donates products such as quilts, pillows and sleeping bags for tombola or raffle prizes.

Education: The company operates work experience schemes for pupils and teachers.

Exclusions

Unsolicited appeals are not welcome, nor are large national appeals, denominational appeals, political appeals, appeals from individuals, overseas projects or advertising in charity brochures.

Applications

In writing to the correspondent.

Brixton Estate plc

22–24 Ely Place, London EC1N 6TQ
0171-400 4400; Fax: 0171-405 1630

Correspondent: Celeste Watling, Secretary, Charity Committee

Chief officers: *Chairman:* D F Gardner; *Managing Director:* T J Nagle

Year end	Turnover	Pre-tax profit
31/12/97	£83,715,000	£37,865,000

Nature of company business
Principal activities: property investment and development and some property dealing.

UK employees: 54

Charitable donations

1997: £60,000
1996: £60,000
1995: £60,000
1994: £60,000
1993: £60,000

Community support policy

Charitable donations: Priority is given to charities in the geographical areas in which the company operates and to national charities. Preference is also given to appeals where a member of staff is involved. Typically, grants are in the range £100 to £1,000. Donations are made mainly through the Brixton Estate Charitable Trust. The trustees are Sir R B Wilbraham, D F Gardner, D E Marlow and S J Owen (all directors of the company).

The trust receives £60,000 a year from the company under deed of covenant. In 1997/98, grants totalled £61,000. Unfortunately, no further information was available for this year and the most recent year for which a grants list was available was 1994/95. In this year, only three of the grants were for over £1,000, with £2,000 going to two Lord Mayor's Appeals, one for St Paul's Cathedral and one for the British Heart Foundation. The other larger grant was £1,500 to BBC Children in Need Appeal.

There were 23 grants for £1,000, with the remainder for £250 to £500. Recipients of £1,000 included Alzheimer's Disease Society, Bomber Command Association, Chichester Cathedral Trust, Congleton Youth Project, King George's Fund for Sailors, National Trust, Save the Children Fund and Worshipful Company of Masons Craft Fund. Most grants were to health and welfare charities, with youth, children and service/ex-service organisations also benefiting.

Exclusions

Support for registered charities only. No support for individuals, students, fundraising events, local appeals not in areas of company presence, local branches of national charities and charities whose main aim is to support other charities.

Brixton Estate undertakes no secondment or sponsorship of the arts.

Applications

In writing to the correspondent. Grant decisions are made by the committee which meets quarterly.

BTP plc

Hayes Road, Cadishead, Manchester M44 5BX
0161-775 3945; Fax: 0161-775 3970

Correspondent: Creightan Twiggs, Group Company Secretary

Chief officers: *Chairman:* J H B Ketteley; *Chief Executive:* S J Hannam

Year end	Turnover	Pre-tax profit
31/3/98	£439,000,000	£43,000,000

Nature of company business
The principal activities are the manufacture and distribution of speciality chemical products and the manufacture, assembly and distribution of technical safety systems.

Main subsidiaries include: Lancaster Synthesis Ltd; Nipa Laboratories Ltd; AB Vickers Ltd; AP Chemicals Ltd; Hodgson Chemicals Ltd; Hodgson Specialities Ltd; Barrow Hepburn Sala Ltd; Protecta International Ltd; IN-CAL Ltd; Reverex Chemicals Ltd.

UK employees: 3,386

Charitable donations

1998: £60,255
1997: £47,982
1996: £21,570
1995: £12,983
1994: £9,705

Community support policy

Donations are given to local charities in areas of company presence. Although there are about 50 companies within the BTP group each of which can make charitable donations, we were informed that in practice few do.

Applications

Appeals should be addressed to the appropriate company or branch manager.

BTR plc

BTR House, Carlisle Place, London SW1P 1BX
0171-834 3848; Fax: 0171-834 3879
Website: www.btrplc.com

Correspondent: David Stevens, Company Secretary

Chief officers: *Chairman:* E O M Eilledge;
Chief Executive: I C Jackson

Year end	Turnover	Pre-tax profit
31/12/97	£8,091,000,000	£1,293,000,000

Nature of company business
The company is involved in construction, energy and electrical products, industrial goods, transportation and consumer-related activities. It is responsible for the Dunlop Slazenger, Carlton and Puma sports ranges, and Wm Lawrence, Rest Assured and Bridgecraft furniture and bedding.

Main subsidiaries include: Dunlop Holdings Ltd; Hawker Siddeley Group Ltd.

UK employees: 110,498

Charitable donations

1997: £593,197
1996: £168,085
1995: £145,157
1994: £284,560
1993: £283,581
Membership: *BitC*

Community support policy

BTR companies and their employees give time, energy and resources to support local, national and international causes. Most of the donations budget is distributed by head office, the remainder by the subsidiaries which make grants independently of head office. There has been a large increase in the level of giving over the past year.

Charitable donations: The company gives preference to national appeals, charities which have an affinity to industries in which the company is involved and projects in which a member of staff is involved. Preferred areas of support are: the arts; children/youth; education; elderly people; enterprise/training; environment/heritage; medical research; religious appeals; sickness/disability; social welfare and science/technology.

Employee involvement: In addition to various fundraising activities (such as the annual BTR raft race, which raises over £10,000 each year) many employees support charities through the payroll giving scheme.

Education: The company seeks to promote industry and education links through various schemes. It provides student sponsorships, organises factory visits for staff and students, has carried out work on a school's new technology course and seconded staff to act as business advisers to a group of local sixth-form students engaged in extracurricular activity to set up and run their own business.

In 1990, the group initiated an annual educational grant in support of a joint-training programme with the UK Foreign and Commonwealth Office to fund scholarships for Australian postgraduates at UK universities.

Exclusions
No response to circular appeals. No support for fundraising events, advertising in charity brochures, appeals from individuals, animal welfare, purely denominational (religious) appeals, local appeals not in areas of company presence or overseas projects.

Applications
In writing to the correspondent. An appeals committee meets as necessary at head office. Local appeals are only considered if they are close to company locations, and should be directed to the local subsidiary.

Advice to applicants: The correspondent states that the volume of mail is getting too large to handle and therefore only relevant appeals should be sent. Many appeals are badly researched, badly presented and are sent to the wrong people, thus reducing their chance of success.

Other information: A formal staff charity fund does not exist, but ad hoc arrangements operate in specific instances. The company reports on its involvement in its annual report.

H P Bulmer Holdings plc

The Cider Mills, Plough Lane, Hereford HR4 0LE
01432-352000

Correspondent: George Thomas, Public Relations Manager

Chief officers: *Chairman:* J E Bulmer;
Chief Executive: M J Hughes

Year end	Turnover	Pre-tax profit
24/4/98	£298,228,000	£21,100,000

Nature of company business
An international alcoholic drinks business with a particular focus on cider, including the Strongbow and Woodbecker brands.

Main subsidiaries include: Symonds Cider & English Wine Company Ltd; Inch's Cider Ltd.

Main brands include: Strongbow; Woodpecker; White Lightning; Scrumpy Jack.

UK employees: 870

Charitable donations

1998: £35,000
1997: £33,000
Total community contributions: £40,000

Community support policy

The company mainly supports local charities, particularly in Hereford and Herefordshire, and specific trade-related charities. Local fundraising events may also be supported. In addition to making cash donations, support is provided through arts and good cause sponsorship and gifts in kind.

Donations may be given in the following areas: animal welfare charities, the arts, children and youth, elderly people, environment/heritage, medical research, sickness/disability charities and social welfare.

Bunzl

Exclusions
No response to circular appeals. No support for advertising in charity brochures, local appeals not in areas of company presence, large national appeals or overseas projects.

Applications
In writing to the correspondent.

Bunzl plc

110 Park Street, London W1Y 3RB
0171-495 4950; Fax: 0171-495 4953

Correspondent: Julia Battyll, Public Relations Consultant

Chief officers: *Chairman:* A Habgood;
Managing Director: D Williams

Year end	Turnover	Pre-tax profit
31/12/97	£1,753,200,000	£125,900,000

Nature of company business
Principal activities: distribution, conversion and light manufacture, primarily of paper and plastic based products for a wide variety of end-user products.

Main subsidiaries include: Fine paper: Alba Paper (Manchester); Mason's Paper (Ipswich, Cambridge, Norwich, Hornchurch); Donald Murray (Paper) (Glasgow, Aberdeen, Edinburgh, Bristol, Belfast, Newcastle); Michael Jackson (Preston); Powell & Heilbron (Liverpool); Rothera & Brereton (Leeds, Sheffield, Nottingham); Southern Counties Paper (Camberley, Brentford); Southern Paper (Shoreham, Croydon, Chatham, Canterbury, Southampton); Thom & Cook (London); Dixon & Roe (London, Hatfield, Leicester); Europoint; Papermark; Rapid Reel. Plastic products: Morane (Banbury); Toolmak (Manchester); Moss Plastic Parts (Kidlington/Witney); The Stewart Company; Laminex.
Paper and plastic disposables distribution: ACS (Morden); Alpha Supplies.
Cigarette filters: Filtrona (Harpenden, Jarrow, Milton Keynes); Filtrona Instruments & Automation.

UK employees: n/a

Charitable donations
1997: £153,000
1996: £144,000
1995: £138,000
1994: £135,000
1993: £132,000
Membership: *BitC*

Community support policy

The group maintains a community relations programme which supports a cross-section of charitable organisations on a national basis, mainly in the areas of healthcare, social welfare, disability, education and enterprise.

The Foundation for Children with Leukaemia has received long-term support, with funds given to buy research equipment and an annual donation to buy materials needed to keep the machines in operation. In the field of disability, the group has sponsored the Bunzl Print Training Workshop at Dorincourt Industries – a supported factory operated by Queen Elizabeth's Foundation for Disabled People, and supported the Jubilee Sailing Trust appeal for a second sailing boat. The Homework Haven was an education initiative supported by the company at a secondary school close to one of its major sites. The scheme provides the school with a resource centre which students can use throughout the day and after school. The group is also involved in a programme with the Foreign & Commonwealth Office and Cranfield University, offering bursaries to foreign students.

Group companies also support charities within their own localities, and those which have the support of employees. Typical grants have been about £1,000.

Enterprise: The company is a member of Business in the Community.

The arts: Bunzl supports selected areas of the arts.

Exclusions
No response to appeals from individuals, to political appeals or appeals outside areas of company presence. No advertising in charity brochures.

Applications
In writing to the correspondent. Subsidiaries have a donations budget independent of head office and should be contacted directly.

BUPA Ltd

BUPA House, 15–19 Bloomsbury Way, London WC1A 2BA
0171-656 2000
Website: www.bupa.co.uk

Correspondent: The Corporate Communications Director

Chief officers: *Chairman:* Sir Bryan Nicholson;
Chief Executive: Val Gooding

Year end	Turnover	Pre-tax profit
31/12/97	£1,460,000,000	£68,100,000

Nature of company business
Principal activities: operation of health insurance funds and the provision of health care facilities and services including ownership and management of hospitals, care homes, homecare and health screening services.

UK employees: 40,000

Charitable donations
1997: £1,065,000
1996: £916,000
1995: £790,000
1994: n/a
1993: £227,000
Membership: *BitC %Club*

Community support policy

BUPA is a member of the PerCent Club and Business in the Community and supports a range of mainly medical charities, especially medical research. Children/youth charities are also supported, as are arts organisations, education, elderly people, social welfare and sport. Payments are usually made via Gift Aid. The donations figure of just over £1 million included a total of £513,000 to the medical charity (The BUPA Foundation) which it established. In addition, the company has made further commitments of £1.6 million over the next three years.

The BUPA Foundation aims to promote the advancement of health care through research. In 1997, it donated over £500,000 in grants to medical research projects. In 1997, support was given to Chain of Hope, Council for Music in Hospitals, Duke of Edimburgh's Award, National Asthma Campaign, and Counsel and Care for the Elderly. The foundation also rewards excellence in medical research, patient empowerment and education through its annual awards event. Five awards of £10,000 each are made.

Non-cash support is usually given in areas such as community fitness events through good cause sponsorship, gifts in kind and training schemes.

In 1996/97, support was given to the Prince's Trust/Business in the Community – Invest in Futures – by seconding a full-time manager, the Gateway Training Centre with a cash donation and furniture for training and study facilities, and the Refuge Centre where the company has provided rent-free accommodation for three years.

Exclusions

The company does not support appeals from individuals, political appeals or religious appeals.

Applications

In writing to the correspondent.

Burmah Castrol plc

Burmah Castrol House, Pipers Way, Swindon SN3 1RE
01793-614 094

Correspondent: Secretary to the Appeals Committee

Chief officers: *Chairman:* Jonathan Fry;
Chief Executive: Tim Stevenson

Year end	Turnover	Pre-tax profit
31/12/97	£2,936,000,000	£237,700,000

Nature of company business
Principal activities: the international manufacture and marketing of specialised oil and chemical products.
Main subsidiaries include: Castrol Ltd; Veedol International.
Main brands include: Castrol GTX.
Main locations: Swindon, Pangbourne (Reading), Marlow, Crayford, Chesham, Broadstairs, Tamworth, Market Drayton, Stanlow, Hyde and Glasgow.
UK employees: n/a

Charitable donations

1997: £200,000
1996: £170,000
1995: £212,000
1994: £195,000
1993: £228,000
Membership: *BitC %Club*

Community support policy

Charitable donations: Burmah Castrol is a member of the PerCent Club, annually giving about £200,000 in charitable donations, although presumably giving in the region of £1 million to fulfil its PerCent Club commitment.

The company receives hundreds of requests each year for financial assistance, so support is given **only** to projects which are close to areas of company presence either in the UK or overseas (ie. within 20 miles of one of the company's larger operating units, generally Wiltshire, Broadstairs and Stanlow).

Support is only given to specific projects and mainly concentrated on health, welfare and educational organisations. Preference is given to charities in which a member of staff is involved. Donations have also been given to charities concerned with the arts and overseas aid/development. Grants to national organisations range from £500 to £3,500. Grants to local organisations from £50 to £3,000.

Under its policy of aid for UK-based charities working in developing countries, the company has continued to support ActionAid and Save the Children, and extended its funding to HelpAge International and the International Childcare Trust.

All the group's companies and staff are encouraged to support local charities and community projects. The company also gives gifts in kind (surplus office furniture and equipment, etc.), free professional advice from staff and the use of company facilities free of charge. Grants are also given to top-up employee fundraising efforts.

Employee involvement: Priority may be given to projects in which a member of staff is involved. Similarly, it sometimes operates a matching funds scheme for employee fundraising, employee participation and payroll giving, and encourages active involvement by employees in their local communities. Employees at various company locations around the world have established charity fundraising groups. In the main, each group supports projects in its own locality. Further information can be obtained from the correspondent.

Enterprise: The company is a member of Business in the Community, various chambers of commerce and local enterprise agencies.

Education: Local links are maintained at school, technical and university level. Examples include teacher placements and work experience.

Environment: The company supports environmental projects through separate budget allocations: sponsorship and charity. In **all** cases, the project must be close to one of the company's operating locations. Requests for sponsorship should be directed to the Community Relations Executive, Burmah Castrol Trading Ltd, while charitable requests should be directed to the correspondent.

The arts: Burmah Castrol is a member of the Royal Academy of Arts. Arts projects can be supported from either the sponsorship or the charity budget. Projects supported from the sponsorship budget are ones which:

- are likely to gain good media coverage
- are likely to provide medium to long-term corporate exposure
- have logical synergy with other parts of Burmah Castrol's community relations activities
- encourage excellence in arts practice
- provide corporate hospitality opportunities
- include benefits to Burmah Castrol employees.

Projects supported from the charitable donations budget generally provide little or no corporate exposure, but are likely to meet the objectives of:

- providing greater opportunities for people with disabilities to have access to the arts
- using arts-based projects for therapeutic and/or educational purposes.

Support is restricted to projects in areas of company presence. Sponsorship applications should be made to the Community Relations Executive, Burmah Castrol Trading Ltd, and charitable appeals to the correspondent.

Exclusions

Support is given only to specific projects; no 'general' appeals are supported. No response to circular appeals. No support for fundraising events, advertising in charity brochures, appeals from individuals, purely denominational (religious) appeals, local appeals not in areas of company presence, large national appeals, political organisations, third parties, expeditions, exchanges and study tours, or individual schools, playgroups and mother/toddler groups – except where special schemes are announced.

Applications

In writing to the correspondent. The initial application need not be too detailed but should include a summary of the project, its objectives and costs. If you have any queries about the eligibility of a project, a preliminary telephone call would be advisable.

Information available: The company publishes information on its community affairs in its annual report and in occasional articles in employee newsletters. It has published a leaflet entitled *Burmah Castrol – Charitable Donations Guidelines*, copies are available on request from the correspondent.

C & A Stores

20 Old Bailey, London EC4M 7BH
0171-629 1244; Fax: 0171-409 2257

Correspondent: Chris Williams, The Secretary

Chief officers: n/a

Year end	Turnover	Pre-tax profit
28/2/97	n/a	n/a

Nature of company business
C & A operates fashion retailing stores in the main towns and cities across the UK.

UK employees: n/a

Charitable donations
1997: £279,270
1996: £280,728
1995: £278,492
1994: £301,369
1993: £300,862
Membership: *BitC*

Community support policy

All donations are made through the C & A Charitable Trust (Charity Commission number 269881) which was established in 1975. It operates primarily through local committees composed of C & A staff representatives in 119 stores, five distribution centres and head office. These local committees take the initiative both in selecting the small number of registered charities to benefit in their area and in helping to raise further funds for them. (From 1992 to 1997, employees raised over £550,000.) The management committee considers the local recommendations and also assesses national charitable appeals.

It prefers organisations and projects which aim at improving the quality of life of disadvantaged people living in the neighbourhood of local C & A stores. Donations should benefit the local area rather than forming part of a large national or international appeal.

A proportion of the trust's budget continues to be reserved for central donations. Beneficiaries in recent years have included: Down's Syndrome Association, Childline, East London Trust for Children with Special Needs, Cancer Relief Macmillan Fund and the Cot Death Society.

In 1996/97, the trust had an income of £344,000 (£305,000 in 1995/96) and made 211 grants totalling £279,000 (252 grants totalling £281,000 in 1995/96). These grants were broken down by the trust as (1996 figures in brackets):

Direct relief of poverty .... £187 .... (£348)
Housing aid .... £1,546 .... (£2,200)
Health and disability .... £214,625 .... (£243,863)
Recreation and youth .... nil .... (£400)
Community centres .... £5,000 .... (£1,000)
Deprived children and families ...... £45,810 ...... (£19,143)
Elderly .... £2,750 .... (£4,661)
Rehabilitation of offenders/victims .. nil .... (£2,184)
Addiction and suicide .... £180 .... (£2,702)
Environment .... £600 .... (£1,401)
Swiftflow Distribution .... £8,579 .... (£2,826)

Around 80% of the grant total is given in the health and disablement category, which in 1996/97 included 150 to 200 donations. Many of the organisations supported were local branches of national charities, some of which were supported by committees from across the country, such as Cot Death Society (which was supported by 26 stores and received 14% of the category total) and Whizz-Kidz (support from 14 stores).

Purely local charities/organisations were were also supported such as hospitals in Bolton and Blackpool (£1,500 each) and Darlington Area Playscheme for Handicapped Children – DASH (£1,100). 12 sites gave a main donation of more than £2,500, to organisations which included British Kidney Patient Association, Cobalt Unit Appeal Fund, Cystic Fibrosis Trust, Glenfield Hospital, Institute of Child Health, Shopmobilty – Highlands. Most grants ranged from £500 to £1,500, and these included grants to Eden Valley Hospice (Carlisle), Kent Air Ambulance Trust (Tunbridge Wells), Rainbow Family Trust (Chester) and SANDS (Harlow).

The next most favoured category was deprived children and families which received 10 grants totalling £46,000 (17% of total grants up from 7% in 1996). Childline received nearly £40,000 in three grants (almost all from the head office), with other recipients including Southend Women's Aid (£2,300), Instant Neighbour (Aberdeen – £1,100), NSPCC (Warrington – £900 and Hemel Hempstead – £200) Mayor's Charity (head office £1,000), Stevenage Community Trust (£900) and Crawcrook Children's Home (Gateshead – £150).

Grants in other categories included:

Projects for elderly people (£2,750 in 14 grants): Cottage Homes received grants of £50 to £150 from 14 stores in the South East, around the Greater London area and Help the Aged received two grants totalling £1,250.

Community centres: one grant of £5,000 to Bereaved Families Fund – Dunblane from the head office.

Environment: two stores each gave the RNLI £300.

Exclusions
The trust does not respond to unsolicited appeals, appeals from individuals, animal welfare, the arts, environment/heritage, overseas projects, political or religious appeals, sport or science/technology. Brochure appeals are not supported.

Applications
The trust states that it no longer considers unsolicited applications.

Local charities are selected by store charity committee members asked to complete a short application form. This, with any supporting information, is forwarded to the central trust administrator for approval by the management committee.

Cable & Wireless plc

124 Theobalds Road, London WC1X 8RX
0171-315 4000; Fax: 0171-315 5000
Website: www.cwplc.com

Correspondent: Ms Swati Patel, Community Investment Manager

Chief officers: *Chairman:* Dr N Brian Smith; *Chief Executive:* Richard H Brown

Year end	Turnover	Pre-tax profit
31/3/98	£7,001,000,000	£2,184,000,000

Nature of company business
Telecommunications. Mercury Communications Ltd is 85% owned by the company.
Main subsidiaries include: MPC 92 Ltd.

UK employees: 46,550

Charitable donations
1998: £1,600,000
1997: £1,600,000
Membership: ABSA BitC

Community support policy
The company is no longer a member of the PerCent Club, though still a member of ABSA and Business in the Community.

In its 1998 annual report the company states: 'In the United Kingdom £1.6 million was donated for charitable purposes. Worldwide, including the United Kingdom, the total expenditure in donations and sponsorship for the benefit of the community amounted to £4.9 million'.

The company aims to build mutually beneficial links with the communities in which its businesses are based. Support is focused on the arts, education and science/technology. Charities applying for support should be able to show where their interests coincide with those of the company.

In 1998, in addition to the company's existing support for community projects, a special employee community scheme was launched to mark the 125th anniversary.

Exclusions
No support for circular appeals, advertising in charity brochures, appeals on behalf of individuals, local appeals not in areas of company presence, economic research, political organisations, or religious or sectarian causes.

Applications
In writing to the correspondent.

Cadbury

Cadbury Schweppes plc

25 Berkeley Square, London W1X 6HT
0171-409 1313
Website: www.cadburyschweppes.com

Correspondent: The Cadbury Schweppes Foundation

Chief officers: *Chairman:* Sir Dominic Cadbury; *Chief Executive:* John Sunderland

Year end	Turnover	Pre-tax profit
31/12/97	£4,173,000,000	£987,000,000

Nature of company business
Principal activities: the manufacture and marketing of confectionery and soft drinks.

Main subsidiaries include: Cadbury; Reading Scientific Services; Schweppes; Trebor Bassett.

Main brands include: Additional to those products marketed under the Cadbury's, Schweppes and Trebor Bassett brand names are: Canada Dry, Sunkist, Dr Pepper, 7 Up, Motts Apple Juice, Clamato, Kia-ora, Roses Lime Juice, Holland House, Crush and A&W.

Main locations: Bournville (Cadbury); Maple Cross, Hertfordshire (Trebor Bassett); plus operating sites throughout the UK.

UK employees: 10,052

Charitable donations

1997: £1,251,878
1996: £1,036,000
1995: £760,000
1994: £670,000
1993: £650,000

Total community contributions: £3,850,000 (1996)

Membership: *BitC %Club*

Community support policy

Selected secondments and provision of company facilities for community use represent a significant part of the company's total contribution to the community on top of cash donations. In 1996, community contributions totalled £3,850,000.

Charitable donations: The company is a member the PerCent Club. Most requests for charitable donations are channelled through the Cadbury Schweppes Foundation – the company's charitable trust in the UK. This has no endowment but is funded by grants from the company each year.

Grants are made at the discretion of the trustees whose current focus is on selected projects and organisations in the fields of:

- education and enterprise
- health and welfare
- environment.

The trust plans its giving in advance for each year; unsolicited appeals are not encouraged. Preference is given for charities relevant to company business, in areas of company presence and with company staff involvement. Grants to national organisations range from £10,000 to £75,000, and to local organisations from £1,000 to £5,000. In 1996, major grant recipients included Business in the Community (£70,000), The Confectioners Benevolent Fund (£55,000) and Young Enterprise (£35,000) – regularly the main beneficiaries. Relate (£35,000), Mencap and British Red Cross (£25,000 each) were the next main beneficiaries during the year.

Employee involvement: The company operates a payroll giving scheme. It also encourages employee fundraising with matched giving by the company for specific projects. Staff are encouraged to become school governors and have been seconded full-time to community-based organisations.

Enterprise: The company is a member of Business in the Community and a major supporter of enterprise initiatives. A senior manager has been seconded to the Prince's Youth Business Trust as part of a major commitment to this area.

Education: Regular links are maintained with over 50 schools through work experience, work shadowing, collaborative projects and provision of school packs. 25 schools are now assigned a links person or industrial governor.

Exclusions

In view of the policy of concentrating grants behind selected projects most ad hoc appeals have to be declined and are therefore not encouraged. No support for circular appeals, large national appeals, fundraising events, advertising in charity brochures, appeals from individuals, purely denominational (religious) appeals, local appeals not in the areas of company presence, requests for company products for fundraising events and projects outside the criteria listed above.

Normally support has not been for projects outside the UK since it is policy to provide support through local businesses in the many countries around the world where Cadbury Schweppes has operations.

Applications

As indicated above, appeals outside the criteria defined are not encouraged as most grants are committed in advance on an ongoing basis. Any correspondence should be addressed to: The Cadbury Schweppes Foundation at the above address.

Cadogan Estates Ltd

18 Cadogan Gardens, London SW3 2RP
0171-730 4567; Fax: 0171-730 5339

Correspondent: Sue Wizard, Secretary to Lord Cadogan

Chief officers: n/a

Year end	Turnover	Pre-tax profit
31/12/95	£81,814,000	£12,807,000

Nature of company business
The principal activity of the group is property investment. Subsidiaries are involved in the manufacture and distribution of menswear, upholstered furniture and protective workplace clothing, and the retailing of furniture.

Main subsidiaries include: Chelsea Land Ltd; Oakley Investment Ltd; Christy & Co Ltd; Michelsons Ltd; Holliday & Brown Ltd; Multifabs Ltd; Oakley Leisure Parks Ltd; Furniture Village PLC.

UK employees: n/a

Charitable donations
1995: £50,000
1994: n/a
1993: £181,000

Community support policy
We have not been able to update this entry since the last edition of the guide, other than to check the correspondent details. The company gave £50,000 in charitable donations in 1995, but was unwilling to give any further information.

The company stated: 'One of our shareholders has a charitable trust and the bulk of our donations are now made that way'. Presumably this is The Cadogan Charity (registered charity number 247773) which gives grants of about £150,000 a year, but we are not sure if the company gives a donation directly to the trust for distribution. (Further details on the trust can be found in *A Guide to Major Trusts Volume 2.*)

Applications
In writing to the correspondent.

Caledonia Group Services Ltd

Cayzer House, 1 Thomas More Street, London E1 9AR
0171-481 4343; Fax: 0171-488 0896

Correspondent: Major M G Wyatt, Deputy Chairman

Chief officer: *Chairman:* Peter N Buckley

Year end	Turnover	Pre-tax profit
31/3/98	£68,000,000	£41,000,000

Nature of company business
A diversified trading and investment company, its holdings are in four sectors: financial, industrial and services; leisure; property and general; and investment trusts.

Main subsidiaries include: Abacus Self Storage Ltd; Amber Industrial Holdings PLC; Edinburgh Crystal Glass Co Ltd.

UK employees: 993

Charitable donations
1998: £71,000
1997: £73,000
1996: £69,000
1995: £75,416
1994: £67,000

Community support policy
The company donates a total of about £70,000 to charities. It has a preference for appeals relevant to company business and charities in which a member of company staff is involved. There is also a preference for education, environment/heritage, arts and enterprise/training. Grants to national organisations from £200 to £2,000.

Exclusions
No grants for fundraising events, advertising in charity brochures, purely denominational (religious) appeals, local appeals not in areas of company presence, large national appeals, overseas projects or circular appeals, and absolutely no individual sponsorship of college/university students.

Applications
In writing to the correspondent.

Camellia plc

25 Upper Brook Street, London W1Y 1PD
0171-629 5728; Fax: 0171-629 4484

Correspondent: D M Bacon, Managing Director

Chief officers: *Chairman:* G Fox; *Managing Director:* D M Bacon

Year end	Turnover	Pre-tax profit
31/12/97	£233,883,000	£26,211,000

Nature of company business
The company is the holding company of an agricultural, industrial and financial services group. The main activities of its subsidiaries are: agriculture and horticulture (production of tea, coffee, citrus fruits, edible nuts and general farming); private and merchant banking services; food trading; trading and agency; cold storage, transport and warehousing; engineering; chemical and pharmaceuticals production; property leasing; dealing in fine art.

Main subsidiaries include: J Benett Ltd; W G White Ltd; British Traders & Shippers Ltd; Highland Fuels Ltd; Lawrie Plantation Services Ltd; AJT Engineering Ltd; Unochrome Industries Ltd; JPL Fine Arts Ltd; Lumley Cazalet Ltd; David Field Ltd; W D G Properties Ltd; Duncan Lawrie Ltd; Associated Cold Stores & Transport Ltd; Assam-Dooars Holdings Ltd; Associated Fisheries PLC; Bordure Ltd; Lawrie Group PLC; Linton Park PLC; Sterling Industrial Securities Ltd; Walter Duncan & Goodricke Ltd; Western Dooars Tea Holdings Ltd.

UK employees: under 50

Charitable donations
1997: £32,772
1996: £40,000
1995: £22,139

Community support policy
Despite increased pre-tax profits of over 40% compared to last year, the total charitable donations of the company decreased to under £33,000, from £40,000 in 1996. The policy has also changed slightly from last year.

The company supports local and national charities across the UK, especially in the fields of children and youth, elderly people, medical research, environment/heritage and sickness/disability. Grants may be for up to £500. However, the company stated that it tends to give support to the same charities each year, and only in very

Camelot

exceptional circumstances would any new causes be added to the existing list.

Exclusions

No support for fundraising events, advertising in charity brochures, appeals from individuals, political appeals, purely denominational (religious) appeals, local appeals not in areas of company presence, large national appeals, enterprise/training, science/technology, medical research, sport, social welfare, education, animal welfare charities or overseas projects. Sponsorship is not undertaken.

Applications

In writing to the correspondent, but please note the above policy.

Camelot Group plc

Tolpits Lane, Watford WD1 8RN
01923-425000

Correspondent: The Camelot Foundation

Chief officers: *Chairman:* Sir George Russell; *Chief Executive:* Tim Holley

Year end	Turnover	Pre-tax profit
31/3/98	£4,723,000,000	£70,800,000

Nature of company business
The principal activity of the company is the operation and promotion of the National Lottery. The licence to run the lottery expires on 30 September 2001.

The shareholders of the company are *Cadbury Schweppes plc*, *De La Rue plc*, *International Computers Ltd* and *Racal Electronics plc*.

UK employees: 667

Charitable donations

1998: £3,500,000
1997: £3,200,000
1996: £550,000

Total community contributions: £3,900,000

Membership: *BitC*

Community support policy

The company gave £3.9 million in community contributions in 1997/98. This included a payment of £3 million to the Camelot Foundation (Charity Commission number 1060606). The remaining £0.9 million comprised contributions in cash and in kind to community and charitable organisations, of which £0.5 million related to direct donations to charities.

Other support included undertaking a limited amount of good-cause sponsorship and advertising in charity brochures. The company allows staff time off to volunteer and the use of the company's meeting rooms, at the regional offices. The company also operates the Give As You Earn payroll giving scheme.

The Camelot Foundation

The Camelot Group launched The Camelot Foundation in November 1996. The period ending 30 September 1997 was its first year of operation, during which it received £5 million from the company.

The aim of the foundation is to support organisations which help disabled or disadvantaged people play a fuller role in the workplace and the community.

In the period February to September 1997, grants totalling £2.9 million were made to voluntary organisations throughout the UK. In November 1997, the largest award to date was announced: £1,212,000 to The Prince's Trust to establish the Young People Leaving Care project. A further £202,000 was awarded to 'Reaching Young People Beyond the Fringes of the State' initiative led by a consortium of Centrepoint, Save the Children, Pilotlight, NCVO and Demos. These initiatives focus on helping disadvantaged young people into the community.

The annual review of the foundation states, 'Unlike some donors, our funding policy is not restricted to capital funding or simply to project funding. We recognise voluntary organisations' increasing need for core funding, contributing towards their running costs in difficult times. We also support the effective operation of voluntary groups by enabling them to recruit, pay for and train key staff – many of our awards from our Community Support Programme have gone towards staff and office expenses, the purchase of computer equipment or the specialised training of key staff'.

There are three programmes:

Community Support Programme
This gives small grants to voluntary organisations and community-based organisations. Grants normally range from £500 to £5,000, exceptionally up to £10,000.

Funding is spread across a broad range of themes and schemes within the foundation's overall aim. A total of 3,776 applications were received in this category of which 929 were successful, receiving a total of £1.69 million.

A full list of all the grants made in 1997 including the amount awarded and the purpose of the grant was provided by the foundation.

Following what the foundation described as phase one of this programme and discussions with the voluntary sector, phase two is now in operation, concentrating on very small organisations that deal with specific issues relating to disability and disadvantage. The foundation is particularly keen to ensure it meets the needs of those organisations within the community who are currently receiving little or no help. The following is taken from the foundation's guidance notes for applicants for this programme.

Grants will be made to groups working with people aged 16 and over. Grants are only awarded for one year at a time and are available for the following:

- equipment
- training for project users, staff, volunteers and committee members
- volunteer expenses (for example, travel)
- running costs

- requests that have an effect on the quality of life of people who use the service such as trips out, holidays or respite care (for example a carer taking a temporary break).

The main focus of the disadvantage theme of the programme will be on:
- Alzheimer's disease and other dementias
- carers
- people leaving care
- domestic violence
- refugees
- local transport schemes in rural areas
- programmes which help people to find work.

The main focus of the disability theme of the programme is:

to provide resources to organisations where disabled people form a clear majority of both voting members and the governing committee. However, organisations run for disabled people rather than by disabled people will be eligible for a grant if the project is aimed at getting more disabled people to take part in the running of the organisation.

Under both themes, the foundation will concentrate on funding organisations who have a strong belief in self-help and getting users involved in running and managing the organisation if appropriate.

Charitable Projects Programme

Under this programme, support is given to a small number of major innovative charitable projects. 'In order to find suitable major projects, we don't just assess applications – we actively talk to specialists within the voluntary sector and to groups who have innovative and strong ideas.'

Seven major projects were approved during the first year, all within the disability or disadvantaged sectors. They were:

Spinal Injuries Association: up to £100,000 over two years to set up support groups to assist people transferring from full-time care to home-based care.

Revolving Doors: up to £180,000 over two years to a project working in three areas which help people with mental health problems when they are dealt with by the police.

Dalston Youth Project: up to £365,000 over two years for expansion into a disadvantaged area of Manchester.

Release: £195,000 over two years to help establish a national specialist education consultancy.

Dark Horse Venture: £50,000 over three years for a pilot project in the north of England, aimed at helping older people break out of isolation through music, dance and drama.

Give 5 – Make it Happen: £58,850 to this Channel 5 project enabling small and regionally based voluntary organisations to get the best out of the channel's week long campaign in September 1997.

Training for Trainers: £41,500 for a pilot scheme aiming to enable people with impairments and disabilities to develop their skills as trainers and to allow greater employment opportunities in the hospitality industry.

Employee Participation Programme

This programme builds on the fundraising activities of Camelot's employees, and coordinates the provision of employees resources and office facilities for use by voluntary sector organisations across the UK.

The foundation operated a double match-funding programme in 1997, donating £2 for every £1 raised by an employee to a charity of their choice. The total given by the foundation under this scheme was £223,000.

Employees are also allowed a paid half day off work every month to support charities of their choice.

The trustees of the foundation include the Chief Executive of the company and two non-executive directors, Mary Baker and Sir Peter Imbert. The other trustees are Trevor Phillips, Usha Prashar, Jane Tewson and Sir Clive Whitmore.

Exclusions

Under the Community Support Programme the following are not funded:

- organisations who spend more than £100,000 a year
- organisations whose free reserves are more than their running costs for one year
- projects aimed at children or young people under 16
- salary costs
- buying minibuses
- requests for more than £10,000
- contributions to major building projects
- general appeals
- schools, colleges, hospitals
- individuals
- promoting religion
- trips abroad
- services run by statutory or public authorities
- medical research or equipment.

Applications

Applications should be made on a form available from The Camelot Foundation. Applications are dealt with on receipt.

Canon (UK) Ltd

Canon House, Manor Road, Wallington, Surrey SM6 0AJ
0181-773 6000; Fax: 0181-773 2156

Correspondent: G Thorn, Public Relations Manager

Chief officer: *Managing Director:* M Laws

Year end	Turnover	Pre-tax profit
31/12/96	£508,481,000	£16,123,000

Nature of company business
Marketing of electronic business machines.

Main subsidiaries include: Joe Walker Ltd; Central Systems and Business Machines Ltd; Libra Business Services Ltd; Partyseal Ltd.

UK employees: 2,951

Caparo

Charitable donations
1996: £188,000
1995: £218,000
1994: £246,000
1993: £207,000
Membership: *BitC %Club*

Community support policy

The company is a member of the PerCent Club and gave a report on its community involvement in the 1998 Annual Report of that organisation. It has established a CARE Programme, made up of company employees, which decides which appeals to support.

It allocates available funds as follows:
Business and community 30%
Education 20%
Arts 20%
General humanitarian charities 20%
Environment 10%

Financial help or equipment may be given, but an important part of the package may also be the expertise and involvement of staff. The *Business and community* category covers projects that include promoting growth in employment opportunities through business enterprise programmes, community business group support and local community events.

Exclusions
No support for overseas projects, religious or political appeals, individuals or advertising in charity brochures.

Applications
In writing to the correspondent.

Caparo Group Ltd

Caparo House, 103 Baker Street, London W1M 1FD
0171-486 1417; Fax: 0171-935 3242

Correspondent: Elizabeth Allan, Assistant to the Chairman

Chief officers: *Chairman:* Lord Paul; *Chief Executive:* A Paul

Year end	Turnover	Pre-tax profit
31/12/97	£515,000,000	£4,000,000

Nature of company business
The company activities are in engineering and industrial services.
Main subsidiaries include: Nupac Ltd; Osborne Hotel Torquay Ltd.

UK employees: 3,921

Charitable donations
1997: £430,000
1996: £469,000
1995: £465,000
1994: £460,000
1993: £443,000
Membership: *%Club*

Community support policy
The company is a member of the PerCent Club and continues to support the education and training of young people through contributions to national charities such as Youth Clubs UK, Voluntary Service Overseas and the Prince's Trust.

At London Zoo it sponsors the Ambika Paul Children's Zoo and the new Pygmy Hippo project.

Grants to national organisations range from £10 to £1,000. Grants to local organisations from £10 to £500. There is a preference for charities local to the West Midlands and Humberside, for example it has supported the West Midlands Police Children's Safety Books, the University of Hull and the Caparo League for under 12's in Scunthorpe. Other projects supported include Bharatiya Vidya Bhavan, One World Action, Women's India Association and the Budhrani Cancer Institute. A number of small grants have been made to educational, arts and children's charities in the UK and India.

Employees volunteering/charitable activities are supported financially and by giving company time off to volunteer.

Exclusions
No support for advertising in charity brochures; animal welfare charities; appeals from individuals; elderly people; environment/heritage; fundraising events; overseas projects; political appeals; religious appeals or sickness/disability charities. Sponsorship is not undertaken.

Applications
In writing to the correspondent.

Caradon plc

Caradon House, 24 Queens Road, Weybridge, Surrey KT13 9UX
01932-850850
Website: www.caradon.com

Correspondent: Derek Burningham, Assistant Group Secretary

Chief officers: *Chairman:* A P Hichens; *Chief Executive:* P J Jansen

Year end	Turnover	Pre-tax profit
31/12/97	£1,716,600,000	£129,000,000

Nature of company business
Principal activities: the manufacture of branded building products.
Main brands include: Stelrad; Henrad; Ideal; Twyfords; Doulton; Mira; MK Electrical Products; Everest; Terrain; Celuform; Catnic.

UK employees: n/a

Charitable donations
1997: £43,760
1996: £59,000
1995: £61,750
1994: £66,655
1993: £53,816
Membership: *BitC*

Community support policy

We have very little information available on the policy of this company. It has a preference for local charities in areas of company presence and appeals relevant to company business. The company is a member of Business in the Community.

Applications

In writing to the correspondent.

Cargill plc

Knowle Hill Park, Fairmile Lane, Cobham, Surrey KT11 2PD
01932-861000; Fax: 01932-861200

Correspondent: R Rawling, The Charities Committee

Chief officer: *Managing Director:* Graham Secker

Year end	Turnover	Pre-tax profit
31/5/97	£1,723,824,000	£25,426,000

Nature of company business
Principal activities: commodity trading and shipping, and the processing and distribution of foodstuffs.
Main subsidiaries include: Sun Valley Poultry Ltd; Sun Valley Foods Ltd.

UK employees: 6,384

Charitable donations

1997: £165,107
1996: £210,112
1995: £236,934
1994: £165,000
1993: £127,000
Membership: %Club

Community support policy

The company is a member of the PerCent Club, with the main area of non-cash support being gifts in kind.

In the previous edition of this guide we stated that the policy regarding charitable support was currently under review. This still appears to be the case and the following policy information may therefore change.

The company has a preference for local charities in areas of company presence (Lincolnshire) and charities in which a member of company staff is involved, the latter being given priority. The Charity Committee at Cobham decides guidelines for Cargill PLC's charitable giving. Currently, these are that 40% of donations should go to alleviating social hardship, 40% for medical causes, both patient care and research, and 20% for all other causes. Local units are encouraged to support their local communities, but to abide by the above guidelines.

'Other causes' can include children/youth, education, elderly people, enterprise/training, environment/heritage, fundraising events, science/technology, sickness/disability charities and sport.

In 1996, main beneficiaries include Whisby Natural World (£10,000), North Muskham County Primary School (£2,000), Lincoln University (£50,000). Registered charities receive donations in the form of Charities Aid Foundation (CAF) vouchers. Donations to non-registered charities need prior approval from the Charities Committee. Grants to national organisations range from £50 to £5,000. Grants to local organisations range from £50 to £3,000.

Employee involvement: Cargill encourages its employees to get involved personally with charities. The Cobham Committee will normally match funds raised for registered charities by employees on a one-for-one basis up to £500. (Prior approval is required.)

Exclusions

No grants for advertising in charity brochures, appeals from individuals, local appeals not in areas of company presence, overseas projects, the arts, animal welfare charities, intermediary bodies or grant-making trusts, religious organisations and political parties.

Applications

The company will be selecting the charities it wishes to support and unsolicited applications are unlikely to be successful. In addition to the contact listed above, there is a separate contact in Lincoln: Sarah Oliver, Charity Co-ordinator at Cargill PLC, Camp Road, Swinderby, Lincoln LN6 9TN (01522-550100; Fax: 01522-868244).

Carlton Communications plc

25 Knightsbridge, London SW1X 7RZ
0171-663 6363; Fax: 0171-663 6300
Website: www.carlton.co.uk

Correspondent: Beverley Matthews, Personal Assistant to the Chairman

Chief officers: *Chairman:* Michael Green;
Managing Director: June de Moller

Year end	Turnover	Pre-tax profit
30/9/97	£1,750,000,000	£316,000,000

Nature of company business
Carlton Communications is engaged in the processing, enhancement and display of visual images, principally for the television industries in Europe and the United States. Carlton Television started broadcasting on January 1 1993 in the London franchise region.

Main subsidiaries include: Central Independent Television PLC; Cinema Media Ltd; CTE Ltd; Selec TV Cable Ltd; Technicolor Distribution Services Ltd; Technicolor Video Services Ltd; The Moving Picture Company Ltd; Quantel Ltd; Solid State Logic Ltd; C.D.S.S. Ltd; Westcountry Television Ltd; Rank Film Distributers Ltd; Metrocolor London Ltd.

UK employees: n/a

Carlton

Charitable donations
1997: £1,100,000
1996: £1,600,000
1995: £1,400,000
1994: £1,345,000
1993: £915,000
Membership: *ABSA*

Community support policy

The company is no longer a member of the PerCent Club. The charitable donations of £1.1 million in 1997, included £500,000 donated to the Carlton Television Trust (see below). Regional donations by Central Television totalled about £430,000, with £50,000 given by Westcountry Television. Support is given for:

- *Education/training:* Special interest in media fields. There is a general preference for educational establishments rather than individuals' programmes.
- *The community:* Disadvantaged young people and homeless people.
- *The arts:* Both Carlton and Central support the National Film and Television Archive, the National Film and Television School, and Ravensbourne College. Both also aim to encourage creative talent. For example, Carlton is the principal sponsor of the Donmar Warehouse Theatre and funds courses in screen writing, television acting, directing and producing.
- *Health:* Medical research, victims of disease, illness and people with physical/mental disabilities.

There is a preference for appeals relevant to company business and charities in which a member of company staff is involved. Grants range from £100 to £5,000.

Support is also given through donation of stock or equipment, professional services and the use of in-house facilities either free of charge or at cost price.

Carlton Television Trust

The Carlton Television Trust was set up in 1993 with the purpose of benefiting the community within the Carlton television transmission zone. This includes Greater London, and part of the counties of Essex, Hertfordshire, Buckinghamshire, Bedfordshire, Oxfordshire, Berkshire, Surrey, East and West Sussex and Kent.

Over 100 grants are made each year to a variety of registered charities providing help to disadvantaged children in a broadly educational way. Grants vary from £200 to £30,000 (average £4,000) and are given towards capital or revenue costs. The trust's sole source of income is a grant from Carlton Broadcasting Ltd who have pledged to commit £500,000 a year. In 1997, 120 projects were supported with grants. The largest was for £30,000 and went to the Royal Academy of Dramatic Arts. This was the first of four instalments towards rebuilding premises, establishing a trust fund to secure their financial position and an endowment fund to provide scholarships for talented but poor students. Together with 20 other donations of between £10,000 and £20,000, it accounted for a total of £159,000, 31% of grant expenditure. Nearly all other grants were for under £5,001. £20,000 donations went to the Sports Aid Foundation in Camden (to provide training grants), and to Mencap in the City of London (towards the salary of a family adviser).

Summary of grants made in 1993 to 1997

Training and employment projects ... 110 .... £583,000 ..... 26%
Educational establishments and projects .... 137 .... £505,000 ..... 22%
Arts organisations and projects .... 101 .... £413,000 ..... 18%
Young people's activities .... 65 .... £258,000 ...... 11%
Play and minded care projects .... 112 .... £245,000 ...... 11%
Support for families .... 38 .... £232,000 ..... 10%
Miscellaneous .... 15 .... £43,000 .... 2%
Total .... 578 .... £2,285,000

The trust describes its policy: 'We will consider applications from properly constituted non-profit making voluntary organisations and organisations registered as charities in the UK. Grants are only paid to registered charities so non-registered groups must find a charity willing to endorse their application and receive any grant on their behalf. Lower priority is given to appeals from statutory services and local authorities. Although the trustees may consider support for individuals through charities which can speak for their families' social and economic circumstances, no such grants have yet been made.

'Capital or project grants are considered. Grants for two or three years may be made in exceptional circumstances only for salaries and running costs for registered charities. This type of grant should be to establish new ways of meeting need or to enable an organisation to move to a new level of effectiveness. No two or three year grants have yet been made (although posts in some charities have been supported for more than one year following repeat applications). All projects must be of educational benefit to children and young people who have special needs or are disadvantaged in other ways. We will only consider the provision of transport and transport costs for young people with physical and/or learning disabilities. There are no set minimum or maximum levels for grants which have ranged in size from £200 to £30,000 in any year.

'Grants have been awarded for such purposes as tutors' fees, salaries and costs for education/training posts, toys and books and play equipment, drugs education packs, IT courses, drama and dance workshops, and courses on parenting skills.'

The following is a typical section of the trust's excellent grants list (1997), which describes the beneficiary and the specific purpose for the grant:

'*Mirage Children's Theatre Company, Kensington and Chelsea.* Multicultural children's theatre company which aims to take high quality entertainment, especially theatre and puppetry, to children who would not normally get the opportunity to experience it. £4,950 towards production of dual language tapes of traditional stories used in most nursery and infant schools. Many refugee children can't understand the original material so restricting their ability to participate. The tapes will benefit six groups: Somalis, Kurds, Tamils, Bosnians, Vietnamese and Farsi speakers.

'*National Pyramid Trust, Ealing.* Uses screening, inter agency co-operation and therapeutic activity groups

(Pyramid Clubs) to promote resilience and self-esteem in vulnerable children.

'*New Assembly of Churches, Wandsworth*. Group of black-led churches working with young offenders and those in danger of offending. Includes a pre-release course and post-release support for inmates at Feltham YOI. £5,000 towards the development of the pre-release course at Feltham to include more training in basic skills and greater coverage of life and work skills. The grant will be used towards the salary of the principal tutor.

'*Mencap, City of London*. Provides services for people with learning disabilities including housing, employment and leisure opportunities. £20,000 towards the salary of a Family Advisor for Southwark, who will offer information, advice and direct support for young people with learning disabilities, aged 14 to 18. The primary concern will be education helping with the transitory period when a child leaves school.

'*London Connection, Westminster*. Day centre for young homeless people offering a wide range of services. £10,000 towards salary of the Playspace Project Worker, the parenting skills project providing education and support to around 300 young homeless families. Introduces them to constructive play, positive discipline techniques and child development issues.'

In the five-year review, the Chairman wrote:

'The goals are to help those within the community who are disadvantaged through social and economic deprivation, homelessness, unemployment, disability or because they have special needs, including, for example, refugees or ex-offenders.

'In order to encourage the widest possible range of organisations to apply, we have sought to spread awareness of the trust through the national, local and voluntary sector press, local authorities and entries in funding directories, as well as through Carlton's regional programmes. Each year at least half the proposals came from first-time applicants.

'We review our criteria and policies each year to ensure that we take into account changes within the sector we support, and regularly exchange views with other funders. In some cases our grants provide pump-priming for new projects which have surpassed all expectations; in others they help maintain existing services which are examples of good practice. We usually arrange an opportunity every 12 months or so to meet with representatives of some of the organisations we have assisted.'

Exclusions

No response to circular appeals. No grants to appeals from individuals, local appeals not in areas of company presence, overseas projects, appeals for building or general administrative costs or political appeals.

Carlton Television Trust will not support:
- trips abroad
- projects outside the Carlton Television transmission area – please contact the trust if you are uncertain of the area covered
- unspecified expenditure
- general appeals
- deficit funding and repayment of loans
- distribution to other organisations
- retrospective funding of projects which will take place before applications can be processed
- the relief of statutory responsibilities
- conferences and seminars
- ongoing salaries and running costs (see note on grants for two or three years under 'Applications').

Applications

In writing to the correspondent.

For Carlton Television Trust:
Funds are disbursed once a year only. Application forms are available between April and early June **only** and an A4 sae (postage for 75 grammes) should be sent to: Carlton Television Trust, PO Box 1, London W12 8UB.

The closing date for receipt is shown on the form. Organisations may submit only one application per calendar year for projects due to take place from November onwards. Decisions will be made by 30 November.

Applications must come from properly constituted non-profit making organisations in the Carlton transmission area. Grants will be made payable only to organisations registered as charities. Each application must be endorsed by a management committee member, and an independent referee, or the registered charity supporting the request and acting as a conduit for the funds. Very low priority will be given to applications from statutory services and local authorities.

Grants may be considered for individual children and young people if the applications come from organisations which apply on their behalf and which can speak about the family's financial circumstances. (Applications are not accepted from private individuals or parents, nor from teachers or other welfare professionals on behalf of their clients.)

Applications for educational equipment or mobility/communication aids must:
- enclose a professional assessment from a relevant consultant or therapist
- confirm that the organisation will take responsibility for matters relating to safety regulations, insurance and maintenance
- explain any loan system and its criteria (if administered).

Grants for two to three years are exceptional. An organisation applying for salary costs for up to three years must be a registered charity in its own right. Such grants should establish new ways of meeting need or to enable new levels of effectiveness to be met.

The guidance leaflet provides more useful guidance about transport requests.

The trustees meet in September to shortlist applications and in November to decide the allocation for grants.

Celtic

CEF Holdings Ltd

1 Station Road, Kenilworth, Warwickshire CV8 1JJ
01926-858127; Fax: 01926-850448

Correspondent: Mrs Una Wynne, Secretary

Chief officer: *Chairman:* R H Thorn

Year end	Turnover	Pre-tax profit
30/4/97	£454,870,000	£20,983,000

Nature of company business
Principal activity: electrical wholesalers and manufacturers.
Main subsidiaries include: City Electrical Factors Ltd; Dennis Vanguard International Ltd.

UK employees: n/a

Charitable donations
1997: £259,000
1996: £174,000
1995: £269,057
1994: £107,550
1993: £162,000

Community support policy

The company covenants its donations to the Janet Nash Charitable Trust and has recently covenanted to a London hospital. The trust usually prefers to support children's and sickness/disability charities, especially those local to the company's main sites. The company has given gifts in kind and rewired charities' properties on special occasions. The Janet Nash Charitable Trust (Charity Commission number 326880) had an income of £250,000 in 1996/97, from 'donations and gifts' received. Presumably most, if not all, of this was from the company.

Grants made by the trust totalled £209,000. Most of the grants and £161,000 of the grant total was given for the medical treatment of individuals. Other grants, totalling £41,500 in 1996/97 were given mostly to medical-related organisations, particularly in the West Midlands and Warwickshire areas. Five grants were given during the year, to Warwick Castle Park Trust (£20,000), Acorns Children's Hospice (£10,000), Macmillan Cancer Relief (£5,000), Dyslexia Institute (£4,000) and Warwickshire Care Services Newlands House (£2,500).

Applications
In writing to the correspondent.

Celtic Group Holdings Ltd

Heol Ty Aberaman, Aberdare, Mid Glamorgan CF44 6LX
01685-874201; Fax: 01685-878104

Correspondent: Julie El-Kayekh, Technical Services Secretary

Chief officer: *Chairman:* D W Kendall

Year end	Turnover	Pre-tax profit
30/3/96	£140,663,000	£8,675,000

Nature of company business
The main activities are opencast coal mining and associated activities.

Main subsidiaries include: Celtic Energy Ltd; Celtic Mining Ltd.

UK employees: 291

Charitable donations
1996: £96,000

Community support policy

This company took over British Coal's South Wales operations. It has an extensive community programme focused mainly on the local communities around the company's sites. Support is given in three ways.

1. Initial support on setting up a new site. Each time the company establishes a new site, it makes a substantial donation to local community trusts or to the local borough council for distribution to the community. These funds can exceed £100,000.

2. Support for local liaison funds at each of the company's four sites in South Wales. Each site donates £400 to £500 a month to these local funds. These are then distributed to local voluntary organisations by local staff.

3. Support from a central community budget. These donations are used to support organisations that fall outside the remit of the local liaison funds. This budget allows the company to respond to more general appeals, although still with a South Wales bias. About £40,000 is available each year, although discretionary payments are also made which may be in excess of this. Grants typically range from £50 to £500, and exceptionally can be as high as £5,000.

For all three categories, the company tends to support local schools, youth groups and disability organisations. National charities are only ever supported where they are working specifically in the area of the company's sites.

The company also has an educational programme, distributing information packs to schools on opencast mining, and encourages pupils to visit its operations.

Applications
In writing to the correspondent.

Celtic PLC

Celtic Park, 95 Kerrydale Street, Glasgow G40 3RE
0141-551 4276; Fax: 0141-554 5389
Website: www.celticfc.co.uk

Correspondent: Peter McLean, Public Relations Manager

Chief officer: *Chairman:* Fergus J McCann

Year end	Turnover	Pre-tax profit
30/6/98	£27,821,000	£7,156,000

Nature of company business
The principal activity of the company continues to be the operation of Celtic Football Club.

Main subsidiaries include: Protectevent Ltd; Glasgow Western Developments Ltd; The Celtic Football and Athletic Company Ltd.

UK employees: n/a

Charitable donations
1998: £280,000
1997: £100,000
1996: £47,000
1995: £20,000

Community support policy

The founding aim of the football club in 1888 was to raise money to provide food for the poor of the East End of Glasgow and to encourage positive social integration between the Scottish and Irish people living in Glasgow.

The club's policy today reflects this and it prefers to support charities in the three principal areas of

(a) children

(b) drug-related and

(c) promoting religious and ethnic harmony.

It also supports three subsidiary areas: (i) homelessness, (ii) unemployed people and (iii) alleviation of suffering caused by illness and famine and to aid innocent families within areas of war.

In addition to the £280,000 given to charity by Celtic Football Club, a further £120,000 was raised from Celtic supporters, staff and directors, the players, corporate clients, the general public and club funds for distribution through the Celtic Charitable Fund. In addition to the cash donations, hundreds of signed footballs and complimentary tickets are also given away for charitable purposes.

In 1997/98, beneficiaries included: St Vincent De Paul (founded in 1833) who carry out work assisting the homeless, the elderly, and the physically disabled; Social Responsibility, the caring arm of the Church of Scotland, and offer social care across Scotland; Northern Ireland Children's Events – Big Day Out is the largest children's day out in Great Britain with 1,200 children being brought together with the aim of helping to alleviate poverty in the most deprived areas of Northern and Southern Ireland, bringing children of divided communities together to learn trust, respect, and to appreciate each others cultures. Other organisations who have benefited include: the Parkhead Youth Project for their efforts to advance education, relieve poverty, improve health, provide facilities, and ease the unemployment situation in the East End of Glasgow; and the Scottish Asian Sports Association whose integrated football team aims to promote the sport in ethnic minority communities and encourage social integration.

Applications

If you wish to apply to the Celtic Charitable Fund for donations an application form should be requested in writing. Decisions regarding donations are made in July of each year.

Centrica plc

Charter Court, 50 Windsor Road, Slough SL1 2HA
01753-758000; Fax: 01753-758011
Email: Community@centrica.co.uk
Website: www.centrica.co.uk

Correspondent: Jo Bayliss, Community Relations Co-ordinator

Chief officer: *Chief Executive:* Roy Gardner

Year end	Turnover	Pre-tax profit
31/12/97	£7,383,000,000	(£623,000,000)

Nature of company business
Centrica is a supplier of energy and services to homes and businesses in Great Britain. This includes sale of gas and electricity, gas production from the Morecambe fields, central heating installation and maintenance, and 240 high street shops selling gas and electrical products. The group trades as British Gas in England and Wales and Scottish Gas in Scotland. It is developing a range of products using the Goldfish brand.

Main subsidiaries include: Accord Energy Ltd; British Gas Energy Centres Ltd; British Gas Services Ltd; British Gas Trading Ltd; Hydrocarbon Resources Ltd.

UK employees: 15,423

Charitable donations
1997: £1,750,000
Membership: *BitC %Club*

Community support policy

The company is a member of the PerCent Club. In 1997, it contributed £1.75 million to a range of projects throughout England, Scotland and Wales.

Projects focused on the following areas:

- practical assistance to older and disabled people
- promoting the efficient use of energy
- job creation.

Over £500,000 of the total was given to local community projects, including:

SchoolEnergy 'Cashback' – a rebate programme for schools who develop specialised energy efficiency measures, in partnership with the Energy Saving Trust.

Powersavers – an energy efficiency competition and teaching programme for primary and secondary schools in partnership with the Department of the Environment, Transport and the Regions and the Energy Savings Trust.

Disability in Business – working with charities to raise awareness of disability issues and to acknowledge businesses who provide facilities for disabled people, their families and carers. Awards programmes in 1998 included The Ease of Access, Service and Employment, and Open to All awards.

Welfare to Work – providing work training and job opportunities for disabled people and carers in the British Gas offices in the north west of England.

Carers National Association – helping to fund the national helpline for carers. British Gas is also the major sponsor for National Carers Week.

National Energy Action – a range of national and local projects to deliver tangible benefits to communities through initiatives that focus on low income households.

Scottish Gas Youth Challenge – run jointly with the East End Partnership in Glasgow, to provide personal development programmes for young people.

Exclusions
Due to key areas of project focus it is not usually possible to consider requests relating to individuals, animal welfare organisations, building projects or research. This also applies to requests for support from political or denominational groups, the arts or sports organisations. Advertising or sponsorship are only considered if they form part of a specific project with which the company is already involved.

Applications
In writing to the correspondent.

CGU plc

St Helen's, 1 Undershaft, London EC3P 3DQ
0171-283 7500
Website: www.commercial-union.co.uk/cu

Correspondent: Miss J Miller, The Appeals Officer

Chief officer: *Chairman:* Pehr Gyllanhammar

Year end	Turnover	Pre-tax profit
31/12/97	n/a	£568,000,000

Nature of company business
Principal activities: insurance and life assurance other than industrial life, and other financial services. The group also invests in stocks, shares, properties, loans and mortgages and carries on the business of trading in property.

UK employees: n/a

Charitable donations
1997: £303,997
1996: £300,803
1995: £265,267
1994: £221,558
1993: £213,582
Membership: *ABSA BitC*

Community support policy
Following the merger of Commercial Union and General Accident the company is now called CGU plc. The figures given above are for Commercial Union only. The comparable figures for General Accident for charitable donations are: 1994, £395,800; 1995, £400,000; 1996, £448,000.

The company's charitable funds are allocated mainly in the form of long-term support to a carefully selected group of charities in categories ranging from medical research and care to arts and conservation and from welfare of the elderly to education and support for the young. Local charities are dealt with by local branches; many appeals are then referred to head office. The company gives financial support to employees volunteering.

Enterprise: The company is a member of both Scottish and English Business in the Community and gives support to enterprise/training projects.

Sponsorship: The company has sponsored a number of larger initiatives in the UK including the Natural Breaks Programme run by the British Trust for Conservation Volunteers, Crime Prevention & Community Awards and the World Wheelchair Games. The company is also a patron of ABSA. It has sponsored a range of national arts organisations including the English Chamber Orchestra, London Philharmonic Orchestra, Monteverdi Trust and Royal Opera House, as well as the National Festival of Music for Youth and the School Prom concerts in Cardiff and London.

Exclusions
No support for circular appeals, advertising in charity brochures, animal welfare charities, appeals from individuals, fundraising events, overseas projects, political or religious appeals.

Applications
Due to the company's committed support to a selected group of charities, very few donations are allocated to charities that apply in writing.

Charnos plc

Corporation Road, Ilkeston, Derbyshire DE7 4BP
0115-932 2191; Fax: 0115-932 0722

Correspondent: Amanda Godber, Personal Assistant to the Chairman

Chief officer: *Chairman:* R Noskwith

Year end	Turnover	Pre-tax profit
31/12/96	£91,749,000	£4,087,000

Nature of company business
The group manufactures stockings and tights, texturised yarn, lingerie and knitwear.

Main subsidiaries include: Adria Ltd; Cityprime Ltd.

UK employees: n/a

Charitable donations
1996: £83,735
1995: £64,657
1994: £54,809
1993: £85,190
Membership: *%Club*

Community support policy
The company is a member of the PerCent Club. It prefers to support local charities in the areas of company presence (Derby/Nottingham area) and appeals relevant to company business. Donations are made through the company's charitable trust.

Preferred areas are children and youth, medical, environment and heritage, and the arts. Typical grants to national organisations range from £50 to £2,000, and to local organisations from £10 to £100. 1996 was the company's diamond jubilee year and most of the money was allocated to the building of a Family Support Centre at Ilkeston.

Exclusions

Generally no support for circular appeals, advertising in charity brochures, year books, etc., purely denominational (religious) appeals, large national appeals or overseas projects.

Applications

In writing to the correspondent.

Charter plc

7 Hobart Place, London SW1W 0HH
0171-838 7000; Fax: 0171-259 5112
Email: Lynda_Treacy@charterplc.com
Website: www.charterplc.com

Correspondent: Lynda Treacy, Public Affairs Officer

Chief officers: *Chairman:* J W Herbert;
Chief Executive: N W R Smith

Year end	Turnover	Pre-tax profit
31/12/97	£1,114,000,000	£64,000,000

Nature of company business
The company is an international engineering company. The group's activities are concerned with welding and cutting, air and gas handling, and specialised engineering. Products are manufactured internationally to meet customer requirements across a wide range of industries around the world. Subsidiaries include: Esab, Howden and Pandrol.
Main subsidiaries include: Howden Sirocco Ltd; Howden Compressors Ltd; Pandrol International Ltd; Airscrew Howden Ltd; Howden Aircontrol Ltd.

UK employees: n/a

Charitable donations

1997: £230,000
1996: £314,000
1995: £337,000
1994: £326,000
1993: £389,000
Membership: *BitC %Club*

Community support policy

The company is a member of the PerCent Club, although it has seen a fall in its level of donations by about 25% in the last year. This is presumably related to a fall in profits the previous year (from 1995 to 1996). However, profits increased again in 1997, so there may well be a corresponding increase in donations in 1998. The company is also a member of Business in the Community.

Charitable donations: The charity programme has been devised to ensure each donation, whether large or small, has maximum impact. Care has been taken to select only one charity in each of the areas the company considers important and to make fairly long-term commitments to each.

Among the wide range of charities supported are: six schools, the engineering faculty at Bristol University, Thrombosis Research Institute, Bath Festivals Trust and Royal Opera House. The weighting of donations is heavily in favour of educational causes which together receive half the total.

Many group employees raise funds or work directly with charities and a portion of the charities budget is allocated to back up this work with financial support.

Donations may also be given to special projects in areas of company presence or those related to the company businesses. Donations are only given to registered charities.

The arts: Charter undertakes arts sponsorship. It has sponsored the Royal Opera House and Bath Festival.

Exclusions

No support for circular appeals, advertising in charity brochures, appeals from individuals or local appeals not in areas of company presence.

Applications

In writing to the correspondent. Many more applications are received than can be supported, and applicants are advised to consider if there is any particular reason why their appeal should be supported by the company. All applications will be answered.

Charterhouse plc

1 Paternoster Row, St Paul's, London EC4M 7DH
0171-248 4000
Website: www.charterhouse.co.uk

Correspondent: Secretary, Charterhouse Charitable Trust

Chief officers: *Chairman:* M V Blank;
Chief Executive: M L Hepher

Year end	Turnover	Pre-tax profit
31/12/96	n/a	£40,400,000

Nature of company business
The company, a subsidiary of European Corporate Finance Holding SA which is jointly owned by Berliner Handels und Frankfurter Bank KG and Credit Comercialde Francais SA, is a holding company co-ordinating the activities of its subsidiary companies which are engaged in providing a range of banking and other financial services.

UK employees: n/a

Charitable donations

1996: £84,250
1995: £87,550
1994: £68,117
1993: £60,000
Membership: *BitC*

Chelsfield

Community support policy

Most of the company's donations are made through the Charterhouse Charitable Trust (Charity Commission number 210894), which supports registered charities only, particularly national charities or those operating in areas where the company has a presence (Liverpool and London). A payroll giving scheme is in operation.

In 1996/97, the trust had assets of £1.1 million and an income of £133,000 including £50,000 covenant from Charterhouse plc, £5,000 covenant from Charterhouse Bank Ltd, and £78,000 from investment income.

The trustees report stated that, 'All donations normally:
- make a meaningful contribution to a deserving charity
- support a charity which is either nationwide or based in an area where the Charterhouse Group has a presence.

'The trust's income is distributed between:
1. Inner city welfare including homelessness and drug or alcohol dependency
2. Major educational charities
3. Fixed annual donations
4. Miscellaneous donations in response to appeals.

'During the year the trustees had under consideration several proposals for major endowments in the educational sector and since the year end have agreed, in principle, to make donations over a period of time of: £111,000 to The Environmental Change Unit, University of Oxford, in connection with a solar energy project, and £90,000 to the Judge Institute, University of Cambridge, to fund three Charterhouse Research Studentships.'

The larger grants given in 1996/97 were to London Connection (£30,000), Macmillan Cancer Relief and St Mary's 150th Anniversary Appeal Charity (both £10,000), Wellbeing (£7,500) and the City of London Endowment for St Paul's Cathedral (£4,000). There were a further 21 grants of 31,000 with recipients including Cot Death Society, Crimestoppers Trust, Fairbridge, Fight for Sight, Liverpool Royal Court Theatre Foundation and RSPB. There were 17 smaller grants of £250 or £500.

Enterprise: The company is an active member of Business in the Community.

The arts: The company has been the principal sponsor of the Orchestra of the Age of Enlightenment for the last seven years.

Exclusions

No support for: advertising in charity brochures; appeals from individuals; fundraising events; political appeals; religious appeals; science/technology; sickness/disability charities; sport; national charities.

Applications

All appeals should be in writing, and not by telephone, to the correspondent. The charitable trust meets formally four times a year, but suitable appeals are considered by the trustees on a monthly basis.

Chelsfield plc

67 Brook Street, London W1Y 2NJ
0171-493 3977; Fax: 0171-629 0971

Correspondent: I Osborne, Company Secretary

Chief officers: *Chairman:* E Bernerd; *Managing Director:* W N Hugill

Year end	Turnover	Pre-tax profit
31/12/97	£86,711,000	£24,634,000

Nature of company business
The main activities are the investment in and development of property assets, and the ownership and management of asset backed leisure operations including an indoor tennis club and the Wentworth golf and country club. Major property locations, in addition to central London, include Ascot, Edgbaston, Bristol, Dudley and Stanmore.

Main subsidiaries include: Evans Row Property Co Ltd; London Fields Ltd; Kingsyard Management Ltd; The Vanderbilt Racquet Club Ltd; Wentworth Group Holdings Ltd; Westbury Hotel Ltd.

UK employees: n/a

Charitable donations
1997: £157,300
1996: £90,200
1995: £51,830
1994: £15,930

Community support policy

The company's level of charitable giving has steadily increased over the last four years. The only information we have been able to obtain on its policy is that it prefers to support local charities in areas of company presence or those which have a member of company staff involved.

Applications

In writing to the correspondent.

Chevron UK Ltd

Woodhill House, Westburn Road, Aberdeen AB16 5XL

Correspondent: Ruth Mitchell, Public Affairs Co-ordinator

Chief officer: *Managing Director:* R K Connon

Year end	Turnover	Pre-tax profit
31/12/96	£1,311,187,000	£269,524,000

Nature of company business
Principal activity: oil and gas exploration and production on the UK Continental Shelf. The company is part of the Chevron Corporation based in San Francisco.

Main subsidiaries include: Gulf Oil Ltd; Pelmans Petroleum Ltd; Gulf Oil Refining Ltd; Telegraph Service Stations Ltd; Curran Petroleum Ltd; De La Pena Lubricants Ltd; Gulf Service Stations Ltd.

UK employees: 860

Charitable donations
1996: £90,103
1995: £116,705
1994: £112,000
1993: £95,700
Membership: *ABSA*

Community support policy

Charities should note that the majority of causes supported by the company are predetermined and therefore few additional requests for assistance are likely to be successful. Donations and sponsorship are spread across the arts, education, environment and social welfare, in north-east Scotland. There is a preference for local charities in areas of company presence, appeals relevant to company business and charities in which a member of company staff is involved. Grants to local organisations and to local sections of national organisations range from £50 to £1,000.

Beneficiaries have included the Prince's Youth Business Trust, Scottish Wildlife Trust, Thames Salmon Trust, Art in Nature and support for various universities.

The arts: The company is a member of ABSA. It has supported the New London Orchestra, Royal Scottish National Orchestra, Scottish Ballet, Polka Children's Theatre and the Contemporary Dance Trust.

Exclusions

No support for circular appeals, individuals, local appeals not in areas of company presence, large national appeals or overseas projects.

Applications

In writing to the correspondent.

Christie's International plc

8 King Street, St James', London SW1Y 6QT
0171-839 9060; Fax: 0171-839 1611

Correspondent: Mrs Robin Hambro, Charities Department

Chief officers: *Chairman:* Lord Hindlip;
Chief Executive: C M Davidge

Year end	Turnover	Pre-tax profit
31/12/97	£261,212,000	£35,306,000

Nature of company business
Christie's International is the holding company of a group engaged primarily in the business of fine art, wine and philatelic auctioneering, and runs a fine arts course in London. The group also owns printing works in Perth. Auctioneering is conducted principally from major and secondary salesrooms in London and New York and from salesrooms in Glasgow, Amsterdam, Melbourne and Rome.

Main subsidiaries include: Spinks & Son Ltd; White Bross Ltd; Studio SMK Ltd; CI Property & Investments Ltd.

UK employees: n/a

Charitable donations
1997: £395,000
1996: £375,000
1995: £295,000
1994: £283,000
1993: £281,000
Membership: *%Club*

Community support policy

'Christie's sponsorship and donations policy is based on the ethos that the arts are of prime importance to the cultural life of the community. Therefore, the major portion of the charitable donations goes to underwriting a broad scope of arts-related causes and projects on all economic levels. These range from the conservation of paintings and the fabric of small country churches to the sponsorship of major exhibitions in national museums, arts centres or on the Christie's premises at King Street.

'One of the important areas of sponsorship is the underwriting of art exhibition catalogues. Christie's believes the recording of research on known and lesser-known art works is important for future generations of art historians, students and the interested general public. In addition to underwriting the work of a great many health, community, youth and educational projects, Christie's also uses its autioneering expertise to raise money for both health and arts-related charities. This consistent level of charitable support has made Christie's UK a member of the PerCent Club.'

Exhibitions sponsored in the UK:
New English Arts Club Annual Exhibition 1989 to 1995
John Channon & Brass Inlaid Furniture Exhibition at the Victoria & Albert Museum 1994.

Exhibitions mounted by Christie's:
Copplestone Warre Bampfylde 1995
James Smeatham Exhibition 1995
Foundations for the Future 1995 – an exhibition looking at the past and future of Cambridge University.

Catalogue sponsorship includes catalogues for:
The Victoria & Albert Museum
The Fitzwilliam Museum, Cambridge
Series of catalogues of art in British Embassies abroad.

Charitable exhibitions include those held in aid of:
British Field Sport Society Art in Academia
African Medical & Research Foundation
Wardour Chapel Appeal
William Heath Robinson Trust.

Bursaries, funds, education:
The National Gallery Furniture Fund
British Library Manuscript Conservation Fund
Royal Holloway & Bedford New College Bursary
Centre for the Study of Victorian Art and Architecture.

European sponsorship:
International Castles Institute
Europa Nostra
World Monument Fund.

Ciba

Awards:
The Garden of the Year Award in conjunction with the Historic Houses Association 1985-1995
The Europa Nostra Restoration Award
Christie's South Kensington and Christie's America also run many of their own charitable events.

Charitable donations: The company prefers to support charities working in the fields of heritage, arts, conservation, health and child care, education and the environment. It also has a preference for specifically London charities (rather than those which happen to be based in London), for appeals relevant to company business and for charities in which a member of staff is involved. Regional offices of the company do have a limited budget which they can use as they wish, and local representatives have an input into the decision-making process at head office. Grants to national organisations range from £200 to £5,000. Grants to local organisations range from £100 to £500.

Employee involvement/in kind support: Staff are encouraged to become volunteers in their own time. Staff time and expertise are made available to prepare catalogues or to officiate at charity auctions, and the company's galleries are loaned to organisations. The company also gives catalogues and expert advice on arts-related subjects. It operates a payroll giving scheme.

Education: The company provides educational materials for schools and work experience schemes for pupils. The Christie's Education Trust sponsors scholarships, research, exhibitions and conservation projects and provides support in cases of financial hardship to students who apply for Christie's courses.

Environment: The company supports rural conservation and environment programmes. It is involved in the Westminster Council conservation activities.

Exclusions
No grants are given to circular appeals, appeals from individuals or purely denominational (religious) appeals.

Applications
In writing to the correspondent. Those with particular reference to the company's charitable programme are submitted to a committee which makes grant decisions. The correspondent states that too often applications are badly written by hand, are addressed to the wrong person or mis-spell the chairman's name or other names that are clearly written in Christie's catalogues.

Information available: Christie's reports on its involvement in *Christie's International Magazine* and staff newsletters.

Ciba Specialty Chemicals PLC

Charter Way, Macclesfield, Cheshire SK10 2NX
01625-421933; Fax: 01625-619002

Correspondent: Mrs S A Seed, Head of Communications

Chief officer: *Regional President:* B G Kerr

Year end	Turnover	Pre-tax profit
31/12/97	n/a	n/a

Nature of company business
Ciba Specialty Chemicals was formed at the beginning of 1997 following the merger of Ciba and Sandoz – and the subsequent spin-off of their specialty chemical operations into a separate entity.

Main locations: Macclesfield; Clayton (Manchester); Duxford (Cambridgeshire); Paisley (Scotland); Bradford; Grimsby.

UK employees: 4,000

Community support policy
The former Ciba-Geigy plc gave almost £70,000 in 1995, unfortunately we have no financial information on the new company.

The company gives some support for medical and educational charities where staff take part in fundraising but most support is concentrated where the company has a presence (see above). Other areas of support are: youth, education, science and technology and social welfare.

The arts: Support for local events where the company has a presence but this has lower priority as preference is given to events and organisations with a science-education focus.

Exclusions
No support for appeals from areas that are not located near to a Ciba Specialty Chemicals site, nor applications from individuals.

Applications
In writing to the Communications Department.

Citroen UK Ltd

221 Bath Road, Slough SL1 4BA
0870-606 9000; Fax: 01753-812120

Correspondent: Marc Raven, Public Affairs Director

Chief officers: *Chairman:* C Satinet;
Managing Director: C Gobenceaux

Year end	Turnover	Pre-tax profit
31/12/95	£771,084,000	£4,000

Nature of company business
The main activity of the company is vehicle importers and distributors.

UK employees: n/a

Charitable donations
1995: £41,163
1994: £41,317
1993: £28,236

Community support policy
Although the company responded to our survey, no updated financial information was provided. The only information we have on the policy of the company is that both UK and local (presumably the Slough area) causes are supported.

Applications
In writing to the correspondent.

Claremont Garment Holdings plc

1 Stephenson Road, Peterlee, County Durham SR8 5AX
0191-586 2281; Fax: 0191-586 2686

Correspondent: Personnel Department

Chief officers: *Chairman:* P M Wiegand;
Chief Executive: J M Gilliatt

Year end	Turnover	Pre-tax profit
27/12/97	£185,944,000	(£12,011,000)

Nature of company business
The design and manufacture of clothing almost exclusively to Marks & Spencer.

Main subsidiaries include: Bellrise Fashions Ltd; Columbus Swimwear Ltd.

UK employees: 6,342

Charitable donations
1997: £126,000
1996: £134,000
1995: £153,000
1994: £154,000
1993: £95,000
Membership: %Club

Community support policy
In 1995, support was given to Marie Curie, Barnardo's and Childline. Unsolicited appeals are dealt with on an ad hoc basis.

No further information was available except that the company has continued its support for its 'Claremont School of Tailoring' initiative based in Kentish Town. The scheme trains young, unemployed school-leavers to be sewing machinists, with the company's commitment including running costs as well as two full-time instructors.

Applications
In writing to the correspondent.

Clerical Medical Investment Group Ltd

Narrow Plain, Bristol BS2 0JH
0117-929 0290; Fax: 01275-552667

Correspondent: Carol Morris, Charities Administrator

Chief officers: *Chairman:* John Wood;
Chief Executive: Robert Walther

Year end	Turnover	Pre-tax profit
31/12/97	n/a	n/a

Nature of company business
Financial services.

UK employees: 2,000

Charitable donations
1996: £50,000
1995: n/a
1994: n/a
1993: £47,738
Total community contributions: £90,000

Community support policy
Clerical Medical is part of the Halifax Group and separate financial information was not available. However, the company continues to administer requests in the South West.

Grants are mainly given to local organisations and usually range from £50 to £5,000. The main areas of assistance are debt counselling, homelessness, medical, disabled, education, job creation, elderly, environmental, arts and sports. Preference is also given to organisations in which members of staff are involved.

Exclusions
No response to circular appeals. No support for advertising in charity brochures, appeals from individuals, religious appeals or large national appeals.

Applications
In writing to the correspondent.

Clinton Cards Plc

The Crystal Building, Langston Road, Loughton, Essex IG10 3TH
0181-502 3711; Fax: 0181-502 0295

Correspondent: Mrs Gumbrell, Secretary to the Chairman

Chief officers: *Chairman:* D J Lewin;
Managing Director: C S Lewin

Year end	Turnover	Pre-tax profit
1/2/98	£152,790,000	£7,676,000

Nature of company business
Main activity: specialist retailing of greeting cards and associated products. The group has nearly 500 branches nationwide.

UK employees: 3,720

Clydesdale

Charitable donations
1997: £149,350
1996: £45,959
1995: £22,234
1994: £21,586

Community support policy
We have no information on the charitable donations policy of the company.

Applications
In writing to the correspondent.

Clydesdale Bank PLC

30 St Vincent Place, Glasgow G1 2HL
0141-248 7070; Fax: 0141-204 0828

Correspondent: Mrs Brenda Blackwood, Public Relations Coordinator

Chief officers: *Chairman:* Lord Nickson;
Chief Executive: John Wright

Year end	Turnover	Pre-tax profit
30/9/97	£522,939,000	£146,299,000

Nature of company business
The company is a wholly owned subsidiary of National Australia Bank Ltd. It offers a full range of banking services through 280 branches in Scotland, Cumbria and London.

UK employees: 5,409

Charitable donations
1997: £80,000
1996: £76,000
1995: £82,000
1994: £98,000
1993: £71,000
Membership: *ABSA*

Community support policy
The bank prefers to support Scottish organisations concerned with medicine, sickness and disability, the arts, elderly, enterprise and training, heritage, social welfare, education and youth, environment and local natural disasters (ie. in Scotland). National grants range from £100 to £10,000. Local grants range from £50 to £500.

Major grant recipients in previous years have included Princess Royal Trust for Carers, National Trust of Scotland, Scottish Association of Citizen's Advice Bureaux, Disability Scotland, Imperial Cancer Research Fund Scotland and National Museum Scotland.

Employee involvement: Staff are encouraged to become volunteers in their own time. A payroll giving scheme is operated by the company.

Enterprise: The company is a member of Business in the Community. It gives non-financial support to enterprise agencies and advisory support to local economic development initiatives.

Sponsorship: The bank sponsors the arts, sport, and environment and business-related organisations/events. The typical sponsorship range is from £100 to £25,000. National arts bodies sponsored include Scottish Ballet, Scottish Opera, National Galleries of Scotland and the Royal Scottish Academy.

Exclusions
No response to circular appeals. No grants for fundraising events, purely denominational (religious appeals), local appeals not in areas of company presence, large national appeals, overseas projects, political activities or individuals. Non-commercial advertising is not supported. It does not sponsor individuals or travel.

Applications
In writing to the correspondent. Applications are considered by a charitable donations committee.

Co-operative Bank plc

1 Balloon Street, Manchester M60 4EP
0161-832 3456; Fax: 0161-839 4220
Website: www.co-operativebank.co.uk

Correspondent: Chris Smith, Group Public Affairs Manager

Chief officers: *Chairman:* Alan Prescott;
Chief Executive: Mervyn Pedelty

Year end	Turnover	Pre-tax profit
10/1/98	n/a	£55,024,000

Nature of company business
Principal activity of the group: the provision of banking and financial services in the UK. The Co-operative Bank is the only UK clearing bank to publish an ethical stance whereby it clearly tells its customers where it will, and will not, invest its customers money.

Main subsidiaries include: Roodhill Leasing; First Pioneers Leasing; Larchvale.

UK employees: 3,930

Charitable donations
1997: £1,054,080
1996: £638,312
1995: £597,000
1994: £594,000
1993: £190,009

Total community contributions: £1,956,089

Membership: *BitC %Club*

Community support policy
The bank's partnership approach demonstrates a commitment to working with, and acknowledging its responsibilities towards, all partner groups on which its business has any direct or indirect impact.

In the latest PerCent Club Annual report it states: 'The Bank's Partnership Report, published in 1998, identifies seven stakeholders within the business: shareholders, customers, staff and their families, suppliers, local communities, national and international society, and past and future generations of co-operators. The Partnership Report, which is independently audited, communicates the values, processes and outputs of the Bank's community involvement to all stakeholders together with a commitment to developing best practice, and a critical evaluation of its activities'.

Community contributions were valued at over £1.9 million in 1997, over 3.5% of pre-tax profits. This included donations, sponsorship, its 'Customers Who Care' scheme (in which the bank donates a proportion of its VISA income to charities – VISA customers vote on how the money raised should be shared among nominated organisations) and Affinity Partnerships. An audit in 1996 of other in kind contributions showed an additional value of £224,000 and it is believed similar figures applied for 1997.

The bank supports community groups, particularly those involved in ethical, ecological and co-operative ventures. Generally the bank makes only small charitable donations. Support may also be given to other charities in the fields of inner city regeneration, equal opportunities, education, children and youth, animal welfare, overseas projects, sickness/disability and social welfare.

Main beneficiaries in 1997 included Christian Aid, National Centre for Business & Ecology, Princess Royal Trust for Carers, Mines Advisory Group, Macmillan Cancer Relief and Credit Unions.

Banking services: The bank offers 'Charities Direct', a low-cost interest-bearing current account for charities with balances up to £2 million. For larger charities, banking services are negotiated on an individual basis with the bank's Charities Unit. The bank offers a preferential banking service to business customers who meet stringent ecological criteria.

Employee involvement: Staff are involved in their local communities both on a professional basis and through voluntary work in their own time, eg. as school governors. The Give As You Earn payroll giving scheme is operated for staff. The company is currently reviewing the area of how it will support employees' volunteering/charitable activities.

Non-cash support: This has increased through a rise in gifts in kind, joint promotions and good-cause sponsorship. Non-cash support to community groups includes accommodation, donations/use of office equipment, professional expertise, fundraising and work experience.

Enterprise: The bank supports Co-operative enterprises, credit unions, institutions promoting the alternative option of worker co-operatives and business founded on the principles of employee participation.

It supports such organisations as Agency for Economic Development, East Manchester Partnership, North West Business Leadership Team and North West Business & Industry Awards. It is a member of Business in the Community. The bank also supports two community loan schemes: Bolton Business Ventures and Oldham Business Development Loan Fund.

Exclusions
No support is usually given to appeals from individuals, the arts, medical research, political appeals, religious appeals, sport projects or local appeals not in areas of company presence.

Applications
In writing to the correspondent.

Co-operative Insurance Society Ltd

Miller Street, Manchester M60 0AL
0161-837 5898; Fax: 0161-837 4048

Correspondent: T H Webb, Assistant Secretary

Chief officers: *Chairman:* W Tucker; *Chief Executive:* D S Hollas

Year end	Turnover	Pre-tax profit
31/12/97	£1,315,000,000	£223,500,000

Nature of company business
Insurance.

UK employees: 11,400

Charitable donations
1997: £102,465
1996: £108,655
1995: £113,000

Community support policy
For its major giving, the company prefers to support charities operating nationally or throughout the North West. For a four-year period to the end of 1997, the Society had a covenant with CAF where by charitable giving was set at a fixed level. In 1998, rather than establish another covenant and following the approval of a 12 month budget, use was made of the Gift Aid scheme. It is likely, however, that the Society will undertake a serious re-examination of its charitable giving policy in the near future.

The Society uses the United Trusts of Greater Manchester for its charitable giving. Preference is given to projects in the fields of: medical research, children, elderly people, environment and social welfare. Support may also be given to causes involving: the arts; education; enterprise and training; heritage; overseas projects and sickness/disability charities.

Grants to national organisations range from £1,000 to £4,000. In 1997, main grant beneficiaries included: British Lung Foundation, Community Trust for Greater Manchester, Royal Exchange Theatre, Corda and Research into Ageing.

In addition to cash donations, the society gives gifts in kind. A Community Award Scheme has been introduced to support and encourage employee fundraising.

Exclusions
Generally no support for fundraising events, advertising in charity brochures, individuals, purely denominational

Co-operative

appeals, animal welfare charities, science/technology, sport or local appeals not in areas of society presence.

Applications
In writing to the correspondent.

Co-operative Retail Services Ltd

Sandbrook Park, Sandbrook way, Rochdale, Lancashire OL11 1SA
01706-713000; Fax: 01706-891411

Correspondent: David Boardman, Corporate Communications Manager

Chief officers: n/a

Year end	Turnover	Pre-tax profit
25/1/97	£1,500,000,000	(£13,000,000)

Nature of company business
Retail of food and household goods.

UK employees: 25,000

Charitable donations
1997: £50,000

Community support policy

The overall value of the society's support is not known. The figure quoted above is for one specific initiative – Co-operative partnerships – detailed below.

Other support is given through cash donations, arts and good-cause sponsorship, gifts in kind and joint promotions. The society also supports its employees activities through financial support and matching employee fundraising.

The preferred areas of support for charitable donations are children and youth, environment and heritage and overseas projects. In 1996/97, main beneficiaries of support included Oxfam, Woodcraft Folk, NCH Action for Children and Diana, Princess of Wales Memorial Fund.

Co-operative partnerships

This is a community award scheme launched in 1996. In its first year it was aimed to enable established voluntary groups to put into action a particular idea they may have to improve the local environment. It provides small-scale financial help to get things moving. Grants range between £200 and £2,000 depending on the size and nature of the project, and totalled around £50,000. To qualify, the environmental projects had to be in the vicinity of a Co-operative store (between two and ten miles depending upon the type of Co-operative outlet).

The theme for 1998 was children and young people, again aimed at small-scale community initiatives.

Applications
On a form available from the correspondent.

Coats Viyella plc

1 The Square, Stockley Park, Uxbridge, Middlesex UB11 1TD
0181-210 5000
Website: www.coats-viyella.com

Correspondent: Patricia Lane, Office Manager

Chief officers: *Chairman:* Sir David Alliance; *Chief Executive:* Michael S Ost

Year end	Turnover	Pre-tax profit
31/12/97	£2,358,500,000	£33,300,000

Nature of company business
Principal activities: manufacture, processing and distribution of sewing thread for industrial and domestic use, home furnishings, fashionwares, knitwear and garments, handknittings and precision engineering products.

Main subsidiaries include: The British Van Heusen Company; Coats; Corah; CV Home Furnishings; Dynacast; William Hollins & Company; Jaeger Holdings; Pasolds; Patons & Baldwins; Tootal Group; Vantona Viyella; Coats Patons; J & P Coats.

Main brands include: Aero; Anchor; Beehive; Jaeger; Milwards; Nomotta; Patons; Red Heart; Penelope; Viyella; Aertex; Allen Solly; Berghaus; Byford; Chilprufe; Dalkeith; Peter England; Ladybird; Matchplay; Louis Phillipe; Rocola; Van Heusen; Aptan; Chain; Drima; Dual Duty; Duet; Epic; Koban; Super Sheen; Trident Chortex; Diana Cowpe Rhapsody Towels; Dorma; Royal Ascot; Vantona.

UK employees: 21,637

Charitable donations
1997: £136,000
1996: £168,000
1995: £193,000
1994: £199,000
1993: £175,000
Membership: *ABSA BitC %Club*

Community support policy

The company is a member of the PerCent Club, Business in the Community and ABSA.

Charitable donations: Charities which the appeals committee would ordinarily support come under the following headings: education, the community, the arts, medical research and healthcare, and the environment. Beneficiaries are almost invariably closely associated with the company and its associates. Typical grants to national organisations range from £2,000 to £10,000 and to local organisations from £1,000 to £10,000.

Monies raised by employee fundraising are matched by the company for certain selected charities.

Enterprise: The company seconds staff to local enterprise agencies and initiatives dealing with youth employment.

Education: The company supports several academic appointments in a number of educational centres.

The Coats Viyella Foundation

Though this trust (Charity Commission number 268735) has the company name and strong links with the company, it has assets of £1.4 million with no investments in the company. Neither does it appear to receive donations from the company. However, the company does bear all the administration and management expenses.

The objects of the trust are:

- relief of aged, impotent and poor
- advancement of education
- provision in the interest of social welfare, of facilities for recreation or other leisure time occupation.

The income in 1996/97 was £62,000 and grants totalled £38,000, ranging from £500 to £5,000.

Exclusions
No support is given to circular appeals or to local appeals not in areas of company presence.

Applications
In writing to the correspondent.

Cobham plc

Brook Road, Wimborne, Dorset BH21 2BJ
01202-857651; Fax: 01202-849304
Email: smartr@cobham.com
Website: www.cobham.com

Correspondent: Roger Smart, Group PR Executive

Chief officers: *Chairman:* Sir Michael Knight; *Chief Executive:* G F Page

Year end	Turnover	Pre-tax profit
31/12/97	£323,000,000	£52,000,000

Nature of company business
Design and manufacture of equipment, specialised systems and components used primarily in the aerospace, defence, energy and electronics industries and the operation and maintenance of aircraft, particularly in relation to special mission flight operations.
Main subsidiaries include: Flight Refuelling Ltd; ML Aviation Ltd; ML Lifeguard Equipment Ltd; Slingsby Aviation Ltd; Slingsby Engineering Ltd; Westwind Air Bearings Ltd; Chelton Ltd; FSB Ltd; FR Aviation Ltd; FRA Serco Ltd.

Charitable donations
1997: £51,210
1996: £51,642
1995: £46,816
1994: £28,895
1993: £51,838

Community support policy
The company restricts its charitable support to causes in the Dorset area where it is based. No further information was available.

Applications
In writing to the correspondent.

Coca-Cola Great Britain

Charter Place, Vine Street, Uxbridge, Middlesex UB8 1ST
01895-844834; Fax: 0181-237 3700

Correspondent: Ian Muir, Manager of External Affairs

Year end	Turnover	Pre-tax profit
31/12/96	£111,027,000	£61,434,000

Nature of company business
Principal activity: production of soft drinks.

Although we obtained the financial information above from Companies House, the company stated that they do not relate to the activities of Coca-Cola Great Britain and include income received through a holding company. (Presumably, Coca-Cola Holdings (United Kingdom) Ltd, at the same address.)

Charitable donations
1995: £41,884
1994: £52,000
Membership: *BitC %Club*

Community support policy
The company is a member of the PerCent Club, although we have not been able to obtain recent figures for the company's level of charitable giving.

It prefers to support young people, especially in the area of education and training. Currently, support is mainly given to Special Olympics UK, Variety Club of Great Britain, Outward Bound Trust and Community Action Network. The Coca-Cola Youth Foundation, set up at the end of 1995, supports the Duke of Edinburgh Awards, the Scout Association, National Playing Fields Association and YouthNet UK. Much of Coca-Cola's community support is classified under 'cause-related marketing' and thus does not feature in any donations account. Product and services continue to be provided in-kind, although no figure was given to cover this.

Employee involvement: The company encourages staff involvement in community activities and a payroll giving scheme is also operated.

Enterprise: Coca-Cola Great Britain is a member of Business in the Community.

Sponsorship: The company sponsors both national and local events in the sport, entertainment and environment fields. It concentrates on two specific environmental issues: (a) recycling through various areas, and (b) litter through support for the Tidy Britain Group, especially in the sponsorship of their People and Places Programme. Educational activities have also tended to cover environmental matters with sponsorship either in whole or in part of such publications as 'Finding Out About Packaging', 'Finding Out About Managing Waste', the 'Dustbin Pack' and ' Wise up to Waste'. More recently, 'Our World, Our Responsibility', an environmental guide for schools produced by the RSPB under the auspices of the Council for Environmental Education has been translated into Welsh.

Applications
In writing to the correspondent.

Colgate-Palmolive Ltd

Guildford Business Park, Middleton Road, Guildford, Surrey GU2 5LZ
01483-302222; Fax: 01483-303003

Correspondent: Jeanette Sindle, Charities Co-ordinator

Chief officer: *Chairman:* Karen Guerra

Year end	Turnover	Pre-tax profit
31/12/95	£157,413,000	£6,435,000

Nature of company business
Principal activity: household and personal care products.

UK employees: 699

Charitable donations
1995: £44,117
1994: £50,000

Community support policy
Unfortunately we have not been able to update the figures for this company. The last information available was for 1995, when donations to charity totalled just over £44,000.

The company has told us previously that it has a preference for local charities in areas of company presence (ie. Guilford and Salford) and charities in which a member of company staff is involved. Support is normally given to causes concerned with: the arts; children/youth; education; elderly people; environment/heritage; fundraising events and sickness/disability charities.

Exclusions
The company will not take advertising in charity brochures/souvenir programmes nor take out deeds of covenants for large amounts (exceptional requests would be considered but are unlikely to be supported). No support for circular appeals, religious appeals, overseas projects or political appeals.

Applications
In writing to the correspondent.

Compaq Computer Group Ltd

Hotham House, 1 Heron Square, Richmond, Surrey TW9 1EJ
0181-332 3000; Fax: 0181-332 1961

Correspondent: Peter Wogan, Marketing Manager

Chief officers: n/a

Year end	Turnover	Pre-tax profit
31/12/96	£2,889,769,000	£189,481,000

Nature of company business
The company manufactures microcomputers.

UK employees: 1,927

Charitable donations
1996: £191,879
1995: £198,168
1994: £189,350
1993: £357,146

Community support policy
In each of the years 1994 to 1996, the company gave just under £200,000 in charitable donations. Figures for 1997 were unavailable, but we have no reason to suppose there has been any dramatic change.

However, there has been a change in the company's policy, following the merger with Digital and due to the many requests from the company's own employees to help their personally chosen charities. The company has combined its charity responsibilities within the Association of Compaq Employees regional structure, and is now concentrating funding on employee participation events by way of sponsorship and matched funds, not on a straight donation basis.

Exclusions
The above format is strictly adhered to. No requests for donations will be considered from any individuals, groups or charities once selection has taken place.

Applications
Due to the change in the policy as outlined above, unsolicited requests are no longer considered.

Compass Group plc

Queen's Wharf, Queen Caroline Street, London W6 9RJ
0181-741 8900; Fax: 0181-741 1088
Website: www.compass-group.com

Correspondent: John Greenwood, UK Managing Director

Chief officers: *Chairman:* J M Thomson;
Chief Executive: F H Mackay

Year end	Turnover	Pre-tax profit
30/9/98	£4,213,800,000	£159,100,000

Nature of company business
The principal activities are the provision of food services to business and industrial organisations.

Main subsidiaries include: Select Service Partner Ltd; Eurest; Letheby & Christopher Ltd; Select Service Partner Airport Restaurants Ltd; Payne & Gunter Ltd; National Leisure Catering Ltd.

Main brands include: Upper Crust; Cafe Select; Caffe Ritazza.

UK employees: 40,000

Charitable donations
1998: £313,000
1997: £352,000
1996: £207,000
1995: £19,000
1994: £49,000
Membership: *BitC*

Community support policy

The company reports on its community involvement in its annual report from where the following information is taken.

In September 1996, the company launched a worldwide initiative to recognise its staff who work to combat long-term youth unemployment. The group makes awards to successful participants and financial grants to support their projects. Over 100 projects were launched in the first year, of which 30 received grants. In the UK these included providing mentoring and work experience to youngsters from areas of particularly high unemployment.

Charitable initiatives to benefit from support during the year included:

- Co-operation with sheltered homes for young people with disabilities – including St Michael's House in Ireland.
- Participation by Eurest in a number of local community projects from head teacher business mentoring to youth employment programmes.
- Involvement with the Prince's Trust in the UK with SSP, providing a 12-week course of community project work and team building courses to help young unemployed people into education or employment.
- Funding for colleges and trade schools in the USA to provide scholarships, together with particpation in student exchange programmes.
- Providing training facilities through SSP airport restaurants worldwide for local schools. This includes offering on-the-job training for students and unskilled people, acting as tutor and teaching students how to write a curriculum vitae and apply for jobs.

Applications

In writing to the correspondent, or Ron Morley, Group Company Secretary, at Compass Group PLC, Cowley House, Guildford Street, Chertsey, Surrey KT16 9BA.

Congregational & General Insurance plc

Currer House, Currer Street, Bradford BD1 5BA
01274-700700; Fax: 01274-370754

Correspondent: Roger Williams, Marketing Manager

Chief officers: *Chairman:* Michael F Taylor;
Managing Director: David J Collett

Year end	Turnover	Pre-tax profit
31/3/97	n/a	£984,000

Nature of company business
The transaction of general insurance business, in the form of the insurance for fire and other damage to property.

UK employees: 57

Charitable donations
1998: £399,996
1997: £447,122
1996: £400,000

Community support policy

The company is a wholly owned subsidiary of The Congregational & General Charitable Trust. During 1997/98 the gross amount payable under the deed of covenant to the trust was £399,996.

The trust was established to 'promote the Christian religion and in particular United Reformed Church and Congregational denominations and other churches which are of the protestant tradition'.

The latest accounts on file at the Charity Commission were those for 1995/96, when the total income was £523,000 including £400,000 from the company. (The assets increased markedly the previous year, when the company covenanted £848,000 to the trust and expenditure totalled only £185,000.) The assets of the trust stood at over £2 miilion by the year end.

Grants in 1995/96 totalled £344,000. Unfortunately, no list of grants was included with the accounts. However, the previous year probably gives an indication of the usual distribution of grants. Of the £156,000 distributed in that year, £142,000 went in 'individual grants to churches'. The remainder went to other organisations associated with United Reformed and Congregational churches.

Applications
In writing to the correspondent.

Conoco Ltd

Conoco Centre, Warwick Technology Park, Gallows Hill, Warwickshire CV34 6DA
01926-404804

Correspondent: Loraine Bartlett, Secretary of UK Contributions Committee

Chief officer: *Chairman:* D O Kem

Year end	Turnover	Pre-tax profit
31/12/97	n/a	n/a

Nature of company business
Conoco UK is the UK subsidiary for the US-based Conoco oil company, which is part of E I Du Pont de Nemours. In the UK its petrol is marketed under the Jet brand name.

Main subsidiaries include: Du Pont Ltd; IDAC UK Ltd; Camtax Ltd; DUK Shipping Ltd; Jet Petroleum Ltd; Ronady Ltd.

UK employees: n/a

Charitable donations
1997: £536,000
1996: £456,000
1995: £500,000
1994: £450,000
1993: £266,213

Total community contributions: £561,000

Membership: *BitC*

Cookson

Community support policy

The company supports a wide range of local charities in areas of company presence, ie. Aberdeen, Warwick and Humberside. The company produces the *Conoco in the Community* leaflet which states that Conoco has a strong commitment to the economic and social welfare of the communities in which it operates. It breaks down its charitable support as follows.

Environment

The company have: produced a book and CD-ROM – *Understanding our Environment*, a teaching programme (in seven languages) for schools which helps pupils learn about the natural world; refurbished a nature observatory at Cleethorpes Discovery Centre and the Conoco Natural History Centre to incorporate University of Aberdeen's Natural History Museum and Cruickshank Botanic Garden. There are plans to support South Humber Bank Landscape Initiative to improve the area. Other environmental groups receiving support include Lincolnshire & South Humberside Trust for Nature Conservation, BTCV, RSPB, Wildlife Trusts, Wildfowl & Wetlands Trust, Marine Conservation Society and World Wide Fund for Nature.

Education

The company supports staff, students, courses, equipment and special projects such as marine research in 24 departments at British universities. At a local level Conoco's various operating groups provide regular funding for a variety of educational initiatives in schools, colleges and universities, generally in support of young people. Special needs education is supported, eg. long-standing support for Paddington Integration Project in London to help people with severe learning difficulties to get more out of life. Support is also given to Understanding Industry, Education Business Partnerships, Drive for Youth and Young Enterprise.

Employees

The company has an annual Community Service Award, which gives up to £500 to organisations that have company staff, or long-term contractors involvement. Staff are engaged in fundraising at sites and through the sports and social clubs for local charities.

In the Community

Support is given to a wide range of causes. Examples include: crime reduction and victim support programmes; recycling projects benefiting charities such as Oxfam and Help the Aged; Jet fuel sponsorship for charity events such as Children in Need Round Britain Rally; emergency services such as RNLI and funds towards holidays for deprived or disabled children. Cash donations are usally modest, but gifts in kind are also given such as advice, donating surplus equipment, raffle prizes and help with photocopying.

Jet People Awards recognise ordinary members of the community who give their time, energy and enthusiasm to help those less fortunate than themselves.

Health – support is given towards hospital equipment, hospices, elderly people and medical research. British Red Cross receives support from this category.

Arts sponsorship helps Aberdeen International Youth Festival and the Warwick and Leamington Arts Festival, as well as smaller more local festivals, concerts and exhibitions nationwide.

Other areas of support may include children/youth, elderly people, enterprise/training, fundraising events, science/technology and social welfare.

The main areas of non-cash support are good-cause sponsorship and gifts in kind.

Exclusions

No support for: advertising in charity brochures; appeals from individuals; overseas appeals; political appeals; religious appeals; science/technology; sport or national charities.

Applications

In writing to the correspondent.

Cookson Group plc

The Adelphi, 1–11 John Adam Street, London WC2N 6HJ
0171-766 4500; Fax: 0171-747 6600
Website: www.cooksongroup.co.uk

Correspondent: Mrs Pat Dowton, Appeals Administrator

Chief officers: *Chairman:* Sir Bryan Nicholson; *Chief Executive:* S Howard

Year end	Turnover	Pre-tax profit
31/12/97	£1,721,000,000	£91,000,000

Nature of company business
The Cookson Group is a holding company for an internationally-based group of companies principally engaged in the manufacture of specialist industrial materials. The group is divided into four divisions: electronic materials, ceramics, plastics and engineered products. The group is located mainly in the UK, North America and Western Europe.

Main subsidiaries include: Alpha Fry Ltd; Focas Ltd; Flogates Ltd; KSR InternationaL Ltd.

UK employees: n/a

Charitable donations

1997: £696,565
1996: £202,889
1995: £211,719
1994: £152,868
1993: £164,327
Membership: *BitC*

Community support policy

The company supports both national and local charities, with a preference for those based in the City or its environs. Preferred areas of support include: homelessness (especially regarding young people); advertising in charity brochures; animal welfare charities; children/youth; education; elderly people; environment/heritage; medical research; overseas projects; and sickness/disability charities. During the year ending December 1996, main grant beneficiaries included: Sightsavers; The Bede

Foundation; CBI Education Foundation; Council for Industry & Higher Education; Barnardo's Ball (brochure advertising); Crisis.

Exclusions
No support for appeals from individuals; the arts; enterprise/training; fundraising events; political appeals; religious appeals; science/technology; social welfare or sport.

Applications
In writing to the correspondent, no telephone approaches.

Cooper Gay (Holdings) Ltd

International House, 26 Creechurch Lane, London EC3A 5EH
0171-480 7322; Fax: 0171-204 4997

Correspondent: A Mason, Secretary to the Cooper Gay Charitable Trust

Chief officer: *Chairman:* M Jones

Year end	Turnover	Pre-tax profit
30/9/97	£14,296,000	£399,000

Nature of company business
Insurance brokers.

UK employees: 135

Charitable donations
1997: £110,000
1996: £114,000
1995: £110,000
1994: £172,000
1993: £133,000

Community support policy

The company appears to make donations through the Cooper Gay Charitable Trust. This trust has the following objects:

(a) to make grants/donations for provision or maintenance of facilities in hospitals, homes or other bodies/organisations

(b) to promote research and results of research to the public.

The trustees in 1996/97 were: M D Conway; S M Gillick; D A Allen; A A Mason; D G Staplehurst. The trustees' report stated that grants were reduced by £30,000 on the previous year and substantially down on the peak of over £200,000 in 1994. It also stated that the number of applications received increased annually and 'therefore in order to donate to new, worthy causes we have further reduced the preferred list'. This list consists of charities which receive regular support from the trust.

The trust also encourages staff of the company and its subsidiaries to submit applications for charities in which they have a particular interest.

The income was £106,000 in 1996/97, including £105,000 in donations presumably from the company. Grants totalled £85,000. 47 grants were made ranging from £500 to £5,000.

The largest went to Churchill Hospital Research Department and the Mountbatten Centre – Kent & Canterbury Hospital. Grants of £3,000 went to Down's Syndrome Association, Evelina Children's Unit, Guillain-Barre Syndrome Support Group, Hospice of Our Lady & St John, Institute of Cancer Research, National Ankylosing Spondylitis Society, Petersfield Society for Handicapped Children, Robert Owen Foundation, Royal British Legion (Lloyds Branch), RNLI and St Francis Hospice, Romford. The smaller grants given were to similar organisations, with a few exceptions such as Southwark Playground Trust, Spitalfields Farm Association Ltd and Thurrock Womens Refuge Association.

Exclusions
Only registered charities are supported. No support for students.

Applications
In writing to the correspondent. Applications are considered twice a year.

Cordiant Communications Group plc

121–141 Westbourne Terrace, London W2 6JR
0171-262 4343

Correspondent: Letitia Brecher, Administration Manager

Chief officers: *Chairman:* Charles Scott; *Chief Executive:* Michael Bungey

Year end	Turnover	Pre-tax profit
31/12/97	£4,206,200,000	£34,600,000

Nature of company business
A holding company with subsidiaries providing a range of advertising and marketing services on a worldwide basis. On 14 December 1997 the company demerged, transferring the assets and liabilities of the Saatchi & Saatchi network to Saatchi & Saatchi plc and subsequently changing its name from Cordiant plc to Cordiant Communications Group plc.

Main subsidiaries include: Bates Dorland.

UK employees: 509

Charitable donations
1997: £58,000
1996: £34,000

Community support policy

The company has a preference for community-based organisations, mainly in Greater London, and to charities for homeless people and those providing for children and young people. Preference may be given to projects in which a member of staff is involved. Grants range from £125 to £2,000.

Exclusions
No response to circular appeals. No support for individuals, religious appeals, local appeals not in areas of company presence, large national appeals, animal welfare

Cornhill

charities, bricks and mortar appeals, research organisations or overseas projects.

Applications
In writing to the correspondent.

Cornhill Insurance plc

32 Cornhill, London EC3V 3LJ
0171-626 5410; Fax: 0171-929 3562
Website: www.cornhill.co.uk

Correspondent: C Kiddle-Morris, Company Secretary

Chief officers: *Chairman:* Lord Walker of Worcester; *Chief Executive:* W R Treen

Year end	Turnover	Pre-tax profit
31/12/97	n/a	£58,800,000

Nature of company business
The group undertakes all classes of insurance business. It has 13 UK branches.

Main subsidiaries include: British Reserve Insurance Co Ltd; Domestic Insurance Services Ltd; Fine Instruments Finance Ltd; Cornhill Trustee Ltd; Trafalgar Insurance PLC; Pet Plan Ltd; Ajax Insurance Association Ltd.

UK employees: 2,870

Charitable donations
1997: £80,000
1996: £81,250
1995: £31,042
1994: £29,217

Community support policy

Areas of non-cash support include gifts in kind and joint promotions.

The company makes most of its donations to registered charities through the Charities Aid Foundation. There is a preference for charities where the business is located and in which a member of staff is involved, and for charities working in the fields of children and youth, social welfare, education, elderly people, enterprise/training, sickness/disability charities, medical, and environment. Grants range up to £1,000 for national and local organisations.

The company operates the Give As You Earn payroll giving scheme, and may match employee fundraising.

Main beneficiaries in 1997 included The Stroke Association, Children in Need, Phyllis Tuckwell Hospice, Great Ormond Street and Leukaemia Research.

Pet Plan Ltd, a subsidiary company, has an associated charitable trust. This trust, the Pet Plan Charitable Trust (Charity Commission number 1032907), receives its income from policy holders of the company and the company itself. In 1996/97, it made donations totalling £245,000 to support dogs, cats and horses through funding clinical vetinary investigation, education and welfare projects. Further details can be found in *A Guide to the Major Trusts Volume 2*.

Exclusions
No response to circular appeals and no support for fundraising events, advertising in charity brochures, appeals from individuals, political or religious appeals, science/technology, sport, the arts, animal welfare charities, local appeals not in areas of company presence or overseas projects.

Applications
The correspondent above should be contacted to obtain policy guidelines and an application form.

Courtaulds Textiles plc

13–14 Margaret Street, London W1A 3DA
0171-331 4500; Fax: 0171-331 4600
Website: www.courtaulds-textiles.com

Correspondent: P J Aubusson, Head of Corporate Affairs

Chief officers: *Chairman:* J D Eccles; *Chief Executive:* Colin Dyer

Year end	Turnover	Pre-tax profit
31/12/97	£912,000,000	£38,000,000

Nature of company business
Textile and clothing manufacture with four divisions: international fabrics; lingerie and hosiery; casualwear and underwear; and furnishings.

Major brands include: Aristoc, Berlei, Georges Rech, Gossard, and Lyle & Scott.

UK employees: 16,000

Charitable donations
1997: £120,000
1996: £92,000
1995: £133,000
1994: £111,000
1993: £158,000

Community support policy

All of the company's donations are made through individual businesses and consequently concentrate support on charities, mainly in the East Midlands, that are considered to be of most relevance to company employees and their communities. Appeals should be addressed to individual businesses within the group.

Exclusions
No response to circular appeals. No grants for advertising in charity brochures, animal welfare charities, appeals from individuals, religious or political appeals, local appeals not in areas of company presence or overseas projects.

Applications
Appeals should be made in writing to individual businesses within the group.

Coutts & Co

440 Strand, London WC2R 0QS
0171-753 1000

Correspondent: Mrs P A Varga, Administrator, The Coutts Charitable Trust

Chief officers: *Chairman:* Sir E A J Fergusson; *Chief Executive:* H Post

Year end	Turnover	Pre-tax profit
31/12/95	n/a	£42,236,000

Nature of company business
Banking and allied financial services. The ultimate holding company is the National Westminster Bank. The bank's main location is in London.

UK employees: 1,756

Charitable donations

1997: £172,000
1996: n/a
1995: £158,000
Membership: *ABSA BitC*

Community support policy

The company's support is, in the main, directed towards charities involved with homeless, disadvantaged and disabled children and adults, those dealing with rehabilitation and teaching self-help, youth organisations, the relief of poverty, medical research and sickness/disability. Support may also be given for fundraising events. Where possible, the trustees continue support for those charities to which they have traditionally given over a number of years and they also prefer to support organisations in areas where the bank has a presence.

Coutts Charitable Trust

Some charitable donations are given through the Coutts Charitable Trust, which only supports registered UK charities. All appeals are considered on their merits.

The trust operates on a different financial year to the bank, therefore the figures are different to those quoted for the company. 1997/98 figures were not on file at the Charity Commission at the time of compiling this information. In the year 1996/97, the bank covenanted a sum of £148,000 to the trust.

This trust is funded by the bank under a deed of covenant equivalent to one half of 1% of the bank's pre-tax profit with a minimum of £50,000.

In 1996/97, the trust had a total income of £152,000 and gave donations totalling £117,645 (£109,000 in 1995/96). The trust sumarises its donations as follows (1995/96 figures in brackets):

Aged	£6,225	(£3,200)
AIDS/HIV research support	£500	(nil)
Alcohol/drug addiction	£1,600	(£2,350)
Animal welfare	£250	(nil)
Arts	£750	(nil)
Arts/culture	£5,450	(£4,350)
Benevolent	£250	(£550)
Blind	£2,400	(£2,300)
Building/restoration/premises	£200	(nil)
Cancer care	£600	(£850)
Cancer research	£2,550	(£3,350)
Children	£7,070	(£7,750)
Children/youth	£1,550	(£900)
Deaf	£1,200	(£1,550)
Disabled physical/mental	£12,800	(£15,620)
Education	£13,100	(£5,650)
Emergency services	£250	(£200)
Environment	£2,150	(£1,300)
Heritage	£950	(£1,400)
Homeless	£7,500	(£7,700)
Hospices	£1,000	(£970)
Hospitals	£2,300	(£2,790)
Housing	£1,150	(£3,650)
International fellowship	£750	(£1,250)
Job creation/training	£1,200	(£450)
Job training	£250	(£250)
Law and order	£150	(£450)
Medical research	£11,050	(£7,100)
Mental health	£1,300	(£700)
Mentally handicapped	£950	(£850)
Overseas aid	£400	(£1,500)
Physically disabled	£1,900	(£6,400)
Prison aid	£150	(nil)
Rehabilitating offenders	£850	(£1,100)
Religious	£3,600	(£2,250)
Service charities	£1,400	(£1,650)
Social welfare	£11,050	(£9,900)
Sports and recreation	£250	(nil)
Sundry	£3,900	(£3,500)
Youth organisations	£6,700	(£5,000)

Most of the grants were for £250 or less. The largest grants were to John Grooms Association for the Disabled (£10,000), Reeds School (£5,000) and Almshouse Association (£3,000).

Donations from the trust are made on a daily basis where amounts of £500 or less are felt to be appropriate. The trustees meet quarterly to consider larger donations.

Coutts Foundation

This foundation was set up to mark the bank's tercentenary in 1992. The foundation had a total income of £64,000 in 1996/97 and gave donations totalling £55,000. It is thought that the accumulated fund stood at over £1.1 million. This foundation distributes most of the total income each year to a small number of selected charities. In 1996/97, those supported were Peabody Trust – Bruce House Project, St Mungo's and Hodgkins Disease & Lymphona Association.

Other support

The company operates the Give As You Earn payroll giving scheme. In addition, with its TESSA (the tax exempt savings account) the bank has offered the option of a

Cummins

slightly lower interest rate with the difference going to charity. It states that nearly 10% of customers opening a TESSA have chosen this option. The company is a member of Business in the Community and ABSA.

Exclusions

No response to circular appeals. No support for appeals from individuals or overseas projects.

Applications

Applications to the Coutts Charitable Trust should be addressed to the correspondent above. Sponsorship proposals should be directed to the Sponsorship and Events Manager.

Cummins Engine Co Ltd

Yarm Road, Darlington, County Durham DL1 4PW
01325-556000; Fax: 01325-368040

Correspondent: Janette Mottram, Secretary to the Trustees

Chief officer: *Chairman:* J M Pottinger

Year end	Turnover	Pre-tax profit
31/12/97	£527,026,000	£23,707

Nature of company business
The principal activity is the manufacture, sale, distribution and servicing of diesel engines and components. The company is a subsidiary of Cummins Engine Company, Inc (US).

UK employees: 2,157

Charitable donations

1997: £38,589
1996: £75,367
1995: £96,114
1994: £53,860
1993: £50,000
Membership: *BitC*

Community support policy

The company supports projects local to the company's manufacturing plants and offices (north east England, Glasgow/Edinburgh, Northamptonshire, West Yorkshire, Lincolnshire and Kent). It prefers to support education/experience for young people, and especially charities in which a member of staff is involved.

Grants to national organisations range from £500 to £3,000. Grants to local organisations are up to £10,000.

The main areas of non-cash support are secondments, gifts in kinds and training schemes. The company is a member of Business in the Community.

Applications

In writing to the Secretary to the Trustees at the address above. The company's head office is at: 46–50 Coombe Road, New Malden, Surrey KT3 4QL (0181-949 6171).

Cussons International Ltd

Cussons House, Bird Hall Lane, Stockport SK3 0XN
0161-491 8000

Correspondent: Janice Armstrong, Secretary to the Chairman

Chief officers: *Chairman:* A J Green;
Managing Director: C N Green

Year end	Turnover	Pre-tax profit
31/5/97	£350,348,000	£30,186,000

Nature of company business
Principal activities: manufacture of soap, toiletries, cleaning agents, pharmaceuticals and associated products.

Main subsidiaries include: Cussons Group; Fragrance Chemicals; Parnon; P C Products (1001).

Main brands include: Cussons; Pearl; Imperial Leather; Morning Fresh; Freshness!; Racasan; 1001.

UK employees: n/a

Charitable donations

1997: £50,000
1996: £50,000
1995: £50,000
1994: £50,000
1993: £50,000

Community support policy

The company gives £50,000 each year to charities. It has a preference for local charities in areas of company presence, particularly projects involving children and youth, social welfare, medical, education, recreation and disabled people. Donations usually range from £50 to £1,000.

Exclusions

Generally no support for circular appeals, fundraising events, advertising in charity brochures, individuals, denominational appeals, large national appeals or overseas projects.

Applications

The charities committee only meets once a year in May. Appeals should be addressed to Mrs A Bacchus, Secretary to the Chairman, at head office.

Other information: The Zochonis Charitable Trust made grants of £927,000 in 1996/97 for general charitable purposes. Its income is derived almost exclusively from share holdings in the company, but acts independently. Further details can be found in *A Guide to the Major Trusts Volume 1*. The correspondent of the trust is The Secretary to the Trust, at the above address.

Daejan Holdings plc

Freshwater House, 158–162 Shaftesbury Avenue, London WC2H 8HR
0171-836 1555; Fax: 0171-379 6365

Correspondent: B Freshwater, Chairman

Chief officer: *Chairman:* B S E Freshwater

Year end	Turnover	Pre-tax profit
31/3/98	£38,843,000	£27,101,000

Nature of company business
Property investment and trading, with some development. 62% of the group's properties are in Central London. Daejan Holdings is a member of the Freshwater Group of Companies.

Main subsidiaries include: Astral Estates Ltd; Bampton Holdings Ltd; Brickfield Properties Ltd; City and Country Properties Ltd; Chilon Investments Co Ltd; Hampstead Way Investments Ltd; Limebridge Co Ltd; Pegasus Investment Co Ltd; Rosebel Holdings Ltd; Seaglen Investments Ltd; St Leonards Properties Ltd; The Bampton Property Group Ltd; The Cromlech Property Co Ltd; The Halliard Property Co Ltd.

UK employees: n/a

Charitable donations

1998: £120,000
1997: £60,000
1996: £60,000
1995: £60,000
1994: £60,000

Community support policy

The company gives £60,000 a year to charities. It mainly supports orthodox Jewish charities, especially in the educational and medical fields, in the USA, Britain and Israel. Support is also given to organisations concerned with the relief of poverty. The company channels its giving through the Charities Aid Foundation and operates the Give As You Earn payroll giving scheme. The Freshwater Group is also associated with two or three other substantial private charitable companies, whose policy is similar to that of Daejan Holdings.

Exclusions

Organisations dealing with professional fundraisers, large overhead expenses and expensive fundraising campaigns are avoided. Support is not given to the arts, enterprise or conservation.

Applications

In writing to the correspondent (who is also the contact for the payroll giving scheme). There is no donations committee.

Daily Mail and General Trust plc

Northcliffe House, 2 Derry Street, London W8 5TT
0171-938 6000; Fax: 0171-938 4626
Website: www.dmgt.co.uk

Correspondent: V Harmsworth, Director of Corporate Affairs

Chief officers: *Chairman:* Rt Hon. Viscount Rothermere; *Chief Executive:* C J F Sinclair

Year end	Turnover	Pre-tax profit
28/9/97	£1,200,000,000	£144,000,000

Nature of company business
Principal activity: publication and printing of newspapers and periodicals.

Main subsidiaries include: Northcliffe Finance Ltd; Associated Newspapers Ltd; Aberdeen Journals Ltd; The Cheltenham Newspaper Co Ltd; Cornish Weekly Newspapers Ltd; The Courier Printing & Publishing Co Ltd; Derby Daily Telegraph Ltd; Essex Chronicle Series Ltd; Express & Echo Publications Ltd; Gloucestershire Newspapers Ltd; Grimsy & Scunthorpe Newspaper Ltd; Herald Express Ltd; Hull Daily Mail Publications Ltd; The Journal Co Ltd; Leicester Mercury Group Ltd; Lincolnshire Publishing Co Ltd; Llanelli Star Ltd; Northcliffe Retail Ltd; North Devon Journal Herald Ltd; Nottingham Post Group Ltd; The Printworks Ltd; South West Wales Publications Ltd; Staffordshire Sentinel Newspapers Ltd; Westcountry Publications Ltd; The Western Morning News Co Ltd; Euromoney Publications PLC; Century House Information Ltd; Raven Fox Ltd; Harmsworth Media Ltd; Harmsworth Broadcasting Ltd; Arts and Entertainment Programming Ltd; British Pathe PLC; New Era Television Ltd; Teletex Ltd; DMG Exhibition Group Ltd; DMG Business Media Ltd; DMG Angex Ltd; DMG Pinnacle Ltd; DMG Trinity Ltd; DMG Home Interest Magazines Ltd; DMG Antique Fairs Ltd; Metropress Ltd; The Publishing Co Ltd; DMG Radio Ltd; DMG Regional Radio Pty Ltd; Festival City Broadcasters Ltd; Radio Hibernia AB; Hobsons Publishing PLC; John M Newton & Sons Ltd; Lumitron Ltd.

UK employees: n/a

Charitable donations

1997: £718,000
1996: £403,000
1995: £426,000
1994: £334,000
1993: £282,000
Membership: *BitC*

Community support policy

The company gives most of its donations to the Rothermere Foundation. The company supports primarily charities connected with the printing industry and charities local to the company and its subsidiaries (Kensington, Surrey Quays and Rotherhithe). The main donation in 1996 was to the Institute for American Studies, Oxford. Support may also be given to education, environment/heritage and medical research and through arts sponsorship. Donations are generally for £200 to £500, but can be for much more. The company also gives gifts in kind.

Danka

Exclusions

No support for circular appeals, individuals, purely religious or political appeals, science/technology, sickness/disability, social welfare, sport, local appeals not in areas of company presence or overseas projects.

Applications

In writing to the correspondent. A donations committee meets several times a year on an ad hoc basis.

Danka UK PLC

1230 Arlington Business Park, Theale, Berkshire RG7 4TX
0118-928 4900

Correspondent: Helen Berentzen, External Communications Manager

Chief officers: *Chairman:* Mark A Vaughan-Lee;
Chief Executive: D M Doyle

Year end	Turnover	Pre-tax profit
31/3/98	£2,040,074,000	£65,101,000

Nature of company business
The principal operating subsidiary, Danka Industries Inc, and its subsidiary undertakings are engaged in the supply and servicing of business equipment in the USA.

UK employees: n/a

Charitable donations
1998: £131,000
1997: £185,000
1996: £270,000
1995: £105,000
1994: £121,000

Community support policy

Preference is given to local charities in areas where the company operates. No further information was available.

Applications

In writing to the correspondent.

De La Rue plc

De La Rue House, Jays Close, Viables, Basingstoke, Hampshire RG22 4BS
01256-329122
Website: www.delarue.com

Correspondent: Stephen Hoffman Womersley, Head of Corporate Affairs

Chief officers: *Chairman:* Brandon Gough;
Chief Executive: Ian Much

Year end	Turnover	Pre-tax profit
31/3/98	£790,200,000	£87,200,000

Nature of company business
The company is involved in the production of over 150 currencies worldwide and a wide range of security documents. It also supplies cash handling and physical security equipment. In addition it holds a 50% share of Royal Mint Services and 22.5% of Camelot Group.

Main subsidiaries include: Portals Group.

UK employees: 4,100

Charitable donations
1998: £310,000
1997: £302,000
1996: £339,000
1995: £303,000
1994: £72,000
Membership: %Club

Community support policy

Charitable donations: Donations by the company are made through the De La Rue Charitable Trust which aims to direct funds to causes around the world in countries where De La Rue operates. Emphasis is given to educational projects at home and abroad which promote relevant skills, international understanding and bring relief from suffering. Established in 1977, the trust is a member of the PerCent Club and as such makes available for charitable giving either 0.5% of UK profits or 1.0% of dividend per annum.

The chairman of trustees is Sally Field, with four trustees representing head office and each of the three operating divisions (ie. Stephen Hoffman Womersley, Keith Boiston Knox, Terry McWilliams and Nicol McGregor).

Corporate giving on a larger scale will be directed to the following categories:

(a) Well-researched causes in under-developed countries with which De La Rue has significant supplier relationships, if possible through UK charities.

(b) Educational establishments at home and abroad which promote relevant skills and international understanding, including bursaries, funded scholarships, specific educational projects and the sponsorship of disadvantaged students from appropriate countries or sources.

(c) Disaster funds in client countries or De La Rue company locations.

(d) Sponsorship of relevant and/or topical charitable projects which could also enlighten and inform potential customers, local communities and the general public as to the activities, purpose and culture of De La Rue.

(e) Local subsidiary donations to local community projects.

The balance of the available funds will be used for smaller donations which fall under these three categories:

(a) The relief of suffering of De La Rue pensioners and their relatives and dependants, and to relieve suffering in hardship cases brought to the trust's attention through a De La Rue connection.

(b) Towards the setting up costs of new hospices (up to a total of £6,000 over a three-year period) in the vicinity of De La Rue locations.

(c) One-off immediate payments to specifically identified causes perceived as topically important to either the group or individual business units.

In 1997/98, grants totalled around £300,000 with some of the main beneficiaries being: Tear Fund in Mexico; World Vision in Brazil; Starehe School in Kenya; Save the Children in the Philippines; Orbis in Mongolia and Atlantic College UK.

The accounts on file at the Charity Commission for the trust consisted of only three pages, with no grants list. The trust had a balance of over £1 million in 1996/97.

Employee Involvement: The company operates the Give As You Earn scheme and matches employee fundraising.

Exclusions

Generally no support for circular appeals, fundraising events, brochure advertising, individuals, purely denominational (religious) or political appeals, local appeals not in areas of company presence or large national appeals. No telephoned applications can be considered. Applications that do not fall within the above categories will not be considered unless their are extenuating or emergency circumstances. Grant applications made by individuals either in the UK or abroad cannot be considered. All circular appeals will be rejected.

Applications

Appeals, in writing only, should be made to: Miss Charlotte Carroll, Appeals Secretary, De La Rue Charitable Trust. Applications are considered at trustees meetings held in February and July.

Debenhams plc

1 Welbeck Street, London W1A 1DF
0171-408 4444

Correspondent: Gwyneth Letherbarrow, Secretary of Charitable Appeals Committee

Chief officers: n/a

Year end	Turnover	Pre-tax profit
30/8/97	£1,282,800,000	£17,500,000

Nature of company business
Membership: *BitC*

Community support policy

Following its demerger from the Burton Group, the department store has localised its community support. Its new programme, 'Debenhams and the Community', will support communities at a local level. Its annual charitable budget is divided between each of its 90 stores according to their size and used to organise and support staff fundraising activities. Each store will have a fundraising committee of employees who will decide on the activities and charities they wish to support. The only criteria is that they fundraise for a charitable concern which is 'working for the good of the community'. The staff committees may respond to requests for fundraising or they may fundraise for causes employees are already involved in.

In response to the numerous requests for raffle prizes, Debenhams has produced a cuddly bear that staff can use in their fundraising efforts. In addition, the company will match fund, up to a ceiling of £250 a year, employees' individual fundraising efforts carried out in their own spare time.

Debenhams also operates a Give As You Earn payroll giving scheme and is a member of Business in the Community.

Charities should contact the chair of the local fundraising committee. The contact given above will direct them to that member of staff.

Applications

In writing to the correspondent.

Deloitte & Touche

Hill House, 1 Little New Street, London EC4A 3TR
0171-303 7149; Fax: 0171-583 8517
Email: Richard_Stone@deloitte.touche.co.uk
Website: www.deloitte.co.uk

Correspondent: Richard Stone, Director of Community Investment

Chief officers: *Chairman:* Martin Scicluna; *Chief Executive:* John Connolly

Year end	Turnover	Pre-tax profit
30/9/98	£563,000,000	n/a

Nature of company business
Audit, tax, corporate finance, corporate recovery and management consultancy services.

UK employees: 7,000

Charitable donations
1998: £250,000
1997: £250,000
1996: £250,000
1995: £250,000
1994: £250,000
Total community contributions: £294,000
Membership: *ABSA BitC %Club*

Community support policy

Deloitte & Touche is a member of the PerCent Club and commits in excess of 1% of UK pre-tax profit towards its community involvement. In 1997/98, this totalled £294,000.

It is committed to supporting the community at a national and local level through its network of 24 offices throughout the UK. (Each region has a small budget for supporting local charities.) Key projects include Prince's Youth Business Trust mentoring and secondary school student mentoring programmes.

In 1997/98, the firm's charitable fund made donations amounting to £250,000 to a variety of national and local causes. A number of major donations are made each year to selected charities dedicated to areas such as children

Delta

and young people, medicine and research and social deprivation. Major beneficiaries included Sense, Tommy's Campaign, NSPCC, Youth at Risk and Centrepoint.

The firm co-sponsors Business in the Community's Business Bridge project and seconded a manager to the project during 1996/97. The firm also provides services to community projects through Business in the Community's Professional Firms Group and Business on Board programmes.

The charitable fund also matches the contributions made to the staff fund through Give As You Earn. In addition, other initiatives encouraging staff involvement include: Team Challenges – where the firm matches charity fundraising for teams of six or more staff, and Charity of the Year – fundraising for local charities managed by each local office.

Exclusions

No support for animal welfare, environmental, religious, political, and international aid programmes. Individuals are not supported.

Applications

In writing to the Deloitte & Touche Charity Committee. However, few ad hoc or unsolicited requests for funding are approved by the committee.

Delta plc

1 Kingsway, London WC2B 6XF
0171-836 3535; Fax: 0171-836 4511

Correspondent: Alex Wain, Human Resources

Chief officers: *Chairman:* Sir Martin Jacomb;
Chief Executive: J P Scott-Maxwell

Year end	Turnover	Pre-tax profit
3/1/98	£898,000,000	(£23,000,000)

Nature of company business
The main activities of the company are electric cables, circuit protection, engineering and industrial services.
Main subsidiaries include: Schubert & Salzer Ingolstadt-Armaturen.

UK employees: 7,971

Charitable donations

1998: £57,949
1997: n/a
1996: £66,973
1995: £72,127
1994: £80,001

Community support policy

The company supports both national and local organisations, with a preference for those based in areas local to company sites. Support is given to charities covering the fields of medical, disabled people, youth, children's welfare, elderly people, community, social welfare, environment/heritage, service/ex-service and education. Grants range from £100 to £600 to national organisations, and from £25 to £100 to local organisations.

In 1996, the company gave grants to around 35 main beneficiaries including Macmillan Cancer Relief, Acorn Children's Hospice, RNID, RNIB and Anthony Nolan Bone Marrow Appeal.

Exclusions

No response to circular appeals and no support for fundraising events, advertising in charity brochures, appeals from individuals, animal welfare, the arts, enterprise/training, purely denominational (religious) or political appeals, science/technology, sports or overseas projects.

Applications

In writing to the correspondent.

Deutsche Morgan Grenfell Group plc

23 Great Winchester Street, London EC2P 2AX
0171-545 5337

Correspondent: Maria Wright, Secretary to the Charities Committee

Chief officer: *Chairman:* Sir John Craven

Year end	Turnover	Pre-tax profit
31/12/95	n/a	£148,936,000

Nature of company business
Morgan Grenfell Group plc is the holding company of a group providing international merchant banking and investment management services on a worldwide basis to clients including corporations, governments, financial institutions and investors. Major UK subsidiaries are all based in London and operate under the Morgan Grenfell name.

UK employees: 1,824

Charitable donations

1995: £243,873
1994: £228,300
1993: £193,277

Total community contributions: £383,535
Membership: %Club

Community support policy

The group is a member of the PerCent Club. It operates a matched giving programme and the Give As You Earn payroll giving scheme.

Charitable donations: All the group's charitable donations are distributed by head office mainly through the Charities Aid Foundation. Donations are only made to registered charities with support primarily given to national charities but local charities are supported if they are in, or for the benefit of, or have another connection with, the City of London.

National charities donations are usually in the range £500 to £1,000. Local and overseas charities are not usually supported. Within these broad guidelines, the group supports organisations working in the areas of medical research/welfare, arts and music, social welfare, education, environment, disabled people, children and youth, religion, trades and professions and elderly people.

Enterprise: In connection with the 150th anniversary of Morgan Grenfell's foundation, continuing support is given to the East London Small Business Centre Ltd.

Education: The group funds the Morgan Grenfell Chair in Financial Markets at the City University Business School, having committed £350,000 over seven years.

Exclusions

No support for advertising in charity brochures, enterprise/training, small local appeals not in areas of company presence or appeals from individuals.

Applications

In writing to the correspondent. All appeals are reviewed, and grants decisions made, by a charities committee which meets quarterly.

Sponsorship proposals to R P Elliston.

Devro plc

Gartferry Road, Moodiesburn, Chryston, Glasgow G69 0JE
01236-879191; Fax: 01236-872557

Correspondent: Grant Rae, Personnel Manager

Chief officers: *Chairman:* L R Allen;
Chief Executive: Dr G Y Alexander

Year end	Turnover	Pre-tax profit
31/12/97	£284,492,000	£58,011,000

Nature of company business
The principal activity is the production and marketing of manufactured casings for the food industry.

UK employees: 3,740

Charitable donations

1997: £118,000
1996: £156,000
1995: £19,000
1994: £14,000

Community support policy

There was a large increase in the level of charitable giving by the company, from £19,000 in 1995 to £156,000 in 1996. The 1997 figure remains in excess of £100,000, but down on the previous year. The company tends to give a large number of relatively small donations to local charities in and around Glasgow.

The company requested to be taken out of the guide saying that the information was inaccurate. However, we maintain our policy of including all relevant companies. The information is largely taken from the company's own 1997 annual report.

Exclusions

No support for large national appeals or through third-party fundraisers or advertising in charity brochures.

Applications

In writing to the correspondent.

Dewhirst Group plc

Dewhirst House, Westgate, Driffield,
East Yorkshire YO25 6TH
01377-252561

Correspondent: Timothy C Dewhirst, Chairman

Chief officers: *Chairman:* Timothy C Dewhirst;
Chief Executive: David Witt

Year end	Turnover	Pre-tax profit
16/1/98	£363,592,000	£31,506,000

Nature of company business
The principal activity is the manufacture and distribution of clothing and toiletries.

UK employees: 9,928

Charitable donations

1998: £44,115
1997: £38,815
1996: £21,178

Community support policy

The company prefers to support charities local to Driffield, especially those with staff involvement.

Exclusions

No support for national charities.

Applications

In writing to the correspondent.

Dhamecha Foods Ltd

2 Hathaway Close, Stanmore, Middlesex HA7 3NR
0181-903 8181; Fax: 0181-902 4420

Correspondent: P K Dhamecha, Financial Director

Chief officers: n/a

Year end	Turnover	Pre-tax profit
31/3/97	£65,830,000	£706,000

Nature of company business
The principal activities are wholesale food cash and carry, property dealings and the manufacture and sale of paper disposable products.

Main subsidiaries include: London Paper Products Ltd.

UK employees: 124

Diageo

Charitable donations
1997: £50,305
1996: £50,252
1995: £50,875

Community support policy
Although we were unable to speak to anyone concerning the company's donations policy, the named contact was confirmed as correct.

Applications
In writing to the correspondent.

Diageo plc

8 Henrietta Place, London W1M 9AG
0171-927 5200; Fax: 0171-927 4600
Website: www.diageo.com

Correspondent: Geoffrey Bush, Director of Corporate Citizenship

Chief officers: *Chairman:* A A Greener; *Chief Executive:* J B McGrath

Year end	Turnover	Pre-tax profit
30/6/98	£12,029,000,000	£1,943,000,000

Nature of company business
International branded food and drinks company with four main businesses: UDV – spirits and wines; Pillsbury – foods; Guinness – brewing; Burger King – hamburger restaurant chain.

Main subsidiaries include: United Distillers & Vintners; Guinness; Burger King.

Main brands include: Smirnoff; Johnnie Walker; J&B; Gordon's; Pillsbury; Haagen-Dazs; Guinness.

Charitable donations
1998: £8,300,000
Membership: *ABSA BitC %Club*

Community support policy
The company has committed 1% of annual worldwide trading profit to support community activities. In addition to the £8 million donated to charitable organisations in the UK, group companies in the United States made donations totalling £6 million. The UK figure includes payments of £2.5 million to the Thalidomide Trust. Excluding this latter commitment, the total charitable giving by the company is about the same as the combined totals of the former separate companies GrandMet and Guinness.

The Diageo Foundation has been established to provide charitable giving and matching, and longer term social investment. Its work is international and inclusive and complementary to the group's businesses, brands and people. The trustees are from the businesses around the world supported by external advisers on specific focus areas.

The overall policy is to support charitable organisations under the theme of one of Diageo's core values: 'Freedom to succeed'. To quote the company, 'Freedom to succeed is about providing opportunities for people to fulfil this potential. It means giving our businesses, our employees and our community partners the space to be challenging and innovative'.

Support from the foundation concentrates on the following:

- *Local citizens:*

    Culture – with emphasis on local community arts initiatives.

    Local regeneration – in locations where the business has a major presence and it is able to make a difference on issues such as homelessness, unemployment and disability.

- *Our people* – concentrating on employee involvement and matched giving.
- *Skills for Life* – giving people of all ages and cultures practical opportunities to gain skills which enable them to fulfil their potential and improve their life prospects.
- *Water of Life* – Diageo's international humanitarian and environmental initiative supporting projects with a water theme.

Preference will be given to:

- excluded and disadvantaged people who, with support, can help themselves to transform their own lives
- partnerships with community groups, rather than individuals
- causes where company involvement can make a difference
- kick-start funding to get the company and employees involved. There will be a three-year limit on any funding commitment.

Exclusions
The following are outside the foundation's guidelines:

- locations where Diageo does not have a business presence
- organisations which are not registered charities
- individuals
- loans or business finance
- medical charities or hospitals
- promotion of religion
- animal welfare
- endowment funds
- expeditions or overseas travel
- political organisations.

Applications
The foundation requires appropriate reports and evaluation on the outcomes of the project or organisation funded, identifying the effectiveness and benefits to both community and business.

Diamond Trading Company

17 Charterhouse Street, London EC1N 6RA
0171-404 4444; Fax: 0171-430 1821

Correspondent: Alastair Gordon, Secretary to the Oppenheimer Charitable Trust

Chief officers: n/a

Year end	Turnover	Pre-tax profit
3/10/94	n/a	n/a

Nature of company business
Principal activities: mining of gem and industrial diamonds; marketing through the Central Selling Organisation of diamonds produced by the group and other producers; manufacture and marketing of synthetic diamond and related hard materials for use in industry; management of a portfolio of international investments in mining, industrial and finance companies.

UK employees: n/a

Charitable donations
1994: £103,000
1993: £119,000

Community support policy

In 1961, the Oppenheimer Charitable Trust was established to channel the donations of the Diamond Companies of the De Beers Group.

De Beers Consolidated Mines Ltd does not operate in this country and channels its donations through the Anglo American and De Beers Chairmans Fund in South Africa.

The Oppenheimer Charitable Trust is managed by four trustees, who are senior executives of The Central Selling Organisation. In 1996/97, the trust had an income of £80,000 including £46,000 from the company. £75,000 was given in grants, up from £52,000 the previous year. No further information was available for this year, or for the previous year.

In 1994/95, the income was £84,000 all of which was awarded in grants. Only registered charities are supported. Nearly three quarters of the grants are small scale, between £100 and £500. The larger grants went to Victoria & Albert Museum (Jain Exhibition) (£25,000), Benefactors of the Victoria & Albert and Book Aid International (£5,000 each), Royal Opera House Trust (£4,500), Council for Christians & Jews and Commonwealth Society for the Deaf (£2,500 each), and Leonard Cheshire Foundation International (£2,000). There were over 100 smaller grants given in the fields of medicine, heritage, welfare and conservation. Recipients included Artsline, British Museum, Goldsmith's, Silversmith's & Jewellers Benevolent Institution, Institute of Mining & Metallurgy, National Back Pain Association, Riding for the Disabled, SCOPE and Spitalfields Festival.

The trust has no assets or investments. In general, contributions are made for the well-being/benefit of people in areas where the companies of the De Beers group operate. In the UK there is a preference for the London area, particularly causes related to health and welfare.

Applications

Grants are made in three ways: by application to the trustees; by recommendation to the trustees; and on the initiative of the trustees themselves.

Dixons Group plc

Maylands Avenue, Hemel Hempstead, Hertfordshire HP2 7TG
01442-353000

Correspondent: Stephen O'Brien, Corporate Affairs Officer

Chief officers: *Chairman:* Sir Stanley Kalms; *Chief Executive:* John Clare

Year end	Turnover	Pre-tax profit
2/5/98	£2,774,000,000	£219,000,000

Nature of company business
Electronic consumer goods retailers.

Main subsidiaries include: Coverplan Insurance Services PLC; Currys Group PLC; DN Computer Services PLC; DSG Retail Ltd; Mastercare Coverplan Service Agreements Ltd; Mastercare Service & Distribution Ltd; The Link Store Ltd; Byte Computer Superstores Ltd.

Charitable donations
1998: £564,988
1997: £524,874
1996: £450,000
1995: £280,000
1994: £280,000
Membership: *ABSA BitC*

Community support policy

The company gives assistance through financial support, staff time and contributions in kind. The company is a member of Business in the Community and ABSA.

Charitable donations: The company supports all types of charities concentrating on education, medical research, welfare, youth and the arts, enterprise/training and environment/heritage. All giving for the group is centralised. Requests from national charities are administered by the Dixons Foundation Committee. Grants range from £100 to £10,000. Local branches have no budgets for appeals, and local appeals are forwarded to head office. Gift vouchers may be given.

Dixons Foundation is a registered charity (Charity Commission number 1053215). The trustees are Sir Stanley Kalms, Mark Souhami and Geoffrey Budd. The trust was registered in 1996 and in 1997 had an income of £541,000 including £500,000 from the company. The year end is different to that of the company, explaining the slightly different figures.

In 1997, the trust gave a total of £616,000 in over 1,480 grants. The management and administration expenses were only £315 and the balance at the year end was £706,000. The largest grants were £200,000 to London Business School (see education category below) and £100,000 to King's College School of Medicine and Dentistry (to which the company has made a five-year commitment of £500,000). There is an ongoing commitment to support Dixons City Technology College which received £67,500 in 1997.

Other larger grants were to Institute for Policy Research Foundation (£25,000), Breakthrough Breast Cancer (£20,000) and International Shakespeare Globe Centre Ltd (£17,625). Five organisations received £10,000: Oxford Centre for Hebrew & Jewish Studies, Richmond College – The American International University in London, Scout Association, Technology Colleges Trust and Young Enterprise. There were eight grants of £5,000 and a further 23 of £1,000, especially in the fields outlined above. £51,000 was given in smaller grants of less than £1,000.

The company supports CREATE, a training project for long-term unemployed people, by providing end-of-life white goods, which are refurbished by CREATE members. PC World stores operate collection facilities for the recycling of toner cartridges. The proceeds benefit the Cancer & Leukaemia in Childhood Fund.

Education: This remains a priority for the company which continues to sponsor Bradford City Technology college and the Chair of Business Ethics & Social Responsibility at the London Business School. It has also equipped academic staff at the University of North London with laptop computers as part of a £90,000 investment over three years and has implemented a programme to encourage the use of CD-ROM technology in schools. The group is a major sponsor of the IT for All initiative, aimed at bringing information technology to a wider audience. It is planning to sponsor free computer seminars at PC World stores.

Fundraising: The company set up the Dixons Charity Fundraising Scheme in April 1992. In 1996/97, employees raised more than £20,000 for charity which was matched £ for £ by a group donation to Mencap. The sale of badges in-store raised a further £57,000. Macmillan Cancer Relief also benefited from £30,000 as a result of badge sales. Over £34,000 was raised for the Heart of Britain project at the Royal Brompton Hospital through the sale of single use cameras and film processing in Dixons stores.

Employee involvement: A payroll deduction scheme is operated. Staff are allowed time off for activity of community benefit as well as being encouraged to become volunteers in their own time. The company has also seconded staff to enterprise initiatives.

Exclusions

No response to circular appeals. No support for appeals from individuals, overseas projects, single expeditions or secondment.

Applications

All charity requests are put before a committee on a regular basis and should be made in writing to the Secretary to the Dixons Foundation.

Dow Chemical Company Ltd

No 2 Heathrow Boulevard, 284 Bath Road, West Drayton, Middlesex UB7 0DQ
0181-917 5000; Fax: 0181-917 5400
Website: www.dow.com

Correspondent: Jane C Mackey, Public Affairs

Chief officers: n/a

Year end	Turnover	Pre-tax profit
31/12/97	£380,000,000	n/a

Nature of company business
The company is a worldwide manufacturer and supplier of chemicals and performance products, plastics, hydrocarbons and energy, and consumer specialities including agricultural products and consumer products.

UK employees: 358

Charitable donations
1997: £70,000
1996: £71,967
1995: n/a
1994: £60,000
1993: £83,460
Membership: %Club

Community support policy

Dow donates more than $18 million each year worldwide with most support meeting at least one of the following criteria:

- addresses a demonstrated need in a city/community in which the company has a presence
- provides an opportunity for a hands-on science experience for students below the college level, thus improving the pool of talented students from which future employees can be chosen
- supports a university project or programme involving science, engineering, business or other related areas that also improve the pool of talented students from which future employees can be chosen
- enhances the environment.

In the UK, the company is a member of the PerCent Club and has established criteria for donations. The main focus is charities and organisations Dow employees are involved with and the communities where the company has plants and offices. There is some preference, however, for appeals connected with children/youth, education, enterprise/training, environment/heritage, fundraising events, science/technology, sickness/disability and social welfare. The company operates a payroll giving scheme and matches employee fundraising.

A main beneficiary during 1998 was the Queen Elizabeth Foundation for Disabled People.

Exclusions

No response to circular appeals. No support for advertising in charity brochures; animal welfare charities;

appeals from individuals; the arts; elderly people; medical research; overseas projects; political appeals; religious appeals or sport.

Applications

All donations are identified by the company through its donations guidelines. Unsolicited applications/blanket appeal letters and charity advertising will not be considered.

Dresdner Kleinwort Benson

20 Fenchurch Street, London EC3P 3DB
0171-623 8000

Correspondent: Jennifer Emptage, Administrator, Kleinwort Benson Charitable Trust

Chief officer: *Chairman:* Lord Walker

Year end	Turnover	Pre-tax profit
31/12/96	n/a	n/a

Nature of company business
Investment banking.

UK employees: 2,600

Charitable donations
1996: £310,500
1995: £294,000
1994: £310,286
1993: £248,000

Total community contributions: £392,500

Membership: *BitC %Club*

Community support policy

Community contributions include secondments, sponsorship and support for enterprise agencies. The company is a member of the PerCent Club and Business in the Community.

Charitable donations: Grants range from £250 to £1,000. Most grants are channelled through the Kleinwort Benson Charitable Trust. Only registered charities are supported and normally charities will receive no more than one donation within a 12-month period.

The trust was established in 1979. In 1997, it had assets of £57,000 and an income of £263,000, £250,000 of which was from the company. The trust gave over 150 grants totalling £247,000. Donations were principally made in the fields of medicine, welfare, youth, conservation, inner cities and the arts. Support is mainly directed to national charities rather than to local charities and sympathetic consideration is given to charities with which staff members of the Dresdner Kleinwort Benson Group have an active involvement.

There were seven grants of £10,000 or more to: Alzheimer's Disease Society, ChildLine and ME Association (£12,500), Atlantic College (£11,900), Treloar Trust (£11,000), Hackney Music Development Trust (£10,500) and WaterAid (£10,000). Business in the Community and Glyndebourne Festival Opera both received just over £5,000 and LENTA Trust, Imperial War Museum Trust (Holocaust Exhibition) and United Kingdom Historic Building Preservation Trust received £5,000 each.

Over 60 grants were for £1,000 to £3,000, given to a wide range of charities such as Bach Choir, Belfast City Mission, British Brain and Spine Foundation, Centre for Economic Policy Research, Centrepoint, London Wildlife Trust, National Literacy Trust, Neonatal Special Baby Care Fund and Raleigh International. Other grants were for £350 to £750, with most being for £500.

Employee involvement: The company operates the Give As You Earn payroll giving scheme and a matching funds scheme for employee fundraising. Staff are encouraged to become volunteers in their own time, financial support is given to those charities that have company staff involvement.

Enterprise: Kleinwort Benson is a member of Business in the Community. It provides a seedcorn capital fund for the East London Small Business Centre to help new businesses to start up in Tower Hamlets.

The arts: Sponsorship is mainly of events in the City of London, such as the City of London Festival and the Spitalfields Festival. A number of major arts organisations have also been supported. Typical sponsorship range is from £5,000 to £20,000.

Exclusions

The company states that appeals from individuals, or appeals from local charities or branches of national charities are unlikely to receive favourable consideration. No support for overseas projects, political or religious appeals.

Applications

In writing to the correspondent. Grant decisions at head office are made by a charities committee which meets quarterly. No grant decisions are made by subsidiary companies, but overseas grants are handled individually by overseas offices.

Sponsorship is only undertaken on rare occasions, but proposals should be addressed to Miss J A Emptage.

Eastern

Eastern Group plc

Wherstead Park, PO Box 40, Wherstead, Ipswich IP9 2AQ
01473-553409; Fax: 01473-554466
Website: www.eastern.co.uk

Correspondent: Peter Gray, Corporate Relations Manager

Chief officer: *Chairman:* Philip Tuberville

Year end	Turnover	Pre-tax profit
31/3/98	£3,475,000,000	£262,000,000

Nature of company business
Electricity supply, distribution and generation, and gas supply.

UK employees: n/a

Charitable donations

1998: £110,000
1997: £232,056
1996: £264,360
1995: £260,360
1994: £236,677

Total community contributions: £1,512,000

Membership: *ABSA BitC %Club*

Community support policy

In 1997/98, total community contributions (including sponsorships, donations, secondments, placements, staff time and help/gifts in kind) were around £1.5 million. The company is a member of the PerCent Club, Business in the Community and ABSA. The figure for total contributions of £1.5 million is based on the London Benchmarking Group model.

The company tends to favour projects in the following categories:

- the young, especially those with special needs
- older people, especially those with special needs
- the physically, mentally and socially disadvantaged
- those involved in environmental conservation
- sport for people with disabilities
- arts sponsorships.

Donations: Donations to local and national organisations generally range from £50 to £5,000. Typical examples of organisations supported in 1997/98 are: Imperial Cancer Research (£250); National Meningitis Trust (£5,000); National Back Pain Association (£500). The company encourages employee volunteering by matching employee fundraising and allowing company staff time off to volunteer. It also operates the Penny-a-Week Fund.

Sponsorship: Around 240 local and regional sponsorship grants were given in 1997/98. The main beneficiaries were Wildlife Trusts – Special Places programme in the eastern region and a national Wildflower Watch, team building/community-based projects with the National Trust, CSV – Eastern Energy for Action (employee volunteering), and the Woodland Trust – Eastern Group Woodland programme.

Education: The company has links with most of the schools in its region, offering advice and practical support covering topics related to the industry. It has also produced a number of teaching resources, projects and sponsored events.

Exclusions

No support for advertising in charity brochures, animal welfare charities, appeals from individuals, enterprise/training, overseas projects, political appeals, religious appeals, able-bodied sport, or applications for the supply of electricity or gas.

Applications

In order to ensure that all applications are treated fairly and equally, requests are put to one of three committees which operate across Eastern's region. The committees are made up of a cross-section of employees from a range of departments, ensuring that judgement is made in a fair and objective manner.

Committees meet once every three months, with all applicants hopefully being informed of the outcome within five working days.

Policy guidelines for applicants are available from the correspondent to whom applications can be made in writing, or on an application form available upon request. Sponsorship proposals should be addressed to P Gray, Corporate Relations Manager and donations requests to M Faulkner, Secretariat Manager.

Ecclesiastical Insurance Group plc

Allchurches Trust Ltd, Beaufort House, Brunswick Road, Gloucester GL1 1JZ
01452-528533; Fax: 01452-423557
Website: www.ecclesiastical-insurance.com

Correspondent: R W Clayton, Company Secretary

Chief officers: *Chairman:* M R Cornwall-Jones;
Chief Executive: G V Doswell

Year end	Turnover	Pre-tax profit
31/12/96	£207,000,000	£25,000,000

Nature of company business
Principal activity: general and long-term insurance.

UK employees: 680

Charitable donations

1996: £3,040,000
1995: £1,685,000
1994: £1,500,000
1993: £1,500,000

Community support policy

The company is owned by the Allchurches Trust Limited (Charity Commission number 263960) to which all charitable grants made by the company are given. Details of the trust can be found in *A Guide to the Major Trusts Volume 1*.

Briefly, support is given to Christian-related appeals (eg. churches, religious charities, theological colleges or schools promoting Christianity) or to charities recommended by the church, local community and those concerned with the welfare of disadvantaged or disabled people. In 1996, the company gave £3 million to the Allchurches Trust for church and charitable purposes. In the same year, the trust gave almost £2.6 million, during the last five years it has given a total of £11.2 million. The trust planned to give £3.9 million in 1997.

Exclusions

The company does not support animal welfare charities, appeals from individuals, political appeals or overseas projects.

Applications

No applications are considered by the company. Please refer to the entry for the Allchurches Trust in *A Guide to the Major Trusts Volume 1*.

Economist Newspaper Ltd

25 St James's Street, London SW1A 1HG
0171-830 7000; Fax: 0171-839 2968
Website: www.economist.com

Correspondent: Jean Simkins, Charities Liaison Officer

Chief officers: *Chairman:* Dominic Cadbury;
Chief Executive: Helen Alexander

Year end	Turnover	Pre-tax profit
31/3/98	£205,024,000	£25,076,000

Nature of company business
Principal activities: publication of *The Economist* and specialist publications including *European Voice* and, in the United States, *CFO*, *Journal of Commerce*, and *Roll Call*; supply of business information (Economist Intelligence Unit); letting of properties (Ryder Street Properties). The company owns 50% of The Economist's Bookshop.
Main subsidiaries include: Ryder Street Properties Ltd; Redhouse Press Ltd.

UK employees: n/a

Charitable donations

1998: £130,000
1997: £142,000
1996: £96,000
1995: £83,000
1994: £62,000
Membership: %Club

Community support policy

The company is a member of the PerCent Club, with the main area of non-cash support being gifts in kind.

Charitable donations: In 1997/98, the company changed the way donations were made with a view to increasing staff involvement and internal awareness of activities. 'We will respond to causes at national and international levels, concentrate on activities in some way linked to our own (learning and education, business and free enterprise) and make contributions at a sufficiently high level to produce lasting benefits to the charity. We will focus on projects where there is a possibility of monitoring the benefits and where there is scope for personal staff involvement. We have also introduced a matching scheme for individual staff members' fundraising efforts.'

A few large grants are given, but many small and staff-matching ones are made to a wide range of causes. The larger grants were to British Dyslexia Association and Talking Newspaper Association (£15,000 each), Body Positive (£10,000), Nordoff-Robbins Music Therapy (£5,000) and Elias Fawcett Trust (£1,000). Donations fall under four main headings:

(a) charities related to the company by local or business connections

(b) welfare and (usually medical) research, including self-help groups for specific medical and social problems

(c) education – from personal development by volunteering, through to some public education

(d) arts – a small proportion of the total, generally directed to grassroots projects or those overlapping other categories (eg. music for people who are disabled or institutionalised).

Projects with a 'communication' aspect, and appropriate Third World causes are also supported, as are charities concerned with elderly people, enterprise/training, sickness/disability, social welfare, women's refuges, prisoners and victims of torture. Projects are favoured which trigger matching donations from other sources or work several times over. For example, products made by disabled people were purchased through Countrywide Workshops and donated to fundraising events for other charities.

The Economist also supports the visual arts by allowing its premises to be used for exhibitions. There are frequent events throughout the year, allowing up and coming artists to display their work to the general public.

Secondment to charities has occurred in the past, but only for a short period and part-time. The company operates the Give As You Earn payroll giving scheme and matches employee fundraising.

Exclusions

The Economist Charitable Trust does not support appeals from non-charities, circular appeals, applications of a chain-letter type, gala charity events, advertising in charity brochures, appeals from individuals, larger national appeals, church restoration appeals, politically sensitive organisations, organisations of a religious or denominational nature, single service (among forces) charities, arts sponsorship (see above) or appeals from ordinary educational establishments (eg. schools, university building funds). Special schools or projects for disabled students are the exception to this rule.

Applications

In writing to the correspondent at: 4 Parsonage Lane, Bishop's Stortford, Hertfordshire CM23 5BE.

The Economist Charitable Trust is run by a small team of staff volunteers. Applications can be made at any time. No donations are made in December.

The New York and Asia Pacific offices have small independent appeals budgets.

Advice to applicants: The company states that multiple approaches are wasteful and counter-productive, particularly when they are addressed to directors who retired some time ago, indicating use of out-of-date lists. A few applications each year are rejected simply because they are badly presented. Many more fail because their deadlines for events are far too close when they apply. Applicants are also advised that if they are asked for additional information, this is a sign of interest in the project and not the opposite.

EDS International Ltd

Matheson House, Grange Central, Telford TF3 4HQ
01952-290044

Correspondent: Frank Mullin, Manager

Chief officer: *Chairman:* J A Bateman

Year end	Turnover	Pre-tax profit
31/12/96	£819,636,000	(£12,077,000)

Nature of company business
The principal activity is information technology.
Main subsidiaries include: Electronic Data Systems.

UK employees: 9,148

Charitable donations
1996: £97,000
1995: £26,000
1994: £17,000
Membership: *BitC*

Community support policy

The company's charitable donations rose markedly in 1996 to almost £100,000. It supports a wide range of causes but has a preference for local schools, hospitals and appeals and events that could benefit employees or their families. Preference is given to local charities in areas of company presence, appeals relevant to the company's business and charities in which a member of staff is involved.

The main areas of non-cash support are arts sponsorship, good-cause sponsorship and training schemes. Donations of old computers and office machinery are also made.

Exclusions

No support for advertising in charity brochures, appeals from individuals, purely denominational (religious) appeals, overseas projects or local appeals not in areas of company presence.

Applications

In writing to the correspondent.

Eidos plc

Wimbledon Bridge House, 1 Hartfield Road, Wimbledon, London SW19 3RU
0181-636 3000
Website: www.eidos.co.uk

Correspondent: John Davies, Marketing Director

Chief officer: *Chairman:* I Livingstone

Year end	Turnover	Pre-tax profit
31/3/98	£137,234,000	£16,507,000

Nature of company business
The principal activity is the development and publishing of computer and entertainment software. It also continues to be involved in the design, manufacture and sale of video compression and video editing software, and has invested in the business of advanced digital video graphics and record production.

Charitable donations
1998: £162,000
1997: £47,218

Community support policy

The charitable donations have risen substantially over the last year. In 1997, donations totalled £47,218, which according to the company annual report relates to payments of fees and sponsorship for students studying on courses of relevance to Eidos.

Applications

In writing to the correspondent.

Electrocomponents plc

4240 Nash Court, Oxford Business Park, Oxford OX4 2RU
01865-711234; Fax: 01865-783400
Website: www.electrocomponents.com

Correspondent: Jeffrey Hewitt, Group Finance Director

Chief officers: *Chairman:* R C G Cotterill;
Chief Executive: R A Lawson

Year end	Turnover	Pre-tax profit
31/3/98	£662,000,000	£118,000,000

Nature of company business
The main activity is the marketing of electronic, electrical and industrial supplies and services to industrial and commercial customers and retailers.

Main subsidiaries include: RS Components Ltd; Pact International Ltd.

Charitable donations
1998: £39,432
1997: £58,099
1996: £30,815
1995: £37,822
1994: £37,238

Community support policy

Most of the company's support in recent years (about £25,000 a year) has gone to the City Technology College in Corby. A further £6,000 is given to the relevant trade charity, with the remainder, about £8,000 in 1997/98 (£27,000 the previous year), given in small grants to local charities where the company operates and appeals relevant to the company business. Grants to such charities range from £100 to £500.

Exclusions

No support for appeals from individuals, purely denominational (religious) appeals or local appeals not in areas of company presence.

Applications

In writing to the correspondent.

Elementis plc

One Great Tower Street, London EC3R 5AH
0171-711 1400; Fax: 0171-711 1404

Correspondent: Mrs H M Cowin, Elementis Charitable Fund

Chief officers: *Chairman:* J M Fry; *Chief Executive:* W Turcan

Year end	Turnover	Pre-tax profit
31/12/97	£1,919,000,000	(£113,000,000)

Nature of company business
Principal activity of the group is: chemical and industrial.

Main subsidiaries include: Linatex; Elementis Chrome; Elementis Pigments; Elementis Specialities.

UK employees: n/a

Charitable donations

1996: £124,789
1995: £129,673
1994: £104,812
1993: £95,507

Community support policy

Charitable donations: The figures shown are for the group as a whole. Roughly half is dispensed through the Elementis (formerly Harrisons & Crosfield) Charitable Fund (Charity Commission number 277899) and half through subsidiary companies and branches at local level. The company is reviewing its current policy and as such the following information may not be valid in future.

The fund's policy is: 'to support charities providing practical help to disadvantaged people'. Grants are mostly one-off or recurrent for up to four years. There are also some annual donations. Preference is given to charities in which a member of staff is involved. The company prefers to support children/youth, education, elderly people, enterprise/training, overseas projects, sickness/disability and social welfare charities. The main beneficiaries in 1997 were Business in the Community, Macmillan Cancer Relief, John Grooms Association for Disabled People, Carers National Association, RNID and Prince's Youth Business Trust.

Enterprise: The company gives financial support to local enterprise agencies.

Education: The company is involved in local education/business partnerships. It operates work experience schemes for pupils and teachers and provides educational materials for schools.

The arts: The company sponsors the London Philharmonic Orchestra. Applications are not invited for sponsorship.

Exclusions

Applications are not invited from either charities or individuals. Local appeals are rarely considered at group level. The following are NEVER considered: requests for advertising in souvenir brochures, sponsorship of social functions, telephone or written requests from professional fundraisers.

Applications

Applications must be in writing, including a copy of the charity's latest report and accounts, and should be sent to the Elementis Charitable Fund, but note the above.

Elf Petroleum UK PLC

1 Claymore Drive, Bridge of Don, Aberdeen AB23 8GB
01224-233000; Fax: 01224-233838

Correspondent: Public Relations Co-ordinator

Chief officer: *Managing Director:* Pierre Godec

Year end	Turnover	Pre-tax profit
31/12/97	£2,004,000,000	£438,000,000

Nature of company business
Oil and gas exploration and production.

UK employees: n/a

Charitable donations

1997: £451,174
1996: £696,845
1995: £371,751
1994: n/a
1993: £667,260
Membership: *ABSA*

Community support policy

The figures we have obtained from various sources have been for Elf Petroleum UK plc. In 1995, 1996 and 1997, total charitable donations have been £371,751, £696,845 and £451,174, respectively.

On contacting Elf Petroleum UK, we were consistently referred to the Aberdeen office as the company's head office and the office from where donations were made. In the UK, Elf's main operating company is Elf Exploration UK Ltd, based in Aberdeen. However, we were informed that these donations figures did not refer to Elf Exploration UK. It may be that it is the total figure for all Elf companies in the UK, although they operate as separate companies and administer their own donations.

Ellis

Donations policy: Elf Exploration UK PLC has a limited budget used to support local causes. It is committed to supporting the arts, the environment, education and social welfare groups within the communities in which it operates (principally Aberdeen and the Orkney Islands).

Assistance is given to charities in which a member of company staff is involved. Annual major donations range from £1,000 to £20,000. Monthly smaller donations range from £50 to £500.

Exclusions

No response to circular appeals. No support for advertising in charity brochures, appeals from individuals, purely denominational (religious) appeals, local appeals not in areas of company presence, large national appeals or overseas projects.

Applications

In writing to the correspondent.

Other information: Elf Exploration is a subsidiary of Elf Aquitaine, headquartered in France. Elf Aquitaine appears to have four operating companies in the UK, all of which act autonomously. They are: AGAS (Associated Gas Supplies Ltd), Elf Atochem UK Ltd, Elf Exploration UK PLC and Elf Oil UK Ltd.

Ellis & Everard plc

46 Peckover Street, Bradford BD1 5BD
01274-377000; Fax: 01274-377088
Website: www.elliseverard.com

Correspondent: Donna Rothwell, Administrator

Chief officers: *Chairman:* J F Taylor; *Chief Executive:* P S Wood

Year end	Turnover	Pre-tax profit
30/4/98	£732,000,000	£32,100,000

Nature of company business
The principal activities are the sales, marketing and distribution of chemicals and polymers.

Main subsidiaries include: Chemitrade; G Fiske & Co; Distrupol.

Charitable donations

1998: £42,000
1997: £36,000
1996: £40,000
1995: £36,000

Community support policy

Charitable donations are handled by the Charities Aid Foundation, with a preference for children and youth, and medical causes.

Exclusions

No response to circular appeals. No support for appeals from individuals, purely denominational (religious) appeals or local appeals not in areas of company presence.

Applications

In writing to the correspondent.

EMAP plc

1 Lincoln Court, Lincoln Road, Peterborough, Cambridgeshire PE1 2RF
01733-568900; Fax: 01733-312115
Website: www.emap.com/plc

Correspondent: David Grigson, Financial Director

Chief officers: *Chairman:* Robin W Miller; *Chief Executive:* Kevin Hand

Year end	Turnover	Pre-tax profit
31/3/98	£772,600,000	£141,700,000

Nature of company business
Principal activities: publishing consumer magazines, providing business-to-business communications media, and operating radio and cable TV channels.

Main subsidiaries include: Box Television; Kiss FM Radio; Metro Radio; Piccadilly Radio; Radio Aire; Radio City; Radio Hallam; Red Rose Radio; TFM Radio; Viking Radio; CAP Motor Research; Glenigan; Inter Garden Promotions; LGC Communications; MH Holdings (UK); Sewells International; Trade Promotion Services.

Main locations: Aylesbury; Burgess Hill; Kettering; Leamington; Nuneaton; Peterborough.

UK employees: 4,539

Charitable donations

1998: £81,000
1997: £57,000
1996: £64,000
1995: £56,000
1994: £48,000

Community support policy

Recipients of major donations are selected by staff ballot, currently the NSPCC is receiving most of the company's support. Only charities in which a member of company staff is involved will be supported.

In addition, many charitable appeals are supported by the group's magazines, exhibitions and radio stations. This support is not quantified, but presumably would mean that the company is giving more than the above figures would indicate, which is equivalent to 0.06% of pre-tax profits.

Exclusions

If a member of company staff is not involved no support will be given.

Applications

The contact for charitable donations is the correspondent above, but the current policy means that unsolicited appeals are very unlikely to receive support.

EMI Group plc

4 Tenterden Street, London W1A 2AY
0171-355 4848; Fax: 0171-495 1307
Website: www.emigroup.com

Correspondent: Melanie Gant, Head of CCI

Chief officer: *Chairman:* Sir Colin Southgate

Year end	Turnover	Pre-tax profit
31/3/98	£3,309,000,000	£307,100,000

Nature of company business
EMI covers all aspects of the music industry from music recording and publishing through to manufacture, marketing and distribution.

Main subsidiaries include: Chrysalis Records Ltd; Virgin Records Ltd.

UK employees: 5,954

Charitable donations

1998: £2,100,000
1997: £3,700,000
Membership: *ABSA BitC*

Community support policy

EMI Group's charitable donations for 1997/98 in the UK, including the Music Sound Foundation, totalled £2.1 million. Worldwide contributions totalled £3.6 million.

Support is divided between three key areas: employee initiatives, charitable donations and support of the arts. The company is a member of Business in the Community.

'As a permanent record of its 1997 Centenary, EMI established the Music Sound Foundation (Charity Commission number 1055434). The foundation is a multi-million pound charitable trust dedicated to improving access to music by everyone for generations to come. Accordingly, at the start of our new financial year we altered our donations policy to reflect this and all of our donations and sponsorship efforts are now targeted to the Music Sound Foundation.'

The foundation's trustees are: Sir Colin Southgate, Chairman; Jim Beach; William Cavendish; Ruth Edge; Leslie Hall; David Hughes; Steve O'Rourke; Rupert Perry; Ken Townsend. The accounts on file at the Charity Commission cover the 11-month period to 31 March 1997. The objects are the 'promotion and furtherance of education in and knowledge of the art of music. It aims to educate the public and in particular young people in all aspects of music (including without limitation, its composition, the development of musical instruments and methods of sound reproduction and the history of music) and towards the relief of poverty by the provision of grants to enable people in need to buy instruments and music tuition which they would otherwise be unable to afford'.

In 1996/97, the trust received £3.9 million from EMI Group plc, no grants were made.

Criteria

Having altered the company policy to target charitable efforts almost entirely to the Music Sound Foundation, only small ad hoc donations are now made to those projects which relate to the company's business and which create learning opportunities and encourage improved environmental performance.

The criteria are:

- The achievement of a well-balanced programme, which is appropriate to company business and reflects the current needs of today's society and environment. Support is divided between three key areas: employee initiatives, charitable donations and support for the arts.
- To encourage and support the commitment, enthusiasm and participation of employees who are involved in voluntary activities within their local communities, and give consideration to projects which they put forward and in which they become involved. (The company operates the payroll giving scheme, and an employee-matching scheme for UK employees.)
- Financial donations must be tax efficient and therefore of maximum benefit to the recipient and maximum value for the company.'

Our policy relates to those activities supported from the Group's corporate headquarters in the UK. A committee considers all written requests against the above guidelines and on their merit. In addition, EMI Group's businesses decide individually where to focus their own charitable giving and sponsorship resources.'

Categories supported

Music in the Community – support for organisations whose primary activities promote, enhance or increase the understanding of music. The EMI Group is a member of ABSA and a corporate member of several arts organisations including the Royal Albert Hall, Glyndebourne, the Tate Gallery, the ENO and the Royal Opera House.

Education – support for organisations which provide educational or self-development opportunities for disadvantaged young people, including the RSA Campaign for Learning (£25,000) and RSA Leadership Lectures (£14,000).

Environment – support for organisations which seek to promote and raise awareness, educate and strive to improve the environment. Among those supported are Westminster Initiatve (£10,000) and Green Screen (£20,000).

Exclusions

EMI Group will not fund medical research, secondments or individuals seeking sponsorship, expeditions, sporting activities, wildlife, natural disasters or capital building programmes. No donations are made to political, sectarian, religious or racist organisations.

Applications

Applications (including sponsorship proposals) should be in writing to the correspondent.

Empire

Empire Stores Group plc

18 Canal Road, Bradford BD99 4XB
01274-729544; Fax: 01274-843819

Correspondent: F W Oakes, Company Secretary

Chief officer: *Chairman:* J B Tefra

Year end	Turnover	Pre-tax profit
31/1/95	£250,131,000	£12,376,000

Nature of company business
Mail order retailing. The company is part of the French company Pinault Printemps–Redoute.

UK employees: n/a

Charitable donations
1995: £62,000
1994: £15,520
Total community contributions: £81,000

Community support policy

Community contributions in 1995 totalled £81,000 including £19,000 in the form of goods, at cost price, arts sponsorship and support for enterprise agencies. We have been unable to update these figures, although the budget for charity support is now about £100,000 a year. The following information was provided by the company.

The group's policy states that they prefer to deal with registered charities and that cash donations are very rarely made outside the current Gift Aid of £20,000 a year to the Charities Aid Foundation Scheme. Under the scheme, CAF issues cheques/vouchers which the company secretary draws down in favour of successful applicants. About 20 appeals of various types are received each week.

Cash/CAF donations are given to registered charities local to the company's operating sites in Wakefield and Bradford. Preference is given to charities associated with children, teenagers, poverty, family service units, local employment ventures, cancer, deafness, heart disease, kidney problems, blindness and local efforts to raise funds for Third World projects.

In addition (but this is not restricted to registered charities), catalogue goods are donated via a free gift voucher system. This enables donees to 'buy' goods from one of the staff shops in Wakefield and Bradford. The maximum limit for a voucher is £250, but usually £100.

Local registered charities are also offered special Charity Staff Shop cards so they can buy items for fundraising events. Prices are usually 30% off catalogue selling prices.

Exclusions
No support for appeals from individuals, advertising in charity brochures, political or religious appeals, large national appeals or overseas projects. The company generally does not 'sponsor' events connected with general arts or sporting events or fundraising events for one or several charities.

Applications
In writing to the correspondent. Policy guidelines/advice for applicants is available from the correspondent.

English China Clays plc

1015 Arlington Business Park, Theale,
Reading, Berkshire RG7 4SA
0118-930 4010; Fax: 0118-930 9501

Correspondent: Will Verrall, Director of Human Resources

Chief officers: n/a

Year end	Turnover	Pre-tax profit
31/12/97	£845,000,000	£89,000,000

Nature of company business
English China Clays plc is the holding company of a group engaged in the production and sale of industrial mineral pigments and speciality chemicals.

Main subsidiaries include: ECC Overseas Investments Ltd.

UK employees: 6,290

Charitable donations
1997: £300,000
1996: £300,000
1995: £300,000
1994: £300,000
1993: £327,000

Community support policy

Donations totalling £300,000 were paid for charitable purposes and to local causes for the benefit of group employees. This includes a contribution of £50,000 to St Austell China Clay Museum Ltd in support of its ongoing promotion of the history of the china clay industry. Some donations are made through the English China Clays Charitable Trust (Charity Commission number 326184).

Support is given to local charities in areas of company presence (in Cornwall/Devon; applications from Berkshire are forwarded on to Berkshire Community Trust for consideration by the trustees, the company is a founder member), to appeals relevant to company business and to charities in which a member of company staff is involved. Grants range from £200 to £10,000. Preferred areas of support are children/youth, education, elderly people, enterprise/training and environment/heritage. The company also supports fundraising events and advertising in charity brochures.

Main beneficiaries in 1996 included Wheal Martyn Museum, St Stephen-in-Brannel Church Council, Fowey Community School, St Dennis Country Primary School and West of England's Bandsmen's Festival.

Exclusions
No support for any charity not in areas of company presence or which does not have a connection with the company or its employees.

Applications
In writing to the correspondent.

Enterprise Oil plc

Grand Buildings, Trafalgar Square, London WC2N 5ES
0171-925 4000; Fax: 0171-925 4321
Website: www.entoil.com

Correspondent: Mrs Jane Stevenson, Secretary – Donations Committee

Chief officers: *Chairman:* Sir Graham Hearne;
Chief Executive: Pierre Jungels

Year end	Turnover	Pre-tax profit
31/12/97	£947,000,000	£255,000,000

Nature of company business
Principal activities: oil and gas exploration and production, principally on the UK continental shelf, and overseas.
Main subsidiaries include: Saxon Oil Ltd.

UK employees: n/a

Charitable donations

1997: £199,884
1996: £228,300
1995: £196,790
1994: £280,248
1993: £188,401
Membership: *BitC*

Community support policy

Donations are given from head office only. There is a preference for projects in areas where the company operates and appeals where a member of staff is involved. Large national appeals are supported, particularly social welfare, medical, children and youth, elderly, animal welfare charities, education, environment and organisations concerned with disabled people. Occasionally the company may support overseas, religious, sports or science appeals.

During 1997, the group supported a wide range of community organisations, projects and charities. The environment featured strongly, with a prize of £25,000 being presented to the winner of the biennial Enterprise Oil/Heriot-Watt Environmental Award. Support was also given to Forum for the Future, the Oxford Centre for the Environment, Ethics and Society, and the Scottish Wildlife Trust's Web of Life initiative which promotes knowledge of biodiversity in Scotland. The group again supported the Young People's Trust for the Environment, with other beneficiaries including St Wilfrid's Hospice in Chichester, The Urban Mission Centre, Action in Addiction and Mencap.

In addition to community development, the main areas of support are good-cause sponsorship and gifts in kind.

Employee involvement: The company operates a payroll giving scheme. It also matches £ for £ monies raised by employee fundraising. In 1997, for instance, a number of staff took part in a 217-mile ride across Wales on behalf of the Aberdeen Royal Infirmary Leukaemia Research Unit, raising a total of £31,000. Staff fundraising also assisted the Evelina Family Trust and the British Heart Foundation.

The arts: The company sponsors the arts.

Exclusions
No support for advertising in charity brochures, political appeals, fundraising events or appeals from individuals.

Applications
In writing to the correspondent. A donations committee, consisting of the Chairman, Corporate Affairs Director and Secretary meets several times a year.

Essex & Suffolk Water plc

Hall Street, Chelmsford, Essex CM2 0HH
01245-491234; Fax: 01245-350271
Website: www.eswater.co.uk

Correspondent: Roger Griffin, Director of Customer Services

Chief officers: *Chairman:* Antony Haynes;
Managing Director: John Cuthbert

Year end	Turnover	Pre-tax profit
31/12/97	£82,268,000	£24,421,000

Nature of company business
The company is concerned with the treatment and supply of water in parts of the counties of Essex, Suffolk, Norfolk and parts of East London. It is a member of the Suez Lyonnaise des Eaux Group.

UK employees: 706

Charitable donations

1997: £38,857 (nine months)
1997: £52,900
1996: £150,000
1995: £71,000
1994: £37,000

Community support policy

The company states in its 1998 annual report that it has continued to support the local community through charitable donations and continues to emphasise those projects with an environmental theme and those involving young people and education. Donations are generally between £25 and £500.

Applications
In writing to the correspondent.

Esso UK plc

Esso House, Ermyn Way, Leatherhead, Surrey KT22 8UX
01372-222312; Fax: 01372-223222

Correspondent: Stella Crossley, Community Affairs Adviser

Chief officers: *Chairman:* Keith Taylor;
Managing Director: I W Upson

Year end	Turnover	Pre-tax profit
31/12/97	£9,332,900,000	£551,700,000

Eurotunnel

Nature of company business
Principal activities: the exploration for, production, transportation and sale of crude oil, natural gas and natural gas liquids; the refining, distribution and marketing of petroleum products within the UK. The company's interests are spread throughout the UK and include a refinery at Fawley on Southampton Water, a research centre at Abingdon, major terminals in Birmingham, Purfleet and West London, and offices at Leatherhead.

UK employees: 3,399

Charitable donations
1997: £1,497,187
1996: £1,495,351
1995: £1,511,423
1994: £1,541,400
1993: £1,560,000

Total community contributions: £2,719,361

Membership: *BitC*

Community support policy

Total community contributions in 1997 were £2,719,316, just over half of which was given in charitable donations.

The company gives priority to three main areas: environment, education (particularly in the areas of science, technology and maths) and to projects in areas which are near main employing points – New Forest, Abingdon and Leatherhead. Examples of support include animal welfare charities, energy efficiency, social welfare, sickness/disability charities and the arts.

Esso proactively plans its programmes and likes to strike up long-term working partnerships with the organisations it works with in the voluntary sector. Almost all funds are committed at the beginning of the year, therefore unsolicited requests are rarely supported. The company carries out advertising and promotion on behalf of the charities it works with. It gives financial support to employee volunteering schemes and operates a payroll giving scheme (Give As You Earn).

In 1997, main grant beneficiaries included: The National Gallery, Wildlife Trusts, NEA, the Groundwork Trust, and the major millennium campaign for the company – Trees of Time and Place. The company is a member of Business in the Community.

Exclusions
No response to circular appeals. No support for appeals from individuals, fundraising events, religious appeals, political appeals or overseas projects.

Applications
The company responds to all appeals received, but in view of the policy outlined above unsolicited appeals are very rarely successful.

Eurotunnel plc

PO Box 2000, Folkestone, Kent CT18 8XY
01303-272222

Correspondent: Michelle Fox, Public Affairs Manager

Chief officers: *Chairmen:* P Ponsalle; R Malpas; *Chief Executive:* Georges Christian Chazot

Year end	Turnover	Pre-tax profit
31/12/97	£456,155,000	(£611,362,000)

Nature of company business
Tunnel construction.

Main subsidiaries include: The Channel Tunnel Group Ltd; Le Shuttle Holidays Ltd; Orbital Park Ltd.

UK employees: n/a

Charitable donations
1997: £74,823
1996: £120,383
1995: £124,601
1994: £111,000

Community support policy
There is a preference for local charities in areas of company presence and appeals relevant to the company's business. Preferred areas of support are children and youth, education, environment and heritage.

Exclusions
No response to circular appeals. No grants for fundraising events, appeals from individuals, purely denominational (religious) appeals, local appeals not in areas of company presence or large national appeals.

Applications
In writing to the correspondent.

Evans of Leeds plc

Millshaw, Ring Road Beeston, Leeds LS11 8EG
0113-271 1888; Fax: 0113-271 8487
Email: evansofleeds@compuserve.com

Correspondent: Claire White, Personal Assistant to the Personnel Director

Chief officers: *Chairman:* J M F Padovan; *Managing Director:* J D Bell

Year end	Turnover	Pre-tax profit
31/3/98	£30,611,000	£13,866,000

Nature of company business
The principal activities of the group are property investment and development.

Main subsidiaries include: Astra House Ltd; Furnival Estates Ltd; Jangay Investment Ltd; Lichfield Securities Ltd; Lonsdale Properties Ltd; Marchington Properties Ltd; Millshaw Property Co Ltd; Mulgate Investments Ltd; Speylands Ltd; Tern Hill Securities Ltd; White Rose Property Investments Ltd; Redvers Development Enterprises Ltd.

UK employees: 73

Charitable donations
1998: £33,490
1997: £54,149
1996: £25,789
1995: £13,105
1994: £13,341

Community support policy
We have no information on the charitable donations policy of the company. The level of giving has decreased from over £50,000 in 1997, although pre-tax profits are fractionally higher.

Applications
In writing to the correspondent.

Express Dairies plc

Express House, Meridian East, Meridian Business Park, Leicester LE3 2TP
0116-281 6281; Fax: 0116-281 6283
Website: www.express-dairies.co.uk

Correspondent: Susanna Stott, Personnel Department

Chief officers: *Chairman:* C Haskins;
Chief Executive: R C N Davidson

Year end	Turnover	Pre-tax profit
31/3/98	n/a	n/a

Nature of company business
The company is the UK's leading supplier of milk and cream. The company comprises five businesses: Express Dairies Direct Service, Express Dairies Major Retail, Express Dairies Distribution, Express Dairies Ingredients and Express Dairies Ireland.
Main subsidiaries include: Woodgate Farms Dairy.
Main brands include: Dale Farm; Express.
Main locations: Leicester; Wakefield; Ashby de la Zouch; York; Alfreton; Ballymena.
UK employees: 5,458

Charitable donations
1998: £69,231 (three months)
Total community contributions: £175,231

Community support policy
Express Dairies was formed on 1 March 1998 through the demerger of the dairy operations of Northern Foods plc (which has a separate entry in this guide). The first report produced by the group covers the period of three months to 31 March 1998 when charitable donations totalled £69,231. The company's total community contributions for the latest year were £175,231.

The company stated that it is actively pursuing membership of Business in the Community and the PerCent Club. The main focus of the company support programme is providing assistance to community projects with a core element of youth development. Preference is given to local charities in areas where the company operates: Liverpool, Manchester, Wakefield, Nottingham, Kirkcudbright, Nairn, Crediton, Staplemead, Ruislip, Ashby-de-la-Zouch, Middlesbrough, Northallerton, Ballymena, Belfast, Hull, Chester, Stoke-on-Trent, Wythenshawe, Uckfield, Northampton, Holme-on-Spalding-Moor, particularly those proposed by company employees and which offer the opportunity for staff involvement. The company will also support national charities working in the community field with priority being given to youth and social welfare project-based activities which assist these local communities.

Additionally, the company offers backing to Third World projects of a practical nature which help communities to improve their quality of life.

Supported organisations should ideally be registered as a charity.

Exclusions
The company will not normally consider support for animal welfare, elderly people, individuals, fundraising events, medical appeals, health charities, sport, heritage appeals, environmental projects, science and technology or charitable advertising. It will not offer funding for religious and political organisations or general funding to national charities.

Applications
In writing to the Secretary to the Social Responsibility Committee with full support for the application. The committee, comprising directors and senior executives, is scheduled to meet quarterly.

Express Newspapers plc

Ludgate House, 245 Blackfriars Road, London SE1 9UX
0171-928 8000; Fax: 0171-922 7965

Correspondent: Dawn Faulkner, Communications Manager

Chief officers: *Chairman:* Lord Stevens;
Managing Director: Stephen Grabiner

Year end	Turnover	Pre-tax profit
25/12/96	£297,340,759	£8,371,672

Nature of company business
Publishing of newspapers and periodicals.
Main brands include: Daily Express; Sunday Express; Daily Star.
UK employees: n/a

Charitable donations
1996: £304,062
1995: £300,094

Exxon

Community support policy

Support is given mainly to national charities, although local charities are considered. Preferred areas of support are children and youth, social welfare, elderly people, animal welfare, medical, education, environment/heritage, overseas projects, sport, the arts and fundraising events. Grants to national organisations range from £100 to £250 and to local organisations from £50 to £100.

The company also has an employee volunteering scheme.

Exclusions

No support for advertising in charity brochures.

Applications

In writing to the correspondent.

Exxon Chemical Ltd

Cadland Road, Hythe, Southampton SO45 3NP
01489-880880; Fax: 01489-880990
Website: www.exxon.com/exxonchemical/

Correspondent: Delia Ponter, Public Affairs Department

Chief officer: *Chairman:* S M Kennedy

Year end	Turnover	Pre-tax profit
31/12/97	£511,669,000	£61,399,000

Nature of company business
The main activities are the manufacture and marketing of a range of industrial chemicals and other speciality chemical products.

UK employees: 832

Charitable donations

1997: £50,571
1996: £50,995
1995: £26,610
1994: £7,477

Community support policy

The company prefers to support local charities in areas of company presence, especially those in which a member of staff is involved and causes concerned with children and youth, social welfare, medical, education, environment and heritage, and the arts. Grants tend to range from £100 to £2,000.

Exclusions

No support for national appeals, circular appeals, advertising in charity brochures, appeals from individuals, purely denominational (religious) appeals, overseas projects, political appeals or sports clubs.

Applications

In writing to the correspondent.

Favermead Ltd

Nour House, 6 Hill Street, London W1 7FU
0171-493 4241

Correspondent: Sally Chancellor, Secretary

Chief officers: n/a

Year end	Turnover	Pre-tax profit
31/3/95	£99,173,000	£7,762,000

Nature of company business
Property.

UK employees: n/a

Charitable donations

1995: £143,667

Community support policy

We have very little information on this company and no information on its donations policy. The figures given above were obtained from Companies House. On contacting the company we were told that any correspondence should be addressed to the Director, and charitable appeals would be considered.

Applications

In writing to the company.

Fenwick Ltd

39 Northumberland Street, Newcastle upon Tyne NE99 1AR
0191-232 5100; Fax: 0191-232 2367

Correspondent: I J Dixon, Company Secretary

Chief officer: *Chairman:* M A Fenwick

Year end	Turnover	Pre-tax profit
31/1/98	£249,368,039	£30,096,000

Nature of company business
Department stores.

UK employees: 1,937

Charitable donations

1998: £131,765
1997: £119,785
1996: £107,772
1995: £91,042

Community support policy

The company has seen a small but steady increase in its level of charitable giving over the last four years. It gives support mainly to projects in areas where it has a presence (ie. the North East, North Yorkshire, East Midlands and South East). There is a preference for: the arts; children/youth; education; elderly people; medical research; sickness/disability charities and social welfare.

The arts: Arts sponsorship has included grants to the Northern Sinfonia Orchestra, Royal Opera House Trust and Royal Shakespeare Theatre Trust.

Exclusions

No support for circular appeals, advertising in charity brochures, political appeals, overseas projects or small purely local appeals not in areas of company presence.

Applications

In writing to the correspondent. Local stores have an independent budget for appeals.

FI Group plc

Campus 300, Marylands Avenue, Hemel Hempstead, Hertfordshire HP2 7TQ
01442-233339; Fax: 01442-238400
Website: www.figroup.co.uk

Correspondent: Marion Clyde, Community Affairs Manager

Chief officers: *Chairman:* Sir Peter Thompson; *Chief Executive:* Mrs H M Cropper

Year end	Turnover	Pre-tax profit
30/4/98	£161,595,000	£10,670,000

Nature of company business
The supply of computer software services.

Charitable donations

1998: £17,018
1997: £14,572

Total community contributions: £102,500

Membership: *BitC %Club*

Community support policy

The company is a member of the PerCent Club and allocates 1% of pre-tax profits to its community programme. This totalled £102,500 in 1997/98 including £17,000 in cash donations.

The programme is focused on education and helping young homeless people by developing partnerships with voluntary organisations and schools. Staff are encouraged to contribute by volunteering their skills, experience and energy and by fundraising for charitable and educational causes.

FI operates nationwide and all offices have established programmes of support for a local community group or school. Specialist IT and business skills are provided in response to specific requests from community partners. One initiative is the development of a mentoring scheme for young homeless people following on from a similar scheme with schoolchildren.

The group also recycles office equipment into the community and provides work placements for candidates identified by its community partners.

Applications

In writing to the correspondent.

Fiat Auto (UK) Ltd

Fiat House, 266 Bath Road, Slough, Berkshire SL1 4HJ
01753-511431; Fax: 01753-536166

Correspondent: Peter Newton, Public Relations Director

Chief officer: *Managing Director:* M Blades

Year end	Turnover	Pre-tax profit
31/12/96	£704,328,000	£30,836,000

Nature of company business
Principal activity: Fiat car distributors.

UK employees: n/a

Charitable donations

1996: £78,750
1995: £64,146
1994: £53,134
1993: £42,156

Community support policy

The company has a preference for organisations working with children and youth. Donations are made through the Fiat Auto (UK) Charity (Charity Commission number 1059498). In 1997, this charity had an income of £163,000 and gave grants totalling £192,000. The main beneficiary was the Children's Society which received £100,000 with £57,000 given to the trade charity – the Motor Trade Benevolent Fund.

Exclusions

Generally no support for circular appeals, appeals from individuals, purely denominational appeals, local appeals not in areas of company presence or overseas projects.

Applications

In writing to the correspondent.

Field Group plc

Misbourne House, Badminton Court, Rectory Way, Old Amersham, Buckinghamshire HP7 0DD
01494-720200; Fax: 01494-431138
Email: marketing@fieldgroup.com

Correspondent: Anne Bond, Personnel Administrator

Chief officers: *Chairman:* F W Knight; *Chief Executive:* K Gilchrist

Year end	Turnover	Pre-tax profit
4/4/98	£245,030,000	£24,062,000

Nature of company business
The principal activity is the production of consumer packaging, specialising in the design, manufacture and sale of printed cartons, composite containers, printed labels, printed leaflets and packaging machinery systems.

Main subsidiaries include: Alvax Supplies; Field, Son & Co; Ethical Print & Packaging; E F Taylor; Tudor Labels.

Main locations: Amersham; Bradford; Bedford; Bellshill; Bourne; East Kilbride; Newcastle; Nottingham; Portsmouth; Tewkesbury; Thatcham; Yatton.

UK employees: 2,196

Filtronic

Charitable donations
1998: £43,488
1997: £40,419
1996: £38,962
1995: £36,099

Community support policy

Charitable support is mainly undertaken by local offices. In addition to the head office in Amersham, the company has sites at East Kilbride, Belshill, Newcastle upon Tyne, Bradford, Nottingham, Bourne, Bedford, Tewkesbury, Yatton, Thatcham and Portsmouth.

There is a preference for charities local to those sites/offices working in the fields of children/youth, sick and elderly people, and crime prevention. Nationally the company supports printers' charities.

The company also has a ten-year sponsorship programme with the Department of Colour Chemistry at Leeds University, ending in 2005.

Exclusions

No response to circular appeals and no support for fundraising events, advertising in charity brochures, appeals from individuals, purely denominational (religious) appeals, local appeals not in areas of company presence, large national appeals or overseas projects.

Applications

In writing to the correspondent.

Filtronic plc

The Waterfront, Salts Mill Road, Saltaire, Shipley,
West Yorkshire BD18 3TT
01274-530622; Fax: 01274-531561

Correspondent: Emma Fearnley, Personnel Assistant

Chief officer: *Chairman:* Prof J D Rhodes

Year end	Turnover	Pre-tax profit
31/5/98	£94,093,000	£11,012,000

Nature of company business
The principal activity is the design and manufacture of microwave products for cellular telecommunication systems.

UK employees: 309

Charitable donations
1998: £53,000
1997: £41,000
1996: £12,167
1995: £4,851

Community support policy

The company currently has two main charities which it supports and which are also supported by employee fundraising events. These are the Kidney Research Fund and Candlelighters. Any other support given to charities is likely to be local and small scale. There are three manufacturing sites in the UK: Shipley, Wolverhampton and Stewarton.

Applications

In writing to the correspondent.

Fine Art Developments plc

Burley House, Bradford Road, Burley-in-Wharfedale,
West Yorkshire LS29 7DZ
01943-864686

Correspondent: D Hale

Chief officers: *Chairman:* Keith Chapman; *Chief Executive:* D Anthony Johnson

Year end	Turnover	Pre-tax profit
31/3/98	£217,058,000	£7,888,000

Nature of company business
Principal activities: the sale of greeting cards, paper products, gifts and educational supplies through mail-order catalogues and the provision of trading services to national charities.

Main subsidiaries include: Care Cards; Club Centre; Collisons; Express Gifts; James Galt & Co; Home Farm Hampers; Premier Educational Supplies; Webb Ivory (Burton).

UK employees: 3,279

Charitable donations
1998: £138,176
1997: £128,663
1996: £184,167
1995: £174,068
1994: £170,571

Community support policy

The company's annual report states, of the year's contributions of £138,176, £62,518 was recharged to Creative Publishing plc in accordance with demerger arrangements.

Donations are spread by the company among more than 200 organisations with particular emphasis on those working with children and disabled people, including many less well-known charities. Donations are generally in the range of £100 to £500, although in special circumstances they can be larger.

The group also provides support to a large number of local charities through donating gifts of merchandise for fundraising purposes.

Applications

In writing to the correspondent.

FirstGroup plc

395 King Street, Aberdeen AB24 5RP
01224-650100; Fax: 01224-650140

Correspondent: Shona Byrne, Marketing Manager

Chief officers: *Chairman:* T Smallwood;
Chief Executive: M Lockhead

Year end	Turnover	Pre-tax profit
31/3/98	£795,000,000	£73,000,000

Nature of company business
The provision of passenger transport services primarily through provision of local bus and coach services and passenger railways.

Main subsidiaries include: First Aberdeen; First Badgerline; First Beeline; First Bradford; First Calderline; First Centre West; First CityLine; First Cymru; First Eastern Counties; First Eastern National; First Glasgow; First Huddersfield; First Leeds; First Leicester; First Lowland; First Manchester; First Midland Bluebird; First Midland Red; First Northampton; First PMT; First Provincial; First Southampton; First Thamesway; First Wessex; First Western National York; First Great Eastern; Great Western Trains; North Western Trains; Bristol International Airport.

UK employees: 22,819

Charitable donations
1998: £60,200
1997: £36,000
1996: £34,000
Membership: *BitC*

Community support policy
In the company's latest annual report it states: 'FirstGroup looks for sponsorship and charitable opportunities which involve working with local communities or people from them'. It has maintained its involvement as a Patron Company with Outward Bound and in June 1998 sponsored a further 30 children taking part in a week-long Outward Bound course in the Scottish Highlands. It has also established training bursaries with Save the Children and the Princess Royal Trust for Carers.

At a local level, subsidiary companies give support to local community projects. For example, First Aberdeen is undertaking a programme of fundraising events to raise £50,000 for two local and two national charities as part of its centenary celebrations.

Applications
In writing to the correspondent.

The Albert Fisher Group plc

C Sefton Park, Bells Hill, Stoke Poges,
Buckinghamshire SL2 4HS
01753-677877; Fax: 01753-664481

Correspondent: Mary Sweeney, Group Company Secretary

Chief officer: *Chief Executive:* N England

Year end	Turnover	Pre-tax profit
31/8/97	£1,280,000,000	£42,000,000

Nature of company business
Principal activity: food distribution and services.

Main subsidiaries include: Fisher Chilled Foods; Howard Long International; Jacques Onoa & Co; Macfish; Rahbeck-Food; Saphir Produce; SPIA Wood & Sons (Detling); Wentworth Import & Export.

UK employees: n/a

Charitable donations
1997: £59,000
1996: £125,000
1995: £157,000
1994: £110,000
1993: £79,000
Membership: *BitC*

Community support policy
The company's donations have more than halved in the last year, although pre-tax profits of the company remained about the same level. Support is given to charities involved with the food industry (eg. nutritional research) and certain local causes, which it supports through the Berkshire Community Trust. Grants to national organisations range from £1,000 to £25,000.

Gifts in kind may be given (the company is now only producing tinned, dried and frozen foods).

Exclusions
Generally no support for appeals from individuals, purely denominational appeals or local appeals not in areas of company presence.

Applications
In writing to the correspondent.

FKI plc

West House, Kings Cross Road, Halifax HX1 1EB
01422-330267; Fax: 01422-330084
Website: www.fki.co.uk

Correspondent: Mike Porter, Company Secretary

Chief officers: *Chairman:* J Whalley;
Chief Executive: R G Beeston

Year end	Turnover	Pre-tax profit
31/3/98	£1,286,839,000	£145,083,000

Nature of company business
The principal activity of the group is manufacturing through four divisions: material handling; hardware; automotive; engineering.

Fleming

Main subsidiaries include: Bridon International Ltd; Huwood International Ltd; Parsons Chain Co; Premier Stamping; British Babcock Ltd; Brush Electrical Machines Ltd; Brush Transformers Ltd; Clarkson Osborn; Froude Consine; Hawker Siddeley Switchgear Ltd; Laurence, Scott & Electromotors Ltd; South Wales Transformers; Whipp & Bourne; Bridon Overseas Holdings Ltd; Bridon PLC; West House Insurance Ltd.

UK employees: 16,370

Charitable donations
1998: £50,000
1997: £40,020
1996: £36,100
1995: £30,000
1994: £29,200

Community support policy
The company has a charitable budget allocated in March each year. This is distributed in April. Recently support has been given mainly to children's charities.

Applications
In writing to the correspondent.

Robert Fleming Holdings Ltd

25 Copthall Avenue, London EC2R 7DR
0171-638 5858; Fax: 0171-588 7219

Correspondent: D Pocknee, Secretary, Charity Committee

Chief officers: *Chairman:* P J Manser;
Chief Executive: D W J Garrett

Year end	Turnover	Pre-tax profit
31/3/98	£343,006,000	£136,120,000

Nature of company business
Merchant banking. The principal subsidiary in addition to those trading under the Robert Fleming name is the Save & Prosper Group (see separate entry).

Main subsidiaries include: Save & Prosper Group.

UK employees: 2,728

Charitable donations
1998: £305,170
1997: £261,000
1996: £177,372
1995: £270,000
1994: £225,715

Community support policy
Each charity appeal received by the company is considered on its merits. Preference is given to local charities in areas of company presence (ie. London) and charities in which a member of staff is involved. Areas of support include animal welfare charities, the arts, children/youth, education, elderly people, environment/heritage, medical research, religious appeals, science/technology, sickness/disability charities, social welfare and sport.

Typical grants to national organisations range from £200 to £500, and to local organisations from £100 to £300. Main beneficiaries in 1997/98 included the British Museum, Book Aid, Mencap, the Royal Society and the Samaritans.

Exclusions
No support is given to circular appeals, fundraising events, appeals from individuals, enterprise/training, political appeals, overseas projects, local appeals not in areas of company presence or for advertising in charity brochures.

Applications
In writing to the correspondent.

Flextech plc

160 Great Portland Street, London W1N 5TB
0171-299 5000; Fax: 0171-299 6000
Website: www.flextech.co.uk

Correspondent: Nicola Howson, Vice President of Corporate Affairs

Chief officers: *Chairman:* Adam Singer;
Chief Executive: Roger Luard

Year end	Turnover	Pre-tax profit
31/12/97	£110,638,000	(£6,200,000)

Nature of company business
The holding company of a group engaged in broadcast media activities with investments in satellite, cable and terrestrial television and programming.

Main subsidiaries include: Starstream Ltd; Bravo TV Ltd; Maidstone Broadcasting; UK Living Ltd; Maidstone Studios Ltd.

UK employees: 364

Charitable donations
1997: £36,000
1996: £14,426
1995: £12,000

Community support policy
The only information available on the company's charitable support is that it has a preference for media-related appeals.

Applications
In writing to the correspondent.

Ford Motor Company Ltd

Room 661, Eagle Way, Brentwood, Essex CM13 3BW
01277-252551; Fax: 01277-252429
Website: www.ford.co.uk

Correspondent: R M Metcalf, Director, Ford of Britain Trust

Chief officers: *Chairman:* I G McAllister;
Chief Executive: I G McAllister

Year end	Turnover	Pre-tax profit
31/12/97	£6,876,000,000	£60,000,000

Nature of company business
The Ford Motor Company Ltd is a wholly owned subsidiary of the Ford Motor Company of Dearborn, Michigan, USA. Principal activity: the manufacture of motor cars and commercial vehicles, component manufacture and associated leasing and hire purchase activities. The company and its subsidiaries operate principally in the UK and the Republic of Ireland. It is part of an integrated vehicle manufacturing group of Ford companies throughout Europe. It has 21 plants in Britain, with assembly in Dagenham, Halewood and Southampton, engine manufacture in Bridgend and Dagenham, pump production in Belfast and a research and engineering centre at Dunton, Essex.

Main locations: Dagenham; Halewood; Southampton; Bridgend; Belfast; Dunton, Essex.

UK employees: 28,700

Charitable donations

1997: £650,200
1996: £1,638,900
1995: £898,000
1994: £307,000
1993: £203,000

Total community contributions: £1,769,200

Membership: *BitC*

Community support policy

In addition to the donations figure above, the company funds the Ford of Britain Trust (Charity Commission number 269410), a charitable organisation wholly supported by company contributions. The main areas supported by the Ford of Britain Trust are outlined below. Recipient organisations should preferably be registered charities. The majority of donations are one-off grants to local charities in the areas where the company has a presence. There is also a preference for charities in which a member of staff is involved. Within these guidelines preference is given to organisations concerned with children and youth, social welfare, training, medical (but not research), education, science/technology, recreation, road safety, environment and the arts. Typical grants to national organisations range from £500 to £5,000 and to local organisations from £50 to £5,000.

The objects of the trust are the 'advancement of education, and other charitable purposes beneficial to the community'. The trust pays particular attention to organisations located near to Ford plants, or where a substantial percentage of Ford employees reside.

The salary of the Director and his assistants is paid for by Ford Motor Company. The trust's income consists of donations from the company, and interest earned on these donations.

Grants awarded in 1997/98 were £399,487 (£440,506 in 1996/97). These were categorised by the trust as follows:

Arts	£4,050	1.0%
Community service	£123,283	30.9%
Education	£25,835	6.5%
Environment	£3,450	0.8%
Disability	£50,974	12.8%
Hospitals	£14,440	3.6%
Professional and trade	£1,500	0.4%
Grants to schools	£82,445	20.6%
Special schools	£9,680	2.4%
Youth service	£82,330	20.6%
Other	£1,500	0.4%

The proportions given in each category are similar to previous years.

In kind support: Examples of in kind support include: donations of surplus equipment and a community bus scheme which provides nine Transit buses at its major locations around the country. Free bus loans are made to charitable organisations, groups for the disabled, schools and churches within local plant areas. A volunteering agency for Ford retirees placed 450 people in voluntary positions during the past three years. The company allows employees company time off for some voluntary activities, gives financial support to employees volunteering and gives contributions to employee fundraising.

The company also undertakes good-cause sponsorship.

Enterprise: The company is a member of Business in the Community and supports local enterprise agencies. Support is given in the form of youth training, resources, equipment or management expertise.

Education: Ford has established a Professorship at the Loughborough University of Technology, concerned with advanced automatic engineering. The position is endowed at a cost of £50,000 a year. It also sponsors engineering professorships at the University of East London, Anglia Polytechnic University, Bradford University and Liverpool John Moores University. These posts are endowed with £20,000 each. The company sponsors undergraduates at universities and business schools, and supports the development of national schools programmes, Technical and Vocational Educational Initiatives and the Certificate of Pre-Vocational Education.

Environment: Ford organises the Henry Ford European Conservation Awards which has a total prize fund of $500,000 and participants from 23 countries across Europe. It is operated in association with the Conservation Foundation, UNESCO and other leading conservation agencies in all participating countries.

Exclusions

For the Ford of Britain Trust: national charities are rarely supported, except for specific local projects in Ford areas. Generally no support for circulars, fundraising events, brochure advertising, individuals, purely denominational

Foster

appeals, political appeals, local appeals not in areas of company presence or overseas projects.

Applications
Applications to the Ford of Britain Trust should be addressed to the Director. The trustees met on three occasions in the year to 31 March 1997: July, January and March.

Foster Wheeler Ltd

Foster Wheeler House, Station Road, Reading RG1 1LX
0118-958 5211; Fax: 0118-939 6333

Correspondent: G J Rimer, Company Secretary

Chief officer: *Chairman:* I M Bill

Year end	Turnover	Pre-tax profit
31/12/97	£346,988,000	£21,091,000

Nature of company business
Principal activity: industrial services and equipment.

UK employees: 2,166

Charitable donations
1997: £52,000
1996: £42,743
1995: £43,072
1994: £48,061
1993: £37,141

Total community contributions: £78,000

Membership: *%Club*

Community support policy
The company is a member of the PerCent Club with support for the community totalling £78,000 in 1997, of which £52,000 was given in charitable donations. The company has divided its charitable giving into three sections:

1. National charities with strong representation in areas where the company operates in the UK (Reading, Glasgow and Teesside). Two charities are chosen each year in January.
2. Support for the arts centred mainly on Berkshire.
3. Support for the local community, by means of a five-year commitment to the Berkshire Community Trust, by direct grants to local organisations.

Support is only given to local charities in areas where the company operates (ie. the Reading area, Teesside, and Glasgow), with a charity committee deciding who benefits. There is a preference for appeals relevant to company business and charities in which a member of company staff is involved. Preferred areas of support are the arts; children/youth; education; elderly people; enterprise/training; environment/heritage; medical research; science/technology; sickness/disability; social welfare and sport. Main beneficiaries included Reading Youth Orchestra, Ryeish Green School (Reading), Berkshire Multiple Sclerosis Centre, British Heart Foundation and Compact – Teesside.

The Foster Wheeler Sports & Social Club has also made donations to Barnardo's, Guide Dogs for the Blind and Macmillan Nurses.

In addition to cash support, the company undertakes good-cause sponsorship and donates gifts in kind.

Exclusions
No response to circular appeals. No grants for advertising in charity brochures; animal welfare charities; appeals from individuals; fundraising events; overseas projects; religious or political appeals; local appeals not in areas of company presence; or large national appeals.

Applications
In writing to the correspondent.

Friends' Provident Life Office

Pixham End, Dorking, Surrey RH4 1QA
01306-740123

Correspondent: Roger Whiffin, Deputy Secretary

Chief officers: *Chairman:* D K Newbigging;
Chief Executive: K Satchell

Year end	Turnover	Pre-tax profit
31/12/97	£1,589,000,000	n/a

Nature of company business
Long-term insurance.

Main subsidiaries include: Preferred Assurance Co Ltd; Larpent Newton & Co Ltd; Box Hill Investments Ltd; London Capital Holdings Ltd; Regional Properties Ltd.

UK employees: 4,233

Charitable donations
1997: £73,000
1996: £62,000
1995: £61,800
1994: £82,232
1993: £61,800
Membership: *ABSA BitC*

Community support policy
The company does not normally respond reactively to appeals, having channelled its funds into the establishment of a Friends Provident Research Fellowship to be administered by the British Heart Foundation. Any additional support would be for medical research, religious appeals (Quaker only) and sickness/disability charities. Donations may also be given to local charities in the vicinity of the Head Office.

In addition to the British Heart Foundation, beneficiaries in 1997 included St Catherine's Hospice; Insurance Benevolent Fund; Stroke Association; Mental Health Foundation; Research into Ageing; and Imperial Cancer Research Fund.

The company operates the Give As You Earn payroll giving scheme, matching contributions by employees.

The arts: Friends Provident supports local (to company presence) organisations such as Salisbury Arts Festival.

Exclusions
No support is given to circular, telephone or fax appeals, fundraising events, appeals from individuals, denominational appeals (except Quaker), local charities outside company head office areas, overseas projects, animal welfare charities, children/youth, education, elderly people, enterprise/training, environment/heritage, social welfare, sport or for advertising in charity brochures.

Applications
In writing to the correspondent.

Gallaher Group Plc

Members Hill, Brooklands Road, Weybridge KT13 0QU
01932-859777; Fax: 01932-832792
Website: www.gallaher_group.com

Correspondent: Mrs C Taylor, Secretary, Charities Committee

Chief officers: *Chairman:* P M Wilson;
Chief Executive: P M Wilson

Year end	Turnover	Pre-tax profit
31/12/97	£4,415,000,000	£382,000,000

Nature of company business
An international group whose business is in tobacco.

Main subsidiaries include: Benson & Hedges Ltd; JR Freeman & Son Ltd; The Galleon Insurance Co Ltd; The Schooner Insurance Co Ltd.

Main brands include: Benson & Hedges; Silk Cut; Berkeley; Condor; Hamlet.

Main locations: Cardiff; Hyde (Cheshire); Ballymena (N Ireland); Perivale (Middlesex); Weybridge (Surrey).

UK employees: n/a

Charitable donations
1997: £322,546
1996: £315,182
1995: £346,312
1994: £470,832
1993: £479,136
Membership: ABSA   BitC

Community support policy

Charitable donations: The company gives mainly to large national charities, and to smaller organisations working in areas of company presence. Preference is given to organisations concerned with social welfare, enterprise/training and disabled people, and also to charities where a member of staff is involved. Typical grants to national organisations range from £500 to £1,000 and to local organisations from £100 to £500. Local branches are given guidelines and a budget for making their own donations.

The company operates the Give As You Earn payroll giving scheme, with employees' donations being matched by the company.

Enterprise: It supports local enterprise agencies and initiatives and is a member of Business in the Community.

The arts: Gallaher is a member of ABSA. It sponsors the Ulster Orchestra and its recordings. Requests for sponsorship will not be considered.

Exclusions
No support for circular appeals, telephone appeals, fundraising appeals, purely denominational (religious) appeals, local appeals not in areas of company presence or for advertising in charity brochures.

Applications
Appeals, relating to Gallaher Ltd only, should be addressed to the correspondent. Applications are considered by the appeals committee which meets occasionally, usually three or four times a year. Regional contacts for local appeals only are:

Ms J Kennedy, J R Freeman & Son, PO Box 54, Freeman House, 236 Penarth Road, Cardiff CF1 1RF.

R Richardson, Virginia House, Weston Road, Crewe, Cheshire CW1 1GH.

W Parkinson, 201 Galgorm Road, Lisnafillan, Gracehill, Ballymena, Co Antrim, N Ireland BT24 1HS.

Subsidiary companies have their own budgets for charities, and their charitable giving is autonomous, although budget levels are agreed with the parent company.

Gardner Merchant Services Group Ltd

Kenley House, Kensey Lane, Kenley, Surrey CR8 5ED
0181-763 1212; Fax: 0181-763 1044

Correspondent: David Ford, Managing Director

Chief officers: *Chairman:* J G Hawkes;
Managing Director: David Ford

Year end	Turnover	Pre-tax profit
31/8/96	£1,121,191,000	£37,767,000

Nature of company business
The provision of catering management services to clients in commercial, industrial, educational, healthcare and other establishments. Activities also include catering at special events, sporting, leisure and public locations, vending services, supply of catering equipment, facilities management, design and allied services.

Main subsidiaries include: Kelvin International Services Ltd; Sodexho Services UK Ltd; Gilmour & Pether Ltd; Town & County Catering Ltd; Ring & Brymer Holdings Ltd; Wheatsheaf Catering Ltd.

UK employees: n/a

Charitable donations
1996: £61,405
1995: £197,134
1994: £89,490
1993: £57,253

General

Community support policy

We have not been able to obtain any information on the company's charitable donations policy. After noting in the previous edition of this guide that the figure for 1995 was for a seven-month period, it appeared the level of the company's giving had risen substantially. However, this appears to have been an exceptional year, with donations decreasing in 1996, despite an increase in pre-tax profits of £10 million.

Applications
In writing to the correspondent.

General Electric Company plc

One Bruton Street, London W1X 8AQ
0171-493 8484; Fax: 0171-4931974
Website: www.gec.com

Correspondent: C B Wheatley, Assistant Secretary

Chief officers: *Chairman:* Sir Roger Hurn;
Chief Executive: Lord Simpson

Year end	Turnover	Pre-tax profit
31/3/98	£6,269,000,000	£1,055,000,000

Nature of company business
GEC is Britain's largest manufacturing company and a world leader in electronics, electrical and power generation apparatus and systems. Its products range from defence systems to household appliances.
Main subsidiaries include: Avery Berkel; GDA; Gilbarco; Marconi Communications; Marconi; Picker; Videojet; Woods Air Movement.
Main locations: Camberley; Chelmsford; Colchester; Coventry; Edinburgh; Hatfield; Leeds; Liverpool; Nottingham; Peterborough; Portsmouth; Rochester; Stafford; Stevenage; Stanmore.

UK employees: 44,323

Charitable donations
1998: £986,000
1997: £824,000
1996: £1,121,000
1995: £815,000
1994: £541,000
Membership: *ABSA   BitC*

Community support policy
The company has formed the GEC Community Service, which in addition to making charitable donations and supporting voluntary agencies, is 'intended to respond to national needs and to stimulate community activities wherever GEC has operating units'.

Charitable donations: The main areas of charitable support are:

- advancement of education, science and engineering
- encouragement of young people to undertake engineering as a career
- the environment
- support for the communities in which the company is involved
- charities concerned with social issues.

Preference is given to local charities in areas of company presence, appeals relevant to company business and charities in which a member of staff is involved. Direct support is preferred. Grants to national organisations range from £1,000 to £5,000 and to local organisations from £500 to £2,000. Grant recipients during 1998 included: ABSA, Relate, British Dyslexia Association, The Reserve Forces Ulysses Trust and Employers Forum on Disability.

In addition to cash donations, the company provides in kind support through its local operating units. It also has a small number of mostly pre-retirement secondees and allows time off for activity of community benefit. Matching funds schemes are operated by some of the local companies.

Education: GEC continues to encourage education, the advancement of science and engineering. Grants given during 1998 towards the advancement of education included the following: Women into Science and Engineering, Business in the Community, Salters Horner Advance Physics Project, Engineering Council for Britain and the Royal Society – Clifford Paterson Lecture.

Enterprise: GEC is a member of Business in the Community.

The arts: The company is a supporter of ABSA. Most support is for 'educational' arts mainly at a local level rather than national.

Exclusions
No support for circular appeals, advertising in charity brochures, appeals from individuals, fundraising events, purely denominational (religious) appeals, building appeals or local appeals not in areas of company presence.

Applications
Appeals (other than local appeals) should be made in writing to the correspondent and are considered by a donations committee which meets as required. Applications for local support should be made in writing to your local GEC operating unit in the UK. These subsidiaries and operating units have their own grants budgets. Some of the units also operate a staff charity fund, where the staff collect and distribute money to charity on their own initiative.

Information available: The company reports briefly on its community objectives in its annual report.

S R Gent plc

Dodworth Road, Barnsley, South Yorkshire S70 6JE
01226-241434; Fax: 01226-735339

Correspondent: John H Whitmore, Human Resources Director

Chief officers: *Chairman:* P M Wolff; *Chief Executive:* M Stakol

Year end	Turnover	Pre-tax profit
30/6/96	£153,393,000	(£11,128,000)

Nature of company business
Principal activity: the manufacture of ladies' and children's clothing.

UK employees: 2,979

Charitable donations
1996: £165,000
1995: £98,000
1994: £179,000
1993: £181,642

Community support policy
The emphasis of the company's community support is on industry-related training including involvement in the Clothing and Allied Products Industry Training Board. This promotes the industry in schools and provides supportive training. The company is also involved in the development of local Training and Enterprise Councils. No further information was available.

Exclusions
No support for individuals or for overseas projects.

Applications
In writing to the correspondent.

Gerrard Group plc

4th Floor, Atrium Building, Cannon Bridge, 25 Dowgate Hill, London EC4R 2GN
0171-337 2800; Fax: 0171-337 2801

Correspondent: J Shelmerdine, Secretary

Chief officers: *Chairman:* R B Williamson; *Chief Executive:* M E T Davies

Year end	Turnover	Pre-tax profit
31/3/98	£835,271,000	£35,452,000

Nature of company business
The main activities are futures buying, stockbroking, discount house, and fund management.
Main subsidiaries include: GNI Holdings Ltd; Greig Middleton Holdings Ltd; King & Shaxson Bond Brokers Ltd; Lombard Street Research Ltd.

UK employees: 1,625

Charitable donations
1998: £44,817
1997: £103,744
1996: £43,455
1995: £70,953
1994: £63,334

Community support policy
The level of the company's giving has more than halved from the peak of over £100,000 in 1997. In the PerCent Club's 1998 annual report, Gerrard & National are listed as a member.

The company has a preference for charities concerned with children and youth, social welfare, medical, education, environment/heritage, the arts and enterprise/training.

Exclusions
No support for advertising in charity brochures, appeals from individuals or purely denominational (religious) appeals.

Applications
In writing to the correspondent. A charity committee meets once every two months at which any appeals received are considered.

GGT Group plc

82 Dean Street, London W1V 6HA
0171-437 0434

Correspondent: Victoria Cooper, Financial Director

Chief officer: *Chairman:* M E Greenlees

Year end	Turnover	Pre-tax profit
30/4/97	£416,076,000	(£81,000)

Nature of company business
GGT Group is an advertising agency.
Main subsidiaries include: Option One; RM Communications; BDH Advertising.

UK employees: n/a

Charitable donations
1997: £117,000
1996: £68,000
1995: £36,000
1994: £51,000
1993: £22,000

Community support policy
The company is continuing to concentrate its support on charities associated with children. No further information was available.

Applications
In writing to the correspondent.

Gillette

Gillette Industries plc

Gillette Corner, Great West Road, Isleworth TW7 5NP
0181-560 1234; Fax: 0181-847 6165

Correspondent: Gloria Couché, Personal Assistant – Charities Committee

Chief officer: *Chairman:* A Boath

Year end	Turnover	Pre-tax profit
30/11/96	£612,435,000	£44,699,000

Nature of company business
Principal activity: development, manufacture and sale of a wide range of products for personal care or use. Major lines include blades and razors, toiletries and cosmetics, stationery products, Braun electric shavers and small appliances, and Oral-B care products.
Main brands include: Braun; Oral-B.

UK employees: 2,653

Charitable donations
1996: £120,000
1995: £99,000
1994: £99,000
1993: £70,700

Total community contributions: £137,288

Community support policy

The company is a wholly owned subsidiary of Gillette in the USA. Worldwide the company sets aside 1% of pre-tax profits each year for donations. It aims to contribute to the educational, cultural and social services of the communities in which it operates.

The main areas of non-cash support are good-cause sponsorship, gifts in kind and allowing staff company time to help run an IT mobile training unit in local high unemployment areas.

Charitable donations: In the UK, Gillette concentrates its support in the Brentford, Ealing, Hounslow and Reading areas. Support is given to local charities in these areas and to local branches of national organisations. Preferred areas of support are: animal welfare charities; children/youth; education; elderly people; enterprise/training; environment/heritage; fundraising events; medical research; and sickness/disability charities.

Grants range from £10 to £10,000 with previous beneficiaries including: Computer Coach Trust, Middlesex Young Peoples Clubs, Brentford & Chiswick Victim Support and Watermans Development – Brentford.

Exclusions
No response to circular appeals. No grants for appeals from individuals, advertising in charity brochures, purely denominational (religious) appeals, local appeals not in areas of company presence, large national appeals (see above) or overseas projects.

Applications
In writing to the correspondent.

GKN plc

PO Box 237, West Malling, Kent ME19 4DR
01732-520082

Correspondent: Miss Joanne Sutton

Chief officers: *Chairman:* Sir David Lees; *Chief Executive:* C K Chow

Year end	Turnover	Pre-tax profit
31/12/97	£2,834,000,000	£406,000,000

Nature of company business
An international company involved in automotive and agritechnical products, aerospace and special vehicles and industrial services.

Charitable donations
1997: £385,000
1996: £353,000
1995: £548,000
1994: £148,000
1993: £174,534

Total community contributions: £1,038,000

Membership: *%Club*

Community support policy

The main emphasis of GKN's community involvement continues to be on education. The company is a member of the PerCent Club. In the UK, it continued its core support of both the Technology Tree and Young Enterprise schemes for primary and secondary schools, respectively. The group also contributed towards the refurbishment of a travelling engineering laboratory for Women in Science and Engineering.

In 1997, community contributions totalled £1,038,000 including £385,000 in charitable donations. Some of the company's beneficiaries have been The Engineering Education Scheme, The Year in Industry, Motor & Allied Trades Benevolent Fund (BEN) and City Technology College Kingshurst.

Charitable donations: The company lists its main areas of charitable support as education, the community, health and welfare. This includes children/youth, education, enterprise/training, medical research, science/technology, sickness/disability charities and social welfare. Preference is given to appeals from local and community organisations in areas where the company has a branch (particularly local to the GHQ in Redditch, Worcestershire). Donations are made through the Charities Aid Foundation.

Employee involvement: Employees are involved in community projects, notably through fundraising. Staff fundraising at GHQ is matched £ for £ by the company. Preference is given to supporting charities in which a member of staff is involved. Staff are allowed company time off to volunteer. The company operates the Give As You Earn payroll giving scheme.

Enterprise: The company supports enterprise agencies with their main support in this area being given to The Prince's Trust.

Education: In addition to company support as mentioned above, employees are involved as school governors and a number of young people are undertaking work experience. The company provides support for City Technology Colleges.

The arts: Support is given to the Ironbridge Gorge and Black Country Museums.

Exclusions

No support for circular appeals; animal welfare; appeals from individuals; political appeals; religious appeals; or local appeals not in areas of company presence.

Applications

Appeals, in writing, should be addressed to the Company Secretary at the address shown above. Local appeals should be sent to local branches. Subsidiary companies make small grants independently of head office.

Advice to applicants: As a substantial proportion of the company's charitable budget is already committed to community projects/charities, only a small proportion remains for donations to individual appeals. Applicants should therefore ensure that they send only appropriate appeals.

GlaxoWellcome plc

GlaxoWellcome House, Berkeley Avenue, Greenford, Middlesex UB6 0NN
0171-493 4060; Fax: 0181-966 8330
Website: www.glaxowellcome.co.uk

Correspondent: Ruth Seabrook, Manager – Charitable Contributions

Chief officers: *Chairman:* Sir Richard Sykes;
Chief Executive: Robert Ingram

Year end	Turnover	Pre-tax profit
31/12/97	£7,980,000,000	£2,686,000,000

Nature of company business
Glaxo Wellcome is a research-based company whose people are committed to fighting disease by bringing innovative medicines and services to patients throughout the world and to healthcare providers who serve them.
Main brands include: Zantac; Imigran; Zovirax; Zofran; Zinnat; Ventolin; Serevent; Becotide.
Main locations: Barnard Castle, County Durham; Beckenham, Kent; Dartford, Kent; Greenford, Middlesex; Montrose, Tayside; Speke, Liverpool; Stevenage, Hertfordshire; Stockley Park, Middlesex; Ulverston, Cumbria; Ware, Hertfordshire.

UK employees: n/a

Charitable donations
1997: £6,000,000
1996: £6,000,000
1995: £9,700,000 (18 month period)
1994: £6,500,000
1993: £6,000,000

Total community contributions: £7,000,000

Membership: *ABSA BitC %Club*

Community support policy

In 1997, GlaxoWellcome's total community contributions of £7 million were equivalent to around 2.7% of that share of group pre-tax profit proportional to the UK contribution to group turnover. The company is a member of Business in the Community and a founder member of the PerCent Club. It runs a programme of charitable support along the following lines.

Charitable donations: All charitable donations made in the UK are agreed by the Group Appeals Committee, which is a Committee of the Board of GlaxoWellcome plc. The company considers appeals that fall within the following categories:

(a) *Healthcare in the UK* – to include medical infrastructure, medical research and the relief of suffering. In this latter category a particular healthcare problem is chosen by the Committee each year and one, or a group of projects relating to that chosen theme are supported. In previous years Children in Care and Learning Difficulties have been selected as themes; however, a new theme is selected annually.

(b) *Education* – the promotion of education, particularly in science at the tertiary level includes a programme of academic endowments, the improvement of scientific infrastructure in higher education and the continuing education of healthcare professionals.

(c) *International healthcare* – the committee seeks to support innovative projects, which contribute to healthcare significantly in the country concerned, and which have the potential to be replicated elsewhere.

(d) *Environment* – projects are supported both in the UK and internationally.

(e) *Arts support* – to enable or facilitate the performance, display or establishment of worthy arts projects.

(f) *Social research projects.*

GlaxoWellcome's policy places particular emphasis on the first two categories. Donations were made to two infrastructure projects within the NHS, the largest of which was a donation of £750,000 for a new cardiothoracic unit at the Central Middlesex Hospital. Within education the company launched a new fellowship scheme – GlaxoWellcome Fellowships, aimed at encouraging medically qualified individuals to continue a career in academic medicine, with the purpose of building bridges between the laboratory and the hospital ward. Other major beneficiaries included the University of Portsmouth – Chair in Healthcare of Elderly (£200,000) and the National Autistic Society (£200,000).

In international healthcare GlaxoWellcome donated £216,000 to UNAIS (International Service) to assist with its leprosy eradication programme in the most rural areas of Amazonas, Brazil which is undertaken in association with the Institute Alfredo da Matta. MERLIN (£105,000) and United National High Commission for Refuges – Refaid (£122,400) also received support.

Glencore

As part of the company's environmental support £250,000 was donated to fund a millennium seed bank at the Royal Botanic Gardens, Kew which aims to collect seeds from the entire UK flora and one tenth of the world's flora.

In the arts the company has supported the exhibition at the National Gallery 'Degas as a Collector' which was visited by over 160,000 people and is a major sponsor of Music for Youth which aims to keep music alive in schools through a festival of music involving regional concerts. The company is also a member of a number of organisations, including the British Museum, the Royal Academy of Arts, the Science Museum, the Natural History Museum and the Royal Philharmonic Orchestra.

It is company policy to support projects with clear tangible objectives from organisations which can demonstrate that the company's contribution will be efficiently used to achieve the desired purpose.

Community support: In addition to charitable contributions the group's operating companies make donations directed to helping with community projects, particularly in the localities of their sites.

The company operates the Give As You Earn payroll giving scheme, and it occasionally matches employee fundraising and giving.

Exclusions

No support for appeals from individuals. For example, the company is unable to provide support for individual students or Operation Raleigh applicants, but does support organisations such as the British Medical Association Charity Trust, which in turn provides financial assistance to medical students. No support for fundraising events, advertising in charity brochures, purely denominational (religious) appeals, political appeals or sport.

Applications

Appeals for charitable support on a national scale should be addressed in writing to the correspondent. Arts sponsorship proposals should be sent for the attention of the Corporate Events Manager, GlaxoWellcome House, Berkeley Avenue, Greenford, Middlesex UB6 0NN. Organisations seeking support for community projects within the locality or region of GlaxoWellcome sites should contact the relevant site to request the correct company contact.

Applicants are asked to supply a concise summary of their aims, objectives and funding requirements together with a copy of their most up-to-date audited accounts.

Information available: The company publishes a statement of its charitable and community support policy, in the form of a booklet, which is available on request from the Manager, Charitable Contributions.

Glencore UK Ltd

49 Wigmore Street, London W1H 0LU
0171-935 4455; Fax: 0171-487 5431

Correspondent: James Boxer, Secretary to the Glencore Foundation

Chief officer: *Chairman:* W Strothotte

Year end	Turnover	Pre-tax profit
31/12/96	US$1,988,825,000	US$27,401,000

Nature of company business
Commodity traders.

Main subsidiaries include: Inomex Ltd.

UK employees: n/a

Charitable donations

1996: US$3,318,000
1995: n/a
1994: n/a
1993: £202,225

Community support policy

The company gave $3,318,000 worldwide in community contributions during 1996. Donations are made through the Glencore Foundation (Charity Commission number 1041859) which states its principal objectives are 'to contribute to the education and welfare needs of society, principally in Israel'. According to the trust's correspondent, it also gives grants to non-Jewish organisations.

The company itself only supports local charities in areas of company presence (it has regional offices at Stracathro, Inverness, Thame and Wymondham). There is a preference for children and youth; medical; education; arts. Preference is also given for supporting charities in which a member of staff is involved.

In addition, the company operates a payroll giving scheme and a matching scheme for fundraising by employees.

The Glencore Foundation

In practice, grants are given throughout the world to Jewish organisations. In 1996, the total income of the foundation was £3.3 million and grants totalled £2.64 million. Three organisations received most of the grant total with £1 million going to the Solon Foundation in Switzerland, £125,000 to the School for Educational Leadership and £120,000 to Children of Chernobyl. Further details can be found in *A Guide to Major Trusts Volume 1*.

Exclusions

No support for circular appeals, fundraising events, advertising in charity brochures, appeals from individuals, local appeals not in areas of company presence or overseas projects. Appeals in the following areas are not supported: culture and recreation, education and research, environment and heritage.

Applications

In writing to the correspondent.

Glynwed International plc

Headland House, 54 New Coventry Road, Sheldon, Birmingham B26 3AZ
0121-742 2366; Fax: 0121-742 0403
Website: www.glynwed.com

Correspondent: J C Blakley

Chief officers: *Chairman:* Gareth Davies; *Chief Executive:* Tony Wilson

Year end	Turnover	Pre-tax profit
27/12/97	£1,241,500,000	£76,200,000

Nature of company business
The principal activities of the group are the processing of metals and plastics.

Main subsidiaries include: Aga-Rayburn; Falcon Catering Equipment; Flavel-Leisure; Leisure (Sinks); Wholesale Catering Equipment; Capper; Durapipe-S&LP; Viking Johnson; Victualic Systems; VIP-Heinke; Ductile Stourbridge Cold Mills; Dudley Port Rolling Mills; Firth Cleveland Steel Strip; GB Steel Bar; George Gadd & Co; HUB; JB&S Lees; Longmore Brothers; Macreadys; Monmore Tubes; Newman-Tipper Tubes; W Wesson; Ansell Jones; Lindapter International; Paul Fabrications; Steelway-Fensecure; Aalco; Amari Contract Services; Amari Special Alloys; Amari Transport Products; Baigent Stock Alloys; Cashmores.

UK employees: 12,582

Charitable donations

1997: £84,000
1996: £118,470
1995: £101,196
1994: £120,356

Community support policy

During 1997 the group gave £84,000 for charitable purposes in the UK. The 1997 company annual report states: 'Amongst the principal beneficiaries were organisations concerned with medical research, the elderly, people with physical or mental disabilities and inner city projects. The group's charitable giving is one aspect of its relationships with the communities within which it works: importance is attached to those relationships, which encompass the provision of help and support, in financial and other ways, not just to the organisations as already mentioned, but also in the fields of education, the arts and sport.' Both local and national charities are supported. The company also sponsors certain organisations with particular reference to youth, education and the arts in Birmingham and wider West Midlands area. For example, Birmingham Royal Ballet and the Ironbridge Gorge Museum.

In addition, much support is given at local level to charitable and community organisations by the many individual operating units in the group, for instance through gifts-in-kind and the efforts of employees in fundraising or volunteering.

Applications

In writing to the correspondent.

The Go Ahead Group PLC

Cale Cross House, Pilgrim Street, Newcastle upon Tyne NE1 6SU
0191-232 3123; Fax: 0191-221 0315
Website: www.go-ahead.com

Correspondent: Martin Ballinger, Managing Director

Chief officers: *Chairman:* Prof Sir Frederick Holliday; *Managing Director:* Martin Ballinger

Year end	Turnover	Pre-tax profit
27/6/98	£414,287,000	£36,877,000

Nature of company business
The company undertakes the operation of buses, coaches, and taxis in the north east of England, Brighton and Oxford. The group also owns and controls a number of public houses in the North East.

Main subsidiaries include: Brighton & Hove Bus and Coach Company; City of Oxford Motor Services; Gateshead & District Omnibus Company; Grandforce; London Central Bus Company; Mokett; Northern General Transport Company; Northern National Omnibus Company; OK Motor Services; Sunderland & District Omnibus Company; Tynemouth & District Omnibus Company; Tyneside Omnibus Company; Visitauto; Wycombe Bus Company; Victory Railway Holdings; Thames Trains; Govia; Thameslink Rail; Brighton Transport.

UK employees: n/a

Charitable donations

1998: £128,000 (community contributions)
1997: £107,000 (community contributions)
1996: £66,000
1995: n/a
1994: £55,000

Community support policy

Support is given to charities in areas of company presence. Each branch has its own budget and policy.

The company's annual report states: 'The group supports local communities' events in which its employees participate. The group is a member of the PerCent Club in the North East and commits a proportion of its pre-tax profits to community activities principally in the fields of education and training. Charitable donations, sponsorship and community support amounted to £128,000.'

Applications

In writing to the correspondent. Charities should contact their local branch/subsidiary. The contact for the North East is Paul Matthews at 117 Queen Street, Gateshead, Tyne and Wear NE8 2UA.

Grampian Holdings plc

Stag House, Castlebank Street, Glasgow G11 6DY
0141-357 2000; Fax: 0141-334 8709
Website: www.grampian.co.uk

Correspondent: John Douglas, Deputy Company Secretary

Chief officer: *Chairman:* W Y Hughes

Year end	Turnover	Pre-tax profit
30/1/98	£244,282,000	£25,572,000

Nature of company business
Transport, sports goods, pharmaceuticals and retail.

Main subsidiaries include: The Edinburgh Woollen Mill Ltd; W H Malcolm Ltd; Wm Wilson & Sons Ltd; Malcolm Plant Ltd.

UK employees: n/a

Charitable donations
1998: £44,063
1997: £48,575
1996: £56,000
1995: £55,000
1994: £50,000

Community support policy

The company stated that it had undergone several changes in the last few years which means that it has slimmed down to two divisions. Changes have included the takeover of Edinburgh Woollen Mill and Scottish Woollens Group Ltd. Its policy on charitable donations, 'although not having changed in this period, has had to take a back seat'.

The figures declared in the company's annual report would indicate that the level of charitable giving has stayed about the same. The following policy information is therefore reprinted from the previous edition of this guide.

Preference for local charities in the areas of company presence, charities in which a member of staff is involved and appeals relevant to company business. Preferred areas of support: children and youth, social welfare, medical and recreation. Grants to national organisations range from £250 to £5,000 and to local organisations from £100 to £2,000.

Previous major grant recipients have included Macmillan Cancer Relief (£5,000); Glasgow Opportunities Enterprise Trust (£1,000); Leukaemia and Cancer Children's Fund (£500); Friends of Russian Children (£400); and Cystic Fibrosis Trust (£250). The group's subsidiary companies may give gifts in kind.

Exclusions
No grants for fundraising events, advertising in charity brochures or purely denominational (religious) appeals.

Applications
In writing to the correspondent.

Granada Group PLC

Stornaway House, 13 Cleveland Row, London SW1A 1GG
0171-451 3000

Correspondent: G J Parrott, Commercial Director

Chief officers: *Chairman:* G Robinson; *Chief Executive:* C Allen

Year end	Turnover	Pre-tax profit
26/9/98	£4,031,000,000	£773,000,000

Nature of company business
The four UK divisions are media (television broadcasting and programme production), restaurants, hotels and rental (television and video rental). The company now owns four ITV licenses: Granada, LWT, Yorkshire and Tyne Tees. The company owns 50% of British Digital Broadcasting (trading as ONdigital), 33.3% of MUTV Ltd and 35% of The Home Shopping Channel.

Main group locations: Bedford, London, Manchester, Teddington.

Main subsidiaries include: LWT (Holdings); Forte (UK); UK Consumer Electronics; Heritage Hotels; Meridien Hotels; Posthouse Hotels; UK Consumer Electronics; UK Retail.

UK employees: n/a

Charitable donations
1998: £800,000
1997: £600,000
1996: £500,000
1995: £500,000
1994: £300,000
Membership: ABSA BitC

Community support policy

The four licencees, Granada, LWT, Yorkshire and Tyne Tees, concentrate support in their franchise areas, through cash donations, help with resources and support for staff involved in charitable activities. Examples of initiatives undertaken by the different operating companies are given in the company's annual report, from where the following examples were taken.

Live Challenge '99 (following the success of the Granada Community Challenge) is a partnership between Granada Television, Border Television and six commercial radio stations. Teams of executives from 22 major businesses have been challenged to raise £22 million for children and young people's charity projects.

The LWT Talent Challenge was completed in 1998. This programme involved 1,000 young people from some of London's most disadvantaged boroughs in a programme of arts activity and training. The scheme was delivered in partnership with four other major companies who assigned teams of managers to develop projects with local arts and educational organisations.

Yorkshire Television's Action Time encourages the public to put practical skills and resources to good use in their community, responding to challenges set by charitable organisations and groups. For example, in 1998, a memorial garden at a maternity unit in Pontefract was created, following a challenge by the Forget-Me-Not group.

Aside from the challenges all the media businesses continue to support a wide range of charitable causes in their local areas, with donations to meet specific needs as well as by building long-term relationships.

The Granada Media and Education Partnership provides financial and vocational support to five colleges in the North West, while in February 1998, Granada Television and Granada Studios tour launched Inside The Box – an information pack on careers in the media, distributed to every school in the North West. In the South, LWT has had a close relationship with Ravensbourne College of Design & Communication for many years, providing an annual grant as well as regular advice to tutors, staff secondments to assist with training and work placements for students.

Other support for the arts includes Granada Media's three-year funding agreement for the new Live Youth Theatre in Newcastle and Tyne Tees Television's support of the Northern Screen Commission.

Other examples of local businesses supporting local causes include: Granada Technology's support for a day centre for the homeless in Bedford by donating crockery, cutlery and kitchen equipment; Granada Motorway Services involvement in the Albany Taxi Run – providing gifts for the children being taken on a day out by London taxi drivers; Forte's Signature Hotels' staff raising money for research into genetic disorders.

One of the more unusual activities was the linking of Granada Motorway Services with The Global Wildlife Trust and the Sunday People newspaper to raise funds for tiger conservation in Sumatra and India (in the Chinese year of the tiger). The motorways division is hoping to support other such campaigns.

The Granada Foundation

In addition, support is given by the Granada Foundation to encourage and promote the following: the study, practice and appreciation of the fine arts including drawing, architecture and landscape architecture, sculpture, literature, music, opera, drama, ballet, cinema, and the methods and means of their dissemination. There is a clear preference for organisations working in the Granada Television transmission area (the North West of England).

In 1998, the trust had assets of £4.4 million generating an income of £145,000. A total of £148,000 was given in 32 grants.

Exclusions

Generally no support for circular appeals, appeals from individuals, purely denominational (religious) appeals, local appeals not in areas of company presence, medical research, animal welfare, religious or political appeals or overseas projects. Brochure advertising, fundraising events, science/technology, sport or large national appeals will rarely be supported. No sponsorship of charity events.

Applications

Applications should be sent to the correspondent.

William Grant & Sons Distillers Ltd

Strathclyde Business Park, Phoenix Crescent, Bellshill ML4 3AN
01340-820373; Fax: 01340-820805

Correspondent: The Chairman

Chief officers: *Chairman:* A G Gordon; *Managing Director:* G G Gordon

Year end	Turnover	Pre-tax profit
30/12/96	£323,294,000	£54,490,000

Nature of company business
Distillers of scotch whisky.

Main subsidiaries include: Quality Spirits International Ltd; The Grangestone Grain Company Ltd; Channel Islands Cream Liqueurs Ltd.

Main brands include: Glenfiddich; Grants.

UK employees: 897

Charitable donations

1996: £70,000
1995: £97,000
1994: £97,000
1993: £34,000

Community support policy

The company prefers to support local charities across a broad spectrum of causes. In addition, it undertakes sponsorship of arts and environmental projects including Glenfiddich Fiddle Championships, Glenfiddich Piping Championships and Glenfiddich Living Scotland awards.

Exclusions

Large national appeals and brochure advertising are not generally supported. Glossy brochures are not favourably regarded.

Applications

Applications for cash should be addressed to the Chairman at the address above and applications for bottles to Eileen Hemmings, at Glenfiddich Distillery, Dufftown, Banffshire AB55 4DH (01340-820373; Fax: 01340-820805).

Applications from outside Scotland should be addressed to the Public Relations Manager, Independent House, 84 Lower Mortlake Road, Richmond, Surrey TW9 2HS.

Great Portland Estates plc

Knighton House, 56 Mortimer Street, London W1N 8BD
0171-580 3040; Fax: 0171-631 5169

Correspondent: Sally McLaren, Secretary to the Chairman

Chief officer: *Chairman:* Richard Peskin

Year end	Turnover	Pre-tax profit
31/3/98	£114,070,000	£44,678,000

Greenalls

Nature of company business
The main activity of the company is property development and investment.

Main subsidiaries include: City and Corporate Holdings Ltd; Collins Estates Ltd; Courtana Investments Ltd; Ilex Ltd; Jekyll Properties Ltd; JLP Investments Co Ltd; Knighton Estates Ltd; Petra Investments Ltd; Pontsarn Investments Ltd; Queen's Arcade Ltd; B & HS Management Ltd; Limco Group PLC.

UK employees: 70

Charitable donations
1998: £62,000
1997: £60,000
1996: £58,000
1995: £60,000
1994: £59,172

Community support policy
The company trust gives support to 'deserving causes'. It has no real preferences, apart from charities concerned with housing/homelessness (eg. Shelter) and medical charities. Donations are paid in CAF vouchers. It tries to donate to different causes each year.

The company also forward applications to the Corah Samuel Charitable Trust and Basil Samuel Charitable Trust which have substantial shareholdings in the company (see entries in *A Guide to the Major Trusts Volume 1 & Volume 2*). These trusts share the same address as the company and the chairman of the company is also a trustee of the Basil Samuel Charitable Trust.

Applications
In writing to the correspondent.

The Greenalls Group plc

Wilderspool House, Greenalls Avenue, Warrington WA4 6RH
01925-651234; Fax: 01925-413137

Correspondent: A W A Spiegelberg, Company Secretary

Chief officers: *Chairman:* A G Thomas;
Chief Executive: Lord Daresbury

Year end	Turnover	Pre-tax profit
26/9/97	£1,142,164,000	£137,652,000

Nature of company business
The main activities are the operation of public houses, hotels and off-licences.

Main subsidiaries include: De Vere Hotels Ltd; Village Leisure Hotels Ltd; Tavern Group Ltd; Stretton Leisure Ltd.

UK employees: 20,862

Charitable donations
1997: £128,000
1996: £122,000
1995: £134,712
1994: £98,000
1993: £128,000
Membership: BitC

Community support policy
The company is involved with Business in the Community and seeks to serve the community in the main areas where its employees live and work, particularly in the North West. There is a preference for charities in which a member of company staff is involved and environmental projects.

Small donations of around £10 (eg. for Operation Raleigh or a bottle for a fundraising event) are distributed regularly. Larger donations are considered by a charitable appeals committee two/three times a year. Donations can be for £100 to £10,000 and may be given by deed of covenant.

Applications
In writing to the correspondent.

Greggs plc

Fernwood House, Clayton Road, Jesmond, Newcastle upon Tyne NE2 1TL
0191-281 7721

Correspondent: Ms Jenni Wagstaff, Charity Administrator

Chief officers: *Chairman:* Ian Gregg;
Managing Director: Mike Darrington

Year end	Turnover	Pre-tax profit
27/12/97	£265,900,000	£18,035,000

Nature of company business
Principal activity: manufacture and sale of bread, flour confectionery, sandwiches and savoury products. Shop and bakery locations: Birmingham, Enfield, Gosforth, Leeds, Manchester, Rutherglen and South Wales.

Main subsidiaries include: Charles Bragg (Bakers); Olivers (UK); J R Birkett & Sons.

Main brands include: Baker's Oven.

UK employees: n/a

Charitable donations
1997: £197,000
1996: £151,000
1995: £138,000
1994: £106,000
1993: £63,310

Community support policy
The company gives 1% of pre-tax profits in charitable donations, mainly through the Greggs Trust.

Greggs Trust
(Charity Commission number 296590).

The trust's current policy, due to be revised in 2000, is as follows: to support projects which aim to alleviate poverty and social deprivation. Projects working in areas such as the arts, environment, conservation, education and health will be considered if they have a social welfare focus or are based in areas of deprivation. The trust mainly supports causes in the North East but also in other areas where Greggs businesses operate. Priority is given to local, and in certain cases regional, projects and organisations. Grants are also given to individuals experiencing hardship through a small number of approved agencies.

Applications are encouraged 'from disadvantaged groups of all kinds including ethnic minorities, people with disabilities and other minorities, without prejudice as to racial origin, religion, age, gender or sexual orientation'.

'Recent grants have included support for work with homeless people, older people, young people, children and women, fathers, including the unemployed, and for people with disabilities and ethnic and multi-cultural groups.

'Applications from small community-led organisations and self-help groups are more likely to be successful than those from larger and well-staffed organisations and those which have greater fundraising capacity. Exceptions may be made where innovative work is being developed by established agencies or where such agencies are providing services to smaller or local groups.' It is not necessary to be a registered charity to apply.

Grants can be for core costs, running costs, projects, start-up costs, buildings, capital other than building (computers, etc), recurring costs, and salaries, and are usually one-off. Large grants are for £1,000 or more and small grants are usually not more than £500.

In 1998, the funds were allocated as follows (figures in brackets are the allocation for 1999):

£140,000 (£184,000) in large grants, approved at twice-yearly meetings

£60,000 (£75,000) in small grants mostly of £500 or less, approved on a monthly basis

£50,000 (£55,000) for 'hardship' grants distributed on a continuous basis

£100,000 (£120,000) for the Charity Committees which are established in the Divisional areas of Greggs plc (for distribution to local charitable causes) which includes funds to match employee giving through the Give As You Earn scheme. These committees distribute funds within guidelines consistent with the trust's policies and tend to support a relatively large number of projects with small grants.

In 1998, the largest grants approved were Links, Hexham (£10,000 a year for three years) and Consett Churches Detached Youth Project (£10,000 a year for two years). The following organisations were approved a one-off grant of £10,000: Stepping Stones, Gosforth; SHAID – Single Homeless Action Initiative in Derwentside, Stanley; Children North East, Newcastle; Churches Acting Together, Whitley Bay; and Scotswood Area Strategy, Newcastle. Other major grants were approved as follows:

Grants between £5,000 and £10,000 to: North East Prison After Care Service – NEPACS, Durham City (£7,500); Tyneside Cinema, Newcastle (£7,200); East Community Care Centre, Old People's Project, Sunderland, Hebburn Neighbourhood Advice Centre, Hebburn and Them Wifies, Newcastle (all £5,000 a year for three years); Age Concern, Newcastle (£5,000 a year for two years); Beacon Lough Baptist Church, Gateshead, Escape Family Support, Blyth and The Samaritans of Tyneside (each £5,000).

Grants over £1,000 to under £5,000 to: The Rights Project, Newcastle (£4,400); Mentor – submitted by the Centre for Innovation in Social Policy & Practice, Newcastle (£3,000); North Tyneside Advocacy Project, North Shields (£2,500); Tyneside Women's Health Project, Gateshead (£2,100); and Live Theatre, Newcastle and The Learning Disabilities Federation, North Shields (both £2,000).

Grants of £1,000 to: Abuse Counselling & Training Centre, Ashington; Age Concern, Gateshead; Brunswick Young People's Project, Newcastle; Byker Bridge Housing Association, Newcastle; Disability North, North East; Durham Wildlife Trust; FRADE (Furniture Reclamation & Delivery Enterprise); Gateshead Council on Disability; Newcastle Council for Voluntary Service; Phoenix House, South Shields; South Shields Activity Centre; South Tyneside Women's Aid; Transport Unlimited, Gateshead; Who Cares? North East; and Unity Organisation, Sunderland.

No further financial information was available for 1998 at the time of going to print.

In 1997, the trust had assets of £5 million and an income of £583,000 mainly derived from the profits of Greggs plc and from the donations of major share holders. Grants totalled £499,000.

A total of £129,000 was given in 25 large grants, ranging from £1,000 to £10,000. 'Special major grants' were given to Tyne & Wear Foundation for the South East Northumberland Project (£30,000 over three years); The Diana, Princess of Wales Memorial Fund (£17,000 for UK based charities); and The Woodlands Trust (£10,000 for planting trees at Longhirst, Northumberland in memory a former trustee).

A total of 130 small grants amounting to £50,400 were given to local projects in the North East. Details of the beneficiaries were not available.

A total of 500 hardship grants amounting to £52,000 were given to individuals, to families or individuals referred by Social Services, Probation Services and other welfare agencies.

The Divisional Charity Committees gave over 230 grants amounting to £86,000, mostly for under £1,000.

Exclusions

No sponsorship is undertaken. Grants will not be made for the following purposes other than as specified:

- academic research
- animal welfare
- capital appeals or running costs of fee-charging residential homes and nurseries
- commercial charity reference books/directories
- conferences/seminars/exhibitions/publications
- festivals, performances and other arts and entertainment activity, unless of specifically educational value and involving groups from areas of greater social need or disadvantaged by low-income or disability
- foreign travel/expeditions/holidays and outings other than for disadvantaged groups
- fundraising organisations, general fundraising appeals, fundraising events and sponsorship
- hospitals, health service trusts, medically related appeals and medical equipment

- loans, repayment of loans or retrospective funding
- national appeals and general appeals of established regional organisations
- medical research
- minibuses and vehicles, other than community transport schemes which serve a combination of groups in a wide geographical area
- overseas projects or organisations working abroad
- purchase, conversion and restoration of buildings other than community-based projects serving areas of greater social need and/or particularly disadvantaged or at risk groups
- religious advancement or religious buildings, community aspects of church-based or other religious projects may be considered if projects show outreach into the community and provide services of benefit to the community as a whole or to particularly disadvantaged or at risk groups
- restoration and conservation of historic buildings and the purchase or conservation of furnishings, paintings, other artefacts or historic equipment
- school appeals, other than for projects at LEA schools in areas of greater social need, eg. after school clubs and activities promoting parental and community involvement
- sports buildings, equipment and sporting activities other than where particularly disadvantaged groups are involved and where the activity is ongoing rather than 'one-off'
- statutory agencies and activities that are primarily the responsibility of statutory agencies
- uniformed organisations (scouts, guides, sea cadets etc.) and organisations associated with the armed services other than areas of greater social need where projects involve outreach into the community and wider community benefit.

Applications

The trustees meet twice a year, usually in May and November. Applications for major grants may be submitted at any time, but if they are to be assessed in time for these meetings they should be sent no later than mid-March or mid-September. There are no application forms Applicants for small grants are asked to note the guidance relating to major grants, and advised to use their discretion in providing sufficient information to support their case.

Applicants for major grants are asked to set out their application briefly in a letter, giving full address, phone/ fax number and a contact name, the purpose of the application, the amount requested, details of any other applications for the same purpose and responses if available. More information about the project or work proposed may be provided in supporting documents.

Applications must include the following:

- latest audited accounts or financial report required by the Charity Commission and, if a period of three months or more has passed since the year end, a certified statement of income and expenditure for the period
- latest annual report or, if not available, a summary of current work
- the applicant organisation's equal opportunities policy and practice
- details of constitutional status (actual documents need not be included); charity registration number if applicable; organisational structure; composition of management committee; management arrangements for the project for which application has been made; details of staff and volunteers
- budget for the organisation as a whole for the current year and costings for the project for which application is made
- if support for a salaried post or posts is requested, the job-description for the post(s)
- details of the organisation's policy and provision for training of management body, staff and volunteers
- details of how it is intended to evaluate the work for which a grant is requested.

The trust aims to respond to applications for small grants within about two months and to acknowledge applications for major grants in the same period. Applicants will be informed if their application has not been selected for further consideration. If an application has been selected for further assessment the administrator may be in touch to request further information or to arrange a visit.

R Griggs Group Ltd

Cobbs Lane, Wollaston, Wellingborough, Northants NN29 7SW
01933-665381; Fax: 01933-664088
Email: andrew_borge@airwair.co.uk

Correspondent: Andrew Borge, Head of Communications and Corporate Affairs

Chief officers: *Chairman:* Stephen W Griggs; *Managing Director:* Frank M Duffy

Year end	Turnover	Pre-tax profit
31/3/97	£247,810,000	£34,100,000

Nature of company business
Manufacturers and distributors, through Airwair Limited, of Dr Martens footwear.

Main subsidiaries include: Airwair Ltd; Dr Martens Dpt Store Ltd; Dr Martens Sport and Leisure Ltd; Ferrersmere Estates Ltd; Wollaston Vulcanizing Ltd.

Main brand: Dr Martens.

UK employees: 3,400

Charitable donations

1997: £316,977
1996: £309,886
1995: £341,102

Total community contributions: £1,467,809

Membership: *ABSA BitC*

Community support policy

The company has regularly supported the arts, music, charity (in the fields of children/youth, education and enterprise/training) and sport. The company is a member of ABSA. Support is given to both local and national charities especially those based in Northamptonshire, Leicestershire and Somerset. Last year the company's contributions totalled almost £1.5 million including £317,000 in charitable donations.

In addition, the company sponsors the premiership football team West Ham United and owns Rushden & Diamonds FC.

Children and youth: There has been an on-going programme of practical and financial support in many different youth-related initiatives. Prominent amongst these is the support given to The Prince's Youth Business Trust and Shelter.

Arts: Griggs Group is also heavily involved in music and the arts, providing funding for a variety of projects including help for performers and sponsorship of theatres, dance companies, festivals and bands including Portabello Festival in London, New Works Festival in Leicester, the National Youth Theatre Summer Season in Edinburgh, Tinderbox in Belfast, the Derngate in Northampton, The Castle in Wellingborough and the Jazzxchange dance company.

Sport: Dr Martens Sport & Leisure represents the sporting interests of the Griggs Group. Most sponsorship is commercial, but the company also sponsor the West Ham United FC Football in the Community programme.

Other support: Non-cash support is given through gifts in kind and joint promotions as well as arts and good-cause sponsorship.

Exclusions

No support for advertising in charity brochures, animal welfare charities, appeals from individuals, elderly people, environment/heritage, medical research, overseas projects, political appeals, religious appeals, science/technology or sickness/disability charities.

Applications

In writing to the correspondent.

GTECH UK Corporation

Roseberry House, 4 Farm Street, London W1X 7RA
0171-495 8765

Correspondent: Joanna Manning-Cooper, Director of Public Relations for UK & Europe

Chief officers: n/a

Year end	Turnover	Pre-tax profit
n/a	n/a	n/a

Nature of company business
Computerised online lottery products and services.

Charitable donations
1997: £150,000
Membership: *BitC*

Community support policy

The world's leading supplier of computerised online lottery products and services donated £150,000 to a variety of community projects, mostly centred around its UK sites in Watford, Liverpool and Blackburn.

Its criteria for support in these areas is educational projects which link with the technology and communications nature of the company. For example, it donated £1,000 to Watford schools through the police charity, Child Victims of Crime, which dealt with safety, drugs and bullying. In addition, it donated £90,000 to the first hospice for children in the North West and £50,000 to develop an IT network for social entrepreneurs, called the Community Action Network.

It also has a worldwide Reach Out scheme which gives staff one paid day off each year to volunteer for the organisation of their choice and has just launched 'Dollars for Doers', which contributes $250 to an organisation when a GTECH employee volunteers at least 25 hours a year with that organisation.

Applications

In writing to the correspondent.

Guardian Media Group plc

164 Deansgate, Manchester M60 2RR
0161-832 7200
Website: www.guardian.co.uk

Correspondent: A V Townsend, Company Secretary

Chief officers: *Chairman:* Robert Gavron; *Chief Executive:* Robert Phillis

Year end	Turnover	Pre-tax profit
29/3/98	£367,560,000	£53,039,000

Nature of company business
Newspaper and magazine publishing. The group has newspapers in the North West, the North East, Bristol, Surrey, Glasgow, Edinburgh and London.

Main subsidiaries include: Manchester Evening News Ltd; Diverse Media Ltd; G & A N Scott Ltd; Lancashire and Cheshire County Newspapers Ltd; Surrey Advertiser Newspaper Holdings Ltd; Berkshire Press Ltd; Auto Trader Ltd (Various); Broadcast Communications plc.

Main brands include: The Guardian; The Observer; Manchester Evening News; Auto Trader; Bazal.

UK employees: n/a

Guardian

Charitable donations
1998: £140,000
1997: £132,000
1996: £91,600
1995: £242,000
1994: £207,000
Membership: *ABSA*

Community support policy

The company covenants its donations to a number of charities and trade associations. There is a preference for charities local to Manchester and London, then the North West and South East. Smaller appeals are considered every three months, when around 200 appeals are considered and about 10 receive donations of £50 to £200.

The company also sponsors the arts, especially theatre, music, modern arts, film and dance. For example, the London Film Festival, National Film Festival and Serpentine Gallery have been supported recently.

The company established the Guardian Foundation (Charity Commission number 1027893) in 1993. This foundation has undertaken to promote the development of journalism particularly in Eastern European countries and to support free speech. In 1995/96, the latest year for which accounts were on file at the Charity Commission, the income was £65,000 from 'donations received'. Expenditure included charitable donations (£21,000) and expenses re charitable projects (£28,000).

Exclusions
No support for political or religious appeals.

Applications
In writing to the correspondent. Appeals sent directly to individual papers are dealt with separately.

Guardian Royal Exchange plc

Royal Exchange, London EC3V 3LS
0171-283 7101
Website: www.gre-group.com

Correspondent: C V Foster, Appeals Secretary

Chief officers: *Chairman:* Lord Hambro; *Chief Executive:* John Robins; *Managing Director:* John Sinclair

Year end	Turnover	Pre-tax profit
31/12/97	n/a	£872,000,000

Nature of company business
Guardian Royal Exchange plc is the holding company of the Guardian Royal Exchange Group which carries on insurance, financial services, healthcare and investment business in the UK and throughout the world.

Main subsidiaries include: Atlas Assurance Co; Caledonian Insurance Co; Guardian Pensions Management; Guardian Insurance; Guardian Assurance; Guardian Health; Guardian Direct; Orion Personal Insurances; PPP Healthcare; RAC Insurance Direct; Bruton Property Holdings; Compass Securities; Guardian Investment Holdings; Guardian Asset Management; Guardian Mortgage Services; Guardian Properties; Metropolitan Trust.

UK employees: 7,335

Charitable donations
1997: £424,331
1996: £287,272
1995: £291,933
1994: £281,969
1993: £218,764
Membership: *BitC %Club*

Community support policy
GRE is a member of the PerCent Club and Business in the Community. Total charitable donations have increased by about 30% in 1997, from 1996.

Charitable donations: Grants are channelled through the Guardian Royal Exchange Charitable Trust, which was established in 1982. The trustees are: Hon. G E Adeane, J R W Clayton, Sir Paul Newall and J Sinclair. Support is considered for local charities where the company has a presence and UK charities with single-purpose objectives in the areas of medical and research, welfare, the environment and the arts. The trustees favour a broad span of smaller donations rather than a few larger donations.

In 1997, the trust had an income of £259,000 (£251,000 in 1996), £205,000 of which was covenanted from the company including the associated tax refund. It gave 275 grants totalling £234,000. About half the grants were for £750 to £3,000 (the majority of which were £750 to £1,000) and the other half were mostly for £500. Grants were mainly for welfare and then medical charities.

The main donations were to: Royal Academy of Music and British Heart Foundation (£3,000 each), Royal Academy of Dancing, Lord Mayor's Appeal for St Paul's Cathedral, British Home & Hospital for Incurables, Police Convalescence and Rehab Trust (£2,500 each) and GAP Activity Projects Ltd (£2,000).

More typical, were the grants of around £1,000 to £1,500, which included Corporate Action Trust – Spinal Regeneration Strategy, Order of St John, NSPCC, Tower of London – Organ Appeal and Felixstowe Volunteer Coastal Patrol Service. Smaller grants of around £500 included: Glasgow Museums, Mencap – Egypt Cycle Ride, Stoneham Housing Association, The Haemophilia Society, Royal School for the Blind and Think Children.

Employee involvement: The company operates a payroll giving scheme. Matching support is given to selected causes chosen by members of staff.

Enterprise: The group is involved with Community Relations Councils, and supports projects associated with the transition from school to work, including work-experience programmes for disabled young people in Ipswich.

Exclusions

The group does not support appeals from individuals, nor will it support local appeals not in areas of company presence, circular appeals, fundraising events, animal welfare, purely denominational (religious) appeals or overseas projects. The company does not support non-commercial advertising and does not welcome proposals for arts sponsorship.

Applications

All appeals should be made via the secretary of the GRE Charitable Trust for consideration by the trustees. Appeals must be in writing stating the objectives of the registered charity, together with a copy of the most recent accounts. Grant decisions are made by a donations committee which meets on a regular basis.

Advice to applicants: Any appeal made to a GRE group company is considered by GRE Charitable Trust, thus there is no point in writing to more than one company.

Halifax plc

Trinity Road, Halifax, West Yorkshire HX1 2RG
01422-333413/6; Fax: 01422-333007
Email: communityaffairs@halifax.co.uk
Website: www.halifax.co.uk

Correspondent: Victoria Soye, Community Affairs Manager

Chief officers: *Chairman:* Jon Foulds; *Chief Executive:* James Crosby

Year end	Turnover	Pre-tax profit
31/12/97	n/a	£1,649,000,000

Nature of company business
The Halifax is the UK's largest mortgage lender as well as providing savings and other financial services to 21 million customers via 897 branches and 1,002 agencies.

Main subsidiaries include: HCM Holdings Ltd; Clerical Medical Investment Group Ltd.

UK employees: n/a

Charitable donations

1997: £2,001,626
1996: £1,860,396
1995: £1,888,945
1994: £1,073,918
1993: £953,153

Total community contributions: £3,051,327

Membership: ABSA BitC

Community support policy

Total community contributions in 1997 were £3.05 million, including over £2 million in charitable donations.

The community affairs department aims to help community-based charities and organisations in areas of company presence and charities in which a member of staff is involved. A programme has been established covering the broad categories of children and youth, social welfare, medical, education initiatives, environment, enterprise/training, homelessness, elderly and disabled people, sports and arts.

The main beneficiaries in 1997 were Centrepoint, Money Advice Trust, RSA, National Council for Voluntary Organisations and British Trust for Conservation Volunteers.

The main areas of non-cash support are secondments, gifts in kind and training schemes. Support may be given in whichever form is most appropriate to the particular need. The company's Community Development Circles are a staff initiative encouraging Halifax staff to work together to benefit both team members and local charities. Over £750,000 has been raised through this initiative for projects such as refurbishment of hostels, support of local hospices and the development of programmes to reduce drug and alcohol abuse.

Additionally, over £1 million will be made available to the three charities (British Heart Foundation, Imperial Cancer Research and Mencap) involved in the Halifax Visa Charity Card.

Types of support

Charitable donations: Donations are made mainly on a local basis in areas where the company has a presence. Typical grants range from £500 to £5,000.

In kind support: Obsolete furniture or equipment, training courses for charity managers, promotional materials and a donations collection service for major appeals, are all provided free of charge.

Employee involvement: Staff are encouraged to become volunteers in their own time and to participate in the Duke of Edinburgh Award Scheme. A payroll giving scheme is operated by the company, which also runs a matching scheme for employee fundraising.

Policy guidelines

The following information is taken from a booklet recently published by the company. Please note that the company prefers to provide funding for specific project costs and equipment rather than capital, revenue or salary costs (volunteers' expenses will be considered). The general maximum limit is £10,000 for each appeal, which may be exceeded in some cases. However, most donations are about £1,000. The following information refers to Halifax's five main categories for support.

Homelessness

Money is donated to national organisations and small, local projects that help and advise those in need. Many homelessness charities have received support including Centrepoint and Shelter. The following types of project are considered:

- those supplying the basics, such as food and clothing for people living on the streets
- short-stay hostels and resettlement projects
- opening day centres and advice schemes
- those offering assistance with education and employment issues.

Hallmark

Education
Halifax aims to:
- help with mainstream education in a number of ways, from the purchase of equipment or training aids that benefit large numbers of students to supporting schemes that cover issues of great significance to youngsters
- encourage projects that help people prepare for the working environment, especially schemes for young people, the disabled, people with learning difficulties and ethnic minorities
- fund projects that help people in inner city and high unemployment areas to find employment (such as youth training, vocational or life-skills training) and training in new skills for people re-entering the workforce.

For example support has been given to Devon Schools Library Service, encouraging teenagers to read more and to Southwark Children's Foundation enabling them to offer four Saturday morning band lessons to local children.

Community
The company is committed to helping community groups and organisations which provide practical support at grass roots level. Current support ranges from day centres and hospital radio stations, to junior football teams and YMCA centres. Halifax welcomes applications from groups working to improve the lives of people in their area, perhaps by providing equipment or services. Help is also given to deal with problems in other ways, for example, by backing schemes to rehabilitate people who are addicted to drugs or alcohol.

Quality of Life
Halifax helps with projects that supply caring people when they are needed most. Help is given to:
- support groups and counselling schemes to provide sympathetic and experienced carers for the sick and bereaved
- workshops and leisure activities for disabled people of all ages
- schemes to provide company for the elderly through day centres and home visits
- schemes to purchase and fit smoke alarms and other security measures in their homes
- appeals concerned with preventative medicine, enhancing the quality of life and the alleviation of suffering where it can be shown that the community benefits directly.

Environment
Halifax supports a range of local projects to conserve the environment. Support is given to:
- as many local environmental schemes as possible, from drystone walling and woodland management to clearing derelict land and creating inner-city gardens
- promote projects involving communities, where local people contribute and have an interest in the success of their ideas.

Exclusions
No support for circular appeals, fundraising events, third-party funding, individuals, purely denominational appeals, science/technology, political appeals, military appeals (although ex-service charities may be supported in some cases), animal welfare, academic research, overseas projects (although a funds collection service is available where appropriate) or for advertising in charity brochures.

Applications
The company produce their own guidelines and application form (available from the correspondent). From 1 January 1999, applications to the Halifax Community Affairs programme can only be accepted for specified categories on a quarterly basis:

Quarter one (1 January to 31 March) Community

Quarter two (1 April to 30 June): Education and environment

Quarter three (1 July to 30 September): Quality of life and community

Quarter four (1 October to 31 December): Homelessness

Applications are received and assessed as follows:

First month of quarter: applications received and acknowledged

Second month of quarter: applications assessed and visits/contact made where appropriate. Queries regarding applications made in this quarter cannot be handled during this time.

Third month of quarter: organisations informed of decision and donations made where appropriate.

Applications are acknowledged within 28 days. If you are unsuccessful, you will be able to apply again for a donation during the following year's programme.

Hallmark Cards (Holdings) Ltd

Hallmark House, Station Road, Henley-on-Thames, Oxon RG9 1LQ
01491-578383

Correspondent: Denise Phillipps, Personnel Department

Chief officer: *Chief Executive:* Ian Bant

Year end	Turnover	Pre-tax profit
31/12/97	£91,275,000	£5,702,000

Nature of company business
The principal activity is the manufacture and sale of greetings cards.

UK employees: n/a

Charitable donations
1997: £29,030
1996: n/a
1995: n/a
1994: £44,784
1993: £13,180

Community support policy

Hallmark has previously stated that only one charity is supported each year. The Children's Society used to be the only charity supported, now all donations are given to Sue Ryder Homes.

In 1998, the company took over Creative Publishing plc, formerly part of Fine Art Developments plc. Creative Publishing gave donations totalling just over £80,000 in 1997/98 and was committed to donating 0.5% of pre-tax profits to charity. It focused its support on medical and children's charities in Yorkshire especially Bradford.

It remains to be seen whether Hallmark will continue this support, or in deed increase its current level.

Applications

In view of the policy of the company to support a single charity each year, applications are unlikely to be successful.

Hambros PLC

41 Tower Hill, London EC3N 4HA
0171-480 5000; Fax: 0171-702 4424

Correspondent: Miss Rosemary Hyland, Corporate Communications

Chief officers: *Chairman:* Lord Hambro;
Chief Executive: Sir Chips Keswick

Year end	Turnover	Pre-tax profit
31/3/97	n/a	£64,700,000

Nature of company business
Banking, retail financial services and direct investments, throughout the UK and in many parts of the world.
Main subsidiaries include: Berkeley (Insurance); Cunningham, Hart & Co (Holdings); Network Security Management.

UK employees: n/a

Charitable donations

1997: £171,000
1996: £277,000
1995: £352,000
1994: £289,000
1993: £295,000

Community support policy

The company has recently been taken over by Societe Generale and the policy details below may therefore change, but no updated information was available at the time of going to print.

Charitable donations: Most of the charitable donations are made by head office, with grants ranging from £500 to £5,000. The company prefers to support organisations working in the fields of education, health and medical care, environment/heritage and the arts. The company supported the Fairbridge Drake Society for four years giving at least £12,500 a year. Support has also been given to Victoria & Albert Museum, National Art Collections Fund and Home Farm Development Trust.

Preference is also given to local organisations in areas of company presence and projects in which a member of staff is involved. Local grants range from £50 to £500.

The company operates the Give As You Earn payroll giving scheme.

Exclusions

No response to circular appeals. No support for appeals from individuals, purely denominational (religious) appeals or local appeals not in areas of company presence.

Applications

Appeals to head office should be addressed to the correspondent. Grant decisions are made by the chairman or the whole board once a month. Local appeals should be sent to the appropriate regional office. Corporate sponsorship proposals to Mrs L Blake, Corporate Communications Manager.

Hammerson plc

100 Park Lane, London W1Y 4AR
0171-887 1000; Fax: 0171-887 1010

Correspondent: Stuart Haydon, Company Secretary

Chief officers: *Chairman:* G Maitland Smith;
Chief Executive: R R Spinney

Year end	Turnover	Pre-tax profit
31/12/97	n/a	£61,700,000

Nature of company business
Property investment and development. 66% of the company's property assets are in the UK, with the remainder in Canada, France and Germany. Within the UK, the property portfolio is mainly in London, with other interests in Birmingham, Grimsby, Reading, Romford, Slough, Stockport and Woking.

UK employees: 100

Charitable donations

1997: £65,418
1996: £47,763
1995: £40,744
1994: £45,375
1993: £15,016
Membership: *ABSA*

Community support policy

The total donations made by the company in 1997 were £123,568 of which £65,418 was given in the UK.

Donations policy: A wide range of local and national charities are supported including projects in areas of company presence. The company supports children/youth, education, elderly people, enterprise/training, environment, medical research, science/technology, sickness/disability and social welfare. Arts sponsorship is also undertaken.

The company encourages employees volunteering/charitable activities with financial support.

Hanover Acceptances Ltd

16 Hans Road, London SW3 1RS
0171-581 1477; Fax: 0171-5893542

Correspondent: Sandra Poole, Personal Assistant to the Chairman

Chief officers: n/a

Year end	Turnover	Pre-tax profit
31/12/96	£271,850,000	£7,079,000

Nature of company business
The main activities of the company are property investment, management and trading.

Main subsidiaries include: Dorrington Holdings PLC; Tamoa Ltd; Pride Foods Ltd; British Consolidated Investments Corpn Ltd; Dorrington Investments PLC; Dorrington Properties PLC; Fineman Lever and Co Ltd; Gerber Foods International Ltd; Gerber Foods Soft Drinks Ltd; Hanover Management Services.

UK employees: 1,497

Charitable donations
1996: £65,000
1995: £53,363
1994: £64,000
1993: £63,000

Community support policy
Unfortunately, we still have very little information on this company's charitable donations policy. Donations are generally to smaller local London-based charities and are usually for £100 to £500, but in exceptional circumstances may be for up to £15,000.

There is a preference for arts-based projects, with the Tate Gallery and the Whitechapel Arts Centre having been supported in the past. The Royal Marsden Hospital has also been a major beneficiary.

Applications
In writing to the correspondent.

Hanson plc

1 Grosvenor Place, London SW1X 7JH
0171-245 1245; Fax: 0171-245 1293
Website: www.shareholdernews.com/han

Correspondent: Maureen Nixon, Corporate Secretary

Chief officers: *Chairman:* Christopher Collins; *Chief Executive:* Andrew Dougal

Year end	Turnover	Pre-tax profit
31/12/97	£5,211,000,000	£848,900,000

Nature of company business
Hanson is an industrial management company with operations mainly in the UK and US.

Main subsidiaries include: ARC; Cornerstone; Hanson Brick; Grove Worldwide.

Main locations: Bristol; Stewartby, Bedford.

UK employees: 21,000

Charitable donations
1997: £1,247,000
1996: £1,382,000
1995: £1,058,000
1994: £971,000
1993: £894,000

Total community contributions: £5,510,000 worldwide (1996)

Membership: *ABSA*

Community support policy
The company stated in the 1996 annual report: 'Donations this year to education, medical research, youth sport and the arts totalled £5.5 million'. Of this £1,382,000 was given in the UK, with the total falling slightly to £1,247,000 in 1997.

Initiatives have included the creation of a Hanson Environment Fund for the Wildlife Trust, support for the Prostate Cancer Charity project at Hammersmith Hospital and to the appeal by the Royal College of Radiologists. Support has usually been concentrated on major educational and medical projects, leaving very little money available for general appeals.

The company is a member of ABSA.

Exclusions
No support is given to circular appeals, fundraising events, appeals from individuals or for advertising in charity brochures.

Applications
In writing to the correspondent.

Hays plc

Hays House, Millmead, Guildford, Surrey GU2 5HJ
01483-302203; Fax: 01483-300388

Correspondent: Alison Adams, Benefits Manager

Chief officers: *Chairman:* R E Frost;
Managing Director: J A Napier

Year end	Turnover	Pre-tax profit
30/6/98	£1,549,000,000	£197,000,000

Nature of company business
The company and its subsidiaries form a business services group which provides a range of specialist services for commercial, industrial and professional customers. Its three core activities are: distribution, personnel (staff recruitment agencies) and commercial (office support services).

Main subsidiaries include: DEI Group Ltd; Securicor Omega Office Services Ltd; Delta Medical Express Group.

UK employees: n/a

Charitable donations
1998: £113,597
1997: £85,028
1996: £93,103
1995: £51,594
1994: £91,000

Community support policy
Generally the company supports small local charities which have no access to national funds. Particular emphasis is given to charities which provide for older people and the very young, especially disability charities. National support is given to the arts. Grants to national organisations, where given, range from £250 to £2,500. Grants to local organisations from £50 to £500.

Exclusions
Generally no support for circular appeals, advertising in charity brochures, purely denominational (religious) appeals, local appeals not in areas of company presence, large national appeals or overseas projects.

Applications
In writing to the correspondent.

Hazlewood Foods plc

Slack Lane, Rowditch, Derby DE1 1NB
01332-295295; Fax: 01332-292300

Correspondent: Neil Chalk, Company Secretary

Chief officers: *Chairman:* Peter Barr; *Chief Executive:* John Simons (UK); Tom Van Gurp (Continental)

Year end	Turnover	Pre-tax profit
31/3/98	£774,200,000	5£32,300,000

Nature of company business
The main activity is the manufacture of ready meals and convenience foods.

Main subsidiaries include: Breadwinner Foods Ltd; F H Lee; R & B Group Ltd; Van Heyningen Brothers Ltd.
Main locations: Basildon, Bedford, Bristol, Derby, Dunstable, London, Plymouth, Sheffield, Warrington, Wisbech, Worksop.

UK employees: 9,171

Charitable donations
1998: £56,031
1997: £42,121
1996: £41,730
1995: £44,892
1994: £42,678

Community support policy
The company gives support to a few specified national charities and to local organisations in its area. However, a large part of its community support is to allow access to its expertise in training and business practice to small non-competing businesses and in support of undergraduate business focused training in a number of universities.

Applications
In writing to the correspondent.

Heath Group plc

133 Houndsditch, London EC3A 7AH
0171-234 4000; Fax: 0171-234 4111
Website: www.heathgroup.com

Correspondent: N Rowe, Company Secretary

Chief officers: *Chairman:* M H Kier;
Managing Director: J G MacKenzie Green

Year end	Turnover	Pre-tax profit
31/3/98	£111,832,000	£7,297,000

Nature of company business
A holding company whose subsidiaries trade in the businesses of international insurance and reinsurance broking.

Main subsidiaries include: Amberly Cleave 4 Ltd; Boniface Insurance Services Corporation; Collins Halden (Scotland) Ltd; Hughes Aubrey & Partners Ltd; Independent Medical Insurance Consultants Ltd; Sino-Heath Ltd.

UK employees: 1,680

Charitable donations
1998: £51,843
1997: £61,761
1996: £66,787
1995: £82,161
1994: £75,879

Community support policy
The company prefers to support capital and medical research projects aimed at the relief of human suffering, science/technology and overseas/national emergencies. Preference for national charities and charities in areas of company presence. Grants range from £1,000 to £2,000.

Heinz

Grants are made through the Erycinus Charitable Trust (Charity Commission number 265100), which was established by the company with the principal purpose of making donations to any charitable body or institution engaged in medical research. The trustees are M H Kier, N Rowe and T P Newbery.

In 1996/97, the trust gave a total of £31,000 in grants having received a £20,000 covenant from the company. It gave 10 grants of £3,000 with none of the recipients having been supported the previous year. They were Karim Centre for Meningitis Research, Lupus UK, Pain Relief Foundation, DEBRA, Asthma Allergy & Inflammation Research Trust, Covent Garden Cancer Research Trust, JLOF Royal Marsden Hospital, National Osteoporosis Society, IBS Appeal and Royal Hospitals Neurosurgical Research Fund. In 1997/98, the main beneficiary was Polish Flood Emergency Aid.

Exclusions

No grants for appeals from individuals, purely denominational (religious) appeals and local appeals not in areas of company presence.

Applications

In writing to the correspondent.

H J Heinz Company Ltd

Hayes Park, Hayes, Middlesex UB4 8AL
0181-573 7757; Fax: 0181-848 2325

Correspondent: Mrs Ann Banks, Corporate Affairs Manager

Chief officer: *Chairman:* Malcolm Richie

Year end	Turnover	Pre-tax profit
26/4/97	£608,179,000	£55,106,000

Nature of company business
Principal activities: the manufacture, processing, growing and distribution of food.
Main subsidiaries include: Sous Chef Ltd; Single Service Ltd; Flexi-Pak Ltd.

UK employees: n/a

Charitable donations
1997: £130,000
1996: £115,000
1995: £94,000
1994: £105,000
1993: £140,000

Community support policy

Charitable donations: The H J Heinz Co Ltd Charitable Trust was set up in 1983 to handle all requests made to the company for financial assistance. It is funded by the company who pay annually a sum agreed by the board. The trust confines its giving to purposes accepted in law as charitable. It gives priority to:

- the maintenance and enhancement of its reputation for good citizenship in the local communities in which the company operates
- support for the medical aspects of nutrition and health, with particular emphasis on paediatrics
- maintenance and enhancement of its reputation for leadership and social responsibility as a major employer in the food manufacturing industry.

The trustees are Mrs D Heinz, Dr A J F O'Reilly, A Beresford, A G M Ritchie, B R Purgavie and M Cook. In 1997, the trustees' report stated 'the trustees have responded to appeals for assistance from organisations in the fields of community relations, education, international causes, welfare, medical and the arts'.

The income of the trust in that year was £115,000 and grants totalled £84,000. 35 grants were made ranging from £100 to £20,000, with 17 of £1,000. The larger grants went to Holding Hands Appeal (£20,000), Royal College of Paediatrics & Child Health (£15,000), The Wildlife Trust (£10,00)) and Diana, Princess of Wales Memorial Fund and ICAN (both £5,000). Other grant recipients included The American Ireland Fund, Ireland Fund of Great Britain, Brittle Bone Society, Cumbria Deaf Association, Mayhew Animal Rescue Home, National Grocers' Benevolent Fund, Royal Academy of Arts and Tools for Living.

In kind support: The company gives goods to raise money for local charities. It also donates to overseas disaster appeals.

Enterprise: Heinz is one of the sponsors for Wigan New Enterprise Ltd, particularly the Youth Enterprise Centre.

Education: The company is involved in local education/ business partnerships and provides educational materials for schools. It has also sponsored research at Surrey University into the cholesterol properties of certain fibre foods.

The arts: The company undertakes arts sponsorship on a national and local level. For example it has sponsored the 'Orchestra of the Mill', a community orchestra in Wigan.

Exclusions

No support is given to circular appeals, purely denominational (religious) appeals, political appeals, individuals undertaking educational or vocational studies, individuals or groups for sponsored events. No commercial sponsorship or advertising in charity brochures is undertaken by the trust.

Applications

In writing to the correspondent. Applications should include a short, general description of the society and/or project, with a statement of aims together with any supporting material. The trustees meet once a year, usually in July or August. However, a sub-committee who are authorised to grant funds up to a limit agreed by the trustees, meets four times a year. This committee also selects applications to be considered by the trustees at their annual meeting. One of the trustees is David Cook who can be contacted at the same address and whose telephone number is 0181-848 2282.

Corporate sponsorship proposals should be addressed to M Sargent, General Manager, Corporate Communications & Public Affairs.

Information available: The company reports on its involvement in its annual report.

Henderson plc

3 Finsbury Avenue, London EC2M 2PA
0171-638 5757; Fax: 0171-410 4414

Correspondent: Catherine Bellinger, Secretary to the Chairman

Chief officers: *Chairman:* B H B Wrey; *Managing Director:* D M Eadie

Year end	Turnover	Pre-tax profit
31/3/97	n/a	n/a

Nature of company business
Principal activities: investment advisory and management services. UK principal offices: London.

UK employees: 950

Charitable donations
1997: £86,300
1996: £83,000
1995: £72,584
1994: £65,000
1993: £64,401

Community support policy

Support is given to charities in which a member of company staff is involved, local to the City of London or local to branch offices. Preference for causes concerned with: the arts; children/youth; education; elderly people; enterprise/training; environment/heritage; fundraising events; medical research; sickness/disability charities and social welfare. Main beneficiaries in 1996/97 included Community Links, Cancer Research and BKPA.

A payroll giving scheme is operated (Give As You Earn), and the company partially matches employee fundraising.

Exclusions
No support for animal welfare charities; appeals from individuals; overseas projects; political appeals; religious appeals or sport.

Applications
In writing to the correspondent.

Hewlett-Packard Ltd

Cain Road, Bracknell, Berkshire RG12 1HN
01344-360000; Fax: 01344-363344
Website: www.hp.com

Correspondent: Director, Communications & Public Affairs

Chief officer: *Managing Director:* John Golding

Year end	Turnover	Pre-tax profit
31/10/97	£2,007,542,000	£205,311,000

Nature of company business
Hewlett-Packard Ltd is a subsidiary of the Hewlett-Packard Company incorporated in the USA. The principal activities of the group are the design, manufacture and marketing of measurement and computation products and systems.

Main subsidiaries include: Computer Peripherals & Research Centre; Telecommunications Division & Microwave Operation.

Main locations: Bristol; South Queensferry, West Lothian.

UK employees: n/a

Charitable donations
1997: £140,000
1996: £129,000
1995: £96,000
1994: £74,000
1993: £95,000

Total community contributions: £450,000 (1996)

Membership: *BitC*

Community support policy

Charitable donations: All charities supported are selected from nominations by employees, with preference given to those which employees give their time and efforts to or which directly benefit employee families or friends.

Support is given to a wide variety of organisations, particularly local, community-based charities (within a 25-mile radius of the company's factories) and selected national charities.

Preferred areas of support are children and youth, social welfare, medical, education, enterprise/training and environment and heritage. Recipient organisations must be registered charities and donations are given through the Charities Aid Foundation.

The company also donates equipment to selected higher education establishments. For donations of equipment/gifts in kind apply to the Personnel Division at the address above.

The company complements staff donations to charity under the 'money match' scheme.

Enterprise: Hewlett-Packard is a member of Business in the Community and seconds staff to some agencies.

Environment: The company seeks to promote awareness of wider environmental issues. It currently sponsors the Margaret Mee Amazon Trust and BTCV.

Exclusions
No applications for support of political activities are considered and no support is given to advertising in charity brochures, fundraising events, appeals from individuals, large national appeals, purely denominational (religious) appeals or overseas projects.

Applications
All charities are nominated by company employees. Sponsorship proposals should be addressed to the correspondent.

Highland Distillers plc

West Kinfauns, Perth PH2 7XZ
01738-440000; Fax: 01738-628167

Correspondent: F S Morrison, Assistant Company Secretary

Chief officers: *Chairman & Chief Executive:* B G Ivory

Year end	Turnover	Pre-tax profit
31/8/98	£211,000,000	£43,000,000

Nature of company business
Malt whisky distillers.

Main subsidiaries include: Matthew Gloag & Son Ltd; Glenturret Distillery Ltd; Gordon Graham & Co Ltd; The Macallan Distillers Ltd; HRB Investments Ltd; HS Distillers Ltd; Alfred Dunhill Scotch Whisky Ltd.

Main brands include: The Famous Grouse; The Macallan; Highland Park; Tamdhu; Bunnahabhain; Glenturret; Gloag's Gin; Black Bottle.

UK employees: 435

Charitable donations

1998: £149,000
1997: £133,000
1996: £119,000
1995: £110,000
1994: £103,000
Membership: %Club

Community support policy

The company is a member of the PerCent Club. It supports a variety of local charities and community activities preferably in Scotland and particularly in the more remote areas where its distilleries are located. Support is given to environment/heritage, sickness/disability and social welfare, the arts, advertising in charity brochures, animal welfare charities appeals from individuals, children/youth, elderly people, fundraising events, medical research, science/technology, sport, job creation, educational opportunities for young people, inner city projects and research into alcohol abuse. Donations are usually for £100 to £1,000, but can be larger in exceptional circumstances.

The main beneficiaries in 1998 were Prince's Trust in Scotland (£20,000), Piping Centre Trust (£52,000), Princess Royal Trust for Carers (£10,000), Glasgow Academy Millenium Fund and St Giles Cathedral Fund. The company's main area of non-cash support is good-cause sponsorship. It also allows employees company time off to volunteer and matches employee fundraising.

Enterprise: The company is a member of Scottish Business in the Community.

Exclusions

Limited support for overseas charities. No support for political or religious appeals.

Applications

In writing to the correspondent.

Hillsdown Holdings plc

Hillsdown House, 32 Hampstead High Street, London NW3 1QD
0171-794 0677; Fax: 0171-433 6409

Correspondent: Sandra Fagelson, Charities Administrator

Chief officer: *Chairman:* Sir John Nott

Year end	Turnover	Pre-tax profit
31/12/97	£3,094,100,000	£110,000,000

Nature of company business
Principal activities: food processing and distribution; fresh meat and bacon; poultry and eggs; furniture; housebuilding and property; and specialist operations.

Main subsidiaries include: Chivers Hartley Ltd; F E Barber Ltd; H L Foods; Premier Brands Ltd; Henry Telfer Ltd; Pinneys of Scotland Ltd; Smedleys Foods Ltd; MBM Produce Ltd; Buxted Chicken Ltd; Buxted Foods Ltd; Daylay Foods Ltd; Devon Crest Poultry Ltd; Moorland Poultry Ltd; Premier Poultry Ltd; Ross Breeders Ltd; Ross Poultry Ltd; Carleton Furniture Group Ltd; Christie Tyler PLC; Fairview New Homes PLC; J J Yates & Co Ltd; Walker & Homer Group Ltd.

UK employees: 31,223

Charitable donations

1997: £300,000
1996: £300,000
1995: £300,000
1994: £500,000
1993: £300,000
Membership: ABSA %Club

Community support policy

The company supports a variety of charities/projects both directly and through the Hillsdown Charitable Trust. The company is very committed to medical research and substantial support has been given towards the Help Appeal of the Royal College of Physicians and the Cancerkin Unit at the Royal Free Hospital. The company says that donations are made at the discretion of the chairman. Subsidiaries have their own donations budgets.

The arts: The company sponsors arts, including the London International Opera Festival. It is a member of ABSA and a corporate member of the Royal Opera House Trust.

Applications

In writing to the correspondent.

Honda Motor Europe Ltd

Caversham Bridge House, Waterman Place, Reading, Berkshire RG1 8DN
01189-566399; Fax: 01734-554772

Correspondent: Mrs Margaret Hooper, Site Services Manager

Chief officer: *Chairman:* K Ito

Year end	Turnover	Pre-tax profit
31/3/98	£2,809,000,000	(£3,000,000)

Nature of company business
The principal activity of the company is the importation and distribution of motor vehicles, parts and accessories.

UK employees: 2,694

Charitable donations
1998: £76,000
1997: £85,000
1996: £48,000
1995: £34,000
1994: £27,000

Total community contributions: £200,000

Membership: *BitC*

Community support policy

Community contributions amounted to about £200,000, of which £76,000 was given in charitable donations. The main areas of non-cash support are good-cause sponsorship, support for enterprise agencies and gifts in kind. Employees are allowed time off to volunteer.

The company prefers to support national charities in the fields of: children/youth, education, enterprise/training, environment/heritage, science/technology and sport. Support for fundraising events and advertising in charity brochures may also be undertaken.

Exclusions

No support for animal welfare, appeals from individuals, political appeals, religious appeals and large national charities.

Applications

In writing to the correspondent.

House of Fraser PLC

1 Howick Place, London SW1P 1BH
0171-963 2000; Fax: 0171-828 8885

Correspondent: Peter Hearsey, Company Secretary

Chief officers: *Chairman:* B D McGowan;
Chief Executive: J Coleman

Year end	Turnover	Pre-tax profit
31/1/98	£812,000,000	£29,000,000

Nature of company business
Department store operators. The group's 49 stores trade under the following names: Army & Navy, Arnotts, Barkers, Binns, Cavendish House, David Evans, D H Evans, Dickins & Jones, Dingles, Frasers, Jolly's, Hammonds, House of Fraser, Howells, Kendals, Rackhams and Schofields.

UK employees: n/a

Charitable donations
1998: £66,499
1997: £91,117
1996: £77,401
1995: £64,853
1994: £144,089

Membership: *BitC*

Community support policy

The company chooses three charities (primarily associated with the retail trade) to support via covenanted donations. Therefore other donations tend to be given to local charities in areas where the company's stores are located in the fields of children and youth, social welfare, medical, environment and heritage, enterprise/training, education and the arts. Non-cash support is in the form of joint promotions. In 1998, the main beneficiaries included Cottage Homes, Purley Children's Trust and Duke of Edinburgh Award.

Exclusions

Support is not generally given to circular appeals, appeals from individuals, purely denominational (religious or political) appeals, local appeals not in areas of company presence or overseas projects.

Applications

In writing to the correspondent. Local charities are supported at the discretion of local store managers.

Household International UK Ltd

North Street, Winkfield, Windsor, Berkshire SL4 4TD
01344-890000; Fax: 01344-890014

Correspondent: Trudi Hunter, Corporate Communications Co-ordinator

Chief officers: *Chairman:* David Keys;
Managing Director: Gary Gilmer

Year end	Turnover	Pre-tax profit
31/12/96	£261,881,000	£57,718,000

Nature of company business
Banking and insurance.

Main subsidiaries include: HFC Bank PLC; DLRS Ltd; Hamilton Insurance Co Ltd; Hamilton Life Assurance Co Ltd; Hamilton Financial Planning Services Ltd.

UK employees: 1,873

Charitable donations
1996: £68,176
1995: £71,650
1994: £65,000
1993: £64,908

HSBC

Community support policy
No information was available other than that the company supports both local and national charities.

Applications
In writing to the correspondent.

HSBC Holdings plc

10 Lower Thames Street, London EC3R 6AE
0171-260 0500; Fax: 0171-260 0501
Website: www.hsbcgroup.com

Correspondent: Amanda Combes, Community Relations Manager

Chief officers: *Chairman:* Sir William Purves; *Chief Executive:* J R H Bond

Year end	Turnover	Pre-tax profit
31/12/97	£22,876,000,000	£4,971,000,000

Nature of company business
The group provides banking and related financial services.

Main subsidiaries include: The British Bank of the Middle East; James Capel & Co Ltd; East River Savings Bank; Eversholt Holdings Ltd; First Direct; Forward Trust Ltd; Midland Bank Ltd; Midland Life Ltd; Samuel Montagu & Co Ltd.

UK employees: 441

Charitable donations
1997: £10,146,000 (worldwide)
1996: £2,805,000
1995: £3,817,000
1994: £4,420,000
1993: £5,345,000
Membership: %Club

Community support policy
HSBC Holdings plc are responsible for creating a unified image for members of the HSBC Group; hence the demise of the Midland griffin and its replacement by HSBC's hexagon symbol on our high streets. We understand that as a consequence of this move national charitable donations and policy decisions previously taken by the Midland are now being made by HSBC. Requests for local funding, however, may still be made to local Midland Bank branches.

Unfortunately, despite requests for information updates from both parties the 'listening bank' has chosen to turn a deaf ear and details of any new (unified?) policy have not been forthcoming. Even reference to the group's website failed to turn up any community support information, and in this respect it compares unfavourably to other leading UK bank websites. As a major giver in the UK this lack of availability of clear guidelines does not help charities correctly identify possible sources of support.

In order to provide some information, the following is taken from the 1998 PerCent Club Annual Report, and refers to Midland Bank plc only. It should be read bearing in mind the comments on policy above.

'Midland Bank contributes to a range of national and local voluntary and charitable activities throughout the UK, helping to enhance its reputation as a community bank.

'Midland's three-year partnership with Shelter, Age Concern and the National Deaf Children's Society continued successfully with the launch of the Sheltercard at Shelter's first National Supporter's convention and the distribution of the Teacher's Guide... giving important information to young people on homelessness within national curriculum guidelines. Age Concern launched a further five Safe and Warm Schemes giving elderly people energy advice for the winter and The Listening Bus made its 100th visit in February by which time it had been visited by over 12,000 people.

'Midland's commitment to education and sport was demonstrated by its continued support of Young Enterprise and Schools Tennis. Over 900 staff currently act as advisers or area board members for Young Enterprise throughout the country.

'Midland Bank was once again the leading supporter of grassroots tennis in schools. Over 40,000 young players took part in the Midland Bank Schools Tennis Programme, including team competitions for all ages and abilities and free coaching and equipment to encourage school players to join their local club. The Match Points Scheme enabled schools to obtain free tennis equipment.... .

'Midland also sponsored "Ooh Ah Showab Khan", the sequel to the award winning anti-racism play, "Kicking Out". To date the play has been seen by over 50,000 secondary school children. Special gala performances also brought awareness of the issues discussed in the play to the attention of business leaders, schools and education experts in the UK's towns and cities.

'All these initiatives underlined Midland's long-standing links with local communities and charitable organisations which continue[d] in 1998.'

Applications
In writing to the correspondent.

Hunting plc

3 Cockspur Street, London SW1Y 5BQ
0171-321 0123; Fax: 0171-839 2072
Email: anna.bw@hunting.plc.uk
Website: www.hunting.plc.uk

Correspondent: Ms Anna Blundell-Williams, Personal Assistant to the Chairman

Chief officers: *Chairman:* R H Hunting; *Chief Executive:* K W Miller

Year end	Turnover	Pre-tax profit
31/12/97	£1,317,000,000	£39,000,000

Nature of company business
The principal activities are defence engineering, oil services and military support.

Main subsidiaries include: EA Gibson Shipbrokers Ltd; AWE PLC; Irvin Aerospace Ltd; Gibson Petroleum Co Ltd.

UK employees: 12,744

Charitable donations
1997: £91,000
1996: £59,000
1995: £38,000
1994: £82,000
1993: £42,000

Community support policy
In addition to the £91,000 given to charities in the UK, a further £91,000 was given to overseas charities. Charitable donations are generally made through the Hunting Charitable Trust, which supports UK charities involved in welfare and medicine.

Local charities are usually only supported by subsidiaries if a member of staff has a particularly close connection with the charity. Subsidiaries also have their own sponsorship budgets.

The company sponsors the Hunting Art Prizes Competition.

Exclusions
No support for environment or heritage charities.

Applications
In writing to the correspondent. The trustees of the Hunting Charitable Trust meet once a year, generally in November.

Huntleigh Technology plc

310–312 Dallow Road, Luton, Bedfordshire LU1 1TD
01582-413104; Fax: 01582-402589
Website: www.huntleigh-technology.com

Correspondent: Julian Schild, Group Finance Director

Chief officers: *Chairman:* R Schild; *Managing Director:* D Schild

Year end	Turnover	Pre-tax profit
31/12/97	£83,566,000	£11,492,000

Nature of company business
The principal activity is the design, manufacture, distribution and rental of equipment, instrumentation and control systems for medical applications.

UK employees: 950

Charitable donations
1997: £60,000
1996: £27,000
1995: £17,457

Community support policy
The company prefers to support charities in Bedfordshire and other parts of the UK where it has sites including south Wales and the West Midlands. It supports charities in the fields of children/youth, fundraising events, medical research, science/technology, sickness/disability, social welfare, sport and the arts, education and enterprise and training. Recent beneficiaries include the Arkwright Scholarships, Duke of Edinburgh Award – Shield Project, St John's Hospice and the University of London.

Exclusions
No support for animal welfare, appeals from individuals, environment/heritage, overseas projects, political appeals or religious appeals.

Applications
In writing to the correspondent.

Hyder plc

PO Box 295, Alexandra Gate, Rover Way, Cardiff CF2 2UE
01222-500600; Fax: 01222-585600
Email: hyder.plc@hyder.com

Correspondent: Karen Welch, Public Relations Officer

Chief officers: *Chairman:* John Robins; *Chief Executive:* Graham Hawker

Year end	Turnover	Pre-tax profit
31/3/98	£1,185,100,000	£168,500,000

Nature of company business
The group is principally engaged in utility management and the provision of infrastructure services. The group provides electricity distribution and electricity and gas supply services, as well as water and sewerage-based services.

Main subsidiaries include: Welsh Water; South Wales Electricity.

UK employees: 8,994

Charitable donations
1998: £99,000
1997: £63,000
1996: £30,000
1995: £51,000
1994: £53,190

Total community contributions: £850,000

Membership: *BitC %Club*

Community support policy
In addition to the quoted charitable donations figure of £99,000, the company annual report for 1997/98 states that the group supports a vast range of community initiatives, together with a very substantial investment of employee time. In all, cash and in kind support for the year totalled £850,000, up from £340,000 the previous year. Some of the current initiatives being undertaken by Hyder in the community include the following:

Employee volunteering initiative – Support is given to employees who wish to carry out projects and activities for the benefit of the wider community in Wales, on a voluntary basis and largely in their own time. As well as making small donations and grants, Hyder provide vehicles, facilities, equipment and other resources.

ARENA Network – Launched as a Business in the Community project in 1993, the Network is managed by a senior Hyder manager, and has grown into an independent company with charitable status. It provides guidance, information and practical assistance to companies in Wales on business and environmental issues.

Educational activities – Both SWALEC and Dwr Cymru Welsh Water provide a comprehensive service to schools and colleges, including in-service teacher training and curriculum development.

Challenge Carol – A team building exercise based on Challenge Anneka, staff ingenuity and energy was used to raise money and redecorate a community centre for underprivileged children in a multi-cultural area of Cardiff. The success of this initiative has led to other similar projects being undertaken.

Preferred areas of sponsorship are: the arts; children/youth; education; older people; environment/heritage; medical research; science/technology; projects promoting the Welsh language. Preference for charities in areas of company presence, although national (UK) charities may be supported.

Exclusions
No support for individuals; branches of organistaions; overseas projects – except WaterAid; advertising in charity brochures; animal welfare charities.

Applications
In writing to the correspondent.

IBM United Kingdom Holdings Ltd

IBM UK Trust, South Bank, 76 Upper Ground, London SE1 9PZ
Website: www.uk.ibm.com/community/comm2.html

Correspondent: Peter Wilkinson

Chief officer: *Chairman:* Carl G Symon

Year end	Turnover	Pre-tax profit
31/12/97	£4,956,900,000	£351,000,000

Nature of company business
IBM United Kingdom Ltd is the UK subsidiary of IBM Corporation. It is involved in the provision of information technology services and solutions, and the development, production and supply of advanced information technology products.

UK employees: 16,833

Charitable donations
1997: £511,000
1996: £550,746
1995: n/a
1994: n/a
1993: £1,422,000

Total community contributions: £1,800,000

Membership: *ABSA BitC %Club*

Community support policy
In 1997, IBM's total contribution in the UK was valued at over £1.8 million, through a combination of all the resources at its disposal, from equipment and software, to consultancy, employee time, student placements and financial donations.

IBM's focus for community relations is to help educational and training institutions across the world to deliver their services in innovative ways by the application of technology for education and training. The aim is to support change at systematic level and raise educational standards, and contributions are made primarily through IBM's *Reinventing Education* and *Training for Work* programmes.

Reinventing Education
This is a worldwide initiative launched by IBM in 1994 to refocus schools systems on high academic standards. The programme offers a core of innovative technology solutions housed in a framework called Wired for Learning and developed by IBM and educators across the world. In Europe, IBM is contributing $1 million to Ireland's school system and has other projects in development.

Training for Work
IBM's *Training for Work* programme helps institutions across the world to deliver their services in innovative ways to people who would otherwise be excluded from training and jobs. In Europe, a series of projects has been launched in seven countries which will, over the next three years, investigate how the innovative use of information technology can really improve the training and learning process. Two projects are being supported in the UK as part of the programme to develop new approaches to training the disadvantaged. Knowsley Community College is introducing an NVQ course in multimedia which will equip young people with the skill for jobs in this new industry and Brunel University Centre for Lifelong Learning is increasing access to training by setting up facilities for remote learning in a community centre, a rugby club and through home learning groups.

Contributions are also made to support the raising of educational standards and the 1998 programmes in the UK included several new projects to develop use of IT in schools. In Hampshire, in partnership with a teacher training college, trainee teachers have been given a portable PC during their practice placements, to promote collaboration and reduce isolation. In Newcastle, IBM installed a suite of networked PCs for a homework club at a school concerned to raise student attainment. The facility is used for both students and parents who also may have a need to develop basic skills.

Employee involvement: IBM encourages and supports IBM employees and retirees to undertake voluntary work. To further this objective, IBM developed Volbase, a Lotus Notes software programme, which matches prospective employee volunteers to volunteering opportunities identified by the company through its contacts with voluntary organisations. The Volbase programme has now been adopted by Business in the Community for its volunteering initiatives.

The company operates the Give As You Earn payroll giving scheme.

Exclusions

No support for building projects, political, religious or sectarian organisations, animal charities, individuals (including students), overseas activities such as expeditions, recreational and sports clubs, or appeals by third parties on behalf of charities or individuals.

The company does not currently offer full-time secondments of employees to voluntary organisations.

Applications

The majority of support is given through specific programmes identified and developed by IBM with identified partner organisations. Very few unsolicited requests can be considered. There is no formal application process. All requests should be in writing and include a brief resume of the aims of the organisation and details of the assistance required.

Information on IBM's community programmes within the UK is available on the internet at http://www.uk.ibm.com/community/comm2.html. Any correspondence or enquiries should be addressed to Peter Wilkinson, IBM UK Trust, PO Box 9108, London SW14 8ZN (0181-288 1845; Fax: 0181-287 6580).

Arts and sports sponsorship enquiries should be addressed to: Peter Wilkinson, Peter Wilkinson Associates, at the address above.

Iceland Group plc

Second Avenue, Deeside Industrial Park,
Deeside, Flintshire CH5 2NW
01244-830100

Correspondent: Barbara Crampton, Public Relations Manager

Chief officer: *Chairman:* Malcolm C Walker

Year end	Turnover	Pre-tax profit
3/1/98	£1,566,400,000	£43,500,000

Nature of company business
Iceland is a multiple retailer of frozen food groceries, chilled products and domestic appliances.

Main subsidiaries include: Bejam Group; Burgundy; Woodward Foodservice.

UK employees: 18,784

Charitable donations

1997: £119,000
1996: £307,000
1995: £409,000
1994: £360,000
1993: £334,818

Community support policy

In 1996, the company and its employees donated over £300,000 to a variety of causes including UNICEF, Duke of Edinburgh Award, Tacade and Juvenile Diabetes Foundation. 1996 was the first year of a three-year partnership with the Cancer Research Campaign during which the company has committed to communicate health messages to consumers, as well as donating and raising funds for the charity.

Exclusions

The company does not support appeals from non-charities, advertising in charity brochures, circular appeals, small purely local appeals not in areas of company presence or overseas projects. The company does not generally undertake arts sponsorship or secondment.

Applications

The company states that at the time of going to print it is reviewing its strategy for charity support with a view to being more community focused. In the interim unsolicited approaches are not required.

ICL plc

Observatory House, Windsor Road,
Slough, Berkshire SL1 2EY
01753-516000

Correspondent: Martin Archer, Director of Marketing Communications

Chief officers: *Chairman:* M Naruto; *Chief Executive:* Keith Todd

Year end	Turnover	Pre-tax profit
31/12/97	£2,477,000,000	£30,000,000

Nature of company business
Principal activity: information technology.

UK employees: n/a

Charitable donations

1997: £51,000
1996: £44,000
1995: n/a
1994: n/a
1993: £230,000
Membership: *BitC*

Community support policy

The company gives support to some educational establishments or organisations, usually only for particular causes such as encouragement of young people towards careers in science or technology. Several universities and schools are supported. Certain causes chosen by ICL staff, industry charities and charities local to ICL sites of operation are also supported.

Exclusions

Charitable advertising and appeals from outside the areas indicated are unlikely to be supported. No other appeals will be considered.

Applications

In writing to the correspondent.

IMI plc

PO Box 216, Witton, Birmingham B6 7BA
0121-356 4848; Fax: 0121-331 1736

Correspondent: Elaine Morgan, Secretary, IMI Charitable Appeals Committee

Chief officers: *Chairman:* Sir Eric Pountain; *Chief Executive:* G J Allen

Year end	Turnover	Pre-tax profit
31/12/97	£1,434,000,000	£146,500,000

Nature of company business
IMI is a diversified engineering group operating in the areas of building products, drinks dispense, fluid power and special engineering. It manufactures and sells internationally and has major plants in the UK, North and South America, Continental Europe and Australia.

Main locations: Birmingham, Liverpool, Manchester, Yorkshire.

UK employees: 7,145

Charitable donations

1997: £301,000
1996: £313,000
1995: £257,000
1994: £223,000
1993: £267,000

Total community contributions: £380,000

Membership: *BitC*

Community support policy

The community contributions totalling £380,000 in 1997 include charitable donations, in kind support, non-commercial advertising, and arts sponsorship (£75,000). The main areas of non-cash support are secondments and allowing charities to use some of the company's office space. In addition, non-cash support will be provided by many of IMI's subsidiary companies throughout the UK, but this is not quantified.

Charitable donations: The majority of group donations are distributed by head office through the Charities Aid Foundation. The balance is distributed by the main operating subsidiaries which have their own separate budgets for charitable donations. There is a preference for charities of direct or indirect benefit to the business in the West Midlands, Lancashire and Yorkshire, those which benefit or are likely to benefit employees (present, past and potential) and charities located and working in areas where the company has its major interests (see above).

IMI prefers to support organisations working in the following areas: children/youth, elderly people, social welfare, animal welfare, arts and culture, health and medical care, education, religious appeals, science/technology, sickness/disability and sport. Support is also given to enterprise/training and environment/heritage appeals.

National grants generally range from £250 to £5,000, and local grants from £25 to £5,000. 260 grants were given in 1997. The main grants were to Birmingham Children's Hospital, National Youth Orchestra, Foundation for Conductive Education, Princess Royal Trust for Carers and Business in the Community. Typical beneficiaries included the Prince's Youth Business Trust (£5,000 a year for four years), Birmingham Young Volunteers (£300) and Elms Farm Primary School (£25).

Employee involvement: Preference is given to charities in which a member of staff is involved and staff are allowed time off for activity of community benefit. Support for employee charitable activity is provided at subsidiary level and is therefore not quantified in the overall company's community contribution.

In kind support: Office accommodation is provided for use by Opportunities for People with Disabilities and Birmingham Children's Hospital Appeals Office.

Enterprise: IMI is a member of Business in the Community. It offers support to organisations local to head office.

Education: The company gives a substantial amount of money to the City Technology College in Birmingham. It also operates work experience schemes for pupils and provides student sponsorships.

The arts: Although the company is not a member of ABSA, it does sponsor the City of Birmingham Symphony Orchestra, Birmingham Royal Ballet, Birmingham Hippodrome and Symphony Hall and supports the Royal Society of Arts. The typical sponsorship range is from £250 to £25,000, with a preference for local projects or organisations.

Exclusions

Company policy is to give direct to charities and not to organisations which are themselves collecting for charity. No support for circular appeals, advertising in charity brochures, small purely local appeals not in an area of company presence, appeals from individuals, fundraising events, circular appeals, political appeals, large national appeals or overseas projects.

Applications

In writing to the correspondent. Corporate sponsorship proposals should be addressed to the company secretary. Grant decisions are made by an appeals committee which meets on an ad hoc basis. Local appeals should be sent to the relevant local plant or branch.

Advice to applicants: The company welcomes appeals from charities but its appeal mail is getting too large to handle. Applicants should therefore ensure that they can establish some link with the company. Appeals should, where applicable, give details of the total amount to be raised and a description of how the money is to be spent. If possible, the latest statement of accounts should accompany the appeal. The company correspondent complains that many appeals are poorly presented and some not even signed.

Imperial Chemical Industries plc

Imperial Chemical House, 9 Millbank, London SW1P 3JF
0171-834 4444; Fax: 0171-834 2024
Website: www.ici.com

Correspondent: Paul Patten, Administrator – Appeals Committee

Chief officers: *Chairman:* Charles Miller Smith; *Chief Executive:* Brendan R O'Neill

Year end	Turnover	Pre-tax profit
31/12/98	£9,286,000,000	£293,000,000

Nature of company business
The principal activities of the company are applications oriented coatings, materials and specialty chemicals businesses.

UK employees: 16,900

Charitable donations

1998: £2,800,000
1997: £1,900,000
1996: £700,000
1995: £800,000
1994: £900,000
Membership: *ABSA*

Community support policy

The responsibility for ICI's charitable giving in the UK rests with the Appeals Committee of the ICI Board, based at ICI Group Headquarters at the address above. Donations to registered charities are normally paid through the ICI Charity Trust. ICI regional businesses also provide support at local level to the communities in which they operate. ICI's priority areas of giving are education, social welfare, youth, disability groups and the environment, with a preference for national organisations (grants usually range from £500 to £20,000) or those located in communities where the company has a strong presence (grants usually range from £250 to £1,000). In addition to ICI's support for local UK communities, the individual subsidiary businesses of ICI worldwide have their own programmes of local support.

ICI Group's worldwide charitable donations for 1998 totalled £2.8 million, of which £1.7 million was spent in the UK. ICI also supports academic development, and encourages its employees to give their time and expertise as secondees and volunteers in local community activities.

The company produce a leaflet: *Our Approach to Charitable Giving in the UK*. This gives details of 'the guidelines we use in meeting our responsibilities as a good corporate citizen through the programme of charitable giving'. There is a preference for:

- Youth organisations in areas where the company has a strong presence or where the organisations operate nationally. Groups dealing with young people who are unemployed or socially disadvantaged are preferred.
- Education initiatives may be given support where they are closely associated with the company's activities and interests, particularly in relation to the encouragement of science.
- Mentally and physically disabled people are supported locally and nationally, especially in areas where the company has a strong presence.
- Environment organisations that make a positive contribution to the improvement of the environment are supported.
- National medical charities and projects are supported, especially if there is some relevance to the company's activities.
- Local arts organisations or projects are supported, especially those that involve young or disabled people. The company is a member of ABSA.
- Major national sports organisations or projects which are not requests for commercial sponsorship are considered.
- Churches of any denomination are considered if they are in the vicinity of an ICI site or are of national or historical significance.
- Only the main service charities which use smaller charities for the distribution of their funds are supported. No support for benevolent funds or individuals.
- Expeditions sponsored by learned societies may be considered.
- Natural disasters and emergencies are only supported if these directly affect ICI sites or employees.
- Building appeals will only be considered for buildings of national or historical importance.

In kind support: Dulux Paints are donated under the well-established Dulux Community Projects Scheme. Around £180,000 worth of paint is given away each year. The scheme is designed to 'provide help and encouragement to recognised voluntary groups who wish to carry out painting projects for the benefit of the community'. The only requirement is that the painting is done by unpaid volunteers. In addition, cash awards are made to 20 selected projects which offer 'the greatest potential in terms of creativity and benefit to the community'.

Applications should be on the official application form (available on receipt of a 49p A4-sized sae) which specify exact requirements in terms of type of paint, colour and quantity. The form is available from Easter to May with the closing date for receipt of application forms being the end of May/early June.

Please contact: The Dulux Community Projects Office, PO Box 343, London WC2E 8RJ.

Advertising: Requests for advertising space are normally referred to the Group Public Relations department. It will consider taking advertising space only if it is justified from the company's commercial or public relations point of view.

Exclusions

No donations are given to individuals, political parties, religious bodies or profit-making organisations. An appeal which is the same as, or similar to, one which has been refused within recent years will be refused.

Generally, only one donation will be given to any organisation within a 12-month period.

Imperial

Applications

In writing to the correspondent including the aims and objectives of the organisation, and outline details of the project requiring funding where appropriate. Applicants should include a current copy of their Annual Report and Accounts.

Appeals of a local nature originating near to ICI operations should be addressed to the relevant ICI business directly. National, Westminster and other requests should be addressed to the Appeals Committee Administrator at the address above.

Imperial Tobacco Group PLC

PO Box 244, Hartcliff, Bristol BS99 7UJ
0117-963 6636; Fax: 0117-966 7405

Correspondent: Sue Tudor, Secretary, Charity Appeals Committee

Chief officers: *Chairman:* Derek Bonham; *Chief Executive:* Gareth Davis

Year end	Turnover	Pre-tax profit
26/9/98	£4,029,000,000	£325,000,000

Nature of company business
Tobacco. The group acquired Rizla International in January 1997.
Main subsidiaries include: Sinclair Collis Ltd; Douwe Egberts, Van Nelle Tabacco.
Main brands include: Castella; Embassy; Golden Virginia; John Player; Lambert & Butler; Panama; Regal; St Bruno; Tom Thumb.

UK employees: 2,666

Charitable donations

1998: £412,000
1997: £225,000

Community support policy

The company states in its annual report that the group made charitable donations in the UK of £202,000; the comparable figure for 1997 was £25,000. In addition, the group provided a further £210,000 for charitable purposes to be distributed through the Charities Aid Foundation in accordance with the company's charities policy.

It supports local causes in the communities in which it operates and encourages employee participation in community affairs.

Unfortunately no further information was available on the types of causes favoured.

Applications

In writing to the correspondent.

Inchcape plc

33 Cavendish Square, London W1M 9HF
0171-546 0022; Fax: 0171-546 0010

Correspondent: Mary MacLennan, Group Communications Officer

Chief officers: *Chairman:* Sir Colin Marshall; *Chief Executive:* Philip Cushing

Year end	Turnover	Pre-tax profit
31/12/97	£5,931,400,000	£89,600,000

Nature of company business
Following the restructuring of the group in 1999, Inchcape is the world's largest independent importer and distributor of motor vehicles operating in around 30 countries worldwide. Its operations also encompass Motors Retail in the UK, and financial services. The latter including consumer and dealer finance, and insurance and warranty products.
Main subsidiaries include: CJ Imports; Toyota GB; Wadham Kenning Motor Group; Mann Egerton Vehicle Contracts; Kenning Leaseline.

UK employees: n/a

Charitable donations

1997: £381,000
1996: £305,000
1995: £401,000
1994: £443,000
1993: £471,000

Total community contributions: £780,000 (worldwide)

Membership: *ABSA*

Community support policy

Inchcape's corporate community involvement policy is to concentrate the majority of its funding on one international charity where it can make a significant difference and enable the charity to achieve its own objectives. From 1995, about £1.25 million, plus goods and services, has been committed in an initial five-year partnership with Raleigh International entitled 'The Inchcape Initiative'. The only other donations made in the UK, at group level, are for long-standing charitable commitments.

The group programme is supplemented locally, by a variety of sponsorships, donations and fundraising and fundraising activities by individual businesses. Wherever possible, the company seeks to involve its employees and business partners in community activities.

In 1997, the UK charitable donations made by the group totalled £381,000. The total charitable donations worldwide were £780,000.

The arts: The company is a member of ABSA.

Exclusions

Appeals which do not conform to Inchcape's policy.

Applications

In writing to the correspondent.

Independent Insurance Group plc

5th Floor, 2 Minster Court, Mincing Lane, London EC3R 7BB
0171-623 8877; Fax: 0171-283 8275

Correspondent: Malcom Ayling, Assistant Company Secretary

Chief officers: *Chairman:* G M Ramsay;
Chief Executive: M J Bright

Year end	Turnover	Pre-tax profit
31/12/97	£439,000,000	£65,000,000

Nature of company business
Insurance and related services.

Main subsidiaries include: VBA Management Ltd; New Scotland Services Ltd; Property & Casualty Services Ltd; Environmental Risk Services Ltd; Kite Property Holdings Ltd; The Insurance Club Ltd.

UK employees: 1,461

Charitable donations
1997: £60,934
1996: £67,584
1995: £47,000

Community support policy
The company supports both national (UK) charities (mainly Children in Need) and local charities, with a preference for those concerned with children/youth, medical research, and sickness/disability. Appeals from individuals will also be considered when backed-up by relevant support material.

The company supports employees' volunteering/charitable activities financially including matching employee fundraising.

Exclusions
No support for advertising in charity brochures, fundraising events, political appeals, religious appeals or sport.

Applications
In writing to the correspondent.

Intel Corporation UK Ltd

Pipers Way, Swindon SN3 1RJ
01793-696000; Fax: 01793-644660
Website: www.intel.com

Correspondent: The Charities Committee (ISW 60)

Chief officer: *Chairman:* K Chapple

Year end	Turnover	Pre-tax profit
27/12/97	£1,585,158,000	£154,092,000

Nature of company business
Integrated circuits and systems.

UK employees: n/a

Charitable donations
1997: £111,310
1996: £231,694
1995: n/a
1994: n/a
1993: £119,783

Community support policy
Most of the company's donations are given through the Wiltshire Community Foundation, to which it has covenanted £80,000 a year for four years.

The company also give gifts in kind, primarily to local charities in areas of company presence, with preference for charities in which a member of company staff is involved. Preferred areas of support are children and youth, social welfare, medical and education.

Further details on the Wiltshire Community Foundation are available in *A Guide to Local Trusts in the South of England*.

Exclusions
No support for appeals from individuals, purely denominational (religious) appeals, local appeals not in areas of company presence, large national appeals or overseas projects.

Applications
In writing to the correspondent.

Interpublic Ltd

4 Golden Square, London W1R 3AE
0171-734 7116

Correspondent: See below

Chief officer: *Chairman:* E P Beard

Year end	Turnover	Pre-tax profit
31/12/96	£1,560,565,000	£11,814,000

Nature of company business
Holding company for advertising and related service companies.

UK employees: n/a

Charitable donations
1996: £201,000
1995: n/a
1994: £223,589

Community support policy
As far as we are aware, the company is not a member of organisations such as the PerCent Club, Business in the Community or ABSA and has provided no information on its charitable policy for this guide. However, it appears that the company is still giving in excess of £200,000 a year in donations. The only information provided previously is that the company's donations are made by subsidiary companies rather than the group.

Jaguar

Applications
Appeals should be made to subsidiaries, not to the group. Applications to Lintas, 84 Eccleston Square, London (0171-822 8888); or to McCann-Erickson Advertising Ltd, 36 Howland Street, London W1A 1AT (0171-580 6690).

Jaguar Cars Ltd

Browns Lane, Allesley, Coventry CV5 9DR
01203-202058; Fax: 01203-203364
Website: www.jaguarcars.com

Correspondent: Mrs Val King, Secretary to the Jaguar Charities Committee

Chief officer: *Chairman:* Nick Scheele

Year end	Turnover	Pre-tax profit
31/12/97	n/a	n/a

Nature of company business
The design, development, manufacture and marketing of luxury cars and specialist sports cars.
Main locations: Birmingham; Coventry.

UK employees: n/a

Charitable donations
1997: £33,347
1996: n/a
1995: n/a
1994: £41,576
Membership: ABSA BitC

Community support policy
The figure given for charitable donations above is that for the Charities Fund and does not include company donations. The budget for 1999 for the company is expected to be about £50,000.

Charitable donations: The company was a founder member of the PerCent Club, but is not listed as a member in the PerCent Club's 1998 annual report. It gives support, through its charitable trust, exclusively for local charities in areas of company presence and charities in which a member of staff is involved. Within these geographical constraints, which are strictly adhered to, the company prefers to support organisations concerned with children and youth, social welfare and medical. The company will support national charities if they have a local branch, or can in some way, benefit the groups' employees and their families.

Employee involvement: Preference is also given to charities in which a member of staff is involved. The company operates a payroll giving scheme for employees, matching donations £ for £.

Enterprise: The company is a member of Business in the Community and supports Coventry Business Centre, Spirit of Coventry and Coventry Common Purpose.

Education: The company is involved in local education–business partnerships and operates work experience schemes for pupils.

Environment: Financial support has been given to help set up a jaguar reserve in Belize, in conjunction with the World Wide Fund for Nature.

Sponsorship: The group has a preference for prestige sports, arts and similar events. A major objective is to provide hospitality opportunities for dealers, and the group is not necessarily looking for TV exposure or press coverage. Typically, the group will spend up to £5,000 on an event sponsorship, or up to £10,000 on an exhibition. It prefers to be the sole or main sponsor.

Support in previous years has been given to Birmingham Royal Ballet, British Academy of Film & Television Arts, Royal Scottish Opera and the Royal Academy of Arts.

Exclusions
No support is given to fundraising events, advertising in charity brochures, appeals from individuals, purely denominational (religious) appeals, large national appeals or overseas projects.

Applications
In writing to the correspondent. Decisions are made by a donations committee which meets quarterly. The contact for arts sponsorship is Alan Hodge, Promotions Department. Applicants should note that the group receives up to 15 proposals each day.

Jardine Lloyd Thompson Group Services

Jardine House, 6 Crutched Friars, London EC3N 2HT
0171-528 4444; Fax: 0171-528 4185

Correspondent: Amy Martin, Finance Department

Chief officers: *Chairman:* R J O Barton; *Chief Executive:* K Carter

Year end	Turnover	Pre-tax profit
31/12/97	£336,349,000	£42,349,000

Nature of company business
The company is a holding company of an international group of insurance broking companies and a Lloyd's members' agency.
Main subsidiaries include: Colburn French and Kneen Ltd; Specialty Risk Broking Ltd; Traveltest Ltd; JIB Group PLC.

UK employees: n/a

Charitable donations
1997: £217,000
1996: n/a
1995: £161,000
1994: £177,000
1993: £155,000

Community support policy
We have not been able to obtain any details on the company's charitable giving, although total donations have now risen to over £200,000.

The company's major donations are given through deeds of covenant and are probably long-term commitments.

Other donations are usually for £100 to £250 and are paid in Charities Aid Foundation vouchers.

Exclusions

No grants for fundraising events, advertising in charity brochures, appeals from individuals or large national appeals.

Applications

In writing to the correspondent. The Charities Committee meets four times a year.

Johnson Matthey Plc

2–4 Cockspur Street, Trafalgar Square, London SW1Y 5BQ
0171-269 8400; Fax: 0171-269 8433
Email: godwini@matthey.com
Website: www.matthey.com

Correspondent: I Godwin, Public Relations Manager

Chief officers: *Chairman:* M Miles; *Chief Executive:* C R N Clark

Year end	Turnover	Pre-tax profit
31/3/98	£3,267,100,000	£130,200,000

Nature of company business
The company is involved in advanced materials and precious metals technology, with the following operating divisions: catalytic systems, electronic materials, precious metals, and ceramic materials.

UK employees: 3,000

Charitable donations

1998: £213,000
1997: £234,000
1996: £229,000
1995: £362,000
1994: £414,000
Membership: *ABSA BitC*

Community support policy

The company gave donations totalling £272,000 in 1997/98, of which £213,000 was in the UK. It does not have a sponsorship policy, but apportions its support across a wide range of charities grouped under the following main categories: medical, welfare, young people, education, environment and the services. Charitable donating is reviewed in March each year to set the programme for the following financial year beginning in April. Any application should be made in writing. The company encourages employee involvement by matching any money they have raised for the nominated 'charity of the year'.

Donations are made through the Charities Aid Foundation and direct giving is preferred rather than, for example, giving through advertising in charity brochures. The company continues to support the Royal London Society for the Blind – an association which dates back to 1838. Others beneficiaries included The Samaritans, Prince's Youth Business Trust and Macmillan Cancer Relief.

Charitable donations: Preference is given to charities which have some connection with the company's activities, for example the Jewellery Benevolent Fund and cancer charities (the company makes cancer drugs) and those near the company's operating locations (north Hertfordshire, Enfield area, Stoke-on-Trent area). Support is also given to appeals from projects in which a member of staff is involved. Areas of support include advertising in charity brochures, the art, children/youth, elderly people, environment/ heritage, fundraising events, medical research, overseas projects, sickness/disability charities.

Johnson Matthey Plc Educational Trust

To mark Johnson Matthey's 175th anniversary in 1992, a donation of £175,000 was made to the Johnson Matthey Plc Educational Trust (Charity Commission number 313576). The company and the trust appear to be closely linked, with the chairman of the trust being a director of the company. The expenses of the trust are met by Johnson Matthey plc. The objects of the trust are as follows:

1) provision of financial or other assistance for the education or training of children, students or trainees whose parents are connected to the precious metals industry

2) establishment of professorships, lectureships or other teaching posts

3) promotion of research into any scientific or academic subject

4) general promotion and advancement of education.

Applications are invited for scholarships. Student awards are usually paid for three years. In 1996/97, the income was £25,000 all from investments. The trust currently makes awards to 50 university students.

Enterprise: The company has supported enterprise agencies in the past. It is also a primary sponsor of the Prince of Wales Business Leaders Forum and a member of Business in the Community.

The arts: The company became a corporate member of ABSA in 1996. Its arts programme has included sponsorship of Glyndebourne Festival Opera, Monteverdi Trust, National Gallery and Royal Opera House.

Exclusions

No support for appeals from individuals; enterprise/training; fundraising events; political; appeals; religious appeals; science/technology or sport.

Applications

In writing to the correspondent. A donations committee meets quarterly.

Johnson Wax Ltd

Frimley Green, Camberley, Surrey GU15 6AJ
01276-852000

Correspondent: Marie McCanna, Consumer Services Manager

Chief officers: *Chairman:* S C Johnson;
Chief Executive: W Perez; *Managing Director:* M Loeb

Year end	Turnover	Pre-tax profit
30/6/98	£129,561,000	£1,622,000

Nature of company business
The company manufactures waxes, polishes and cleaning products for the consumer and industrial markets.
Main brands include: Goddards; Brillo; Mr Muscle; Glade; Pledge; Sparkle; Raid; Shout.

UK employees: 520

Charitable donations
1998: £174,000
1997: £240,000
1996: £240,000
1995: £240,000
1994: £240,343
Membership: ABSA %Club

Community support policy

The company is a member of the PerCent Club and gives 3–4% of pre-tax profits (in Britain) for charitable purposes each year. The company prefers to support local charities in areas of company presence, mainly in Hampshire and Surrey, especially in the fields of children and youth, social welfare, the arts, medical, and particularly the environment.

Main beneficiaries in the year were Blackwater Valley Enterprise Agency, Business in the Community, National Trust, Business in the Environment, British Trust for Conservation Volunteers, Disability Initiative, Tomlinscote School and Frimley Park Hospital.

Typical grants to national organisations range from £1,000 to £25,000, and to local organisations from £25 to £50,000.

Employee involvement: From its charitable trust the company matches monies raised by employees for local activities (ie. small local groups or local branches of national bodies). Staff are encouraged to become volunteers in their own time and to become school governors.

Education: Initiatives supported by the company include the provision of educational materials for schools, and work-experience schemes for pupils and teachers.

Exclusions
No support for fundraising events, advertising in charity brochures, individuals, elderly people, medical research, overseas projects, political appeals, purely denominational (religious) appeals, science/technology, sport or local appeals not in areas of company presence.

Applications
Marie McCanna is in charge of charitable donations.

Jupiter Asset Management

1 Grosvenor Place, London SW1X 7JJ
0171-412 0703

Correspondent: Angela Hudson, Secretary to the Chairman

Chief officers: *Chairman:* J L Duffield;
Managing Director: M Heathcoat Amory

Year end	Turnover	Pre-tax profit
31/12/94	n/a	£14,616,000

Nature of company business
Investment managment and banking.

UK employees: n/a

Charitable donations
1994: £51,943
1993: £24,600

Community support policy
The company has no set policy regarding its charitable donations and we have not been able to obtain any financial information since that for 1994.

Applications
In writing to the correspondent.

Kalon Group plc

Ploughland House, 62 George Street, Wakefield, West Yorkshire WF1 1DL
01924-330100; Fax: 01924-330102
Website: www.kalon.com

Correspondent: Mike Hennessy, Managing Director

Chief officers: *Chairman:* Rt Hon Lord Wakeham;
Managing Director: M J Hennessy

Year end	Turnover	Pre-tax profit
31/12/97	£472,047,000	£45,160,000

Nature of company business
The main activities are the manufacture and distribution of branded and own label decorative paints.
Main brands include: Leyland; Vallance; Deval; Johnstone's; Manders.

UK employees: 4,683

Charitable donations
1997: £41,864
1996: £70,000
1995: £14,000
1994: £12,000
1993: £59,000

Community support policy
The company supports the Foundation for Conductive Education as its main charity. In addition, employees are asked to nominate charities they would like the company

to support and donations of £500 are made to those selected on a one-off basis.

Exclusions
No support for local appeals not in areas of company presence.

Applications
In writing to the correspondent.

Kellogg's

The Kellogg Building, Talbot Road, Manchester M16 0PU
0161-869 2601

Correspondent: C H Woodcock, Manager, Corporate Affairs

Chief officer: *Managing Director:* T P Mobsby

Year end	Turnover	Pre-tax profit
31/12/97	£688,041,000	£70,116,000

Nature of company business
The company is a manufacturer of breakfast foods.

Main locations: Manchester; Wrexham.

UK employees: 2,261

Charitable donations
1997: £485,000
1996: £484,000
1995: £414,000
1994: £501,000
1993: £460,000

Total community contributions: £880,000

Membership: *BitC* %Club

Community support policy

The company is a founder member of the PerCent Club, and consistently meets its commitment of 1% of previous year's pre-tax profits. Total community contributions in 1997 were £880,000 including £485,000 in charitable donations.

The company is committed to involvement in the communities in which it operates, especially the local communities, recognising this as a part of responsible corporate citizenship. It targets resources on local community development and economic regeneration, the welfare of disadvantaged people and learning opportunities for children. Most of Kellogg's UK community support is focused on the north west of England and Clwyd (in the Manchester and Wrexham areas in particular where it operates major manufacturing facilities), although support is also given to relevant national initiatives. 'The company is distinctly biased in favour of organisations helping those at greatest disadvantage in society.' In addition to charitable donations, community contributions include in kind support, with very little towards non-commercial advertising.

Charitable donations: Between 50% and 60% of the community support which the company provides is by way of carefully considered cash donations, with particular emphasis on projects in the fields of community-based regeneration, welfare and education. Over two-thirds of total community support is focused on north west England and Wrexham, the balance being spread nationally.

Preferred areas of support include children/youth, education, elderly people, enterprise/training, environment/heritage, sickness/disability charities, social welfare and community-based regeneration.

Some main beneficiaries in 1997 were Weston Spirit – Liverpool, Emmaus – Greater Manchester, Rathbone CI – national, Development Trust Association and Moss Side and Hulme Community Development Trust.

In kind support: Support includes: considerable executive, managerial, professional and clerical time and expertise; limited secondment; surplus office equipment and furniture; access to facilities and premises; small quantities of product and promotional items. In kind support is given particularly to inner city-related projects often to add value to cash donations. It is also given in relation to people with disabilities and through links with local schools.

Employee involvement: The company also supports charitable activities undertaken by employees in their own time. In particular, it matches £ for £, to a maximum of £500 (or £1,000 if a group of employees participate), funds raised by employees for charities of their choice. Employees are encouraged to become school governors and business advisors to Young Enterprise Companies.

Enterprise: Kellogg's is a member of Business in the Community. Its activities centre on the regeneration of Trafford Park and inner city areas of north west England, including in particular the Moss Side and Hulme area of Manchester. The company leads the Moss Side and Hulme Business Support Group and is represented on the board of the Moss Side and Hulme Community Development Trust. The company is actively involved in the Moss Side & Hulme Initiative. Kellogg's also provides active support and funding to a number of local enterprise agencies in the North West.

Education: Kellogg's has well-developed industry/education liaison programmes, including the operation of work-experience schemes for pupils and teachers.

Environment: The company is a registered supporter of the Environment Council's Business and Environment Programme and represented on the board of trustees of Groundwork Trusts in Salford and Trafford, Manchester and Wrexham.

Exclusions
Donations will not normally be given to circular appeals, fundraising events, the arts, purely denominational appeals, small local appeals not in areas of company presence, appeals from individuals, animal welfare charities, political appeals, religious appeals, science/technology, able-bodied sport, medical research, overseas projects or for advertising in charity brochures.

Kimberly

Applications

All applications should be addressed in writing to the correspondent. Grant decisions are made by a donations committee which deals with applications when received. Appeals received by local plants are passed to head office with any comments that the local management wish to make. Each year the company receives over 4,000 applications of which about 300 are successful. It makes a point of replying to all applicants, whether or not successful, but of necessity most replies are by way of standard letters – together with a one-page summary of *Kellogg's Approach to Community Involvement*.

Information available: There is a leaflet explaining the Moss Side and Hulme Business Support Group. Kellogg's approach to community involvement was cited as an example of good practice in a detailed research report by the Policy Studies Institute, published in 1991 under the title *Profitable Partnerships*. The research was funded by the Inner Cities Directorate of the Department of the Environment.

Kimberly Clark Ltd

1 Tower View, Kings Hill, West Malling, Kent ME19 4HA
01622-616000; Fax: 01622-718280

Correspondent: Edwin Mutton, Promotions Manager

Chief officers: *Chairman:* J A Van Steenberg; *Managing Director:* R W Huggins

Year end	Turnover	Pre-tax profit
31/12/95	£430,772,000	(£96,171,000)

Nature of company business
The principal activity is the manufacture and marketing of tissue products for household, commercial, institutional and industrial uses, and related products.
Main brands include: Kleenex; Kotex; Huggies; Andrex.

UK employees: n/a

Charitable donations
1995: £82,363
1994: £92,946
1993: £56,935
Membership: *BitC*

Community support policy

Local sites support local charities in areas of company presence, in particular those concerned with children and youth, social welfare, education and medical.

In addition to charitable donations, the company undertakes joint promotions.

Exclusions
No support for circular appeals, appeals from individuals, purely denominational (religious) appeals, large national appeals or overseas projects.

Applications
In writing to the correspondent.

Kingfisher plc

North West House, 119 Marylebone Road, London NW1 5PX
0171-724 7749; Fax: 0171-724 1160
Website: www.kingfisher.co.uk

Correspondent: David Marshall, Public Affairs Manager

Chief officers: *Chairman:* Sir John Banham; *Chief Executive:* Sir Geoffrey J Mulcahy

Year end	Turnover	Pre-tax profit
31/1/98	£6,409,400,000	£520,500,000

Nature of company business
Retailing and property interests.

Main subsidiaries include: B&Q; Chartwell Land; Comet Group; Entertainment UK; Music & Video Club (MVC); Superdrug Stores; Time Retail Finance; Woolworths.

Main locations: Croydon; Eastleigh; Harrow; Hayes; Hull; Leeds; London; Middlesex.

UK employees: n/a

Charitable donations
1998: £1,343,207
1997: £987,793
1996: £558,413
1995: £914,567
1994: £940,863

Total community contributions: £1,762,765

Membership: *BitC*

Community support policy

The company and its subsidiaries are contributors to a number of community projects, either in cash, in kind or by donation of human resources. The company estimates the value of these resources to have been £1,762,765 in 1997/98. Additionally, charitable fundraising activities of employees contributed £392,892.

The company focuses its activities on supporting opportunities which:

- are pioneering and innovative
- fit well with and contribute directly to Kingfisher's mainstream business activities, customers and products
- allow the company to add real value
- give scope for company employees to become involved, develop their full potential or gain new skills and experiences
- involve developing longer term relationships.

Efforts are concentrated on issues affecting the home and family and in particular:

- education/youth and child development
- older generation
- community safety and crime prevention
- environment
- equal opportunities.

In all these areas the company works with government and national voluntary organisations to pinpoint areas where group expertise and resources can help most. In 1996/97, the main beneficiaries were the Scout

Association, Childline, Age Concern, Entente Cordiale and Crime Prevention.

Corporate Centre

Support is given to:
- equal opportunities – including support for organisations such as Business in the Community, Opportunity 2000, Disability Forum and Employers for Childcare
- crime prevention eg. sponsorship of a Retail Crime secondment
- education eg. support has been given to Entente Cordiale.

B&Q

The main objective is to link in the social responsibility fund with activities that directly relate to the business. The total social responsibility budget allocated from the Marketing Department is £200,000. Initiatives include:

B&Q Hands on Training Scheme (HOTS): piloted in 1996, a DIY training scheme for Age Concern volunteers in 10 towns across Britain (a further 20 Age Concern groups were expected to be offered this programme in 1997). The aim is to give adequate DIY and safety training for volunteers so that they are able to visit the homes of elderly people and carry out basic tasks such as fitting grab rails, smoke alarms, security equipment, change lightbulbs, tap washers, fuses, etc. The B&Q Hands on Training Scheme fits neatly with B&Q's over 50s employment policy and over 60s club card and meets Age Concern's objectives of keeping elderly people independent in their homes.

B&Q Stores Grant: as part of B&Q's environmental '1000 day countdown to the new millennium' B&Q stores have been encouraged to be more involved in local environmental issues by being offered a 'green grant', if the store has reached certain environmental criteria. This grant may be used on the store site or linked with another organisation eg. school, community centre, local authority, WWF or other locally based conservation organisation. The grants will typically be in the low £100s, but the amount will depend on the project.

WWF Education Project: B&Q is working on a CD-ROM package aimed at GNVQ students, hoping to be launched to over 2,000 schools and colleges.

B&Q also raises money for a charity the Wednesday before Christmas. In 1996, it raised over £20,000 for Macmillan Cancer Relief. In 1997, it supported Age Concern. The company also funds a PhD studentship and is involved in schemes in India and the Philippines.

Chartwell Land

Chartwell Land concentrates on charities that are relevant to the construction industry, homelessness and that are specific to selected investment/development properties in order to generate local publicity. It also provides sponsorship to employees and business contacts who are raising money for charities of their choice. A budget of £12,000 has been allocated.

Where possible, the company responds to requests from business contacts and possibly staff for donations for purely charitable purposes. The company does not support sporting or other social activities or 'cold callers'.

Chartwell has a limited budget for placing advertisements in charity programmes or brochures, usually at the request of staff.

Support is given to equal opportunities/Opportunity 2000 through the Women Into Property sponsorship scheme. Candidates will receive £1,000 per year while they are studying and one student each year will be given work experience within Chartwell Land. Last year included far more pupils from State schools than in previous years.

Comet

The main objective of Comet's support is to build an infrastructure to support Comet and demonstrate its commitment to the community and the environment in each local market.

One initiative was the production of a multimedia education pack aimed at 8 to 11 year olds. The pack includes a competition element for the pupil and for the school. Over 10,000 schools have already received the pack. The pack is intended as an 'icebreaker' for stores to contact local schools and set up basic multimedia workshops. The project is being extended in-store to parents and adults.

EUK

A charity fund is set up each year to support selected schools and charities with cash and fundraising gifts. Most of its income comes from selling CDs to staff that are unsaleable in stores and through staff fundraising.

Woolworths

In 1997/98, Woolworths had a budget of £100,000. In 1997, its main support was for Barnardo's (which received £50,000 to sponsor the Woolworths Big Toddle in Aid of Barnardo's) and Whizz-Kidz (in 1996, over £300,000 was raised via staff fundraising activities eg. raft races, cycle rides, etc).

Additionally, the public relations department makes financial and product donations to a huge variety of children's or staff related causes (eg. sick children, hospitals, schools, coffee mornings, raffles etc).

Exclusions

No response to circular appeals. No grants for animal welfare charities; appeals from individuals; the arts; enterprise/training; heritage; fundraising events; medical research; overseas projects; political appeals; religious appeals; science/technology; sickness/disability charities; social welfare; sport or local appeals not in areas of company presence.

Applications

In writing to the correspondent. Shortlisted applications are considered by the Social Responsibility Committee. Applications to operating subsidiaries should be addressed to the contacts listed below and local appeals to the appropriate branch or retail outlet. Sponsorship proposals should be addressed to the group company secretary or to the marketing directors of the individual operating subsidiaries.

Kodak

Contacts for charity and community involvement in the individual operating companies: Alan McWalter, Marketing Director, Woolworths plc, Woolworth House, 242–246 Marylebone Road, London NW1 6JL.

Ms Sandie Skevington, Corporate Communications Manager, Comet Group plc, George House, 67–73 George Street, Hull HU1 3AU.

Stephen Robertson, Marketing Director, B&Q plc, Portswood House, 1 Hampshire Corporate Park, Chandlers Ford, Eastleigh, Hampshire SO53 3YX.

Stephen Round, Marketing Director, Superdrug Stores plc, 40 Beddington Lane, Croydon, Surrey CR0 4TB.

Kodak Ltd

PO Box 66, Hemel Hempstead, Herts HP1 1JU
01442-261122; Fax: 01442-845180
Website: www.kodak.com

Correspondent: Public Relations Department

Chief officer: *Chairman:* A O'Neill

Year end	Turnover	Pre-tax profit
31/12/97	£1,195,000,000	£3,000,000

Nature of company business
Principal activities are the manufacture, supply and distribution of photographic film, paper, chemicals, digital imaging equipment, together with services associated with these activities. The company is a wholly owned subsidiary of the Eastman Kodak Company.

Main subsidiaries include: Cinesite Ltd; Miller Bros Hall & Co Ltd; Taylors Developing & Printing Works Ltd.

UK employees: 7,063

Charitable donations
1997: £328,265
1996: £393,136
1995: £442,542
1994: £882,364
1993: £508,500
Membership: *ABSA*

Community support policy

The company states that its underlying philosophy is to improve the quality of life in the communities in which it has its main company sites (ie. Harrow, Hemel Hempstead; Annesley, Notts; and Kirkby, Merseyside).

Charitable donations: The company prefers to support registered charities working in the areas of local community services, medicine, conservation and the environment, the arts, education, elderly and young people, fundraising events, science/technology and sickness/disability charities. Consideration is also given to other projects within the local community.

Exclusions
Kodak does not support advertising in charity brochures, purely denominational appeals, large national appeals, purely local appeals not in areas of company presence, appeals from individuals, overseas projects or circulars.

Applications
All appeals, including local appeals, should be sent to the correspondent.

Advice to applicants: The company welcomes appeals from charities, but it is receiving a large amount of mail. Applicants should therefore take note of the main areas of interest of the company as stated above.

KPMG

8 Salisbury Square, London EC4Y 8BB
0171-311 1000; Fax: 0171-311 4242

Correspondent: James Forte, Director, KPMG's Community Broking Service

Chief officers: *Chairman:* Mike Rake;
Chief Executive: Gary Williams

Year end	Turnover	Pre-tax profit
30/9/97	£726,400,000	£36,100,000

Nature of company business
Principal activities comprise audit, accountancy, tax advice, corporate finance, corporate recovery and management consulting.

UK employees: 8,944

Charitable donations
1997: £500,000
1996: £500,000
1995: £500,000
Total community contributions: £1,700,000
Membership: *ABSA BitC %Club*

Community support policy

KPMG's Community Broking Service focuses on volunteering programmes supporting education, employment and enterprise as well as children and young people. Major volunteering programmes are undertaken in partnership with Business in the Community, Community Service Volunteers and the Prince's Youth Business Trust. These are supported by KPMG's Community Bank of Time for its employees. KPMG support also extends beyond these sectors to elderly people, distress, social welfare, the arts and heritage, in particular the development of a volunteering programme in partnership with the Association for Business Sponsorship of the Arts.

KPMG is the global advisory firm whose aim is to turn knowledge into value for the benefit of its clients, its people and its communities. KPMG's Community Broking Service supports this by contributing fully to its communities in partnership with private, public and voluntary sector organisations. By meeting its social responsibilities, KPMG's Community Broking Service provides learning opportunities for KPMG people, adds to the firm's knowledge and positively enhances KPMG's reputation.

KPMG gives to appeals supported by its staff and where there is staff involvement. In 1996/97, KPMG gave £0.5 million in cash donations to UK charities. Other support valued at £1.2 million comprising community investment (volunteering support and project specific short-term and development assignments) and subsidies was provided.

KPMG is a member of the PerCent Club, BitC, ABSA, Prince of Wales Business Leaders Forum and Concorde Club (BitC/Ashridge).

Exclusions
No support for political and religious appeals.

Applications
In writing only, to KPMG's Community Broking Service.

Kraft Jacobs Suchard Ltd

St George's House, Bayshill Road, Cheltenham, Gloucester GL50 3AE
01242-236101; Fax: 01242-512084

Correspondent: Jill Mould, Communications Manager

Chief officer: *Managing Director:* Brian Carlisle

Year end	Turnover	Pre-tax profit
14/12/97	£704,148,000	£80,967,000

Nature of company business
The principal activity of the company is food manufacture.

UK employees: 3,351

Charitable donations
1997: £69,000
1996: £75,000
1995: n/a
1994: £43,000
1993: £20,000

Community support policy
The company gives donations of cash and gifts in kind to a wide variety of charities in areas local to its factories and head office. It has a preference for children's charities, schools and local communities.

Exclusions
No support for appeals from individuals, political or religious appeals.

Applications
In writing to the correspondent.

Kwik-Fit Holdings plc

17 Corstorphine Road, Murrayfield, Edinburgh EH12 6DD
0131-337 9200; Fax: 0131-337 0062
Email: info@kwik-fit.com
Website: www.kwik-fit.com

Correspondent: C Grant, Marketing Director

Chief officer: *Chairman:* T Farmer

Year end	Turnover	Pre-tax profit
28/2/98	£472,800,000	£55,100,000

Nature of company business
Principal activity: tyre, exhaust and car repair centres.

Main subsidiaries include: Superdrive Motoring Centres; Budget Tyre Plus Autoservice; Preston Paints; Tyre Sales (Birmingham); Avon and Wiltshire Properties; Autospeed Tyres (Western); Ebley Tyre Services; Humphries Tyre & Exhaust Centres; Tyreplus Autoservice; Ecology Tyre Collections.

UK employees: n/a

Charitable donations
1998: £400,000
1997: £400,000
1996: £410,000
1995: n/a
1994: £400,000

Community support policy
Previously unco-operative in our requests for information on community support, Kwik-Fit now gives over four pages in its annual review to its involvement with the community. Most of the following is taken from the 1998 review.

The company and its employees continued to support financially and in kind a wide range of activities in 1997. More than 200 organisations benefited, with the emphasis on initiatives that support community development, road safety, enterprise and young people.

The largest single fundraising activity in 1997/98 was the campaign for NCH Action for Children which raised over £60,000. Other smaller charities also received support from employees commitment to the communities in which they operate.

Other activities included maintaining links with local schools, colleges and universities through Scottish Business in the Community, acting as business advisors to students participating in the Young Enterprise Scheme, sponsoring local community events and competitions for local schoolchildren. One example of this is sponsorship of a local boys football team in Beverley.

Employees participate in community assignments as part of their training and development, and can spend up to three months on secondment to a range of community-based initiatives, through the Prince's Trust – Volunteers scheme. The company is also a Charter Founder Member of the Duke of Edinburgh's Award.

The company has been involved in many road safety initiatives, the most recent being its 'Safer Roads for Children' programme. This includes study cards and fact-sheets for schools, a 'Kids Code for the Road' for adults

Ladbroke

and children, and sponsorship of a Teenage Pedestrian Road Safety Project. The company regularly sponsors Tyre Safety Weeks.

Exclusions

No response to circular appeals. No grants for advertising in charity brochures or appeals from individuals.

Applications

In writing to the correspondent. Potential applicants please note the company states: 'Our budgets are fully committed and we do not wish to solicit further applications at this time'.

Ladbroke Group PLC

Maple Court, Central Park, Reeds Crescent, Watford WD1 1HZ
0171-856 8000; Fax: 0171-856 8463
Website: www.ladbrokegroup.com

Correspondent: Stephen Devany, Head of Corporate Affairs

Chief officers: *Chairman:* John Jackson;
Chief Executive: Peter George

Year end	Turnover	Pre-tax profit
31/12/97	£3,816,000,000	£203,000,000

Nature of company business
Principal activities: hotels, betting and gaming.

Main subsidiaries include: Hilton International Hotels Ltd; Ladbroke Racing Ltd; Ladbroke & Co Ltd; Vernons Pools Ltd; Ladbroke Group Finance PLC; Town & County Factors Ltd.

Main brands include: Hilton; Ladbrokes.

UK employees: 42,878

Charitable donations

1997: £461,000
1996: £414,000
1995: £241,000
1994: £269,000
1993: £153,000

Total community contributions: £660,000
Membership: *BitC %Club*

Community support policy

Total community contributions in 1997 were £660,000. The main areas of non-cash support are gifts in kind, training schemes and provision of premises. Ladbroke Group is a member of the PerCent Club and Business in the Community. During 1997, in addition to donations made by overseas companies, UK companies donated £461,000 to charitable organisations.

Charitable donations: Ladbroke has no donations policy as such, but it has a preference for children/youth, elderly people, enterprise/training, sickness/disability charities and sport. Grants to national organisations range from £10 to £50,000. Grants to local organisations range from £10 to £10,000. The company is also involved in various enterprise and education initiatives.

During 1997, the group made donations to over 480 charities around the world. In the UK, some of the largest grants included those to Crimestoppers Trust, NEST-United Kingdom, Corporate Action Trust and Refuge.

In kind support: The company organises race nights for fundraising. It has continued to provide premises to the Homeground Partnership in Liverpool, which provides accommodation, counselling and job training for young people on Merseyside.

Employee involvement: The group actively encourages its employees to undertake fundraising activities and employees of each division have a long history of supporting both national and local charities.

During 1997, employees in each division raised more than £220,000 for charity. Ladbroke Racing employees in the UK adopted the Animal Health Trust as their main charity, but also supported a number of the other charities.

Enterprise: The company is involved in local initiatives through staff involvement. Ladbroke Racing is actively involved with the Youth Enterprise Council.

Education: Hilton National offers the National Vocations Qualifications (NVQ) Scholarship Scheme which gives work experience for a year to NVQ students.

Exclusions

No support is given to appeals from individuals, circular appeals, small purely local appeals not in an area of company presence, political or religious appeals or for advertising in charity brochures.

Applications

All appeals for charitable donations, community involvement and sponsorship should be addressed in writing to Stephen Devany, Head of Corporate Affairs. Donation decisions are evaluated on a regular basis.

Laird Group plc

3 St James's Square, London SW1Y 4JU
0171-468 4040; Fax: 0171-839 2921

Correspondent: D Hudson, Company Secretary

Chief officers: *Chairman:* J A Gardiner;
Chief Executive: I M Arnott

Year end	Turnover	Pre-tax profit
31/12/97	£1,058,000,000	£67,000,000

Nature of company business
The principal activities are sealing systems, service industries, transport.

Main subsidiaries include: Linear Ltd; Ventrolla Ltd; Cego Frameware Ltd; Euromond Ltd; EWS Ltd; Feneseal Ltd; Permacell Finesse Ltd; Reynolds Ltd; Stanton Rubber & Plastics Ltd; Fullarton Computer Industries Ltd; RH Technical Industries Ltd; Verichrome Plating Services Ltd.

UK employees: n/a

Charitable donations
1997: £59,000
1996: £37,000
1995: £53,000
1994: £39,000
1993: £49,000

Community support policy
Regular annual support is given to a few selected charities. Grants range from £100 to £5,000. The company also sponsors worthwhile activities on a one-off basis.

Exclusions
No support for political appeals.

Applications
In writing to the correspondent.

Lambert Fenchurch Group plc

Friary Court, Crutched Friars, London EC3N 2NP
0171-560 3000; Fax: 0171-560 3502

Correspondent: Robin Merttens, Group Solicitor

Chief officers: *Chairman:* Sir Robert Clark; *Chief Executive:* David Margrett

Year end	Turnover	Pre-tax profit
31/3/98	£137,800,000	£14,700,000

Nature of company business
Holding company for insurance brokers.

Main subsidiaries include: Protection House Insurance Services; Thatchowners (Insurance Agency); Architects & Professional Indemnity Agencies; Kininmonth Lambert; RIBA Insurance Agency.

UK employees: 1,916

Charitable donations
1998: £86,289
1997: £64,857
1996: £59,454
1995: £55,809
1994: £31,439

Community support policy
Preference for charities in which a member of company staff is involved and charities close to the network of offices. Preferred areas of support are: advertising in charity brochures; appeals from individuals; children/youth; fundraising events and sickness/disability charities. Grants range from £25 to £1,000.

Non-cash support takes the form of arts sponsorship, good-cause sponsorship and gifts in kind. The company also provides financial support for employees' volunteering.

Applications
In writing to the correspondent.

Land Securities PLC

5 Strand, London WC2N 5AF
0171-413 9000; Fax: 0171-925 0202

Correspondent: P M Dudgeon, Company Secretary

Chief officers: *Chairman:* Peter Birch; *Chief Executive:* Ian Henderson

Year end	Turnover	Pre-tax profit
31/3/98	£484,000,000	£266,000,000

Nature of company business
Land Securities is the largest UK property group, involved in both property development and investment.

Main subsidiaries include: Ravenseft Properties; Ravenseft Industrial Estates; The City of London Real Property Co; Ravenside Investments.

UK employees: 577

Charitable donations
1998: £127,000
1997: £125,000
1996: £135,000
1995: £128,000
1994: £108,000
Membership: BitC

Community support policy
The company has given about the same in donations for the past four years. It has no set policy, but it is unlikely that appeals from local charities outside areas of company presence will be successful. Preference for children and youth charities, and medical appeals. Other areas of support may include the arts, education, elderly people, enterprise/training, environment/heritage and sickness/disability charities.

The company is a member of Business in the Community.

Exclusions
No support for advertising in charity brochures, animal welfare charities, appeals from individuals, overseas projects or political appeals.

Applications
In writing to the correspondent. The company receives 80 to 90 applications every six weeks, when the charity committee meets to choose the most suitable applications.

Laporte plc

Nations House, 103 Wigmore Street, London WC1H 9AB
0171-399 2440; Fax: 0171-399 2401
Website: www.laporteplc.com

Correspondent: Mrs N Geairns, Office Manager

Chief officers: *Chairman:* George Duncan; *Chief Executive:* Jim Leng

Year end	Turnover	Pre-tax profit
31/12/97	£830,300,000	£76,400,000

LASMO

Nature of company business
Laporte is a British-based international chemicals group engaged in the development, manufacture and marketing of speciality chemicals.

Main subsidiaries include: Compugraphics International; Fine Organics; Micro-Image Technology.

UK employees: 1,698

Charitable donations
1997: £77,000
1996: £81,000
1995: £95,000
1994: £82,000
1993: £57,000

Community support policy

In addition to cash donations which in 1997 totalled £77,000, the main areas of support are good-cause sponsorship and gifts in kind.

Charitable donations: The company prefers to support local charities and projects in the vicinity of its industrial sites which are mainly located in the Midlands and the north of England, with major national charities where central support is more appropriate. Each appeal is considered separately by a donations committee who try to spread donations as widely as possible over many different deserving groups.

The company prefers to support national charities serving people who are disabled or disadvantaged. Grants are also given to medical research, youth vocational training, charities linked to the chemical industry, education, environment/heritage, social welfare and the arts. Previous beneficiaries have included the Institute for Citizenship Studies, Westminster Cathedral Centenary Appeal, Industry and Parliament Trust, Charities Aid Foundation and Catalyst Museum. Cancer Relief, Mencap, Royal Commonwealth Society for the Blind and MacIntyre Schools have also recently been supported. Typical grants to national organisations range from £100 to £5,000, and to local organisations from £25 to £500.

Employee involvement: The company operates the CAF payroll giving scheme and matches both employee giving and fundraising.

The arts: The company undertakes arts sponsorship 'to a diminishing degree'. The total budget for arts support and sponsorship was £14,000 in 1996, with a preference for regional musical events.

Exclusions

It is company policy not to take advertising space in souvenir brochures or programmes in aid of charitable events, nor to purchase tickets for charity performances. No support is given to individuals, circulars, fundraising events, purely denominational (religious) appeals, overseas projects, small purely local appeals not in areas of company presence or in the form of secondment.

Continuous support is not generally given to any one organisation within a category. The committee does not give twice to any organisation in a 12-month period, however worthy the cause.

Applications

A donations committee meets quarterly. Appeals must be in writing and should be directed to the correspondent.

LASMO plc

101 Bishopsgate, London EC2M 3XH
0171-892 9000; Fax: 0171-892 9292

Correspondent: Nina Hamilton, Public Affairs Adviser

Chief officers: *Chairman:* R Agnew; *Chief Executive:* J Darby

Year end	Turnover	Pre-tax profit
31/12/97	£722,000,000	£154,000,000

Nature of company business
Oil and gas exploration and production.
Main locations: London; Aberdeen.

Charitable donations
1997: £137,596
1996: £132,024
1995: £137,183
1994: £154,500
1993: £147,000

Total community contributions: £225,000

Community support policy

Total community contributions in 1997 were £225,000 including £138,000 in charitable donations.

Charitable donations: To receive consideration by the appeals committee, appeals should be directed towards national causes or local charities in areas where the company has operations ie. Aberdeen (through the Elf Consortium) and London. Favoured areas of support are: community projects, education, elderly people, environment/conservation, sickness/disability charities, medical research, mental health and youth. Typical grants to national organisations range from £250 to £5,000, and to local organisations from £100 to £1,000. Typical ad hoc fund grants range from £250 to £1,000. Main beneficiaries in 1997 included Scottish Wildlife Trust and Macmillan Cancer Relief.

The company's charitable budget for Scotland is paid into the Elf Consortium which supports a wide range of concerns in the arts, social welfare, education, and the environment. Support is principally given to Aberdeen and the Orkney Islands. Projects falling within these guidelines should apply for funding to: The Public Relations Coordinator, Elf Caledonia Ltd, 1 Claymore Drive, Bridge of Don, Aberdeen AB23 8GD.

Employee involvement: The company encourages staff to be involved in community projects through the LASMO volunteers support scheme. This provides cash grants to charity and volunteering projects in which employees and/or their families are involved. A payroll giving scheme is operated and matching schemes for employee giving and fundraising are also in place.

Education: The company provides work-experience schemes for pupils and student sponsorships. Sponsorship proposals: LASMO is pro-active in selecting sponsorship projects, with funds largely committed at the beginning of each year. Organisations supported include the English National Opera, New Shakespeare Theatre Co., Camerata Scotland, World Conservation Monitoring Centre, VSO and the LASMO Arts Trust (music competition for advanced students only). Unsolicited appeals are rarely considered and individuals are not sponsored.

Exclusions

No grants to organisations/projects already receiving support from the company in other ways. No support is given to circular appeals, local appeals not in areas of company presence, advertising in charity brochures, institutions/organisations whose proper source of funds is through public channels, political, sectarian or purely religious organisations/activities or appeals from individuals for sponsorship/funding.

Applications

Applications are considered half yearly in June and December. No progress report can be given outside of these review dates. Charitable appeals and sponsorship proposals should also be addressed to the correspondent.

Information available: In addition to the statement of UK donations in its annual report, the company reports on its community involvement in the staff newsletter.

Lazard Brothers & Co Ltd

21 Moorfields, London EC2P 2HT
0171-588 2721

Correspondent: Elisabeth Brown, Secretary to the Lazard Charitable Trust

Chief officer: *Chairman:* M Michael Baughan

Year end	Turnover	Pre-tax profit
31/12/97	n/a	n/a

Nature of company business
Banking, capital markets, corporate finance.

UK employees: 614

Charitable donations

1997: £200,000
1996: £200,000
1995: £200,000
1994: n/a
1993: £200,000

Community support policy

The charity has a donations budget of about £200,000 a year given through the Lazard Charitable Trust (Charity Commission number 1048043). The trustees are M Michael Baughan, Mrs Frances Heaton and Mrs Charlotte Syder. In 1997, the total income of the trust was £207,000 and grants totalled £156,000. The balance was £169,000 at the year end.

It prefers to support local charities in areas of company presence, charities in which a member of staff is involved and charities in inner cities and areas of deprivation. Preferred areas of support are children and young people, elderly people, social welfare and sickness/disability charities. Fundraising events may be supported and the trust matches fundraising efforts of staff. Grants to national and local organisations range from £100 to £1,000.

Main beneficiaries in 1997 were Children Nationwide, DEBRA, Equal Play Adventure, ChildLine and Queen Elizabeth Hospital for Sick Children.

Exclusions

No response to circular appeals. No support for advertising in charity brochures, animal welfare charities, appeals from individuals, the arts, education, enterprise/training, environment/heritage, medical research, overseas projects, political appeals, religious appeals, science/technology or sport.

Applications

In writing to the correspondent.

Legal & General plc

Temple Court, 11 Queen Victoria Street, London EC4N 4TP
0171-528 6200; Fax: 0171-528 6222

Correspondent: Jackie Quantock, Social Responsibility Manager

Chief officers: *Chairman:* Sir Christopher Harding; *Chief Executive:* David Prosser

Year end	Turnover	Pre-tax profit
31/12/97	n/a	£610,000,000

Nature of company business
Legal & General's core businesses are life and pensions business, general insurance and investments. 80% of the group's business comes from the UK. The most important areas of operation overseas are Australia, USA and Europe.

Main subsidiaries include: Fairmount Group PLC; Gresham Insurance Company Ltd.

UK employees: 6,065

Charitable donations

1997: £683,000
1996: £461,103
1995: £464,750
1994: £477,750
1993: £466,500

Total community contributions: £1,000,000

Membership: *ABSA BitC %Club*

Community support policy

Sponsorship and donations programme: Legal & General gives up to 1% of pre-tax profits to support activities which benefit the community, with an increase of over £200,000 in charitable donations in the last year. The long-term aim of the programme is to build a better quality of life.

Levi

The company believes that the best way to do this is to give significant long-term support to a small number of projects which are directly related to the group's core businesses. Local programmes are used to support the community in places where large numbers of employees live and work. The company is a member of the PerCent Club, Business in the Community and ABSA.

National programme: The group's policy is to support identifiable work in five defined areas, with donations or sponsorships of between £25,000 and £100,000 a year, usually for two or three years.

The company has an established, long-term programme which is run proactively, in that the company looks for organisations that meet its criteria. Unsolicited appeals are not welcome, although information about organisations which work in the relevant areas is always useful. The programme covers the following areas:

(a) social welfare
(b) medical research
(c) environment
(d) crime prevention
(e) equal opportunities for women.

Local programmes: Local programmes fund a wide range of community activities in areas where employees live and work. Preference is given to projects in which employees are involved. Local programmes are run in the following areas: Brighton and Hove, Cardiff, and Surrey.

Current initiatives include work with Princess Royal Trust for Carers; Living Earth; Crime Concern; Prostate Cancer Charity; The Prince's Youth Business Trust.

In kind support: The group's main in kind support is given to enterprise agencies.

Employee involvement: Although there is no formal employee involvement policy, employees are encouraged to support charitable activities and to become school governors. The Give As You Earn payroll giving scheme is promoted through the staff newsletter.

Secondment: No secondments are being made at present.

Environment: Legal & General is working with Living Earth on a schools/business basis.

The arts: Support for the arts is focused on eight regional sponsorships. This is an established programme which means it is difficult to make new commitments.

Exclusions

Nationally, Legal & General does not advertise in brochures or programmes, and does not support purely denominational appeals, small local appeals and community-based projects, appeals from individuals, fundraising events, large national appeals, overseas projects, animal wefare charities or circulars.

Applications

Information about national charities which meet the group's guidelines should be sent to the correspondent. Appropriate local appeals should be sent to:

Brighton & Hove: Gianna Dodd, Community Affairs, Legal & General, 2 Montefiore Road, Hove, East Sussex BN3 1SE.

Cardiff: Lynne Sheeney, Community Affairs, Legal & General, Knox Court, 10 Fitzallan Place, Cardiff CF2 1TL.

Surrey: Rob Catt, Community Affairs, Legal & General, Legal & General House, St Monicas Road, Kingswood, Tadworth, Surrey KT20 6EU.

National decisions are made by the Group Communications Division; local appeals are considered by individual offices. Legal & General does not have a charities committee. Overseas grants are handled by the subsidiary company in each country.

Information available: Articles on charitable activities are published in the *Gazette*, a monthly newspaper for employees and company pensioners.

Levi Strauss (UK) Ltd

100 New Bridge Street, London EC4 V 6JA
0171-439 3933; Fax: 0171-437 1232
Website: www.levi.com

Correspondent: Emily Riley, Corporate Affairs Manager

Chief officer: *Managing Director:* Jack Cosgrove

Year end	Turnover	Pre-tax profit
30/11/96	£205,221,000	£18,193,000

Nature of company business
Clothing manufacture and marketing under the Levi's brand. UK locations are:

England: LSUK Northampton, Moulton Park, Northampton NN3 1QG

Scotland: Levi Strauss (UK) Ltd, Bellshill North Industrial Estate, Bellshill, Lanarkshire ML4 3J

Levi Strauss (UK) Ltd, Block 31, Dunsinane Avenue, Kingsway Industrial Estate, Dundee DD2 3J

Levi Strauss (UK) Ltd, Murraysgate Industrial Estate, Whitburn, West Lothian EH47 0LD.

Main subsidiaries include: Retail Index Ltd; Farvista Ltd.

UK employees: 1,674

Charitable donations

1996: £315,580
1995: £355,463
1994: £304,256
1993: £196,556

Total community contributions: £497,000

Membership: *ABSA*

Community support policy

Levi Strauss aims to show its commitment to the communities in which it operates by encouraging employee volunteering, making cash and non-cash contributions to non-profit organisations and working in partnership with others in pursuit of community benefit. In the UK, Levi's community support is focused on the communities of Northampton, Dundee, Belshill, near Glasgow, and Whitburn in West Lothian (its main UK sites).

Charitable donations

The company supports:
- job creation and community-based development
- job training, placement and access strategies
- community leadership development
- care for AIDS/HIV positive sufferers and risk education
- childcare
- general social welfare.

Grants range from £300 to £15,000. Examples of support given include: providing a counsellor training facility for Childline (Scotland); buying a van for an organisation offering support services to AIDS patients; providing start-up funding for an organisation developing community leadership skills; funding a project to place long-term unemployed people in small/medium companies. Organisations supported include The Big Issue, National AIDS Trust, Northampton Women's Network and Nordoff Robbins Music Therapy Trust.

Levi's operate two contributions programmes: *Community Involvement Team* (CIT) grants and *Special Emphasis* grants.

CIT grants are employee directed and are made by teams of employee volunteers who review local community needs and, in consultation with local applicant groups, develop and implement projects to meet those needs. CIT grants can typically be up to £15,000 and those interested should write, outlining the proposal, to the CIT at their local Levi's facility.

The *Community Partnership (special emphasis)* grants programme is intended to support creative and innovative projects, funding higher risk efforts which have little access to traditional sources of funding. The company has a special interest in programmes which address the economic barriers faced by women, ethnic minorities and others who may face special disadvantage. Grants are also made to projects which seek to improve care available to those suffering from AIDS or which improve education about the dangers of the disease. Those interested in Special Emphasis grants should write to the Community Affairs Manager.

Levi's grants rarely exceed £15,000, although multi-year grants are available and may exceed this figure.

Employee involvement: In addition to preference being given to charities in which a member of staff is involved, staff are allowed time off for activity of community benefit and encouraged to become volunteers in their own time. The company operates a matching scheme for employee fundraising.

In kind support: The company may occasionally make some of their products (jeans) available to charitable organisations. Donations of furniture, machines, etc. that are no longer in use may also be made to support the work of an organisation.

Exclusions

The company does not support circular appeals, advertising in brochures, purely denominational appeals, small purely local appeals not in an area of company presence, large national appeals, overseas projects, appeals from individuals, fundraising events, circular appeals, projects for political or sectarian religious purposes and requests for the sponsorship of courtesy advertising, sponsorship of the arts or sporting events.

Applications

Appeals for Community Partnership grants should be addressed to the correspondent. As explained above, requests for Community Involvement Team grants should be directed to the relevant local plant.

Applications from outside the UK should be addressed directly to Emily Riley, Community Affairs Manager, 489 Avenue Louise, 1050 Brussels, Belgium
Tel: 00-32-2-641,62,24.

John Lewis Partnership plc

171 Victoria Street, London SW1E 5NN
0171-828 1000; Fax: 0171-828 4145

Correspondent: Mrs Chris Jones, Secretary to the Central Charities Committee

Chief officer: *Chairman:* S Hampson

Year end	Turnover	Pre-tax profit
31/1/98	£3,460,100,000	£250,300,000

Nature of company business
The company operates 23 department stores and 117 Waitrose supermarkets with ancillary manufacturing activities. The department stores trade under a variety of names including Bainbridge, Bonds, Caleys, Cole Bros, George Henry Lee, Heelas, Jessop & Son, Peter Jones, Knight & Lee, John Lewis, Robert Sayle, Trewins and Tyrrell & Green.

The company has department stores in Aberdeen, Bristol, Cambridge, Cheadle, Edinburgh, High Wycombe, Kingston, Liverpool, London, Milton Keynes, Newcastle, Norwich, Nottingham, Peterborough, Reading, Sheffield, Southampton, Southsea, Watford, Welwyn and Windsor.

Waitrose supermarkets are found throughout southern England, the Midlands and East Anglia. The Partnership is a retail business run on co-operative principles. All the ordinary share capital is held by a trustee – John Lewis Partnership Trust Ltd – on Partners' (employees) behalf. Under irrevocable trusts the balance of profits is available to be shared among all Partners after provision for prudent reserves and for interest on loans and fixed dividends on shares held outside. Management is accountable to the general body of Partners, in particular through elected councils and through the partnership's journalism.

Main subsidiaries include: Waitrose; Cavendish Textiles; Stead, McAlpin & Company; Herbert Parkinson; J H Birtwhistle & Company; Leckford Estate; Leckford Mushrooms.

UK employees: 33,300

Charitable donations

1998: £1,420,000
1997: £1,030,000
1996: £790,000
1995: £699,000
1994: £682,000

Community support policy

The Partnership's Central and Branch Councils are responsible for about half the total donations (£531,000 in 1996/97). It gives to what can be broadly described as 'welfare' organisations, generally with charitable status. Organisations at both national and local level are supported, preferring to give directly to the organisations concerned. National grants range from £250 to £10,000. Individual grants range from £50 to £7,500 and gifts in kind.

The chairman is responsible for the other half of the giving (£497,000 in 1996/97) and gives to organisations which, in broad terms, fall into the categories of the arts, education and the environment. Last year more than half was given in support of musical activities, the rest being divided among the other arts – drama, literature, painting, etc., the conservation of buildings, and the countryside and teaching and research, including museums and natural history.

Exclusions

No support for advertising in charity brochures, appeals from individuals, fundraising events, overseas projects, political appeals, religious appeals, science/technology, or sport. No sponsorship is undertaken.

Applications

In writing to the correspondent. Applications are discussed quarterly. Local charities should deal with their local Partnership department store, production unit or Waitrose branch.

Lex Service PLC

Boston Drive, Bourne End, Buckinghamshire SL8 5YS
01628-843888; Fax: 01628-810294
Email: lex@lex.co.uk
Website: www.lex.co.uk

Correspondent: David Leibling, Head of Corporate Communications

Chief officers: *Chairman:* Sir Trevor Chinn;
Chief Executive: Andrew Harrison

Year end	Turnover	Pre-tax profit
31/12/97	£1,489,800,000	£44,000,000

Nature of company business

Lex Service is a business and vehicle services company operating mainly in the UK. Lex business services cover vehicle management, mechanical handling and inventory management where the goal is to help industrial and commercial customers operate their businesses more efficiently and more profitably. Lex vehicle marketing and motoring services cover vehicle importing and retailing and specialist aftermarket businesses.

Lex provides contract hire, rental and fleet management for cars, trucks and mechanical handling equipment. It imports Hyundai cars, Isuzu trucks, Komatsu, Daewoo and TCM lift trucks and retails a range of different cars and trucks. Motoring services includes servicing and repairs, used car sales and body repairs for all makes of cars.

Main locations: Bedworth (Warks), Bourne End (Bucks), Chorley, Coventry, High Wycombe, Marlow, Northampton, Solihull, Ware.

UK employees: 7,589

Charitable donations

1997: £241,000
1996: £245,000
1995: £232,000
1994: £245,000
1993: £250,000
Membership: %Club

Community support policy

Lex is a member of the PerCent Club, regularly giving about £250,000 a year to UK charities.

Charitable donations: Donations are made to charities serving the arts, education, medicine and social welfare (including children, youth and elderly people). Other areas of support include advertising in charity brochures, enterprise/training and sickness/disability charities. Only registered charities are supported and the programme largely comprises long-term commitments.

Preference is given to national charities, local appeals in areas of company presence, appeals relevant to company business and charities in which a member of staff is involved. Major beneficiaries included the industry charity (BEN) and The Prince's Youth Business Trust.

Employee involvement: The company operates the BEN payroll giving scheme. Staff are allowed time off for activity of community benefit. The company undertakes no secondment.

The arts: Lex is not a member of ABSA but it does undertake some national arts sponsorship. It has supported the Royal National Theatre, Royal Shakespeare Theatre Trust, National Arts Collection Fund, Royal Academy of Arts, Royal Opera House and the English National Opera Company.

Exclusions

No support for animal welfare charities; appeals from individuals; environment/heritage; fundraising events; medical research; overseas projects; political appeals; religious appeals; science/technology or sport.

Applications

In writing to the correspondent. Grant decisions are made by a donations committee which meets every three months. Unsuccessful applicants are not notified.

Liberty International Holdings PLC

40 Broadway, London SW1H 0BT
0171-222 5496; Fax: 0171-222 5554

Correspondent: Alison Barraclough, Personal Assistant to the Chairman

Chief officers: *Chairman:* D Gordon; *Managing Director:* D Fischel

Year end	Turnover	Pre-tax profit
31/12/98	£262,700,000	£126,500,000

Nature of company business
The principal activity is that of an investment company, with financial services including life insurance, pensions, asset management and property investment.
Main subsidiaries include: Capital Shopping Centres PLC; Capital & Counties PLC; Portfolio Fund Management Ltd.

UK employees: 50

Charitable donations
1998: £50,371
1997: £51,250
1996: £35,125
1995: £25,160

Community support policy
We currently have no information on the charitable donations policy of the company, although the total given increased to over £50,000 in 1997.

The company prior to May 1996 was known as TransAtlantic Holdings PLC. It has a 72% interest in Capital Shopping Centres PLC which owns nine regional centres, the largest investments being in Lakeside, Thurrock, The Harlequin, Watford and MetroCentre, Gateshead. The other major subsidiary is Capital & Counties plc which operates commercial and retail properties.

Applications
In writing to the correspondent.

Eli Lilly Group Ltd

Dextra Court, Chapel Hill, Basingstoke RG21 5SY
01256-315000; Fax: 01256-315412
Website: www.lilly.com

Correspondent: D G Anthony, Secretary to the Grants Committee

Chief officers: *Chairman:* S Taurel; *Managing Director:* A Plump

Year end	Turnover	Pre-tax profit
31/12/97	£526,579,000	£62,669,000

Nature of company business
Eli Lilly & Company Ltd is a research-based corporation that develops, manufactures and markets human medicines, medical instruments, diagnostic products and agricultural products. Corporate headquarters are located in Indianapolis, USA.
Main subsidiaries include: Creative Packaging Ltd; Dista Products Ltd; Elanco Products Ltd; Greenfield Pharmaceuticals Ltd.

UK employees: 1,810

Charitable donations
1997: £35,575
1996: n/a
1995: £51,000
1994: £65,000
1993: £82,000

Community support policy
Community contributions made by the company include charitable donations, good-cause sponsorship, in kind support and non-commercial advertising. The company supports national causes and local charities with a preference for those close to its main UK locations in Basingstoke (Hampshire), Speke (Liverpool) and Windlesham (Surrey).

Charitable donations: To receive a grant, registered charitable status is desirable. Support is given to medical and social welfare projects (especially those which benefit children) and charities which have a bearing on agriculture. Grants to national organisations range from £100 to £300, and to local organisations from £50 to £100.

Sponsorship: Sponsorship is very selective at national level (only one scheme is running at present). At a local level some sponsorship up to about £1,000 is undertaken, usually for health-related causes.

Employee involvement: The company operates a payroll giving scheme for employees and preference is given to charities in which a member of staff is involved. Staff are also encouraged to become school governors.

In kind support: The company donates pharmaceutical products to medical charities and causes, but only very rarely and usually for emergency relief overseas.

Enterprise: The company gives support to local enterprise agencies and was a founding supporter of the Basingstoke & Andover Enterprise Centre.

Education: Initiatives include involvement in local education/business partnerships and the provision of work experience schemes for pupils and teachers, and educational materials for schools.

Exclusions
The arts are not sponsored. No support for advertising in charity brochures, appeals from individuals, bricks and mortar appeals or local appeals not in areas of company presence.

Applications
In writing to the correspondent. Decisions on national appeals are made at head office by a grants committee which meets quarterly.

Limit plc

Beaufort House, 15 St Botolph Street, London EC3A 7PA
0171-390 6100; Fax: 0171-390 6110

Correspondent: J G W Agnew, Chairman

Chief officer: *Chairman:* J G W Agnew

Year end	Turnover	Pre-tax profit
31/3/98	n/a	£189,000,000

Nature of company business
Insurance company.

Main subsidiaries include: Bankside Insurance Holdings; CUL Holdings; Janson Green Holdings; Garwyn.

Charitable donations
1998: £55,846
1997: £3,729

Community support policy
The level of giving by the company has risen dramatically in the last year to almost £56,000. Unfortunately, we currently have no information on the charitable donations policy.

Applications
In writing to the correspondent.

Linpac Group Ltd

Evan Cornish House, Windsor Road, Fairfield Industrial Estate, Louth, Lincolnshire LN11 0LX
01507-601601; Fax: 01507-600339

Correspondent: Bob Buxton, Sales & Marketing Director

Chief officer: *Chairman:* M Cornish

Year end	Turnover	Pre-tax profit
31/12/97	£864,857,000	£31,530,000

Nature of company business
Packaging manufacture.

Main subsidiaries include: Aquafilm Ltd; Apex Storage System Ltd; Billoway Engineering Ltd; Salter Paper Group Ltd.

UK employees: n/a

Charitable donations
1997: £77,000
1996: £69,000
1995: £115,000
1994: £162,000
1993: £99,000

Community support policy
The company has stated previously that it does not complete surveys and has not responded to our requests for information on its community support. The only information we have is that a fund had been set up for schools which received all donations made by the company up to 1997. We do not know if this is still the situation.

Applications
In writing to the correspondent.

Littlewoods Organisation PLC

100 Old Hall Street, Liverpool L70 1AB
0151-235 2713; Fax: 0151-476 5118

Correspondent: Jerry Marston, Group Community Affairs Manager

Chief officers: *Chairman:* James Ross;
Chief Executive: J M Barry Gibson

Year end	Turnover	Pre-tax profit
30/4/98	£2,286,000,000	£109,500,000

Nature of company business
The retail and leisure group started by Sir John Moores in 1923 now employs 27,000 people, half of whom are based in the North West, of which 7,000 live and work on Merseyside. It has over 200 chain and catalogue (Index) stores. Littlewoods Leisure runs the football pools operation and lottery scratchcards. New joint ventures are under way with Arcadia to develop niche catalogues and Shop!, the home shopping TV channel with Granada was launched in November 1998.

Main subsidiaries include: The International Import & Export Co Ltd; UKCL Ltd; CDMS Ltd; J & C Moores Ltd; Charities Trust Ltd; Stanley Insurance Services Ltd; Old Hall Insurance Services Ltd.

UK employees: 28,000

Charitable donations
1998: £1,702,000
1997: £1,500,000
1996: £1,500,000
1995: £1,300,000
1994: £1,445,000

Total community contributions: £2,421,000

Membership: *BitC %Club*

Community support policy
The company is a member of the PerCent Club and Business in the Community. During 1997/98, community sponsorships and charitable funding exceeded £2.4 million. In addition, charity beneficiaries of Littlewoods Lotteries received over £11 million, and the Foundation for Sport and the Arts and the Football Trust each received £8.4 million from Littlewoods Pools.

Following a review completed in November 1997, the company has established a new community investment strategy built around the key theme of regeneration. The geographical focus will continue to be the North West, with an emphasis on creating and sustaining jobs and prosperity in targeted communities. Support in many cases is for a number of years, and combines employee expertise and other company resources with cash donations to achieve greater impact. Charities and organisations supporting disadvantaged groups continue to receive funding, and employee fundraising and volunteering are now being more actively structured and promoted.

Examples of projects supported in 1997/98 include:
- significant funding to the Hothouse Project, in partnership with John Moores University, which will provide intensive support to young entrepreneurs
- founding sponsorship of the Groundwork Trust in Liverpool
- long-term funding and other support to two inner city schools, Our Lady's and Shorefields in Liverpool
- support to community economic schemes in disadvantaged neighbourhoods across Merseyside
- funding of the Mersey and Liverpool City Partnerships
- funding of Young Enterprise, and the Prince's Trust Volunteers
- sponsorship of, and employee involvement in, Granada Live Challenge, Comic Relief, KidsOut, Childline, the Weston Spirit and the Roy Castle Foundation
- sponsorship of the Liverpool Tate Gallery's Eye-openers access programme.

Exclusions

The company will not consider applications:
- for support to individuals, for any purpose
- for church-based activities, unless the proposal is separate from core religious activities and non-denominational in its approach
- for support for fundraising initiatives or events, including advertising space
- which are seeking to replace statutory funding
- from national organisations, unless it is for work which is specifically to be undertaken and managed in an area where the company operates
- from schools, hospitals, social services or criminal justice agencies, unless the proposal is community based and independent
- for academic or medical research
- from animal welfare charities.

Applications

The community affairs committee meets four times a year to consider applications under the regeneration programme. Charitable applications are considered on a continuing basis by the Charity Sub-committee, which meets throughout the year. There is no application form. Applications should be limited to two pages of A4, which will go to the committee, and accompanied by appropriate supplementary material – annual reports, accounts, brochures, etc., which probably will not be circulated.

To reduce the amount of unnecessary work by applicants, it is suggested that you call to discuss your proposal in advance of drafting and submitting a detailed application.

Liverpool Victoria Friendly Society

Frizzel House, County Gate, Bournemouth, Dorset BH1 2NF
01202-292333; Fax: 01202-292253

Correspondent: Mrs Coney, Public Relations Department

Chief officers: *Chairman:* A S Noble; *Chief Executive:* R B M Hurley

Year end	Turnover	Pre-tax profit
31/12/97	n/a	n/a

Nature of company business
The society is an incorporated Friendly Society which carries on insurance and financial services business in the UK.

Main subsidiaries include: Frizzell Bank; Frizzell Life & Financial Planning.

UK employees: 2,904

Charitable donations
1997: £268,947
1996: £302,477

Community support policy

The figure stated above is that declared in the Society's annual report as the charitable donations made during 1997. We have no further information on the donations given directly by the Society.

In addition, Liverpool Victoria Charity Challenge (a snooker tournament) raises about £264,000 annually for up to 12 organisations. Charities that apply to the company are encouraged to complete an application form to enter the Challenge. A list of about 30 charities are selected from those that apply. These are then featured in the *TV Times*, with the public invited to vote, to select one charity in each of about six categories. The top 12 are than supported by the Challenge.

Applications
In writing to the correspondent.

Lloyd's of London

One Lime Street, London EC3M 7HA
0171-327 5925

Correspondent: Mrs L Harper, Secretary, Lloyd's Charities Trust

Chief officers: *Chairman:* David Rowland; *Chief Executive:* Ron Sandier

Year end	Turnover	Pre-tax profit
31/12/95	n/a	n/a

Nature of company business
Insurance underwriting market.

Main subsidiaries include: Additional Securities Ltd; Centrewrite Ltd; Lioncover Insurance Co Ltd; Sharedealer Ltd; Syndicate Underwriting Management Ltd.

UK employees: n/a

Lloyds

Charitable donations
1998: £250,000
1997: n/a
1996: n/a
1995: £253,519
1994: £351,750
Membership: *BitC*

Community support policy

Lloyd's supports the community through a charitable trust and through its Community Programme.

The Lloyd's Charities Trust

The trust is funded mainly by voluntary covenanted subscriptions from members of Lloyd's and by interest on its accumulated endowment. The trust has changed its policy and has selected five charities to support over the next three years. They are:

Alzheimer's Research Trust: to help establish an electronic network, linking centres of excellence around the country

CARE International: to help support a peace-building programme in Bosnia and Hercegovina

British Trust for Conservation Volunteers: to support the Thames-Side Project

Save the Children: to support a rural education project in Brazil

Crimestoppers: to support the Bishopsgate Youth Club in the City.

These charities will be supported through donations, gifts in kind including donations of equipment, and by hosting a meeting/event at Lloyd's for each charity.

These charities were selected proactively. Lloyd's requested projects which were then short-listed. The short-listed charities were invited to present to a panel. However, all the charities were known for their work and had received donations in previous years.

The annual budget for the trust is £250,000. Ad hoc income from covenants, bequests and donations, which totalled £353,000 in 1997, is distributed through Lloyd's Patriotic Fund (£90,000) – established to further research into science, technology and business by way of fellowships and PhD business scholarships, Lloyd's Tercentenary Foundation (£180,000) – established to provide financial assistance to ex-servicemen and women and their widows and dependants, and Lloyd's Community Programme (£83,000) – see below.

The Lloyd's Community Programme

This programme was set up 10 years ago in partnership with Business in the Community. It aimed to encourage links between Lloyd's and their neighbours in Tower Hamlets. The programme has now become more independent as it has established strong contacts and links with schools and voluntary sector organisations within Tower Hamlets – in particular Tower Hamlets Education Business Partnership.

The programme supports schools and local businesses in Tower Hamlets. It established a reading partners scheme in 1995 to help local children with reading and communication skills. Nearly 300 volunteers are involved in the scheme. The Lloyd's Loan Fund was established in the mid-1980s to help new businesses in Tower Hamlets who have been unable to raise finance through banks.

The programme is supported by subscriptions from Lloyd's firms and firms closely associated with the market.

Exclusions

Support is NOT given to: advertising in charity brochures, appeals from individuals, the arts, sponsorship, fundraising events, political appeals, religious appeals, science/technology, sport or local appeals not in areas of company presence.

Applications

Due to the current policy unsolicited applications cannot be supported.

Lloyds TSB Group plc

71 Lombard Street, London EC3P 3BS
0171-356 2462; Fax: 0171-356 2403

Correspondent: Jo Willis, Head of Public Affairs

Chief officers: *Chairman:* Sir Brian Pitman; *Chief Executive:* Peter B Ellwood

Year end	Turnover	Pre-tax profit
31/12/97	n/a	£3,162,000,000

Nature of company business
The Lloyds TSB Group is the largest financial services company in the UK, covering retail banking, commercial and corporate banking, mortgages, life assurance and pensions, general insurance, asset management, leasing, treasury and foreign exchange dealing.

Main subsidiaries include: Cheltenham and Gloucester PLC; The Agricultural Mortgage Corpn PLC; Hill Samuel Asset Management Group Ltd; Abbey Life Assurance Co Ltd; Black Horse Financial Services Group Ltd.

UK employees: 82,580

Charitable donations
1997: £21,446,000
1996: £7,690,000
1995: £4,606,000
1994: £1,150,753
1993: £1,131,089
Total community contributions: £30,000,000
Membership: *ABSA BitC %Club*

Community support policy

Lloyds TSB Group is rooted in local communities throughout the UK and believes it has a responsibility to support those communities that it serves as a business.

- The group's charitable donations are channelled through four independent charitable trusts, the Lloyds TSB Foundations.
- Lloyds TSB Group's corporate community investment programme focuses on education, regeneration and staff support for community causes.

The Lloyds TSB Foundations

The Lloyds TSB Foundations are four independent grant-making trusts, covering England and Wales, Scotland, Northern Ireland and the Channel Islands. They are shareholders in Lloyds TSB Group and together receive 1% of the group's pre-tax profits, averaged over three years, instead of the dividend on their shareholding. In 1998, the foundations distributed approximately £21 million to over 4,000 registered charities throughout the UK, and on the basis of the group's current profitability, allowing nothing for further progress, the Lloyds TSB Foundations' annual income by 2000 could exceed £30 million. The Lloyds TSB Foundations are committed to supporting underfunded, grassroots charities that enable people, especially disabled or disadvantaged people, to play a fuller role in society.

The broad objectives are to fund UK registered charities which:
- meet social and community needs
- promote education and training
- support scientific and medical research.

Within these general criteria, each of these foundations has areas of special interest. For the Lloyds TSB Foundation for England and Wales these currently include:
- crime prevention
- creating positive opportunities for disabled people
- family support
- helping homeless people back into mainstream society
- the prevention of substance abuse
- supporting independent living for older people
- the needs of carers
- advocacy.

The foundation for Scotland gives priority to:
- young people
- rural deprivation
- support for elderly people
- alleviation of homelessness
- the prevention of drug and alcohol abuse
- support for minority groups
- creating opportunities for mentally and physically disadvantaged people
- supporting the infrastructure of the voluntary sector. In Northern Ireland, priority is given to cross-community work.

The foundations regularly review their grant-giving criteria and will consider applications for both 'core funding' and 'project funding'. Grants awarded can range from a few hundred pounds to several thousand, but regional grants are typically in the region of £300 to £10,000 and are judged on merit.

Exclusions

The foundations will not support individuals, including students, or organisations which are not registered charities. There is no support for: animal welfare, environment (including geographic/scenic, conservation and protection of flora and fauna), overseas appeals, activities which are primarily the responsibility of local or national government or some other responsible body, mainstream schools, universities and colleges (except when benefiting disabled students), hospitals and medical centres (except for projects which are clearly additional to statutory responsibilities), sponsorship or marketing appeals, restoration of buildings, fabric appeals for places of worship, promotion of religion, activities which collect funds for subsequent redistribution to other charities or individuals, endowment funds, general appeals, fundraising events, corporate affiliation or founder membership of a charity, loans or business finance, expeditions or overseas travel.

Matched giving scheme

The foundations also encourage staff of Lloyds TSB Group to raise funds for community causes through a matched giving scheme. Staff fundraising is matched £ for £ up to a maximum of £500 per staff member, per year, providing funds are raised for recognised charities that fit within the foundations grant-giving criteria. From 1999, the foundations will also donate £5 for every hour's voluntary work given out of work hours, up to a maximum of £100 per staff member, per year. In 1998, more than 1,500 members of staff raised over £1.4 million for community causes with the matched giving scheme. And in 1999, about £1 million has been allocated to support staff fundraising.

Applications

For further details of grant-giving policies and an application form please contact the appropriate Lloyds TSB Foundation for your locality.

Lloyds TSB Foundation for England and Wales
PO Box 140, St Mary's Court,
20 St Mary at Hill, London EC3R 8NA
0171-204 5276
website: www.lloydstsbfoundations.org.uk

Lloyds TSB Foundation for Scotland
Henry Duncan House,
120 George Street, Edinburgh EH2 4LH
0131-225 4555

Lloyds TSB Foundation for Northern Ireland
4 Queens Square, Belfast BT1 3DJ
01232-325599

Lloyds TSB Foundation for the Channel Islands
25 New Street, St Helier, Jersey, Channel Islands JE4 8RG
01534-503052.

Corporate Community Investment

In 1998, the group's community investment totalled nearly £9 million. This comprises support for education, social sponsorships, work experience placements, Business Links, Young Enterprise, Prince's Youth Business Trust, local community support and charitable donations.

Education

Across the group, education emerges as a primary focus for investment.

- *Teaching Awards 1999* – run by the Teaching Awards Trust, the awards aim to recognise excellence in the teaching profession; to raise morale and the profile of teachers. Pupils, parents, governors and head teachers will nominate teachers and winners will be rewarded at a celebratory awards ceremony.

Lofthouse

- *Lloyds TSB Live!* – the Lloyds TSB Live! bus will tour schools to provide young people aged between 11 and 16 with an introduction to Shakespeare, rugby and music. With support from the Royal National Theatre, the Rugby Football Union, the Scottish Rugby Union and Fender, Roland and Steinberg, who provide musical equipment.
- *Work experience* – support for 1,500 students in branches right across the country.
- *School Governors Programme* – the group actively supports more than 600 members of staff who are also school governors; by providing training through regional seminars, a weekend summer school, a national conference and a regular newsletter.
- *Quality in Education programme* – this programme promotes excellence in schools through the use of the Business Excellence Model as a tool for self-assessment. Through a pilot programme, the model has been introduced to more than 800 schools nationwide and the programme is now working with more than 35 local education authorities.
- *The provision of national curriculum materials* – production of literature for personal money management issues and to prepare and help students into higher or further education, eg. the PUSH guide to higher education.

Regeneration and enterprise

- Support of Business Links, Prince's Youth Business Trust, Business Support Groups and enterprise agencies.
- Pilot programme in support of credit unions and community banks.

Employee involvement

- Staff secondments – currently to Business in the Community, the New Deal and Community Banking.
- School Governor Programme – see above.
- Staff participation in schools with schemes such as Young Enterprise, School Banks and Prince's Youth Business Trust.
- Fundraising – through the matched giving scheme and national fundraising campaigns. In 1998, staff raised £1 million for the Cancer Relief Campaign and in 1999 they will be raising money for NCH Action for Children.

Lofthouse of Fleetwood Ltd

Maritime Street, Fleetwood, Lancashire FY7 7LP
01253-872435

Correspondent: Mrs D W Lofthouse, Trustee, Lofthouse Foundation

Chief officers: n/a

Year end	Turnover	Pre-tax profit
31/12/97	£25,680,000 (1995)	£8,570,000 (1995)

Nature of company business
Manufacturers of the famous 'Fisherman's Friend' medicated confectionery.

Main brands include: Fisherman's Friend.

UK employees: n/a

Charitable donations
1997: £350,000
1996: £163,750
1995: £220,000

Community support policy

We have not been able to update information on this company other than from the Charity Commission file for the associated charitable trust, the Lofthouse Foundation (Charity Commission number 1038728).

Through this trust, the company support local charities, generally in the Fleetwood area. There are three trustees, all of whom are members of the Lofthouse family.

The trust was established in June 1994 with general charitable objects for the benefit of Fleetwood and its environs.

In 1997, it had an income of £475,000 including donations received of £352,000 of which £350,000 was from Lofthouse of Fleetwood Ltd and investment income of £123,000. We have assumed this to be the charitable donations figure of the company for this year.

Grants totalled only £82,000 and the trust had a balance of £1.8 million at the year end. Two grants were given for specific projects: £61,000 to Welcome Home Memorial and £10,000 to Fleetwood Hospital. Other grants totalled £11,000, no further information was available on these.

During 1996, the trustees negotiated the funding of a second environmental scheme which was completed during the year. This encompassed paving work on the esplanade at Fleetwood, for which the trust has yet to contribute £70,000.

The first environmental scheme supported by the foundation was in 1994, when £381,000 was granted to enhance the main junction at the entrance to Fleetwood's main shopping centre. The following year a further £21,000 was given to the scheme and the foundation also acquired a freehold property for use by Wyre Community Services at a peppercorn rent.

Applications
In writing to the correspondent.

London Electricity plc

Templar House, 81–87 High Holborn, London WC1V 6NU
0171-242 9050; Fax: 0171-831 0373

Correspondent: Jane Vine, Community Affairs Executive

Chief officers: n/a

Year end	Turnover	Pre-tax profit
31/12/97	n/a	n/a

Nature of company business
Principal activities: licensed distribution and supply of electricity to commercial and residential consumers, the provision of services relating to energy and electrical contracting services.

The company is now a wholly owned subsidiary of a US company.

UK employees: 3,900

Charitable donations
1996: £50,000
1995: £50,000
1994: £37,000
1993: £111,466

Total community contributions: £700,000

Membership: ABSA BitC

Community support policy

Support is given through sponsorship and donations to national charities and charities in the London Electricity areas, particularly to projects which deal with issues of direct concern to Londoners.

The company supports projects in education and training, urban regeneration and the environment. Donations are channelled to a few areas of support, generally around social welfare and have included organisations which assist homeless people, people suffering from drug and alcohol addiction, charities concerned with deaf people and elderly or disabled people and children/youth. Major activities include:

- a biennial awards scheme to encourage Londoners to reward and acknowledge their fellow Londoners whose efforts make the city a better place to live
- Learning Through Landscapes – a charity aiming to eradicate ashphalt playgrounds by the year 2000
- local community relations programme involving operational managers with direct customer interface who support local arts, sports, schools, environment and welfare projects.

The company is particularly keen on projects that have the scope for employee volunteering. It gives financial support to its employees' volunteering and matches employee fundraising. The main areas of non-cash support are in secondments and gifts in kind.

Grants range from £100 to £5,000. Sponsorship projects in the arts, heritage, environment and community involvement are also undertaken. Sponsorships are seen as participative.

Community involvement: The company is a member of Business in the Community. A major community sponsorship is the biennial *Brightening Up London Awards*. These awards recognise individuals, organisations and businesses who have made their contribution to help improve life in London.

Environment: As part of the company's environmental policy, it is sponsoring a three-year project with the London Wildlife Trust called Operation City Greenspace. This is a survey-based project to provide data about London's wildlife from which the trust aims to produce a longer term strategy for London's wildlife.

Exclusions

No response to circular appeals. No grants for advertising in charity brochures, animal welfare charities, appeals from individuals, the arts, children/youth, elderly people, fundraising events, medical research, overseas projects, political or religious appeals, sickness/disability charities, social welfare, sport, local appeals not in areas of company presence, or large national appeals.

Applications

In writing to the correspondent.

London Forfaiting Company PLC

International House, 1 St Katharine's Way, London E1 9UN
0171-481 3410; Fax: 0171-480 7626

Correspondent: Deborah Napolitano, Senior Receptionist

Chief officers: *Chairman:* Jack A G Wilson;
Chief Executive: Stathis A Papoutes

Year end	Turnover	Pre-tax profit
31/12/97	£2,268,841,000	£38,479,000

Nature of company business
The principal activity of the group is the provision of finance in connection with international trade and the arrangement and syndication of transferable loans.

UK employees: 217

Charitable donations
1997: £55,541
1996: £52,731
1995: £32,451
1994: £18,000
1993: £17,510

Community support policy

The company prefers to support charities in the south of England, especially those concerned with children/youth, education, elderly people, medical research, science/technology, sickness/disability charities, social welfare and sport.

Exclusions

No support for advertising in charity brochures, animal welfare charities, appeals from individuals, the arts, enterprise/training, environment/heritage, fundraising events, overseas projects, political or religious appeals.

Applications

In writing to the correspondent.

London Stock Exchange

London EC2N 1HP
0171-797 1000; Fax: 0171-588 3504

Correspondent: Paula Woodrow, Marketing Officer

Chief officers: *Chairman:* J Kemp-Welch;
Chief Executive: Gavin Casey

Year end	Turnover	Pre-tax profit
31/3/97	£191,745,000	£25,258,000

Low

Nature of company business
The organisation and regulation of markets in securities, the provision of associated settlement and information services and the admission of securities to listing. In addition to the UK, the exchange operates in the Republic of Ireland, Australia, South Africa and the USA.

Main subsidiaries include: SE Mutual Reference Ltd; The Birmingham Stock Exchange Buildings Co Ltd.

UK employees: n/a

Charitable donations

1997: £113,000
1996: £113,000
1995: £117,000
1994: £175,000
1993: £166,000

Community support policy

There is a preference for charities within the inner London area and the surrounding boroughs ie. Tower Hamlets and Islington. Generally, the preferred areas of support include: appeals from individuals, the arts, children/youth, education, elderly people, enterprise/training, environment/heritage, fundraising events, science/technology, sickness/disability charities and social welfare. Two recent new beneficiaries were Action for Kids and the Association for All Speech Impaired Children.

More specifically, the Stock Exchange concentrates its charitable giving in six areas:

Arts: Donations are made to charities whose work focuses on creating access to the arts for disadvantaged groups, for example SHAPE (£10,000). The Stock Exchange is a patron of ABSA.

Enterprise: Support is provided for charities who provide advice, support, grants and training to new businesses e.g. Instant Muscle (£10,000).

Local Community: Donations are given to organisations involved in issues of local concern such as Saint Mungo's (homelessness – £10,000), Providence Row (hostel for homeless men in London – £12,000) and APA (Association for Prevention of Addiction – £10,000).

Environment: Donations tend to be made for projects in London whose aim is to improve the city environment or to educate city dwellers on enviromental issues such as 'City Farm'.

Medical: Medical research is not supported, but examples of healthcare support include campaigns for people with speech difficulties.

Education: Support for training for disadvantaged groups.

The company operates an employee volunteering scheme, allows employees time off to volunteer and matches employee fundraising. They promote Give As You Earn, although do not match employee giving through the scheme.

The company's main area of non-cash support is allowing charities the use of facilities at the Stock Exchange for meetings/seminars.

Exclusions

Political, overseas and purely religious charities are not supported.

Applications

In writing to the correspondent.

Low & Bonar PLC

Bonar House, Faraday Street, Dundee DD1 9JA
01382-818171; Fax: 01382-816262

Correspondent: Mrs Ann Henry, Administrative Secretary to the Charitable Fund

Chief officers: *Chairman:* J H Robinson;
Chief Executive: J L Heilig

Year end	Turnover	Pre-tax profit
30/11/97	£438,677,000	£30,231,000

Nature of company business
Plastics, packaging and specialist material manufacture.

Main subsidiaries include: Ex-Press Plastics Ltd; Tufton Ltd; Cole Group Plc.

UK employees: 1,800

Charitable donations

1997: £65,950
1996: £58,100
1995: £58,650
1994: £49,515
1993: £62,800
Membership: %Club

Community support policy

The company is a member of the PerCent Club. Charitable donations are made through the Low & Bonar Charitable Fund which seeks to relieve human suffering generally. Priority is therefore given to charities falling into the following categories:

- medical, encompassing research, treatment and the general welfare of patients including those physically and mentally disabled
- the welfare of the old and infirm
- the protection and welfare of children and young people
- the relief of human suffering where not otherwise covered under the sections above.

These are regarded as the primary objects of the fund, and it is the policy of the trustees that not less than 80% of the funds available for distribution will be devoted to charities falling within the above categories.

If the trustees are satisfied that the stated primary aims of the fund are being met, then consideration will be given to charities meeting social, cultural and environmental needs. Other charities whose work the trustees judge to be of value may then also be supported.

Where the trustees feel that circumstances justify, the fund may make donations to international disaster relief appeals, whether such disasters occur within the UK or overseas.

'In view of the limited resources of the fund and the very substantial number of appeals which it receives, the trustees' policy is to allocate part of its available funds to make donations to selected nationally and internationally based charities, whose activities fall within the primary objects of the fund, and to allocate the balance of its funds to charities based in or especially benefiting Scotland and, in particular, to those working in the Dundee and Tayside area.'

In 1997, main grant beneficiaries included British Heart Foundation, Macmillan Cancer Relief, Cancer Research Campaign, RSPCC and RNLI. Grants to national organisations range from £200 to £1,000 and to local organisations from £100 to £500.

Exclusions
No grants for local appeals not in areas of company presence. Support is NOT given to: advertising in charity brochures, animal welfare, appeals from individuals, enterprise/training, fundraising events, political or religious appeals, science/technology, overseas projects or sport.

Applications
In writing to the correspondent. The trustees of the fund meet quarterly.

Lowe Group

Bowater House, 68–114 Knightsbridge, London SW1X 7LT
0171-584 5033

Correspondent: Caroline Lewis, Personal Assistant to the Creative Director

Chief officers: *Chairman:* Paul Weinberger; *Managing Director:* T Lindsay

Year end	Turnover	Pre-tax profit
31/12/94	n/a	n/a

Nature of company business
Principal activities: advertising. Subsidiaries are based in 12 European countries, USA and Canada.
Main subsidiaries include: Lowe Howard-Spink; Brompton Agency; Orbit International.

UK employees: 275

Charitable donations
1994: £58,000
1993: £53,000

Community support policy
Most of the charitable budget is allocated to 'industry' charities, mainly NABS and D&AD. Any remainder is given to a charity chosen by staff (after a vote).

Support may also be given for advertising in charity brochures, to large national appeals (such as the NSPCC) and to the arts. The company gives preference to projects in which a member of staff is involved but not necessarily to projects in areas of company presence.

Exclusions
No support for individuals, circular appeals or small, purely local appeals not in areas of company presence.

Applications
In writing to the correspondent, but note the above policy implying that very little support, if any, is available for unsolicited appeals. The company does not have a donations committee. Appeals are decided by one of the directors.

LucasVarity plc

46 Park Street, London W1Y 4DJ
0171-647 0610; Fax: 0171-647 0624

Correspondent: Nicholas Jones, Director of Group Corporate Relations

Chief officers: *Chairman:* Ed Wallis; *Chief Executive:* Victor Rice

Year end	Turnover	Pre-tax profit
31/1/98	£4,681,000,000	£316,000,000

Nature of company business
The group provides advanced technology systems, components and services to the world's automotive and aerospace markets.
Main subsidiaries include: Perkins Group Ltd.

UK employees: 23,794

Charitable donations
1997: £177,554
1996: £102,940
1995: £309,077
1994: £409,659
1993: £360,600
Membership: *BitC %Club*

Community support policy
The company has recently joined the PerCent Club and Business in the Community. Community support comprises a 'macro' and 'micro' programme. The former has the heading 'LucasVarity Drive for Engineering Excellence', under which each of the company's operating divisions is developing programmes with secondary schools near their principal operational locations, designed to encourage excellence in teaching and learning of engineering or other technical subjects.

Under the 'micro' programme, operating divisions and the corporate centre have smaller sums available with which to support local voluntary organisations.

Grants are no longer made through the Joseph Lucas Charitable Trust (Charity Commission number 274952).

Exclusions
The company does not support appeals from individuals.

Applications
In writing to the correspondent.

M & G

M & G Group plc

3 Minster Court, Great Tower Street, London EC3R 7XH
0171-626 4588; Fax: 0171-623 8615
Website: www.lll.co.uk/m_g

Correspondent: Adrian Sharp, Charities Secretary

Chief officers: *Chairman:* D L Morgan;
Managing Director: M G A McLintock

Year end	Turnover	Pre-tax profit
30/9/97	£167,650,000	£67,400,000

Nature of company business
Unit and investment trust management.

UK employees: 845

Charitable donations
1997: £91,843
1996: £88,712
1995: £72,223
1994: £35,300
1993: £38,288

Community support policy

Preference for local charities in areas of main operation (ie. City of London and Essex), appeals relevant to company business and charities in which a member of staff is involved. Preferred areas of support are: advertising in charity brochures; the arts; children/youth; education; elderly people; enterprise/training; environment/heritage; fundraising events; sickness/disability charities and social welfare. Grants generally range from £250 to £2,500. The company also operates a payroll giving scheme (Give As You Earn) and matches employee fundraising.

Exclusions
Generally no support for circular appeals, appeals from individuals, overseas appeals, political or religious appeals.

Applications
In writing to the correspondent. The address for the Charities Secretary is M & G Group plc, M & G House, Victoria Road, Chelmsford CM1 1FB.

Makro Self-Service Wholesalers Ltd

Emerson House, Albert Street, Eccles, Manchester M30 0BS
0161-707 1585

Correspondent: Diane Carr, Secretary to the Managing Director

Chief officer: *Chairman:* P Fentener Van Vlissingen

Year end	Turnover	Pre-tax profit
31/12/95	£872,890,000	(£6,370,000)

Nature of company business
Cash and carry merchandising.

UK employees: n/a

Charitable donations
1996: £74,000

Community support policy

Donations totalled at least £74,000 in 1996, but we have not been able to update this figure.

The company has stated previously that it nominates one charity to support each year. Most donations in 1996 were to the hospice movement, but local stores may make small donations to local charities. Direct giving is preferred rather than support for advertising in brochures or fundraising events.

Applications
In writing to the correspondent.

E D & F Man Plc

Sugar Quay, Lower Thames Street, London EC3R 6DU
0171-285 3000; Fax: 0171-285 3665

Correspondent: Ann Cuttill, Trustee, Charitable Trust

Chief officers: *Chairman:* Michael Stone;
Managing Director: Harvey McGrath

Year end	Turnover	Pre-tax profit
31/3/98	£267,400,000	£119,000,000

Nature of company business
The company has two main businesses: the supply of agricultural products and the provision of financial services.

UK employees: 650

Charitable donations
1998: £280,000
1997: £235,000
1996: £205,000
1995: £164,704
Membership: *BitC %Club*

Community support policy

The company is a member of the PerCent Club and Business in the Community, and has shown a steady increase in its level of giving over the last four years.

Charitable donations: Most donations are made through the E D & F Man Limited Charitable Trust, which was established in 1978. Support is given to enterprise initiatives in East London and to charities concerned with underprivileged and disabled young people at home and abroad. In particular, the company prefers to support national charities and local charities that have company staff involvement.

In 1996/97, the E D & F Man Ltd Charitable Trust had an income of £165,000 (£114,000 of which was given directly by the company), and gave grants totalling £235,000. 96 grants were given ranging from £150 to £12,000. The largest grants were: £12,000 to Atlantic College, with £10,000 each to East London Partnership, East London Small Business Centre Ltd, Keith O' Hana Memorial Fund,

NCH Action for Children, London Federation of Clubs for Young People, VSO, National Hospital Development Fund, Queen Elizabeth's Foundation for Disabled People, MERLIN, Commonwealth Society for the Deaf, RAFT and James House Hospice Trust.

Other grants of £5,000 or more were given to: Business in The Community, Royal National Theatre, St Edward's School and the Lord Mayor's Appeal for Cancer Research Campaign.

The remaining grants went to a wide range of charities including: Teenage Cancer Trust, Orchestra of the Age of Enlightenment, CRISIS, Thriftwood School, Breath of Life and Mozambique & Angola Anglican Association.

The company's overseas subsidiaries support causes in their country of operation.

Applications
In writing to the correspondent.

Manchester Airport plc

Wythenshawe, Manchester M90 1QX
0161-489 3000
Email: trust.fund@manairport.co.uk
Website: www.manairport.co.uk

Correspondent: Mrs Wendy Sinfield, Community Relations Manager

Chief officers: *Chairman:* Cllr S R Oldham; *Chief Executive:* Geoff Muirhead

Year end	Turnover	Pre-tax profit
31/3/98	£230,950,000	£33,052,000

Nature of company business
International airport operation.
Main locations: Manchester.

UK employees: 2,187

Charitable donations
1998: £100,000
1997: £100,000
1996: £190,000
1995: £165,538
1994: £101,515

Total community contributions: £600,000 (1996)

Membership: *ABSA BitC*

Community support policy

The Airport Company established the Manchester Airport Community Trust Fund in 1997 as a community-based initiative to promote, enhance, improve, protect and conserve the natural and built environment in areas which are affected by the activities of Manchester Airport.

Each year the airport will pay £100,000 plus all income from environmental fines imposed on noisy operators into the fund. The latter amounted to £91,157 in 1997. Support is only given to organisations within a 20-mile radius of Manchester Airport (ie. South Manchester, Altrincham, Bramhall, Stockport, Wilmslow, Borough of Congleton (excluding the town of Congleton), Borough of Macclesfield (excluding the town of Macclesfield), and up to, but not including, the town of Northwich. However, exceptionally local branches of national charities may also receive help.

The trust will support projects which:

- encourage tree planting, forestation, landscaping and other works of environmental improvement or heritage conservation
- promote or advance social welfare for recreation, sport and leisure, with the object of improving the conditions of life for those living or working in, or visitors to, the area of benefit
- provide better appreciation of the natural and urban environment, and ways of better serving, protecting and improving the same. This may include education and training
- promote the use of the natural environment as a safe habitat for flora and fauna of all kinds.

Projects must be for the benefit of the whole local community or a substantial section of it, and not groups of an exclusive nature. Preference will be given to projects that have considered the needs of the disabled or elderly people within the community.

Priority will be given to schemes where the trust's grant will be at least matched by funding from other sources eg. an organisation's own fundraising or another grant. The trust will especially welcome partnership schemes or schemes forming part of an agreed overall plan or programme.

The funding is divided between large and small projects as follows: (i) Large projects costing from £5,000 to £25,000, may be funded over a maximum of three years. In any given year, funding for a large scale project will not be allowed to exceed £50,000; (ii) Small projects may receive grants to a maximum of £5,000. These projects will be for one year only.

In 1997, community projects supported included the Woodhouse Park Family Centre, Mersey Basin Water Watch and Quinta Arboretum.

Non-cash support has previously taken the form of sponsorship of the arts (initiatives have ranged from support for the Hallé Orchestra World Tour, to local community-based arts and drama projects) and the provision of training schemes. The company is a member of ABSA. It is not clear, however, whether this will continue under the new arrangements.

Exclusions
No support for appeals from individuals, commercial organisations, those working for profit, or for organisations outside of the trust boundary.

Applications
Policy guidelines are provided on the application form which is available to organisations upon request. Applicants should obtain the fund's brochure to make sure they fit the criteria. The administrator may also visit the project or proposed site or the applicant may be asked to visit the airport, to provide further details. The trust liaises

with local environmental organisations such as Cheshire Wildlife Trust, Cheshire Landscape Trust, Manchester Wildlife Trust and the Groundwork Trust Network; their advice may be asked when projects are being evaluated.

If a large grant is being applied for it will be necessary to check whether funding is available from the year's allocation for large projects. All applications must show clear financial records. Trustees meet quarterly in the first weeks of April, July, October and January. A minimum of one month should be allowed for applications to be processed. Applications must be received by the Administrator no later than the first week of the month preceeding the above meeting times. However, early submission of your application will ensure that any queries can be dealt with before passing it to the trustees.

Manweb plc

Manweb House, Kingsfield Court, Chester Business Park, Chester CH4 9RF
01244-652093; Fax: 01244-652119

Correspondent: Alison MacLeod, Corporate Communications

Chief officers: *Chairman:* Mike Kinski; *Chief Executive:* Charles Berry

Year end	Turnover	Pre-tax profit
31/3/97	£755,100,000	£135,000,000

Nature of company business
Principal activities: electricity distribution and supply. The company is now a subsidiary of ScottishPower plc, but administers its own community support.

UK employees: 2,757

Charitable donations

1995: £85,638
1994: £79,592
1993: £76,158

Total community contributions: £250,000

Membership: *ABSA BitC %Club*

Community support policy

The company is a member of the PerCent Club. Its funding policy is to 'donate resources equal to 1% of dividends to the community'. In 1996/97, its community contributions totalled £250,000 (no separate cash donations figure is available since the company's takeover by ScottishPower). The main areas of non-cash support are in good-cause sponsorship, secondments, and gifts in kind.

The company does report on its community activities in the 1998 Per Cent Club annual report, but this refers as much to the ScottishPower group as to Manweb.

Charitable donations: Priority is given to:

- projects in the Manweb area (Merseyside, North Wales, Cheshire and parts of Lancashire, Greater Manchester, Staffordshire and Shropshire)
- projects to help work creation and new enterprises
- support of the fundraising efforts of employees through Manweb plc's Charity Chest
- projects to help elderly and disabled people
- projects to help encourage electricity-related curriculum and syllabus development in educational establishments.

A limited number of cultural events across the region will also be supported. Grants generally range from £10 to £1,000. Among the largest donations during 1996/97 were: Royal National Institute for the Blind's North West Transcription Centre (£10,000), Cycling Project for the North West (£11,000), and Wales Council for Voluntary Action (£10,000). The Manweb/Chronicle Community Champions Awards recognised the significant contributions of the Cheshire and North Wales community; NEA was supported to improve home energy efficiency; and 'Live Music Now!' brought live music to special schools, hospitals and day-care centres in England and Wales. Activities that encourage the setting up of new businesses and the growth of existing ones, and projects to help work creation are also supported.

In kind support: The company gives many gifts in kind. As part of the campaign against hypothermia, room thermometers were donated to caring agencies for distribution to those people most at risk.

Employee involvement: The company seconds employees to enterprise and education initiatives, which it may also give financial support to. It also matches fundraising by employees and employee giving.

Education: The company is developing links with local schools and has produced classroom resources including information on electricity and supply.

The arts: The company is a member of ABSA with sponsorship limited to two or three events a year, planned well in advance. The Welsh National Opera, Royal Liverpool Philharmonic Orchestra, International Eisteddfodd and Chester Summer Music Festival have all been supported recently.

Sponsorship for sporting events and advertisements in publications, etc. will normally only be considered commercially in terms of potential advertising benefits. Sponsorship of the arts will be limited to two or three events a year, planned well in advance. Sponsorship proposals should be addressed to Mrs Gaynor Kenyon, Head of Communications.

Exclusions

No support is given to appeals from individuals, national charities (unless the fund is used solely for a local project), preservation of historic buildings, research, expeditions, political or military organisations, circular appeals, advertising in charity brochures, animal welfare charities, religious appeals, local appeals not in areas of company presence or overseas projects.

Applications

In writing to the correspondent.

Marconi Marine

Barrow-in-Furness, Cumbria LA14 1AF
01229-823366

Correspondent: Malcolm J Cookson, Secretary, Charities Committee

Chief officers: *Chairman:* Lord Chalfont;
Chief Executive: C N Davies

Year end	Turnover	Pre-tax profit
31/3/95	£428,772,000	£64,517,000

Nature of company business
Principal activities: the design, development and production of submarines, surface warships, armaments and combat systems, all backed by comprehensive post-delivery support services. The group also manufactures high-quality specialist engineering components. Other activities include the design, manufacture, sale and service of equipment for the oil and gas industries.
Principal subsidiaries include: Vickers Shipbuilding & Engineering; Seaboard Lloyd.
Locations: Barrow-in-Furness and Cumbernauld.

UK employees: 5,950

Charitable donations

1996: c.£100,000
1995: £143,739
1994: £136,924
1993: £129,737

Community support policy

Formerly VSEL, which was taken over by General Electric Company, and is now part of the Marconi group, the company continues to support local charities in Barrow-in-Furness. It prefers those which help disadvantaged people and appeals relevant to company business. Donations usually range from £50 to £400, but have been significantly larger.

The company has stated that 'most charitable and sponsorship requests are turned down, as a result of the need to reduce costs to improve competitiveness in non-defence markets following government reductions in defence spending'.

The company supports employee volunteering and operates a Give As You Earn payroll giving scheme (giving a 20% top-up of the amount donated by staff). It raises a further £30,000 from that each year.

Its main area of non-cash support is to enterprise agencies.

Exclusions

No support for local appeals not in areas of company presence, large national appeals, overseas projects, appeals from individuals, advertising in charity brochures, educational causes or purely denominational (religious) appeals.

Applications

In writing to the correspondent, but note the above.

Marks and Spencer plc

Michael House, Baker Street, London W1A 1DN
0171-935 4422; Fax: 0171-268 2260
Website: www.marks-and-spencer.co.uk

Correspondent: Mrs Y Pennicott, Manager, Community Involvement

Chief officer: *Chairman:* Sir Richard Greenbury

Year end	Turnover	Pre-tax profit
31/3/98	£8,243,300,000	£1,168,000,000

Nature of company business
The principal activity is retailing: the group sells clothing, footwear, household goods and foods under the St Michael trade mark in its chain of Marks & Spencer stores in the United Kingdom, France, Belgium, Germany, Spain, Holland, Canada, Hong Kong and Eire, and through the Brooks Brothers and Kings Supermarket chains in USA and Hong Kong. St Michael merchandise is also sold for export in 85 franchise stores in Europe and the Far East.

UK employees: 59,352

Charitable donations

1998: £6,000,000
1997: £5,500,000
1996: £4,900,000
1995: £4,635,000
1994: £4,345,000

Total community contributions: £10,100,000

Membership: *ABSA BitC %Club*

Community support policy

The following information was largely taken from the company's website, where the objective for the company's community involvement is stated as:

'Whilst responsible to shareholders, customers, employees and suppliers, the Company's philosophy has always maintained a belief in supporting the communities in which we operate, thus creating a more prosperous and self-sufficient society. Being a good corporate citizen and sharing our success with charities and other voluntary sector organisations is as important to us as the principles we hold on quality, value and service.

'In addition, to the above, there are excellent commercial reasons for our activity. Our Community Involvement programme is one of "enlightened self-interest". By supporting those communities where we operate we bring added value, create safer living and working environments, better educated young people, more effective small businesses, and an enriched cultural life and a healthier nation. In turn, this creates a more prosperous and self-sufficient society, which is obviously good for business. Put simply, "healthy back streets lead to healthy high streets".'

The Community Involvement programme uses the following resources:

- cash donations and sponsorships
- secondment of staff – both full and part-time programmes
- gifts in kind eg. redundant equipment, date expired foods from stores

Marks

- employee fundraising – matched £ for £
- Helping Hands Award Scheme – whereby staff, who are volunteering in their local community, are able to apply for a grant of up to £250 per year to benefit the charity or organisation that they are involved with
- provision of advice, information and expertise eg. our staff are management committee members, members of chambers of commerce, school governors, etc.
- facilitated customer giving – sale of charity Christmas cards – in 1997/98, £318,000 was donated to charity
- Hanger Recycling Scheme – in 1997/98, £300,000 was donated to local environmental projects
- communication of issues which we feel are important to those who can bring about change
- encouragement and advice to other companies on how to become involved.

In 1997/98, the company committed £10.1 million. In 1998/99, with the inclusion of specific donations resulting from initiatives such as the hanger recycling project and the commitment to the Children's Promise, community expenditure is estimated at £14m. These figures, however, exclude any attempt to quantify the cost to the business of the time and resource put into many activities eg. work experience placement, committee membership.

Marks & Spencer was a founder member of Business in the Community and instrumental in establishing the PerCent Club in the UK.

How does the programme work?

The Community Involvement budget is agreed by the Board of Directors each year based on recommendations made by the Community Involvement department and the committees who manage the Community Involvement budgets. There are three major committees:

Community Involvement committee – meets three times a year to discuss trends and policy issues, to review budgets and to debate/approve major appeals of £100,000 or more.

Health & Care and *Community & Cultural Opportunities* committees take responsibility for the two policy areas (see details below). They meet three to four times a year and review policy, budgets, secondments and appeals over £25,000 for their specific area. Each committee member comes from a wide range of roles within the business and serve for approximately three years, so increasing the knowledge base of our activities throughout the company.

Donations of £25,000 and below are agreed by the management of the Community Involvement department which is part of the Personnel and Corporate Affairs Group.

The total cash donations budget for 1998/99 is £5.5 million.

Criteria for support have been developed over many years and individual policies are reviewed regularly to ensure that the needs of the community continue to be met. In deciding which causes to support, the company policy is to help a wide spectrum of charities rather than make very large donations to a favoured few. 10,000 appeals are received into Head Office each year and currently about 1400 organisations throughout the UK are supported. The average donation is £4,500 – the range extends from £40 upwards.

How do stores support?

The company regards store involvement in the community as very important 'as employees know their own communities far better than anyone'.

Stores support the community in a number of ways:

- they have their own local budget to respond to small requests
- they can recommend a higher level of funding to the community involvement department at head office for appeals sent to stores
- they can investigate appeals and make recommendations when the approach has been direct to head office
- they can present cheques to organisations when support has been agreed
- they can establish local links
- they can take part in the company's matching funds scheme which benefits everyone – the local charity and the employees who have fun in the process.

The company estimates that in 1998/99, £375,000 will be raised and matched by the company to make £750,000. Date-expired food is another way in which we strengthen our links within the community. Once date-expired food has been removed from the shelves and sold to staff, it is then given away to local charities. Each store has links with organisations who collect the date expired food and re-distribute. There are strict guidelines regarding the onward dispersal and agreements are drawn up and charities regularly monitored to ensure they are handling the food correctly.

'We encourage our staff to get involved in the community through volunteering and we have launched a national award scheme whereby staff who give up their own time are eligible to apply for a grant of £250 for the particular charity that they are involved with.'

Health & Care

The primary aim of this policy is to support projects which:

- focus on the health and social welfare needs of those affected by disability, ill-health and the breakdown of traditional family support structures
- give preference to projects which are likely to have direct benefits to company staff/ retired staff
- emphasis is given to community-based projects rather than research. There are seven main areas of support:

People Care

Focuses on projects which aim to:

- enhance the quality of lie for elderly people in the community, preferably within their own homes
- provide information/ advice, support and relief to people suffering from illness or disease
- support carers through both information/ advice services and the provision of respite care
- provide training for specialists.

Disabilities

Focuses on projects which aim to:

- enhance the quality of life for those people who have a disability

- support disabled people in the community
- support carers through both information/ advice services, and the provision of respite care
- provide leisure and sport activities, and those which aim to increase mobility
- develop education, training and employment opportunities, and those which encourage independent living
- bring art forms to disabled, elderly and institutionalised people acting both as a stimulus and an education tool.

Mental Health
Focuses on the commonest causes of mental health problems from depression to dementia, from young people to old. The company achieve this by supporting:
- care and counselling programmes for suffers of mental illness, their carers and families
- information/ advice services for those affected by a mental illness
- projects connected with the identification and relief of stress
- schemes to integrate mentally ill people into the community and into work.

Families and Parenting Issues
Focuses on issues relating to the breakdown of the traditional family support structure. The company achieve this by supporting:
- information/ advice services which aim to prevent family breakdown occurring
- counselling and support services for individuals in personal crisis through either partnership breakdown, domestic violence, bullying or abuse.

Addictions
Focuses support on:
- health education projects both in schools as well as outreach and peer education programmes
- rehabilitation and self-help initiatives for people who misuse drugs and other substances as well as support for their families.

Homelessness
Focuses support on:
- projects which provide emergency and practical support for those who are homeless, covering both rural and urban areas of the UK
- education, training and employment opportunities, and those which encourage independent living.

Children
Focuses support on:
- the provision of both medical and complementary equipment or specialist units through the UK
- projects which assist families with seriously ill children through the provision of short-term accommodation.

The millennium
In addition, to mark the millennium, and as part of the company's sponsorship of the 'Millennium Experience', it will be leading the 'Children's Promise' – a major nationwide fundraising initiative. Working in a unique partnership with seven of the UK's major charities that work for children – Barnardo's, BBC Children in Need, Childline, The Children's Society, Comic Relief, NCH Action for Children and the NSPCC – the 'Children's Promise' will encourage everyone in the country to donate their final hours earnings of this millennium to help create a better future for the 'Children of the next Millennium'. For more information contact 0870-6071999.

Community & Cultural Opportunities
The primary aim of this policy is to support projects which:
- enhance community life, such as those addressing employment opportunities, crime reduction, and extend participation in the arts and cultural activities
- encourage people in both rural and urban areas to care for, and make improvements to, their own surroundings within the areas of environment and heritage.

Within 'community', there are four main areas of support:
- education, training and employment
- crime reduction and victims of crime
- community services
- environment.

Education, Training & Employment
Focuses on initiatives which aim to:
- create opportunities for people to help themselves to produce more employable, motivated and responsible citizens
- supplement the education needs of those with a lack of basic literacy and numeracy skills
- try to change peoples' attitudes by making education more accessible and relevant to an individuals' needs
- develop the self-esteem and confidence of individuals to realise their potential.

Crime Reduction, and Victims of Crime
Focuses on initiatives which aim to:
- provide young people at risk with meaningful activities which will deter them from becoming involved in crime
- support the rehabilitation of ex-offenders to give them the necessary skills to obtain employment
- provide counselling and support services for individuals in distress who either live in fear of crime or have been victims of crime.

Community Services
Focuses on initiatives which aim to:
- support those organisations who help to enhance the operational/ managerial skills of other charitable bodies
- assist national community organisations who support the community through local offices
- support specific organisations in disadvantaged areas who have need for improved community facilities.

Environment
Focuses on initiatives which aim to:
- consider, protect and improve the environment placing emphasis on urban rather than rural areas
- provide impartial information and a signposting service to other projects to enhance and build on that knowledge

Marley

- educate young people
- promote sustainable regeneration including recycling, waste and energy conservation
- make positive use of neglected environments
- reduce air/water pollution, and encourage more environmentally friendly transport
- support animal welfare placing emphasis on wildlife rather than domestic pets

Cultural

There are six main areas of support:

- performing arts
- festivals
- written word
- visual art – including crafts, film, photography and new media
- heritage
- corporate membership.

Within these areas, classical, contemporary work and a combination of art forms are comprehensively covered.

The focus is on initiatives which aim to:

- encourage, develop and support both participation and enjoyment in cultural activities or people of all ages
- reach out to people within local communities making art accessible to a wider audience
- raise awareness and enthusiasm for arts and heritage, and for those which assist artists and craftsmen to develop, as well as enhance their skills
- support staff involvement in artistic projects through corporate membership and events
- provide training for people in the skills and understanding of our cultural heritage which enable the community to continue to enjoy both buildings and artefacts.

Secondment

The secondment programme represents a major aspect of the company's involvement. In 1998/99, it will second on a full-time basis 25 full-time employees of management staff, on full pay and benefits, to work with charities and voluntary sector organisations. In addition to this, over recent years the company have developed part-time programmes with Business in the Community and The Prince's Trust Volunteers and this year over 300 members of staff will be participating in them. These secondments will cost the business £2.3 million. The company gives the following reasons for seconding:

'In a well-managed secondment programme everyone gains:

- the individual has the experience of working in a different organisation, the challenge of developing new skills and of making a difference
- it is a totally broadening experience and gives people increased confidence in their abilities while at the same time making a positive contribution to the community
- the organisation has access to professional expertise and skills (which it may not be able to afford), the experience of a large commercial organisation, a fresh approach and ultimately a job achieved
- the company has an employee returning with enhanced capability, a retiree with a new venture and challenge, a practical investment in and increased knowledge of the community, and not least an enhanced image and profile
- projects are identified across all fields of our community involvement programme as well as more recently some assignments to government and commercial activities e.g. town centre managers
- the programme is now recognised as one for career development as well as end of career/pre-retirement. Half of the current full-time and all of the part-time secondees are completing assignments for their own development.'

Exclusions

No response to circular appeals. No support for endowment funds, expeditions, sports (except for people with special needs), fundraising events, appeals from individuals, political/religious appeals, medical research, or overseas charities.

Applications

All applications for funding must fall within current policy criteria. In addition they should:

- be received by post (applications by e-mail or the internet will not receive a response)
- include the aims and objectives of your organisation and specific details of the project for which you are seeking funds, together with a detailed breakdown of costs
- an indication of what funding has already been secured for this particular project
- a copy of your recent annual report and audited accounts.

Please send your application to: Community Involvement – D147, at the above address.

Marley plc

7 Oakhill Road, Sevenoaks, Kent TN13 2DS
01732-455255; Fax: 01732-740694
Website: www.marleyplc.com

Correspondent: D J A Musgrave, Assistant Company Secretary

Chief officers: *Chairman:* A G L Alexander; *Chief Executive:* D A Trapnell

Year end	Turnover	Pre-tax profit
31/12/97	£682,000,000	£54,000,000

Nature of company business
Principal activities: manufacture and sale of building materials, plastic leisure and decorative products. The range of products extends from plastic plumbing, flooring and moulding products to traditional concrete and clay goods and aerated blocks.

Main subsidiaries include: Greenwool Air Management Ltd; Phetco Ltd; Thermalite Holdings Ltd; Bracknell Roofing Co Ltd; New Fields Management Ltd; Mainstay Ltd.

UK employees: 3,000

Charitable donations
1997: £35,000
1996: £44,000
1995: £74,000
1994: £78,000
1993: £77,000

Community support policy
The only information we have on the company's policy is this statement in the latest annual report: 'The Group continues to support some national charities but it remains Group policy to concentrate financial support on smaller charitable organisations and support groups which serve the communities in which the Group companies principally operate'.

Applications
In writing to the correspondent.

Marlowe Holdings Ltd

PO Box 1, Edmundson House, Tatton Street, Knutsford, Cheshire WA16 6AY
01565-633811

Correspondent: Company Secretary

Chief officer: *Managing Director:* D T McNair

Year end	Turnover	Pre-tax profit
31/12/96	£549,180,000	£25,668,000

Nature of company business
Distributor of electrical, DIY and garden products.

UK employees: 2,912

Charitable donations
1996: £755,112
1995: n/a
1994: n/a
1993: £744,000

Community support policy
Although the company gives in excess of £750,000 in charitable donations, we have been unable to obtain any information about the company's policy.

Applications
In writing to the correspondent.

Mars UK Ltd

3D Dundee Road, Slough, Berkshire SL1 4LG
01753-693000

Correspondent: Jenny Ward, Charities Administrator

Chief officers: n/a

Year end	Turnover	Pre-tax profit
31/12/95	£1,655,304,000	£40,569,000

Nature of company business
Food manufacture. Major subsidiaries and locations include: Slough (Mars Confectionery); Melton Mowbray (Pedigree Petfoods); Kings Lynn (Master Foods); Batley (Thomas's); Wokingham (Mars Electronics); Basingstoke (Four Square).

UK employees: n/a

Charitable donations
1995: £209,474
1994: £224,084
1993: £541,980
Membership: *ABSA BitC*

Community support policy
Mars have consistently declined to provide information for our guides and we have been unable to obtain information from other sources on the company's UK support. This lack of transparency appears to be specific to Mars UK, as the US parent company and its operating divisions in other countries provide details of their community support on the internet.

The contact above is for Mars UK, which supports mainly national charities. The subsidiary companies tend to support charities local to their sites. For example, Mars Confectionery supports charities in the categories of health, education, youth, elderly and environment, within the Slough area.

The following information was provided by the company a few years ago and may well have changed since.

In kind support: Confectionery products, petcare products, main meal food products, drinks, office furniture (occasionally) and office stationery supplies may all be supplied free of charge by the company for the following: charitable use such as raffle prizes, children's parties, university expeditions, fundraising by schools, pet shows and sporting events.

Employee involvement: Subsidiaries in the group may provide staff secondment or volunteering for activity of community benefit, if there is an opportunity for staff team-building. Staff are encouraged to become volunteers in their own time and to become school governors.

Enterprise: The company supports local enterprise agencies and local initiatives such as Melton Business Club, MIDAS (Melton Industrial Development Award Scheme) and North Lynn Development Club.

Education: The company is involved in local education/ business partnerships. It provides work experience schemes for pupils and teachers, and educational materials for schools. Improved links between education and industry are sought through involvement with universities and student sponsorships.

Environment: The company is a member of the British Trust for Conservation Volunteers and local ecology trusts. It sponsors the Mars Awards for Environmental Achievement and the Mars Environment Awards for schools in Slough.

Sponsorship: The company sponsors national and local activities including the arts, environment and other good causes. The typical sponsorship range is from £25 to £10,000.

Marsh

The arts: The company is a member of ABSA, and supports a range of activities in the visual and performing arts.

Exclusions

No support for advertising in charity brochures, appeals from individuals, fundraising events, overseas projects, political appeals, or religious appeals.

Applications

In writing to the correspondent. Approaches from local charities should be made directly to operating companies. The appeals committee meets four times a year.

The contact for Mars Confectionery for local charities in Slough is Valerie Eyre, External Relations Department at the address above.

J & H Marsh & McLennan Ltd

Aldgate House, 33 Aldgate High Street, London EC3N 1AQ
0171-377 3309; Fax: 0171-397 3199
Email: victoria_secretan@sedgwick.com

Correspondent: Victoria Secretan, Community Programmes Manager, Sedgwick Group

Chief officer: *Chairman:* H M J Ritchie

Year end	Turnover	Pre-tax profit
31/12/97	£212,000,000	£30,300,000

Nature of company business
Insurance brokers (a member of the Marsh & McLennan Companies Inc).

Main locations: Birmingham; Bristol; Edinburgh; Glasgow; Leeds; London; Newcastle; Southampton.

UK employees: 2,999

Charitable donations

1997: £150,000
1996: £150,000
1995: n/a
1994: £150,000

Total community contributions: £500,000

Membership: ABSA   BitC   %Club

Community support policy

NOTE: As Sedgwick Group joined Marsh & McLennan at the end of 1998, the two companies are integrating their approach to community involvement and charitable giving. No new commitments are likely to be entered into in 1999.

The company is a member of the PerCent Club (as is Sedgwick), with community contributions totalling £500,000 in 1997 including £150,000 in charitable donations. The main areas of non-cash support are secondments and training schemes.

Charitable donations: Recipient organisations must be registered charities. The company prefers to give to national or local charities in areas where there is employee involvement, and to appeals relevant to company business. There is also a preference for charities in the areas of youth, enterprise and training, social welfare, medicine and the arts. Charities concerned with conservation have also been suppported. Donations are made through the company's charitable trust.

J & H Marsh & McLennan (Charities Fund) Ltd
The trustees are H M J Richie (Chairman), W K Hayes, V M Secretan, Miss A M Stephens and J Oatley. In 1997, the trust had an income of £162,000 including £156,000 received from the group. It gave almost 300 grants totalling £163,000, just under two thirds of which were recurrent from 1996. A wide range of organisations were supported with those receiving over £1,000 being Leonard Cheshire Foundation (£3,000), Macmillan Cancer Relief (£2,600), Help the Hospices, Special Trustees of Guy's Hospital and University of Buckingham (all £2,000), Cancer Research Campaign (£1,800), Abbeyfield Society and Business in the Community (both £1,500) and East London Partnership and East London Small Business Charity (£1,250 each).

There were a further 21 grants of £1,000, including those to ABSA, All Hallows by the Tower, Insurance Benevolent Fund, NSPCC and Tower Hamlets Mission. Many of the organisations supported were national charities, with a few grants to local causes, especially London, though not exclusively. Examples include Boys' & Girls' Clubs of Scotland, Carlisle Cathedral Development Trust, Lagan College – Northern Ireland, Liverpool School of Tropical Medicine, Northumberland National Park Search & Rescue Team and Birmingham Children's Hospital.

In kind support: The company has provided redundant furniture and accommodation to charities free of charge.

Employee involvement: The company gives preference to charities in which a member of staff is involved and allows time off for activity of community benefit. It operates a payroll giving scheme. Fundraising by employees has also been matched in the past, to a set limit. The company may also consider seconding members of staff to charities and supporting training schemes.

Enterprise: The company is a member of Business in the Community which it supports directly and through secondments. Support has been given to enterprise agencies and to the Lloyd's Community Programme (see separate entry for Lloyd's of London) in the Spitalfields area of London.

Education: The company is involved in local education/business partnerships, and runs work-experience schemes for pupils and teachers.

The arts: The company is a member of ABSA, supporting the arts rather than sponsoring them. It has supported London City Ballet and the Young Musicians Symphony Orchestra.

Exclusions

Donations are not made to individuals, schools, churches, or for expeditions. The company does not support circular appeals, advertising in charity brochures, purely denominational appeals or local appeals not in areas of company presence.

Applications

In writing to the correspondent. The company does not welcome unsolicited appeals from charities as the charitable budget is too limited.

Information available: In addition to the statement of total UK donations in the company annual report, occasional reports are given in the employee newsletter.

Matsushita Electric (UK) Ltd

Pentwyn Industrial Estate, Cardiff CF2 7XB
01222-540011; Fax: 01222-549308

Correspondent: Ian Coughlin, Corporate Affairs

Chief officer: *Chairman:* C Toda

Year end	Turnover	Pre-tax profit
31/3/95	£330,672,000	n/a

Nature of company business
Television set and microwave manufacture. The main brand is Panasonic. The sales company (Panasonic UK) operates independently and has a separate entry in this guide.

UK employees: 2,400

Charitable donations

1995: £200,000
Total community contributions: £230,000

Community support policy

The only figure we have for the company's charitable giving is that for 1995, when it gave £200,000. The company has a focused approach to charitable donations and currently is working on two large-scale community-based activities namely: the Panasonic Student Innovation Awards, and a long-term programme with the Prince's Youth Business Trust. The former, although taking the brand name, is an initiative of Matsushita Electric UK (manufacturing) and not Panasonic UK (sales).

Other preferred areas of support are: education; enterprise/training; and science/technology. There is a preference for charities in Wales.

In addition to charitable donations, the company gave a further £30,000 through other contributions including secondments, joint promotions and training schemes.

Exclusions

Support is NOT given to: brochure advertising; animal welfare; individuals; the arts; children/youth; elderly people; environment/heritage; fundraising events; medical research; overseas projects; political appeals; religious appeals; sickness/disability charities social welfare; or sport.

Applications

In writing to the correspondent.

Bernard Matthews plc

Great Witchingham Hall, Norwich NR9 5QD
01603-872611; Fax: 01603-871118

Correspondent: D M Reger, Company Secretary

Chief officers: *Chairman:* B T Matthews; *Managing Director:* D J Joll

Year end	Turnover	Pre-tax profit
28/12/97	£371,818,000	£12,185,000

Nature of company business
The principal activities of the group are the production and marketing of turkey and red meat products, oven-ready turkeys, day-old turkeys and fish products.

UK employees: n/a

Charitable donations

1997: £226,344
1996: £271,457
1995: £257,094
1994: £238,150
1993: £218,414
Membership: %Club

Community support policy

The company is a member of the PerCent Club. It has a preference for local charities in the areas where it operates (Norfolk and Suffolk), especially those concerned with children, youth, environment and the arts. As well as cash donations the company donates gifts in kind.

A wide range of small organisations are supported locally, for example local churches, village halls and playgroups. The Caistor Lifeboat and Norfolk Air Ambulance have received significant support.

Human resources as well as cash support is given to youth activities. The Duke of Edinburgh Award Scheme has been supported for several years and support is also given to the Prince's Trust and local schools.

Support for the environment is a major consideration and a tree planting programme has been ongoing around the East Anglian sites, including a 30-acre future wood.

Support for the arts has included contributions to several arts festivals, local museums and exhibitions.

Exclusions

No support for circular appeals, advertising in charity brochures, appeals from individuals, local appeals not in areas of company presence, large national appeals, political appeals or overseas projects.

Applications

In writing to the correspondent.

Mayflower

Mayflower Corporation plc

Mayflower House, London Road, Loudwater, High Wycombe, Buckinghamshire HP10 9RF
01494-450145; Fax: 01494-450607

Correspondent: David Donnelly, Group Managing Director

Chief officers: *Chairman:* R N Hambro;
Chief Executive: J W P Simpson

Year end	Turnover	Pre-tax profit
31/12/97	£393,000,000	£33,000,000

Nature of company business
The principal activities of the group are the design, engineering and manufacture of bodies for cars, light truck and sport utility vehicles and commercial vehicle cabs; the design, engineering and manufacture of buses; vehicle conversions; and the production of synthetic webbing.
Main subsidiaries include: Walter Alexander (Falkirk); Walter Alexander (Belfast); Ribbons.

UK employees: 3,944

Charitable donations
1997: £38,490
1996: £21,191
1995: £9,424

Community support policy
We currently have no information on the charitable donations policy of the company.

Applications
In writing to the correspondent.

McBride plc

McBride House, Penn Road, Beaconsfield, Buckinghamshire HP9 2FY
01494-607050; Fax: 01494-607055
Website: www.mcbride.co.uk

Correspondent: Malcolm Allan, Personnel Director

Chief officers: *Chairman:* Lord Sheppard of Didgemere;
Chief Executive: Mike Handley

Year end	Turnover	Pre-tax profit
30/6/98	£468,400,000	£34,100,000

Nature of company business
The principal activity of the group is the manufacture of private label and minor brand household and personal care products.

UK employees: 2,374

Charitable donations
1998: £37,000
1997: £27,000
Membership: BitC

Community support policy
In common with many companies ongoing support is given to several charities, with other appeals considered if they are of particular interest or have some kind of link with the company, such as geographical.

Applications
In writing to the correspondent.

McCain Foods (GB) Ltd

Havers Hill, Scarborough, North Yorkshire YO11 3BS
01723-584141; Fax: 01723-581230

Correspondent: Mrs L Baker, Secretary to the Charities Committee

Chief officer: *Chairman:* C H A McCarthy

Year end	Turnover	Pre-tax profit
30/6/97	£220,761,000	£20,701,000

Nature of company business
The main activities are the manufacture and selling of frozen foods and dry goods, buying and selling of agricultural and industrial handling equipment, operation of cold stores and selling of dairy products.
Main subsidiaries include: PAS Ltd; SSHP Holdings Ltd; Dansco Dairy Products Ltd; Tolona Pizza Products Ltd; Everest Foods PLC; Everest Frozen Foods Ltd; Britfish Ltd.

UK employees: 2,045

Charitable donations
1997: £124,000
1996: £147,000
1995: £398,256
1994: £120,564
1993: £157,364

Community support policy
The company prefers all cash donations to be given locally (mainly in Yorkshire and particularly Scarborough). Large national charities are supported through local fundraising events. There is a preference for appeals relevant to company business. Preferred areas of support: children and youth; medical; education; recreation/sport; environment and heritage; the arts; enterprise/training. The company stated that only a small part of the quoted figure of £124,000 is made up of cash donations. The majority consists of gifts in kind, sponsorship etc.

Exclusions
Generally no support for circular appeals; fundraising events; advertising in charity brochures; appeals from individuals, purely denominational (religious) appeals or local appeals not in areas of company presence.

Applications
In writing to the correspondent.

Sponsorship proposals should be addressed to:
Mrs Leivers, Marketing Director.

McDonald's UK

11–59 High Road, East Finchley, London N2 8AW
0181-700 7000; Fax: 0181-700 7068

Correspondent: Stephen Hall, Corporate Community Affairs Manager

Chief officers: *Chairman:* Paul Preston; *Chief Executive:* Andrew Taylor

Year end	Turnover	Pre-tax profit
31/12/97	n/a	£100,154,000

Nature of company business
The activity of the company is quick service restaurants.

UK employees: 39,058

Charitable donations
1997: £378,046
1996: £731,245
1995: £287,753
1994: £357,993

Total community contributions: £1,034,729

Membership: *BitC %Club*

Community support policy

The company is a member of the PerCent Club and Business in the Community, with community contributions totalling just over £1 million in 1997. Over one-third of this was given in charitable donations.

The company gave details of its support in the 1998 PerCent Club annual report, from which the following information is taken.

The company focuses support on child welfare, the environment, education and youth-related social issues. It encourages employees to use company time, products and premises to support the local communities in which it operates and to raise funds for charity. Ronald McDonald Children's Charities (RMCC) is the main recipient of donations and funds raised by McDonald's employees, suppliers and customers. Since 1989, RMCC has raised over £8 million for causes benefiting children in areas of healthcare, education and welfare. Its principal contribution has been towards building three Ronald McDonald Houses, at Guy's, Alder Hey and Yorkhill Childrens' Hospitals, providing home from home accommodation for parents of children undergoing treatment.

Since 1994, RMCC's Big Smile Appeals have raised £2 million for hundreds of local childrens' causes selected by staff at each McDonald's restaurant. The company is an Environment Council member and supports environmental initiatives including Groundwork and Tidy Britain Group's national spring-clean campaign.

Support for education includes the provision of study materials, and conference support. 1993 saw the creation of McDonald's Education Service, which offers restaurants as resources to their local communities through Education Business Partnerships.

Local support: Local giving is very much on a smaller basis and business related. Links with charities are usually on the basis of making support a 'fun event'. For example, the marketing department handles bookings for Ronald McDonald to appear at charity events. Demand is heavy and bookings are made one year in advance.

Orange drink and cups may be provided and dispensers loaned at no charge. Meal vouchers can also be given as charity prizes.

Exclusions
No grants for appeals from individuals, purely denominational (religious) appeals or overseas projects.

Applications
In writing to the correspondent. Regional and local appeals should be directed to the appropriate communications departments in London, Manchester (Salford) or Birmingham (Sutton Coldfield). The contact for RMCC is Melvyn Lynch, Head of RMCC. Specific education-related requests should be made to James Graham, Head of McDonald's Education Service.

MCL Group Ltd

77 Mount Ephraim, Tunbridge Wells, Kent TN4 8BS
01892-510088; Fax: 01892-538547
Email: sroberts@mclgroup.co.uk

Correspondent: Sharon Roberts, Communications Controller

Chief officers: *Chairman:* M Karsube; *Managing Director:* D Heslop

Year end	Turnover	Pre-tax profit
31/12/96	£371,206,000	£10,808,000

Nature of company business
Vehicle importers.

Main subsidiaries include: Mazda Cars (UK) Ltd; Kia Cars (UK) Ltd; Autocheck Services Ltd; Autoflow Services Ltd.

UK employees: n/a

Charitable donations
1997: £51,186
1996: £47,000
1995: £45,000
1994: £55,000
1993: £51,000

Total community contributions: £58,166

Membership: *%Club*

Community support policy

The company is a member of the PerCent Club. It maintains a policy of concentrating its support upon good causes and appeals within the local community ie. Kent. Nevertheless more than 100 diverse charities, many of which are national, receive assistance in one form or another from the group during any one year.

The group adopts one charity annually to receive particular support, both financial and otherwise. This is selected by staff who fundraise for the charity. In 1998, the MCL Group Youth Development Team researched,

Medeva

designed, financed and built a new senior playground for a local Barnardo's School.

The company also has an ongoing relationship with Tunbridge Wells International Young Artists Competition, which it has supported for over 15 years.

Preference for appeals relevant to company business and charities in which a member of company staff is involved. Preferred areas of support: appeals from individuals; the arts; children/youth; education; elderly people; environment/heritage; fundraising events; medical research; sickness/disability charities; social welfare; sport. Grants to national organisations range from £5 to £10,000. Grants to local organisations from £25 to £3,000.

Main grant beneficiaries in 1997 included: Hospice in the Weald, BEN, Tunbridge Wells International Young Concert Artists, Barnardo's, Prince Michael Road Safety Awards.

Gifts in kind, such as obsolete equipment and money raised from recycled materials are made available to the community. Office facilities are made available for meetings and social gatherings.

Exclusions

No support for advertising in charity brochures, animal welfare charities, enterprise/training, overseas projects, political or religious appeals, or science/technology.

Applications

In writing to the correspondent.

Medeva plc

10 St James's Street, London SW1A 1EF
0171-839 3888; Fax: 0171-930 1514

Correspondent: Mark Hardy, Corporate Development Director

Chief officers: *Chairman:* J W Baker;
Chief Executive: Dr W Bogie

Year end	Turnover	Pre-tax profit
31/12/97	£355,000,000	£111,000,000

Nature of company business
The principal activities are the development, manufacture and marketing of prescription pharmaceutical products.
Main subsidiaries include: Evans Healthcare Ltd; IMS Ltd.

UK employees: 1,000

Charitable donations

1997: £46,000
1996: £46,000
1995: £36,000
1994: £48,000
1993: £14,000

Total community contributions: £79,898

Community support policy

The group's contributions to the community in 1997 totalled £80,000 with over half of this amount given in charitable donations.

Group policy is to make donations only in the field of healthcare (national and local charities) with a preference for appeals local to sites of company presence. Other community contributions, such as gifts in kind, may be made through subsidiary companies. The main areas of support may also include children/youth, education, elderly people, medical research, science/technology, sickness/disability charities and social welfare where the company has a local presence.

In 1997, main grant beneficiaries included: British Lung Foundation, Eating Disorders Association, SANE, Home Start, and Children Nationwide.

Exclusions

No support for advertising in charity brochures, animal welfare charities, appeals from individuals, the arts, elderly people, enterprise/training, environment/heritage, fundraising events, overseas projects, political appeals, religious appeals, or sport.

Applications

In writing to the correspondent.

Medical Insurance Agency Ltd

Hertlands House, Primett Road, Stevenage, Hertfordshire SG1 3EE
01438-742828

Correspondent: Ms Alex Colman, Corporate Services Manager

Chief officers: n/a

Year end	Turnover	Pre-tax profit
31/12/96	n/a	n/a

Nature of company business
Medical insurance.

UK employees: n/a

Charitable donations

1996: £200,000

Community support policy

In 1996, the company made a donation of £200,000 to the Medical Insurance Agency Charity. The total income of the charity for the year was £266,000. It supports institutions, hospitals and individuals for the general benefit of the field of medicine and dentistry. Grants made by the charity in 1996 totalled £233,000, but unfortunately no grants list was available for this or previous years at the Charity Commission.

The grant total in 1996 was actually lower than the previous two years. In 1995, grants totalled £348,000 and in 1994, £460,000. The income in these two years was £42,000 and £197,000, respectively, with accumulated surplus used to fulfil grant commitments.

Applications

In writing to the correspondent.

John Menzies plc

Hanover Buildings, Rose Street, Edinburgh EH2 2YQ
0131-225 8555; Fax: 0131-459 8111
Website: www.john-menzies.co.uk

Correspondent: Miss M Scott, Secretary to the Charities Committee

Chief officers: *Chairman:* G B Reed;
Chief Executive: D J Mackay

Year end	Turnover	Pre-tax profit
2/5/98	£1,543,000,000	£34,000,000

Nature of company business
Principal activities: distribution services.
Main subsidiaries include: Jones Yarrell; THE / THE Games; Early Learning Centre; Samas Universal Office Supplies; Concorde Express; AMI; London Cargo Centre.
Main locations: Edinburgh; Newcastle-under-Lyme; Eastleigh; Crawley; Swindon; Birmingham.

UK employees: 8,500

Charitable donations

1998: £158,000
1997: £165,000
1996: £155,000
1995: £153,000
1994: £145,000
Membership: %Club

Community support policy

The group is a member of the PerCent Club and in 1997/98, donated £158,000 to various charitable, community and arts organisations. It prefers to support charities in the fields of job creation, health/welfare, youth/sport, the services and environmental charities. Particular support is given to Scottish charities and charities in areas of company presence. The group prefers to give support on a long-term covenanted basis. Products may also be donated to local fundraising events. Community contributions are also made through secondment of managers to voluntary organisations.

In addition to the above group donations figure, Early Learning Centre supported Save the Children Fund by the donation of £53,000 raised through product sales.

Employee involvement: The John Maxwell Menzies Community Fund distributes funds to organisations in which company staff are directly involved. Every employee (retired and present) receives *The Reporter*, the groups monthly newspaper, which gives details of employees' community activities.

The arts: The company presently supports the Museum of Scotland Project, Edinburgh International Festival, National Art Collection Fund, Scottish National Orchestra, Scottish Opera, Pitlochry Festival and Perth Festival.

Exclusions

No support for advertising in charity brochures, or overseas projects.

Applications

In writing to the correspondent.

MEPC plc

Nations House, 103 Wigmore Street, London W1H 9AB
0171-911 5300; Fax: 0171-499 0605
Email: mepc@dial.pipex.com
Website: www.mepc.com

Correspondent: Miss Matita Glassborrow, Secretary to the Charities Committee

Chief officers: *Chairman:* Sir John Egan;
Chief Executive: J L Tuckey

Year end	Turnover	Pre-tax profit
30/9/97	£350,000,000	£84,000,000

Nature of company business
Property investment, development and trading.
Main subsidiaries include: Caledonian Land Properties Ltd; Castlecourt Investments Ltd; DGI Ltd; English Property Corpn PLC; Escort Property Investments Ltd; FOC Holdings Ltd; Lansdown Estates Group Ltd; Louisville Investments Ltd; The London County Freehold and Leasehold Properties Ltd; Manchester Commercial Buildings Co Ltd; Marathon Properties Ltd; Marcus Estates Ltd; The Metropolitan Railway Surplus Lands Co Ltd; Nonpareil Securities Ltd; The Oldham Estate Co PLC; PSIT PLC; PSIT Properties Ltd; Sovmots Investments Ltd; Threadneedle Property Co Ltd.

UK employees: n/a

Charitable donations

1997: £48,600
1996: £116,000
1995: £143,000
1994: £306,000
1993: £325,839

Community support policy

The company more than halved its level of giving to charities in 1996/97 and has seen a steady decrease since 1993. It supports a range of charities in the area of London and UK as a whole. Each application is considered on its merit. Preferred areas of support are children/youth, education, elderly people, enterprise/training, sickness/disability and social welfare.

The main beneficiary in 1997 was Centrepoint, with donations of between £100 and £1,000 given to several charities.

Exclusions

No support for advertising in charity brochures, animal welfare charities, appeals from individuals, the arts, environment/heritage, fundraising events, medical research, overseas projects, political or religious appeals, science/technology and sport.

Applications

In writing to the correspondent. The charities committee meets quarterly.

Merck

Merck Sharp & Dohme Ltd

Hertford Road, Hoddesdon, Hertfordshire EN11 9BU
01992-467272; Fax: 01992-467270

Correspondent: External Affairs Manager

Chief officers: n/a

Year end	Turnover	Pre-tax profit
31/12/96	£283,502,000	£5,996,000

Nature of company business
Merck Sharp & Dohme Ltd is the UK subsidiary of Merck & Co. Inc., a research-driven pharmaceutical and services company. It discovers, manufactures and markets a broad range of innovative products to improve human and animal health.

UK employees: 1,544

Charitable donations

1996: £50,861
1995: £49,070
1994: £31,193
1993: £17,500
Membership: *BitC   %Club*

Community support policy

The company is a member of the PerCent Club and has maintained its level of giving at about £50,000. Unfortunately we have no new policy information and can only repeat the rather general information that appeared in the last edition of this guide.

MSD Ltd and its parent company have formed many partnerships with a wide range of charities and aid organisations at international, national and local levels. Depending on specific requirements of each case, the company's involvement may include financial support, product donations and/or provision of services. In addition to these partnerships, there are very limited funds available and priority is given to local causes.

Applications

In writing to the correspondent.

Mercury Asset Management Group Ltd

33 King William Street, London EC4R 9AS
0171-280 2800; Fax: 0171-280 2820

Correspondent: Chris Georgiou, Assistant Director

Chief officers: n/a

Year end	Turnover	Pre-tax profit
31/3/98	£409,856,000	£147,644,000

Nature of company business
The holding company of a group engaged in the provision of investment management and advisory services. The company was taken over by ML Invest PLC, a wholly-owned subsidiary of Merrill Lynch Europe & Co, at the end of 1997 and delisted from the London Stock Exchange in March 1998.

UK employees: 1,313

Charitable donations

1998: £150,000
1997: £300,000
1996: £275,000
1995: £235,000
1994: £230,000
Membership: *ABSA   BitC*

Community support policy

The company is involved in ABSA matching schemes and is a member of Business in the Community. It used to be a member of the PerCent Club. Total donations halved from 1997 to 1998, following the takeover by Merrill Lynch.

The company assists specific projects and charities supported by their clients and their own members of staff. Areas receiving support in 1996/97 included the arts, inner-city projects, sports aid, medical research/equipment and hospices/care.

In kind support is provided through gifts in kind (supply of used computers and office equipment) and the provision of advice to charities on fundraising ideas and activities. The company has a payroll giving scheme in operation (Give As You Earn) and matches employee fundraising/giving.

Exclusions

No support for appeals from individuals, overseas projects or political appeals.

Applications

In writing to the correspondent.

The Mersey Docks & Harbour Company

Maritime Centre, Port of Liverpool, Liverpool L21 1LA
0151-949 6000; Fax: 0151-949 6300

Correspondent: Bill Bowley, Secretary to the Dock Charitable Fund

Chief officers: *Chairman:* G H Waddell;
Chief Executive: P T Furlong

Year end	Turnover	Pre-tax profit
31/12/97	£168,501,000	£34,577,000

Nature of company business
The principal activities of the group are the operation and maintenance of port facilities on the Rivers Mersey and Medway, provision of cargo handling and associated services, and the conservancy and pilotage of the Ports of Liverpool and Medway.
Main subsidiaries include: Coastal Container Line; Medway Ports; Neptune Insurance; Portia Management Services.

UK employees: 1,222

Charitable donations

1997: £62,993
1996: £22,420
1995: £10,290

Community support policy

The company has a preference for local charities in the areas of company presence and appeals relevant to company business. Preferred areas of support are children and youth, social welfare and medical.

The £63,000 given in charitable donations included £50,000 to the Dock Charitable Fund (Charity Commission number 206913), which gives grants annually to certain local charities. The trustees of this charitable trust are the board of directors of the company. The trust was set up with three objectives:

- reward of people assisting in the preservation of the life of the crew of any ship wrecked in the port of Liverpool or in the preservation of the ship or cargo or in the preserving or endeavouring to preserve people from drowning
- relief of sick, disabled or superannuated men in the dock service or the families of such men who were killed in service
- benefit of charities in the town or port of Liverpool.

The trust has a different financial year to the company and in 1996/97 had an income of £27,500. This was up from £10,000 the previous year and appears to have risen substantially again the following year. Grants in 1996/97 totalled £21,000, with nine of the 25 grants made being recurrent. The largest two grants, accounting for almost half the grant total, were £5,000 to both Fairbridge in Merseyside and the Royal Liverpool Philharmonic Society (Diamond Jubilee). Mersey Mission to Seamen received £1,600 while four organisations received £1,000: City of Liverpool Macmillan Nurses Appeal, ICU Warrington General Hospital, North West Cancer Research Foundation and Roy Castle Cause for Hope Foundation.

Other grants were made to a range of organisations within the above criteria including Brunswick Youth Club, Firwood Birtle Cricket Club, Greenbank Project, River Mersey Inshore Rescue Service and Salvation Army.

Exclusions
No support for circular appeals, fundraising events, advertising in charity brochures, appeals from individuals, purely denominational (religious) appeals, local appeals not in areas of company presence, large national appeals or overseas projects.

Applications
In writing to the correspondent.

Meyer International plc

Aldwych House, 81 Aldwych, London WC2B 4HQ
0171-400 8888; Fax: 0171-400 8700

Correspondent: Amanda Burton, Company Secretary

Chief officers: *Chairman:* Tony Palmer; *Chief Executive:* Alan Peterson

Year end	Turnover	Pre-tax profit
31/3/98	£1,254,100,000	£53,400,000

Nature of company business
Principal activities: the merchanting of building materials and timber and the distribution of laminates and specialist timber products.

Main subsidiaries include: Jewson; Harcros Timber & Building Supplies; H W Morey & Sons.

UK employees: 7,089

Charitable donations
1998: £64,200
1997: £49,300
1996: £49,500
1995: £50,000
1994: £51,000

Total community contributions: £170,000

Membership: %Club

Community support policy

Most of the group's community contributions in 1997/98, amounting to £170,000, were made up of donations in kind, the remainder (£64,200) being given in charitable donations. The company is a member of the PerCent Club.

Charitable donations: Support is given to national charities and charities local to the company's operations and appeals where a member of the group's staff is involved. There is a preference for those activities and projects concerned with children/youth, enterprise/training, environment/heritage – especially the preservation of buildings of national importance, education and overseas projects. The company gives around 50 grants to national and local organisations ranging from £50 to £5,000, grants to local organisations are usually up to £2,000.

The grants list for 1994/95 was broken down as follows:

Environmental – 16 grants totalling £6,800.

Development and housing – six grants totalling £13,700.

Social services – six grants totalling £6,500.

Arts – Only one grant of £500 to New Art Gallery – Tate, St Ives.

Preservation of buildings – six grants totalling £8,800.

Education and research – five grants totalling £3,700.

Business and professional – three grants totalling £5,350, £5,000 of which was to ProShare.

Donations are made through the Charities Aid Foundation. A payroll giving scheme for employees is operated by the group.

In kind support: The main area of non-cash support has been in kind giving, especially supplying building materials, usually at cost price. Support is also given by matching employee giving.

The company's subsidiaries in Holland and USA support charities in their own areas of operation.

Exclusions
The company will not fund individuals, denominational (religious) appeals, major overseas or national appeals. Support is not now given to the arts.

MFI

Applications
In writing to the correspondent. Telephone applications cannot be accepted.

Information available: The company gives a brief summary of its community involvement in its annual report.

MFI Furniture Group plc

Southon House, 333 The Hyde, Edgware Road, Colindale, London NW9 6TD
0181-200 8000; Fax: 0181-200 8636

Correspondent: Claire Weedon, Public Relations Officer

Chief officers: *Chairman:* D S Hunt; *Chief Executive:* John Randall; *Managing Director:* John O'Connell

Year end	Turnover	Pre-tax profit
25/4/98	£895,000,000	£60,000,000

Nature of company business
Principal activities: manufacture and sale of furniture.

Main subsidiaries include: Hygena Ltd; Hygena Packaging Ltd; Schreiber Furniture Ltd; Howden Joinery Ltd; Southon Insurance Co Ltd.

UK employees: n/a

Charitable donations
1998: £72,486
1997: n/a
1996: £176,688
1995: £166,692
1994: £89,413

Community support policy
The total charitable donations given by the company has more than halved since 1996, to just over £70,000. Most donations by the company are made through the Charities Aid Foundation. There is a preference for children and youth charities, with the National Children's Home being the main beneficiary of support. The small remaining budget is given to a wide range of other appeals, but generally in areas of company presence. Grants tend to range from £50 to £250.

The company operates the Give As You Earn payroll giving scheme.

Exclusions
No grants for purely denominational (religious) appeals, local appeals not in areas of company presence or overseas projects.

Applications
In writing to the correspondent.

Michelin Tyre plc

Campbell Road, Stoke-on-Trent, Staffordshire ST4 4EY
01782-402081; Fax: 01782-402011
Website: www.michelin.co.uk

Correspondent: P Niblett, Internal Communications Manager

Chief officers: *Chairman:* M Caron; *Managing Director:* P Lepercq

Year end	Turnover	Pre-tax profit
31/12/97	£636,010,000	£15,215,000

Nature of company business
Principal activities: the manufacture and sale of tyres, tubes, wheels and accessories.

Main locations: Ballymena; Burnley; Dundee; Stoke-on-Trent.

UK employees: 6,194

Charitable donations
1997: £44,812
1996: £41,566
1995: £63,000
1994: £19,000
1993: £26,000

Community support policy

Charitable donations: The company has a strong preference for local charities (ie. Stoke-on-Trent, Burnley, Ballymena, Dundee and Watford), especially those in which a member of staff is involved and appeals relevant to the company's business. These three stipulations form the basis of the company's donating philosophy, but the company considers all appeals presented. In particular it supports charities concerned with children and youth, social welfare, enterprise and education and training. Grants range from £10 to £500.

Employee involvement: As well as preference being given to charities in which a member of staff is involved, staff are encouraged to become involved in the local community through acting as volunteers in their own time and becoming school governors. The Give As You Earn payroll giving scheme is operated by the company, and there is a matching scheme for employee fundraising.

In kind support: The company provides its sports and social facilities free of charge for local school sports events and training for local organisations such as the police and fire brigade.

Enterprise: The company gives support to local enterprise agencies, and last year had three employees on full-time secondment to enterprise projects.

Education: The company is involved in local education/business partnerships and links have been developed through the provision of educational materials for schools, work experience schemes for pupils and teachers, and through student sponsorships.

Environment: The company is involved in local schemes to improve wasteland and school playgrounds, as well as running tree-planting schemes at factory locations.

Sponsorship: In addition to sponsorship of national and local activities associated with company products (eg. rallying and cycle racing) the company has sponsored local theatre and musical events. However, arts sponsorship is rarely undertaken.

Exclusions
No support for circular appeals, overseas projects, political appeals, religious appeals or local appeals not in areas of company presence.

Applications
In writing to the correspondent.

Midlands Electricity plc

MEB Whittington, Whittington, Worcester WR5 2RB
01905-613191; Fax: 01905-727187
Website: www.meb.co.uk

Correspondent: Sue Heritage, Corporate Relations Officer (Community)

Chief officers: *Chairman:* Fred Hafer; *Chief Executive:* Mike Hughes

Year end	Turnover	Pre-tax profit
31/3/98	£1,337,500,000	£165,800,000

Nature of company business
The ultimate controlling companies are Cinergy Corp and GPU, Inc both of the USA, each of which hold a 50% stake. The holding company is Avon Energy Partners Holdings which carries out all its operational activities through Midlands Electricity plc.

Principal activities: electricity distribution and supply, power generation, supply of natural gas and electrical contracting. Through its subsidiary Midlands Power International, the group owns and operates power stations at Hereford and Redditch, and holds investments in Teesside Power and Humber Power.

UK employees: n/a

Charitable donations
1998: £474,452
1997: £419,416
1996: n/a
1995: £1,625,000
1994: £141,961
Membership: ABSA BitC

Community support policy

Charitable donations: Preference is given to local charities in the Midlands, national charities and charities in which a member of staff is involved. Preferred areas of support include: the arts, children/youth, education, elderly people, enterprise/training, environment/heritage, fundraising events, medical research, science/technology, sickness/disability charities, social welfare and sport.

Donations are made through the Charities Aid Foundation. Grants to national organisations usually range from £250 to £5,000, grants to local organisations from £50 to £5,000. In 1997/98, the company continued its partnership with Neighbourhood Energy Action with a further contribution of £250,000 (included in the figure above).

The company's main area of non-cash support is in the form of good-cause sponsorship, secondments and gifts in kind. A variety of local events are sponsored, including arts and music festivals.

Secondments: The company encourages employee volunteering by giving cash support to employee volunteering and by matching employee fundraising. Managers have been seconded to Business in the Community and Opportunities for People with Disabilities.

The arts: A range of organisations are supported within the company's operating area. Recently this includes Symphony Hall Birmingham, Birmingham Rep, Cheltenham Festivals, Birmingham Readers & Writers Festival and the English String Orchestra. The company is a member of ABSA.

Exclusions
No support is given to circular appeals, appeals from individuals, purely denominational (religious) appeals, local appeals not in areas of company presence, large national appeals or overseas projects.

Applications
In writing to the correspondent. The company reports on its community involvement in its annual report.

Mirror Group plc

One Canada Square, Canary Wharf, London E14 5AP
0171-510 3000; Fax: 0171-293 3360

Correspondent: Paul Vickers, Company Secretary

Chief officers: *Chairman:* Victor Blank; *Chief Executive:* David Montgomery

Year end	Turnover	Pre-tax profit
28/12/97	£559,000,000	£80,000,000

Nature of company business
Production and distribution of media products. The group has six divisions: national newspapers, regional newspapers, Scottish newspapers, television, magazines and exhibitions, and sports.

Main subsidiaries include: Scottish Daily Record and Sunday Mail Ltd; Century Press & Publishing Ltd; Saltire Press Ltd; Live TV Ltd.

Main brands include: The Mirror; Sunday Mirror; The People; Daily Record; Sunday Mail; Birmingham Evening Mail; Racing Post.

UK employees: 5,645

Charitable donations
1997: £140,000
1996: £227,000
1995: £274,000
1994: £112,000
1993: £60,000

Community support policy

The company normally only donates money to UK registered charities that are either, based in the local communities around its office and print sites (especially those in the Isle of Dogs, Manchester, Watford and Glasgow areas) or are connected to the newspaper,

Mobil

printing or advertising industries. Exceptions to the last rule are occasionally made if the charity committee feels a cause is sufficiently deserving.

There is a preference for groups working with people who are disabled, ill, elderly or young and also to hospices, cancer research and those with a newspaper industry link.

The group also run the Man of the People Appeal Fund in conjunction with news stories and appeals for readers donations. Money is raised towards the end of the year, trustees meet in March and make payments in April. Donations are given to major disaster appeals. In 1998, the fund had an income of £18,000 and gave out £30,000.

The group's main area of non-cash support is good cause sponsorship. The company encourages employee involvement through matching employee fundraising and giving company time off to volunteer.

Exclusions

No support is given to environment/heritage, sport, religious or political appeals, overseas projects, medical research and appeals for individuals.

Applications

In writing to the correspondent.

Mobil Holdings Ltd

Witan Gate House, 500–600 Witan Gate, Central Milton Keynes MK9 1ES
01908-853000; Fax: 01908-853999

Correspondent: R C Newstead, Manager, Media Relations

Chief officer: *Chairman:* G H G Ellis

Year end	Turnover	Pre-tax profit
31/12/95	£1,656,565,000	(£47,530,000)

Nature of company business
The main activities are the transportation, import and refining of crude oil and the manufacture and marketing of petroleum products.
Main subsidiaries include: Prime Garages Ltd; Vacuum Oil Company; Fountain Real Estate Ltd.

UK employees: 4,048

Charitable donations
1995: £71,317
1994: £78,864
Membership: ABSA

Community support policy

The company is currently reviewing its community activities in the UK. No up-to-date financial information was available.

Previously, it only supported registered charities, with areas of support being the arts, children/youth, education, elderly people, enterprise/training, environment/heritage, medical reserach, science/technology, sickness/disability charities and social welfare. Priority is given to charities in areas of company presence ie. Milton Keynes, south Essex and Wirral.

The company is a member of ABSA and has supported the Mobil Touring Theatre and Greenwich Music Festival.

Exclusions

No support for advertising in charity brochures, animal welfare charities (except birds), appeals from individuals, fundraising events, overseas projects, political appeals or religious appeals.

Applications

In writing to the correspondent.

Monsanto plc

PO Box 53, Lane End Road, High Wycombe HP12 4HL
01494-474918; Fax: 01494-447872

Correspondent: Karen Tait, Public Relations Manager

Chief officer: *Chairman:* M Ford

Year end	Turnover	Pre-tax profit
31/12/96	£357,450,000	£40,603,000

Nature of company business
The main activities are the manufacture and sale of herbicides for agriculture, prescription pharmaceutical products, the sweetener Canderel and food ingredients.

UK employees: 1,813

Charitable donations
1996: £35,557
1995: £37,000
1994: £68,000
1993: £65,000

Community support policy

The company supports local charities in areas of company presence, national charities and charities in which a member of company staff is involved. There is a preference for charities working with the very ill and disabled people, children and youth, education and enterprise/training. The company tries to help self-supporting projects. It has strong links with schools and education. Grants to national organisations range from £250 to £1,000. Grants to local organisations range from £20 to £100.

Most grants are given to local organisations and charities especially in Wales, but also High Wycombe and Morpeth. Beneficiaries have ranged from national charities such as Age Concern and National Federation for the Blind to Cefn Mawr Musical Society, Llangollen Cottage Hospital and Wrexham Groudwork Trust.

The company matches donations raised for charities by employees and allows staff time off for activity of community benefit.

Exclusions

No grants for fundraising events, advertising in charity brochures, purely denominational (religious) appeals, local appeals not in areas of company presence, large national appeals, animal charities, overseas projects or circular appeals.

Applications

In writing to the correspondent. The charity committee meets four times a year and tends to exclude the more well-known charities.

Morgan Crucible Company plc

Morgan House, Madeira Walk, Windsor, Berkshire SL4 1EP
01753-837000; Fax: 01753-850872

Correspondent: D J Coker, Company Secretary

Chief officers: *Chairman:* Dr E B Farmer; *Managing Director:* I P Norris

Year end	Turnover	Pre-tax profit
4/1/98	£891,000,000	£112,000,000

Nature of company business
This is the holding company of more than 120 subsidiary and related companies engaged in the manufacture and/or marketing of specialised materials and components for application in a wide range of industries and services.
Main subsidiaries include: Rocol Group Ltd; Centronic Ltd; MBM Technology Ltd; Mini Instruments Ltd.

UK employees: 3,307

Charitable donations
1997: £229,814
1996: £147,178
1995: £114,670
1994: £99,566
1993: £91,075

Community support policy

The company states that its main support goes to relatively small, 'niche' charities in the fields of medical care and research. Some limited support is given to the arts in areas of company presence. Grants usually range from £100 to £500, and are distributed by the Morgan Crucible Company plc Charitable Trust. In 1996/97, the trust categorised its donations as follows:

Medical development & research £6,178
Care (including holidays) of people physically or mentally disabled £15,800
Care (including holidays) of young people in deprived or undesirable circumstances £5,850
Adventure or training holidays or courses for character development £3,950
Local (Windsor area) good causes £4,900
Character reform £2,008
Arts £2,800
Education £1,900
Community services £1,275
Director sponsored £15,160

The total is £60,000, so presumably some of the company's donations are made directly to charities. Grants are made nationally, but primarily in Wirral, Leeds, South Wales, South London, Worcester and Thames Valley. Subsidiary companies do have their own budgets for appeals, but no figures are available.

The arts: Morgan Crucible undertakes a very limited amount of support for the arts in areas where it is an employer.

Exclusions

No support for animal welfare charities; appeals from individuals; overseas projects; political appeals; religious appeals; science/technology or sport.

Applications

In writing to the correspondent. Grant decisions are made by a donations committee which meets quarterly.

Morgan Stanley & Co International Ltd

25 Cabot Square, Canary Wharf, London E14 4QA
0171-513 8000; Fax: 0171-425 8984

Correspondent: Mrs Heather Bird, Secretary, Morgan Stanley International Foundation

Chief officers: n/a

Year end	Turnover	Pre-tax profit
31/12/97	n/a	n/a

Nature of company business
Principal activities: finance, investment and savings.

UK employees: n/a

Charitable donations
1997: £875,000

Community support policy

The company makes its charitable donations through the Morgan Stanley International Foundation (Charity Commission number 1042671), to which it donated £875,000 in 1997.

The foundation makes grants 'towards non-profit social service, educational, cultural and healthcare organisations, which provide a benefit to the local (ie. East End) Morgan Stanley community', as outlined in its guidelines for applicants. The East End is defined as the London boroughs of Tower Hamlets, Newham and Hackney.

Grants are focused on organisations operating in the following areas:

'*Arts and culture*
Support for major museums and cultural institutions.

'*Hospitals/health*
Support for major hospitals in the beneficial area of giving. As a rule, the foundation does not support organisations involved in the research of specific diseases.

Morrison

'*Social welfare*
Support for major social welfare organisations involved in the following sectors:

- services for youth – organisations of which the primary mission is providing educational and leadership activities for young people
- job training/remedial education/handicapped support – for adults and young people in order to prepare these people to become self-supporting
- housing/hunger – organisations providing food and shelter to adults and families in need of assistance. The foundation is particularly interested in organisations working to develop creative and long-term solutions to these problems
- multi-service centres/community development – agencies working on behalf of the entire community, from infants to the elderly, and addressing a variety of neighbourhood issues. Also, community organisations involved in economic development activies.'

In 1997, the amount available for grant distribution was £625,000 and grants totalled £487,000, up from £276,000 in the previous year. The balance of £250,000 was designated by the company to be used to establish a permanent endowment. Grants over £1,000 were listed in the trust's annual report and were made to 87 organisations. Grants less than £1,000 totalled about £2,000.

The largest grant of £88,000 to NSPCC, was given under a matching contribution agreement. The charity was the firm's Charity of the Year in 1997/98.

The trust has undertaken a major commitment of £217,000 to the Isle of Dogs Community Foundation of £50,000 a year, until 2001, with £17,000 given in 1997. Other larger grants were £41,000 to Community Links, £15,000 to both The De Paul Trust and Whitechapel Art Gallery, £13,000 to Royal London Hospital, £12,000 to London Chest Hospital, and £10,000 each to Bromley by Bow Centre, Mencap, Mudchute Park and Farm, Spitalfields Festival and Woodland Centre Trust.

Another 20 grants were between £5,000 and £7,500 and the remaining 55 were smaller, averaging £2,400. These grants were to a wide range of charities, including BIA Quaker Social Action, British Dyslexia Association, City of London Festival, Fern Street Settlement, Good Shepherd Mission, Hackney Music Development Trust, Jubilee Sailing Trust, London Children's Ballet, Neighbours in Poplar, Ragged Schools Museum Trust, Save the Children, Tower Hamlets Victim Support and Write Away.

Exclusions

'As a rule, grants will not be made to either international or national charitable organisations unless they have a project in this local area. In addition, grants will not be made to either political or evangelistic organisations, "pressure groups", or individuals who are seeking sponsorship either for themselves (eg. to help pay for education) or for onward transmission to a charitable organisation.'

Applications

In writing to the correspondent, from whom guidelines to applicants are available.

Morrison Construction Group Ltd

Morrison House, 12 Atholl Crescent, Edinburgh EH3 8HA
0131-228 4188; Fax: 0131-337 1880

Correspondent: Stewart MacLeod, Director

Chief officers: *Chairman:* A F Morrison; *Managing Director:* K M Howell

Year end	Turnover	Pre-tax profit
31/3/98	£383,200,000	£20,800,000

Nature of company business
Construction industry and related services.

UK employees: n/a

Charitable donations

1998: £28,575
1997: £23,908
1996: n/a
1995: £74,951
1994: £24,823

Total community contributions: £70,000

Community support policy

In 1997/98, over £41,000 was given through non-cash support including gifts in kind and training schemes. The company also support employees' volunteering/charitable activities by providing financial help and company time off to volunteer. A payroll giving scheme is also in operation and the company matches employee fundraising.

Donations policy: Each subsidiary and area head office makes its own donations and decides its policy. Before sending in an application, charities should approach a subsidiary or area office to find out if they have a policy that will support them.

The Scottish area offices appear to prefer to support Scottish charities with preference for causes connected with the arts, education, environment/heritage, medical research, religious appeals and sickness/disability charities. Major grant beneficiaries in 1997/98 included: Sargent Cancer Fund for Children, Princess Royal Trust for Carers and Scottish Prison Fellowship.

Exclusions

No support for advertising in charity brochures, animal welfare charities, elderly people, enterprise/training, fundraising events, overseas projects, political appeals, science/technology, social welfare or sport.

Applications

In writing to the correspondent.

Wm Morrison Supermarkets plc

Hillmore House, Thornton Road, Bradford BD8 9AX
01274-494166; Fax: 01274-494831

Correspondent: Jean M Sowman, Charitable Trust Secretary

Chief officer: *Chairman:* K D Morrison

Year end	Turnover	Pre-tax profit
1/2/98	£2,296,996,000	£151,360,000

Nature of company business
Principal activity: retail through supermarkets.

Main subsidiaries include: Farmers Boy Ltd; Farock Insurance Co Ltd; Holsa Ltd; Neerock Ltd; W Todd Ltd.

Charitable donations
1998: £135,000
1997: £122,000
1996: £785,000
1995: £212,000
1994: £69,000
Total community contributions: £472,000

Community support policy

Each year a single (usually national) charity is nominated, which is supported throughout the stores through fundraising and collection points. The company also contributes to this cause, although no figure was given. In 1998 the nominated charity was Marie Curie Cancer Care.

In addition to cash donations, the company's community contributions amounted to £350,000. Main areas of non-cash support are gifts in kind, joint promotions and training schemes.

Other appeals are supported through the Wm Morrison Charitable Trust which received £40,000 from the company in 1996/97. The total income was £48,000 and 86 grants were made totalling £122,000. Support is given to a wide range of other charities, but no further information was available. However, there may be a preference for advertising in charity brochures, animal welfare charities, appeals from individuals, elderly people, fundraising events, medical research sickness/disability charities and social welfare.

Main beneficiaries of grants in 1996/97 included: Bradford Cancer Support Centre; The Lord Mayor of Bradford's Appeal; The Lord Mayor Of Leeds Appeal; NSPCC; and The Carer's Resource – Harrogate.

Each store also has a small budget for local community causes.

Exclusions
No response to circular appeals or support for the arts, overseas projects, or political appeals.

Applications
In writing to the correspondent.

Napier Brown Holdings Ltd

International House, 1 St Katherines Way, London E1 9UN
0171-335 2500

Correspondent: Sue Crabtree, Personal Assistant to the Chairman

Chief officer: *Chairman:* P G Ridgwell

Year end	Turnover	Pre-tax profit
29/3/97	£387,426,000	£10,881,000

Nature of company business
The main activities are the processing, packing and distribution of sugar, dried fruit, nuts and various chilled products.

Main subsidiaries include: Borland & Sclanders Chalice Foods Ltd; Solway Foods Ltd; Trent Foods Ltd; Whitworths Ltd.

UK employees: 1,647

Charitable donations
1997: £33,098
1996: £40,831
1995: £35,041
1994: £34,716
1993: £48,000

Community support policy
The company has stated previously that all support is given to one cancer-related charity through a long-term deed of covenant. Unsolicited appeals cannot be supported.

Applications
See above.

National Express Group plc

Worthy Park House, Abbotts Worthy, Winchester SO21 1AN
01962-888888; Fax: 01962-888898

Correspondent: Phil White, Chief Executive

Chief officers: *Chairman:* A M Davies; *Chief Executive:* P M White

Year end	Turnover	Pre-tax profit
31/12/97	£1,134,000,000	£55,000,000

Nature of company business
The principal activities of the group are the provision of passenger transport services in four areas: coaches, buses, airports and trains.

Main subsidiaries include: West Midlands Travel; Taybus Holdings; Travel Merryhill; East Midlands International Airport; Bournemouth International Airport; Midland Main Line; Gatwick Express; Silverlink Train Services; Central Trains; ScotRail Railways; Scottish Citylink Coaches; Highland Country Buses; Fregata Travel.

Charitable donations
1997: £51,118
1996: £10,343

National Grid

Community support policy

The group provided the following information regarding its charitable giving.

'The group operates a devolved management system which means that its subsidiary businesses have day-to-day responsibilities for their operations. This includes their involvement with the communities they serve. The group does not consider that it is appropriate to control this activity as we have a high number of businesses spread throughout the UK. Local community groups should contact their nearest local National Express Group business.

'National Express Group's Head Office selects certain charities or sponsorships at the time of setting its budget, usually during the autumn. In view of the group's geographic coverage, it prefers to select a national rather than local initiative, although we welcome contact with local groups in the Hampshire area and will assess each on their merits.'

In general, organisations supported will be:

- well-run and publish annual reports of their spending and success
- registered, if a charity
- capable of offering a well-balanced programme of activities which reflect the current needs and trends in society.

The group is also keen to encourage staff in any contributions, voluntary or otherwise, which they make to their own communities.

Exclusions
No support for political or religious appeals.

Applications
In writing to the correspondent.

The National Grid Group plc

National Grid House, Kirby Corner Road, Coventry CV4 8JY
01203-537777; Fax: 01203-423678
Website: www.ngc.co.uk

Correspondent: Trevor Seeley, Sponsorship Manager

Chief officers: *Chairman:* David Jefferies; *Chief Executive:* David Jones; *Managing Director:* Roger Urwin

Year end	Turnover	Pre-tax profit
31/3/98	£1,519,300,000	£574,800,000

Nature of company business
Principal activity: own and operate the high-voltage electricity transmission system in England and Wales.

Main subsidiaries include: Energy Settlements & Information Services Ltd; Energy Pool Funds Administration Ltd.

Charitable donations
1998: £363,298
1997: £2,300,000
1996: £1,056,209
1995: £478,000
1994: £327,624

Total community contributions: c. £1,000,000
Membership: *ABSA BitC*

Community support policy

The National Grid Group (NGG) has an extensive community relations programme, with particular emphasis on environmental and educational partnerships. It supports some national charities and local charities in areas of company presence. Local donations may cover a wider range depending on the needs of the local community. The company is a member of Business in the Community and ABSA.

The level of charitable giving has fallen dramatically over the last year. Even comparing the 1998 total community contributions figure of £1 million (rather than the £363,000 charitable donations figure declared in the company annual report), to the previous year's figure donations of £2.3 million, the decrease is well over £1 million.

In addition to the figure quoted above, a one-off charitable donation of £162,195 was made during the year. This sum arose from an error in calculating the value of fractions of shares left over following the share consolidation. The amounts unpaid to individual shareholders ranged from 2p to 45p. Rather than despatch individual cheques for these small amounts, the company donated the total unpaid sum to the group of charities supported by staff through the Give As You earn scheme.

Education: NGG is involved in a number of liaison activities with schools and universities. It also supports educational materials for schools through the Electricity Association's 'Understanding Electricity' service.

Environment: NGG supports beneficial environmental initiatives, both on its own land and elsewhere. The company has established a major network of environmental education centres, with the active involvement of local education authorities. The company has three large national sponsorships, in partnership with the Local Government Management Board (National Grid Community 21 Awards Scheme), the Tree Council (National Grid Tree Warden Scheme) and the British Trust for Conservation Volunteers (National Grid for Wildlife hedgerows campaign).

Employee involvement: The company operates a payroll giving scheme (matching employee giving) and matches £ for £ employees fundraising up to £1,000.

Exclusions
Support is not given to circular appeals, religious appeals, political causes, and local appeals not in areas of company presence. Also, the company rarely sponsors individuals.

Applications
A leaflet on NGG's sponsorship and donations policy is available on request. Sponsorship proposals should be addressed to Trevor Seeley, Sponsorship Manager. Appeals for donations to Sue Tyler, Donations Co-ordinator.

National Magazine Co Ltd

National Magazine House, 72 Broadwick Street,
London W1V 3BP
0171-439 7144; Fax: 0171-439 5093

Correspondent: Cecile Barnett

Chief officers: *Chairman:* F A Bennack;
Managing Director: T G Mansfield

Year end	Turnover	Pre-tax profit
31/12/97	£258,107,000	£17,418,000

Nature of company business
The main activities are the publishing and distribution of magazines and periodicals.
Main brands include: Cosmopolitan; Company; Good House Keeping; Country Living; Harpers & Queen; Esquire; House Beautiful; She.

UK employees: 856

Charitable donations
1997: £47,000
1996: n/a
1995: £39,000
1994: £21,000
1993: £44,000

Community support policy
The group has a preference for medical research and women's organisations. It makes some small cash donations, advertises in charity brochures and donates a year's magazine subscription.

Each magazine also takes on a charity to support each year.

Applications
In writing to the correspondent.

National Power PLC

Windmill Hill Business Park, Whitehill Way, Swindon, Wiltshire SN5 6PB
01793-877777; Fax: 01793-893861
Website: www.national-power.com

Correspondent: Catherine Springett, Assistant Company Secretary

Chief officers: *Chairman:* Sir John Collins;
Chief Executive: Keith Henry

Year end	Turnover	Pre-tax profit
31/3/98	£3,354,000,000	£720,000,000

Nature of company business
Electricity generation and supply.

UK employees: 3,216

Charitable donations
1998: £413,784
1997: £419,322
1996: £384,905
1995: £377,282
1994: £354,584
Membership: *BitC %Club*

Community support policy
The company is a member of the PerCent Club and Business in the Community. Charitable donations are routed through The National Power Charitable Trust. The company operates the Give As You Earn payroll giving scheme and matches employee fundraising.

The figures given above for charitable donations actually refer to the trust and not the company. This is the figure quoted in the company annual report.

The National Power Charitable Trust
The National Power Charitable Trust (Charity Commission number 1002358) was established in 1991 with a donation of £1 million from the company and a total of £1.7 million during the subsequent period. The trustees are Mrs A Ferguson, J W Baker, G A W Blackman and M G Herbert.

The trust supports a wide range of community, health and social causes, particularly initiatives which aim to alleviate suffering and deprivation and for the promotion of self-help and voluntary work in the community. Support is particularly given to charities with local outlets near company sites or with company staff involved.

The trust has three main areas of support:
- major support for Barnardo's
- range of national organisations encompassing a broad spread of charitable causes
- ad hoc support in response to appeals, particularly community initiatives. In addition, the promotion and matching £ for £ of staff fundraising activities.

The trust has supported Barnardo's with £50,000 a year for six years, and also contributed the same amount as raised by company staff in support of charity, up to a maximum of a further £50,000 a year. The report states that 'The association has proved extremely successful with good relationships built up at both corporate and local level'.

The trust has continued its support for several national charities including health, welfare and medical causes. In 1998, these included Diana, Princess of Wales Memorial Fund (50,000), British Occupational Health Research Foundation (£12,500) and Mencap (£10,000).

The trust is keen to support community initiatives and funding was given to organisations linked with community self-help programmes and voluntary work. In particular, the trust continued to provide substantial contributions to the Wiltshire Community Foundation, as well as to CSV Learning Together initiative and The Green Hut – a Swindon-based charity providing support to homeless people in the area.

In 1996/97, the income of the trust was £617,000, including £592,000 from the company and £25,000 interest on bank deposits. The previous year no income was received from the company. Grants for the year totalled £419,000 with a corresponding increase in the funds carried forward from £681,000 to £879,000.

Nationwide

The trust broke down its grants by size as follows (1996 in brackets):

£50,000–100,000 .... 1 .... (1)
£20,000–49,999 .... 1 .... (1)
£15,000–19,999 .... 0 .... (0)
£10,000–14,999 .... 7 .... (5)
£5,000–9,999 .... 17 .... (10)
£1,000–4,999 .... 86 .... (67)
£0–999 .... 30 .... (18)

Exclusions

Support is NOT given to: advertising in charity brochures; animal welfare charities; appeals from individuals; the arts; environment/heritage; fundraising events; political appeals; religious appeals; science/technology; or sport.

Applications

In writing to the correspondent. Sponsorship proposals should be addressed to: Sponsorship Manager, Corporate Communications.

Nationwide Building Society

Nationwide House, Pipers Way, Swindon SN38 1NW
01793-455143; Fax: 01793-455858
Website: www.nationwide.co.uk

Correspondent: Karen Johnson, Community Affairs Manager

Chief officers: *Chairman:* Charles Nunneley;
Chief Executive: Dr Brian Davis

Year end	Turnover	Pre-tax profit
4/4/98	n/a	£372,300,000

Nature of company business
The group provides a comprehensive range of personal financial and housing services.

UK employees: 10,727

Charitable donations

1998: £2,781,642
1997: £606,741
1996: £544,464
1995: £550,485
1994: £664,108

Community support policy

The dramatic increase in the company's level of charitable giving was due to a donation of £2 million in 1998 to The Nationwide Foundation. This foundation was established during the year.

There are four broad themes within Nationwide's Community Affairs strategy and any activities should normally embrace at least one of these themes:

- *Homes* – housing initiatives.
- *Initiative* – training, youth projects, education/schools/preparation for life.
- *Caring* – counselling and advice, disabled support/access, health, discrimination (various).
- *Heritage/environment* – saving things (as well as money), green issues, conservation/recycling.

There is a preference for projects with the potential for staff involvement. Support is given to national and local charities. Nationwide operates the Give As You Earn payroll giving scheme and supports employee fundraising in various ways. As part of the company's 150th anniversary celebrations, it launched the Nationwide Awards for Voluntary Endeavour in January 1998. This scheme, run in conjunction with the National Council for Voluntary Organisations and The Newspaper Society, is designed to give 'local heroes' in the UK who help out in the community the recognition they deserve. The first awards were presented in October 1998.

The company will also normally consider supporting causes concerned with the arts, children/youth, elderly people, fundraising events, and sport.

Non-cash support in the form of equipment, consultancy, furniture, prizes/merchandise, and print/design, is also provided.

Exclusions

No response to circular appeals. No support for advertising in charity brochures, animal welfare charities, appeals from individuals, medical research, overseas projects, political appeals, religious appeals, science/technology, or for commercial (as opposed to community related) sponsorship.

Applications

Applications for donations or sponsorship should be sent to the correspondent above. On a local basis, giving depends on the local area managers, who have small budgets for local community projects.

NatWest Group

2nd Floor, 41 Lothbury, London EC2P 2BP
0171-726 1000 ; Fax: 0171-726 1573
Website: www.natwestgroup.com

Correspondent: Community Relations Officer

Chief officers: *Chairman:* Robert Alexander;
Chief Executive: Derek Wanless

Year end	Turnover	Pre-tax profit
31/12/97	n/a	£1,011,000,000

Nature of company business
NatWest Group provides an extensive range of financial services in the UK and internationally.

Main subsidiaries include: Retail Banking Services; Corporate Banking Services; Card Services; Mortgage Services; NatWest Insurance Services; Lombard Group; Ulster Bank Group; Global Financial Markets; Hawkpoint Partners; Coutts Group; NatWest Life and Regulated Sales; Gartmore; NatWest Equity Partners; Greenwich NatWest; Gleacher NatWest.

UK employees: 70,000

Charitable donations

1997: £2,400,000
1996: £2,300,000
1995: £2,793,833
1994: £2,789,472
1993: £1,588,665

Total community contributions: £14,300,000 (worldwide)

Membership: *ABSA BitC %Club*

Community support policy

NatWest Group is a leading corporate contributor to community issues. In 1997, the group invested more than £14 million in cash and in kind in communities in which it operates. The company is a member of ABSA, Business in the Community and the PerCent Club.

The group's community investment initiatives are designed to complement business activity and focus on three areas where its resources can make the most impact:

- *Financial literacy* – helping children, adults and organisations develop personal money management and enterprise skills.
- *Developing communities* – promoting economic health and local opportunities by supporting small businesses, community groups, charities and the arts.
- *Helping staff give time and money* – encouraging staff to give their time, skills, and expertise to local comunities.

Employee-led involvement initiatives

NatWest maintains its wider roots in the community by supporting causes and organisations where NatWest staff are involved. More than 8,000 employees make monthly donations to charities through Charity Plus, NatWest's payroll giving scheme, matched up to £10 per employee per month by NatWest. And, if a NatWest employee is a regular volunteer with your organisation, NatWest can support their efforts by making a cash donation to you under its staff Community Action Awards. Nearly 5,000 organisations benefited in this way in 1997.

Employer-led involvement initiatives

In addition to the group initiatives encouraging voluntary involvement, each business has its own structured programme which has been developed to reflect employee profile, business needs, location and markets. Initiatives include mentoring or secondment programmes, development assignments, staff challenges, team fundraising events and tailored community investment activities.

For instance, NatWest Face 2 Face With Finance is an award-winning programme of practical learning experiences which help schools teach money management and enterprise skills within the curriculum. Since 1994, 3,940 NatWest staff have worked with 2,359 secondary schools in England and Wales. Over 120,000 young people have benefited from the programme to date.

In any one year more than 30 staff are on full-time secondment to a charity or voluntary organisation with the aim of helping these organisations benefit from essential resource and sound management which would otherwise be unavailable. Secondees build new skills and knowledge, develop valuable local networks, and gain understanding of the local market place by managing projects in a new environment.

Taking a lead with other organisations

NatWest Group is committed to sharing best practice, bringing the benefits of a structured investment programme to communities across the UK.

The group helps employers support staff and encourages involvement in the management of arts-based charities and community groups through ABSA's NatWest BoardBank. BoardBank recruits and trains employees, giving them the skills to serve on the boards of local arts organisations, and brokers placements.

Through its charitable trust, NatWest supports a wide range of programmes which contribute to community regeneration in specific areas. All these projects are monitored and evaluated in order to share lessons learned with other voluntary organisations, policy makers, businesses, academics and others. In 1997, NatWest Group received the Lord Mayor of London's Dragon Award for its contribution towards developing opportunities for disadvantaged young people in the changing world of work – managed through its trust's grants programme.

NatWest promotes new services for community organisations as it strongly believes that corporate grants and donations can never be a reliable and sustainable source of income for the 'Not for Profit' sector. As the major business partner in the Local Investment Fund (run by Business in the Community), NatWest encourages loans for projects which benefit communities as well as earning income, which traditional banking has been unable to support. NatWest helped CAF set up Investors in Society, which also provides loans to smaller community organisations, and works with NCVO to develop training for financial management for charities.

Exclusions

NatWest Group does not invite unsolicited applications and prefers to seek and develop partnerships with organisations on a proactive basis.

Support is not given for advertising in charity brochures, animal welfare charities, appeals from individuals, fundraising events, medical research, political appeals, or religious appeals.

Applications

The focus of the central programme means that most resources are committed to long-term relationships. New partnerships are agreed through proactive approaches, with specific criteria and guidelines for new funding themes developed and promoted through targeted organisations.

At local level, support is given to projects which meet defined local criteria. However, NatWest is unable to support all of the thousands of strong requests it receives each year.

Applications for local support should be directed to the local NatWest branch in the first instance.

Enquiries about the central programme should be directed to NatWest Group Community Relations, 41 Lothbury, London EC2P 2BP.

… Nestlé

Nestlé UK Ltd

York YO1 1XY
Fax: 01904-603461

Correspondent: Peter J Anderson, Community Relations Manager

Chief officer: *Chairman:* P H Blackburn

Year end	Turnover	Pre-tax profit
31/12/97	n/a	n/a

Nature of company business
Manufacture and sale of food products and associated activities.

Main brands include: Chambourcy; Cross & Blackwell; Findus; Kit Kat; Libby's; Nescafé.

UK employees: 14,281

Charitable donations

1997: £932,000
1996: £980,000
1995: £864,000
1994: £1,079,000
1993: £847,000
Membership: *ABSA BitC %Club*

Community support policy

The company is a member of the PerCent Club, it's charitable donations figure of £932,000 in 1997 representing 1.6% of UK pre-tax profit. It makes donations to registered charities through the Nestlé Charitable Trust and also supports non-registered good causes locally. There is a preference for charities that have company staff involvement and Employee Volunteer Awards to a total of £50,000 a year are given to those actively involved in their local community. In addition to cash donations its main area of non-cash support is gifts in kind – the company providing product, furniture and equipment donations to local good causes.

Charitable donations: Company charitable donations are considered at a national level by a representative group of managers at the head office in Croydon. There are also local management groups at the main factories, which consider applications from local charities and good causes.

The company considers donations in various fields which relate to arts and culture, community development, education, enterprise, environment, health (medical), or young people's sport. Support is given to properly managed activities of high quality in their particular field.

However, a relevant link or connection with the company's business is usually looked for. This may be geographic (within the catchment area of company factories, there are over 20 locations throughout the UK), related to the food industry or through connections with university departments or employee activities. Employees involved with local voluntary groups may apply for a grant of up to £1,500.

Sporting events supported include the Nestlé Junior Tennis Ladder Tournament and Yorkshire Cricket Clubs 'Enjoy Cricket Scheme'.

Major beneficiaries in 1997 included Kids Club Network, London Mozart Players, Confectioners Benevolent Society, Children Nationwide, British Nutrition Foundation and Young Enterprise.

Support is also given to local events, performances, sporting occasions and festivals which involve communities and enrich the lives of both participants and spectators. The company is especially keen to support an event when this will help raise additional money for charitable causes, encourage local community involvement and bring greatest benefit to the community as a whole. Many of the events may be termed sporting or artistic, but they are not merely competitive or passive. Examples include: York Early Music Festival, music and dance in the local community, and Race the Sun – an army event to raise funds for local good causes.

Education: Educational development in the broadest sense has been one of the company's priorities. It is sympathetic to requests for help from pupils, teachers and education advisers from the communities in which it operates. Support has included curriculum advice, specialised training courses for heads and senior teachers and the provision of information on nutritional and general business matters in schools. The company are major supporters of the British Nutrition Foundation's educational initiative, 'Food: A Fact of Life', to teach children about food, nutrition and health. The company is also interested in the development of international awareness of young children and the development of foreign language teaching via the North Yorkshire 'Tous Ensemble' Project. York Schools and Youth Trust was selected as the company's millennium project.

Enterprise: The company is one of the main sponsors of Young Enterprise, providing management advisers seconded to schools to give practical and expert advice. Training and Enterprise Councils (TECs) and Education Business Partnerships are also supported. The company is a member of Business in the Community and the Nestlé Charitable Trust supports several registered charities in the enterprise field.

Environment: Support is given to organisations ranging from The British Trust for Conservation Volunteers, to a trust in Halifax which offers low interest loans for companies wanting to improve the appearance of their properties in the inner city, and providing a little money to convert a school's grounds into environmental areas.

The arts: The company is a member of ABSA. Support has been given to Glyndebourne Festival Society, London Mozart Players, and York Early Music Festival.

Exclusions

No support for advertising in charity brochures, appeals from individuals (including students), local appeals not in areas of company presence, political organisations or overseas projects. Overseas aid is controlled by the head office in Vevey, Switzerland.

Applications

Applications for support of local good causes should be made to the Manager of the nearest Nestlé location, but for large-scale donations or national charities the request should be sent to Community Relations Department, Nestlé UK Ltd, Haxby Road, York YO1 1XY.

The company supports about 3,000 of the 17,000 requests received each year.

Neville Russell

24 Bevis Marks, London EC3A 7NL
0171-377 1000

Correspondent: John Chastney, Partner

Chief officers: n/a

Year end	Turnover	Pre-tax profit
31/12/95	n/a	n/a

Nature of company business
Chartered accountants.

UK employees: n/a

Charitable donations
1995: £85,250
1994: n/a
1993: £101,000
Membership: *BitC %Club*

Community support policy

The company is a member of the PerCent Club and Business in the Community. In the 1998 PerCent Club annual report, the figure given for the company's total community investment is £104,000 equivalent to 4.9% of pre-tax profit.

Resources have been made available to drug and alcohol rehabilitation and AIDS care and research.

The N R Charitable Trust

Support is given through the N R Charitable Trust in the form of time and money to a wide range of charities concerned with the advancement of the Christian faith and general charitable purposes. The correspondent stated that resources are committed almost entirely to charities known to the partners of the firm. It is very unlikely that unsolicited appeals will be considered.

This trust gave grants totalling £127,000 in 1997 from an income of £141,000. The income was virtually all from covenants and Gift Aid donations received from the particpating partners of Neville Russell based on their profits in the year end December 1996. 22 grants were made including four of £15,000 to Carmel House at Victoria School, Emmaus (Cambridge), Mildmay International and Spurgeon's College. Other beneficiaries included the Chartered Accountants Benevolent Fund, IFES, Little Haven Children's Hospice, Lupus UK and Operation Mobilisation.

The arts: The company has supported St George's Music Trust.

Exclusions

Support is NOT given to: advertising in charity brochures; animal welfare charities; appeals from individuals; the arts; enterprise/training; environment/heritage; political appeals; science/technology or sport.

Applications

In writing to the correspondent. Andrew Russell, Chairman of the management committee stated: 'For the present, and foreseeable future, it appears that the funds available for distribution by the trust will be fully absorbed by charitable projects with which the partners in Neville Russell have personal contact and it is therefore extremely unlikely that "cold calls" from other charities will receive consideration.'

Newarthill plc

40 Bernard Street, London WC1N 1LG
0171-837 3377

Correspondent: Alex Wardrope, Charity Co-ordinator

Chief officer: *Chairman:* Sir John Hedley Greenborough

Year end	Turnover	Pre-tax profit
31/10/97	£324,822,000	£7,064,000

Nature of company business
Principal activities: construction, property and investment.

UK employees: n/a

Charitable donations
1997: £132,000
1996: £68,000
1995: £57,000
1994: £54,000
1993: £78,000

Community support policy

The company has a preference for local charities in areas where it operates and charities in which a member of company is involved. Preferred areas of support are children and youth, and education. We have not been able to obtain any further information on the company's support, although total charitable donations almost doubled in the last year.

This is the parent company of Sir Robert McAlpine Ltd. McAlpine have two associated charitable trusts.

The Robert McAlpine Foundation

This gives to organisations supporting children and people who are deaf or elderly. Support is also given for education, hospices, medical research and social welfare. The foundation receives about 1,000 applications each year, but we are not sure how many are successful or the size of the grants given. The trustees meet in July and November; successful applicants are informed at the end of the year. Applications should be address to the Secretary of the Trustees of the Robert McAlpine Foundation, at the address above.

The McAlpine Educational Endowment

This trust is for 13 to 18 year olds, who have sound academic ability, show leadership potential and are facing financial hardship. The trust favours 10 particular schools, with referals coming from the headmasters. Applications should be address to the Secretary of the Trustees of the McAlpine Educational Endowment, at the address above.

Applications

In writing to the correspondent.

Newcastle Building Society

Portland House, New Bridge Street,
Newcastle upon Tyne NE1 8AL
0191-244 2000; Fax: 0191-244 2002
Website: www.newcastle.co.uk

Correspondent: Rachel Dodd, Corporate Communications Manager

Chief officers: *Chairman:* A A E Glenton;
Chief Executive: R J Hollinshead

Year end	Turnover	Pre-tax profit
31/12/97	n/a	£11,554,000

Nature of company business
Building society.

Main subsidiaries include: Adamscastle Ltd; Adamson Newcastle Ltd; Bank of Newcastle Ltd; Newcastle Bank Ltd.

UK employees: 543

Charitable donations
1997: £48,900
1996: £47,425
1995: £51,629
Membership: %Club

Community support policy
In its 1997 annual report the society stated that: 'over and above the substantial support given through our sponsorship programme, the society made donations to charities amounting to £48,900. There is a preference for charities in the North East. Preferred areas of support are the arts, children/youth, education, elderly people, sickness/disability charities, and sport'.

In addition to charitable donations, support is given through gifts in kind, joint promotions, and advice and mentoring.

The company is a member of the PerCent Club in the North East.

Exclusions
No support for advertising in charity brochures, animal welfare charities, appeals from individuals, overseas projects, political or religious appeals.

Applications
In writing to the correspondent.

News International plc

PO Box 495, Virginia Street, London E1 9XY
0171-782 6641; Fax: 0171-895 9020

Correspondent: Peter Rimmer, Community Affairs Manager

Chief officers: *Chairman:* K R Murdoch;
Chief Executive: A A Fischer

Year end	Turnover	Pre-tax profit
30/6/96	£1,007,100,000	£415,900,000

Nature of company business
Main activity: the printing and publishing of national newspapers. Other activities include television broadcasting by satellite and newsprint storage and distribution.

Main subsidiaries include: News Group Newspapers; Times Newspapers Holdings; The Times Supplements; Convoys; Broadsystem; British Sky Broadcasting (40%).

UK employees: n/a

Charitable donations
1996: £1,005,849
1995: £800,000
1994: £1,900,000
1993: £1,789,000
Total community contributions: £1,492,419

Community support policy
Unfortunately we were unable to obtain any up-to-date financial information for the company, the only figures available being for the News Corporation as a whole and not the UK company.

News International's programme aims to achieve a balance between national projects and those in areas where the company has a presence. Support for communities close to company locations is normally given by the local company. In the case of Wapping support is also given given through the St Katherine & Shadwell Trust (details of which can be found in *A Guide to the Major Trusts Volume 1*). In addition to Wapping, the main locations are Glasgow, Knowsley (Merseyside) and Peterborough.

Group policy: Donations to registered charities only. Preference for: newspaper related industry causes; literacy/education/training; environment; local projects in areas above.

Subsidiary companies: Local appeals are dealt with by the company's plants in Glasgow (contact – Tracey Crawford), Knowsley (contact – Kath Johnson), and Peterborough (contact – Jane Hamill). Local projects in Wapping are dealt with by the ECC charities sub-committee (contact – Kathleen Herron).

Total community contributions: In order to determine more accurately the company's overall level of charitable support, the Charities Aid Foundation were asked to carry out an audit in September 1996. As a result, a number of previously unrecorded fundraising activities were traced. Besides cash donations of about £1 million and good-cause sponsorship/gifts in kind to a value of about £400,000, an additional £2.5 milliion in 'facilitated fundraising' was identified. This was mainly accounted for by donations from readers to fundraising campaigns promoted by the company through free advertisements and editorials in their newspapers. Whilst we applaud, and would include the cost of providing free promotional space as part of community contributions, we feel it is misleading to include reader donations within this. All four newspapers devote editorial and advertising space to causes which are chosen to reflect their readers' concerns and priorities. The company also provides rent-free accommodation to the St Katherine & Shadwell Trust.

Subsidiary companies (including the plants already mentioned) are encouraged to pursue their own community affairs programmes within this policy framework.

Charitable donations: *Group community affairs policy* – preference is given to literacy, education and training; the local community in areas of company presence; the environment and newspaper industry causes. The company receive an average of about 60 applications each month from around the country, about 10 to 12 of which are supported. Grants range in size from £250 to an annual grant of £50,000 to the Prince's Youth Business Trust. The company does not, as a rule, take out advertisements on behalf of charitable causes.
Subsidiary companies – the policy and priorities are the same for subsidiaries as for the rest of the company. However, fundraising campaigns run by newspapers often reflect their readers' concerns and priorities rather than the company's policy, and the recipient causes are therefore chosen by the editor and editorial team.

Employee involvement: Preference is given for supporting charities in which a member of staff is involved. Staff are encouraged to become volunteers in their own time and to become school governors. A payroll giving scheme is operated. Part-time secondees from subsidiary companies have worked in an advisory capacity to government programmes.

In kind support: The group donates books, atlases and T-shirts for charitable raffles, auctions, etc.

Enterprise: The group supports The Prince's Youth Business Trust with £50,000 a year. The Times Supplements sometimes support enterprise agencies in an advisory capacity.

Education: The group sponsors the Rupert Murdoch Chair in Language and Communications at Oxford and a Lectureship in Management at Birbeck College in the University of London. It also provides educational materials for schools. Subsidiary companies are involved in local education/business partnerships. They provide educational materials for schools, student sponsorships, work-experience schemes for pupils and speakers for training and careers seminars.

Environment: The group has been involved with an initiative in Knowsley in conjunction with Groundwork Trust called Greenforce. It aims to improve the landscape within Knowsley, utilising help and assistance from local residents, schools and businesses as well as financing projects itself.

Exclusions

No support for fundraising events, advertising in charity brochures, appeals from individuals, religious or political appeals or local appeals not in areas of company presence. As a general rule the company does not make contributions to capital or building projects

Applications

In writing to the correspondent. The charities committee meets regularly. Unsuccessful applicants are given reasons and the corporate policy explained. Appeals to subsidiary companies should be made to managing directors, managing editors or editors. In some cases larger requests are referred to the charities committee. Sponsorship proposals to the group should be addressed to the Director of Marketing, News Group Newspapers or the Director of Marketing, Times Newspapers.

Next plc

Desford Road, Enderby, Leicester LE9 5AT
0116-286 6411

Correspondent: Ms Karen Bird, Charities Co-ordinator

Chief officers: *Chairman:* Lord Wolfson; *Chief Executive:* David Jones

Year end	Turnover	Pre-tax profit
31/1/98	£1,176,800,000	£184,000,000

Nature of company business
The principal activites of the group are high-street retailing, home shopping, customer services management and financial services.
Main subsidiaries include: Club 24; Vetura; Clydesdale Financial Services; Callscan.

UK employees: 12,743

Charitable donations

1998: £426,000
1997: £407,000
1996: £194,000
1995: £90,000
1994: £203,000
Membership: *BitC*

Community support policy

In addition to charitable donations totalling £426,000, the company also gives support to the community through good-cause sponsorship, joint promotions and gifts in kind. Support can be given in the form of gift vouchers, samples as prizes, faulty/old stock given to charities and staff time/involvement with projects.

Next continues to support charities in three ways:

Annual subscriptions

The company subscribes annually to the following national organisations:

Princess Royal Trust for Carers – Next is represented on both the regional and national committees. It sponsored a Leicestershire Carers centre.

Duke of Edinburgh Award – the company has formalised its relationship with the Duke of Edinburgh's Award, Charter for Business, and has informed all employees how they can become involved if they wish.

Business in the Community – the company is formalising plans to help/organise community-related projects within Leicestershire. Next are also considering opening up this opportunity to Store Managers to volunteer their own time, with projects initiated by themselves in their own communities.

Cottage Homes – a four-year covenant to improve the safety and quality of life of retired staff covered by the Mill Hill Cottage Appeal.

Retired and Senior Volunteer Programme – Next backed the production of a video to increase awareness of RSVP. The company will extend its support in showing the video at pre-retirement seminars and staff council meetings.

The company also donates office space to Homestart (UK) in Garfield House, London.

Next staff charity committee

The staff at Next have a charity committee which raises money. The committee has decided, after discussion with the different Staff Councils (and through them with employees), to have two social events a year to raise money for local organisations. The Sports & Social Committee will run the events with the Charity Committee providing support.

Future events will raise funds for local charities suggested by staff. Employees wishes will be taken into consideration following the results of a questionnaire distributed to staff. The committee is also looking at collection points for a variety of objects and is already committed to organising a toy appeal for Romania.

Small donations

A number of smaller donations are given to charities who write in. Priority is given to organisations local to the head office in Leicestershire and the warehouses in Leeds and Bradford in the form of cash or gift vouchers/samples to help with fundraising activities. The company also responds to emergency appeals with one-off cash donations, or by giving less than perfect clothing returned by the stores. The company has also recently established a 'Room to Care' policy by which a total of 6–8 rooms a year in hospitals/charities, chosen in line with the above guidelines, are furnished with Next interior products.

Local charities are supported by the branches where possible, who also have a budget for such purposes. This budget is held at head office by the Charity Co-ordinator, not in the stores.

Other support

Sponsorship – The company undertakes limited good cause and arts sponsorship (it sponsors the Royal Society of Arts).

In kind support – The company sometimes gives some of its merchandise or gift vouchers to charities free of charge as prizes or to help refugees.

Enterprise – The company is a member of Business in the Community but does not support enterprise agencies, nor is it involved in any local economic development initiatives.

Education – The company is involved in work experience schemes for school pupils.

Exclusions

It does not second staff to voluntary organisations. No support is given to political causes and the company prefers not to give for adverts in publications and/or sponsorship of an event or individual – the companies involvement in these areas is limited.

Applications

All donation requests should be sent to the Personnel Department where they will be carefully considered, with priority being given to local charities, ie. local to Leicester and Leeds (this is where the majority of employees are based). A budget has been specifically allocated for this purpose. As such all letters and telephone requests should be directed to the Charity Co-ordinator on ext 2872 and she will reply.

Full details of the company's involvement are carefully recorded and further information can be obtained from the correspondent. Details of charitable donations will be presented to the Board and be available for all members of the Charity Committee.

NFC plc

The NFC Foundation, The Merton Centre, 45 St Peter's Street, Bedford MK40 2UB
01234-272222; Fax: 01234-261884
Email: val.corrigan@nfc.co.uk
Website: www.nfcplc.com

Correspondent: Valerie Corrigan, Director of Community Affairs

Chief officers: *Chairman:* Sir Christopher Bland; *Chief Executive:* Gerry Murphy; *Managing Director:* Terry Stockley

Year end	Turnover	Pre-tax profit
30/9/97	£2,412,000,000	£88,000,000

Nature of company business
The activities of the group comprise international logistics and moving services.

Main subsidiaries include: Tradeteam Ltd; Pickfords Ltd.

Main brands include: Excel Logistics; Tankfreight; Tradeteam; Pickfords.

UK employees: 19,500

Charitable donations

1998: £550,000
1997: £500,000
1996: £386,000
1995: £599,000
1994: £951,000

Total community contributions: £1,200,000

Membership: BitC %Club

Community support policy

Charitable giving is channelled through the NFC Foundation. The company is a member of the PerCent Club, and gives a percentage of pre-tax profits to the foundation. The foundation was also given 1% of the company's equity in 1988. The NFC Social Responsibilities Council supports 'enlightened and caring employment policies… the stability of UK society and… the care of its employees into retirement'. Money is given in North America and Australia in response to requests from employees and shareholders there.

In 1997/98, total community contributions were £1.2 million including £550,000 in charitable donations. In addition to the latter, the main areas of support are through gifts in kind, storage and training schemes. The company operates payroll giving schemes and matches employee fundraising. Staff are allowed company time off to volunteer.

The company supports national charities and local charities throughout the UK. Preference for causes concerned with: children/youth; education; elderly people; enterprise/training; sickness/disability; and social welfare. Support may also be given to local charities connected with road safety. Grants to national organisations range from £250 to £10,000 and to local organisations from £50 to £500.

In 1997/98, the foundation received £550,000 from NFC plc and £353,000 in dividend income on its investments. Grants totalled £656,000 with a further £350,000 charitable expenditure. 'During the year, the foundation adopted a new strategy for its charitable support and became more focused on transportation and mobility issues.' This included support for the NFC Young Drivers Scholarship and Truck and Child Safety.

Grants included £473,000 from unrestricted funds, including £92,000 in matching funds for employee, pensioner and shareholder fundraising. A further £183,000 of restricted funds was granted, primarily to The Royal National Institute for the Blind.

In 1997, the largest donations were to Airborne (£60,000); Motability (£45,000); Furniture Resource Centre (£40,000); RNIB (£100,000) and Avon and Somerset Police (£20,000).

Pensioners' Association: The main focus of support by the foundation is for former employees of the company. It finances pensioner visitors, the association's 70 branches, and publication of a pensioners' magazine.

Education: NFC encourages links with education.

Road safety: NFC promotes safer roads through its 'Truck and Child Safety' programme, and the NFC Young Drivers Scholarship.

Exclusions

No support for advertising in brochures, animal welfare charities, appeals from individuals, the arts, environment/heritage, fundraising events, medical research, overseas projects, political appeals, religious appeals, science/technology or sport.

Applications

Application should be made in writing using the guidelines available from the correspondent.

Other information: Appeals are too numerous for all to have a positive outcome, so prospective applicants should ensure that their appeals fall within the company's donations policy. Charities are also advised to send a copy of their latest audited accounts. The company is largely employee owned and confers with shareholders as to which charities should be supported.

Information available: The company reports on its community involvement in its annual report.

Norcros plc

Ladyfield House, Station Road, Wilmslow, Cheshire SK9 1BU
01625-549010; Fax: 01625-549011

Chief officers: *Chairman:* M E Doherty; *Chief Executive:* J Matthews

Year end	Turnover	Pre-tax profit
31/3/98	£240,000,000	£6,000,000

Nature of company business
The principal activities are in two divisions: ceramics; print and packaging.

Main subsidiaries include: H & R Johnson Tiles Ltd; Triton PLC; Norprint International Ltd; Norprint Labelling Systems; Magnordata International; Autotype International Ltd.

UK employees: 3,567

Charitable donations

1998: £36,000
1997: £44,000
1996: £22,000
1995: £52,000
1994: £45,000

Community support policy

The company rarely supports national charities, preferring to support charities in Berkshire, Stoke-on-Trent, Nuneaton and Wilmslow (its main areas of operation) and charities that have an industrial link with the company. Preferred areas of support are children/youth, education and medical research.

Exclusions

No support for circular appeals, brochure advertising, campaigning work by charities, appeals from individuals, school expeditions, denominational (religious) appeals, local appeals not in areas of company presence, large national or overseas appeals. Arts sponsorship is not undertaken.

Applications

In writing to the correspondent.

Nortel plc

1b Portland Place, London W1N 3AA
0171-291 3066

Correspondent: Catherine Bailey, Manager Government Relations UK

Chief officer: *Chairman:* D Ball

Year end	Turnover	Pre-tax profit
31/12/97	£1,211,700,000	£67,400,000

Nature of company business
The company's main activity is telecommunications and electronics.

UK employees: 8,495

North

Charitable donations
1997: £184,700
1996: n/a
1995: £174,700
1994: £157,000
1993: £52,347
Membership: *ABSA BitC*

Community support policy
The company only supports charities local to areas of company presence and those relevant to the company's business. There is a preference for education, enterprise/training and science/technology. The main beneficiary in 1997 was the Princess Royal Trust for Carers. The company has several branches in the UK, which adminster their own donations budgets. Applications sent to the address above will be forwarded to the appropriate location. The company sites include Central London, Harlow, Maidenhead, New Southgate, Paignton, South Wales and Wakefield.

In addition to charitable donations of £184,700, the main areas of support are gifts in kind, training schemes and education sponsorship.

The company is a member of Business in the Community and ABSA. It operates the CAF payroll giving scheme.

Exclusions
No support for appeals from individuals, elderly people, overseas projects, advertising in charity brochures, animal welfare charities, the arts, environment/heritage, fundraising events, medical research, social welfare, sport, political appeals or religious appeals.

Applications
In writing to the correspondent.

North West Water Ltd

Dawson House, Liverpool Road, Great Sankey,
Warrington WA5 3LW
01925-234000

Correspondent: Sharon King, Community Partnership Officer

Chief officers: *Chairman:* Sir Christopher Harding; *Chief Executive:* Derek Green; *Managing Director:* Harry Croft

Year end	Turnover	Pre-tax profit
31/3/98	£894,700,000	£238,700,000

Nature of company business
The provision of water and waste water services in the north west of England.

UK employees: 5,000

Charitable donations
1998: Nil
1997: Nil
1996: n/a
1995: £103,025
Total community contributions: £2,000,000
Membership: *ABSA BitC*

Community support policy
The company provides the majority of its community support in projects relating to its business of water and waste water, and through long-term partnerships with organisations operating in the North West.

In 1996, a community partnership policy was set up (as a response to stakeholder consultation) with four focus areas:

- education
- environment
- enterprise skills and regional leadership
- extra needs.

The company has contributed £2 million a year to this programme for the last two years.

Community partners include: the Lake District National Park, RNIB, RNID, Age Concern, and British Trust for Conservation Volunteers. The company gives gifts in kind, operate the WaterAid payroll giving scheme, and support employee volunteering/charitable activities by allowing company time off.

Education: The company has a network of Environmental Education Centres, which offer free of charge facilities and resources to all schools and colleges in the North West.

Enterprise skills & regional leadership: The company works with organisations such as North West Business Leadership Team, North West Tourist Board, and a number of private/public sector partnerships. The company is a member of Business in the Community and provides offices to the organisation.

Exclusions
North West Water does not support advertising in charity brochures, appeals from individuals, political or religious appeals, the arts, medical research, overseas projects, sport, or any activities outside the north west of England. Long-term partnerships relating to, and resulting in, mutual benefit for community, business and employees are favoured over one-off sponsorships.

Applications
In writing to the correspondent. Full details of what to include in a partnership proposal are in the community policy leaflet. To obtain a copy telephone: 01925-233032.

Northern Electric plc

Carliol House, Market Street, Newcastle-upon-Tyne NE1 6NE
0191-221 2000; Fax: 0191-235 2109
Email: corporate.affairs.@northern-electric.co.uk
Website: www.northern-electric.co.uk

Correspondent: Julian L Kenyon, Community Affairs Officer

Chief officers: *Chairman:* David Sokol;
Chief Executive: Greg Abel

Year end	Turnover	Pre-tax profit
31/3/98	£980,400,000	£109,600,000

Nature of company business
Principal activities: electricity and gas distribution and supply, and electrical and gas appliance retailing.

Main subsidiaries include: Northern Trading and Collection Services Ltd; Gas UK Ltd; Northgas Ltd; Northern Transport Finance Ltd; Northern Metering Services Ltd; Northern Utility Services Ltd; Northern Information Systems Ltd; Combined Power Systems Ltd; Sovereign Exploration Ltd.

UK employees: 3,500

Charitable donations

1998: £223,000
1997: £223,000
1996: £223,000
1995: £200,000
1994: £229,000

Total community contributions: £1,000,000

Membership: *ABSA BitC %Club*

Community support policy

The company has produced detailed and clear information on its community programme and policies. It states: 'our overriding objectives are to help create facilities of benefit to the community, to assist in economic growth and to widen opportunities for local people. We will give support in cash, kind and employee time to projects which improve the quality of life of people in this region through community regeneration, training and personal development, job creation, the arts, sport and recreation and through initiatives to improve opportunities for young people and people with disabilities.' Areas of support also include elderly people, environment/heritage and fundraising events.

Community contributions (£1 million in 1997/98) include in kind support, secondments and staff time, award schemes and community festivals, in addition to charitable donations. The company is a member of the North East PerCent Club and Business in the Community.

Charitable donations: The company supports only local charities in its area of operation (ie. Northumberland, Tyne & Wear, Cleveland, Durham and North Yorkshire) and of perceived value to the community. Grants to local organisations usually range from £200 to £15,000. Main beneficiaries in 1997/98 included the three community foundations in the area (the Cleveland Community Foundation, County Durham Foundation and Tyne & Wear Foundation) as well as Marie Curie Cancer Care and Coalition Against Crime.

Other community support: In kind support has included the provision of office furniture and computer equipment either free of charge or at cost price to the voluntary sector, provision of trade-in electrical appliances to voluntary organisations and for training in workshops for disabled people, vehicles mainly to training organisations and the printing of literature by in-house printing unit.

Employee involvement: Staff are also allowed time off for activity of community benefit and are encouraged to become volunteers and school governors in their own time. A payroll giving scheme is operated by the company, which also runs a matching scheme for employee fundraising, contributing about £10,000 in total last year.

Enterprise: The company supports local enterprise and development agencies such as Wearside Initiative, Project North East and Northern Development Company. The company supports Business in the Community. It seconds staff to enterprise and other projects and has supported the Wearside Opportunity and Hartlepool Enterprise Agency.

Education: Support includes financial support for local educational institutions, work placements for local school pupils, teaching resources for special-needs education, and bursaries, industrial experience and vacation training for undergraduates.

Environment: In addition to the company's own initiative to promote awareness of environmental issues and initiatives to promote energy efficiency, a range of local environmental organisations are supported including the Botanic Centre at Middlesbrough, Washington Wildlife Centre, local civic societies and wildlife trusts.

The arts: The company is a member of ABSA and sponsors a range of activities, with an important element being the opportunity to provide for education outreach work. Support in the form of sponsorship has included the Royal Shakespeare Company in Newcastle and the Northern Electric Arts Awards.

Exclusions

No support for circular appeals, advertising in national charity brochures, appeals from individuals, purely denominational (religious) appeals, local appeals not in areas of company presence, large national appeals, science/technology, animal welfare charities or overseas projects.

Applications

In writing to the correspondent.

Information available: The company reports on its community support in its annual report and in a booklet, *Energy for People*.

Northern Foods plc

Beverley House, St Stephen's Square, Hull HU1 3XG
01482-325432; Fax: 01482-226136
Website: www.northern-foods.co.uk

Correspondent: Mrs Helen Bray, Social Responsibility Committee

Chief officers: *Chairman:* C R Haskins; *Chief Executive:* A J Stewart

Year end	Turnover	Pre-tax profit
31/3/98	£1,832,200,000	£151,600,000

Nature of company business
Manufacturer and distributor of chilled foods, meat and convenience foods, biscuits and savoury pastry products.
Note: In March 1998, the company demerged Express Dairies which has a separate entry in this guide.

Main subsidiaries include: Cavaghan and Gray; Batchelors (Ireland); Bowyers; Elkes Biscuits; Evesham Foods; Fenland Foods; Fox's Biscuits; Grain D'or; Gunstones Bakery; Walter Holland & Son; Kara Foods; NFT Distribution; Palethorpes; Park Cake Bakeries; Paynes; Pennine Foods; Pork Farms; Rawmarsh Foods; Riverside Bakery; Smiths Flour Mills; Trafford Park Bakery; Matthew Walker.

UK employees: 20,655

Charitable donations

1998: £796,000
1997: £727,000
1996: £702,000
1995: £695,000
1994: £710,000
Membership: *ABSA BitC %Club*

Community support policy

Northern Foods is a member of the PerCent Club, Business in the Community and ABSA. It commits a page of its latest annual report to reporting on its community involvement, including listing 36 of the charities it supports.

Recipient organisations should normally be registered charities. Resources are concentrated on three areas: relief of deprivation in inner cities (including enterprise and training); sustainable aid to the Third World; and selective education projects. There is a preference for children/youth and social welfare, especially for local charities in areas of company presence eg. Sheffield, Manchester, Nottingham and Batley. Grants to national organisations range from £5,000 to £10,000 and to local organisations from £25 to £5,000.

The following is a sample of the charities listed in the annual report: Barnardo's, Challenge for Youth, Corporate Responsibility Youth Project, National Council for One Parent Families, National Mentoring Consortium, Opera North Community Education, Scope Fast Track, South Yorkshire Community Foundation, St Anne's Shelter & Housing Action, and Theatre in Prisons Project.

In inner cities and towns the company supports projects tackling unemployment, homelessness, youth crime and vandalism. Organisations supported include: Prince's Youth Business Trust, QED – Bradford, Rathbone Community Industry and Runnymede Trust.

The company's links with the Third World go back over many years. It has consistently supported Oxfam since the 1950s, and also supports One World Action, Intermediate Technology, and the Get Ahead Foundation in South Africa.

Support for education includes financial support and gifts in kind to schools and universities, particularly those close to its companies or from which it recruits staff. It is also involved with a number of industry-education links including Compacts and support for CRAC and UBI.

The Northern Foods Association covers all employees. Through primarily a sports and social club its activities include fundraising for charities, which is encouraged by the company. Employees at many of the companies are involved in charitable and community activities and a number have participated in short assignments or longer term secondments to community projects. A number of directors and senior managers serve as trustees, advisers or non-executive directors of these groups. The Give As You Earn payroll giving scheme is operated.

Other community support: The company is a member of Business in the Community and supports enterprise agencies. In kind support is given in the form of stock or equipment and the provision of professional services free of charge.

Exclusions

The company does not generally support the larger national charities, religious or political bodies. Support given to health charities and the arts is extremely limited. No grants for circular appeals, advertising in charity brochures, animal welfare charities, appeals from individuals, elderly people, environment/heritage, fundraising events, medical appeals, science/technology, sickness charities or sport.

Applications

In writing to the committee, including supporting information. Applications are considered by a committee comprising Directors and Executives which meets on a quarterly basis.

Northern Rock plc

Northern Rock House, Gosforth,
Newcastle upon Tyne NE3 4PL
0191-285 7191; Fax: 0191-284 8470
Website: www.nrock.co.uk

Correspondent: Christopher Jobe, Group Secretary

Chief officers: *Chairman:* Robert Dickinson; *Chief Executive:* Leo Finn

Year end	Turnover	Pre-tax profit
31/12/97	n/a	£148,500,000

Nature of company business
The main purpose of the group is the provision of housing finance, savings and a range of related personal financial and banking services.

Main subsidiaries include: Regency Care Homes; Kingsclear Homes.

UK employees: 4,521

Charitable donations

1997: £2,000,000
Membership: *ABSA %Club*

Community support policy

The conversion of Northern Rock Building Society into a public company was completed on 1 October 1997. An integral part of this was the formation of a charitable body, the Northern Rock Foundation. This was launched in January 1998 and is entitled to receive a covenant of about 5% of annual pre-tax profits of Northen Rock plc.

The main aim of the foundation is to help improve the conditions of those disadvantaged in society by age, infirmity, poverty or other circumstances. The contribution for 1997 amounted to £2 million. Based upon the 1997 results, and assuming no exceptional costs, a full year's covenant would have amounted to £9.4 million. The foundation holds a special category of shares which are non-dividend bearing and non-voting. In the event of a change of control of the company the covenant would cease, and the shares held by the foundation would be converted into 15% of the company's ordinary shares, thus creating an endowment. In the first half of 1998, the company gave £5.1 million, and expenditure on grants by the foundation in 1998 was expected to be about £6 million.

The Northern Rock Foundation

The policy of the foundation will be to support charitable causes mainly, but not exclusively, in the North East of England. Applications will be considered from Scotland, Cumbria, the North West and Yorkshire. Grants will be given for limited capital, core or project funding and for varying periods of time. For any type of grant it must be clear what the organisation's plans are, following the end of funding from the foundation. It is also preferable to show support from other funders which helps to 'establish confidence in your project'. The foundation states: 'We wish to encourage cooperation and partnership between organisations'.

The foundation has launched two major programmes for 1999 on:
- help for disabled people (£3 million)
- small grants up to £10,000 for welfare and community groups (£1 million).

There are also three pilot programmes (with initial budgets up to £200,000) and operating to begin with only in Tyne & Wear, Northumberland, Durham and Teesside. During 1999, they may be prolonged or extended, geographically or financially. These are outlined below.

Programme for disabled people and carers

The first programme of grants, which is still running, was concerned exclusively with charities working for people with disabilities and carers. The programme aims to improve the quality of life of people with disabilities and carers by promoting independence, raising disability awareness and enabling disabled people to play a full and active role in society. The foundation is keen to support self-managed and self-help organisations, especially those which involve members of the beneficiary group.

It is interested in applications from projects which remove barriers preventing disabled people from becoming involved in work, social, leisure and personal development opportunities. Projects in the following areas will be considered:
- independent living
- physical access improvements
- improved services in rural communities
- improving information
- removing barriers from social/leisure opportunities
- adult education and training
- personal development programmes
- employment opportunties
- housing initiatives.

Applicants must demonstrate how they will consult and involve disabled people in the design and provision of improvements and how they will ensure good use of the facilities or services they want to provide.

Applications from carers groups are also welcomed for projects to assist carers in maintaining their own health, skills and access to social and cultural opportunities. This can include respite care and assisting hospices.

Small organisations and projects

A scheme for small organisations and small projects for requests from £1,000 to £10,000. It is designed to support the following: projects with a limited life span, core funding lasting up to four years (the total amount not exceeding £10,000) and capital or equipment purchase.

This small grants scheme will not contribute to large capital appeals. Organisations requesting core funding must have an annual turnover of no more than £25,000. Larger organisations can apply for a new project that has a clearly separate budget. An item or amount for capital work should not cost more than £15,000. It is particularly interested in supporting the following areas:
- caring – the provision of respite and care
- disability
- homelessness – prevention, support and access to housing
- improvements to the quality of life for older people
- money management schemes
- self-help schemes to enable communities to improve their living environment
- young people at risk, especially initiatives offering alternatives to crime.

For this scheme it is not necessary to be a registered charity. You must show that your organisation has a legal framework, is established for public benefit and has purposes that are recognised by law as charitable. Evidence in the form of a written constitution or other legal document will need to be provided. It must be arranged for a registered charity to receive any grant on your behalf.

Northern Rock

Pilot programmes

During 1998/99, a pilot is being conducted in the North East for the second grants programme (Tyne and Wear, Northumberland, Durham and Teesside only). This is titled: *Developing our communities* and covers the following headings: Promotion of good parenting, Development of Literacy, and Community Self-Help.

Promotion of good parenting

To promote parenting skills among existing and prospective parents. The foundation welcomes applications from organisations or initiatives that:

- help parents in difficulty through stress, unemployment, family break-up or other causes to develop or improve their parenting skills
- support parents in dealing with difficult or challenging behaviour in their children
- help prepare young people for parenthood – with preference given to initiatives outside the formal education system
- promote better parenting by fathers including those living apart from their children
- help new partners of parents, or step-parents, find an appropriate parenting role in a new family
- advocate conditions that nurture good parenting eg. the promotion of policies in buildings, work and leisure opportunities, etc., designed to recognise and support parental responsibility.

In all cases, the aim must be to help parents reach a state where they are confident in their own abilities to bring up their children. This programme is not intended for initiatives helping parents of children with disabilites: proposers of such schemes are directed to the Disability and caring programme (see above).

Development of literacy

To assist projects that help those who have emerged from the education system without literacy skills. Projects addressing the needs of adults, either employed or not, and young adults and recent school leavers will be welcomed. In addition to accepting applications from agencies or organisations specialising in the promotion of literacy, approaches from other non-specialists who have innovative ideas or proposals to tackle this subject will be considered. In such cases, partnerships that include experts in the field are preferred.

This programme is not designed to support either mainstream educational needs or the special needs of school age children with disabilities and/or communication problems.

Community self-help

To support voluntary groups in creating local solutions to local problems. Applications are invited from groups intending to tackle, for example, poverty, social exclusion, vandalism, local crime, the absence of basic amenities, or other sources of disadvantage from which they suffer themselves. Groups may have been created specifically to address the problem or may already exist, but in both cases they are likely to be small and not to have paid workers.

Grants may be provided for equipment or running costs. Salaries are unlikely to be met. Projects begun by the beneficiaries themselves will be strongly favoured over those initiated by outside agencies. Applicants should:

- explain what is the problem they are trying to solve
- outline what their proposed solution is
- describe how they arrived at the scheme they propose
- describe how they will go about their activities including a timetable if possible
- provide some evidence to show that they are the right people to take on the task or describe who will help them
- explain how much money they need and show what it will be spent on
- tell us how they will know whether or not they have succeeded.

Groups must show that their purposes are charitable and should provide two referees who can vouch for them. Grants must be made to or through a registered charity, therefore groups may need to seek advice or help from their Council for Voluntary Service or Voluntary Organisations Development Agency.

Exclusions

These include:

- organisations which are not registered charities (see small grants scheme)
- charities which trade, have substantial reserves or are in serious debt
- national charities which do not have a strong significance in the North East and the North
- open-ended funding agreements
- general appeals, sponsorship and marketing appeals
- retrospective grants
- endowment funds
- replacement of statutory funding
- activities primarily the responsibility of central or local government, including local education, health authorities and National Health Trusts
- individuals, including students and animal welfare
- mainstream educational activity
- medical research, hospitals (other than hospices) and medical centres
- environmental projects which do not accord with the main objectives of the foundation
- buildings other than charitable schemes for housing individuals
- promotion of religion
- fabric appeals for places of worship
- corporate applications for founder membership of a charity
- loans or business finance expenditure
- overseas travel.

Applications

On a form obtainable from the Grants Manager, 21 Lansdowne Terrace, Gosforth, Newcastle upon Tyne NE3 1HP
0191-284 8412; Fax: 0191-284 8413

For applications over £10,000: A brief supporting statement should be added (no more than two pages of A4) which should include the following:
- a timetable for the project
- details of how the project meets the foundation's objectives
- the organisation's aims and procedures which enable it to carry out the project
- amount requested, the overall project budget and information about applications to other funding sources
- how the project will be evaluated. A copy of your current year's budget and most recent management accounts and a copy of your most recent annual report and audited accounts should be attached.

Applications are assigned to one member of staff whose name you will be given, a result would normally be given in three months. The assessment process will include a telephone conversation or a visit in person.

For applications under £10,000: These will be dealt with on a 'fast track' basis. As much as is practical of the above information should be provided. The application may still be followed up in the same way as stated above.

Making your application as clear and concise as possible will normally lead to a quicker result. The foundation aims to acknowledge straight away applications which are ineligible.

Northern & Shell Group Ltd

Northern & Shell Tower, City Harbour, London E14 9GL
0171-308 5090

Correspondent: R C Desmond, Chairman

Chief officers: *Chairman:* R C Desmond;
Managing Director: M S Ellice

Year end	Turnover	Pre-tax profit
30/6/94	£15,559,415	(£1,313,681)

Nature of company business
Publishing and investment.

Main subsidiaries include: Export Magazine Distributors; Fitzroy; OK Magazines; Sightline Publications; Sorse Distribution; Green Magazine Company.

UK employees: 127

Charitable donations
1994: £67,716
1993: £117,376

Community support policy

Unfortunately, we have not been able to obtain any financial information on the company since that for 1994 and do not know if the company has maintained its level of charitable giving. It previously provided the following information on its donations policy.

The focus of support is on: young people; elderly people; and the publishing community's own charity – Old Ben. In addition to charitable donations the company produces brochures and catalogues for many charities.

Applications
In writing to the correspondent.

Northumbrian Water Group plc

Abbey Road, Pity Me, Durham DH1 5FJ
0191-383 2222

Correspondent: John Mowbray, Customer Relations Manager

Chief officers: *Chairman:* Sir Michael Straker;
Chief Executive: David Cranston

Year end	Turnover	Pre-tax profit
31/3/95	£509,600,000	£147,400,000

Nature of company business
Water supply and sewage services.

UK employees: n/a

Charitable donations
1997: £134,660
1996: n/a
1995: £95,691
1994: £96,000
1993: £193,000
Membership: *ABSA BitC %Club*

Community support policy

The company is a member of the PerCent Club and Business in the Community. It supports local charities in its area of operation and appeals relevant to company business. Preferred areas of support are children and youth, education, enterprise, environment and heritage. Grants range from £50 to £10,000, although most are for less than £1,000, averaging around £200 to £300. The three community foundations in the area all receive support ie. the Tyne & Wear Foundation, Cleveland Foundation and County Durham Foundation.

The above figure also includes sponsorship, with emphasis on educational projects relevant to the water industry such as engineering scholarships. Three educational establishments, Durham Business School, Sunderland University and Newcastle University are all receiving long-term sponsorship. Local schools also benefit with CD-ROMs and teaching packs.

The company has established two funds: the Kick-Start Fund, helping in the creation of jobs and in 1997, the Northumbrian Water Environmental Trust, to take advantage of landfill tax legislation.

The arts: The company is a member of ABSA, it has sponsored the RSC over the last three years.

Exclusions

No support for circular appeals, advertising in charity brochures, local appeals not in areas of company presence,

Norwich

large national appeals or overseas projects (other than support for WaterAid).

Applications

In writing to the correspondent.

Norwich Union plc

Surrey Street, Norwich NR1 3NG
01603-622200; Fax: 01603-687253
Website: www.norwich-union.co.uk

Correspondent: Group Corporate Affairs

Chief officers: *Chairman:* G W Paul; *Chief Executive:* R J Harvey

Year end	Turnover	Pre-tax profit
31/12/97	n/a	£590,000,000

Nature of company business
The transaction of all classes of insurance business (other than industrial insurance) and associated investment activities.

Main subsidiaries include: Haven Insurance Policies Ltd; Hill House Hammond Ltd; Maritime Insurance Co Ltd; Scottish Union & National Insurance Co; Security Insurance Group Ltd; The General Practice Finance Corpn Ltd.

UK employees: 12,263

Charitable donations

1997: £290,000
1996: £276,000
1995: £249,000
1994: £257,000
1993: £253,000

Membership: *ABSA BitC %Club*

Community support policy

Norwich Union is a member of the PerCent Club and ABSA. Non-cash support is provided through sponsorship, secondments and training schemes, eg. sponsorship of St John Ambulance to provide the public with training in First Aid. Local sponsorship in the Norwich, Sheffield and Eastleigh areas falls into two broad categories: staff-led initiatives – where the company aims to supply resources to aid community projects staff are already involved with and projects with links to education (through a number of schools) and the environment.

Charitable donations: The company has a preference for appeals relevant to company business, community projects in the Norwich, Sheffield and Eastleigh areas, and charities in the fields of crime prevention, and health and safety. For the foreseeable future, the company is focusing its program on fewer 'key' charities. Main grant beneficiaries during 1997 included: St John Ambulance, Childline, Help the Aged, Crime Stoppers and Norfolk Accident Rescue Service.

Main areas of support are children/youth, education, elderly people, enterprise/training, environment/heritage, fundraising events (only through the company's staff charity of the year and its voluntary staff award scheme), sickness/disability charities, causes with a link to protection and social welfare. Under the staff voluntary award scheme, Norwich Union staff who are actively involved with a registered charity in their local community can apply for a donation.

A payroll giving scheme (Give As You Earn) is in operation, while the company matches employee fundraising for its Charity of the Year, which in 1998 is Childline.

Enterprise: The company is a member of Business in the Community and supports enterprise agencies.

Education: The company contributes to national education in industry initiatives including Industry in Education, Young Enterprise and Business in the Community eg. Aim High.

Environment: The company has an environmental policy and actively supports a number of conservation initiatives.

Exclusions

No support for brochure advertising, animal welfare, individuals, teams, fundraising events, overseas projects, political appeals and religious appeals.

Applications

In writing to the correspondent. Sponsorship proposals should be addressed to: Catherine Demicco, Group Corporate Affairs, 25–27 Surrey Street, Norwich NR1 3TA.

Nycomed Amersham plc

Amersham Place, Little Chalfont, Buckinghamshire HP7 9NA
01494-544000; Fax: 01494-542266

Correspondent: Matthew Butler, Director of Corporate Affairs

Chief officers: *Chairman:* Johan Fr Odfjell; *Chief Executive:* W M Castell

Year end	Turnover	Pre-tax profit
31/12/97	£568,100,000	£78,900,000

Nature of company business
This company was formed through the merger of Amersham International plc with the Norwegian company Nycomed ASA. Development, manufacture and sale of specialised products for research-based biotechnology supply and for the diagnosis and treatment of disease. It also operates a pharmaceutical business. Major UK locations are Amersham and Cardiff.

Main subsidiaries include: Amersham Pharmacia Biotech.

UK employees: n/a

Charitable donations

1997: £44, 898 (nine months)
1996: £87,463
1995: £63,000
1994: £56,932
1993: £52,857

Total community contributions: £117,335

Membership: *BitC %Club*

Community support policy

The company is a member of the PerCent Club, Business in the Community and The Environment Council. In addition to charitable donations, the company gave over £70,000 in other contributions, including gifts in kind and expertise put at the service of community programmes. The company also reported briefly on its community and environmental initiatives in its latest annual report.

Charitable donations: At local (in areas of company presence), national and international level, the company directs its giving towards healthcare, education and the environment. Company operating sites in the UK are south Buckinghamshire, Cardiff and Gloucester. Other causes occasionally supported include: children/youth; elderly people; enterprise/training; fundraising events; medical research; sickness/disability; social welfare; science/technology. The company occasionally advertises in charity brochures.

Employee involvement: The company supports employee initiatives and during 1997 provided matching funds for the British Heart Foundation.

Education: The company is a member of Buckinghamshire and South Glamorgan Education Business Partnerships and other local schemes. A more recent initiative is a programme called SET to Help, which is linked to the national science, engineering and technology scheme, with a focus on the promotion of science education in primary schools; a network of employee volunteers is offering practical help to local primary school teachers, starting with a science workshop.

Exclusions

No support for appeals from individuals, the arts, sport, overseas projects, political or religious appeals.

Applications

In writing to the correspondent.

Oakhill Group Ltd

1st Floor, Seacourt Tower, Westway, Oxford OX2 0JG
01865-204300; Fax: 01865-388400

Correspondent: E McCabe, Managing Director

Chief officer: *Managing Director:* E McCabe

Year end	Turnover	Pre-tax profit
30/11/97	£779,305,000	(£6,861,000)

Nature of company business
Car and commercial vehicle distribution.

Main subsidiaries include: Hartwells Garages Ltd; Hartford Motors Ltd; Hartwell Property Investment Co Ltd; Oxford Property Co Ltd; Trimoco Holdings PLC.

UK employees: n/a

Charitable donations
1997: £263,375
1996: £185,927
1995: £42,395
1994: £196,257

Community support policy

The company has increased its level of giving markedly over the last two years. It supports both national and local charities with a preference for those concerned with education.

The company also has employee volunteering and payroll giving schemes.

Applications

In writing to the correspondent.

Ocean Group plc

Ocean House, The Ring, Bracknell, Berkshire RG12 1AN
01344-302000; Fax: 01344-710031

Correspondent: M Edgar, Human Resources Manager

Chief officers: *Chairman:* N M S Rich;
Chief Executive: J M Allan

Year end	Turnover	Pre-tax profit
31/12/97	£1,164,000,000	£302,000,000

Nature of company business
The main activities of the group are international logistics management, contract logistics, marine services and environmental services.

Main subsidiaries include: MSAS Cargo International; Marken; McGregor Cory; Cory Environmental; Cory Towage; Mercury Holdings.

Charitable donations
1997: £186,000
1996: £7,000
1995: £11,000
Membership: *BitC   %Club*

Community support policy

The company is a member of the PerCent Club and following two years when the declared donations figure was exceptionally low, has seen a dramatic increase in its level of giving.

The only information we have on the company's policy is that it contributes to charities on a national and local basis, with a preference for local charities in areas of company presence.

Exclusions

No support for advertising in charity brochures, purely denominational (religious) appeals, local appeals not in areas of company presence or capital appeals.

Applications

In writing to the correspondent.

Orange

Orange plc

St James Court, Great Park Road, Almondsbury Park, Bradley Stoke, Bristol BS12 4QJ
01454-624600; Fax: 01454-618501

Correspondent: Siobhan McBrien, Sponsorship Manager

Chief officers: *Chairman:* C Fok; *Managing Director:* H R Snook

Year end	Turnover	Pre-tax profit
31/12/97	£914,000,000	(£139,000,000)

Nature of company business
The main activities are the provision of wirefree personal communications services. In addition to Orange services, in the UK the group operates Hutchison Cellular Services and Hutchison Paging.

Main subsidiaries include: Hutchinson Ltd.

UK employees: 4,586

Charitable donations
1997: £261,500
1996: £257,500
1995: £7,000
Membership: *BitC*

Community support policy

The figure above (£261,500) again included £250,000 to the Millennium Seed Bank Appeal (a registered charity) organised by the Royal Botanic Gardens, Kew, the second of ten annual payments of £250,000. One of the most ambitious international conservation projects ever undertaken, the project aims to store seeds from all of the UK's flora and from 10% of the worlds 250,000 plant species by the year 2010.

In addition to the above, the group made charitable cash donations of £11,500 and provided support through sponsorship and gifts in kind to various community projects in Bristol, Hertford, and Darlington totalling around £130,000.

Employees charitable fundraising activities contributed £15,000 to various causes including NCH Action for Children, Children in Need, and the Falciu Orphange in Romania. Employees are also encouraged to donate their time and experience, particularly to educational projects.

Applications
In writing to the correspondent.

Osborne & Little plc

49 Temperley Road, London SW12 8QE
0181-675 2255; Fax: 0181-673 8254

Correspondent: Becky Metcalfe, Public Relations Manager

Chief officer: *Chairman:* Sir Peter Osborne

Year end	Turnover	Pre-tax profit
31/3/98	£36,051,000	£5,255,000

Nature of company business
The main activities are the design and distribution of fine furnishing fabrics and wallpapers.

Main subsidiaries include: Tamesa Fabrics Ltd.
Main brands include: Osborne & Little; Nina Campbell; Liberty Furnishings.

UK employees: 248

Charitable donations
1998: £67,351
1997: £60,698
1996: £33,061
1995: £26,108
1994: £29,023

Community support policy

The company prefers to support local charities where it operates, appeals relevant to its business and those where an employee is involved. Preferred areas of support are children and youth, education (design) and arts (design).

Recently, the main charity supported has been Trinity Hospice in Clapham.

Exclusions
The company does not advertise in charity brochures.

Applications
In writing to the correspondent.

Oxford Instruments PLC

Old Station Way, Eynsham, Witney OX8 1TL
01865-881437; Fax: 01865-881944
Email: kate.nayler@oxinst.co.uk

Correspondent: Kate Nayler, Secretary to the Chairman

Chief officer: *Chairman:* P M Williams

Year end	Turnover	Pre-tax profit
31/3/98	£199,300,000	£15,800,000

Nature of company business
Advanced instrumentation manufacture.

Main subsidiaries include: Medical Systems; Accelerator Technology; Industrial Analysis; Microanalysis; NMR Instruments; Plasma Technology; Research Instruments.

UK employees: 1,173

Charitable donations
1998: £75,000
1997: £74,300
1996: n/a
1995: £64,400
1994: £34,207
Membership: *BitC %Club*

Community support policy

The company is a member of the PerCent Club and Business in the Community. It mainly supports local initiatives in the fields of education, children/youth, elderly people, enterprise and training, science and technology, medical research, social welfare and healthcare in the Oxford area. Decisions to fund projects are made both by head office and by individual business units.

In particular, the company continues to support the 'Education plus' programme at Peers School and Bartholomew school and has an ongoing commitment to community work on the Blackbird Lees housing estate. Support has also been given to New Century which works to bring Japanese scholars to study at Oxford University. Individual subsidiaries operate their own payroll giving schemes.

Exclusions
No response to circular appeals. No support for fundraising events, purely denominational appeals, local appeals not in areas of company presence, large national appeals, overseas projects, purely political appeals, advertising in charity brochure, the arts, environment/ heritage, overseas projects, religious appeal or sport.

Applications
In writing to the correspondent.

P & O Steam Navigation Company

79 Pall Mall, London SW1Y 5EJ
0171-930 4343; Fax: 0171-930 6042
Website: www.p-and-o.com

Correspondent: Michael Owen, Deputy Company Secretary

Chief officers: *Chairman:* Lord Sterling; *Managing Director:* Sir Bruce MacPhail

Year end	Turnover	Pre-tax profit
31/12/97	£5,917,600,000	£433,900,000

Nature of company business
The company operates in the passenger and cargo shipping, transport, building and construction, property development and service sectors.

Main subsidiaries include: Princess Cruises; Swan Hellenic; Larne Harbour; Three Quays International; Containerbase (Holdings); Pandoro; Earls Court & Olympia; Beeton Rumford; Bovis Wyseplant; Chelsea Harbour; Cheverell Estates; Connaught Estates; Laing Estates; Midland City Properties; Vector Investments; Charlwood Alliance Holdings; Centreville Holdings.

UK employees: 9,593

Charitable donations
1997: £717,000
1996: £725,000
1995: £448,000
1994: £596,000
1993: £445,000

Community support policy
P & O is a decentralised group of companies and support is given accordingly. There is long-standing support for charities such as King George's Fund for Sailors, but a wide range of other charities are also given help.

Applications
In writing to the correspondent.

Pall Europe Ltd

Europa House, Havant Street, Portsmouth, Hampshire PO1 3PD
01705-753545; Fax: 01705-831324

Correspondent: Sharon Thomas, Personnel Administrator

Chief officer: *Chairman:* D T D Williams

Year end	Turnover	Pre-tax profit
31/7/97	£169,464,000	£32,186,000

Nature of company business
The main activity is the supply of proprietary fine and ultra-fine filters and ancillary equipment.

UK employees: 1,664

Charitable donations
1997: £18,199
1996: £150,996
1995: £11,324
1994: £66,769
1993: £73,485

Community support policy
The level of charitable donations varies markedly from year to year, rising to £150,000 in 1996, it fell again to just under £20,000 in 1997. The company prefers to support medical charities or causes local to Portsmouth. Previously donations were stated to range from £10 to £400, although it may be that larger grants are given with the increased level of giving.

Exclusions
The company rarely sponsors people or events or advertises in charity brochures.

Applications
In writing to the correspondent.

Palmer & Harvey McLane Ltd

Vale House, Vale Road, Portslade, East Sussex BN41 1HG
01273-420042; Fax: 01273-421324

Correspondent: C Osmond, Charities Administrator

Chief officers: *Chairman:* J H Chedzoy; *Managing Director:* P Hudson

Year end	Turnover	Pre-tax profit
31/3/96	£2,334,805,000	£12,852,000

Nature of company business
The main activity of the company is tobacco and confectionery distribution.

Main subsidiaries include: Snowking Ltd.

UK employees: n/a

Panasonic

Charitable donations
1996: £39,871
1995: £48,799
1994: £39,472
1993: £38,246

Community support policy

Other than support for certain trade charities, the company has no set policy, although it prefers to support 'people charities' local to its branches.

Applications

In writing to the correspondent.

Panasonic UK Ltd

Panasonic House, Willoughby Road, Bracknell RG12 8FP
01344-862444; Fax: 01344-861656
Website: www.panasonic.co.uk

Correspondent: Gary Thomson, Personnel Director

Chief officer: *Managing Director:* S Ushimaru

Year end	Turnover	Pre-tax profit
31/3/97	£812,427,000	£28,814,000

Nature of company business
The ultimate holding company is Matsushita Electric Industrial whose seven main businesses are: video equipment, audio equipment, home appliances, communication and individual equipment, electronic components, kitchen-related products, and others.

Main brands include: Panasonic; Technics.

UK employees: 803

Charitable donations
1997: £285,289
1996: £214,934
1995: £178,241
1994: £158,147
1993: £181,865
Membership: *ABSA BitC*

Community support policy

Each office/site has its own budget to support local charities in their area. Predominantly, Panasonic supports causes local to its main office in Bracknell and its other regional sites in Wakefield and Northampton. In general no cash donations are made by the company. Instead it prefers to donate equipment for either office use or fundraising purposes wherever possible and responds to requests received accordingly. (The figures given above are the cost of this.)

Currently, the company's charitable giving is directed towards the following categories:

(i) General – charities and groups which assist those in need, particularly disadvantaged, disabled, sick and elderly people, plus local schools and playgroups

(ii) Cause related – charities with a theme chosen by staff

(iii) Key project – support for one or two major projects per year within the immediate local area.

The company is patron of the Berkshire Community Trust, an independent community foundation serving the wider community where it is based. The Panasonic Trust, administered by the Royal Academy of Engineering, funds the re-training of professional engineers by giving grants towards attendance of approved courses.

The company is a member of Business in the Community and ABSA.

Exclusions

The company does not normally respond favourably to unsolicited requests. No support for advertising in charity brochures, animal charities, appeals from individuals, the arts, medical research, overseas projects, political appeals, religious appeals, science/technology or sport.

Applications

In writing to the correspondent.

Other information: the company produces a leaflet, *A Guide to Panasonic UK's Corporate Citizenship Activity*, which details the criteria used for the selection of projects to benefit from assistance.

Pannell Kerr Forster

New Garden House, 78 Hatton Garden, London EC1N 8JA
0171-831 7393; Fax: 0171-405 6736

Correspondent: Sheena Sullivan, Business Development Manager

Chief officer: *Chairman:* R J C Pearson

Year end	Turnover	Pre-tax profit
30/4/94	£80,100,000	n/a

Nature of company business
Principal activities: chartered accountants and management consultants.

UK employees: 1,800

Charitable donations
1993: £316,500
Membership: *BitC %Club*

Community support policy

The company is still a member of the PerCent Club and Business in the Community, but unfortunately we have not been able to update the financial or policy information. Community contributions include free professional advice, cash donations and support for the arts. The company supports national charities and local charities near regional offices.

Charitable donations: Contributions are controlled by individual local offices. In Scotland the firm has supported Abbeyfield Homes, Citizen's Advice Bureaux, Starlight Foundation, Camphill Rudolf Steiner Schools, Royal Scot Memorial and the Samaritans. In England support has been given to organisations such as Age Concern, Citizen's

Advice Bureaux, Starlight Foundation and the Samaritans, and a variety of assistance to benevolent societies, housing associations and hospital-related appeals.

In Wales support has been given to the Maritime Museum, Disabled Trusts Support Centre and the Wales Railway Centre.

The arts: Donations and sponsorship have been given to Royal National Theatre and Millstream Touring.

Exclusions

No support for circular appeals, fundraising events, advertising in charity brochures, individuals, purely denominational (religious) appeals, local appeals not in areas of company presence, large national appeals or overseas projects.

Applications

In writing to the correspondent.

Pearl Assurance plc

The Pearl Centre, Lynch Wood, Peterborough PE2 6FY
01733-470470; Fax: 01733-472300

Correspondent: Caroline Collard, Community Relations Manager

Chief officers: *Chairman:* Malcolm Bates; *Managing Director:* Richard Surface

Year end	Turnover	Pre-tax profit
31/12/96	£706,600,000	n/a

Nature of company business
Principal activity: life, pensions and general insurance.

UK employees: 8,390

Charitable donations

1996: £217,000
1995: £352,165
1994: £534,403
1993: £328,331
Membership: *%Club*

Community support policy

The company is a member of the PerCent Club with charitable donations during 1996 of £217,000. This was distributed to charities concerned with medical research and care for people with disabilities such as CORDA, the Papworth Trust, the Association of Wheelchair Children, and Research into Ageing. Pearl's community involvement also included support in kind for small local groups and charities, and extended to other areas such as arts.

The company has been reviewing its community relations policy to line up future projects and partnerships with Pearl's brand and values. In August 1997, as part of the review, Pearl launched its Employee Community Support Programme and donated over £130,000 to various groups and charities across the UK by supporting the efforts of the employees.

In 1998, Pearl joined Kids Club Network to run a pilot with a view to getting involved on a national level for a period of three to four years.

Exclusions

No response to circular appeals or to sponsorship requests for individuals. No support for fundraising events; advertising in charity brochures; religious appeals; overseas projects.

Applications

In writing to the correspondent.

Pearson plc

3 Burlington Gardens, London W1X 1LE
0171-411 2000; Fax: 0171-411 2390
Website: www.pearson.com

Correspondent: Clare Chalmers, Communications Manager

Chief officers: *Chairman:* Sir Dennis Stevenson; *Chief Executive:* Marjorie Scardino

Year end	Turnover	Pre-tax profit
31/12/97	£2,293,000,000	£129,000,000

Nature of company business
The company is an international media group. The group also owns 50% of Lazard Brothers & Co Limited (see separate entry).

Main subsidiaries include: Financial Times Group Ltd; Addison Wesley Longman Ltd; The Penguin Publishing Co Ltd; Thames Television Ltd.

UK employees: 8,287

Charitable donations

1997: £1,267,000
1996: £568,000
1995: £792,000
1994: £486,000
1993: £722,000
Membership: *ABSA BitC %Club*

Community support policy

The company is a member of the PerCent Club and Business in the Community.

Charitable donations: Pearson responds to causes at national level where it concentrates on activities that are in some way linked to its own, and to which it can make contributions at a sufficiently high level to produce lasting benefits. Preference is also given to projects where there is a possibility of monitoring the benefits and where there is scope for personal involvement of the company's staff. Most support is given in the field of education.

The Pearson Charitable Trust was established in 1995, (Charity Commission number 1045393), with the only accounts on file at the Charity Commission being those for 1996. In that year the trust received £462,000 from the company and gave £479,000 in grants. By far the largest grant went to the Bodleian Library which received £100,000. The next largest grant was £30,750 to the British Dyslexia Association and the National Manuscripts

Pennon

Conservation Trust received £14,000. Harlow Council received £12,500 with six organisations benefiting from £10,000, London School of Economics, Institute for Public Policy Research, Demos, British Film Institute, Atlantic College and Social Market Foundation.

There were a further 82 grants of £1,000 to £8,000 including those to Starlight Foundation, Blackfriars Settlement, Writers & Scholars Educational Trust, Isle of Dogs Charitable Trust, South East London Community Foundation, County Durham Foundation, Sussex Wildlife Trust, Science Museum, Glyndebourne Festival Society, University of Cape Town Trust and Society of Portrait Sculptors. Other grants ranged from 350 upwards.

The operating companies respond to trade and local causes, through cash and in kind donations. The main area of non-cash support is through gifts in kind.

Overseas causes are also supported. Subsidiaries overseas also support charities in their areas of operation, namely France, Spain and the USA.

Employee involvement: Wherever possible, employees are encouraged to become involved in charitable work in their local communities. The company often matches the amounts of money that are raised by employees as well as operating the Give As You Earn payroll giving scheme in most subsidiaries.

Education: In 1989, the group established the post of New Media Librarian at the Bodleian Library, Oxford with an endowment of £1 million over 10 years.

The arts: Pearson is a patron of ABSA. In 1997, it sponsored the Seurat exhibition at the National Gallery.

Exclusions
No support for advertising in programmes/brochures, medical charities, religious appeals or sport.

Applications
Appeals to head office should be addressed to Jill Finch. Decisions are made by a donations committee. Local and trade appeals should be sent directly to the relevant subsidiary company.

Pennon Group plc

Peninsula House, Rydon Lane, Exeter EX2 7HR
01392-219666; Fax: 01392-434966

Correspondent: Ken Woodier, Group Company Secretary and Solicitor

Chief officer: Chairman: K G Harvey

Year end	Turnover	Pre-tax profit
31/3/98	£382,000,000	£107,000,000

Nature of company business
The provision of water and waste engineering, waste management and environmental instrumentation.

Main subsidiaries include: South West Water; Haul Waste Group; Environmental Instrumentation Group; T J Brent.

UK employees: 3,420

Charitable donations
1998: £38,000
1997: £30,000
1996: £32,000

Community support policy
The company's total donations rose to £38,000 in 1997/98, though this is still less than 0.05% of pre-tax profit.

Formerly South West Water Group, the company is now known as Pennon Group. It only gives to local charities in areas where it operates, ie. Devon and Cornwall. Preferred areas of support are children and youth, education, fundraising events, sickness/disability charities, social welfare and environment/heritage. Grants range from £500 to £1,000.

Exclusions
No support for circular appeals, advertising in charity brochures, animal welfare charities, appeals from individuals, the arts, elderly people, enterprise/training, medical research, political appeals, purely denominational (religious) appeals, science/technology, local appeals not in areas of company presence, large national appeals or overseas projects.

Applications
In writing to the correspondent.

Pentland Group plc

The Pentland Centre Lakeside, Squires Lane, Finchley, London N3 2QL
0181-346 2600; Fax: 0181-346 2700

Correspondent: Stephen Rubin, Chairman

Chief officers: Chairman: R S Rubin; Chief Executive: A K Rubin

Year end	Turnover	Pre-tax profit
31/12/97	£755,000,000	£42,000,000

Nature of company business
The main activities of the subsidiary companies are footwear, clothing and sports, consumer products and international trading.

Main subsidiaries include: Airborne Footwear Ltd; Airborne Leisure Ltd; Berghaus Ltd; Brasher Boot Co Ltd; Ellesse Ltd; Kangaroos International Ltd; Pony International Ltd; Pony UK Sports Ltd; Red or Dead Ltd; Speedo International Ltd; Sportsflair Ltd.

Charitable donations
1997: £309,000
1996: £305,000
1995: £221,000
Membership: *BitC %Club*

Community support policy
The company is a member of the PerCent Club. Its charity and community efforts are spread across a wide range of organisations and projects around the world, associated with the group's products and business activities and

projects local to their offices and factories. They are also particularly keen to provide seed corn funding for projects that have a multiplier effect in generating money for a charity from other sources. These have included sports projects, charities involving families and young people, medical charities, cultural activities and support for organisations.

Examples of such projects are the group's sponsorship, through Speedo, of the Annual House of Lords vs House of Commons Charity Swim which raises substantial sums for Women Caring trust; sponsorship of the Language Centre at Hendon School; sponsorship, through Berghaus, of the abseiling wall at the Ideal Home Exhibition in aid of the Cystic Fibrosis Trust; and the sponsorship of the Finchley Carnival in which its employees particpate and which raises money for local charities. New activities in 1997 included a resource centre for autistic children in North London, and support by Ellesse International for the victims of the earthquakes in Italy.

Applications
In writing to the correspondent.

Perkins Foods plc

Trinity Court, Trinity Street, Peterborough PE1 1DA
01733-555706; Fax: 01733-558499

Correspondent: Mandy Nash, Personal Assistant to the Chief Executive

Chief officer: *Chairman:* A M Davies

Year end	Turnover	Pre-tax profit
31/12/97	£627,000,000	£28,000,000

Nature of company business
The main activity of the group is the manufacture and distribution of frozen, chilled and fresh foods.

Main subsidiaries include: Brookfield Foods; Studleigh-Royd.

UK employees: 2,524

Charitable donations
1997: £39,000
1996: £36,000
1995: £29,000

Community support policy
Although the company's main donations are to the Macmillan Nurses Appeal and the Injured Riders Fund, small donations of £50 to £100 may be given in support of advertising in charity brochures, appeals from individuals, the arts, children/youth, education, environment and heritage, fundraising events, medical reearch, overseas projects, sickness/disability charities and sport.

Exclusions
No support for animal welfare, elderly people, enterprise/training, political appeals, religious appeals, science/technology or social welfare.

Applications
In writing to the correspondent.

Perpetual plc

Perpetual House, Station Road, Henley-on-Thames, Oxon RG9 1AF
01491-417000; Fax: 01491-416000

Correspondent: Linda Sanderson, Personal Assistant to the Chairman

Chief officers: *Chairman:* Martyn Arbib; *Chief Executive:* David S Mossop

Year end	Turnover	Pre-tax profit
30/9/97	£1,275,682,000	£59,556,000

Nature of company business
The main activities are investment and unit trust services.

UK employees: 490

Charitable donations
1997: £208,816
1996: £154,270
1995: £62,900
1994: £40,259
1993: £38,428
Membership: *BitC*

Community support policy
The company's level of giving has continued to increase and in 1997 was over £200,000. It supports local charities in the Henley and south Oxfordshire area, and national charities with a clear link to that area. The company is a member of Business in the Community.

Applications
In writing to the correspondent.

Persimmon plc

Persimmon House, Fulford, York YO19 4FE
01904-642199; Fax: 01904-610014

Correspondent: G Grewer, Company Secretary

Chief officers: *Chairman:* Duncan Davidson; *Chief Executive:* John White

Year end	Turnover	Pre-tax profit
31/12/97	£525,462,000	£83,783,000

Nature of company business
Principal activities: residential building and development. Persimmon Homes is based in Anglia, Midlands, North East, North West, Scotland, South Coast, South East, South West, Thames Valley, Wales, Wessex, and Yorkshire.

Main locations: Beverley; Blaydon-on-Tyne; Exeter; Fareham (Hampshire); Gerrards Cross (Buckinghamshire); Hamilton; Llantrisant (Mid-Glamorgan); Leicester; Leigh; Lowestoft; Malmesbury (Wiltshire); Norwich; Northampton; Peterborough; Weybridge; York.

UK employees: 1,698

Peugeot

Charitable donations
1997: £92,000
1996: £72,000
1995: £65,000
1994: £71,000
1993: £32,542
Membership: %Club

Community support policy

The company is a member of the PerCent Club. In addition to charitable donations, the company provides in kind support and good-cause sponsorship. Typical sponsorship range is from £50 to £1,000. Employee involvement in charitable activities is encouraged by the company providing financial support, matching employee giving, and matching employee fundraising.

Charitable donations: The company has a policy of supporting local charities in those areas where it has a presence in addition to which it gives support to a few national charities. At the present time, the company has a specific relationship with the Macmillan Nurses Cancer Relief Fund. Donations are paid directly to registered charities and a wide range of different causes are considered.

Areas of support include advertising in charity brochures, animal welfare charities, appeals from individuals, children/youth, education, elderly people, enterprise/training, environment/heritage, fundraising events, sickness/disability charities, social welfare and sport.

In 1998, two major grants were given in York, £20,000 to York Minster and £35,000 to the York Millennium Bridge Trust.

Enterprise: The company gives support to enterprise agencies, including £500 annually to York Enterprise Ltd and Young Business Project.

Exclusions

No support for the arts, overseas projects, political appeals or religious appeals.

Applications

In writing to the correspondent. Each application is considered on its merits.

Peugeot Motor Company PLC

Aldermoor House, PO Box 227, Aldermoor Lane, Coventry CV3 1LT
01203-884000; Fax: 01203-884001
Website: www.peugeot.com

Correspondent: S T E Fenn, Secretary to the Charitable Trust

Chief officers: *Chairman:* M F Saint-Geours;
Managing Director: R D Parham

Year end	Turnover	Pre-tax profit
31/12/96	£2,123,000,000	£31,000,000

Nature of company business
Motor vehicle manufacture.
Main subsidiaries include: Talbot Exports Ltd; Robin & Day Ltd.
UK employees: 5,286

Charitable donations
1997: £304,000
1996: £323,000
1995: £64,000
1994: £215,000
1993: £219,000
Total community contributions: £762,000
Membership: *BitC* %Club

Community support policy

Peugeot Talbot is committed to the community of Coventry and neighbouring Warwickshire. Virtually all the company's charitable donations are directed to organisations within the Coventry area and the company and many of its employees play an increasingly 'hands on' part in furthering the interests of the Coventry community. The company is a member of the PerCent Club and in the 1998 report of the club, gave a total community investment figure of £762,000 (equivalent to 1.5% of pre-tax profit). Non-cash support is mainly concentrated on good-cause sponsorship, gifts in kind and training schemes. The company encourages employee volunteering through allowing company time off to volunteer.

Charitable donations: The company only supports charities local to Coventry or those associated with the motor industry. Some support is given through the Peugeot Talbot Motor Company Charity Trust (Charity Commission number 266182). In 1995/96, the trust had an income of £46,000 of which £43,000 was received from the company. Grants during the year totalled £49,000 to 127 organisations. A full list was included with the accounts which showed that most grants were for £50 to £100 and all were to local or motor industry-related causes.

The trustees' report also stated: 'There has been a high level of calls on the charity's fund from deprived areas of Coventry and this has been augmented by the company's policy of providing a minibus for short-term loan to small organisations unable to fund the facility themselves and the provision of vehicles at a very reasonable cost for the use of various concerns throughout Coventry'

11 grants are listed in the accounts as being of a more substantial nature. These included those to BEN (£20,000), Coventry Cyrenians (£5,000), Belgrade Theatre (£4,500) and Coventry Common Purpose (£2,500). The other seven were for £500 including those to Birmingham Children's Hospital, Helen Ley Home, Rugby Mencap Hostel and St Lawrence Church Hall.

Employee involvement: Throughout the year, employees help to raise many thousands of pounds for local organisations, covering a wide range of charitable and voluntary work for young, elderly and disabled people. A payroll giving scheme is run by the company, which matches employee giving £ for £. Several employees hold office in youth organisations, the magistracy and Coventry City Council. Staff are allowed time off for activity of community benefit.

Enterprise: The company is involved in a number of local initiatives such as Coventry & Warwickshire Training & Enterprise Council, Coventry Compact, Coventry Young Enterprise, Coventry Apprentices Association, Coventry Common Purpose, Training Access Trust and Understanding Industry. It is a member of Business in the Community.

Education: Formal links have been developed with several Coventry schools, the University of Warwick, Tile Hill College and Coventry University. Work experience schemes for pupils are provided and support is given to City Technology Colleges. A number of employees are school governors.

Sponsorship: The company sponsors local events or organisations.

Exclusions

No support is given for advertising in charity brochures, or to purely denominational (religious) appeals or overseas projects. Charities outside Coventry are not considered.

Applications

In writing to the correspondent.

Pfizer Group Ltd

Ramsgate Road, Sandwich, Kent CT13 9NJ
01304-616161; Fax: 01304-616221

Correspondent: Corporate Contributions Manager

Chief officers: *Chairman:* W J Wilson;
Managing Director: P N Gray

Year end	Turnover	Pre-tax profit
30/11/96	£278,978,000	£201,598,000

Nature of company business
Pfizer Inc is a worldwide, research-based company with businesses in healthcare, agriculture, speciality chemicals, materials science and consumer products all trading under the Pfizer name.
Main subsidiaries include: Howmedica International Ltd; Unicliffe Ltd; Shiley Ltd.

UK employees: n/a

Charitable donations

1996: £148,750
1995: £180,000
1994: £194,724
1993: £170,871
Membership: *BitC*

Community support policy

Despite giving about £150,000 a year in charitable donations, the company has consistently stated that it has no strict donations policy. However, education, health and community projects are favoured. The company is a member of Business in the Community.

Exclusions

No support for overseas appeals, which will be supported by Pfizer companies in their country of operation. Support is unlikely to be given to religious appeals, service charities, political appeals or individuals.

Applications

In writing to the correspondent.

Philips Electronics UK Ltd

59 Russell Square, London WC1B 4HJ
0181-781 8405; Fax: 0171-631 0603

Correspondent: Roger Woods, Director of Corporate Relations

Chief officer: *Chairman:* D Jordan

Year end	Turnover	Pre-tax profit
31/12/94	£1,500,000,000	n/a

Nature of company business
Production and sale of electrical goods.

UK employees: 7,500

Charitable donations

No figures available
Membership: *BitC*

Community support policy

Philips aims to act as a responsible member of the local communities within which it operates. Donations are therefore targeted at the regions which have operating units and that reflect local priorities. All unsolicited requests are reviewed, but only a small proportion are considered. The company is a member of Business in the Community.

Applications

All applications must be forwarded to Philips in writing, outlining the nature and purpose of the request. These will then be reviewed and a decision will be made as to any donation which might be forthcoming. However, due to a high demand on limited resources, less than 10% of all enquiries end in a donation. All applications will be acknowledged and should be addressed to either Roger Woods, Director of Corporate Relations, or Justin Leahy, Charity and Sponsorship Officer.

PIC International Group PLC

5th Floor, Bond Street House, 14 Clifford Street, London W1X 2JB
Website: www.pic.com

Correspondent: B E Gandy, Company Secretary

Chief officers: *Chairman:* B F Baldock;
Chief Executive: Dr P J David

Year end	Turnover	Pre-tax profit
30/6/98	£3,260,300,000	£225,900,000

Pilkington

Nature of company business
The principal activity is the supply of improved pig breeding stock. The company, formerly known as Dalgety, sold its pet food manufacture, food manufacture and distribution and agricultural supplies business during 1998.
Main subsidiaries include: Pig Improvement Group.
Main locations: Oxfordshire.

UK employees: n/a

Charitable donations
1998: £136,000
1997: £208,000
1996: £273,000
1995: £222,000
1994: £262,000

Community support policy
Preference for local charities in areas of company presence (ie. Oxfordshire), appeals relevant to the company's business and charities in which a member of company staff is involved. Preferred areas of support are: animal welfare charities; children/youth; education; elderly people; enterprise/training; environment/heritage; medical research; science/technology; sickness/disability charities; social welfare and sport. The company also matches employee fundraising.

Grants to national organisations range from £500 to £2,500; grants to local organisations from £500 to £1,000.

Exclusions
No response to circular appeals. No support for advertising in charity brochures; appeals from individuals; the arts; fundraising events; overseas projects; political appeals; religious appeals or local appeals not in areas of company presence.

Applications
In writing to the correspondent.

Pilkington plc

Prescot Road, St Helens, Merseyside WA10 3TT
01744-28882; Fax: 01744-692660
Website: www.pilkington.com

Correspondent: David Roycroft, Head of Corporate Affairs

Chief officers: *Chairman:* Sir Nigel Rudd;
Chief Executive: Paolo Scaroni

Year end	Turnover	Pre-tax profit
31/3/98	£2,701,000,000	(£100,000,000)

Nature of company business
Producer of glass and related products worldwide.
Main subsidiaries include: Triplex Safety Glass Ltd.
Main locations: St Helens; St Asaph; Doncaster; Kings Norton.

UK employees: 8,200

Charitable donations
1998: £177,000
1997: £109,236
1996: £204,000
1995: £217,000
1994: £199,000

Total community contributions: £1,576,671
Membership: *BitC %Club*

Community support policy

Charitable donations: 'Pilkington supports local educational activities, employment programmes, the arts and charitable work in the communities where it operates, especially St Helens and Merseyside.' Preference for charities in which a member of company staff is involved.

The company supports a wide range of charities/projects/applications: advertising in charity brochures, animal welfare, the arts, children/youth, education, elderly people, environment/heritage, fundraising events, religious appeals, science/technology, sickness/disability charities, social welfare and sport. The main areas of support are the arts, social welfare, health and medical care and particularly disability, education, scientific research and enterprise projects. Grants range from £50 to £2,000. In addition, the company provides non-cash support through arts sponsorship, good-cause sponsorship and gifts in kind. The Give As You earn payroll giving scheme is also in operation.

The company pays particular attention to the community of St Helens where its major site is located. It has agreed to provide private funding of about £1.2 million for the 'World of Glass' museum and heritage centre. The Grants Committee gives donations generally of £50 to £5,000. These donations totalled £109,235 in 1996/97 and increased to £177,000 in 1997/98.

Pilkington is a founder member of the PerCent Club.

The full donations list to 31 August 1997 was provided by the company and is summarised below.

Business contacts
   Konigswinter Conference £2,000
Ecological
   Mersey Basin £10,000
Education (university)
   John Moores University Trust £6,250
Education (miscellaneous)
   The CBI Education Foundation £1,000
   Liverpool City of Learning £1,250
Sport
   St Helens Mayors Appeal Fund £100
Welfare
   CSRF £50
   Fund for refugees in Slovenia £500
   King George's Fund for Sailors £100
Youth
   Prince's Trust Trading Ltd £700
   Child of Achievement Trust Fund £750
   The Citizenship Foundation £1,000
   Young Achiever of the Year Award £110
   Charities Aid Foundation £100,000
TOTAL £124,000
   less 1996/97 accrual of £15,000 = £109,000

Enterprise: The company is a member of Business in the Community. In St Helens it supports activities which help create jobs, attract investment, promote urban renewal and help smaller local businesses. Support is given to the Community of St Helens Trust. The Pilkington Community Programme Agency employs about 200 people and has helped elderly people in St Helens with home improvement schemes.

The company has helped in the formation of NIMTECH-NW and of QUALITEC, the St Helens Training and Enterprise Council.

The company works with the Ravenhead Renaissance Consortium, developing previously derelict industrial areas of the town.

Education: The company helps schools and colleges in the St Helens area and universities in the North West. Particular emphasis has been on setting up a project to improve the science and technology education in primary schools St Helens.

The arts: Pilkington is a regular supporter of Tate Gallery, Liverpool.

Exclusions
No support for appeals from individuals, enterprise/training, overseas projects, political appeals, or religious appeals.

Applications
In writing to: Chairman, Grants Committee, Pilkington plc, Prescot Road, St Helens, Merseyside WA10 3TT.

Polypipe plc

Broomhouse Lane, Edlington, Doncaster,
South Yorkshire DN12 1ES
01709-770000; Fax: 01709-869000

Correspondent: Andrew Hurst, Publicity Manager

Chief officer: *Chairman:* Kevin McDonald

Year end	Turnover	Pre-tax profit
30/6/98	£273,000,000	£34,600,000

Nature of company business
Principal activity: manufacture of plastic pipes, profiles and fittings for the plumbing and building industries.

Main subsidiaries include: Derwent MacDee Ltd; Mason Pinder Ltd; Oasis Leisure Products Ltd; Midland Stom Ltd; TDI Ltd; Celmac Group Ltd; Effast Ltd; Premier Profile Ltd; Stephens Umbrellas Ltd.

UK employees: n/a

Charitable donations
1998: £133,863
1997: £157,046
1996: £118,986
1995: £184,715
1994: £107,636

Community support policy
The company support a wide range of charities in areas of company presence, appeals relevant to the company's business and charities in which a member of company staff is involved. Preferred areas of support are children and youth, medical and education. Elsewhere, hospitals are also supported.

Exclusions
No response to circular appeals. No support for appeals from individuals, purely denominational (religious) appeals, local appeals not in areas of company presence, large national appeals or overseas projects.

Applications
In writing to the correspondent.

THE POST OFFICE

The Post Office

148 Old Street, London EC1V 9HQ
0171-250 2243; Fax: 0171-250 2729

Correspondent: Howard Brabrook, Head of Community Affairs

Chief officers: *Chairman:* Sir Michael Heron; *Chief Executive:* John Roberts

Year end	Turnover	Pre-tax profit
31/3/98	£6,759,000,000	£651,000,000

Nature of company business
The Post Office comprises a number of operating divisions and subsidiary companies of which the principal ones are: Royal Mail – the letters business; Parcelforce Worldwide – parcels and consignments; Post Office Counters – the retail arm; SSL – telebusiness operators.

UK employees: 193,633

Charitable donations
1998: £2,030,000
1997: £2,100,000
1996: £1,973,000
1995: £1,820,000
1994: £1,350,000
Membership: *BitC*

Community support policy
'In order to maximise the effectiveness of our community involvement we concentrate our resources in a number of areas, for example: literacy and technology in education, helping and sustaining local communities and assisting those entering or re-entering the world of work (especially the disabled).

'However, we are not a grant-making trust nor a charitable foundation. We regret therefore that we cannot consider unsolicited applications for grants or donations but we are always pleased to keep up-to-date with what voluntary organisations are doing in the areas of interest to us.

'If we think that your project or activities are relevant we will write to you seeking more information and we may consider inviting you to participate in our community programme. We do not want, however, to raise expectations – we receive many thousands of requests and enquiries each year from voluntary organisations and sadly, very few match our criteria.'

Education: The Post Office Education Service (currently located at the University of Warwick) provides a range of educational materials widely used in schools. The Education Service can be contacted at: The Post Office Education Service, The Centre for Education & Industry, Warwick University, Coventry CV4 7AL (01203-523951).

Employee involvement: The Post Office actively supports those of its employees who undertake voluntary action work in the community. Within Royal Mail there is a network of Community Action Managers. They provide practical support and advice to employee volunteers.

The Post Office operates payroll giving through a scheme managed on its behalf by Charities Trust and currently 55,000 employees donate over £2 million a year. Permission to enter Post Office buildings in order to promote such schemes to staff can only be given by local managers and organisations wishing to do this must apply in writing to the appropriate Post Office manager at the specific location. The Community Affairs Unit at headquarters cannot grant such permission. General enquires about the payroll giving scheme can be directed to Charities Trust, 14th Floor, Sir John Moores Building, 100 Old Hall Street, Liverpool L70 1AB (0151-286 5129).

There is an active programme of secondments to voluntary organisations and in addition, staff at all levels are involved on a part-time basis in the voluntary sector. For example, as school governors, business advisers and helping to organise and manage voluntary organisations and charities. In certain circumstances The Post Office allows time off to participate in these activities and may provide support in-kind as well as some financial assistance. The Post Office also provides selected specialist training for employees who are active in the voluntary sector, for example training is given to school governors and trustees of charities and other organisations.

In-kind support: This is normally limited to large disaster appeals. Community contributions include help with accommodation (this is limited and obviously there are security and operational constraints given the nature of the groups work) and the provision, in selected cases, of a secondee with appropriate skills on a full-time basis. Surplus office equipment can be donated when and where it is available.

Exclusions

Only those organisations which fit The Post Office's policy criteria can be considered for inclusion in its community affairs programme. Detailed guidelines are available on application in writing, but no support can be provided for charities which assist animal welfare, the arts, elderly people, medical research, overseas projects, political or religious appeals, social welfare or sport.

The Post Office does not buy advertising space, nor can it undertake to sponsor individuals for education or research projects. It is regretted, but fundraising appeals by telephone cannot be accepted and only a limited amount of support can be given to general fundraising appeals.

No free, or reduced rate Post Office services can be offered, nor can advertising or display facilities be provided in post offices (there are, however, special arrangements for posting articles for the blind and further details can be obtained by telephoning 0345-950950).

The Post Office cannot undertake to promote a particular charity or its activities to their staff by distributing raffle tickets or displaying posters.

The Community Affairs Unit does not handle applications for sponsorship where the proposal is aimed at supporting or marketing brands, products or services.

Applications

Initially a letter should be addressed to the Community Affairs Unit of The Post Office at the address given above. Further details together with an application form will be sent to the applicant. All applications are assessed against policy criteria, but amounts in excess of £500 have to be approved by a committee which meets every three months.

Local appeals: These can be sent to local offices of The Post Office, but budgets for such appeals are very limited since it is Corporation policy for the bulk of its charitable giving to be undertaken at corporate level. Please note that local managers are not able to offer free or reduced rate Post Office services as a way of supporting charitable appeals.

Advice to applicants: Please read carefully the Post Office's criteria. They receive many thousands of requests each year, most of which fall outside the scope of their present policies. It is strongly recommended that all applicants write in the first instance for policy details, giving a brief outline of their proposal. The Post Office can then advise whether the appeal can be considered and, if so, how such applications can be set out and the type of information they require in order to give proper consideration to your request for help.

Initial requests will be replied to as quickly as possible. If you subsequently receive and complete an application form, the aim is to assess this within 28 working days. You will then receive a reply indicating whether you have been successful, or whether your application is to be considered by their charities committee.

Powell Duffryn plc

Powell Duffryn House, London Road, Bracknell, Berkshire RG12 2AQ
01344-666800; Fax: 01344-666811

Correspondent: Mrs Gillian Clark, Charity Committee Secretary

Chief officers: *Chairman:* Sir Noel Davies; *Chief Executive:* Barry Hartiss

Year end	Turnover	Pre-tax profit
31/3/98	£721,000,000	£38,000,000

Nature of company business
Principal activities are engineering, ports and shipping services.

Main subsidiaries include: Tees and Harlepool Port Authority Ltd; Humberside Holdings Ltd; H & L Garages Ltd; Hamworthy Marine Ltd; Belliss & Morcom Ltd; PDE Geesink Ltd.

UK employees: 4,979

Charitable donations
1998: £42,000
1997: £43,000
1996: £45,000
1995: £53,000
1994: £34,000

Total community contributions: £48,000

Membership: *%Club*

Community support policy
Total community contributions by the company in 1997/98 were £48,000 including £42,000 in charitable donations.

It prefers to support charities local to areas of company business. The company supports charities with donations varying between £50 and £500. Preferred areas of support include youth/education, sport, services, medical research and disabled/elderly people. However, support is also given to enterprise/training; environment/heritage; local fundraising events; science/technology; sickness/disability charities; social welfare.

Exclusions
No support for advertising in charity brochures, animal welfare charities, political appeals or religious appeals.

Applications
In writing to the correspondent.

PowerGen plc

Westwood Way, Westwood Business Park,
Coventry CV4 8LG
01203-424000
Website: www.pgen.com

Correspondent: Pam Staff, Sponsorship & Communications Affairs Manager

Chief officers: *Chairman:* E A Wallis ; *Managing Director:* D I King

Year end	Turnover	Pre-tax profit
29/3/98	£2,932,000,000	£211,000,000

Nature of company business
Principal activity: generation and sale of electricity. The company has also taken over East Midlands Electricity.

Main subsidiaries include: Ergon Insurance Ltd; Kinetica Ltd; Wavedriver Ltd; East Midlands Electricity; DR Investments.

UK employees: 3,456

Charitable donations
1998: £290,889
1997: £254,444
1996: £1,002,670
1995: £372,000
1994: £339,000

Membership: *ABSA BitC %Club*

Community support policy
PowerGen is a member of the PerCent Club, although the charitable donations figure quoted above from the company's annual report represents only 0.14% of pre-tax profit. Presumably, an additional £700,000 is given in other forms of community support.

Community support is focused on areas relevant to its business activities, in particular education; science; technology and engineering; and the environment. The company also supports the arts, and is a member of ABSA and Business in the Community.

In addition, PowerGen's operating locations are active in developing links with local schools and colleges through sponsorship, visits to sites and work-experience placements.

In 1996/97, main grant beneficiaries included: Drive for Youth, Groundwork, Going for Green, National Energy Action and Birmingham Royal Ballet.

For 1998/99, the company hoped to have established an employee payroll giving scheme, together with various other initiatives to support employee fundraising activities.

Exclusions
No support for advertising in charity brochures; animal welfare charities; appeals from individuals; children/youth; elderly people; enterprise/training; fundraising events; medical research; political appeals; religious appeals; sickness/disability charities; or sport.

Applications
In writing to the correspondent.

PricewaterhouseCoopers

Southwark Towers, 32 London Bridge Street,
London SE1 9SY
0171-939 3000; Fax: 0171-378 0647

Correspondent: Claire Gardner, Business Advisory Services

Chief officers: n/a

Year end	Turnover	Pre-tax profit
n/a	n/a	n/a

Nature of company business
Principal activities: chartered accountants and business advisers.

Charitable donations
No figures yet available
Membership: *BitC %Club*

Community support policy
PricewaterhouseCoopers was formed by the merger of Price Waterhouse and Coopers & Lybrand. Both these companies were members of the PerCent Club and reported on their involvement in the community in its

Procter

latest annual report. No figures are yet available for the merged firm's community support.

Generally the firm is proactive in selecting initiatives in the following fields:
- raise educational achievement in primary and secondary schools, particularly within areas of deprivation
- support disadvantaged youth and help create employment for long-term unemployed people
- encourage social and economic community regeneration.

The firm also operates a volunteering award scheme and employee fundraising and Give As You Earn programmes.

In the PerCent Club 1998 annual report, the then separate firms valued their total community support at £2,053,000 (Coopers & Lybrand) and £1,000,000 (Price Waterhouse). In addition to direct charitable donations, wide-ranging support is given in the form of trade-related sponsorships, staff secondments and the provision of professional services.

Exclusions
No support for circular appeals, fundraising events, advertising in charity brochures, individuals, religious or political appeals, sport or local appeals not in areas of company presence.

Applications
In writing to the correspodent. Donations are approved after consideration by a charities committee.

Procter & Gamble UK

PO Box 1EE, Gosforth, Newcastle upon Tyne NE99 1EE
0191-279 2000; Fax: 0191-279 2282

Correspondent: Mrs P E Dodds, Community Relations Manager

Chief officers: *Chairman:* J E Pepper;
Managing Director: C de Lapuente

Year end	Turnover	Pre-tax profit
30/6/97	n/a	£137,400,000

Nature of company business
Procter & Gamble UK is a wholly owned subsidiary of The Procter & Gamble Company, USA. The principal activities of the company and its subsidiaries are the manufacture and marketing of detergents, health and personal care and allied products, with associated research and development services.
Main brands include: Ariel; Bold; Daz; Fairy; Flash; Lenor; Pampers; Pantene.
UK employees: 5,406

Charitable donations
1997: £76,000
1996: £74,000
1995: £72,000
1994: £65,000
1993: £62,000

Total community contributions: £2,600,000

Membership: *BitC %Club*

Community support policy
The company is a member of Business in the Community and the PerCent Club, with contributions to the community totalling £2.6 million in 1996/97, of which £76,000 was in cash donations to charities. Other support is given to education, economic regeneration (including health and welfare) and culture.

The company also contributes through gifts in kind, training schemes and provision of employee time/expertise eg. marketing, finance, etc. to community projects. Company employee skills and expertise are used by over 50 Tyneside community projects in the areas of education, economic regeneration, special social projects and the arts. Additionally, employees doing voluntary work in their own time can apply to the company for grants of up to £500 to support this work. The company operates an Employee Benevolent Fund payroll giving scheme.

Charitable donations: The company only supports local charities in areas of company presence including the North East, especially the Gosforth area of Newcastle, and Weybridge in Surrey, across a wide range of causes including education, health, welfare, culture and the environment. National charities are also supported for work in the above areas. Support may also be given to the arts, children/youth, elderly people, environment/heritage, sickness/disability charities and social welfare.

Exclusions
No support is given to circular appeals, fundraising events, appeals from individuals, political or religious appeals, medical research, science/technology, sport, local appeals not in areas of company presence, animal welfare charities, overseas projects or for advertising in charity brochures.

Applications
Applications by letter only should be addressed to the correspondent. For financial grants on Tyneside, only call the 'P&G Fund' at Tyne & Wear Foundation (0191-222 0945) or write to The Procter & Gamble Fund, Tyne & Wear Foundation, Cale Cross House, 156 Pilgrim Street, Newcastle upon Tyne NE1 6SU.

Provident Financial plc

Colonnade, Sunbridge Road, Bradford BD1 2LQ
01274-731111; Fax: 01274-727300
Website: www.providentfinancial.co.uk

Correspondent: Sandra Larmour, Community Relations Manager

Chief officers: *Chairman:* John Van Kuffeler;
Chief Executive: Howard Bell

Year end	Turnover	Pre-tax profit
31/12/97	£444,173,000	£136,502,000

Nature of company business
Personal credit and insurance.
Main subsidiaries include: Greenwood Personal Credit Ltd; Colonnade Insurance Brokers Ltd.
UK employees: 3,755

Charitable donations

1997: £103,000
1996: £72,000
1995: £51,000
1994: £49,697
1993: £38,000

Total community contributions: £449,000

Membership: *ABSA*

Community support policy

The company's policy states: 'We concentrate our giving where possible on a small number of causes and organisations. The community programme operates nationally and in West Yorkshire where we have our main offices.'

The total community contributions by the company were £449,000 including £103,000 in cash donations. The main areas of non-cash support are arts and good-cause sponsorship and gifts in kind. The company has an employee volunteering scheme and matches employee fundraising.

Currently there are four strands to the community programme.

National charity partner

In 1998, the NSPCC and its sister charity in Scotland, Children 1st, were selected as National Charity Partners. Support over the next two years will include general financial support, support of selected projects across the country, sponsorship of events and publications, and staff fundraising.

Provident in the Community

This is a nationwide programme which provides practical support to small community projects identified by the company's agents and employees. In 1997, over 150 activities were helped through the programme. Requests for support should be submitted through an employee or agent of the group.

The arts

The long-established Provident Financial arts programme supports living artists with a Yorkshire connection by buying work for the Provident Financial Art Collection. This now has over 400 works displayed at the offices in West Yorkshire. Support is also given locally through the sponsorship of the annual Leeds Art Fair and the Provident Financial Triennial Exhibition. Community-based arts projects, especially in the visual arts, are also supported. For example, in 1998, Free Form, a charity working with local communities to improve their local environment using visual arts was sponsored.

West Yorkshire programme

Each year the company selects community organisations in West Yorkshire which it will support. In 1998, these included charities working with drug abuse, a refuge for homeless women and a theatre company working with Asian young people. Substantial support has been given to West Yorkshire Playhouse for its SPARK project which provides after-school clubs in inner-city Leeds working with Leeds FC and Leeds Rugby League Rhinos. They are corporate members of Opera North and the Alhambra Theatre.

Exclusions

No support for advertising in charity brochures, animal welfare, appeals from individuals, elderly people, medical research, overseas projects, political appeals, religious appeals, science/technology, sickness/disability charities and sport.

Applications

In writing to the correspondent.

Prudential Corporation plc

142 Holborn Bars, London EC1N 2NH
0171-583 1415; Fax: 0171-548 3725
Website: www.prudentialcorporation.com

Correspondent: Mrs Jill Fowler, Community Affairs Manager

Chief officers: *Chairman:* Sir Martin Jacomb;
Chief Executive: Sir Peter Davis

Year end	Turnover	Pre-tax profit
31/12/97	n/a	£1,169,000,000

Nature of company business
Prudential's main businesses are life and general insurance, pensions, investment management, unit trusts and direct banking. It has more than nine million customers and is one of Britain's biggest institutional investors.

Main subsidiaries include: Scottish Amicable Life plc.

UK employees: 18,350

Charitable donations

1997: £1,400,000
1996: £1,400,000
1995: £1,700,000
1994: £1,224,000
1993: £844,000

Membership: *ABSA BitC %Club*

Community support policy

Prudential has supported carers and safer communities since 1993 when it launched two five-year partnership initiatives. The Prudential Carers Initiative involved working with The Princess Royal Trust for Carers and Crossroads Caring for Carers to extend the network of local services available to carers. Prudential has also worked in partnership with Crime Concern, the national crime prevention organisation, to establish more Youth Action Groups and empower young people as partners in community safety.

Although the initial partnerships are now concluded, support for these two issues continues into 1999 with the emphasis on raising awareness and extending services and the company is unable to consider any other requests.

Prudential encourages employees to support these two initiatives and operates a Give As You Earn payroll giving scheme.

Psion

Non-cash help is also provided to charity partners through the provision of office space and equipment, legal advice and promotional material.

The arts: Prudential is sponsoring the Creative Britons. This is an awards scheme administered by ABSA to recognise six individuals who have made an outstanding contribution to the arts in the United Kingdom. A total of £200,000 in prize money will be given to the arts organisations nominated by the winners.

Other projects sponsored by Prudential in 1998/9 are Sadler's Wells Theatre, Rambert Dance Company and the Tate Gallery. Prudential also has corporate membership of a number of organisations.

The company is a member of the PerCent Club and in the latters 1998 annual report the total community investment figure given is £2,880,000 equivalent to 0.6% of UK pre-tax profit. It appears that half of this was given in charitable donations.

Exclusions

No support for: animal welfare charities, organisations whose activities are based primarily outside the UK, political organisations, fundraising events, circular appeals, appeals from individuals, purely denominational (religious) appeals for sponsorship of individuals or groups, advertising in charity brochures, education, elderly people, enterprise/training, environment/heritage, medical research, overseas projects, science/technology, sickness/disability charities or social welfare.

Applications

Applications for cash donations cannot be considered (see above).

Enquiries concerning arts sponsorship should be sent to Jackie Dawson, Sponsorship Executive at head office.

Psion plc

Alexander House, 85 Frampton Street, London NW8 8NQ
0171-262 5580; Fax: 0171-258 7343

Correspondent: Jo Downey, Marketing Assistant

Chief officers: *Chairman:* D E Potter;
Managing Director: N S Myers

Year end	Turnover	Pre-tax profit
31/12/97	£142,012,000	£11,426,000

Nature of company business
Development, manufacture and supply of mobile, digital communication and computing technology.

UK employees: n/a

Charitable donations

1997: £59,000
1996: £122,000
1995: £89,000
1994: £40,000
1993: £21,000
Membership: *BitC %Club*

Community support policy

Psion is a member of the PerCent Club and Business in the Community. It focuses its support principally on activities closely related to mobile computing and communications, southern African education and development. Psion also supports organisations local to its production sites in Didcot, Milton Keynes and Greenford (Middlesex).

Applications

In writing to the correspondent.

Racal Electronics plc

Western Road, Bracknell, Berkshire RG12 1RG
01344-483244; Fax: 01344-388061
Website: www.racal.com

Correspondent: Irene Bradley, Secretary, Racal Charitable Trust

Chief officers: *Chairman:* Sir Ernest Harrison;
Chief Executive: David C Elsbury

Year end	Turnover	Pre-tax profit
31/3/98	£1,144,414,000	(£207,180,000)

Nature of company business
Principal activities: professional electronics, telecommunications, and data communications.

Main subsidiaries include: NCS International; Josef Heim KG.

UK employees: 9,400

Charitable donations

1998: £148,000
1997: £86,000
1996: £146,000
1995: £118,000
1994: £123,000
Membership: *BitC*

Community support policy

The charitable donations figure quoted above comprises £143,000 contributed to charitable foundations and £5,000 to support a university project. The company's annual report states: 'Registered charities active in the field of medical research received a major contribution, the rest was shared mainly by organisations supporting children, the sick and the aged'.

The company's policy is to relieve poor, needy, sick and disabled people, and to support those who are engaged in work, including research, to this end. Thus 70% of the budget is spent on health and medical care, 20% on social welfare and 5% on community services. Support is also given to organisations concerned with the environment and heritage.

About 300 national and 50 local grants are made annually. Grants to national organisations range from £100 to £10,000; grants to local organisations from £50 to £100 and are distributed through the Racal Charitable Trust (Charity Commission number 1000162).

Non-cash support is given through secondments, gifts in kind and training shemes. Financial help and company time off are given in support of employees' volunteering/charitable activities.

Exclusions

No support for circulars, individuals, expeditions, advertising in charity brochures, fundraising events or small purely local events in areas of company presence. Unless there are exceptional reasons the trustees prefer to deal directly with a charity rather than with intermediaries.

Applications

All appeals for charitable donations should be sent to the correspondent. Grant decisions are made by a donations committee which meets quarterly. No appeals are considered independently of head office.

Advice to applicants: Racal states that it welcomes appeals from charities, but that mail is getting too large to handle. Thus, applicants should consider the nature and relevance of their appeal and the following advice from the charitable trust. Applicants are advised to apply at the same time every year. No reply is sent to unsuccessful applicants, and it is seldom worth repeating an appeal regularly if it has been rejected. The main complaints about charitable appeals are that there is too much duplication, too much expensive literature included in categories which the trust regards as marginal to its objects, appeals go to subsidiaries which have no authority to respond, and some successful applicants fail to acknowledge a positive response.

Railtrack Group PLC

Railtrack House, Euston Square, London NW1 2EE
0171-557 8000; Fax: 0171-557 9000
Website: www.railtrack.co.uk

Correspondent: Caroline Oakley, Corporate Communications Manager

Chief officers: *Chairman:* Sir Robert Horton; *Chief Executive:* G Corbett

Year end	Turnover	Pre-tax profit
31/3/98	£2,467,000,000	£388,000,000

Nature of company business
The main activities are the provision of train operators with access to track, maintenance and renewal of the infrastructure and undertaking of major capital programmes, and management of timetabling, train planning and signalling.

UK employees: 10,700

Charitable donations

1998: £671,498
1997: £22,632
1996: £2,000

Total community contributions: £1,500,000

Membership: ABSA BitC

Community support policy

The community contributions budget for 1998/99 is £1.5 million, including cash donations. The main theme for support continues to be disability, with the secondary theme being disadvantaged communities.

There are seven partners in this programme. With both the National Trust and National Trust for Scotland support was given for projects to improve access for disabled people on Trust property. These have included sponsoring braille guides and making footpaths more accessible. For RADAR, funding was provided for the salary of an information helpline officer and an employee is also helping the charity set up a website. Special Olympics received funding for new clubs in each of the company's zones. (The company has seven zones plus headquarters.). An employee from each zone was placed on a Prince's Trust Volunteers scheme and eight employee teams took part in Business in the Community challenges for the community. The other partner is ADAPT Trust.

Donations are also made to unsolicited requests on the disability theme, from £50 upwards.

In addition, Railtrack supports employees who write in and request a corporate donation to a charity of their choice. These range from £100 to £1,000 and do not have to fit within the disability theme. Employees are encouraged to take up to five days company time for volunteering with one of the partners mentioned above. Employee giving (through Give As You Earn) and employee fundraising are both matched £ for £.

Applications

In writing to the correspondent. Regional contacts are the Public Affairs Managers.

Raine's Dairy Foods Ltd

Raine House, Crown Road, Enfield EN1 1TX
0181-804 8151; Fax: 0181-805 4211

Correspondent: Bill Ratcliffe, Personnel Manager

Chief officer: *Managing Director:* Mrs Jacobs

Year end	Turnover	Pre-tax profit
27/9/97	£113,892,000	£1,462,000

Nature of company business
The main activity is the manufacture and sale of dairy produce.

UK employees: n/a

Charitable donations

1997: £49,601
1996: £41,352
1995: £75,278
1994: £60,376
1993: £46,893

Community support policy

The only information we have on the policy of the company is that it tends to support one charity a year. Any applications received are therefore unlikely to be successful.

Ramco Energy plc

4 Rubislaw Place, Aberdeen AB10 1XN
01224-622614; Fax: 01224-622610
Website: www.ramco-plc.com

Correspondent: Lisa J Newman, Public Relations Manager

Chief officer: *Chairman:* S E Remp

Year end	Turnover	Pre-tax profit
31/12/97	£6,158,000	£484,000

Nature of company business
Oil exploration and production in the Caspian Region and Eastern Europe. The company also has an oil services business.
Main subsidiaries include: Medusa Oil & Gas.

UK employees: c. 100

Charitable donations
1997: £40,000
1996: £2,000
1995: £4,800

Community support policy
Although based in Scotland, the company operates in Azerbaijan, Georgia, the Czech Republic, Poland and Montenegro. Although charitable donations totalled only £2,000 in 1996, this increased sharply to £40,000 in 1997.

The company supports overseas projects (in the countries where it operates) and fundraising events. For example, support was given for the victims of flood damage in Georgia.

Exclusions
No support for causes other than those stated above.

Applications
In writing to the correspondent at: The Old House, 142 South Street, Dorking RH4 2EU (01306-888809; Fax: 01306-743504; e-mail: lisa@ramco-plc.com).

The Rank Group Plc

6 Connaught Place, London W2 2EZ
0171-706 1111; Fax: 0171-402 4164
Website: www.rank.com

Correspondent: Charles B A Cormick, Company Secretary

Chief officer: *Chairman:* Sir Denys Henderson

Year end	Turnover	Pre-tax profit
31/12/97	£2,012,000,000	£260,000,000

Nature of company business
The Rank Group supplies products and services to the film and television industries, owns holidays and hotel businesses and operates organised recreation and leisure facilities in the UK and overseas. Rank has a joint investment with MCA in the Universal Studios motion picture theme park at Orlando, Florida.
Main subsidiaries include: Butlins Ltd; Haven Leisure Ltd; Hard Rock Cafe; Warner Holidays Ltd; Mecca Bingo Ltd; Odeon Cinemas Ltd; Tom Cobleigh Plc.
Main brands include: Hard Rock.

UK employees: 31,432

Charitable donations
1997: £169,000
1996: £372,000
1995: £239,000
1994: £258,946
1993: £278,344
Membership: *BitC*

Community support policy
Cash donations fell from over £370,000 in 1996, to £169,000 in 1997.

The company is revamping its charity policy to make it easier to administer and more cohesive. Currently support is given to a broad range of charities in the categories of: children and youth, social welfare, medical, education, environment/heritage and the arts. Grants to national organisations range from £500 to £15,000 and to local organisations from £100 to £500. Some support is ongoing for up to five years. The company has moved away from sponsorship towards direct giving to charities.

The correspondent estimates that a further £50,000 to £60,000 is given in community contributions through things such as allowing their theatres to be used for charity premieres and giving educational assistance to community projects.

Exclusions
No response to circular appeals. No support for individuals – students, expeditions etc. No grants for fundraising events, advertising in charity brochures, appeals from individuals, local appeals not in areas of company presence or overseas projects. Support is not usually given to church roof or similar appeals.

Applications
In writing to the correspondent, who receives 50 to 70 applications each week, most of which cannot be supported.

Raychem UK Ltd

Faraday Road, Dorcan, Swindon, Wiltshire SN3 5HH
01793-528171; Fax: 01793-572516

Correspondent: Neil Madle, Public Relations Manager

Chief officers: *Chairman:* Dr Richard Kashnow; *Chief Executive:* Peter Ewart

Year end	Turnover	Pre-tax profit
30/6/97	£146,449,000	£11,829,000

Nature of company business
The principal activities are: plastics, wire and cable manufacture.

UK employees: n/a

Charitable donations
1997: £45,000
1996: £45,000
1995: £41,440
1994: £39,345
1993: £28,203

Community support policy

The company supports educational and health initiatives within a 30-mile radius of Swindon, the UK headquarters. Preference for appeals and/or proactive fundraising which allow for staff involvement, especially in support of needy groups.

Exclusions

No support for dangerous fundraising activities; controversial organisations; animal charities; or appeals from individuals.

Applications

In writing to the correspondent.

Reader's Digest Association Ltd

11 Westferry Circus, Canary Wharf, London E14 4HE
0171-715 8000; Fax: 0171-715 8181

Correspondent: The Charities Administrator

Chief officer: *Managing Director:* S N McRae

Year end	Turnover	Pre-tax profit
30/6/97	£105,061,000	(£10,162,000)

Nature of company business
Reader's Digest is a magazine and mail-order book publisher. It is based in London and Swindon.

Main subsidiaries include: Berkeley Magazines Ltd; David & Charles PLC; Reader's Union Ltd; New Country Developement Ltd.

UK employees: 820

Charitable donations
1997: £75,000
1996: £177,196
1995: £182,000
1994: £262,540
1993: £197,697

Community support policy

Charitable donations and community contributions are channelled through The Reader's Digest Trust (Charity Commission number 283115). The company favours donating to a specific project rather than 'blanket' funding. Preference is given by the trust to UK organisations who:

- foster a spirit of enterprise and self-help, particularly in the fields of education, arts/culture, environment or health education; and
- are involved in problem solving in the area of communications (eg. dyslexia, adult literacy, sub-titling, deafness, blindness, speech and learning difficulties). In addition, applications from charities connected with periodical, book or music publishing will be considered.

The trustees are looking for:

(a) the commitment of the people making the application to achieve their stated aims
(b) clear and realistic objectives
(c) a degree of volunteer involvement
(d) evidence of long-term plans and future funding.

The trust gives support to appeals from Swindon and East London where it has a presence but otherwise local appeals are not generally supported. Projects in which members of staff are involved are more likely to receive support. Grants made by the trust totalled £75,000 in 1996/97, which included £42,000 to match employee Give As You Earn contributions. Typical grants to national organisations range from £500 to £15,000, while local grants range from £250 to £2,500.

Employee involvement: The company operates matching funds schemes for employee payroll giving. The introduction of the Give As You Earn payroll giving scheme and the policy to match these donations will reduce the trust's disposable monies by approximately a third.

The arts: Appeals for arts sponsorship are welcomed where relevant.

Exclusions

No support for: particular charities year after year; individuals; charities with primarily sectarian aims; charities operating outside the UK; grants for the repair, maintenance and purchase of vehicles; expeditions; exchanges and study tours; state funded organisations such as schools and hospitals; fundraising events for charity (except by the provision of Reader's Digest products as prizes, or by giving advertising support).

Applications

On a form available from the correspondent, who also decides smaller grants. The trustees meet quarterly. Local appeals should be made to head office as local branches do not have an independent policy or budget.

Other information: The company's main complaints about appeals are that some are too broad, are inadequately researched, are not clear or are too lengthy. Too many appeals are received each year so the following advice should be taken into consideration when appealing: appeals should be short, summarising the charity's aims, operations and revenue and should specify a particular project (costed out) where the trust might be associated. Positive benefits for the company, where these exist, should be spelled out clearly.

Reckitt & Colman plc

67 Alma Road, Windsor, Berkshire SL4 3HD
01753-835835; Fax: 01753-835830

Correspondent: P D Saltmarsh, Company Secretary

Chief officers: *Chairman:* A J Dalby; *Chief Executive:* V L Sankey

Year end	Turnover	Pre-tax profit
3/1/98	£2,196,600,000	£302,500,000

Nature of company business
Principal activities: the manufacture and sale of household, toiletry and pharmaceutical products.

Main brands include: Harpic; Haze; Airwick; Dettox Cleaners; Robin; Woolite; Mr Sheen; Mansion; Cardinal; Brasso; Silvo; Duraglit; Windolene; Zip; Sunny Jim; Steradent; Immac; Down to Earth; Dettol; Codis; Disprin; Junior Disprol; Disprin Solmin; Lemsip; Gaviscon; Fybogel.

Main locations: Chiswick; Hull; Derby.

UK employees: 1,000

Charitable donations
1997: £326,000
1996: £371,000
1995: £224,000
1994: £320,000
1993: £298,000

Total community contributions: £550,000

Membership: *BitC* %Club

Community support policy

Total commmunity contributions in the UK in 1997 were £550,000 including £326,000 in charitable donations. Its main areas of non-cash support is through gifts in kind and secondments. The company has recently become a member of the PerCent Club.

Recipient organisations should be registered charities. There is a preference for appeals linked to areas where the company has its main UK offices and manufacturing units (Hull, Derby, Windsor and Chiswick), though national charities are also supported, and appeals relevant to company business, especially related to children and youth, education or crime, health and hygiene. Other areas of support may include: advertising in charity brochures, enterprise/training, environment/heritage, medical research, social welfare and overseas projects.

The main beneficiaries in 1998 included Headteachers into Industry, Hull Compact Awards, Business in the Community, Hull Children's University, Outward Bound Trust and Prince's Trust.

The company's subsidiaries around the world support charitable causes in their own areas of company presence. Employee fundraising is matched by the company and employees are allowed company time off to volunteer.

Exclusions
No grants for animal welfare charities; appeals from individuals; elderly people; fundraising events; political appeals; religious appeals; the arts; science/technology; sickness/disability charities or sport.

Applications
In writing to the correspondent. Applications are considered by the community involvement committee which meets at least six times a year. In addition to authorising donations, the committee is concerned with the implementation of policy relating to the company's community programme. The committee consists of one executive director, the company secretary, the director of human resources and the head of group communications.

Redrow Group plc

Redrow House, St David's Park, Flintshire CH5 3PW
01244-520044; Fax: 01244-520720

Correspondent: David Bexon, Marketing Director

Chief officer: *Chairman:* S P Morgan

Year end	Turnover	Pre-tax profit
30/6/98	£307,233,000	£48,158,000

Nature of company business
The principal activities are housebuilding and commercial development.

Main subsidiaries include: Bates Business Centre; Harwood Homes; Poche Interior Design.

UK employees: 867

Charitable donations
1998: £257,453
1997: £104,675
1996: £20,204
1995: £17,000
Membership: *BitC*

Community support policy

The company's charitable donations have risen markedly in the last two years. Each year one local and one national charity are nominated for support on a regional basis. These organisations are chosen at the discretion of the acting managing director in the region. Preferred areas of support are children and youth, social welfare and medical charities. Grants to local organisations range from £500 to £3,000.

Exclusions
No support for circular appeals, advertising in charity brochures, purely denominational (religious) appeals, large national appeals, overseas projects or local appeals not in areas of company presence.

Applications
In writing to the correspondent.

Reed Executive plc

Bedford House, Madeira Walk, Windsor, Berkshire SL4 1EU
01753-850441; Fax: 01753-841688

Correspondent: Roger Burn, Acting Personal Assistant to the Chairman

Chief officer: *Chairman:* A E Reed

Year end	Turnover	Pre-tax profit
28/12/97	£226,926,000	£14,022,000

Nature of company business
The company is an employment agency. Subsidiaries include: Reed Accountancy; Reed Employment; Reed Industrial; Reed Nurse; Reed Computing; Reed Insurance; Reed Care; Reed Paramedic.
Main subsidiaries include: Flexistaff Ltd.

UK employees: n/a

Charitable donations
1997: £375,761
1996: £335,269
1995: £224,211
1994: £106,930
1993: £106,930
Membership: *BitC %Club*

Community support policy

The company is a member of the PerCent Club and Business in the Community. The charitable donations figure in 1997 of £375,761 is equivalent to 2.6% of UK pre-tax profit. The company gives 50% discounts on charity personnel recruited through Reed.

Charitable donations: Donations are covenanted to charity via the Charities Aid Foundation. The company is concentrating its charitable support on helping women in the Third World. It also supports organisations which help women in need in the UK, both nationally and locally.

Financial support is given to employees' volunteering and the company match employee fundraising and giving.

The company reports on particular initiatives in the 1998 PerCent Club annual report, these include:

Reed Re-start project – providing inmates of HMP Holloway with work experience and running a training course on interview and communication skills. This programme has been extended to HMP Eastwood Park and a similar project for homeless people in London

At *Royal Holloway University* the company has established a chair in organisational behaviour and continues to sponsor the Leadership, Innovation and Enterprise Studies course

Support for Ethiopiaid, which launched its millennium Appeal in 1997Support for Women@Risk, part-funded by the Reed Charity.

Other recipients of donations included Prisoners Abroad, Guys and St Thomas's Kidney Patients Association and the Teenage Cancer Trust.

Exclusions
No support for appeals from non-charities, campaigning work by charities, appeals from individuals, advertising in charity brochures, fundraising events, circular appeals and small purely local appeals not in an area of company presence.

Applications
In writing to the correspondent. Donations decisions are made continuously. All grant decisions are made at head office.

Other information: Reed Charity, registration number 264728, has over 10% of the company's capital.

Renishaw plc

New Mills, Wotton-under-Edge, Gloucestershire GL12 8JR
01453-524524; Fax: 01453-524901
Website: www.renishaw.com

Correspondent: David Champion, Chairman, Charities Committee

Chief officer: *Chairman:* D R McMurtry

Year end	Turnover	Pre-tax profit
30/6/98	£92,349,000	£22,380,000

Nature of company business
The main activities are the design, manufacture and sale of advanced precision metrology and inspection equipment, and computer-aided design and manufacturing systems.
Main subsidiaries include: Wotton Travel Ltd.

UK employees: 730

Charitable donations
1998: £40,297
1997: £40,022
1996: £55,322
1995: £24,092
1994: £23,500

Community support policy

The company gives priority to local appeals (ie. within 25 miles of company locations) involving young people, and to local branches of national charities concerned with children/youth. Other preferred causes include: the arts, education, elderly people, enterprise/training, environment/heritage, medical research, religious appeals, science/technology, sickness/disability charities and sport.

Exclusions
No support for brochure advertising, fundraising events for third parties, individuals, overseas projects or political appeals. No sponsorship is undertaken.

Applications
Written appeals only addressed to the Charities Committee, at the above address.

Rentokil

Rentokil Initial plc

Felcourt, East Grinstead, West Sussex RH19 2JY
01342-833022; Fax: 01342-326229
Website: www.rentokil-initial.com

Correspondent: Jim Dowson, Corporate Affairs Executive

Chief officers: *Chairman:* H E St L King;
Chief Executive: Sir Clive Thompson

Year end	Turnover	Pre-tax profit
31/12/97	£2,812,000,000	£417,000,000

Nature of company business
Principal activity: international business services.

Main subsidiaries include: A to Z Couriers Ltd; Portman Recruitment Services Ltd; Sparrow Offshore Services Ltd; United Transport Ltd.

UK employees: 80,000

Charitable donations
1997: £220,000
1996: £180,000
1995: £21,000

Community support policy

The charity budget is reviewed annually and rose substantially from £21,000 in 1995 to £180,000 in 1996, and again in 1997, to £220,000.

The company operates a capped staff matched-giving scheme for all its employees. This means the company will add up to £250 (per individual/group charitable event) to match an amount raised by any staff member(s) who take part in an event for a charitable cause. Charitable institutions the company will consider supporting include registered charities, charitable trusts or non profit-making organisations, which raise funds for charitable causes.

Exclusions
Support is not given to any organisation unless a company employee or a group of employees is involved.

Applications
In writing to the correspondent, but note 'Exclusions' above.

Reuters Holdings PLC

85 Fleet Street, London EC4P 4AJ
0171-250 1122
Website: www.foundation.reuters.com

Correspondent: Stephen Somerville, Director, The Reuter Foundation

Chief officers: *Chairman:* Sir Christopher Hogg;
Chief Executive: Peter Job

Year end	Turnover	Pre-tax profit
31/12/97	£2,882,000,000	£626,000,000

Nature of company business
The company acts as a holding company for Reuters Ltd and its subsidiaries which are principally engaged in the business of an international news organisation publishing general, economic and financial news, providing news retrieval services to subscribers and selling equipment for this purpose.

UK employees: n/a

Charitable donations
1997: £3,000,000
1996: £2,700,000
1995: £2,000,000
1994: £1,500,000
1993: £1,050,000

Total community contributions: £8,400,000 (worldwide)

Membership: *ABSA BitC %Club*

Community support policy

The company is a member of the PerCent Club and ABSA and Business in the Community. The Reuter Foundation, the group's charitable trust, was established in 1982. All the company's charitable donations are given to the Foundation. 90% of the budget is spent outside the UK.

The trustees are the chief executive and two other executive directors of the company.

The Reuter Foundation supports three specific fields:

- *Journalism* – practical training and academic study, with special emphasis on economic and financial news – and assistance for parts of the world most in need. This includes providing fellowships to journalists and photo-journalists from developing countries, at the universities of Oxford, Stanford, Bordeaux and Missouri; fellowships for mid-career journalists to broaden their experience and research; short practical training courses aimed at journalists who 'face the challenge of a world in transition, particularly the developing world and central/eastern Europe'.

- *Education* – co-operation with schools, universities, technical training and research, in the fields of information technology, communications and computer science as well as journalism. The foundation provides scholarships and endowments, resources and school competitions. Support given to arts usually has an educational angle, such as workshops for schools or projects aimed at bringing an appreciation of the arts to wider audiences.

- *Humanitarian causes* – community projects, health care, environmental issues, the arts: an international programme, backing the initiatives of Reuter staff with cash or services in kind. Causes supported are often identified by Reuter staff, and fundraising by staff may be matched by the foundation.

The foundation has also set up AlertNet – a website offering rapid news and communications services for the international emergency relief community. It features the latest Reuters news and background on major disasters as well as a forum for voluntary organisations to exchange information and advice. Available to aid agencies via the internet, membership is free of charge but based on information exchange. Members contribute contact details for current relief operations and can exchange field reports, discuss policy issues, and contact other professionals around the world to plan and coordinate emergency relief operations. It aims to make a practical contribution to the speed and efficiency of humanitarian relief operations.

The foundation also supports: elderly people; enterprise/training; environment/heritage; fundraising events and medical research; science/technology; sickness/disability charities and social welfare. Preference for local charities in areas where the company operates, appeals relevant to company business and charities in which a member of staff is involved.

Other support includes gifts in kind and the services of employees. The company matches employee giving (it operates the Give As You Earn scheme) and employee fundraising.

Exclusions

No support for circulars, unsolicited appeals or advertising in charity brochures. No grants for animal welfare charities; political appeals; religious appeals; or sport (unless fundraising for other causes).

Applications

Appeals should be addressed to John Freeman (national) or to Stephen Somerville (international). Please note: unsolicited requests are discouraged unless there is a strong connection with Reuters staff or business.

Rexam PLC

114 Knightsbridge, London SW1X 7NN
0171-584 7070; Fax: 0171-581 1149

Correspondent: Roddy Child Villiers, Director of Corporate Communications

Chief officers: *Chairman:* Jeremy Lancaster; *Chief Executive:* Rolf Börjesson

Year end	Turnover	Pre-tax profit
31/12/97	£2,002,000,000	£179,000,000

Nature of company business
Rexam PLC is a UK-based holding company for an international group operating in print and packaging, coated products, building and engineering.

Main subsidiaries include: Bowater Business Forms Ltd; Bowater Security Products Ltd; Broadprint Ltd; Business Printing Group; Cox and Wyman; McCorquodale Card Technology; Laser Image Ltd; McCorquodale Engineering Ltd; Essex Business Forms; Cartham Papers; Bowater Windows Ltd; W H S Halo; Staybrite Windows; Zenith Windows TBS.

UK employees: 14,000

Charitable donations

1997: £99,000
1996: £92,000
1995: £67,000
1994: £70,000
1993: £72,000
Membership: *BitC*

Community support policy

In 1997, the company's worldwide donations were £243,000, which included £99,000 in the UK. The company supports registered charities only through the Charities Aid Foundation, particularly those concerned with: children/youth, sickness/disability charities, enterprise/training and social welfare. Major grant beneficiaries in 1997 included Prince's Trust Volunteers; British Occupational Health Research; Bondway Housing Association. Typical grants range from £500 to £20,000. The company is a member of Business in the Community.

The company also operates a payroll giving scheme (through CAF), and provides financial support for employee volunteering/charitable activities.

Exclusions

No support for advertising in charity brochures; animal welfare charities; appeals from individuals; overseas projects; political appeals; religious appeals or sport. Sponsorships are not usually undertaken.

Applications

A donations committee at head office meets on an ad hoc basis, usually in the middle of the year. A shortlist of possible beneficiaries, agreed with CAF, is drawn up before being considered by the committee.

Richer Sounds plc

Richer House, Hankey Place, London SE1 4BB
0171-357 9298; Fax: 0171-357 8685

Correspondent: Fiona Brown, Chief Executive of the Persula Foundation

Chief officers: *Chairman:* Julian Richer; *Managing Director:* David Robinson

Year end	Turnover	Pre-tax profit
31/1/98	£39,187,000	£484,000

Nature of company business
Hi-fi retail.

UK employees: 250

Charitable donations

1998: £106,000
1997: £75,000
1996: £110,000
1995: £108,393
1994: £72,149
Membership: *%Club*

Community support policy

The company is a member of the PerCent Club, but it goes way beyond giving 0.5% of pre-tax profits, giving at least 4% of pre-tax profits to the Persula Foundation. The foundation was set up to handle all Richer Sounds charitable giving. On top of the charitable donations, the company also gave around another £5,000 in gifts in kind towards their own charitable projects.

For example, it helped set up: Charity Media Services, to help charities with public relations; TapeSense, which sells subsidised blank audio cassettes to blind people and groups (non-profit making); On the Right Track, a computerised information service for homeless people.

The company also supports employee volunteering, allowing paid time off work to volunteer and by matching employee fundraising.

The Persula Foundation

The aims of the foundation are:
- to support charities in a cost-effective manner
- to help publicise existing charities and their projects
- to act as a commercial adviser to existing charities
- to research and develop original projects.

The foundation continues to support smaller, less established charities and projects 'which we see as exciting and innovative'. The giving is divided into 'Little and often' and 'Less frequent but more substantial amounts'.

'We will give to charities and the projects which, in our opinion, bring about the greatest benefit and which meet our foundation's criteria – certainly not the best-known ones which traditionally attract most funds.' In addition, the foundation spends considerable time researching the needs of charities to see if there are other ways it can help, eg. business or marketing advice.

The main priorities are human welfare, focusing particularly on homeless and disabled people and human rights, and animal welfare. There may be a preference for appeals with a music element in them. National charities and local charities in areas of Richer Sounds shops are prefered. Grants to national organisations range from £100 to £2,000. Grants to local organisations range from £50 to £500. About £2,500 was given to overseas charities.

In 1995/96, the company donated 5% of its profits to the foundation (£110,000), which together with funds provided during 1994/95 meant £170,700 was available. 229 grants were made totalling £48,375 with expenditure on specific projects totalling £33,000. The latter included several projects completed during the year: a bereavement services video to help raise awareness of the services offered by bereavement organisations while at the same time raising funds for The Compassionate Friends and Cruse Bereavement Care; a video 'Community Mediation' produced by mediation UK to help train their volunteers; a promotional and training video for Live Music Now!; the Taffy Thomas Storytelling Tour – a three-day tour to visit blind organisations in the West Midlands.

Other projects still ongoing include: 'On the Right Track' – which provides a free touchscreen computerised information point for homeless people. Points are now up and running at Victoria Station and inside organisations such as the Big Issue and London Connection; 'Tape Sense' – a mail order service offering subsidised blank audio cassettes to visually impaired people or organisations that support such people; The Charity Media Service, which helps charities, within the area of interest, to secure the best possible media attention. It can write press releases and liaise with national and local media. Help can also be given with management, financial management, cost control and purchasing, marketing/PR, customer service, communications and staff motivation.

Exclusions

No support for circular appeals, advertising in charity brochures, appeals from individuals, the arts, children/youth, education, elderly people, enterprise/training, medical research, overseas projects, political/religious appeals or large national appeals.

Applications

In writing to the correspondent. The foundation produces a useful leaflet that should be read before applying for support.

Rio Tinto plc

6 St James's Square, London SW1Y 4LD
0171-930 2399; Fax: 0171-930 3249

Correspondent: R V Court, Head of Community Affairs

Chief officers: *Chairman:* R P Wilson; *Chief Executive:* L A Davis

Year end	Turnover	Pre-tax profit
31/12/97	£4,711,000,000	£1,210,000,000

Nature of company business
Rio Tinto is one of the world's largest mining companies. Based in the UK, Rio Tinto has substantial worldwide interests in metals and industrial minerals with major assets in Australia, South America, Asia, Europe and Southern Africa.

Main subsidiaries include: Anglesey Aluminium Ltd.

UK employees: 1,300

Charitable donations

1997: £824,000
1996: £1,104,000
1995: £983,000
1994: £692,000
1993: £844,000

Total community contributions: £2,555,000

Membership: *ABSA BitC %Club*

Community support policy

Rio Tinto group companies around the world give active support to their local communities, both directly and through independently managed foundations. Worldwide the companies gave £19.5 million in 1997. In the UK, £2.6 million was given both nationally and in the localities where operating companies are active. The company is a member of Business in the Community and ABSA, as well as the PerCent Club.

The company is currently undertaking a review of its community involvement policy. At the time of going to print, this had not been completed, but the company provided the following extract from the typical message currently being given to those seeking support.

'As you may be aware, the great majority of Rio Tinto operations and employees are overseas. It follows from this that the main focus of our community programmes are those communities overseas who are the direct neighbours of our operations and the priorities which we and our neighbours are able to identify together. This approach is based on our communities policy which stresses the three core principles of mutual respect, active partnership and long-term commitment.

'We need also to concentrate on activities which properly reflect the global nature of the mining business, and on issues where the nature of our business gives us particular responsibilities or enables us to make a distinctive contribution. Examples include bio-diversity, the responsible use of scarce resources such as water, promoting respect for human rights, education and health.

'In the case of the limited funds we have available in the UK, we are looking increasingly to use these to support the approach outlined above. We are currently reviewing all our programmes here to improve their match with these priorities. Not all our programmes in the UK will be of quite the same kind. We will, for example, continue our long-standing support for helping young artists to develop their skills at a range of artistic institutions here. But the greater part of our funding will go to actively-managed and long-term partnerships in the sort of areas described. This effort to concentrate resources and time means that we have to focus on a few partnership-based programmes rather than trying to maintain a large number of funding relationships.'

The following information is taken from the last edition of this guide and the above information should be taken into account before applying. It is likely that some of these programmes continue while some will be changed to fit the new criteria.

The company's community support in Britain was already focused on a limited number of significant projects in specific areas where it believed it could make a distinctive contribution. There is a very focused and proactive approach to the type of organisation the company chooses to support, with the emphasis being on education, the arts, environment, and world affairs.

Education: The aim is to develop people's talents and to broaden their education experience; to improve young people's understanding of science and technology especially in the fields of natural resources, industry and the international economy; to support higher education and research, especially in the mining sector and in assisting young people to reach their potential and to encourage their understanding of development issues.

Major support is given by way of providing bursaries and professional academic positions to the Royal School of Mines at Imperial College, Camborne School of Mines, and the Centre for Petroleum and Mineral Law & Policy at the University of Dundee, the London School of Economics, and the Mining and Environmental Research Network at the University of Bath. Through the Sir Val Duncan and Sir Mark Turner Memorial Trust, the company has supported 87 scholarships to Atlantic College in South Wales.

The company is also providing funding, technical expertise and mineral specimens for display in the Natural History Museum's new earth galleries.

Other educational projects include supplying secondary schools with educational materials, sponsorship of the London International Youth Science Forum and work with Young Enterprise. Youth at Risk is supported through the provision of funds to Fairbridge and Focus.

The arts: To support excellence in the arts, especially through training and nurturing the talents of young people; and to foster international cultural exchange and understanding.

For several years the main initiative was to undertake a scheme to provide funds for training at arts institutions, all of which take part in the company's Arts Season. Each of the arts organisations was given bursary funding to develop young talent in the arts at graduate and postgraduate level. Further funding was available for the Arts Season. The beneficiaries in 1997 were the Guildhall School of Music and Drama, the Royal Academy of Arts, the Royal College of Art, the London Contemporary Dance School and the Royal Academy of Dramatic Art.

The ensemble prize at the Royal Over-Seas League Music Competition is also funded by Rio Tinto.

Environment: To support voluntary initiatives which sustain and improve the physical environment both in the UK and overseas and to encourage debate and discussion on environmental issues.

Support is provided to several major UK environmental organisations. These include: the Conservation Foundation – funding individual field studies and sponsoring a series of environmental master classes hosted by David Bellamy; the World Conservation Monitoring Centre – supporting the study of biodiversity hotspots; Botanic Gardens Conservation Secretariat – supporting the publication of a handbook for botanic gardens around the world wishing to reintroduce plants to the wild. Other initiatives include support for Groundwork Trust's Green IT projects which aims to increase links between schools and local industry through renewal work, as well as support for Earthwatch and British Trust for Conservation Volunteers.

World affairs: Rio Tinto has contributed to a wide range of initiatives to realise the goal of promoting debate and understanding of international affairs. These include sponsorship of the English-Speaking Union's Churchill Lecture and the Atlantic College Lecture, the Royal Institute of International Affairs, and the Royal Commonwealth Society.

Exclusions

No support is given directly or indirectly, to any sectarian, religious or political activity. No funding is provided for building projects or general running costs, nor for advertising in charity brochures. Support is not given to individuals, animal welfare charities or any sporting events.

Applications

In writing to the Community Affairs Assistant, although note the policy changes above.

Information available: The company publishes a booklet *Global Neighbour, Local Partner,* which gives details of the company's community involvement. A brief report on its community involvement is also given in its annual report.

RJB Mining plc

Harworth Park, Blyth Road, Harworth, Doncaster, South Yorkshire DN11 6DB
01302-751751; Fax: 01302-752420

Correspondent: R J Budge, Chief Executive

Chief officers: *Chairman:* Lord Chilver; *Chief Executive:* R J Budge

Year end	Turnover	Pre-tax profit
31/12/97	£1,124,717,000	£172,501,000

RM

Nature of company business
The principal activities of the group are coal mining, opencast and underground, and associated activities.
Main subsidiaries include: Blenkinsopp Collieries Ltd; The Monckton Coke & Chemical Co Ltd; Harworth Insurance Ltd; Coal Supply Ltd.

UK employees: 9,327

Charitable donations
1997: £1,071,082
1996: £1,085,751
1995: £951,678
1994: £22,126
1993: £14,602
Membership: *BitC*

Community support policy
The figure quoted above actually includes £800,000 contributed to the Coal industry's Social and Welfare Organisation (CISWO) in accordance with the agreement with the DTI on privatisation to contribute this amount each year for five years from March 1995. This leaves about £270,000 for other appeals. Other organisations supported include the Coal Trade Benevolent Association, National Coalmining Museum of England, Opera North and school projects.

The company has a preference for supporting charities local to Nottinghamshire and Yorkshire, especially those connected with the arts; children/youth; environment/heritage; fundraising events; medical research; social welfare and sport.

Applications
In writing to the correspondent.

RM plc

New Mill House, 183 Milton Park, Abingdon, Oxfordshire OX14 4SE
01235-826000; Fax: 01235-826999
Website: www.rmplc.net

Correspondent: Lorraine Aspel, Personnel Assistant

Chief officers: *Chairman:* J P Leighfield;
Chief Executive: M D Fischer

Year end	Turnover	Pre-tax profit
30/9/97	£110,200,000	£8,000,000

Nature of company business
The main activities are the supply of IT solutions to educational markets, based upon PC technology and incorporating networking, software and services.
Main subsidiaries include: Research Machines PLC.

UK employees: 750

Charitable donations
1997: £136,000
1996: £97,000
1995: £41,000
1994: £15,000

Community support policy
The company's level of giving has risen steadily over the last four years. In addition to the charitable donations figure quoted above, a further £17,000 was given to locally based community projects.

A wide range of charities are supported, usually with small donations of £100 to £500. Only registered charities are considered.

Applications
In writing to the correspondent.

RMC Group plc

RMC House, Coldharbour Lane, Thorpe, Egham, Surrey TW20 8TD
01932-568833; Fax: 01932-568933

Correspondent: C B Brown, Head of Secretariat

Chief officers: *Chairman:* C Hampson;
Chief Executive: P L Young

Year end	Turnover	Pre-tax profit
31/12/97	£4,330,300,000	£307,600,000

Nature of company business
Principal activities: production and supply of materials for use in the construction industry.
Main subsidiaries include: Great Mills (Retail); Hales Waste Control; Readymix (UK); Rombus Materials.

UK employees: 12,755

Charitable donations
1997: £87,000
1996: £92,000
1995: £75,900
1994: £50,000
1993: £43,000
Membership: *BitC*

Community support policy
Each company in the group tends to support local charities in areas of company presence. Preferred areas of support include: culture and recreation, sickness/disability, social welfare, environment and children/youth.

In addition to charitable donations the company undertakes arts and good-cause sponsorship, both locally and nationally (for example, joint sponsorship of the Building Industry Windsor Half Marathon in aid of charities).

Total contributions are probably well over £150,000 but some areas are not quantified.

Exclusions
No support for circular appeals, animal welfare charities, appeals from individuals or advertising in charity brochures.

Applications
In writing to the correspondent. All appeals are considered by a committee which decides which to support.

Roche Products Ltd

40 Broadwater Road, Welwyn Garden City,
Hertfordshire AL7 3AY
01707-366000; Fax: 01707-391503

Correspondent: Gail Greatwood, Corporate Affairs Officer

Chief officers: *Chairman:* Dr A F Leuenberger;
Managing Director: Dr K M Taylor

Year end	Turnover	Pre-tax profit
31/12/95	£363,630,000	£2,503,000

Nature of company business
Principal activity: the manufacture and sale of pharmaceutical specialities and fine chemicals.
Main subsidiaries include: Bohringer Products Ltd; De Puy Inc.

UK employees: n/a

Charitable donations
1995: £91,000
1994: £63,000
1993: £62,000

Community support policy
The company supports a few national organisations, with a preference for medical/pharmaceutical charities. Local charities and schools in Hertfordshire are supported, as are local environmental, children and youth projects.

Recent beneficiaries have included Action on Addiction, Lords Taverners and Hertfordshire Community Trust. Grants to local organisations range from £50 to £500.

Applications
In writing to the correspondent.

Rockwell International Ltd

Unit 21, Suttons Business Park, Reading RG6 1LA
01189-261111

Correspondent: Phil Stickland, Chairman, Charities Committee

Chief officers: n/a

Year end	Turnover	Pre-tax profit
30/9/95	n/a	£17,048,000

Nature of company business
Principal activity: component manufacturers. The company is part of the US-based Rockwell International Corporation with the following operating businesses in the UK: Allen-Bradley International (Milton Keynes, Sutton Coldfield, Stockport, Bristol, Harrow and Poole); Rockwell Automotive (UK) (based in Alcester, Warwickshire); Rockwell Automotive Body Systems (UK) (Birmingham); Rockwell-Collins (UK) (Reading); Rockwell International – Graphics Systems Division (Hounslow and Preston); Rockwell PMC (Peterborough); ROR Rockwell (Wrexham).

UK employees: 1,661

Charitable donations
1995: £79,000
1994: £87,000
1993: £67,587

Community support policy
The company has stated that 60% of charitable donations made by the company are allocated by Rockwell UK Country Council, a committee made up of representatives of Rockwell's UK business managers. The remaining 40% is allocated locally by individual businesses. The company gives two or three grants of about £10,000 to £15,000 each year, usually including support for the Motor & Allied Trades Benevolent Fund. Smaller grants ranging from £100 to £3,000 are given locally, in the fields of education, health and social welfare.

The Rockwell UK Charitable Trust
The trust (Charity Commission number 1000940) had an income of £81,000 in 1997 with grants totalling £96,000. It appears that the company's giving is routed through the trust.

The three largest grants in 1997 were all to universities, Reading (£30,000), De Montford, Leicester (£16,000) and Birmingham (£15,000). No other grants were over £3,000, with recipients of over £1,000 including Tenovus, New Birmingham Women's Hospital, Foundation for the Study of Infant Deaths and Engineering Education Scheme in Wales.

Exclusions
No support for circular appeals; appeals from individuals; fundraising events; advertising in charity brochures; overseas projects; political appeals or religious appeals.

Applications
In writing to the correspondent.

Rolls-Royce plc

65 Buckingham Gate, London SW1E 6AT
0171-222 9020
Website: www.rolls-royce.com

Correspondent: C E Blundell, Company Secretary

Chief officers: *Chairman:* Sir Ralph Robins;
Chief Executive: John E V Rose

Year end	Turnover	Pre-tax profit
31/12/97	£4,334,000,000	£276,000,000

Nature of company business
Rolls–Royce is an engineering company, supplying aero engines and power systems.

Main locations: Ansty (Coventry); Barnoldswick; Bristol; Derby; Dounreay; East Kilbride; Hillington; Hucknall; London; Newcastle; Sunderland.

UK employees: 31,500

Rothmans

Charitable donations
1997: £338,750
1996: £323,850
1995: £298,800
1994: £248,000
1993: £208,000
Membership: *BitC*

Community support policy

Donations policy: During 1997, the group made charitable donations amounting to £338,750. The annual donations budget is administered by a committee of the Board and by local site committees. The group's policy on donations is to direct its support primarily towards assisting military services' benevolent associations and charities with engineering, scientific or educational objectives, as well as objectives connected with the group's business and place in the community.

National charities with a connection to the company's business are supported at head office level, with grants ranging from £500 to £5,000. Local charities are supported by regional site committees at Ansty, Bristol, Derby, Newcastle and Glasgow, which have independent budgets administered by local site committees. Local grants are from £50 to £1,000.

The company operates a payroll giving scheme.

Applications

In writing to the correspondent. The company annual report states that a list of principal donations made in the latest year is available on written request to the company secretary.

Rothmans International Tobacco (UK) Ltd

Oxford Road, Aylesbury, Bucks HP21 8S2
01296-335000; Fax: 01296-335999

Correspondent: Mrs A E Griffiths, Charities Committee

Chief officer: *Chief Executive:* W P Ryan

Year end	Turnover	Pre-tax profit
31/3/97	£772,000,000	£39,300,000

Nature of company business
The company is involved in the manufacture and sale of tobacco products. Group companies manufacture a wide range of well-known brands of cigarettes, cigars and tobaccos which are sold throughout the world.
Main subsidiaries include: Rothmans of Pall Mall (International) Ltd.
Main brands include: Craven; Dunhill; Rothmans; Peter Stuyvesant.
UK employees: n/a

Charitable donations
1998: £133,000
1997: £241,042
1996: £238,077
1995: £432,766
1994: £441,000

Community support policy

Rothmans does not concentrate its support on any particular area of activity, but it does have a number of arrangements which commits much of its charitable donations to given areas. Support tends to be for national rather than local charities, although support may be given to charities in areas of company presence ie. London, Aylesbury, and the North East. Preferred areas of support are: the arts; education; enterprise/training; environment/heritage; overseas projects and social welfare. Grants to national organisations from £1,000 to £11,000. Grants to local organisations from £100 to £1,000. Main beneficiaries in 1997/98 included County Durham Foundation, Royal National Theatre Foundation, University of Leeds, the Prince's Youth Business Trust and Fairbridge.

The company operates an employee payroll giving scheme and matches employee fundraising.

Exclusions

No response to circular appeals. No support for charities concerned with anti-smoking, advertising in charity brochures, animal welfare charities, appeals from individuals, fundraising events, political appeals religious appeals, children/youth, elderly people, medical research, science/technology, sickness/disability charities or sport. No support for sponsorship events.

Applications

Potential applicants may obtain advice by telephone or letter, if required. Applications should be in writing to the correspondent

N M Rothschild & Sons Ltd

New Court, St Swithin's Lane, London EC4P 4DU
0171-280 5000; Fax: 0171-929 1643

Correspondent: Mary Mitchell, Secretary to the Charities Committee

Chief officer: *Chairman:* Sir Evelyn de Rothschild

Year end	Turnover	Pre-tax profit
31/3/97	£348,171,000	£30,481,000

Nature of company business
The company and its subsidiaries carry on the business of merchants and bankers. The parent company is Rothschild Continuation Ltd and the ultimate holding company is Rothschild Concordia A G, incorporated in Switzerland.

UK employees: n/a

Charitable donations
1997: £632,000
1996: £463,000
1995: £585,000
1994: £494,000
1993: £490,000
Membership: *ABSA BitC*

Community support policy

The main area of charitable support is social welfare, although support is also given in the fields of health and medical care, education, scientific research, and the arts.

About 300 grants to national charities are made each year, ranging from £250 to £1,000. Local grants are not normally given.

The main area of non-cash support is through good-cause sponsorship. The company operates a payroll giving scheme. Financial support is given to employee volunteering. The company is a member of Business in the Community. Its subsidiaries around the world support causes in their areas of operation.

Exclusions

Donations are not normally made to local groups. No response to circular appeals. No grants for advertising in charity brochures; animal welfare charities; appeals from individuals; fundraising events; overseas projects; political appeals; religious appeals or sport.

Applications

In writing to the Secretary to the Charities Committee, which meets quarterly to make grant decisions.

Sponsorship proposals should be addressed to the Group Corporate Affairs Department.

Royal Automobile Club Limited

89–91 Pall Mall, London SW1Y 5HS
0171-930 2345

Correspondent: H Kemlo, Secretary

Chief officer: *Chairman:* B K McGiven

Year end	Turnover	Pre-tax profit
31/12/97	£287,800,000	£11,500,000

Nature of company business
The principal activities of the group are the provision of services and benefits to members of the Royal Automobile Club and the encouragement and development of motoring. It operates motoring services, driver training (acquiring BSM in November 1997), clubhouses and motorsport.

Main subsidiaries include: Motorway Rescue Services Ltd; London Wall Insurance Services Ltd; Bescot Leasing Ltd; British School of Motoring Ltd; MCR Ltd; BSM Holdings Ltd.

UK employees: 4,499

Charitable donations
1997: £55,864

Community support policy

The company has an associated foundation, through which giving appears to be routed. The RAC Foundation for Motoring and the Environment was established in 1990 'to promote for the public benefit awareness and understanding of the environmental problems of the use of motor vehicles, and to research and investigate solutions to these problems'.

In 1995, two research projects were completed. The first, by the Transport Studies Unit at Oxford University on the concept of car dependence. The second on the impact of traffic on the North Yorkshire Moors National Park implementation of experimental measures to address congestion by Oxford Brookes University. It appears that an academic advisory group outlines research programmes for the following year, then puts the proposal out to tender. In 1996, the first proposed project was on the impact of the Okehampton bypass, the report of this study was published in July 1997. The latest project is entitled 'Civilised Cities' and involves several partners including the Civic Trust. The first report from this was due to be published in the spring of 1998.

In 1995, the trust received £45,000 from RAC Motoring Services Ltd. Its expenditure of £80,000 was covered by a surplus the previous year, when in addition to £50,000 from RAC Motoring Services Ltd, it also received £10,000 from Vauxhall Motors Ltd.

We do not know if the figure from the company's annual report, of £56,000 in charitable donations in 1997, was the amount donated to the foundation or whether some or all of it was given to other charities.

Applications

In writing to the correspondent.

The Royal Bank of Scotland Group plc

36 St Andrew Square, Edinburgh EH2 2YB
0131-556 8555; Fax: 0131-558 3573

Correspondent: Jim Bellamy, Head of Sponsorship & Community Programme

Chief officers: *Chairman:* Viscount Younger of Leckie; *Chief Executive:* Dr George Mathewson

Year end	Turnover	Pre-tax profit
30/9/98	n/a	£1,001,000,000

Nature of company business
The Royal Bank of Scotland is one of the UK's leading financial services groups and is engaged in a wide range of banking, insurance and financial services in the UK.

Main subsidiaries include: Adam & Co Group PLC; Direct Line Financial Services Ltd; Tesco Personal Finance Ltd; Direct Line Insurance PLC; Privilege Insurance Co Ltd; Style Financial Services Ltd.

UK employees: 26,670

Charitable donations
1998: £2,277,923
1997: £2,081,352
1996: £1,600,000
1995: £1,124,000
1994: £977,000
Total community contributions: £2,500,000

Membership: *ABSA BitC %Club*

Royal London

Community support policy
The bank is a member of Business in the Community and the PerCent Club and continues its objective of commitment to the communities in which it operates with support of £2.5 million.

The Community Programme supports projects that are national or cover a wide geographical area. Support is targeted on the theme of finance in the community, linking with areas such as education, job creation, social exclusion and the development of small businesses. During 1998, main beneficiaries included the Prince's Scottish Youth Business Trust, Prince's Youth Business Trust and Groundwork Foundation.

The bank is a member of ABSA and prefers to focus on a few selected events each year. Recent support includes the Edinburgh International Festival and the Royal National Theatre's production of *The Prime of Miss Jean Brodie*.

Bank staff are encouraged to commit time and expertise to community projects and grants are made available to staff who are involved in projects which benefit local communities.

Commercial sponsorship and joint business promotions with charitable organisations are not included in the community support figure of £2.5 million.

Exclusions
The bank does not support advertising in charity brochures, animal welfare, appeals from individuals, fundraising events, medical research, overseas projects, political appeals or religious appeals.

Applications
In writing to the correspondent, including if possible, appropriate report and accounts or financial statements. Grant decisions at head office are made by a donations committee which meets quarterly. Local appeals should be sent to local branches.

The bank produces a leaflet advising potential applicants how to apply for a Community Action Programme grant.

Approaches for support should include, where possible, appropriate reports and accounts or financial statements.

The Royal London Mutual Insurance Society Ltd

Royal London House, Middleborough, Colchester, Essex CO1 1RA
01206-761761; Fax: 01206-786980
Website: www.royal-london-ins.co.uk

Correspondent: Stephen Humphreys, Head of Corporate Communications

Chief officers: *Chairman:* Michael Pickard;
Chief Executive: Mike Yardley

Year end	Turnover	Pre-tax profit
31/12/97	n/a	£29,800,000

Nature of company business
Principal activities: the transaction of main classes of insurance business and, through subsidiaries, unit trust and investment management.

Main subsidiaries include: Atrium Management; The Lion Insurance Co.

UK employees: 3,675

Charitable donations
1997: £41,950
1996: £48,752
1995: £44,892
1994: n/a
1993: £46,164
Membership: *BitC*

Community support policy
The company gives about £40,0000 a year, with donations concentrated on aspects of medical research and appeals relevant to its business and local to Essex.

Grants to national organisations range from £250 to £2,000 and to local organisations from £25 to £1,450. In 1998, a review of CCI (Corporate Community Involvement) was undertaken, which is likely to lead to a change of policy.

Exclusions
No support for appeals from individuals, purely denominational (religious) appeals or overseas projects.

Applications
In writing to the correspondent to whom sponsorship proposals should also be addressed.

Royal & Sun Alliance Insurance Group plc

Community Investment Unit, PO Box 144, New Hall Place, Old Hall Street, Liverpool L69 3EN
0151-227 4422; Fax: 0151-224 3787
Website: www.royal-and-sunalliance.co.uk

Correspondent: John Hymers, Community Investment Manager

Chief officers: *Chairman:* Patrick Gillam;

Chief Executive: Robert Mendelsohn

Year end	Turnover	Pre-tax profit
31/12/98	n/a	£400,000,000

Nature of company business
Worldwide insurance company writing all classes of general insurance, life assurance (excluding industrial life) and related financial services.

Main subsidiaries include: Bradford Insurance Company; FirstAssist Group; The Globe Insurance Company; Legal Protection Group Holdings; The London Assurance; The Marine Insurance Company; Royal International Insurance Holdings; Royal Insurance Holdings; Royal Insurance Property Services; Royal Life Insurance; Sun Alliance Life; Sun Insurance Office; Swinton (Holdings).

UK employees: 24,776

Charitable donations

1998: £1,200,000
1997: £899,000
1996: £915,600
1995: £975,600
1994: £148,271

Total community contributions: £2,400,000

Membership: *ABSA BitC %Club*

Community support policy

Total community contributions in 1998 were £2,400,000, half of which was given in cash donations. Royal & Sun Alliance invests in the community because it believes that its responsibility goes beyond the bottom line. Businesses exist within and because of communities; they cannot stand apart from them. The people on whom the group depends – its customers, shareholders, employees and suppliers – are all part of communities. Moreover, company and community depend on each other for their success; companies need healthy communities in which to operate; communities need successful companies if they are to prosper.

The combination of staff involvement, gifts in kind, training schemes, and use of resources (premises and equipment) together with funding demonstrates a significant commitment to the community and helps discharge the company's social responsibility. The company is a member of ABSA, Business in the Community and the PerCent Club.

Royal & Sun Alliance's Community Investment Programme (CIP) is designed to be relevant to the voluntary organisations through which it supports the community, but also to its employees and its business where the company has a presence (London, Horsham, Leeds, Birmingham, Manchester, Liverpool, Glasgow and Belfast).

CIP operates through four strands to give voluntary organisations both the financial and practical support they need whilst giving every chance to employees to support their community in the way that best suits them. The programme concentrates on three priority areas:

- education and training
- safer communities
- health and safety.

Other areas of support are advertising in charity brochures, the arts, children/youth, fundraising events, medical research, science/technology, sickness/disability charities and sport.

The corporate strand focuses on establishing and developing partnerships with charities in each of the three priority areas.

The three other operational strands involve:

- setting up Regional Staff Committees to ensure CIP makes an impact in the local communities in which the group has a significant presence
- community-based Assignment and Secondment opportunities for staff to work with charities on mutually beneficial projects
- through the company payroll, a Give As You Earn scheme to enable staff and pensioners to make tax efficient donations to any charity of their choice, some of which the group matches £ for £.

In 1998, main grant beneficiaries included: Roadrunners; Royal Sun Alliance Panathalon Challenge; Royal Sun Alliance Lifelong Skills Programme; Bromley-by-Bow Centre; Prince's Youth Business Trust and Young Enterprise.

Exclusions

There are few circumstances in which the company is able to provide support outside this policy framework. Therefore, applicants such as political, religious appeals, social or animal welfare, overseas projects or environment/heritage are not considered, nor can charities whose work mainly benefits people overseas or individuals seeking personal or professional sponsorship. Requests received by circular are not actioned.

Applications

Generally applications should be in writing to the correspondent above, or Barbara Harwood, Community Investment Officer, Tricourt House, North Street, West Sussex RH12 1XQ (01403-231161).

Rugby Group plc

Crown House, Rugby, Warwickshire CV21 2DT
01788-542666; Fax: 01788-540256
Website: www.rugbygroup.co.uk

Correspondent: Ken Kitchen, Group Human Resources Manager

Chief officers: *Chairman:* R M Gourlay; *Managing Director:* P M Johnson

Year end	Turnover	Pre-tax profit
31/12/97	£1,065,000,000	£68,000,000

Nature of company business
Building materials.

Main subsidiaries include: Gillingham Portland Cement Co Ltd; Ash Resources Ltd; BCE Cellular Extrusions Ltd; Boulton & Paul.

UK employees: 4,864

Charitable donations

1997: £89,122
1996: £82,595
1995: £53,575
1994: £55,232
1993: £41,627

Community support policy

The company states that it aims to support the community through financial assistance, professional expertise, staff volunteering and donations of products equipment.

National charities are supported from the company's head office. Local companies/sites have their own donations budget to support local charities in their area. Some preference is given to environment/heritage appeals.

Safeway

The group has a benevolent scheme, mainly for past/present employees, but small amounts can be given for other charitable purposes. In kind support is usually given through secondments and training schemes.

Exclusions

No support for advertising in charity brochures, or political appeals.

Applications

In writing to the correspondent.

Safeway plc

6 Millington Road, Hayes, Middlesex UB3 4AY
0181-848 8744
Website: www.safeway.co.uk

Correspondent: Petea Nel, Community Relations Executive

Chief officers: *Chairman:* D G C Webster; *Chief Executive:* Colin Smith

Year end	Turnover	Pre-tax profit
28/3/98	£7,493,600,000	£340,200,000

Nature of company business
Principal activity: food retailing, through the Safeway supermarket chain.

UK employees: 76,096

Charitable donations

1998: £74,000
1997: £46,000
1996: £214,000
1995: £281,000
1994: £343,000

Total community contributions: £357,000 (1996)

Membership: *BitC*

Community support policy

The company's charitable donations in 1997/98 totalled only £74,000, equivalent to 0.02% of pre-tax profit. Unfortunately we have no figure for the company's total community support since that for 1996.

Donations policy: The company supports projects relating to families and children, including education and environmental initiatives. Support is also given to fundraising initiatives organised by national and local charities. There is a preference for national charities and local charities near to trading stores.

Employees are encouraged to play an active role in the community, especially through fundraising activities. 1998 saw the completion of the 'Helping Hand' appeal, which raised £1.6 million for the Pre-School Learning Alliance in England, the Pre-School Play Association in Scotland and the Pre-School Playgroups Association in Wales. For the time being Safeway has decided not to adopt another corporate charity, leaving it up to staff to decide for themselves which charities they wish to support.

Small, local appeals are usually steered through district managers who may then recommend the appeal to head office. Local managers may give some small support to local charities in the form of a prize for a raffle, either in cash or in kind.

Enterprise: The company is a member of Scottish Business in the Community, The Hillingdon Partnership Trust and the Hayes & West Drayton Partnership.

Education: An educational pack entitled 'Learning in Store' is available on loan from all Safeway supermarkets. Safeway also supports the development of vocational qualifications and has continuing strong links with universities. At a local level, Safeway encourages strong links between stores and schools, and many store managers have become governors of their local schools.

Exclusions

The company does NOT support: advertising in charity brochures; animal welfare charities; appeals from individuals; political or religious appeals or sport.

Applications

In writing to the correspondent.

Saga Leisure Ltd

Middelburg Square, Folkestone, Kent CT20 1AZ
01303-711111; Fax: 01303-256676

Correspondent: Peter Bettley, Head of Public Relations

Chief officer: *Chairman:* R M De Haan

Year end	Turnover	Pre-tax profit
31/1/98	£257,696,000	£15,294,000

Nature of company business
Tour operators and financial services.

Main subsidiaries include: Inter-Church Travel Ltd; MetroMail Ltd.

UK employees: 1,200

Charitable donations

1998: £122,000
1997: £95,000
1996: £125,000
1995: £134,000

Total community contributions: £175,000 (1997)

Community support policy

The company has a preference for charities specifically specialising in benefiting the elderly and the hospice movement in Kent. Donations are usually less than £500. In the immediate East Kent area consideration would be given to children, youth groups and education.

In addition to sponsorship of the Saga Book Prize, the company has also sponsored local groups including Bournemouth Orchestras and Folkestone Town Band.

Exclusions

No support for advertising in charity brochures; animal welfare charities; the arts; enterprise/training; environment/heritage; fundraising events; medical research; overseas projects; political appeals; religious appeals; science/technology; sickness/disability charities; social welfare or sport.

Applications

In writing to the correspondent.

J Sainsbury plc

Stamford House, Stamford Street, London SE1 9LL
0171-695 6000; Fax: 0171-695 0097
Website: www.sainsburys.co.uk

Correspondent: Mrs S L Mercer, Sainsbury's Community Affairs Department

Chief officers: *Chairman:* Sir George Bull; *Chief Executive:* D Adriano

Year end	Turnover	Pre-tax profit
8/3/98	£15,496,000,000	£853,000,000

Nature of company business
Principal activity: the retail distribution of food. Other activities include home improvement and garden centres, hypermarkets, and the processing of bacon and pork products. Apart from the Sainsbury supermarket chain (382 stores in England, Scotland and Wales), activities include Shaws Supermarkets Inc USA, a wholly owned subsidiary.

Main subsidiaries include: Savacentre Ltd; Homebase Ltd.

UK employees: 121,565

Charitable donations

1998: £2,400,000
1997: £2,000,000
1996: £2,000,000
1995: £1,400,000
1994: £1,800,000
Membership: ABSA BitC %Club

Community support policy

The company is a member of the PerCent Club and Business in the Community. Community contributions totalled £2.4 million in 1997/98. All stores have a community budget to support local fundraising efforts with raffle prizes. Please write to the store manager. Grants are given via the company's charitable fund.

The main areas of non-cash support are good-cause sponsorship, secondments and gifts in kind.

Projects: The community programme has a proactive approach and supports projects in UK trading areas only. It receives the major project-based appeals. Appeals from organisations working with disabled and elderly people, under-fives and families will be considered.

Other areas of support include the arts, education, elderly people, enterprise/training, environment/heritage, fundraising events and sickness/disability charities.

The company supports national charities and local charities in areas of company presence. Grants range from £50 to £10,000. Grants up to £1,000 are considered weekly. Beneficiaries during 1997/98 included: Northamptonshire Libraries; Craigavon Women's Training Scheme; Young Enterprise; National Asthma Campaign and CSV Literacy Scheme.

Employee involvement: There is an employee volunteering scheme which allows staff time off to volunteer. Sainsburys' gives financial support to these volunteers and matches employee fundraising. The company also operates the 'Sharing the Caring' payroll giving scheme.

Exclusions

No response to circulars. No support for individuals, restoration/fabric of buildings, National Health projects, overseas projects, local appeals not in areas of company presence, political or religious causes, core or pump priming.

Applications

Appeals to head office should be addressed to the correspondent. Applications can be received at any time, and should include details of: aims and objectives, target audience and links with at least one Sainsbury store. Local appeals should be sent to local stores who will then approach the donations committee. This meets quarterly, but a sub-committee meets as and when necessary.

A separate budget exists for small donations to local charities/voluntary groups, administered at store level, in the form of vouchers.

Corporate sponsorship requests should also be addressed to Sainsbury's Community Affairs Department. There are also a number of Sainsbury Family Trusts with major grant-making programmes. These are administered separately (see *A Guide to the Major Trusts Volume 1*), although close contact is maintained with the company's donations programme.

Information available: The company publishes information in its community affairs brochure, its annual report, in articles in the employee journal and in employee reports.

Advice to applicants: Sainsburys' advises applicants to try to avoid stereotyped circulars. All appeals are responded to, but charities often underestimate the time required for consideration of their appeals. So, applicants should be patient!

St James Place Capital plc

27 St James's Place, London SW1A 1NR
0171-493 8111

Correspondent: Mrs Diane R Lovegrove, Administrator, J Rothschild Group Charitable Trust

Chief officer: *Chairman:* Anthony Loehnis

Year end	Turnover	Pre-tax profit
31/12/97	n/a	n/a

St James

Nature of company business
The company is an investment holding company with subsidiaries engaged in investment holding, investment dealing, life assurance, corporate finance and fund management.
Main subsidiaries include: J Rothschild Assurance plc.

UK employees: 67

Charitable donations
1997: £50,000
1996: £66,750
1995: £133,025
1994: £125,000
1993: £125,000
Membership: *BitC %Club*

Community support policy

The company is a member of the PerCent Club. Grants are made through the J Rothschild Group Charitable Trust which establishes a policy with clearly defined areas for support at the start of each financial year. The company now contributes about £50,000 to the trust a year.

The trust has recently changed its accounting period to coincide with that of the company. Grants generally range from £500 to £5,000. Support continues to be given to charities where shareholders and employees are personally involved. A proportion of the budget is also allocated to a number of other charities where the trust is particularly impressed with the work done, or their application.

The trustees are Anthony Loehnis, Lord Rothschild and John Johnston. The trust makes available a detailed report on its charitable donations programme, including a statement of policy and a list of all donations made. The change in the accounting period meant that the 1997 accounts included the final payments in respect of the previous main objective, 'Homelessness'. The target area for 1997 and continuing into 1998 was 'Protection of Youth'.

Policy of the trustees:
- to get the maximum return for the money allocated.
- to support projects where a comparatively small amount of money will do a disproportionate amount of good.
- to identify charities which are not being adequately supported by voluntary and statutory funding, often including what may be regarded as 'neglected' causes.
- to continue to support a number of central charities in their particular areas.
- to 'follow up' on grants given in the major categories area, to assess further needs, and to ensure that the funds are being utilised in the manner intended by the trust.

The trustees report states that they continue to receive numerous applications, but notes that in general they are much better presented, 'with most cases providing the much needed financial information on their situation'. About 10% of applications can be supported.

In 1997, the trust had a total income of £45,000 and gave £56,000 in grants. All the grants made are described in detail in the trust annual report. They were categorised as follows:

Main target areas

Homelessness	£11,000	(7 grants)
Protection of youth	£30,500	(35 grants)
Staff/shareholder appeals	£7,200	(13 grants)
Small grants	£6,950	(18 grants)
Total	£55,650	

Areas supported:

Homelessness: seven grants of £1,000 to £2,500 were given totalling £11,000. Beneficiaries included: Just Ask, to help meet increasing demand for their services; Salvation Army, towards their outreach and resettlement work in London; Eaves Housing for Women, towards a new initiative for a tenant's newsletter.

Protection of Youth: 16 grants of £1,000 to £3,000 totalling £30,500, with a further 19 grants of £500. Major beneficiaries included: East London Schools Fund (£6,000 over a two-year period) to support a school-home support worker at a school in North Islington; Wildside Trust, on-going costs; Mayday Trust, towards an activity/education centre; and St Andrew's Children's Society Ltd, towards its respite care scheme. Other recipients included Back Football and Recreation Club, Burnley Pendle & Rossendale CVS, Edinburgh Cyrenians, Federation of Artistic and Creative Therapy and the Brandon Centre.

Shareholder/staff appeals: small grants to support worthwhile charitable causes in which shareholders and staff of the company take an active personal interest. 13 grants totalling £7,200 and ranging from £200 to £1,000, about half being for £500. Recipients included: Farm Africa, John Grooms Association, Breast Cancer Campaign, Mental Health Foundation and Streatham Youth Centre.

Smaller grants: Typically £200 to £500 grants given in response to the large number of appeals received. 18 grants totalling £6,950 in the fields of health, welfare and disability including DEMAND, Fife Furniture Stockpile, Jericho Community project, Prison Phoenix Trust and Croydon Women's Aid.

At the end of 1997, the company acquired the the outstanding share capital of The J Rothschild Assurance Group (JRA Group). The 1997 annual report for the company included the following information under the heading 'Community Affairs'.

'One of the precepts upon which the JRA Group was established was the belief that a successful commercial organisation has a responsibility to apply some of its profits and energy for the benefit of the less fortunate members of the community. The J Rothschild Foundation was established as a charitable trust and the group has always expressed the intention that, after it moved to a statutory profit, it would contribute a proportion of the profits to the foundation. Equally significantly the foundation has received contributions and voluntary assistance, in terms of time and commitment, from individual members of the partnership and the group's employees.

'In 1997, the foundation made grants in excess of £160,000 to various causes around the UK in accordance with a theme of providing tangible support for pre-teen children suffering from physical or mental disabilities or life-threatening diseases.

'Following the merger of the interests of SJPC and the JRA Group, the Board is developing a coordinated policy for charitable contributions and will, as it did in 1986, present its proposals to shareholders for approval at next year's annual general meeting.'

Exclusions

No response to circular appeals, advertising in charity brochures or individuals. Due to charitable funding being reduced some policy changes have been made: 'Local and disaster fund categories can no longer be supported; charities applying to the trust for funding may be asked to provide evidence that they can obtain the same amount of money from a third party to equal the sum our trust is considering donating; the trust does not undertake sponsorships, corporate advertising or take tickets for charitable and other events.'

Applications

Regular meetings of the J Rothschild Group Charitable Trust are held at which the trustees consider applications. Appeals should be in writing to the correspondent enclosing appropriate financial or other supporting documentation.

Advice to applicants: This company has established a procedure for giving which puts it very much amongst the leaders in the field of corporate charitable giving. By concentrating on specific issues, local action and general appeals of interest to staff and shareholders, the company is able to make a very positive contribution with the funds at its disposal. Any potential applicant should be aware of the company's current policy and appeals falling outside this very clear policy are unlikely to be supported. It should also be noted that, in general, no undertaking of continued support is given when a donation is made.

Salomon Smith Barney Europe Ltd

Victoria Plaza, 111 Buckingham Palace Road,
London SW1W 0SB
0171-721 2000; Fax: 0171-222 7062
Website: www.salomonsmithbarney.com

Correspondent: Elaine Howard, Corporate Relations

Chief officer: *Chief Executive:* P J Middleton

Year end	Turnover	Pre-tax profit
31/12/96	£1,711,000,000	£52,000,000

Nature of company business
The company's main activities are securities, mortgages and asset management. The company was formed in November 1997 through the merger of Salomon Inc with Smith Barney Holdings Inc.

UK employees: 1,376

Charitable donations
1996: £79,429
1995: £73,989
1994: £176,527

Community support policy

This US parent company has a section of its website committed to brief reports on community initiatives. It states that, 'we are unwaveringly committed to community service and diversity'. However, we have not been able to update the figure for the company's charitable support in the UK, the figure above referring to donations made by Salomon Brothers Europe Ltd before its merger. Neither have we been able to obtain any information about what the company supports in the UK.

In the US major initiatives include: support for raising public awareness of women's health issues, including breast cancer; support for civic and minority organisations; involvement with education including training, scholarships and mentoring.

Applications
In writing to the correspondent, for consideration by the charities committee.

Christian Salvesen PLC

500 Pavilion Drive, Brackmills, Northampton NN4 7YJ
01604-662600; Fax: 01604-622605

Correspondent: Jane Lister, Secretary to the Chief Executive

Chief officers: *Chairman:* Jonathan Fry;

Chief Executive: Edward Roderick

Year end	Turnover	Pre-tax profit
31/3/98	£636,000,000	£64,000,000

Nature of company business
Principal activities: logistics and food services.

Main subsidiaries include: Tendafrost Frozen Foods Ltd; Inverleith Insurance Co Ltd.

UK employees: 11,110

Charitable donations
1998: £143,000
1997: £91,000
1996: £78,000
1995: £76,000
1994: £75,000

Total community contributions: £242,000 (1997)

Community support policy

In 1996/97, community contributions totalled £242,000 in terms of cash, employees time and other services to a wide range of charities, community and arts organisations. Charitable donations increased by a further 50% in 1997/98 to over £140,000, from £91,000 in 1996/97.

The company supports education and youth activities, industrial training, and community and environmental charities local to where the company has an operational presence as well as projects where a member of staff is involved.

Main grant beneficiaries in 1996/97 included: NSPCC, Whizz-Kidz, Barnardo's, enterprise trusts, and Young Enterprise.

Samsung

Exclusions
National charities (unless specific to local operational area); circular appeals; advertising in charity brochures; animal welfare charities; medical research; overseas projects; political appeals; religious appeals.

Applications
Apply in writing to the Community Affairs Department. The Group Charities Committee meets quarterly.

Samsung Electronics UK Ltd

Unit 1, Hook Rise Business & Industrial Centre, 225 Hook Rise South, Surbiton, Surrey, KT6 7LD
0181-391 0168; Fax: 0181-397 9949
Website: www.samsungelectronics.co.uk

Correspondent: Kerry Finucane, Human Resources Manager

Chief officers: n/a

Year end	Turnover	Pre-tax profit
31/12/95	£302,401,000	(£5,484,000)

Nature of company business
Samsung electronics manufactures and distributes electronic and electrical goods. In the UK it manufactures fax machines and colour televisions and designs and develops microwave ovens.

UK employees: 787

Charitable donations
1995: £135,000
1994: £100,000

Community support policy
Unfortunately, no new figures were available for the company.

It supports charities local to the Surbiton area, including schools and community projects. In addition to its head quarters in Surrey, the main UK sites are in Telford (distribution centre), Middlesex (research centre) and Wynyard (factory).

Applications
In writing to the correspondent.

Sanofi Winthrop Ltd

One Onslow Street, Guildford, Surrey GU1 4YS
01483-554440; Fax: 01483-554801

Correspondent: Sarah Gant, Head of Communications

Chief officers: n/a

Year end	Turnover	Pre-tax profit
31/12/96	£117,355,000	£4,208,000

Nature of company business
Principal activities: prescription medicines, chemicals.

UK employees: 1,265

Charitable donations
1996: £65,825

Community support policy
The company prefers to support appeals local to its operating sites ie. Guildford and Newcastle. Normally preference is given to support causes connected with: children/youth; education; elderly people; enterprise/ training; medical research; science/technology; sickness/ disability; and social welfare. In 1996 main grant beneficiaries included: Sanofi Winthrop Foundation; Starlight Foundation; Guildford Discovery; British Vascular Foundation and Comic Relief.

The company also operates a payroll giving scheme (Give As You Earn), and supports selected volunteering/ charitable activities by employees' through financial help, matching employee fundraising and matching employee giving. In 1996, the money raised was donated to the corporate chosen charity, Starlight Foundation.

Exclusions
Unsolicited appeals are not supported and no support is given to circular appeals, advertising in charity brochures, animal welfare charities, appeals from individuals, the arts, environment/heritage, overseas projects, political appeals, religious appeals, sport or local appeals not in areas of company presence.

Applications
In writing to the correspondent, to whom sponsorship proposals should also be addressed to the Head of Communications.

Sapalux Ltd

101 Oakley Road, Luton, Bedfordshire LU4 9QQ
01582-491234; Fax: 01582-574255

Correspondent: Christine Askew, Secretary to the Company Secretary

Chief officers: n/a

Year end	Turnover	Pre-tax profit
31/12/94	£803,389,000	£31,680,000

Nature of company business
The principal activities of the company are the manufacture, sale and service of household, commercial, industrial and outdoor products.

Main subsidiaries include: Electrolux Holdings Ltd; Dependable Protection Ltd; Associated Commercial Products Ltd.

UK employees: n/a

Charitable donations
1994: £50,500
1993: £32,000

Community support policy
Unfortunately, we have no information on the donations policy of the company, or any figures since those for 1994.

Applications
In writing to the correspondent.

Save & Prosper Group Ltd

Finsbury Dials, 20 Finsbury Street, London EC2Y 9AY
0171-417 2332; Fax: 0171-417 2300
Website: www.prosper.co.uk

Correspondent: Duncan Grant, Director, Save & Prosper Trusts

Chief officers: n/a

Year end	Turnover	Pre-tax profit
30/4/96	n/a	n/a

Nature of company business
Financial services organisation. The company is a subsidiary of Robert Flemings Holdings Ltd (see separate entry).

UK employees: n/a

Charitable donations
1996: £1,196,000
1995: £1,347,000
1994: £1,734,000
Membership: *BitC   %Club*

Community support policy

The company supports a large number of community and educational projects largely through the Save & Prosper Educational Trust and the Save & Prosper Foundation. The company is a member of Business in the Community and the PerCent Club. The company is based in Romford and Edinburgh and staff support local community projects and national charities with time and fundraising efforts.

Save & Prosper Educational Trust

The trust was established in 1974. The trustee is the Save & Prosper Group Ltd, who have appointed the following management committee: C J Rye (Chairman), D Grant (Director), A G Williams, Mrs L M L Bassett. Its income comes from annuities purchased to pay school fees.

The trust makes grants to educational establishments, education and training in community projects particularly within inner cities, arts education, education for the disadvantaged, and to programmes of scholarships and bursaries. It is interested in supporting 'new and innovative ways of advancing education in the UK'. Grants generally range from £100 to £20,000, with a handful of larger grants given.

Recruitment into this scheme has now ceased, and the income for this trust will therefore be decrease to zero by the year 2014. However, another trust, the Save & Prosper Foundation, is being built up as the old one declines. It received £125,000 during the year.

Further details on the grant-making can be found in *A Guide to the Major Trusts Volume 1*.

Exclusions

No grants for advertising in charity brochures, appeals from individuals, overseas projects, political appeals, religious appeals or large national appeals.

Applications

In writing to the correspondent.

Sponsorship proposals should be addressed to Simon Curtis, Sponsorship Manager.

Savills plc

20 Grosvenor Hill, Berkeley Square, London W1X 0HQ
0171-499 8644

Correspondent: Katie Braithwaite, Personal Assistant to the Managing Director

Chief officers: *Chairman:* Richard Jewson; *Managing Director:* Aubrey Adams

Year end	Turnover	Pre-tax profit
30/4/97	£54,815,000	£7,617,000

Nature of company business
Savills plc is a holding company. Its principal subsidiaries' activities are advising on matters affecting commercial, agricultural and residential property, and providing corporate finance advice, property and venture capital funding and a range of property-related financial services.

Main subsidiaries include: Aubourn Farming; Grosvenor Hill Properties; Property Marketing Company.

UK employees: n/a

Charitable donations
1997: £40,000
1996: £40,000
1995: £44,000
1994: £43,000
1993: £40,000
Membership: *%Club*

Community support policy

The company states in its annual report that the charge to the profit and loss account of donations was £25,000 and the amount paid out of the group's Charities Aid Foundation account was £15,000. The company is a member of the PerCent Club.

It has a preference for local charities in the areas of operation, appeals relevant to company business and charities in which a member of staff is involved. Preferred areas of support are projects involving medicine, enterprise/training and overseas aid/development. Grants to national organisations range from £100 to £500. Grants to local organisations from £50 to £200.

Beneficiaries included Mencap, British Heart Foundation, Macmillan Cancer Relief, NSPCC, British Red Cross and Haven Trust.

Exclusions

Generally no support for advertising in charity brochures, appeals from individuals, purely denominational (religious) appeals or local appeals not in areas of company presence. Unsolicited appeals are unwelcome.

Applications

Appeals should be addressed to local Savills offices, not the head office.

Scapa

Scapa Group plc

Oakfield House, 93 Preston New Road, Blackburn BB2 6AY
01254-580123; Fax: 01254-51119

Correspondent: Mrs Marie Cockayne, Secretary to the Charities Committee

Chief officers: *Chairman:* H Tuley; *Chief Executive:* D M Dunn

Year end	Turnover	Pre-tax profit
31/3/98	£534,000,000	£33,000,000

Nature of company business
A holding company of a group operating in the manufacture and supply of engineered fabrics and roll coverings for the pulp, paper and board industries, filtration products for industry and the environment, industrial textiles, industrial rolls, specialist tapes and cable products.
Main subsidiaries include: Porritt & Spencer; Just Rubber; United Wire; P & S Textiles.
Main locations: Blackburn; Bury; Cwmbran; Edinburgh; Manchester; Rossendale.
UK employees: 2,675

Charitable donations
1998: £76,549
1997: £91,362
1996: £103,266
1995: £77,478
1994: £68,537

Community support policy

There is a preference for charities based in Blackburn and north west England. Donations are given primarily to those organisations with a local, company or personnel connection. Preference for children/youth, medical research, hospices, education, environment/heritage and enterprise/training. The company also covenants to Cancer Research and the Salvation Army. Beneficiaries in 1996/97 included: Christie Hospital NHS Trust; Blackburn and District Childrens Home; The Royal Exchange Theatre, Manchester; and East Lancashire Hospice.

Non-cash support is mainly focused in the areas of enterprise agencies and training schemes.

Exclusions
No support for advertising in charity brochures, fundraising events, overseas projects or political appeals.

Applications
In writing to the correspondent.

Schroders plc

120 Cheapside, London EC2V 6DS
0171-658 6000; Fax: 0171-658 3950

Correspondent: B Tew, Schroder Charity Trust

Chief officer: *Chairman:* W F W Bischoff

Year end	Turnover	Pre-tax profit
31/12/97	£1,686,000,000	£245,000,000

Nature of company business
Schroders plc is the holding company of an international merchant banking and investment group. The group is organised into five principal operating divisions on a worldwide basis: Corporate Finance, Investment Management, Credit and Capital Markets, Treasury, and Trading.
Main subsidiaries include: J Henry Schroder Wagg & Co.
UK employees: n/a

Charitable donations
1997: £660,000
1996: £606,000
1995: £536,000
1994: £505,000
1993: £503,000
Membership: ABSA BitC %Club

Community support policy

The company is a member of Business in the Community and the PerCent Club. In 1997, the group gave £1,100,000 to charities, of which £660,000 was donated to UK charities.

Donations are channelled through the Schroder Charity Trust. Only registered charities are supported, with a tendency to support national appeals. Local branches of national charities may also receive help, but very little money is given to purely local charities. Within these broad areas of preference, each appeal is considered on its merits. Typical beneficiaries include organisations concerned with elderly people, health care, social welfare, education, medical, the environment, overseas and the arts. Currently, particular attention is being given to the country's heritage and a substantial donation was made to the Oxford Bodleian Library campaign. Grants are usually for £500 to £2,000, larger donations may be spread over four or five years.

In 1996, the trustees for the trust were: B L Schroder, J H R Schroder, T B Schroder, C B Mallinckrodt and Mrs C L Fitzalan Howard. The trust had an income of £695,000, £600,000 of which was from Gift Aid and other subscriptions (presumably from the company) and £73,000 dividends on its investments. The latter comprise solely of shares in Schroders with a total market value of £4 million.

Over 350 grants were made with a further 130 in 'matching donations' totalling £588,000. The largest grants included those to Jewish Aid Committee (£16,700), Old Peoples Home (£13,000), WaterAid (£8,800), Westminster Cathedral (£8,300), Duke of Edinburgh Award (£8,000), Bodleian Library (£7,500), Friends of the Elderly, RNLI and Silver Trust (£6,000 each). Five organisations received £5,000: Football Museum, Help the Aged, LSE, Prague Heritage Fund and Save the Children.

Just over half the grants were in the range £1,000 to £5,000. A wide range of charities were supported, mainly national, although a few local causes received support (from Dorset Expeditionary Society to Islay Museums Trust), and a few overseas including Medical Aid for Romania. To illustrate the range of causes supported, the following are beneficiaries under the letters G and H: Galizine St Petersburg Trust, Game Conservancy Trust, Great Ormond Street Children's Hospital, Greater London Fund for the Blind, Gurkha Welfare Appeal, Hackney City Farm,

Hearing Research Trust, Help the Aged, Help the Handicapped Holiday Fund, Help the Hospices, Home-Start UK and Howard League.

The company operates the Give As You Earn payroll giving scheme and supports employee giving and fundraising.

The arts: The company is a member of ABSA and a corporate member of the Liverpool Philharmonic Orchestra, Royal Opera House and Glyndebourne Festival Society.

Exclusions

No support for advertising in charity brochures or appeals from individuals.

Applications

In writing to the correspondent. Grant decisions are made by a committee which meets monthly.

Scotia Holdings PLC

Scotia House, Castle Business Park, Stirling FK9 4TZ
01786-895100; Fax: 01786-895450

Correspondent: G Lafferty, Group Services Director

Chief officers: *Chairman:* Sir James McKinnon;
Chief Executive: Dr Robert Dow

Year end	Turnover	Pre-tax profit
31/12/97	£18,866,000	(£20,659,000)

Nature of company business
This is the holding company providing management services to the group. Scotia Pharmaceuticals Ltd develops and markets pharmaceutical, dietary and health care products.

Main subsidiaries include: Efamol; Callanish.

UK employees: 420

Charitable donations
1997: £77,486
1996: £74,025
1995: £51,021
1994: £34,210
1993: £29,737

Community support policy

We have no information on the company's policy regarding charitable donations, which have increased steadily over the last four years.

Applications

In writing to the correspondent.

Scottish Amicable Life plc

Craigforth, PO Box 25, Stirling FK9 4UE
01786-448844; Fax: 01786-462134
Website: www.scottishamicable.co.uk

Correspondent: Morag McWhinnie, Personal Assistant

Chief officers: *Chairman:* A D Stewart;
Managing Director: R M Nicolson

Year end	Turnover	Pre-tax profit
31/12/96	n/a	n/a

Nature of company business
Life assurance and pensions.

Main subsidiaries include: EuroSALAS Properties Ltd; Cathedral Investment Properties Ltd.

UK employees: 2,274

Charitable donations
1996: £95,495
1995: £113,872
1994: £50,000
1993: £45,656

Community support policy

The society's support is split about half and half between local causes and national causes in Scotland. There is a preference for central Scotland, and mainly for organisations involved with the arts, children/youth, elderly people, enterprise/training, environment/heritage, fundraising events, medical research, sickness/disability charities, social welfare, and sport.

Grants range from £100 for an advertisement at a local event to £10,000 sponsorship of a major Scottish arts body. Usually grants to national organisations range from £250 to £10,000 and grants to local organisations from £50 to £500. Beneficiaries have included: RSNO, Scottish Opera, Scottish Ballet, CBI and Scott Council for Development & Industry.

The company operates a payroll giving scheme, matching employee giving and on occasion matching employee fundraising (matching these takes a large part of the company's charitable donations).

Non-cash support can take the form of equipment, accommodation and use of in-house facilities.

Exclusions

No support for advertising in charity brochures, appeals from individuals, education, overseas projects, political appeals, or science/technology.

Applications

In writing to the correspondent.

Scottish Equitable plc

Edinburgh Park, Edinburgh EH12 9SE
0131-339 9191

Correspondent: Roy Patrick, Company Secretary

Chief officers: *Chairman:* H M Inglis;
Chief Executive: D A Henderson

Year end	Turnover	Pre-tax profit
30/12/96	£2,029,000,000	£49,000,000

Nature of company business
Insurance.

UK employees: 2,200

Charitable donations
1996: £47,317
1995: £41,148
1994: n/a
1993: £35,700

Community support policy

The company makes donations totalling about £40,000 a year. Primarily support is aimed at local and medical charities, mainly supporting staff initiatives. Other preferred areas of support are children and youth, and social welfare. Business-related charities are also supported. Direct support rather than advertising or sponsorship is preferred. Grants to national organisations range from £250 to £2,000. Grants to local organisations range from £50 to £1,000.

The company is also involved in education and enterprise initiatives and sponsors the arts.

Exclusions
No support for circular appeals, fundraising events, advertising in charity brochures, appeals from individuals, purely denominational (religious) appeals, local appeals not in areas of company presence or overseas projects.

Applications
In writing to the correspondent.

Scottish Hydro-Electric plc

10 Dunkeld Road, Perth PH1 5WA
01738-455040; Fax: 01738-455045
Website: www.hydro.co.uk

Correspondent: Carolyn McAdam, Head of Corporate Communications

Chief officers: *Chairman:* Lord Wilson;
Chief Executive: R Young

Year end	Turnover	Pre-tax profit
31/3/98	£1,034,700,000	£213,100,000

Nature of company business
The group's main business is the generation, transmission, distribution and supply of electricity to industrial, commercial and domestic customers. The group holds the generation, transmission and public supply licence for the north of Scotland, and second-tier electricity licences for supply of electricity throughout the rest of Great Britain.

UK employees: 3,205

Charitable donations
1998: £109,900
1997: £77,000
1996: £52,000
1995: £40,000
1994: £40,000

Total community contributions: £379,000 (1997)

Membership: *ABSA*

Community support policy

Hydro-Electric's Community Relations Programme is split into three elements – sponsorship, community fund and charitable donations.

Hydro-Electric's sponsorship programme covers five areas – arts, sport, community, education and environment. The aim of the programme is to bring benefits to the communities Hydro-Electric serves in the north of Scotland, and in particular the remoter communities of the Highlands and Islands. In addition the company supports a number of events Scotland-wide. Special emphasis is given to events involving young people and which have Hydro-Electric as the sole sponsor. The company is a member of ABSA.

The Community Fund supports community and environmental activities within the company's operational area. The aim of this fund is to assist local groups and events throughout the north of Scotland and to generate goodwill among the local communities. The company does not generate visibility from projects it supports through the Community Fund. The remit is very wide and the only criteria is that there must be a clear community benefit from the event.

The Charitable Donations budget supports registered charities active in the north of Scotland as well as a number of national charities which will allocate part of their funding to the north of Scotland. Main beneficiaries in 1997/98 included Scottish Opera, WWF – Bright Sparks Awards, Prince's Trust Youth Cafés, National Children's Youth Orchestra of Scotland and the Happy Gang.

Exclusions
Hydro-Electric does not support individuals, teams or organisations which have political affiliations. It also excludes advertising in charity brochures, research projects including medical research, overseas projects and religious appeals.

Applications
In writing to the correspondent.

Scottish Media Group plc

Cowcaddens, Glasgow G2 3PR
0141-300 3300; Fax: 0141-332 6982

Correspondent: Bob Tomlinson, Head of Public Affairs

Chief officers: *Chairman:* A J Macdonald;
Managing Director: A Flanagan

Year end	Turnover	Pre-tax profit
31/12/97	£197,000,000	£37,000,000

Nature of company business
The main activities are those of licence holder to provide the Channel 3 service for Central Scotland. The group has expanded into newspaper printing and publishing, owning *The Herald* and *The Evening Times* titles among others.

Main subsidiaries include: Caledonian Magazines Ltd; Caledonian Publishing Ltd; Glenburnie Properties Ltd; Grampian Television Ltd; TAS Publishing Ltd.

UK employees: n/a

Charitable donations

1997: £223,054
1996: £321,765
1995: £372,973
1994: £325,345
1993: £436,131
Membership: *ABSA*

Community support policy

The company is a member of the PerCent Club. In addition to cash donations, the company has given support in the form of equipment, expertise and facilities free of charge and arts sponsorship. Staff are allowed time off for activities of community benefit and encouraged to become volunteers in their own time.

Charitable Donations: The company has a policy of providing assistance to professional, community and amateur organisations and individuals concerned with theatrical and musical performances. It will also consider charitable or social organisations undertaking new or special activities. There is a preference for Scottish-based appeals, especially local charities in central Scotland and particularly to those providing an element of training.

Grants usually range from £100 to £15,000. Major recipients in previous years have included Scottish Opera, Scottish Ballet, Edinburgh International Television Festival, Drambuie Edinburgh Film Festival, Celtic Film Festival, Museum of Scotland Projects, National Television Archive, various community festivals, support for young trainee film makers and Comunn Na Gaidhlig.

Social action: The Social Action Broadcast service gives local charities the opportunity to describe their activities and to appeal for volunteers. These last for 40 seconds and receive six transmissions. The Scottish Action programme won awards for work in this field and Action 2000 plays a major role in publicising the work of charities and voluntary organisations.

Exclusions

The company does not undertake sponsorship. No support for fundraising events, advertising in charity brochures, purely denominational (religious) appeals, local appeals not in areas of company presence, large national appeals or overseas projects.

Applications

The Head of Public Affairs deals with donations, while the Comunity Programmes Co-ordinator should be contacted regarding the social action broadcasts.

Scottish & Newcastle plc

Abbey Brewery, Holyrood Road, Edinburgh EH8 8YS
0131-556 2591; Fax: 0131-557 6523
Website: www.scottish-newcastle.com

Correspondent: Linda Bain, Corporate Affairs Manager

Chief officers: *Chairman:* Sir Alistair Grant;
Chief Executive: B J Stewart

Year end	Turnover	Pre-tax profit
3/5/98	£3,352,300,000	£422,000,000

Nature of company business
Scottish & Newcastle has interests in the beer, leisure and retail industries in the UK and Europe. Its beer division, Scottish Courage, is the UK's leading brewer. The retail division comprises some 2,600 pubs, pub restaurants and hotels. The leisure division comprises Center Parcs and Pontins.

Main subsidiaries include: Matthew Brown; Wm Younger & Co; Moray Firth Maltings; Scottish Brewers; Scottish & Newcastle Beer Production; T & R Theakston; Holiday Club Pontins; Centre Parcs; S & N Retail.

Main brands include: Rat & Parrot; Old Orleans; Chef & Brewer; Barras Company; T & J Bernard; Bar 38; John Smith's; Foster's; Kronenbourg; Miller Pilsner.

Main locations: Blackburn; Edinburgh; Manchester; Newcastle; Nottingham.

UK employees: n/a

Charitable donations

1998: £550,000
1997: £525,000
1996: £510,000
1995: £375,000
1994: £356,000

Total community contributions: £5,000,000
Membership: *ABSA BitC*

Community support policy

The company continues to support a wide variety of local and national charities. Support is targeted towards charities working in the company's own communities.

The key categories to receive funding include the arts, heritage, environment, medical, youth, education and social welfare.

In the last year, £550,000 was donated directly to registered charities. This does not include the involvement and fundraising activities of the company's employees and customers. The company's website gave some information on the company's community support, particularly fundraising initiatives rather than the company's direct giving.

Scottish Widows

Previously, the company has provided the following information on its direct support. A charity committee allocates 70% of the total budget with the balance given to divisional companies to support local charities and organisations. Grants range from £50 to £1,000, exceptionally up to £50,000 nationally and up to £5,000, exceptionally £10,000 locally. Beneficiaries of major grants in previous years have included Jubilee Sailing Trust, Scottish Wildlife Trust, British Red Cross, Tyne & Wear Foundation and Scottish Council on Alcohol.

The company is a member of ABSA, sponsoring events and organisations in its areas of operation.

Scottish & Newcastle Retail

One particularly successful event in 1998 was the 'Scottish & Newcastle Lakeland Challenge' where teams from across the UK completed a 24 peak challenge in the Lake District to raise £81,000 for the Children's Aid Direct charity.

Scottish Courage

Charity gala dinners were held throughout the country, and raised over £200,000, to benefit local causes in each region.

An example of cause-related marketing was run by Scottish Courage Brands. Promotional cans of McEwan's Export and Kestrel Lager (with 2p donated to nominated charities for every can sold) raised £100,000 for two national cancer charities.

In the arts field, Scottish & Newcastle has supported Edinburgh International Division for many years.

Scottish & Newcastle Foundation

In recognition of the efforts of employees in their work with local communities and charities, a new initiative was launched in 1998. The Scottish & Newcastle Foundation was introduced to support employees who are actively involved in the community. £50,000 was allocated to the foundation, with the intention of providing enabling grants up to £500 to help make a difference to the success of projects.

Exclusions

No grants for advertising in charity brochures, appeals from individuals, local appeals not in areas of company presence or purely denominational appeals. Overseas projects are not usually supported, but the company's subsidiaries in Europe and the USA support causes in their areas. Sponsorship of individuals, other than company employees, is not undertaken.

Applications

In writing to the correspondent. A charity committee meets quarterly. Local appeals should be directed to the regional office. Sponsorship requests should be addressed to the regional offices.

Advice to applicants: Appeal mail is getting too large to deal with so appeals should be carefully researched and should fall into the company's donations categories. All appeals should be written.

Information available: The company reports on its community involvement in its annual report, but does not have printed policy guidelines.

Scottish Widows' Fund & Life Assurance Society

PO Box 902, 15 Dalkeith Road, Edinburgh EH16 5BU
0131-655 6000; Fax: 0131-667 0901

Correspondent: Carol Lumsden, Personnel Consultant

Chief officers: *Chairman:* L M Urquhart; *Managing Director:* M D Ross

Year end	Turnover	Pre-tax profit
31/12/97	n/a	n/a

Nature of company business
Life insurance, pensions, unit trust management and estate agents.

Main subsidiaries include: Pensions Management Ltd.

UK employees: 2,358

Charitable donations
1997: £88,176
1996: £74,120
1995: £75,000
1994: £74,473
1993: £75,037

Community support policy

In 1996, the company gave nearly £88,000 in cash donations to UK charities; the budget must be spent in furtherance of the interests of company members. The company operate the Give As You Earn payroll giving scheme.

There is a preference for appeals relevant to company business. Appeals with a children/youth, sickness/disability, medical or social welfare aspect are more likely to get support. Geographically the company tries to be even handed, but generally it prefers to give locally in Scotland and avoid the South East where money is more readily available. Previous beneficiaries include Duke of Edinburgh Award, Greater Easterhouse Business, Scottish Council for Development & Industry, Positive Help and Scottish Business in the Community.

Exclusions

No support for advertising in charity brochures; animal welfare charities; appeals from individuals; the arts; education; elderly people; enterprise/training; environment/heritage; fundraising events; overseas projects; political appeals; religious appeals; science/technology or sport.

Applications

In writing to the correspondent.

Sponsorship proposals should be addressed to Beth Kerr, Public Relations Office. As with cash donations the budget must be spent in furtherance of the interests of company members.

ScottishPower plc

1 Atlantic Quay, Broomielaw, Glasgow G2 8SP
0141-636 4560; Fax: 0141-636 4582
Website: www.scottishpower.plc.uk

Correspondent: Josephine Job, Corporate Affairs Director

Chief officers: *Chairman:* Murray Stuart;
Chief Executive: Ian Robinson

Year end	Turnover	Pre-tax profit
31/3/98	£3,128,000,000	£640,000,000

Nature of company business
Principal activity: the generation, transmission, distribution, supply and marketing of electricity, the sale and servicing of electrical appliances, and gas and telecommunications businesses.

Main subsidiaries include: Caledonian Gas Ltd; CRE Energy Ltd; Domestic Appliance Insurance Ltd; Genscot Ltd; Lancastrian Holdings Ltd; Manweb Energy Consultants Ltd; Manweb Gas Ltd; Manweb Generation Holdings Ltd; Manweb Generation Ltd; Manweb PLC; Pinnacle Cellular Ltd; Scotland On-Line Ltd; Southern Water PLC; Teledata Ltd; Telephone International Media Ltd; Telephone Information Services PLC; Demon Internet.

UK employees: 14,356

Charitable donations

1998: £299,766
1997: £484,641
1996: £327,000
1995: £922,000
1994: £591,895
Membership: *ABSA*

Community support policy

The company produced a Community Report 1997/98, from which the following information is taken. The report includes a list of targets the company set itself for its community programme, together with the extent to which those targets were met and further developments for 1998/99. In addition to operating throughout Scotland, the company operates in Merseyside and north Wales through Manweb (see separate entry) and in the south of England through Southern Water.

Programmes during 1997/98 included support for education and employment initiatives, charities and caring organisations representing children and young people, people with disabilities, older people, and the disadvantaged. In addition, the performing arts, sport and recreation were sponsored.

The company has set 10 objectives for the coming year (1998/99). These build upon the major community programmes already in place and provide a focus for activities. They are:

1. Continuing to publish an annual statement of community involvement and activities across the ScottishPower group.
2. Measuring community expectations, auditing current activity, setting targets and monitoring performance against best practice. This will be achieved via membership of the London Benchmarking Group.
3. Directing community investment towards building a vibrant economy, which will benefit everyone in the community.

    The company will provide training places for over 400 unemployed people utilising a range of programmes over the next year. It will work with local councils, enterprise companies, community groups and support agencies to develop training opportunities for the unemployed to be delivered through the New Deal, Employment Zone and Skillseekers programmes.
4. Seeking to develop community partnerships with other key social and economic organisations to ensure the maximum effectiveness of the group's community investment programmes. Through a franchise arrangement with the Prince's Trust Volunteers the company will deliver 25 community projects and provide a range of development opportunities for unemployed young people.
5. Seeking to develop partnerships with charities, local organisations and support groups to help people with special needs. The company is committed to organising five Outward Bound courses for adults with learning disabilities during 1998/99.
6. Extending the range of support programmes and service initiatives aimed at helping customers with special needs. The company will also continue to work closely with community groups and support agencies.
7. Encouraging employees to share their business skills to benefit the wider community. Through support of the Business in the Arts programme the company will aim to place up to 10 staff within an arts organisation to encourage the exchange of their business knowledge. It will also continue to develop relationships between ScottishPower senior managers and head teachers in schools.
8. Encouraging employees to give their time freely to make a difference to the lives of other people, and whenever appropriate, supporting their fundraising activities through the Charitable Trust fund and staff associations.

    The company has set a target of 10,000 community hours within its regional operations for staff in both Scotland and north west England to become involved in community projects. It will also provide materials and resources in support of specific projects where appropriate.

    The company will increase its commitment to its Learn to Swim programme with a target of 250,000, 4–12 year olds successfully completing a programme by 1999.
9. Fostering a responsible interchange of ideas and views on environmental issues and aiming to contain environmental impact of activities to a practicable minimum. Environmental targets for operations have been set and will be delivered through the operational business units.
10. Supporting projects to help encourage utility related curriculum and syllabus development in educational establishments, and the work experience of students. The company will develop working relationships with an additional 25 schools in its operating area.

Through ScottishPower learning, the company will continue to develop initiatives that involve ScottishPower

Seagram

staff in delivering a range of learning-based initiatives within the community.

The report goes on to give information on various projects supported under five headings: serving the community, performing arts in the community, education and employment in the community, enhancing the environment, fitness and health in the community.

The following are just a small sample of the organisations and projects supported: Wheels for All – a cycling project in north west England for people with disabilities; Welsh National Opera – outreach programme; Live Music Now!; establishment of Community Learning Centres at Kirkby, Alloa, Kirkintilloch and Knowsley; Scotland Against Drugs – help to develop an information website and support for its three-year educational project in primary schools; Edinburgh Festival – two-week summer dance school; Young Engineers' Clubs and the Young Engineers of Britain; Enterprise Ayrshire – training opportunities.

Exclusions

Support may not be given in the form of non-commercial advertising. No response to circulars. No grants for advertising in charity brochures; appeals from individuals (other than staff); purely denominational (religious) appeals; local appeals not in areas of company presence.

Applications

In writing to the correspondent.

Seagram Distillers PLC

111 Renfrew Road, Paisley PA3 4DY
0141-531 1801; Fax: 0141-531 1804

Correspondent: Alan McWatters, Finance Director

Chief officers: n/a

Year end	Turnover	Pre-tax profit
30/6/97	£768,925,000	£53,570,000

Nature of company business
The company is a whisky distiller, whose best-known products include Chivas Regal and The Glenlivet whiskies.

Main subsidiaries include: Chivas Brothers; The Glenlivet Distillers; Hill Thomson & Co; Oddbins; Seagram United Kingdom.

UK employees: 2,354

Charitable donations
1997: £167,000
1996: £188,000
1995: £107,000
1994: £116,000

Total community contributions: £200,000

Membership: *BitC*

Community support policy

The company has charity committees to coordinate its charitable giving at each major operating location (there is a preference for charities local to Paisley and West of Scotland; Lothian; Moray District; and Greater London).

The theme adopted by the committees is 'to support those who are disadvantaged', with particular emphasis being given to local, self-help initiatives rather than national charities. Requests for donations should be addressed to the contact above.

Donations usually range from £250 to £5,000. Requests for donations of bottles to support fundraising events should be addressed to Chivas and Brothers Ltd, Reception, at the above address.

Support is also given to employee's volunteering/ charitable activities by matching employee fundraising and giving.

Previously we have published much higher figures for Seagram's charitable giving (over £3 milion). However, the company has now provided UK figures, whereas previous figures were for worldwide support.

Exclusions

Generally no support for advertising in charity brochures, animal welfare charities, the arts, political appeals, overseas projects, science/technology or medical research.

Applications

In writing to the correspondent.

Sears plc

40 Duke Street, London W1A 2HP
0171-200 5999; Fax: 0171-200 5820

Correspondent: J D F Drum, Group Secretary

Chief officers: *Chairman:* Sir Bob Reid;
Chief Executive: L Strong

Year end	Turnover	Pre-tax profit
31/1/98	£1,819,000,000	(£116,000,000)

Nature of company business
Sears has more than 3,500 outlets in the UK and Europe. It concentrates on footwear, department store, fashion and speciality retailing. It has significant investments in property.

Main subsidiaries include: Freemans PLC; Selfridge Retail Ltd; British Shoe Corpn Ltd (including Cable & Co, Curtess, Dolcis, Freeman Hardy Willis, Manfield, Saxone, Shoe City, Shoe Express, Trueform); BSC Footwear Supplies Ltd; Cable & Co Ltd; The Retail Corpn PLC; Broadstoner Holdings PLC.

UK employees: n/a

Charitable donations
1998: £134,000
1997: £181,000
1996: £504,000
1995: £237,000
1994: £226,000
Membership: *BitC*

Community support policy

The company is moving away from small grants to large support for particular projects, usually with national charities. Support is given to medical and healthcare charities and organisations related to the company business such as fitness and health, women and back pain.

Support is also provided for enterprise initiatives and organisations devoted to tackling problems associated with inner city areas. Funds are currently fully committed. The company also fundraises for particular charities. Small grants are £200 to £1,000, large grants can be for anything up to £20,000 to set up and run a project for a year.

About 60% of the company's donations appear to be made through the Sears Foundation (Charity Commission number 283532). In 1996/97, this had an income of £75,000 and grants totalled £72,000.

Almost half the grant total went to Save the Children (£34,000), with £10,000 given to both Action on Addiction and Breakthrough Breast Cancer. Recipients of grants of £1,000 to £4,000 included British Museum Society, Business in the Community, Cottage Homes, Institute of Economic Affairs, Police Foundation and Terence Higgins Trust.

The arts: The company has supported London City Ballet, Glyndebourne Arts Trust and the Royal Opera House Trust.

Exclusions

No support for individuals, students or charities with no company link. No advertising in charity brochures or support for overseas projects.

Applications

The correspondent states that the funds of the Sears Foundation are currently fully committed. The company endeavours to develop projects in partnership with a few major national charities; hence the funds are committed in advance.

Securicor plc

Sutton Park House, 15 Carshalton Road, Sutton, Surrey SM1 4LD
0181-770 7000; Fax: 0181-661 0204
Website: www.securicor.co.uk

Correspondent: Mrs A P Munson, Chair of the Charitable Trust

Chief officers: *Chairman:* Sir Neil Macfarlane;
Chief Executive: R S W H Wiggs

Year end	Turnover	Pre-tax profit
30/9/97	£1,354,000,000	£31,000,000

Nature of company business
Securicor plc is the holding company for the Securicor group of companies. Principal activities of the group include express parcels; warehousing and distribution; container transport, freight forwarding; document delivery; transportation and care of cash and valuables; cash processing; security guards and patrols; mobile communications systems and networks, recruitment agencies.

UK employees: 30,148

Charitable donations

1997: £137,000
1996: £120,000
1995: £115,000
1994: £133,000
1993: £198,000

Community support policy

The company has a preference for supporting community development, job creation/training, arts, music and sport. Donations are in cash and in kind, helping with cash collection/delivery and parcel services.

In 1997/98, the company also donated £54,000 to the Securicor Charitable Trust, which deals with smaller appeals from registered charities, favouring those in the areas of children/youth, social welfare, health, elderly people, sickness/disability, and medical resesarch. The maximum grant is usually £250, although occasionally larger grants are made.

In kind support: Includes occasional provision of cash collections and guards for fundraising events, and occasional delivery services for charities.

The company also undertakes arts and good-cause sponsorship.

Exclusions

Securicor Charitable Trust will offer no support for advertising in charity brochures; fundraising events; animal welfare charities; personal appeals from individuals; requests for educational grants; the arts; enterprise/training; science/technology; overseas projects; political appeals; religious appeals; sport or expeditions.

Applications

In writing to the correspondent. The trustees meet every two months. Only written applications for specific projects will be considered. No telephone calls.

Sponsorship proposals should be addressed to the Group Marketing Manager.

Advice to applicants: Personal applicants should note the excluded areas, in particular educational and expedition grants. Agencies should note that telephone applications will not be considered and the trust does not support charity advertising.

Sedgwick Group plc

Sackville House, 143–152 Fenchurch Street, London EC3M 6BN
0171-377 3456; Fax: 0171-377 3252
Email: victoria_secretan@sedgwick.com
Website: www.sedgwick.com

Correspondent: Ms Victoria Secretan, Community Programmes Manager

Chief officers: *Chairman:* S Riley;
Chief Executive: W R White-Cooper

Year end	Turnover	Pre-tax profit
31/12/97	£334,800,000	£45,400,000

Nature of company business
Sedgwick is one of the world's leading international risk consulting, insurance and reinsurance broking, employee benefits and financial services groups.

Main subsidiaries include: River Thames Insurance Co Ltd.

UK employees: 5,192

Sedgwick

Charitable donations
1997: £198,000
1996: £180,000
1995: £177,000
1994: £159,000
1993: £184,000
Membership: *BitC %Club*

Community support policy

Sedgwick has been a model of openness and good practice, regularly reporting on its community involvement in its annual report as well as producing *Community Partners* a booklet detailing its various activities. The Chief Executive states at the start of this: 'We contribute time, skills and financial support to organisations and projects which help those who have little or no access to the benefits most of us take for granted. We focus on breaking down barriers to education and training, to employment and self-employment, to adequate housing and to personal independence'.

It is to be hoped that this continues under ownership by US-based Marsh & McLennan. Following the annoucement of the takeover, Sedgwick has reaffirmed its commitment to the communities in which it operates, and hopes that increased resources and greater scope may result from this development.

A member of the PerCent Club and Business in the Community, Sedgwick supports national charities and charities local to its offices. Larger offices are in Birmingham, Bristol, Cardiff, Edinburgh, Glasgow, Leeds, Manchester, Norwich, Reading, Slough and Witham (Essex). In particular, Sedgwick has supported organisations in Tower Hamlets where its principal office is based. On a local level, the company participates in a number of community programmes and tends to focus on those which receive little general public attention.

Charitable donations: Preference is given to local organisations in areas of company presence and those in which a member of staff is involved. Preferred areas of support are: education, enterprise/training, environment, disability charities, social welfare, addiction-related charities and crime prevention.

In 1997, organisations to benefit from support included large national charities such as Save the Children (a regular beneficiary), British Red Cross and Macmillan Cancer Relief, as well as St Botolph's, East London Partnership and other small, local agencies such as a victim support trust, a hospice, a hostel and a homework club. Grants to national organisations range from £200 to £5,000 (occasionally up to £10,000) and to local organisations from £100 to £2,500.

Overseas donations given from the UK are to establish long-term development projects in developing countries. Sedgwick is an international member of the Prince of Wales Business Leaders Forum. Sedgwick in the USA has formed a national community partnership with the Red Cross. In China, Sedgwick Noble Lowndes has established an independent and not-for-profit organisation.

In kind support: The main areas of non-cash support have been in training schemes and allowing employees to volunteer in company time. The group is sometimes able to offer contributions of presentations or advice on insurance to enterprise agencies and others. It has also loaned office space rent free to organisations, donated redundant equipment and hosted presentations and meetings.

Employee involvement: 'The group believes that practical help is often more beneficial than financial contributions; it encourages employees to use their skills to help community projects in the areas in which they live and work.' The company also gives support through providing staff time and expertise. It also encourages employee volunteering through financial support, allowing company time off to volunteer, team projects, 100 hour assignments, board membership, etc. For example, the office in Norwich has a team of volunteers which has set up and runs a job club at the local prison. Sports and social club events regularly raise funds and many staff raise money through activities such as sponsored golf tournaments, quizzes and car washing.

A Give As You Earn scheme for employee charity giving, to which the company contributes, was relaunched in 1997. The group makes contributions to staff fundraising efforts and to organisations with which staff are active as volunteers. Volunteering is recognised in staff appraisals.

Enterprise: Sedgwick supports a number of enterprise agencies with grants and practical assistance, has trained enterprise agency directors and counsellors in insurance and has produced a guide to insurance for small businesses.

Education: Support for education ranges from preparing a business study pack on insurance for 16–18 year old students with TVEI, to participating in the Council for Industry and Higher Education and the Windsor Fellowship.

Environment: As well as the environment being one of the areas supported, it operates recycling schemes in its offices with the income generated being donated to local charities and schools. Several offices also take part in Local Agenda 21 environmental initiatives and have joined a number of planting schemes. A series of 'Green Futures' lectures by well-known speakers on environmental issues was sponsored by Sedgwick in conjunction with London Guildhall University and the Corporation of London.

The arts: Sedgwick does not undertake commercial sponsorship but supports a number of arts organisations and events including the Royal Academy, Whitechapel Art Gallery and the City of London Symphonia. A number of festivals have been supported including Spitalfields Festival, East End Festival, the Festival of Bangladesh and those at Norfolk and Norwich. Where possible it chooses to support arts organisations making an additional social contribution to the community, such as ADAPT, which facilitates access to arts venues for people with disabilities, and to Artsline, London's information and advice service for disabled people on arts and entertainment. The Council for Music in Hospitals and the Geese Theatre Company (working in prisons) have also been supported.

Exclusions

No response to circular appeals. No support for advertising in charity brochures, animal welfare charities, appeals from individuals, fundraising events, medical research, overseas projects, political appeals, religious appeals or bricks and mortar appeals.

Applications

The following statement is taken from the company's brochure.

'Sedgwick works in partnership with representatives of the community, central and local government, large national charities and small local initiatives. We choose our partners with care and, where possible, maintain our support for them over several years.

'There is no need to write an elaborate application to obtain support. We need to know who benefits from your work, what you do, what you aim to do and how Sedgwick's help could make a difference. Basic financial information and an annual report or leaflet should be included.

'Remember that Sedgwick may be able to offer time and skills rather than money.'

Grants at head office are decided quarterly by an appeals committee. Applications should be addressed to the correspondent. Local appeals in Norfolk, Essex and East Anglia can be addressed to Debbie Hilton, Public Relations Officer, Sedgwick Ltd, Victoria House, Queen's Road, Norwich N1 3QQ. Sponsorship proposals should be addressed to Miss Julia Fish, Director, Corporate Communications at head office.

Local appeals may also be sent to regional offices – larger offices are in Birmingham, Bristol, Cardiff, Edinburgh, Glasgow, Leeds, Manchester, Norwich, Reading, Slough and Witham (Essex).

Advice to applicants: The group advises applicants that they should write rather than telephone and that information should be concise.

During 1999, following merger with Marsh & McLennan, Sedgwick's policy and process are to be reviewed. No new commitments are likely to be undertaken this year.

SEEBOARD plc

PO Box 639, 329 Portland Road, Hove, East Sussex BN3 5SY
01293-565888; Fax: 01293-657327
Website: www.seeboard.co.uk

Correspondent: Sally Hutchinson, Sponsorship Department

Chief officers: *Chairman:* T J Ellis; *Chief Executive:* John Weight

Year end	Turnover	Pre-tax profit
31/3/96	£836,000,000	£107,000,000

Nature of company business
Principal activities: distribution and supply of electricity to industrial, commercial and domestic consumers; electrical contracting and retailing; supply of gas. Seeboard is a subsidiary of the US company CSW.
Main subsidiaries include: Longfield Insurance Co Ltd; Southern Gas Ltd.

UK employees: n/a

Charitable donations
1996: £164,536
1995: £181,838
1994: £187,253
1993: £134,000
Membership: *ABSA*

Community support policy

Support is concentrated in the company's operating area. This includes most of Kent, all of East Sussex, large parts of West Sussex and Surrey and the London boroughs of Croydon, Kingston and Richmond. It is coordinated under its Community Links programme. There is a preference for charities in which a member of company staff is involved. Grants range from £50 to £5,000.

Support is given in five categories:
- social welfare charities
- education
- environment and countryside projects
- grassroots sports
- the arts, amateur and professional.

Social welfare: Support is given to local charities or local branches of national charities based in the Seeboard area. National charities connected with the electricity industry may also be suported. Grants range from £50 to £10,000, and in kind support is given where appropriate. Activities supported range from care for the elderly to encouragement for young chess players, from hospital donations to fundraising for youth activities. Examples of support include the donation of a dishwasher to a day-care centre, electrical appliances to a residential home and support for the Prince's Youth Business Trust.

Charities with staff involvement will usually receive financial support. In addition to charitable donations the company supports initiatives through secondment and sponsorship.

Education: The company works with schools, colleges and universities. Support ranges from co-sponsorship of a chair of electrical engineering at Brighton University to donation of small prizes for school fundraising events or helping with special projects.

Environment: The company is working with the county wildlife trusts in the South East to encourage volunteer activities. Seeboard has also helped to establish and fund the Alchemist Scrapstore which makes surplus materials from local businesses available for schools and community groups.

The arts: Seeboard sponsors a programme of concerts and primary school projects with the Hanover Band, a locally-based period orchestra. The arts programme also includes support for major arts festivals such as Brighton and Canterbury, and small local projects. The company is a member of ABSA.

Exclusions

No support for circular appeals, individuals, purely denominational (religious) appeals, advertising in charity brochures or local appeals not in the south east of England. Overseas projects are rarely supported.

Applications
Seeboard makes few major sponsorship awards – worth between £5,000 and £20,000 each – in each financial year. Applications for these must be made before the end of the previous December. In most cases these run for one year only, but longer programmes may be considered with an annual review.

Smaller awards are made on a rolling programme. These range from donations of small gifts for fundraising events, through donations of electrical appliances to financial support of up to £5,000. To apply please write, giving brief details of your organisation and your request to the correspondent.

The correspondent stated: 'Seeboard makes every effort to reply to all appeals. We do, however, receive a large number of applications and can support only a small proportion of them.'

Telephone and faxed applications cannot be considered.

Serco Group plc

Serco House, Hayes Road, Southall, Middlesex UB2 5NJ
0181-843 2411; Fax: 0181-843 3907

Correspondent: Ruth Mountford, Group Finance Department

Chief officers: *Chairman:* G G Gray; *Chief Executive:* R D White

Year end	Turnover	Pre-tax profit
31/12/97	£489,018,000	£22,012,000

Nature of company business
The provision of a range of facilities management and systems engineering services.

Main subsidiaries include: NPL Management; Prime Contractors; Salco; Community Leisure Management.

UK employees: 15,999

Charitable donations
1997: £60,000
1996: £35,000
1995: £33,000

Community support policy
The company prefers to support local appeals relevant to the business. Support is given to children and youth, education, medical, overseas aid and development, and forces charities.

Exclusions
No support for large national appeals, circular appeals or purely denominational (religious) appeals.

Applications
In writing to the correspondent.

Seton Scholl Healthcare plc

Tubiton House, Oldham OL1 3HS
0161-652 2222; Fax: 0161-626 9090

Correspondent: Brenda Alexander, Public Relations Officer

Chief officers: *Chairman:* S Wallis; *Chief Executive:* I C D Cater

Year end	Turnover	Pre-tax profit
28/2/98	£117,584,000	£24,002,000

Nature of company business
The manufacture and distribution of healthcare products.

Main subsidiaries include: Brevet Hospital Products (UK); Cupal; Scholl Consumer Products; Pharmatab; Simpla Plastics; Sondico International; Simco; ThackrayCare; Ultra Laboratories.

UK employees: 1,250

Charitable donations
1998: £52,428
1997: £46,334
1996: £73,000

Community support policy
Seton Healthcare and Scholl have recently merged to form this new company. Most of the above figures refer only to Seton; new combined figures will not be available until later in 1999.

The company states that its new policy on charitable giving and community support has still to be formulated following the move of its headquarters.

In the past, Seton Healthcare informed us that in addition to the donations figure quoted, grants are also made through the Stoller Charitable Trust which is based at the same address. Information on this trust can be found in *A Guide to the Major Trusts Volume 2*.

Applications
In writing to the correspondent.

Severn Trent Plc

2297 Coventry Road, Birmingham B26 3PU
0121-722 4544; Fax: 0121-722 4534
Email: audrey.drew@severntrent.co.uk
Website: www.severn-trent.com

Correspondent: Audrey Drew, Community Affairs Executive

Chief officers: *Chairman:* David Arculus; *Chief Executive:* Vic Cocker; *Managing Director:* Brian Duckworth

Year end	Turnover	Pre-tax profit
31/3/98	£1,251,300,000	£374,000,000

Nature of company business
Water and sewerage services, and waste management.

Main subsidiaries include: Biffa Waste Services Ltd; Stoner Associates Europe Ltd; Aztec Environmental Control Ltd; Capital Controls Ltd; Fusion Meters Ltd; Paperflow Services Ltd; Tetra Europe Ltd; Daventry International Rail Freight Terminal Ltd; Charles Haswell & Partners Ltd; Derwent Insurance Ltd.

UK employees: 10,413

Charitable donations
1998: £271,274
1997: £226,725
1996: £218,931
1995: £233,869
1994: £171,137
Total community contributions: £4,294,736
Membership: ABSA BitC %Club

Community support policy

The company is a member of the PerCent Club and ABSA. It has continued its close involvement with Business in the Community where it has worked closely with local business partners on community initiatives. Support is also given to Business in the Environment. Generally support is given to appeals from within the area of the Severn Trent Group operations, but occasionally national charities are considered if they can prove a local link. The company is developing education centres and has six classrooms established in the water company's region, which are used by schools.

In total, community contributions in 1997/98 were £4.3 million (1.2% of UK pre-tax profit) with the main support in addition to cash donations being through secondments and gifts in kind. The latter includes the disposal of old company vehicles, computers and office equipment to charities. The company has also established the Severn Trent Water Charitable Trust Fund, see below.

Charitable donations: Giving is aimed at supporting and supplementing the company's other community activities, carried out through a Charitable Contributions Committee. Normally, support is through a single donation or, if longer-term support is needed, for a maximum of four years. Grants generally range between £500 and £1,000, but can be up to a maximum of £10,000.

There is a preference for charities working in the fields of health, welfare, environment/heritage and arts. Special consideration is given to projects where employees are involved in a fundraising or other voluntary capacity.

- *Local community projects:* support is given to regional or local charities, but a neighbourhood project must operate within areas where there is a significant business presence.
- *Health and welfare:* support for projects which provide help both for people disadvantaged through illness or disability and for their families. Support is also given to projects which provide information and education for sufferers, care workers and the public and to charities working with children.
- *Environment, heritage and the arts:* the company is most interested in supporting the following:
  - national and local conservation groups
  - environmental education
  - projects where employees may participate
  - projects where there are opportunities for people with disabilities to be involved
  - projects in preservation and restoration of historic buildings and monuments
  - helping establish local trusts to manage and maintain historic buildings and machinery.

Major beneficiaries included County Air Ambulance, Princess Royal Trust for Carers, WaterAid, NSPCC and English Symphony Orchestra. Numerous causes are supported either directly by the board Charitable Contributions Committee, or through funds held by area offices. The company gives company time off for staff volunteering and operates the Sharing the Caring payroll giving scheme.

Severn Trent Water Charitable Trust Fund

This trust was established by the company to benefit their own customers. As the trustee's report states, the trust makes 'payouts direct to the organisation to which the amount is owed'. It also states that 'recognising the value of long-term help and support … the trustees have adopted a policy of making limited grants available to organisations who provide money advice services'.

In 1997/98, the company received £2 million in donations from the company and a further £106,000 in investment income. Grants totalling £617,000 were made to water companies ie. Severn Trent Water, and a further £33,000 for a 'variety of bills'. Other direct charitable expenditure totalled £160,000 including £100,000 staff costs, while management and administration costs were £114,000 including £44,000 salary and pension contributions. The assets at the year end stood at £1.15 million with £268,000 transferred to the 'Debt Counselling Fund'.

Exclusions

No support for advertising in charity brochures, appeals from individuals, local appeals not in areas of company presence, medical research, animal welfare charities, enterprise/training, fundraising events, political or religious appeals, expeditions, study tours and cultural exchanges or science/technology.

Applications

In writing to the correspondent. Initial applications to the company need not be too detailed, but should include a summary of the project, its objectives and costs.

Applications to the trust should be made on a form available from: The Severn Trent Water Charitable Trust Fund, Ground Floor, Hammond House, 2259–2261 Coventry Road, Birmingham B26 3PA.

Shell UK Limited

Shell-Mex House, Strand, London WC2R 0DX
0171-257 3000

Correspondent: Miss S K Aylward, Arts and Charities Manager

Chief officer: *Chairman:* Dr C E Fay

Year end	Turnover	Pre-tax profit
31/12/97	n/a	£852,000,000

Nature of company business
The business of the company is the exploration for and production of oil and natural gas, oil refining and chemicals manufacturing, and the marketing of the resulting products.

Shell

Main locations: London; Aberdeen; Cowdenbeath; Chester; Shell Haven (Essex); Stanlow (Merseyside); Wythenshawe; Lowestoft.

UK employees: 6,669

Charitable donations

1997: £1,135,078
1996: £1,024,544
1995: £1,717,978
1994: £2,466,939
1993: £2,200,000

Total community contributions: £4,864,977

Membership: *ABSA BitC*

Community support policy

Total community contributions in 1997 were £4.9 million, including support for various educational, enterprise, environment and arts initiatives. Shell UK offers discounts on fuel cards for registered charities.

A brochure *Shell UK, Investing in the Community*, gives details of the company's Community Investment programmes. Preferred areas of support are children and youth, social welfare, medical, education and environment. Main beneficiaries in 1997, under the programmes as outlined below included NSPCC (£50,000), Step in the Community (£100,000), Occupational Health Research Foundation (£12,500), Rural Forum Scotland (£50,000) and Windsor Fellowship (£21,000).

Charitable donations: The company supports a cross-section of charitable organisations including those with a UK remit, or near a major Shell location (Scotland, north west England and Suffolk), or where a member of staff/retired staff is involved. The furtherance of voluntary endeavour and projects of potential national significance are also favoured. As with general community support, central resources usually benefit national concerns, while local ones aid organisations active within the vicinity of major installations. Typically, national awards can range from £500 to £50,000, while local ones vary from £50 to £5,000.

From 1998, the company has 'themed' its charitable donations at a corporate level over three-year consecutive periods. The first of the themes is *Children and Young People at Risk,* where the company is working with four national charities dealing with different types of risk: NSPCC, Barnardo's, the Foyer Federation and Youth Clubs. This strategy means fewer but more substantial donations to selected charities.

In addition to cash donations, the company provides in-kind support such as the donation of redundant computer equipment, and use of premises for meetings and events. A fuel card is available to registered charities which offers discounts on pump prices and other benefits. For further details of the Shell Gold Card ring 0500-413577.

The company also operates the SMART card charity link, where customers may accrue points for fuel and other purchases and choose the option of donating them to charity. The charities currently benefiting are the RSPCA, Motability and Barnardo's. Customer points are matched financially by the company.

Employee involvement: Through the Shell Employee Action Scheme, grants are made to locally based not for profit organisations and charities in which current and retired members of staff or their spouses are involved. The fund totals £170,000 a year and cash grants are made available from the company for modest scale needs and projects, thus supporting the voluntary efforts of its own people in their local communities. Staff acting as school governors are allowed company time off to volunteer.

Secondment: The company does not currently run a secondment programme.

Enterprise: The company is a member of Business in the Community. Through the Shell Enterprise Unit, a budget of just over £1 million in 1998 was concentrated on two national programmes.

Shell Livewire: gives advice to young people aged 16–30 on setting up their own business. It is co-ordinated under contract by Project North East with staff dedicated to managing an enquiry service, start-up awards competition and development service. Advice is given to an average of 11,000 enquirers a year and some £200,000 is awarded through local, regional and national competitions.

Shell Technology Enterprise Programme (STEP): gives undergraduates the opportunity to experience project work within small firms and voluntary organisations during the summer vacation, and enables the management of these small firms to explore the potential contribution graduates can make to their business. A national network of over 80 agencies is co-ordinated by a contractor, SCOPE Project Management Ltd, to arrange 1,500 placements each year, with the aim of arranging 2,000 by the year 2000.

A development of the Shell Technology Enterprise Programme is *STEP into the Community* which operates along similar lines but offers undergraduates summer project-based placements with voluntary organisations, and STEP into the Environment which concentrates on projects undertaken by undergraduates to encourage awareness in small firms of the business benefits of managing environmental performance, and generally to promote closer integration of environmental and mainstream business issues.

Education: The main area of non-cash support is the Shell Education Service which provides teaching resources for primary and secondary schools.

Environment: On the community environmental front, the main thrust of Shell UK's efforts continues to be concentrated on the Shell Better Britain Campaign, which is now in its 28th year. The campaign encourages 'action by local people to improve the quality of life at neighbourhood level, in ways which respect the Earth's resources', through the provision of information, advice and grant aid.

Arts: Shell UK's support of the arts at corporate level is confined to its long-standing partnership with the London Symphony Orchestra, centred around the annual Shell LSO Music Scholarship for young instrumentalists and the biennial Shell LSO National Tour. Support for the arts at regional level is on a small scale and confined to local partnerships with arts organisations in areas of the company's main installation. The company is a member of ABSA.

Exclusions

No support is given to circular appeals, fundraising events, appeals from individuals, organisations of a sectarian nature, sport, building appeals, local appeals not in areas of major company presence, 'bricks and mortar' appeals, overseas projects, expeditions, or for advertising in charity brochures.

Applications

Enquiries should be addressed to Community Investment, Shell UK Limited, Shell-Mex House, Strand, London WC2R 0DX for attention of the relevant manager.

Contacts:

Arts and charities – Miss S K Aylward; *Enterprise Unit* – Mrs S Saloom; *Environmental Sponsorship* – Miss S Falconer; *Education* – Mr S Smyth.

Shepherd Building Group Ltd

Fulford Moor House, Fulford Road, York YO1 4EY
01904-653040; Fax: 01904-611504

Correspondent: William James

Chief officer: *Chairman:* Paul W Shepherd

Year end	Turnover	Pre-tax profit
30/6/97	£376,000,000	£4,000,000

Nature of company business
The company is involved in building and ancillary activities.

Main subsidiaries include: Computer Skills Ltd; Mechplant Ltd; Portakabin Ltd; Paton Plant Ltd; Yorkon Ltd; Portasilo Ltd.

UK employees: n/a

Charitable donations

1997: £132,000
1996: £84,000
1995: £75,000
1994: £176,000
1993: £130,000

Community support policy

The company's policy is to concentrate support in York and Yorkshire and to avoid contributing to more than one charity or organisation operating in the same field. The main areas of support are children and youth, social welfare, education, medicine, and enterprise and training.

Exclusions

No support for telephone appeals, circular appeals, fundraising events, advertising in charity brochures, appeals from individuals, purely denominational appeals, local appeals not in areas of company presence, large national appeals or overseas projects.

Applications

In writing to the correspondent.

Siebe plc

Saxon House, 2–4 Victoria Street, Windsor SL4 1EN
01753-855411; Fax: 01753-830047

Correspondent: R P A Coles, Company Secretary

Chief officers: *Chairman:* E B Stephens; *Chief Executive:* A M Yurko

Year end	Turnover	Pre-tax profit
4/4/98	£3,670,000,000	£486,000,000

Nature of company business
Principal activities: the design and manufacture of control devices and compressed air equipment.

Main subsidiaries include: Foxboro Great Britain Ltd; APV UK Ltd; Appliance Control Technology Europe Ltd; Coutant-Lambda Ltd; Weir Lambda Ltd; CompAir Holman Ltd; CompAir Reavell Ltd; Tecalemit Garage Equipment Co Ltd; Simulation Sciences Inc; Elctronic Measurement Inc.

UK employees: 6,000

Charitable donations

1998: £136,000
1997: £130,000
1996: £124,000
1995: £130,000
1994: £137,000

Community support policy

The company has consistently given about £130,000 a year in charitable donations (0.03% of pre-tax profit in 1997/98). It prefers to support medical charities, especially the Red Cross, and leukaemia and cancer-related charities.

Siebe has recently merged with BTR, the new company started trading in early Febrary 1999.

Applications

In writing to the correspondent.

Silentnight Holdings Plc

Silentnight House, Salterforth, Barnoldswick, Lancashire BB18 5UE
01282-815888; Fax: 01282-816926

Correspondent: Barry McKenzie, Financial Director

Chief officers: *Chairman:* K Ackroyd; *Chief Executive:* W Simpson

Year end	Turnover	Pre-tax profit
1/1/98	£229,255,000	£16,612,000

Nature of company business
The group manufactures furniture including mattresses, divans, headboards, cabinets and components.

Main subsidiaries include: Layezee Beds; Perfecta Beds; Sealy United Kingdom; Pocket Spring Bed Co; Westminster Pine; Sherbury; Silentlay Felts; Wellhouse Wire Products; Homeworthy Furniture.

Main locations: Barnoldswick, Lancashire; Batley, West Yorkshire; Wombwell, South Yorkshire; Aspatria, Cumbria; Skipton, North Yorkshire; Keighley, West Yorkshire; Wrexham, Clwyd;

Singer

Salterforth, Lancashire; Ossett, West Yorkshire; Mallusk, Northern Ireland; Sunderland.

UK employees: 3,600

Charitable donations
1998: £44,810
1997: £50,051
1996: £51,607
1995: £69,329
1994: £71,268
Membership: *ABSA*

Community support policy
The company has a preference for charities based in the north of England, but will also consider well-established national charities. Donations are usually in the range of £50 to £250, although large donations of up to £2,000 are sometimes made.

Areas of support include the arts, children/youth, education, elderly people, fundraising events, medical research, sickness/disability charities, social welfare and sport.

Exclusions
No support for individual appeals, overseas projects, animal welfare charities, advertising in charities brochures, political or religious appeals, science/technology, enterprise/training and environment/heritage.

Applications
In writing to the correspondent.

Singer & Friedlander Group plc

21 New Street, Bishopsgate, London EC2M 4HR
0171-623 3000; Fax: 0171-623 2122

Correspondent: David Griffiths, Personnel Manager

Chief officers: *Chairman:* A N Solomons;
Chief Executive: J Hodson

Year end	Turnover	Pre-tax profit
31/12/97	£294,388,000	£54,070,000

Nature of company business
The group companies are involved in merchant banking, investment banking, stockbroking, investment management and property investment.

Main subsidiaries include: Gilbert Estates Ltd; Sharepart Ltd; Ancomass Ltd; Collins Stewart Ltd; Rowan & Co Ltd; Sinjul Investments Ltd; Straker Brothers Ltd; Millwalk Ltd; Hillgrove Developments Ltd; Peninsular Park Developments Ltd; Peaston Emerson's Green Ltd; Quinarius Investments Ltd.

UK employees: n/a

Charitable donations
1997: £115,160
1996: £93,400
1995: £62,801
1994: £73,815
1993: £69,640

Community support policy
Although the company has no set policy, there is a preference towards children and youth charities, local charities in areas of company presence and charities where company staff are involved. The company tends to support less well-known charities, especially those in areas of company presence, although some charities outside their areas of operation are supported.

The company's offices are in London, Birmingham, Leeds, Manchester and Nottingham. Some overseas projects are considered.

Applications
In writing to the correspondent.

Slough Estates plc

234 Bath Road, Slough, Berkshire SL1 4EE
01753-537171; Fax: 01753-820585

Correspondent: Air Commodore N Hamilton (Retired), Manager External Affairs

Chief officers: *Chairman:* Sir Nigel Mobbs;
Chief Executive: Derek Wilson

Year end	Turnover	Pre-tax profit
31/12/97	£263,100,000	£93,200,000

Nature of company business
Principal activities: industrial and commercial property development, construction and investment, supply of utility services and the provision of services associated with such activities.

Main subsidiaries include: Allnatt London Properties; Beta Properties; Bredero Properties; Howard Centre Properties; Lewisham Investment Partnership; Pentagon Developments (Chatham); Shopping Centres.

UK employees: 409

Charitable donations
1997: £195,000
1996: £145,250
1995: £161,600
1994: £147,000
1993: £147,000

Total community contributions: £240,000

Membership: *BitC %Club*

Community support policy
The company is a member of the PerCent Club and commits about 1% of dividends to community, charitable and educational causes. In 1997, the group contributed £240,000 in cash and in kind by way of management support.

The company has pledged £500,000 to be managed by the independent Hertfordshire Community Trust. This endowment is to be used for the benefit of causes within the Welwyn Hatfield area.

W H Smith Group plc

Nation's House, 103 Wigmore Street, London W1H 0WH
0171-409 3222; Fax: 0171-514 9635

Correspondent: Andy Finch, Group Corporate Affairs Manager

Chief officers: *Chairman:* Jeremy Hardie; *Chief Executive:* Richard Handover

Year end	Turnover	Pre-tax profit
31/5/97	£2,763,000,000	£124,000,000

Nature of company business
W H Smith is the leading seller of books, newspapers and magazines, music, video, and stationery in the UK.
Main subsidiaries include: John Menzies; Bookshop Co UK.

UK employees: 27,971

Charitable donations

1997: £161,000
1996: £170,000
1995: £172,000
1994: £208,000
1993: £295,000

Total community contributions: £621,000

Membership: *BitC %Club*

Community support policy

The group continues to support the community with a strong focus on education. Community contributions include sponsorship, support in kind, proactive donations, joint promotions, support for staff volunteering and other community support. The group is a founder member of the PerCent Club, with community contributions totalling £621,000 in 1996/97.

Charitable donations: The company's donations policy is proactive and currently focused on support for staff involvement in the community and selected trade/allied charities such as the Newsvendors Benevolent Institution. Grants are made through the W H Smith Group Charitable Trust (Charity Commission number 1013782).

Employee involvement: The company encourages employee volunteering and supports staff fundraising. The staff run their own charity which raises some £100,000 a year. This is distributed with one third of net proceeds going to charities nominated by the staff, and the remaining two-thirds to a charity of the year.

The group operates the Give As You Earn payroll giving scheme.

Education: W H Smith is committed to improving standards of literacy, and to strengthening links between schools and business. In 1997, the group launched a major initiative 'Ready Steady Read', a five-year commitment to improving literacy in over 400 selected primary schools across the UK.

Exclusions
Unsolicited requests.

Charitable donations: The company gives support to a wide range of causes in the fields of art, music and culture; health research and care; youth; old age; education; relief of unemployment; the environment and conservation; welfare and the relief of poverty; fundraising events; animal welfare charities; advertising in charity brochures and sport. There is a preference for local appeals in areas of company presence, principally the Slough area. All cases are considered on their merits. Typical grants range from £25 to £5,000.

Significant donations during the year included support of the Slough and Thames Valley Foyer Appeal and the Army Benevolent Fund. Other beneficiaries of support included Chiltern Cheshire Home, City of London Festival, Groundwork Thames Valley, Royal Academy of Arts and Slough Social Fund.

In kind support: In addition to donations to charities, the main area of support is for enterprise agencies. Equipment and material, professional services and the use of in-house facilities have been donated free of charge for specific purposes.

Employee involvement: The company operates a £ for £ matching scheme for employee giving and fundraising. Secretarial support is given to four charities free of charge.

Sponsorship: The company undertakes arts and good-cause sponsorship on a national level. The main areas supported are art and music, including sponsorship of the annual National Art Collections Fund awards.

Enterprise: The company is a member of Business in the Community and also supports TARGET, Livewire, Instant Muscle and two local enterprise agencies. A total of £7,500 is donated.

Education: Support is given to the University of Buckingham and the professional property education departments of the City University and Reading University (£17,500 in total), and sponsored Hershel Grammar School as a City Technology College. The company operates work-experience schemes for school pupils.

Exclusions
No grants for non-charities; circular appeals; local appeals not in areas of company presence; appeals from individuals; political appeals; religious appeals or overseas projects.

Applications
Decisions are made by a committee which meets quarterly. Air Commodore Nick Hamilton should be contacted for donations and sponsorship. Sir Nigel Mobbs, D R Wilson and D E F Simons are the directors responsible for charitable affairs.

David S Smith

Applications

The group is proactive in identifying potential partners for its community programme. Unsolicited requests, therefore, are not considered.

Information available: The group publishes information on its community affairs in its annual report.

David S Smith Holdings plc

16 Great Peter Street, London SW1P 2BX
0171-222 8855; Fax: 0171-222 8856

Correspondent: Paul Froud, Group Communications Manager

Chief officers: *Chairman:* Alan Clements; *Chief Executive:* J Peter Williams

Year end	Turnover	Pre-tax profit
2/5/98	£1,113,000,000	£51,000,000

Nature of company business
Production of packaging and paper (primarily from waste paper) and the distribution of office products.

Main subsidiaries include: A A Griggs & Co; St Regis Paper Company; Spicers.

UK employees: n/a

Charitable donations

1998: £52,000
1997: £88,000
1996: n/a
1995: £76,000
1994: £50,000

Community support policy

Although the company has no set policy, it does have a preference for the arts, children/youth, education, elderly people, enterprise/training, environment/heritage, fundraising events, medical research, overseas projects, science/technology, sickness/disability charities, social welfare and sport.

Main grant benficiaries in 1996/97 included: British Occupational Health Research Fund, Co-operation Ireland and The Duke of Edinburgh Awards Scheme.

Exclusions

No support for advertising in charity brochures, appeals from individuals, political or religious appeals.

Applications

In writing to the correspondent.

Smith & Nephew plc

2 Temple Place, Victoria Embankment, London WC2R 3BP
0171-836 7922; Fax: 0171-240 7088

Correspondent: Bridget Swanton, Smith & Nephew Foundation – Administrator

Chief officers: *Chairman:* John Robinson; *Chief Executive:* Christopher O'Donnell

Year end	Turnover	Pre-tax profit
31/12/97	£1,048,100,000	£160,700,000

Nature of company business
International healthcare.

Main brands include: Simple; Nivea; Dr White's; Lil-lets.

UK employees: 3,904

Charitable donations

1997: £548,000
1996: £525,000
1995: £552,000
1994: £544,000
1993: £510,000

Total community contributions: £702,000

Membership: *BitC* %Club

Community support policy

In 1997, group contributions to charity amounted to £1,154,000 worldwide. In the 1998 PerCent Club annual report the total UK community investment figure quoted was £702,000 (1.5% of UK pre-tax profit), of which £548,000 was in charitable donations.

Most of the company's UK charitable donations are channelled through the Smith & Nephew Foundation (Charity Commission number 267061), which supports education and research for individuals in the medical and nursing professions. The funding policy is to invite individuals to apply to advertisements. Applications are not considered at any other time. In 1997, the foundation made 159 awards in the UK, 83 to nurses and 76 to doctors, a total investment of £505,000.

Doctors and/or physicians must have qualified in the UK. Nurses, midwives and health visitors must hold an active UKCC number.

The foundation awards grants in the following areas:

Medical Research Fellowships: These are offered once a year and are for postgraduate doctors who have obtained their qualifications in the UK and who wish to undertake one year's research in the UK. They are offered through advertisements in the *BMJ* and *The Lancet*.

Intercalated BSc Degree Bursaries: The foundation pays the fees of medical students throughout the UK to help them undertake intercalated BSc degrees. The funding is done through the Medical Deans of the chosen universities.

Nursing Fellowships: For nurses, midwives and health visitors who either hold or aspire to leadership positions in clinical, management or educational spheres in the nursing professions, who wish to undertake a major research project either in this country or abroad.

Nursing Scholarships: For nurses and midwives working in the UK who wish to undertake shorter periods of professional education or research abroad or in this country.

Nursing Bursaries: For nurses and midwives who wish to improve their clinical practice by undertaking short study programmes or conducting comparative studies in specialist areas.

All the nursing awards are advertised once a year in leading nursing journals.

The company is a member of the PerCent Club and in addition to support given through the foundation, it supports links with educational facilities in areas where its main operations are situated. It also encourages employees to get involved in community activities.

Exclusions

Only applications which fall within the conditions outlined above will be considered.

Applications

All awards are advertised in relevant medical or nursing journals. Any correspondence should be addressed to the Secretary to the Trustees, Smith & Nephew Foundation. Applications are not considered except in response to advertisements for the various awards.

SmithKline Beecham plc

One New Horizons Court, Brentford, Middlesex TW8 9EP
0181-975 2299; Fax: 0181-975 6277
Email: liane.v.catlin@sb.com
Website: www.sb.com

Correspondent: Programme Officer, Community Partnership

Chief officers: *Chairman:* Sir Peter Walters; *Chief Executive:* Jan Leschly

Year end	Turnover	Pre-tax profit
31/12/97	£7,925,000,000	£1,636,000,000

Nature of company business
A leading healthcare company which discovers, develops, manufactures and markets pharmaceuticals, vaccines, over-the-counter medicines and health-related consumer products, and provides healthcare services including clinical laboratory testing, disease management and pharmaceutical benefit management. For company information, visit the website (see above).

Main subsidiaries include: Beecham Group; Horlicks; Smith Kline & French Laboratories; Sterling Health Ltd.

Main locations: Berkshire, Essex, Gloucestershire, Hertfordshire, Irvine (Scotland), Middlesex, Sussex.

UK employees: 8,400

Charitable donations

1998: £1,218,000
1997: £1,100,000
1996: £900,000
1995: £1,350,000
1994: £1,563,000

Total community contributions: £18,324,000 (worldwide)

Membership: *BitC*

Community support policy

'SmithKline Beecham (SB) recognises our interdependence with our communities worldwide. Through visible and sustained investment of the skills and talents of our people, as well as our products and financial resources, we aim to make a real and measurable contribution to improving standards of health for people wherever SB operates.'

Total contributions of cash and products worldwide in 1998 were £18.3 million, including £9.1 million in cash donations. This included £2.5 million in Europe, of which £1.2 million was given in the UK.

'Through our community programmes, SB is committed to establishing partnerships to improve health, with a theme of *SB in the community: Working together to make people healthier.*

'At the heart of SB's Community Partnership strategy is a commitment to bring SB's community activities closer to its business. This is achieved by keeping the following objectives in mind:

- to devote the vast majority of SB's community resources to healthcare issues
- to think globally and act locally: SB's businesses around the world are directly involved in local Community Partnership activities
- to maximise the benefits we bring by working with partners whose skills and resources complement our own
- to act, when appropriate, as a catalyst to bring like-minded parties together
- to be proactive in confronting and solving healthcare issues as they affect communities everywhere
- to achieve as much leverage as possible.

'In January 1996, SmithKline Beecham relaunched its Community Partnership programme, with healthcare as its focus. The programme has been divided between North America, Europe and the rest of the world (International). Each region decides on their individual funding goals. Currently the main focus for Europe is Children's Healthcare Throughout Europe. SmithKline Beecham is unable to respond favourably to unsolicited requests, but proactively seeks partnerships with organisations which reflect this theme and which conform to agreed criteria.

'In Europe, partnerships have been forged with three organisations to reflect the focus of pan-European children's health issues, with a total annual budget of £1.55 million, these include: *Barretstown Gang Camp* – the European Liaison Network Befrienders International, the Reaching Young Europe programme *Project Hope* – paediatric rehabilitation for war-disabled children in Bosnia, and school-based substance abuse prevention and education programme in Russia.

'SB is also working in partnership with the Association for Science Education on the Health Matters School Awards programme; now in its fourth year and expanding from the original UK-based awards programme into the Netherlands, Eire and Belgium.'

In response to the Community Partnership promise to invest the skills and talents of its people, SB launched a new employee involvement programme, called Partners, to all European sites in March 1998 and to North American sites in January 1999. There are plans to make the Partners programme available worldwide in the next few years.

Partners was conceived in Europe to offer the opportunity to all sites, regardless of size, to become involved in children's health-related projects within their own local community, not just financially but by way of employee involvement. Community Partnership offers an initial grant to each site to help them organise activities to benefit their chosen partner, which might be a school for special-needs children, an orphanage or the paediatric oncology unit of a hospital. The list is endless, as are the activities that the employees are undertaking which include re-decorating, sponsored fundraising events and children's outings.

In September 1997, SB launched the first year of its Community Health Impact Award Programme in the UK and Philadelphia area of the US. The awards are innovative in that they recognise achievement in existing work on the part of voluntary organisations working in health, and are designed to promote best practice in the sector. 10 awards of £25,000 will be offered in the UK and 10 of $40,000 in the USA, to smaller voluntary organisations who succeed in making a real difference in their community, usually with very modest resources. In the UK, SB are working in partnership with the King's Fund and appoint a panel to judge applications, which includes external experts in the field of healthcare in the voluntary sector. This is an annual programme.

Exclusions

SmithKline Beecham does not offer support for debt or deficit financing, capital projects, chairs or endowments, multi-year grants, multiple grants in a calendar year, conferences, symposia and related expenses, publications, fundraising events and associated advertising, lobbying to influence legislation, religious organisations, medical research, sporting events, funding for further education, expeditions or individuals.

SB is unable to respond favourably to unsolicited requests for pharmacy only or over-the-counter medicines, but does monitor the distribution of such products, through preferred agencies, to areas where disaster relief is required. In 1997, SB's Manufacture to Give programme distributed $15 million of pharmaceutical products to disaster areas and areas of need throughout the world.

Applications

It is important to note that the overwhelming majority of the Community Partnership work is initiated by SB and does not stem from unsolicited proposals. We would encourage any potential applicant to carefully review our company guidelines before submitting a letter of enquiry.

SB's guidelines form part of the *SB Community Partnership Report* available on request. These details are also included in the Community Partnership pages of the SB website (www.sb.com). There is a brief account in the annual report and accounts, and reports in staff newsletters.

Smiths Industries plc

765 Finchley Road, Childs Hill, London NW11 8DS
0181-458 3232; Fax: 0181-458 4380
Website: www.smiths-industries.com

Correspondent: N Burdett, Assistant Company Secretary

Chief officers: *Chairman:* Sir Roger Hurn;
Chief Executive: K O Butler-Wheelhouse

Year end	Turnover	Pre-tax profit
2/8/97	£1,076,000,000	£192,000,000

Nature of company business
The company is involved in the industrial, aerospace, medical and defence industries.

Main subsidiaries include: SIMS-Portex Ltd; Eschmann Bros & Walsh Ltd; Air Movement Ltd; Lighthome Ltd; Graseby PLC.

UK employees: n/a

Charitable donations

1997: £718,000
1996: £767,000
1995: £730,000
1994: £593,000
1993: £600,000
Membership: *BitC %Club*

Community support policy

The company is a member of the PerCent Club and Business in the Community, with charitable donations representing 0.8% of pre-tax profits in 1997. Support of charities is wide-ranging covering everything from the local village fete to national causes. Appeals are considered on their merits and their relevance to the company's business (ie. medical, industrial and aerospace) and geographical interests.

Some large grants may be donated over several years, for example the company is giving substantial donations to Brooklands Museum (£5,000 each year for four years), Kent Institute of Medical Health Sciences and Royal United Services Institutes. Donations are made through the Charities Aid Foundation and usually range from £500 to £2,500.

The charitable donations figure includes funding for an educational and research programme, particularly in the healthcare field.

Support, other than cash donations, such as gifts in kind and secondments may be provided at a local level by subsidiaries. Support for education and enterprise initiatives is also carried out at local level. For example, Portex Ltd is sponsoring the establishment of a Department of Paediatric Anaesthesia at the Institute of Child Health at Great Ormond Street Hospital.

Applications

In writing to the correspondent. Charities should give their appeals reasonable time to be processed as the company receives about 10 appeals a week and all are considered. A donations committee decides appeals and meets fairly regularly.

Applications should be concise, not too scruffy or glossy and should briefly set out what is wanted and why.

Somerfield Stores plc

Somerfield House, Whitchurch Lane, Bristol BS14 0TJ
0117-935 9359; Fax: 0117-935 0629
Website: www.somerfield.co.uk

Correspondent: Gill Rawlins, Head of Public Relations

Chief officers: *Chairman:* A G Thomas;
Chief Executive: David Simons

Year end	Turnover	Pre-tax profit
26/4/98	£3,484,000,000	(£11,100,000)

Nature of company business
Food retailing within the UK.
Main subsidiaries include: Kwik Save Group PLC.

UK employees: 45,000

Charitable donations
1998: £547,000
1997: £399,000
1996: £768,000
1995: £532,000

Community support policy

The company launched a scratch card in 1997, all proceeds from which go to the Somerfield Community Charity (Charity Commission number 1060297). The charity also receives income from 'brand aid' and other fundraising initiatives. The money is distributed by the trust through its stores.

Each store (of which there are 522) invites customers to nominate local charities/voluntary organisations. The charity with most nominations then receives six month's funding. 1,040 charities receive a grant during the year.

The company also runs a staff lottery which raises about £100,000 a year. This is distributed regionally through a central committee. Recipients tend to be nominated by staff.

The £547,000 quoted as the company's charitable donations is additional to the above, but we have no further information on the allocation of this money.

Exclusions
The company gave no indication of causes it might not support.

Applications
Approaches should be made by nominating causes for support at local stores.

Sony United Kingdom Limited

The Heights, Brooklands, Weybridge, Surrey KT13 0XW
01932-816000; Fax: 01932-817000

Correspondent: Rosemary Small, Public Affairs

Chief officers: *Chairman:* S Foucher;
Managing Director: J Sinyor

Year end	Turnover	Pre-tax profit
31/3/98	£2,173,789,000	£46,909,000

Nature of company business
The company is the distributor in the UK of 'Sony' branded products, which are principally electronic goods for the domestic, leisure, business and professional markets. The company also operates in Bridgend and Pencoed in Wales, where Sony 'Triniton' colour television sets, television tubes, computer monitors and set-top boxes and other key components are manufactured for the domestic and export markets.

UK employees: 5,856

Charitable donations
1998: £81,000
1997: £89,000
1996: £79,000
1995: £86,000
1994: £82,000
Membership: *BitC %Club*

Community support policy

The company is a member of the PerCent Club, commited to giving 0.5% of pre-tax profits in the form of community contributions (ie. at least £235,000 in 1997/98), the main areas of which are arts sponsorship, charitable donations and support for enterprise agencies.

The company prefers to support local charities in areas of company presence (Surrey, Berkshire and Glamorgan), appeals relevant to company business and charities in which a member of staff is involved. There is a preference for children/youth, education, sickness/disability charities and social welfare.

In 1997, the company donated funds and equipment to 300 charity and community organisations through the company's in-house donations committee, and has donated equipment to several educational institutions.

The company supports its employees volunteering with cash and matches employee giving. It also operates the Give As You Earn payroll giving scheme. As well as encouraging the involvement of employees in community projects, managers are encouraged to become school governors, young enterprise advisers and session leaders with Understanding Industry.

Enterprise: The company is a member of Business in the Community and supports enterprise agencies such as Surrey Business Enterprise Agency and Elmbridge Business Partnership.

The arts: The company continues to encourage the arts by supporting and equipping the Royal Society for

South

Encouragement of Arts. Support has also been provided to Glyndebourne, Royal Opera House, and the Design Museum. Local organisations to receive support include Brooklands Museum, Elmbridge Arts Festival and Newbury Spring Festival.

Exclusions
No support for advertising in charity brochures.

Applications
Appeals should be addressed to the correspondent.

South Western Electricity plc

800 Park Avenue, Aztec West, Almondsbury, Bristol BS12 4SE
01454-201101; Fax: 01454-452238

Correspondent: Sharon Cross, Corporate Communications Supervisor

Chief officers: *Chairman:* A W Nicol; *Managing Director:* J J Seed

Year end	Turnover	Pre-tax profit
31/3/97	£826,000,000	£94,000,000

Nature of company business
Principal activities: distribution and supply of electricity to industrial, commercial and domestic consumers, electrical retailing and contracting.
Main subsidiaries include: Aztec Insurance Ltd; Western Gas Ltd.

UK employees: n/a

Charitable donations
1997: £284,000
1996: n/a
1995: £148,000
1994: £147,000
1993: £146,000
Membership: *BitC %Club*

Community support policy
The company supports causes within its local community, ie. areas of company presence, paying particular attention to elderly/young/vulnerable people and those with special needs. Involvement includes support for the arts, education, sport, enterprise initiatives and other deserving causes. Grants generally range from £500 to £3,000.

In kind support: Occasionally electrical appliances are donated to charities which would struggle to survive without them.

Employee involvement: Staff are encouraged to become volunteers in their own time and to become school governors. The company operates a payroll giving scheme and matches monies raised by employees.

Sponsorship: Sponsorship by the company is particularly directed at young people through support of arts and sports events. Typical sponsorship range is from £500 to £12,000.

Enterprise: The company was involved in the formation of South West Enterprise and also supports the Midland Enterprise Fund for the South West.

Education: The company provides work-experience schemes for pupils and teachers, educational materials for schools and student sponsorships.

Exclusions
No grants for appeals from individuals; purely denominational (religious) appeals; overseas projects.

Applications
In writing to the correspondent, between October and December. A committee considers all applications and a decision is based on (a) relevance locally, (b) the nature of the application, (c) geographical spread throughout the South West.

Southern Electric plc

Southern Electric House, Westacott Way, Littlewick Green, Maidenhead, Berkshire SL6 3QB
01628-822166; Fax: 01628-584400

Correspondent: Julian Reeves, Public Relations Manager

Chief officers: *Chairman:* Dr B Farmer; *Chief Executive:* J A Forbes

Year end	Turnover	Pre-tax profit
31/3/98	£1,774,000,000	£249,000,000

Nature of company business
Principal activities: electricity distribution and supply of electricity and gas, generation, electrical and utility contracting and building environmental control systems.
Main subsidiaries include: Thermal Transfer; Southern Electric Gas; Southern Electric Pipelines; MPB.

Charitable donations
1998: £150,000
1997: £232,400
1996: £227,488
1995: £167,450
1994: £127,676
Total community contributions: £400,000
Membership: *BitC*

Community support policy
Total community contributions in 1998 were £400,000 including charitable donations of £150,000, with other support including good-cause sponsorship and gifts in kind. The company is a member of Business in the Community.

Southern Electric supports the community, not just through cash donations, but also by involving its staff – using their expertise to provide practical benefit to community groups in Southern Electric's region (central southern England). It actively supports education business partnerships and provides gifts in kind. The company operates the Barnardo's Winners Club payroll giving scheme.

When considering requests for sponsorship and donations, priority is given to projects which originate and apply within the region. The following information was taken from the company's own leaflet.

'In the case of major sponsorship applications we look particularly at the potential for long-term partnerships which will benefit both the company and the applicant. For this reason we would normally expect to support only a limited number of sponsorship programmes each year.

'However, the majority of applications we receive are for 'community support'.

'These are generally requests for a one-off donation of money, goods or services to local charitable or community groups.

'Before supporting any appeal we first satisfy ourselves that the individual or organisation making the application is reputable and that the project is in line with our sponsorship and corporate giving policy.

'We support as many projects as possible within the funds set aside for this purpose and give priority to activities included in the following list:

- schemes supporting training or increasing the employment prospects of disadvantaged young people
- schemes promoting the welfare and well-being of the young or the elderly, particularly projects related to energy conservation and efficiency
- schemes encouraging safety at work, in homes, schools and in public places
- schemes promoting crime prevention, environmental care and conservation.'

Key projects in the year included the announcement of a three-year partnership with Barnardo's, worth at least £250,000; support for the National Association of Citizen's Advice Bureaux; Schools Resources; EEIBA; Hampshire Fire and Rescue Service and the successful trial of an innovative programme of support for disaffected youngsters who are potentially disruptive or truanting and who are likely to be expelled from school.

Exclusions
No response to circular appeals or appeals from individuals. The company does not generally support unsolicited appeals by large, established charities with substantial fundraising capabilities of their own, fund projects which they consider to be properly the responsibility of the State, or make donations to replace withdrawn or expired statutory funding, donate towards educational bursaries, foreign expeditions, travel or 'adventure' projects, political activity, medical research, purely denominational organisations or advertise in charity brochures or year books.

Applications
In writing to the correspondent, with a brief description of the project and the form of assistance being sought.

The company has produced a leaflet *Southern Electric in the Community* – a guide for charitable and community organisations seeking support.

Spandex plc

1600 Park Avenue, Aztec West, Almondsbury, Bristol BS12 4UA
01454-616444; Fax: 01454-618012
Website: www.spandex.co.uk

Correspondent: C E Dobson, Chairman

Chief officers: *Chairman:* C E Dobson; *Managing Director:* E P Bruegger

Year end	Turnover	Pre-tax profit
31/12/97	£101,347,000	£9,008,000

Nature of company business
Principal activity: computer-aided sign-making equipment.
Main subsidiaries include: Ultramark; Adhesive Products Ltd.

UK employees: 150

Charitable donations
1997: £91,250
1996: £100,850
1995: £88,000
1994: £71,650
1993: £550

Community support policy
The company has a preference for cancer and heart disease related charities in south west England. Support may also be given for advertising in charity brochures; appeals from individuals; medical research and sickness/disability charities.

The bulk of the company's charitable donations are made through the Spandex Foundation (Charity Commission number 800203, also known as the Starfish Trust). The trust's main area of work concerns incurable diseases, with its three main objects being:

1) to provide funding for research and development into incurable diseases such as cancer and meningitis
2) to provide funding for the welfare of sufferers of such illnesses
3) to provide funding for the development and promotion of augmented communication systems, using mainstream technology, to allow sufferers of conditions such as cerebral palsy and after-effects of strokes to communicate with the outside world.

In 1995/96, the income of the trust was £104,000 including donations of £85,000 from Spandex plc; equivalent to 1% of the company's pre-tax profits. Grants totalled £21,000 with a further £29,000 in donated goods and services. The assets of the trust stood at £1.4 million. Four grants totalling £7,800 were listed with the remainder accounted for by the statement: 'the charity distributed £13,600 to three beneficiaries in accordance with the charitable objects'. The grants mentioned were to CLIC – £1,330 (£11,000 in the previous year); Madeline Harding Appeal Fund – £1,200 (£1,500 the previous year); Cancer Care Appeal – £5,000; and Chernobyl Children Cancer Care – £250.

Applications
In writing to the correspondent.

Specialist Computer Holdings Ltd

James House, Warwick Road, Birmingham B11 2LE
0121-766 7007; Fax: 0121-773 3986

Correspondent: The Chairman

Chief officer: *Chairman:* P Rigby

Year end	Turnover	Pre-tax profit
31/3/96	n/a	£16,142,000

Nature of company business
The company and its subsidiaries are dealers, distributers, and retailers of computer systems, accessories and related services.

UK employees: n/a

Charitable donations
1996: £130,000
1995: £90,883
1994: £99,946
1993: £75,387

Community support policy
The company has a preference for charities/causes in the Midlands, especially Birmingham where it is based. No further information was available on the types of causes supported.

Applications
In writing to the correspondent.

Spirax Sarco Engineering plc

Charlton House, Cirencester Road, Cheltenham, Gloucestershire GL53 8ER
01242-521361; Fax: 01242-581470
Website: www.spirax-sarco.com

Correspondent: Jane Husband, Personal Assistant to the Chief Executive

Chief officers: *Chairman:* C J Tappin; *Chief Executive:* T B Fortune

Year end	Turnover	Pre-tax profit
31/12/97	£265,595,000	£47,715,000

Nature of company business
The principal activity is the provision of knowledge, service and products worldwide for the control and efficient use of steam and other industrial fluids.
Main subsidiaries include: Watson-Marlow Ltd.

UK employees: 3,903

Charitable donations
1997: £38,597
1996: £39,685
1995: £39,741
1994: £33,550

Community support policy
The company gives just under £40,000 a year in charitable donations, mainly to local charities in areas where it operates. There is also a preference for appeals relevant to company business and charities in which a member of staff is involved, in particular charities concerned with child welfare, medical research, and education. Grants to national organisations range from £50 to £400 and to local organisations from £20 to £1,000.

Exclusions
No response to circular appeals, and no grants for advertising in charity brochures, purely denominational (religious) appeals, local appeals not in areas of company presence and large national appeals.

Applications
In writing to the correspondent.

Stagecoach Holdings plc

Charlotte House, 20 Charlotte Street, Perth PH1 5LL
01738-442111; Fax: 01738-643648
Email: dscott@stagecoachholdings.com
Website: www.stagecoachholdings.com

Correspondent: D Scott, Company Secretary

Chief officers: *Chairman:* B Souter; *Chief Executive:* M J Kinski

Year end	Turnover	Pre-tax profit
30/4/98	£1,381,500,000	£158,500,000

Nature of company business
Public transport services. Subsidiary companies are spread throughout England and Scotland, but are too numerous to mention.
Main subsidiaries include: East Midland Motor Services Ltd; Bluebird Buses Ltd; Fife Scottish Omnibuses Ltd; East Kent Road Car Co Ltd; Western Buses Ltd; Busways Travel Services Ltd; South East London & Kent Bus Co Ltd; Cleveland Transit Ltd; Cambus Ltd; Greater Manchester Buses South Ltd; Burnley & Pendle Transport Co Ltd; Rhondda Buses Ltd; National Tokens Ltd; PSV Claims Bureau Ltd; South West Trains Ltd; Porterbrook Leasing Co Ltd; Island Line Ltd; Transit International Holdings Ltd; South Yorkshire Supertram Ltd; Prestwick Aviation Holdings Ltd; Glasgow Prestwick International Airport Ltd; East London Bus & Coach Co Ltd.
Main brands include: Stagecoach Express; South West Trains; National Transport Tokens.

UK employees: 22,652

Charitable donations
1998: £798,000
1997: £512,000
1996: £218,000
1995: £163,000
1994: £95,000

Community support policy
The company is committed to giving 0.5% of pre-tax profits in charitable donations. Since 1993, the cash amount given has increased markedly with the current level (1997/98) being £798,000. Further non-cash support

(estimated to be at least an additional 0.2% of pre-tax profits) was made through joint promotions, training schemes such as Understanding Industry, and the Government's New Deal (fares deal and training scheme).

Preferred areas of support are: appeals from individuals, children/youth, education, elderly people, sickness/disability charities, enterprise/training, medical research, and social welfare. There is a preference for supporting charities local to subsidiary operations.

The group continues with its commitment to Save the Children to provide £250,000 over a five-year period, whilst other major beneficiaries include: Imperial Cancer Research Fund; Prince's Trust; Macmillan Cancer Relief; The Princess Trust for Carers, and the Government's Welfare-To-Work New Deal.

The company also supports employee's volunteering/charitable activities by considering, where appropriate, financial help, allowing company time off to volunteer, matching employee fundraising, and loaning equipment/facilities.

Exclusions

No support for advertising in charity brochures; animal welfare; the arts; fundraising events; environment/heritage; overseas projects; religious appeals; political appeals; science/technology or sport.

Applications

In writing to the correspondent.

Standard Chartered plc

1 Aldermanbury Square, London EC2V 7SB
0171-280 7500; Fax: 0171-280 7791
Website: www.stanchart.com

Correspondent: Christopher Makin, Group External Affairs Manager

Chief officers: *Chairman:* Sir Patrick Gilla; *Chief Executive:* Rana Talwar

Year end	Turnover	Pre-tax profit
31/12/97	£2,193,000,000 (net revenue)	£870,000,000

Nature of company business
Standard Chartered is a holding company co-ordinating the activities of its subsidiaries, which are principally engaged in the business of banking and other financial services.

UK employees: 2,500

Charitable donations
1997: £400,000
1996: £300,000
1995: £250,000
1994: £400,000
1993: £249,000
Total community contributions: £1,100,000
Membership: *BitC*

Community support policy

The company produces a booklet, *Standard Chartered in the Community,* from which the following information is taken.

The group has set a budget of £2 million a year for the three years 1998 to 2000, to fund projects to assist those most in need in the communities in which its customers and staff live. (This includes support overseas.) Additionally, it also supports a range of fundraising events, provides advice, secondments and scholarships. UK support in 1997 totalled £1.1 million of which £400,000 was given in cash donations.

There are three focus areas for support:

- *International:* The group's donations are focused on those countries in Asia, Africa and the Middle East where its major operations are based.
- *Youth:* The group concentrates on projects which will assist children and youth.
- *Health and education:* Projects which support health and education have priority.

The following criteria must be met before Standard Chartered can consider making a donation. All donations must:

- reflect the group's focus on youth, health and education
- assist those in the community who are most in need
- support the national aspirations of the country
- be environmentally sound
- support non-governmental organisations involved in charitable or community activities but not political or religious projects, or individuals other than staff
- offer Standard Chartered the opportunity to become involved in the project
- generate mutually beneficial publicity
- represent support for a project rather than for the core funding of charities
- be, where possible, based on a three-year commitment
- support projects with clear and agreed objectives
- ensure all projects are subject and applicable to review, measurement and audit.

Examples of projects supported include: provision of scholarships for students from Botswana, Ghana, Kenya and Zimbabwe to study in Singapore; funding the employment of a therapist for a local paediatric therapy centre; assistance to a centre in Kenya working with HIV positive babies; funding for a Young Learner's Centre in Dhaka; support via the Standard Chartered Community Foundation to a wide range of voluntary organisations in Hong Kong which assist needy young people; a scheme in India whereby a contribution is made to CRY (Child Relief and You) every time a Gold Standard Cardholder uses their card.

Standard Chartered encourages its people to become involved in the communities in which they work. Many participate in a wide range of charitable and community support programmes. In some countries budgets have been established to encourage and support the charitable work of staff.

Stanley

Exclusions

Generally no support for charities in the UK, circular appeals, advertising in charity brochures, appeals from individuals, purely denominational (religious) appeals, local appeals not in areas of company presence or large national appeals. Donations are not made to political parties.

Applications

Please note the following points:

- Ensure that the project for which you are seeking support fits the criteria set out.
- Write a short summary of the project (not more than one page of A4 paper). It should then be sent to the Standard Chartered corporate affairs manager of the country where the project is taking place. Should the group then be able to consider supporting the project a more detailed proposal will be required. The company has operations in over 40 countries in Africa, Asia, the Middle East, and Latin America.
- As donation plans for the year are usually agreed at the end of the year, it is advisable to submit a proposal no later than the third quarter of a given year.
- It is group practice to support a limited number of charities and, where possible, to support them for a period of up to three years. The opportunity for involvement of Standard Chartered and direct support by our people is a key element in gaining funding.

Stanley Leisure plc

Stanley House, 4–12 Marylebone, Liverpool L3 2BY
0151-236 4291; Fax: 0151-227 5068

Correspondent: L Steinberg, Chairman

Chief officers: *Chairman:* L Steinberg;
Chief Executive: C M Kershaw

Year end	Turnover	Pre-tax profit
3/5/98	£454,904,000	£23,935,000

Nature of company business
The main activity of the company is that of betting office and casino operators.
Main subsidiaries include: Gus Carter PLC; James Lane Ltd; Pandashield Ltd; Daniel McLaren Ltd.

UK employees: 4,678

Charitable donations

1998: £107,000
1997: £53,000
1996: £38,603
1995: £26,437
1994: £22,030
Membership: %Club

Community support policy

The company is a member of the PerCent Club, undertaking good-cause sponsorship as well as making cash donations. The latter have doubled in the last year to over £100,000.

It prefers to support local charities in Northern Ireland and the north west of England, especially Merseyside. Preferred areas of support are advertising in charity brochures; animal welfare charities; children/youth; education; elderly people; sickness/disability charities and sport.

Main beneficiaries included children's hospitals, Salford University, Children in Need, Forth AM Help a Child and Thoroughbred Rehabilitation Centre.

Exclusions

No support for appeals from individuals; the arts; environment/heritage; fundraising events; overseas projects; political appeals; religious appeals or science/technology.

Applications

In writing to the correspondent.

Stobart Investments Ltd

Brunthill Road, Kingstown Industrial Estate, Carlisle CA3 0EA
01228-537915

Correspondent: Jonathan Rayson, Sponsorship & Charities

Chief officers: n/a

Year end	Turnover	Pre-tax profit
30/11/96	£65,190,000	£3,560,000

Nature of company business
The company operates a large fleet of freight vehicles nationwide.

UK employees: n/a

Charitable donations

1996: £309,248
1995: £147,000

Community support policy

The company supports a wide variety of causes throughout the UK. There is, however, a preference for charities local to any one of the company's 18 depots.

No further information was available.

Applications

In writing to the correspondent.

Storehouse plc

Marylebone House, 129–137 Marylebone Road, London NW1 5QD
0171-262 3456; Fax: 0171-262 4740

Correspondent: Stephen Pain, Corporate Affairs Director

Chief officers: *Chairman:* A Smith; *Chief Executive:* K Edelman

Year end	Turnover	Pre-tax profit
28/3/98	£1,335,000,000	£127,900,000

Nature of company business
Principal activities: selling by retail and mail order, clothing, household goods, furniture and furnishing. The company operates mainly in the UK, US and Europe.

Main subsidiaries include: Bhs PLC; Mothercare UK Ltd.

Main brands include: Bhs, Mothercare.

UK employees: 21,057

Charitable donations
1998: £126,000
1997: £130,000
1996: £266,000
1995: £338,000
1994: £154,000

Community support policy
Support is given to children/youth, education and medical research, but is concentrated on a range of major charities with preference for children/youth and appeals related to company business. Currently, the major charity supported is Barnardo's.

The company also sponsors the Variety Club of Great Britain's Golden Heart Day. It raised £350,000 through the sale of gold hearts. A similar amount was raised by staff for Children in Need.

In addition to this, the group has undertaken various sponsorships and covenants including the NSPCC and Save the Children Fund. The company encourages employee volunteering through allowing company time off to volunteer, and in-store promotion and support for certain charities.

Bhs is a member of Business in the Community.

Exclusions
Unsolicited appeals are unlikely to be successful. No response to circular appeals. Individual companies in the group have their own charity budgets. Support is NOT given to: advertising in charity brochures, animal welfare charities, appeals from individuals, the arts, elderly people, enterprise/training, environment/heritage, fundraising events, overseas projects, political appeals, religious appeals, science/technology, sickness/disability charities, social welfare or sport.

Applications
In writing to the correspondent, or to the individual companies which do have their own budgets for supporting charitable appeals.

J Swire & Sons Ltd

Swire House, 59 Buckingham Gate, London SW1E 6AJ
0171-834 7717; Fax: 0171-630 0353

Correspondent: Mrs Omar, Secretary

Chief officer: *Chairman:* Edward Scott

Year end	Turnover	Pre-tax profit
31/12/97	£2,444,000,000	£850,000,000

Nature of company business
Principal activities: marine including ship owning and operating, aviation (via Cathay Pacific Airways which is 44% owned by Swire Pacific), cold storage and road transport, industrial and trading activities, plantations and property. The company owns a 30% stake in James Finlay.

UK employees: n/a

Charitable donations
1997: £355,000
1996: £200,000
1995: £345,000
1994: £268,000
1993: £122,000

Community support policy
The worldwide donations of the company were £2,286,000 in 1997, including £355,000 in the UK.

No information is available on the support provided by the company other than that the main areas supported are the arts, medical research, and sickness/disability charities.

Applications
In writing to the correspondent.

Tarmac plc

Hilton Hall, Essington, Wolverhampton WV11 2BQ
01902-307407; Fax: 01902-307408
Website: www.tarmac.co.uk

Correspondent: A C Smith, Group Secretary

Chief officers: *Chairman:* Sir John Banham;
Chief Executive: Sir Neville Simms

Year end	Turnover	Pre-tax profit
31/12/97	£2,773,100,000	£115,200,000

Nature of company business
The group is involved in the UK heavy building materials and construction industries, from the extraction, manufacture and supply of raw materials, through consultancy, design and construction to facilities management.

Main subsidiaries include: Richard Lees Ltd; East Coast Slag Products Ltd; Midland Quarry Products Ltd; Cambrian Stone Ltd; Crown House Engineering Ltd; Castle Plant Services Ltd; Sovereign Harbour Ltd; The Expanded Piling Company Ltd; Centrac Ltd; Schal International Management Ltd; Pasco International Ltd; Stanger Ltd; TPS Consult Ltd; Cimage Enterprise Systems Ltd; Mass CAFM Systems Ltd; TPS Inston Ltd; Cimserve Ltd; Matrix Design Ltd.

UK employees: 16,150

Charitable donations
1997: £264,000
1996: £379,000
1995: £319,000
1994: £181,000
1993: £168,000
Membership: BitC %Club

Tate

Community support policy

The company has previously stated, and continues to state, that it '... do[es] not wish to have any entry in the guide ...', that much of our information is '... hopelessly out-of-date and misrepresents [the] company's position', and that it has '... no intention of updating the same'. However, our policy remains one of including all companies relevant to this guide. Now, as before, much of the information was taken from the company's latest annual report (thoughtfully made available on their website) under a section headed *Tarmac in the Community*, but in view of their comments above we take no responsibility for any inaccuracies contained therein!

'Tarmac and its 25,000 employees are an integral part of the many communities in which its operations are based, in the UK and overseas.

'Tarmac's involvement with its local communities is wide ranging. It includes providing financial and practical help, charitable giving or fundraising for local or national charities, sponsorship of the arts, schools, local interest groups or individuals and direct involvement in education and training projects.

'For 1997/98, Tarmac has chosen Macmillan Cancer Relief as its national charity and is committed to raising £500,000. This involves everyone in the group contributing by organising or participating in events both in the office and out in the field.

'A model of our approach to communities in which we work can be found in Balsall Heath which is one of Birmingham's most rundown areas. Crown House Engineering, which has a regional office there, volunteered to assist in its regeneration in conjunction with Business in the Community, one of the Prince of Wales' trusts, and a local voluntary group, the Balsall Heath Forum. Waste ground was cleared and a park and children's playground were 'adopted' with a pledge to keep it tidy and free of vandalism. This has since encouraged fresh investment and the creation of more employment opportunities.

'Links with local schools, colleges and universities give young people the chance to see and understand what we do. We invest in training our own workforce and for the construction industry generally, through a nationwide network of 14 training centres that work closely with TECs and the CITB to provide training to about 1,000 school leavers and 500 adults every year. Tarmac has also supported the Prince's Youth Business Trust for many years, and received the gold award in 1997 for "outstanding commitment to helping young people succeed through self employment".

'Our commitment to the Arts is strong and demonstrated in our award winning sponsorships of local and national organisations including: the Tate Gallery, the D'Oyly Carte Opera Company, the Birmingham Royal Ballet, the Birmingham Repertory Theatre and the National Youth Orchestra.'

Within the Director's Report section the company declares a charitable donations figure for 1997 of £264,000.

Exclusions

The company has declined the opportunity to provide details of any areas it will not consider for support.

Applications

The company has declined the opportunity to provide any advice to potential applicants.

Tate & Lyle plc

Sugar Quay, Lower Thames Street, London EC3R 6DQ
0171-626 6525; Fax: 0171-623 5213
Email: geoffdown@tateandlyle.com
Website: www.tate-lyle.co.uk

Correspondent: G D Down, Assistant Company Secretary

Chief officers: *Chairman:* Sir David Lees;
Chief Executive: Larry Pillard

Year end	Turnover	Pre-tax profit
26/9/98	£4,466,600,000	£165,400,000

Nature of company business
Principal activities are the processing of carbohydrates to provide a range of sweetener and starch products, animal feed and bulk storage. The company's UK sugar refinery is in London.

Main subsidiaries include: Amylum UK Ltd; Greenwich Distillers Ltd; The Molasses Trading Co Ltd; Kentships; Speciality Sweeteners; FSL Bells; Rumenco; United Molasses; United Storage; UMT.

UK employees: 2,370

Charitable donations

1998: £854,100
1997: £877,000
1996: £792,944
1995: £692,680
1994: £621,000

Total community contributions: £1,583,300 (worldwide)

Membership: *BitC %Club*

Community support policy

Tate & Lyle's main areas of charitable support are education and causes close to where the company operates or those in which an employee is involved. Main locations are Newham, Merseyside, Avonmouth, Hull, Burton-on-Trent and Selby.

The company is a founder member of the PerCent Club and allocates around 0.7% of profit before tax worldwide and 1% of UK pre-tax profits to community projects. Within these overall targets the company aims to contribute to the following sectors:

Education and youth 50%

Civic and environment 25%

Health and welfare 15%

Arts 10%

Registered charitable status is desirable, but not essential, for recipient organisations. Donations are made through the Charities Aid Foundation. Typical grants range from £250 to £5,000. Main beneficiaries in 1998 included National Literary Trust, Reading is Fundamental and Newham Sixth Form College. Non-cash support is given to education business partnerships and to employee volunteering. The company provides some matching to employee giving. Arts and good-cause sponsorship are also undertaken.

Employee involvement: The company operates the Give As You Earn payroll giving scheme. Applications for secondments to enterprise agencies are considered, and executives throughout the group are encouraged to participate in local educational systems. The company operates an employee volunteering scheme, which currently involves 80 employees on a variety of projects.

Enterprise: The company supports Business in the Community and the East London Partnership.

Education: The company's main education activities are the major literacy programmes, Reading is Fundamental and the Newham Literacy Programme. Links are developed with local schools and colleges offering work experience and work shadowing. The Young Enterprise programme is supported by employees and through donations in cash and kind.

Exclusions

No support is given to circular appeals, advertising in charity brochures, individuals, purely denominational (religious) appeals, local appeals not in areas of company presence, animal welfare charities, political appeals, sport or large national appeals.

Applications

All appeals and sponsorship proposals outside the East London area go through head office and should be addressed to the correspondent. Appeals and sponsorship proposals relating to East London should be addressed to M Grier, Tate & Lyle Sugars, Factory Road, Silvertown, London E16 2EW.

Taylor Woodrow Plc

4 Dunraven Street, London W1Y 3FG
0171-629 1201; Fax: 0171-493 1066
Website: www.taywood.co.uk

Correspondent: Ruth Barber, Taylor Woodrow Charity Trust

Chief officers: *Chairman:* C J Parsons;
Chief Executive: K R Egerton

Year end	Turnover	Pre-tax profit
31/12/97	£1,296,000,000	£82,000,000

Nature of company business
The group is engaged in construction, property, housing and trading activities.

Main subsidiaries include: Taywood Homes Ltd; Greenham Trading Ltd.

UK employees: 4,684

Charitable donations

1997: £105,410
1996: £96,000
1995: £66,865
1994: £68,000
1993: £49,457

Community support policy

Charitable donations are made through the Taylor Woodrow Charitable Trust, to which it gave £65,000 in 1998. Preferred areas of support are the arts, children and youth, elderly, enterprise/training, environment/heritage, medical and sickness/disability. The company maintains an active interest in promoting relevant education.

Support is given to national charities with each appeal considered on its merits. There is sometimes a preference for causes in areas of company presence, although donations, when made in such instances, are modest.

The trust had an income of £70,000 in 1997/98, including £50,000 from the company. Grants totalled £67,000 – 'primarily to charities operating at a national level. In addition, a number of special projects were supported during the course of the year relating to charities which provides support for the elderly'. A full grants list was included with the accounts on file at the Charity Commission. The largest were for £5,000 to Age Concern Neighbourly Care Southall, Building Industry Windsor Half Marathon, South Bank Centre and St Mary Battersea Church Building Fabric Trust. Fairbridge received £3,000, with £2,000 given to each of Bedford Mobility Centre, Commonwealth Games Appeal, Victoria & Albert Museum, Wider Share Ownership Educational Trust and Young Enterprise. There were a further 59 grants ranging from £100 to £1,000.

An informal employee volunteering scheme is in operation with company time off being given to volunteer. Any funds raised by employees are matched by the company. A payroll giving scheme is also run by the company.

Exclusions

No support for fundraising events, advertising in charity brochures, political or religious appeals or appeals from individuals.

Applications

In writing to the correspondent.

TBI plc

159 New Bond Street, London W1Y 9PA
0171-355 2345; Fax: 0171-491 2378

Correspondent: Mrs Caroline Price, Financial Director

Chief officers: *Chairman:* G S Thomas;
Chief Executive: K M Brooks

Year end	Turnover	Pre-tax profit
31/3/97	£97,033,000	£19,054,000

Nature of company business
The principal activities are property investment and development and the ownership and management of airport facilities.

Main subsidiaries include: Molyneux Estates PLC; Molyneux Finance PLC; Overgate Centre Ltd; Cardiff International Airport Ltd; Belfast International Airport Ltd; John Cory Ltd.

UK employees: 400

Telegraph

Charitable donations
1997: £41,000
1996: £6,900
1995: £14,756

Community support policy
We have no information available on the donations policy of the company, although there has been a dramatic increase in the company's level of donations.

Applications
In writing to the correspondent.

Telegraph Group Ltd

1 Canada Square, Canary Wharf, London E14 5DT
0171-538 5000; Fax: 0171-538 6242
Website: www.telegraph.co.uk

Correspondent: Katie O'Brien, Corporate Relations Manager

Chief officers: *Chairman:* C M Black;
Chief Executive: D W Colson; *Managing Director:* J W Deedes

Year end	Turnover	Pre-tax profit
31/12/96	£282,409,000	£41,391,000

Nature of company business
Principal activity: publication of national newspapers. Within the UK the company publishes the *Daily Telegraph, Sunday Telegraph, Weekly Telegraph, Electronic Telegraph* and the *Spectator*. Most staff engaged in the publication of the company's titles are employees of the subsidiary Telegraph Publishing Ltd and are not included in the total above.

Main subsidiaries include: The Spectator Ltd; Deedtask Ltd; Creditscheme Ltd.

UK employees: 29

Charitable donations
1997: £150,000
1996: £150,000
1995: £150,000
1994: £195,065
1993: £299,300
Membership: %Club

Community support policy
The company is a member of the PerCent Club. It supports UK charities working in the fields of medical research, hospice care, the disabled, education, the elderly, ex-servicemen appeals, children and youth-targeted projects and newspaper printing and publishing charities. As the company is a member of the PerCent Club, its community contributions should have totalled over £200,000.

The trust makes its grants through the Daily Telegraph Charitable Trust, originally set up in 1944 (Charity Commission number 205296). It receives from the company either one half of 1% of pre-tax profits (excluding any share of associated companies or outside the UK), or £150,000, whichever is the greater.

In 1997, the income was £152,000 (from the company) and grants totalled only £82,000. The trust was carrying forward a balance of £172,000. The largest grants were £10,000 to the Centre for Policy Studies and £8,000 to Newstrade. Other 'material' grants listed in the accounts were as follows: Britain Israel Public Affairs Centre (£6,000), Institute of Economic Affairs, American Museum, Oxford Centre for Hebrew & Jewish Studies, Mudchute Park and Farm and Toynbee Hall (all £5,000). The trustees' report stated that the 'direction in respect of £75,000 per annum lies specifically at the discretion of the chairman of the company'. Appeals from charitable causes located in East London are given special consideration.

Exclusions
Generally no support for circulars with stamped or imprinted signatures, fundraising events, brochure advertising, individuals, political causes or purely denominational (religious) appeals.

Applications
In writing to the correspondent. The appeal committee usually meets quarterly to decide on donations, and these will generally only be made to organisations with recognised charitable status.

Tempus Group plc

1 Pemberton Row, London EC4A 3BA
0171-633 9999
Website: www.tempusgroup.com

Correspondent: Nikki Sedgwick, Personal Assistant to the Group Financial Director

Chief officers: *Chairman:* Chris Ingram;
Chief Executive: David Reich

Year end	Turnover	Pre-tax profit
31/12/96	£1,146,286,000	£4,923,000

Nature of company business
The group operates internationally as media communications specialists providing services related to the planning and evaluation of advertising campaigns and the buying of time and space, primarily in broadcast and published media. The holding company changed its name to Tempus Group plc; it apeared in the last edition of this guide under the name CIA Group plc.

UK employees: n/a

Charitable donations
1996: £44,611
1995: £43,875
1994: £34,000
1993: £30,000

Community support policy
The company is currently reviewing its charitable policy. Previously, the preferred areas of support were children's charities, training and education, youth work and sickness/disability charities. It usually prefers to support national charities and local charities in areas where it operates, mainly London, especially the SE1 area. Grants range from £250 to £4,000.

The company does not support overseas charities; however, overseas subsidiaries support causes in their area of operation.

Exclusions
No response to circular appeals. No grants for advertising in charity brochures, purely denominational (religious) or political appeals, local appeals not in areas of company presence.

Applications
In writing to the correspondent. The company's charity committee meets quarterly.

Tesco plc

Tesco House, Delamare Road, Cheshunt,
Hertfordshire EN8 9SL
01992-632222
Website: www.tesco.co.uk

Correspondent: Linda Marsh, Secretary to the Charitable Trust

Chief officers: *Chairman:* John Gardiner;
Chief Executive: Terry Leahy

Year end	Turnover	Pre-tax profit
22/2/98	£16,452,000,000	£832,000,000

Nature of company business
Tesco is a multiple retailer with superstores and supermarkets in England, Scotland, Wales and Northern Ireland.
Main locations: Throughout the UK.

UK employees: 159,109

Charitable donations
1998: £1,259,000
1997: £1,065,961
1996: £727,000
1995: £403,000
1994: n/a

Total community contributions: £2,886,388 (1996/97)

Membership: ABSA BitC %Club

Community support policy
The company is a founder member of the PerCent Club and a member of Business in the Community. Community contributions for the period 1996/97 totalled about £2.9 million. Mencap was the Tesco charity of the year in 1997 and £1.4 million was raised for the charity. Help the Aged was the 1998 charity of the year. Each year the company gives financial and practical help to hundreds of charities and projects which support children, education, people with disabilities and the elderly in areas local to stores.

Support is given to projects and initiatives whose work falls within the following criteria:

- organisations and projects concerned with children, particularly in the areas of welfare and education
- organisations and projects which support the elderly and people with disabilities.

There is a central committee team in head office who manage national charity and sponsorship activity and set the guidelines for the company's community support. Store managers have responsibility for coordinating and managing the community awards and sponsorship funds for the Tesco stores in their region.

In addition, each store receives an allocation of community vouchers to support requests for raffle prizes, etc. The vouchers may be redeemed at checkouts in the store. A maximum donation of £50 can be made to local organisations through this scheme.

The company differentiates between donations and sponsorship. The former are made through the Tesco Charity Trust, which only supports registered charities or organisations recognised by the Inland Revenue as having charitable status.

Tesco Charity Trust
Support is given to national charities and local community projects in areas of company presence. The Tesco Charity Trust also adds 20% to all money raised for charity by Tesco employees.

Tesco Charity Trust donations are primarily targeted towards educational projects and charities working for the welfare of children, elderly people and people with disabilities. Examples of organisations or projects which could receive support are local hospital wards, hospices, schools, nurseries and pre-schools, community groups, transport for the elderly, disabled or charities concerned with the welfare of children. Grants range from £2,000 to £5,000. A total of £270,000 is awarded through this Community Awards Scheme.

In 1996/97, the Tesco Charity Trust gave major donations to the following charities:

Health and care: Save the Children Fund, Riding for the Disabled Association, Cystic Fibrosis Trust, Hospice Care Servers for East Herts, National Council for One Parent Families, Computability Centre, Muscular Dystrophy Group, Northern Ireland Hospice, Bryson House, Bromley-by-Bow Centre, Mental Health Foundation, Sense, Papworth Trust, Motor Neurone Disease Association, Covent Garden Research Trust, Age Concern England, Age Concern Scotland.

Education and youth: Youth Clubs UK, Cheshunt Outdoor Centre – Youth Mariners Base, Dunblane Primary School, Canterbury Educational Trust, Parent Network.

Other recipients included: Community Action Trust, FRAME, York Minster, Dunblane Appeal Fund, Manchester Lord Mayor's Appeal, REACH, Wines and Spirits Trades Benevolent Fund and National Grocers Benevolent Fund.

Each Tesco store holds a small community budget which they use to help local voluntary organisations in their fundraising activities.

Sponsorship
Tesco defines its sponsorship as the payment of money to a business, charity, local voluntary organisation, school or local council to support a specific project. In return, and unlike donations, the company gets brand recognition as the sponsor. Projects which are supported through Tesco community sponsorship programme could include an education project for a local school, a children's Christmas party, a local fun day or carnival, or a scheme to benefit elderly people.

Tetra

Support for schools
Local schools are supported through visits and work experience placements for pupils. The Computers for Schools scheme runs for a 10-week period each year and by February 1998 had donated £34 million worth of computer equipment to schools.

Exclusions
No support for circular appeals, fundraising events, appeals from individuals, religious appeals, building or refurbishment appeals, or overseas appeals. The trust will not support political appeals, or give grants to other trusts or charities acting as intermediaries.

Applications
In writing to the correspondent.

Other information: The company's Retired Staff Association maintains links with retired employees and through it can offer support and assistance to those in retirement who need it.

Tetra Pak Ltd

1 Longwalk Road, Stockley Park, Uxbridge UB11 1DL
01895-868000; Fax: 01895-868001
Website: www.tetrapak.com

Correspondent: Rosita Whyte, Secretary to the Financial Director

Chief officer: Chairman: H Rausing

Year end	Turnover	Pre-tax profit
31/12/97	£242,584,000	£1,223,000

Nature of company business
The sale and lease of machines for liquid packaging and supply of related packaging materials.

Main subsidiaries include: Choicebond Ltd; Maxicrop International Ltd; Pakcentre Ltd; Beckswift Ltd.

UK employees: n/a

Charitable donations
1997: £209,070
1996: n/a
1995: £434,730
1994: £380,000
1993: £32,000

Community support policy
The company has stated that its charity policy has been determined over many years and efforts are concentrated on a small number of needy charities.

Previously, the company informed us that it had a preference for London, North Wales, Scotland and the Warrington area, with preference for appeals relating to children/youth, education, elderly people, environment/heritage, fundraising events and sickness/disability.

Applications
In writing to the correspondent.

Texaco Ltd

1 Westferry Circus, Canary Wharf, London E14 4HA
0171-719 3000; Fax: 0171-719 5139
Website: www.texaco.co.uk

Correspondent: Paul Bray, Public Relations Manager

Chief officers: Managing Directors: R L Ebert, D Codd

Year end	Turnover	Pre-tax profit
31/12/97	£4,725,309,000	£46,667,000

Nature of company business
The principal activity of Texaco is oil exploration, production, refining and marketing, and petrochemicals. The company is wholly owned by Texaco Inc, based in White Plains, New York.

Main subsidiaries include: Star Service Stations Ltd; Team Fuels Ltd; James D Johnson Ltd; Team Flitwick Ltd.

Main locations: Aberdeen; London; Pembroke; Swindon.

UK employees: 4,149

Charitable donations
1997: £395,000
1996: £54,226
1995: £47,239
1994: £41,674
1993: £25,796
Membership: ABSA BitC %Club

Community support policy
The company is a member of Business in the Community and the PerCent Club. After increasing marginally in recent years, charitable donations dramatically increased in 1997 by about £340,000.

Charitable donations: The company prefers to support local charities in areas where it operates (Aberdeen, Swindon, Pembroke, East London), in the fields of children and youth, education, environment, enterprise/training, science/technology and the arts. It chooses to support activities, projects and organisations which bring long-term benefits. In 1997 main beneficiaries included NCH Action for Children, Business in the Community, Common Purpose, Scottish Conservation Projects Trust and Prince's Trust.

In kind support: The company donates gifts in kind including equipment and materials, professional services, furniture and the use of in-house facilities. Employees are also seconded to organisations and are allowed time off for activity of community benefit. A payroll deduction scheme is operated and the company matches employee fundraising to a limit.

Education: The company has links with local schools on the Isle of Dogs and petroleum engineering universities.

The arts: The company is a patron of ABSA. It undertakes a limited amount of major sponsorship including Young Musician of Wales Competition, Texaco Music Workshops, Texaco Theatre School (Aberdeen) and Texaco Arts Summer School & Outreach programme (Northern Ireland). It prefers to support projects/organisations which aim to develop creativity of young people.

Non-arts sponsorship has included Focus environment competition and exhibition, and Community Links.

Exclusions

No support is given to overseas projects, purely denominational (religious) appeals, circular appeals, individuals, fundraising events, local appeals not in areas of company presence or political appeals. The company does not advertise in charity brochures.

Applications

Applications should be made in writing and sent to Paul Bray at the address above.

Thames Water plc

Customer Centre, PO Box 436, Swindon SN38 1TU
0645-200800
Website: www.thames-water.com

Correspondent: Caroline Glenister, Sponsorship Co-ordinator

Chief officers: *Chairman:* Sir Robert Clarke; *Chief Executive:* Bill Alexander

Year end	Turnover	Pre-tax profit
31/3/98	£1,389,000,000	£419,000,000

Nature of company business
Principal activity: water and waste water services.

Main subsidiaries include: Connect 2000 Ltd; PWR Projects Ltd; Water Project International Ltd; PCI Membrane Systems Ltd; TM Products Ltd; Metro Rod PLC; Morgan Collis Group Ltd; Subterra Ltd; Thames Inceneration and Recycling Ltd; Thames Waste Management Ltd; Isis Insurance Co Ltd; Kennet Properties Ltd; Ham Baker.

UK employees: 5,500

Charitable donations

1998: £125,000
1997: £117,000
1996: £114,000
1995: £112,000
1994: £111,000

Total community contributions: £630,000

Membership: *BitC*

Community support policy

The company gives exclusively to organisations working in its area of operation (Thames Valley) and charities in which a member of staff is involved. National charities are only supported for projects within the company's region. An annual grant totalling one-third of its budget is given each year to WaterAid. The company is a member of Business in the Community.

Charitable donations: Preference is given to appeals relevant to company business and to those in which a member of staff is involved. Preferred areas of support are extra-needs customers, environment and heritage, regional improvement and activities connected with the water business. Grants to local organisations range from £500 to £5,000. Main grant beneficiaries in 1997/98 in addition to WaterAid included: Community Links, Thames Valley Partnership, BBONT, RNLI and Thames Clean 21.

In addition to charitable donations, the company undertakes arts and good-cause sponsorship (£250,000) and gives some support through gifts in kind. Total community contributions were £630,000 in 1997/98. The company has an employee volunteering scheme, which it supports financially. It operates a staff payroll giving scheme and staff fundraising is matched by the company.

In kind support: The company's main area of non-cash support is good-cause sponsorship. It also provides angling permits for raffle and tombola prizes. Facilities for meetings and receptions and the use of in-house facilities and, occasionally, redundant items of equipment free of charge.

Sponsorship: Priority is given to those requests that:

- assist Thames Water projects or operations
- involve employees in communities close to their workplace
- promote access by disabled people to Thames Water's conservation or recreation sites
- support help to customers with extra needs
- improve the environment – particularly that affected by Thames Water's core activities.

Exclusions

No support for advertising in charity brochures, animal welfare charities, appeals from individuals, fundraising events, overseas projects (excluding WaterAid), political appeals or religious appeals.

Applications

The charity committee meets to consider applications in March and October. Applications should be in writing to the correspondent, as should sponsorship proposals at: Thames Water plc, Gainsborough House, RBH3, Manor Farm Road, Reading RG2 0JN.

Thistle Hotels plc

2 The Calls, Leeds LS2 7JU
0113-243 9111; Fax: 0113-244 5555

Correspondent: G P Howden, Company Secretary

Chief officers: *Chairman:* R F Price; *Chief Executive:* I Burke

Year end	Turnover	Pre-tax profit
28/12/97	£319,744,000	£80,564,000

Nature of company business
The ownership and operation of hotels in the UK.

Main subsidiaries include: Arden Hotel (Stratford upon Avon); Avon Hotel (Newcastle); Castle Ross Hotels; Highlife Value Breaks; Kingsmead Hotels; London Park Hotels; Mount Charlotte Hotels; Nijon Investments; Pinewood Hotel; Quay Hotel.

UK employees: 8,554

Charitable donations

1997: £67,590
1996: £9,469
1995: £12,312

Thomson

Community support policy

The company markedly increased its level of giving to charities in 1997, but unfortunately we currently have no information on the charitable donations policy.

Applications

In writing to the correspondent.

The Thomson Corporation plc

The Quadrangle, PO Box 4YG, 180 Wardour Street, London W1A 4YG
0171-437 9787; Fax: 0171-734 0561

Correspondent: Hilary Bateson, Information Manager

Chief officers: *Chairman* (of parent company): Kenneth R Thomson; *Chief Executive* (of parent company): Richard J Harrington

Year end	Turnover	Pre-tax profit
31/12/97	n/a	n/a

Nature of company business
The Thomson Corporation plc is the principal UK subsidiary of The Thomson Corporation, Toronto, Canada. 73% of the common shares of the group are owned by the Thomson family. The company's activities are principally in North America and the UK. Main UK activities of the group are information and publishing.

Main subsidiaries include: Thomas Nelson UK; Jane's Information Group; Gee Publishing Ltd; Sweet & Maxwell Ltd; W Green & Son Ltd; Legal Information Resources Ltd; Primary Source Media; Derwent Information; Institute for Scientific Information; Crossaig.

UK employees: n/a

Charitable donations

1997: £100,000
1996: £100,000
1995: £100,000
1994: £100,000
1993: £100,000

Community support policy

Charitable donations: Donations are made from The Thomson Corporation Charitable Trust (Charity Commission number 1013317). The company prefers to support charities connected with physically, mentally and socially disadvantaged people. Areas of support include children/youth, education, elderly people, medical research, overseas projects, and social welfare. Recipient organisations must be registered charities and audited accounts should be supplied with any application. Some preference is given to national and local charities in the London area and home counties.

The Charitable Trust received £100,000 from The Thomson Corporation PLC in 1996. Donations in the year totalled £95,000. Grants ranged from £100 to £2,000 with most being for £500. Five organisations received £2,000: Arthritis and Rheumatism Council, British Heart Foundation, Derwent House, Hearing Research Trust, Marie Curie Cancer Care and MIND. Medical charities were also the main beneficiaries of other grants of £1,000 or more, with other recipients including APA – Community Drug & Alcohol Initiatives, Help the Aged, National Library for the Blind and Research into Ageing.

In addition to the above, support is also given by the company to The Thomson Foundation which helps develop the media in developing countries by the provision of training courses and consultants.

The arts: The company is not a member of ABSA and it undertakes no arts sponsorship.

Exclusions

Generally no support for fundraising events, appeals from individuals, purely denominational (religious) appeals or political appeals, animal welfare charities, environment/heritage, local appeals not in areas of company presence or advertising in charity brochures. No sponsorships or advertising.

Applications

In writing to the correspondent. Applications are considered by an appeals committee.

Thorn UK

Baird House, Arlington Business Park, Reading RG7 4SA
01189-304000

Correspondent: Charities Committee, Corporate Affairs Department

Chief officers: *Chairman:* Hugh Jenkins; *Chief Executive:* Michael Metcalf

Year end	Turnover	Pre-tax profit
31/3/98	£1,358,000,000	£70,000,000

Nature of company business
The principal activity of the group is consumer rental and rental-purchase.

Main subsidiaries include: Consumer Electronics Insurance Co Ltd.

Main brands include: Radio Rentals; Crazy George's; Easiview.

UK employees: 6,821

Charitable donations

1998: £240,000
1997: £183,000
Membership: BitC %Club

Community support policy

Thorn was formed following the demerger of THORN EMI plc in August 1996. Since then it has been taken over by the investment bank, Nomura International. We are not sure whether or not the policy will change following this development.

The company is a member of the PerCent Club, from where the following information about the company's initiatives was taken.

The company's policy focuses on causes which provide opportunities for economically and socially disadvantaged groups in urban areas. It also promotes programmes which encourage the direct involvement of its employees in community activities.

Its main programme is CREATE (Community Recycling Enterprise and Training for Employment), a community-based initiative opened in Speke, Liverpool in 1995. CREATE recycles end-of-life washing machines and cookers while providing salaried employment and training for long-term unemployed people. The company continues to provide managerial resources and expertise and contributed over £130,000 in 1997.

Other organisations supported include the Starlight Foundation, Diana, Princess of Wales Memorial Fund, Fairbridge and Young Enterprise. In addition, a series of challenges were undertaken by the Crazy George's staff involving refurbishment and furnishing of facilities within the community.

Exclusions

Support is not given for circular appeals, animals, building/restoration programmes (unless for a specific reason such as being part of a project close to a company location), expeditions, individuals, natural disasters, national appeals, political causes, religious groups or sports sponsorship.

Applications

In writing to the Charities Committee. Further information about the company's community and environmental programmes is available from the Corporate Affairs Department.

Thorntons PLC

Thornton Park, Somercotes, Derby DE55 4XJ
01773-540550; Fax: 01773-540842

Correspondent: Ian Samways, Community Affairs Adviser

Chief officers: *Chairman:* C J Thornton;
Chief Executive: R J G Paffard

Year end	Turnover	Pre-tax profit
28/6/98	£132,800,000	£12,600,000

Nature of company business
Principal activity: confectionery manufacture and retailing.

UK employees: 4,084

Charitable donations
1998: £88,000
1997: £80,000
1996: £60,000
1995: £53,000
1994: £88,000
Total community contributions: £130,000
Membership: *BitC   %Club*

Community support policy

The company is a member of Business in the Community and the PerCent Club. It concentrates its support within Derbyshire, upon education, disadvantaged young people, and the environment. During 1998 particular support was given to the Prince's Trust and the Derbyshire Community Foundation. In 1997/98, charitable donations totalled £88,000 with a further £42,000 given by way of other support.

A number of local schools have been supported, for example, Belper School, Ripley Mill Hill School and the Delves Special School in Swanwick. The company's involvement in education was recognised as both a regional and national winner in the 1997 and 1998 'Aim High' Awards organised by Business in the Community. The Cromford Venture Centre for disadvantaged young people continues to be strongly supported and practical help has been given in the formation of the Codnor Park and Ironville Community Trust. The company also supports the Amber Valley Partnership, Groundwork Erewash Valley and the Prince's Trust in Derbyshire.

Small donations of confectionery are made, mainly to local groups, to help with their fundraising. The company also continues to look for opportunities to assist local communities by donation of redundant equipment.

Exclusions

Financial support is limited to local (ie. Derbyshire) charities associated with disadvantaged children, local education and the environment. No support is given for circular appeals, advertising in charity brochures or appeals from individuals. Donations of confectionery are made to small community organisations that fit the above criteria.

Applications

In writing to the correspondent.

3i Group plc

91 Waterloo Road, London SE1 8XP
0171-928 3131; Fax: 0171-928 0058
Website: www.3igroup.com

Correspondent: Sabina Dawson, Assistant Company Secretary

Chief officers: *Chairman:* Sir George Russell;
Chief Executive: Brian Larcombe

Year end	Turnover	Pre-tax profit
31/3/98	£315,000,000	£124,000,000

Nature of company business
Venture capital.

UK employees: 709

Charitable donations
1998: £334,792
1997: £350,000
1996: £350,000
1995: £276,000
1994: £200,000
Membership: *BitC   %Club*

Community support policy

The company is a member of the PerCent Club. In addition to charitable donations it undertakes some arts sponsorship and occasional secondment to charities, as well as contributing through gifts in kind. It devoted a page of its 1998 annual report to reporting on its community activities.

Charitable donations: The company makes its charitable donations through the 3i Charitable Trust (Registered Charity number 1014277), for which there are full accounts on file at the Charity Commission. The trust continues to favour charitable initiatives with which members of staff are personally involved and local charities where 3i has an office. The trust also matches £ for £ giving by staff through the Give As You Earn payroll giving scheme.

The company has offices in the UK in: Aberdeen, Birmingham, Bristol, Cambridge, Cardiff, Edinburgh, Glasgow, Leeds, Leicester, Liverpool, London, Maidstone, Manchester, Newcastle, Nottingham, Reading, Solihull, Southampton and Watford. Each of these offices is allocated a tranche of the company's charitable budget which is administered centrally.

In 1997/98, covenanted income from 3i plc was £310,000 and bank interest was £7,900. Grants from the trust amounted to £466,550. Grants ranged from £15 to £100,000 and were given to 225 charities during the period. 50% of grants went to support local community initiatives and educational causes. Other areas of support include children/youth, elderly people, enterprise/training, religious appeals, science/technology, sickness/disability charities, social welfare and sport.

65 organisations received grants of £1,000 or more. Amongst these were the Youth Cancer Trust, Lambeth Walk-In, Crisis, British Heart Foundation and North Lambeth Day Centre. The main beneficiaries in 1997/98 were Understanding Industry Trust, INSEAD Trust for European Management Education, Royal Opera House Development Appeal, The Cambridge Foundation and Birbeck College.

Education and the environment: 3i is a member of Business in the Environment. During 1997/98, it continued its long-standing support of the Understanding Industry Trust, which it helped establish in 1979 to increase awareness of business issues in schools. 3i have also provided session leaders for Understanding Industry Trust seminars. For a number of years support has been given to Intermediate Technology, a charity which helps rural communities in the Third World to use skills and technologies to become more self-sufficient.

The arts: The company's major involvement continues to be sponsorship of the senior student orchestra of the Royal Academy of Music.

Exclusions

No support to appeals from non-charities, individuals seeking sponsorship, fundraising events, medical research, overseas projects, political appeals, advertising in charity brochures or bricks and mortar projects.

Applications

In writing to the correspondent. A donations committee meets regularly.

3M UK Holdings plc

3M House, PO Box 1, Bracknell RG12 1JU
01344-858000

Correspondent: Tony Bellis, Public Relations Manager

Chief officer: *Chairman:* W W Brown

Year end	Turnover	Pre-tax profit
31/12/97	£586,624,000	£50,392,000

Nature of company business
Principal activity: manufacturing, marketing and distribution of a range of coated materials, pharmaceuticals and other related products and services. The ultimate parent company is Minnesota Mining & Manufacturing Company in the US.

UK employees: n/a

Charitable donations

1997: £167,995
1996: £148,354
1995: £160,548
1994: £125,000
1993: £100,000

Total community contributions: £210,000 (1995)

Membership: *BitC*

Community support policy

Total community contributions made by the company in 1995 were £210,000, including just over £160,000 in charitable donations. This latter figure was at a similar level in 1997.

Donations policy: Support is only given to national charities, local charities in areas of company presence (16 locations nationwide) and appeals relevant to the company's business, with a preference for charities in which a member of company staff is involved. Preferred areas of support are children and youth, medical, education, elderly people, medical research, overseas projects, science/technology, sickness/disability, social welfare, animal welfare, sport and environment/heritage.

Grants to national organisations range from £1,500 to £35,000. Grants to local organisations range from £50 to £5,000.

Support may also be given for individuals and fundraising events. The main areas of non-cash support are secondments, gifts in kind and training schemes. The company encourages employee volunteering by matching employee fundraising and allowing company time to volunteer.

Exclusions

No support for advertising in charity brochures, appeals from individuals, purely denominational (religious) appeals, local appeals not in areas of company presence, or large national appeals.

Applications

In writing to the correspondent. Policy guidelines are outlined in *Corporate Charity & Community Relations Policy*, available from the correspondent.

TI Group plc

Lambourn Court, Abingdon Business Park, Abingdon, Oxon OX14 1UH
01235-555570; Fax: 01235-555818
Email: dsmall@tigroup.com
Website: www.tigroup.com

Correspondent: G M Norris, Deputy Group Secretary

Chief officers: *Chairman:* Sir Christopher Lewinton; *Chief Executive:* W J Laule

Year end	Turnover	Pre-tax profit
31/12/97	£1,704,000,000	£221,000,000

Nature of company business
The group is involved in specialised engineering.

Main subsidiaries include: John Crane UK Ltd; Deep Sea Seals Ltd; Dowty Seals Ltd; Dowty Woodville Polymer; Forsheda Ltd; Lapmaster International Ltd; Bundy UK Ltd; Cambridge Vacuum Engineering; Dowty Aerospace Ltd; Dowty Boulton Paul Ltd; Iloman Engineering Ltd; Thermal Processing Group Ltd.

UK employees: 4,550

Charitable donations

1997: £275,000
1996: £230,000
1995: £216,000
1994: £181,000
1993: £191,000

Membership: ABSA BitC %Club

Community support policy

Charitable donations: Most of the total group donations are distributed by head office, with the remainder being distributed by some of the subsidiary companies. Grants are channelled through the TI Charity Trust. The group's main areas of support are the arts and culture, social welfare, community services, health and medical, conservation and the environment, education, science and enterprise. Within these broad categories, the group is particularly interested in supporting organisations dealing with major social problems, young unemployed people and training and re-training initiatives. Preference is given to community initiatives and causes with an emphasis on education, particularly related to engineering and to appeals from local community organisations in areas where the company has a plant.

In 1996, a new emphasis was placed on medical research and major support was given to heart research at the John Radcliffe Hospital.

Typically, national grants range from £250 to £2,500 and local grants from £100 to £1,000. Main beneficiaries in 1997 included Understanding Industry, Commonwealth Games UK Appeal, The Brain Research Trust, School of St Helen and St Katherine, and Business in the Community.

The arts: TI is a member of ABSA. In the past it has sponsored the City of Birmingham Symphony Orchestra, New Sadlers Wells Opera, Exeter Cathedral Choir and Renaissance Theatre Group.

Exclusions

No support for circular appeals, advertising in brochures, purely denominational appeals, purely local appeals not in areas of company presence, appeals from individuals, animal welfare charities, sport, fundraising events, circulars and Christmas cards.

Applications

All appeals, including local appeals, should be sent to the correspondent. Appeals should be short but give an adequate description of their objects, activities and financial position. Grants decisions are made by a donations committee which meets quarterly. Sponsorship requests should be directed to J B Hutchings at the head office in London.

Tibbett & Britten Group plc

Ross House, 1 Shirley Road, Windmill Hill, Enfield, Middlesex EN2 6SB
0181-367 9955; Fax: 0181-366 7042

Correspondent: Michael Stalbow, Financial Director

Chief officer: *Chairman:* J A Harvey

Year end	Turnover	Pre-tax profit
31/12/97	£924,247,000	£28,203,000

Nature of company business
The provision of transportation and distribution services to the manufacturing and retail industries.

Main subsidiaries include: Fashion Logistics; Transcare Distribution; Axial.

UK employees: 21,535

Charitable donations

1997: £38,664
1996: £30,800
1995: £24,100

Community support policy

We currently have no information on the charitable donations policy of the company.

Exclusions

No support for individuals.

Applications

In writing to the correspondent.

Tioxide Group Ltd

Lincoln House, 137–143 Hammersmith Road, London W14 0QL
0171-331 7777; Fax: 0171-331 7778

Correspondent: D J Busby, Company Secretary

Chief officer: *Chairman:* D A L Coombs

Year end	Turnover	Pre-tax profit
31/12/97	£165,500,000	n/a

TNT

Nature of company business
The manufacture of titanium oxide and titanium compounds.

UK employees: 1,096

Charitable donations

1997: £258,000
1996: £221,000
1995: £325,000
1994: n/a
1993: £220,000

Community support policy

The company has factories in Teesside and Humberside and support is focused on charities local to these sites. It also gives a smaller number of donations to charities in the Hammersmith and Fulham area of London, where the head office is located.

A wide range of causes in these communities are supported, with the preferred areas being children and youth, social welfare, medical and education. Grants usually range from £100 to £1,000, but can be for as much as £6,000. Non-cash support is given in the form of gifts and occasional secondments.

Exclusions

No support for circulars, brochure advertising, local appeals not in areas of company presence, large national appeals, fundraising events or appeals from individuals.

Applications

Teesside charitable appeals to Mrs D Hunter, Tioxide Europe Ltd, Haverton Hill Road, Billingham, Cleveland TS23 1PS.

Grimsby area appeals to M Hinnigan, Tioxide Europe Ltd, Moody Lane, Grimsby, South Humberside DN31 2SW.

Hammersmith & Fulham appeals to D J Busby at the above address.

TNT UK Ltd

PO Box 4, Ramsbottom, Bury, Lancashire BL0 9AR
01706-827511; Fax: 01706-823702
Website: www.tnt.co.uk

Correspondent: Sylvia Gibson, Site Services Manager

Chief officers: n/a

Year end	Turnover	Pre-tax profit
30/6/97	£955,199,000	£63,434,000

Nature of company business
Transportation and logistics, holding company.

UK employees: n/a

Charitable donations

1997: £386,000
1996: £223,500
1995: £158,750
1994: £120,780
Membership: *BitC %Club*

Community support policy

The company is a member of the PerCent Club and Business in the Community. The following information was largely taken from the 1998 PerCent Club annual report and the company's website.

The chairman of the company is also chairman of three charities: Gifts In Kind UK, Transaid Worldwide (which helps reduce transport costs incurred by aid agencies such as Save the Children in developing countries) and Midlands Excellence (which aims to improve competitiveness of organisations in the Midlands). The company provides extensive logistics and financial support for these charities.

Other organisations and projects supported include Prince's Youth Business Trust, Young Enterprise Learning by Doing scheme, Wooden Spoon Society and Valley House Association in Coventry.

Exclusions

No support for motor sports or appeals from individuals.

Applications

In writing to the correspondent.

Tomkins PLC

East Putney House, 84 Upper Richmond Road,
London SW15 2ST
0181-871 4544; Fax: 0181-877 9700
Website: www.tomkins.co.uk

Correspondent: June Evans, Charitable Fund Administrator and Secretary to the Chairman

Chief officers: *Chairman:* G Hutchings;
Managing Director: I Duncan

Year end	Turnover	Pre-tax profit
3/5/98	£5,047,500,000	£500,400,000

Nature of company business
Tomkins is an industrial management company with trading subsidiaries operating in the following sectors: fluid controls, services to industry, professional, garden and leisure products and industrial products.

Main subsidiaries include: Guest & Chrimes Ltd; Hattersley Heaton Ltd; Hattersley Newman Hender Ltd; Pegler Ltd; Shipman & Co Ltd; Alpha Cereals Ltd; Firth Cleveland Engineering; Homer of Redditch Ltd; The Premier Crew & Repetiton Co Ltd; Twiflex Ltd; FH Tomkins Buckle Co Ltd; Hayter Ltd; Tiffany Sharwood's Frozen Foods.

UK employees: n/a

Charitable donations

1998: £398,120
1997: £280,673
1996: £330,276
1995: £619,592
1994: £237,378

Community support policy

The total charitable donations made by the company in the year were £948,000 which included £398,000 in the UK, £538,000 in the United States (including £285,000 from a Tomkins' funded charitable trust) and the remaining £11,500 given by other overseas companies.

The policy of the company is to give little and often in areas of company presence, 'thus enabling our funds to be spread over as wide a field as possible'. Some charities have received support for up to eight years. Some of the company's subsidiaries provide support through product and other in kind donations.

Unfortunately, we have no further information on the company's community policy.

Exclusions

No support for overseas projects.

Applications

Applications should be made to head office.

Toshiba Information Systems (UK) Ltd

Toshiba Court, Weybridge Business Park, Addlestone, Weybridge, Surrey KT15 2UL
01932-841600; Fax: 01932-847240

Correspondent: Helen Cartmell, Corporate Marketing Executive

Chief officer: *Managing Director:* K Hachisu

Year end	Turnover	Pre-tax profit
31/3/96	£276,719,000	£11,750,000

Nature of company business
The sale, marketing and distribution of photocopiers, fax machines, computers and telephone systems.

UK employees: 216

Charitable donations
1996: £65,000
1995: £40,688
1994: £26,233
1993: £24,350

Total community contributions: £100,000

Membership: ABSA BitC

Community support policy

The company has a preference for local charities in Surrey, working in the fields of children and youth, elderly and infirm, education and the arts. Grants range from £50 to £5,000. The main areas of non-cash support are training schemes and gifts in kind.

The company is a member of ABSA and Business in the Community and has supported the Institute of Contemporary Art.

Exclusions

The company does not support appeals from individuals, purely denominational appeals, local appeals not in areas of company presence, large national appeals, overseas projects or circular appeals.

Applications

In writing to the correspondent.

Total Oil Marine plc

Crawpeel Road, Altens Industrial Estate, Aberdeen AB12 3FG
01224-858000; Fax: 01224-858019
Email: mary.dwyer@total-oil-marine.co.uk
Website: www.total.com

Correspondent: Mary Dwyer, Corporate Communications Manager

Chief officers: *Chairman:* Charles Henderson; *Managing Director:* Bernard Vitry

Year end	Turnover	Pre-tax profit
31/12/97	£393,113,000	£162,019,000

Nature of company business
Oil and gas exploration and production.

UK employees: 554

Charitable donations
1997: £79,535
1996: n/a
1995: £61,714
1994: n/a
1993: £44,747

Community support policy

The company has a preference for local charities in areas of company presence ie. Aberdeen and north east Scotland, appeals relevant to company business, or those which have a member of company staff involved. Preferred areas of support are: the arts, youth, education, enterprise/training, environment/heritage, fundraising events and science/technology.

Total also match employee giving and provide 'gifts in kind' such as postage/photocopying. Arts sponsorship is also undertaken.

Exclusions

No support for circular appeals, advertising in charity brochures, animal welfare charities, appeals from individuals, medical research, overseas projects, political appeals, or sport.

Applications

In writing only to the correspondent.

Toyota

Toyota Motor Manufacturing (UK) Ltd

Burnaston, Derbyshire DE1 9TA
01332-282121

Correspondent: Mairi Clifford, Public Affairs Department

Chief officers: n/a

Year end	Turnover	Pre-tax profit
31/12/96	n/a	n/a

Nature of company business
Principal activity: car and engine manufacture.

UK employees: 425

Membership: BitC %Club

Community support policy

The company is a member of the PerCent Club. No figures were available for individual years, but since the start of vehicle production in the UK at the end of 1992, Toyota has contributed more than £300,000 to the communities around the Burnaston and Deeside plants.

Priority is given to projects which add to the welfare of local communities and support or enhance community life. Projects must have some long-term, tangible benefit for the wider community.

Employee involvement in the community is encouraged, and where suitable, the company will offer financial support to member fundraising activities or to local community organisations in which members play an active role. For example, a major fundraising initiative on behalf of the NSPCC in Derbyshire and Deeside raised more than £25,000 in a month.

In 1996, over 150 donations were made to local organsiations including schools, playgrounds and voluntary services. These included support to the National Trust for an environmental project in Snowdonia and the purchase of an ultrasound scanner for the Breast Unit at Derby City General Hospital.

The Toyota Science & Technology Education Fund: This fund was set up in 1992 and is administered by Business in the Community. Its aim is to help improve the quality of science and technology teaching within the framework of the national curriculum. It gives grants of £500 to £1,500 to enable clusters or individual schools to undertake projects with local businesses. The company has invested £1.2 million over six years.

Exclusions

No support for political or religious organisations, overseas aid or local appeals not in areas of company presence. No response to circular appeals.

Applications

In writing to the correspondent. Contributions are determined by an internal committee which meets quarterly to consider more substantial requests and to discuss strategy. Smaller requests are processed monthly against an agreed set of criteria.

Transport Development Group PLC

Windsor House, 50 Victoria Street, London SW1H 0NR
0171-222 7411; Fax: 0171-222 2806

Correspondent: Carol Hui, Group Secretary

Chief officers: *Chairman:* M E Llowarch; *Chief Executive:* A J Cole

Year end	Turnover	Pre-tax profit
31/12/97	£529,101,000	£30,801,000

Nature of company business
Road transport, warehousing and logistics.

UK employees: n/a

Charitable donations
1997: £50,000
1996: £50,000
1995: £54,000
1994: £42,000
1993: £25,000

Community support policy

Company giving is allocated by a charity committee to international, national and local charities. Preference is given to appeals from businesses and employees within the group and in the areas of children, disability, medical research, blind, rehabilitation/teaching/realising potential. Other areas of support include education, elderly people, enterprise/training, overseas projects and social welfare.

Employee fundraising attracts a (capped) matched contribution.

Exclusions

No support for arts, heritage, political appeals or religious appeals.

Applications

In writing to the correspondent. The charity committee meets four times a year.

Travis Perkins plc

Lodge Way House, Harlestone Road, Northampton NN5 7UG
01604-752424; Fax: 01604-587244

Correspondent: John Pitcher, Marketing Manager

Chief officer: *Chairman:* E R A Travis

Year end	Turnover	Pre-tax profit
31/12/97	£555,839,000	£49,680,000

Nature of company business
The marketing and distribution of timber, building and plumbing materials and the hiring of tools to the building trade and industry generally.

Main subsidiaries include: D W Archer; Sherry & Haycock.

UK employees: 4,076

Charitable donations

1997: £54,007
1996: £37,788
1995: £33,323

Community support policy

The company has 200 branches nationwide. The main beneficiary of support is the Groundwork Trust, however, small donations are made to registered charities local to the head office in Northampton. The company may also donate materials.

Exclusions

No grants for appeals from individuals, local appeals not in areas of company presence or large national appeals.

Applications

In writing to the correspondent.

Trinity International Holdings plc

Kingsfield Court, Chester Business Park, Chester CH4 9RE
01244-687000; Fax: 01244-687100

Correspondent: P Graf, Chief Executive

Chief officers: *Chairman:* D K Snedden; *Chief Executive:* P Graf

Year end	Turnover	Pre-tax profit
28/12/97	£324,839,000	£64,060,000

Nature of company business
The main activity of the group is the publication and printing of newspapers both in the UK and overseas.

Main subsidiaries include: Belfast Telegraph Newspapers Ltd; The Chester Chronicle and Associated Newspapers Ltd; Joseph Woodhead and Sons Ltd; The Liverpool Daily Post & Echo Ltd; Newcastle Chronicle and Journal Ltd; North Eastern Evening Gazette Ltd; Scottish and Universal Newspapers Ltd; Western Mail & Echo Ltd.

UK employees: 6,477

Charitable donations

1997: £87,000
1996: £97,000
1995: £32,000
1994: £37,000
1993: £36,000

Community support policy

The only information we have been able to obtain is that charitable giving is carried out by the individual operating companies within the group.

Applications

In writing to the correspondent.

TT Group plc

Clive House, 12–18 Queens Road, Weybridge, Surrey KT13 9XB
01932-841310; Fax: 01932-846724

Correspondent: John Newman, Chairman

Chief officers: *Chairman:* J W Newman; *Chief Executive:* S W A Comonte

Year end	Turnover	Pre-tax profit
31/12/97	£632,000,000	£63,000,000

Nature of company business
The main activities of the company are in two business divisions: electronic components and industrial engineering.

Main subsidiaries include: AB Electronic; Linton and Hirst; Magnet Developments; Neosid; Welwyn Components; AB Automotive Electronics; AB Connectors; AB Electronic Assemblies; AB Stratos; AB Test House; AEI Cables; AEI Compounds; Air Transport Avionics; BAS Components; Burgess Architectural Products; Dawson-Keith; Erskine Systems; F D Sims; Genergy; Houchin Aerospace; James Gibbons Format; The London Electric Wire Company and Smiths; Midland Tool and Design; Munradtech Generators; Rodco; Scorpio Power Systems; Strainstall Engineering Services; Wolsey Comcare; W T Henley; Beatson Clark; Lewis & Towers; United Packaging.

Main locations: Romford; Swindon; Letchworth; Bedlington; Cardiff; Mountain Ash; Newport; Haverhill; Chester-le-Street; Gravesend; Bootle; Colnbrook; Sevenoaks; Hinckley; Havant; Scarborough; Ramsbottom; Filey; Ashford; Wolverhampton; Manchester; Tipton; Coalville; Skelmersdale; Lancing; Cowes; Blyth; Rotherham; Edenbridge; Cleckheaton.

UK employees: 8,621

Charitable donations

1997: £50,000
1996: £30,000
1995: £30,000

Community support policy

We currently have no information on the charitable donations policy of the company.

Applications

In writing to the correspondent.

Tullis Russell Group Ltd

Rothersfield, Markinch, Glenrothes KY7 6PB
01592-753311; Fax: 01592-755872

Correspondent: Isabel Ritchie, Secretary, Charities Committee

Chief officers: *Chairman:* H Browning; *Chief Executive:* J F S Daglish

Year end	Turnover	Pre-tax profit
31/3/95	£95,136,000	£4,796,000

Nature of company business
The main activity is the provision of management services. The group is also involved in manufacturing paper.

Main subsidiaries include: Brittains Ltd; Coated Papers Ltd; Watson Grange Ltd.

UK employees: 1,217

Charitable donations

1997: £56,000
1996: £40,000
1995: £44,000
Membership: %Club

Community support policy

The company is a member of the PerCent Club. It distributes funds by a charity/donations committee made up from employee representatives. Support is only given to local appeals in areas of company presence, covering a wide range of causes. Grants range from £50 to £5,000.

The main areas of non-cash support are arts and good-cause sponsorship, and gifts in kind. Group companies are also involved in local schools, colleges and universities through individual employees and the Paper Federation of Great Britain – Schools Link Programme.

Exclusions

No grants for local appeals not in areas of company presence, large national appeals, enterprise/training, medical research, overseas projects, political appeals, science/technology or sport.

Applications

In writing to the correspondent.

UGC Ltd Unipart Group of Companies

Unipart House, Cowley, Oxford OX4 2PG
01865-778966; Fax: 01865-383763

Correspondent: Patrick FitzGibbon, Group Communications Director

Chief officers: *Chairman:* Lord Shepherd;
Chief Executive: J M Neill

Year end	Turnover	Pre-tax profit
31/12/97	£1,078,441,000	£28,597,000

Nature of company business
Principal activity: the design and manufacture of equipment components and sale and distribution of automotive parts, components, accessories, cellular telephones and airtime.

Main subsidiaries include: UniqueAir Ltd; Advanced Engineering Systems Ltd; Surestock Health Services Ltd; H Burden Ltd.

UK employees: n/a

Charitable donations

1997: £116,000
1996: £99,000
1995: £64,000
1994: £62,000
1993: £44,000
Membership: BitC %Club

Community support policy

The company has a preference for local charities in areas where the company operates, appeals relevant to company business and charities in which a member of staff is involved. The main areas of operation are Oxford, Coventry and Paddockwood (Kent).

Its preferred areas of support are: children and youth; social welfare; medical; education, recreation and enterprise/training. The company matches employee fundraising.

The company is a member of the PerCent Club and in addition to cash donations the company contributes through arts and good-cause sponsorship and gifts in kind.

In the fields of education and enterprise, initiatives have included: support for Schools in Action; setting up Partnership for Youth with the Oxfordshire Association for Young People; and continued support for Young Enterprise.

Exclusions

No grants for purely denominational (religious) appeals, political appeals, overseas projects or animal welfare charities.

Applications

In writing to the correspondent.

Unigate plc

Unigate House, Wood Lane, London W12 7RP
0181-749 8888; Fax: 0181-576 6071
Website: www.unigate.plc.uk

Correspondent: James Burkitt, Company Secretary

Chief officers: *Chairman:* I A Martin;
Chief Executive: R Buckland

Year end	Turnover	Pre-tax profit
31/3/98	£2,311,000,000	£147,900,000

Nature of company business
The company is the holding company of a group engaged in food processing and manufacture, distribution and transport services.

Main subsidiaries include: St Ivel Westway Ltd; St Ivel Ltd; Malton Foods Ltd; Stocks Lovell Ltd; Fermanagh Creameries Ltd; Wincanton Ltd.

UK employees: 27,000

Charitable donations

1998: £292,000
1997: £294,000
1996: £185,000
1995: £181,000
1994: £183,000
Membership: BitC

Community support policy

Unigate's level of giving increased by 50% from 1996 to 1997, maintaining the new higher level in 1998. Substantial support is given to a limited range of charitable causes on a selective basis and unsolicited requests outside the criteria listed below will not succeed.

Most donations are committed on a long-term basis to national charities including the Save the Children Fund, Age Concern and the Duke of Edinburgh's Award Scheme.

In addition, there is a strong preference for local charities in areas of company presence and appeals relevant to the company's business. Areas of support include the arts, children/youth, education and elderly people. Donations are made through a charitable trust.

Non-cash support is given in the form of gifts in kind, secretarial and administrative support, and advice and consultation. The company is a member of Business in the Community.

The company operates payroll giving schemes for employees as well as matching employee fundraising and allowing company time off to volunteer.

Exclusions

No support for brochure advertising, individuals, local appeals not in areas of company presence, overseas projects or political appeals.

Applications

Appeals, where relevant, should be addressed to the correspondent. The trustees of the charitable trust meet four times a year to consider applications.

Unilever

Unilever House, Blackfriars, London EC4P 4BQ
0171-822 5365; Fax: 0171-822 6532
Email: corporate.relations@unilever.com
Website: www.unilever.com

Correspondent: R A Harcourt, Community Affairs Steering Committee

Chief officer: *Chairman:* Niall FitzGerald

Year end	Turnover	Pre-tax profit
31/12/97	£29,766,000,000	£4,723,000,000

Nature of company business
Unilever comprises two parent companies, Unilever plc, London and Unilever NV, Rotterdam, operating in practice as a single company. The greater part of the business is in branded consumer goods (mainly detergents, foods and personal products).
Main subsidiaries include: Arkady Craigmillar; Diversey Lever; Birds Eye Wall's; Elida Faberge; Elizabeth Arden; Lever Brothers; Plant Breeding International Cambridge; UML; Unipath; Van den Bergh Foods; Van den Bergh Professional Foods..
Main brands and locations are too numerous to mention.
UK employees: 16,400

Charitable donations
1997: £4,000,000
1996: £3,000,000
1995: £3,000,000
1994: £2,000,000
1993: £1,836,000
Total community contributions: £5,000,000
Membership: *ABSA BitC %Club*

Community support policy

'In the UK, Unilever's long and successful tradition of working for the well-being of the community goes back more than 100 years to William Hesketh Lever, founder of Lever Brothers and Port Sunlight village. He believed that good citizenship meant good business – improving the environment in which businesses operate and providing a way for the community to share in the company's commercial success. Unilever continues to apply these principles in ways which meet today's needs and take advantage of the company's strengths. It manages this commitment with the same professionalism that is applied to its business activities. The contributions of Unilever and its operating companies are many and varied but always reflect the needs of the regions in which the company operates, concentrating on areas where business involvement is relevant and where Unilever can play an effective part.'

The company is a member of the PerCent Club and Business in the Community. Total community contributions in 1997 were £5 million. The main areas of non-cash support are secondments, gifts in kind and mentoring. The company operates an employee volunteering scheme which it supports financially and gives company time-off to volunteer, within certain guidelines. It also operates a payroll giving scheme. Some employee giving and fundraising is matched. During 1997, the company made financial donations of £4 million to UK charitable organisations and assisted them with a further £1 million of support in other forms.

Charitable donations: The company supports education (science and technology; school leadership; employees as school governors); youth enterprise, sustainable development and the arts. Preference is given to national charities and those in areas where the company has a presence.

About 50% of the charitable contributions are made by the head office. Subsidiaries make smaller grants independently.

In kind support: Additional help for local causes may be provided in other ways such as provision of office space, products, secondees and mentors.

Youth enterprise: Unilever and its operating companies support the development of youth enterprise. The main focus is on preparing young people for the world of work and the company works with a number of organisations such as the Corporate Responsibility Group, enterprise agencies and the Prince's Trust to achieve this.

Education: Unilever is involved in focused education support programmes involving primary and secondary

Unisys

schools, FE colleges, teachers, universities and research institutes. Through its education liaison service, the company sponsors and develops curriculum materials and training on youth enterprise, science and technology, sustainable development and school leadership. Locally, companies are involved in partnerships with schools, education authorities and Business Education partnerships.

Staff are encouraged to serve as governors and many Unilever managers, especially those in the scientific field, lecture at universities.

Sustainable development: Unilever supports a number of environmental projects and organisations in the UK, such as the Mersey Basin Campaign and Forum for the Future. In particular, the company focuses on projects that combine environmental issues with its other priorities of education and youth enterprise.

The arts: The company sponsors a range of artistic activities. Nationally, support is targeted at specific groups and is based on long-term support for a number of organisations such as the Regent's Park Open Air Theatre. Locally, operating companies encourage the arts in a variety of ways, from sponsoring school arts projects to supporting local festivals. The company is a member of ABSA.

The company has subsidiaries in 85 countries around the world that support causes in their areas of operation.

Note: Profit, turnover and donations figures are for Unilever in the UK.

Exclusions

No support for fundraising events, advertising in charity brochures, individuals, religious appeals, political appeals, or local appeals not in areas of company presence.

Applications

In writing to the correspondent. R A Harcourt is responsible for corporate sponsorship while the individual company marketing directors are responsible for brand sponsorship. A donations committee meets quarterly. Local appeals should be addressed to the local plant or branch. A J George is responsible for education liaison.

Information available: A booklet, *A Sense of Community*, gives an indication of the variety and number of projects with which the company is involved (available from external affairs department at head office).

Unisys Ltd

Bakers Court, Bakers Road, Uxbridge UB8 1RG
01895-237137; Fax: 01895-862093
Website: www.unisys.com

Correspondent: Martin Sexton, Director of Corporate Communications

Chief officer: *Managing Director:* Iain Davidson

Year end	Turnover	Pre-tax profit
31/12/96	£279,425,000	£5,050,000

Nature of company business

Principal activities: the development, manufacture, supply and maintenance of information technology systems and related services and supplies. Main UK locations are Milton Keynes and Uxbridge.

UK employees: 2,000+

Charitable donations

1996: £75,836
1995: £106,148
1994: £89,108
1993: £104,480
Membership: *ABSA*

Community support policy

In addition to charitable donations, the company gives support through gifts in kind, arts and good-cause sponsorship, and non-commercial advertising. The charity programme comprises three elements:

- support of a national charity, Help the Aged, by underwriting costs of a national golf clubs championship which runs throughout the year
- support, financial and in kind, for small charities in the local communities in which it has major investments in plant, buildings or people, and where a donation is likely to have a major impact
- an employee matching programme in which the company matches £ for £ monies raised by employees.

Charitable donations: Under the second element above, support tends to be given to local charities such as hospitals and educational appeals. There is a preference for charities in which a member of company staff is involved in Milton Keynes and Uxbridge and appeals relevant to company business. It also supports children and youth, social welfare, education, recreation, environment and heritage and enterprise initiatives. Grants to local organisations are generally from £50 to £1,000, but have been for as much as £10,000. Recently these have focused on safety programmes for local schools organised by public safety organisations (eg. NHS Ambulance, Fire Association, Police).

In kind support: Donations of PC-based equipment and software may be made for general administration purposes, usually free of charge, occasionally at cost price.

Employee involvement: Staff are encouraged to become involved in the local community through becoming volunteers and school governors and through fundraising which the company matches £ for £.

The arts: The company is a patron of ABSA. Support is again focused in those places where the company has a major presence, and which can also be used for client entertainment and public relations. The company has concentrated on music with support given to City of Birmingham Symphony Orchestra, Leeds Festival Chorus, Milton Keynes Chamber Orchestra and The Stables, Milton Keynes.

Exclusions
The company rarely responds to circular appeals. No grants for fundraising events, appeals from individuals, advertising in charity brochures, purely denominational (religious) appeals, local appeals not in areas of company presence, large national appeals, political appeals, enterprise/training or overseas projects.

Applications
In writing to the correspondent. Each appeal is considered by a charities committee which meets once a month.

United Assurance Group plc

Refuge House, Alderley Road, Wilmslow, Cheshire SK9 1PF
01625-605040; Fax: 01625-535955

Correspondent: Wendy Tate, Secretarial Assistant

Chief officers: *Chairman:* J Cudworth;
Chief Executive: Dr G P R Mack

Year end	Turnover	Pre-tax profit
31/12/97	n/a	£227,000,000

Nature of company business
The main activities are life assurance and property insurance.

Main subsidiaries include: Refuge Assurance PLC; Refuge Investments Ltd; United Friendly Asset Management Ltd; United Friendly Life Assurance Ltd; United Friendly Unit Managers Ltd.

UK employees: 5,889

Charitable donations
1997: £60,000
1996: £72,000
1995: £91,000
1994: £56,883

Community support policy
Support is mainly given to small, local charities within 25 to 30 miles of Wilmslow. A wide range of charitable causes are supported, with a preference for medical and caring appeals. Specific projects are preferred to general fundraising, running costs, etc. Individuals are occasionally supported. Grants are usually for about £300, but can be up to £2,000.

Exclusions
No support for sponsored or fundraising events or advertising in charity brochures.

Applications
In writing to the correspondent.

United Biscuits (UK) Ltd

Church Road, West Drayton, Middlesex UB7 7PR
01895-432142; Fax: 01895-432016
Website: www.unitedbiscuits.co.uk

Correspondent: Ken Musgrave, Secretary to the Appeals Committee

Chief officers: *Chairman:* Colin Short;
Chief Executive: Eric Nicoli

Year end	Turnover	Pre-tax profit
3/1/98	£1,549,400,000	£106,200,000

Nature of company business
United Biscuits is a major international food group which produces a wide range of biscuits, snacks, confectionery and frozen/chilled foods.

Main subsidiaries include: McVities Group; UK Foods.

Main brands include: McVities Digestive Chocolate Homewheat; Go Ahead!; Jaffa Cakes; KP Nuts; KP Crisps; KP Hula Hoops; KP Skips; Youngs.

Main locations: Carlisle; Edinburgh; Glasgow; Halifax; Harlesden; Manchester; Ashby-de-la-Zouch; Rotherham; Teesside; Grimsby; Annan; Fakenham; Leamington; Luton; North Thoresby; North Walsham; Okehampton; Redditch.

UK employees: 24,500

Charitable donations
1998: £681,000
1997: n/a
1996: n/a
1995: £569,000
1994: £681,000
Total community contributions: £1,500,000
Membership: *ABSA BitC %Club*

Community support policy
The company's 1997 annual report states: 'We continue to believe that commercial success and social responsibility are inextricably linked. Our community affairs programme is an integral part of our business activity; it helps to develop the potential of our people and our strong commitment to it adds value to our reputation as a leading food manufacturer and employer'.

'Key community objectives are:

- to help society, and the local communities where the group has staff and investments, in ways which will enhance our reputation as a good and socially responsible employer
- to provide a strong environment for the group's future trading by investing in activities which lead to a more stable, prosperous and educated society.'

Priority areas for involvement are:

- training and economic regeneration
- enterprise agencies and trusts
- education
- community initiatives.

Total community contributions in 1997 were £1.5 million. This included the cost of secondments (£600,000), sponsorships (£200,000), in kind support, and charitable

United News

donations (£700,000). The main areas of non-cash support were training schemes, secondments and enterprise agencies. Financial support is also given to employee volunteering schemes. It is company policy to give 1% of UK pre-tax profits in donations, and secondments, to educational and local community initiatives. The company is a founder member of the PerCent Club.

There is an ongoing programme with community partners which includes a mix of financial help, transferable skills and management expertise. The company have seconded 12 managers to organisations in the community. Through education and business links, training initiatives and enterprise programmes the company work with people from all walks of life. There is a preference for people who are young or disadvantaged (unemployed, disabled, etc). The company are encouraging their sites in other areas of Europe (including Eastern Europe) to make the link between commercial enterprise and education.

During 1997, through the Volunteer Award Scheme, 30 awards of £500 were given to charitable groups that had the involvement of company staff. About 60 staff are supported as school governors with annual bursaries. The company supports the Local Investment fund, to assist economically viable, community-based enterprises unable to obtain conventional finance.

The company supports a wide range of education and welfare charities including those caring for children, youth and elderly people. Support is also given to enterprise and training activities in inner city areas. It has a preference for charities where the business is located throughout the UK and in particular where a member of staff is involved.

Charitable donations: Typically, national grants range from £250 to £1,000 and local grants from £250 to £500.

The company has selected four main areas for its support:
- universities, colleges, schools and industry-link organisations;
- youth training and development centres;
- economic development, by support for enterprise agencies;
- local community service. Main donations in 1997 included those to Save the Children, Macmillan Nurses, Samaritans, Prince's Royal Trust for Carers and Workwise in Glasgow.

Employee involvement: The company seconds appropriate managers to community organisations. The length of secondment varies to a maximum of three years.

The company supports community teams at factory and office sites, which undertake projects to assist local community groups. Charitable fundraising by employees is encouraged at many sites. Sites are encouraged to provide facilities for employee payroll giving to charities. The group is registered with the Give As You Earn payroll giving scheme. The company matches employee giving. In 1997/98, the group and staff continued to fundraise for the nominated corporate charity, Save the Children. The commitment is to raise over £1 million for the fund over a nine-year period.

Education: Work with universities, colleges, schools and industry link organisations is designed to create a better understanding of the role of industry in the creation of wealth and the need for people with enterprise in society. The company has links with over 70 schools and is involved in Education Business Partnerships. Initiatives have included curriculum projects, teacher secondments, work experience, training in job applications and interviews, and project time to read *Industry into Education*.

Enterprise: The company is a member of Business in the Community and Scottish Business in the Community. In 30 towns where United Biscuits has a factory or office, the company contributes help and financial support to the local enterprise agency or trust. Community projects supported include Project Rosemary in Liverpool, the Springboard Centre in Coalville and a women's enterprise centre in Stockport.

The arts: United Biscuits is a member of ABSA and supports activities on the basis of their educational, community and cultural links with business locations. Support has been given to Brou Ha Ha Festival, Chatterbox Theatre Company, Edinburgh Festival Theatre, Royal Academy of Arts, Royal Liverpool Philharmonic Orchestra, Royal Opera House and Watermans Arts Centre.

Exclusions

No response to circular appeals. No grants for animal charities, medical research, political appeals, or religious appeals.

Applications

Grant decisions at head office are made by a donations committee which meets quarterly. Appeals should be addressed to the Community Affairs Department. Local appeals should be sent to local branches where donations can be made at the discretion of the local manager.

Information available: United Biscuits publishes information on its community affairs in its Community Links brochure, which can be obtained from the company's community affairs department.

United News & Media plc

Ludgate House, 245 Blackfriars Road, London SE1 9UY
0171-921 5000; Fax: 0171-928 2728
Website: www.unm.com

Correspondent: Elaine Robertson, Public Relations Officer

Chief officers: *Chairman:* Lord Stevens of Ludgate; *Chief Executive:* Lord Hollick

Year end	Turnover	Pre-tax profit
31/12/97	£2,226,000,000	£373,000,000

Nature of company business
United News & Media is an international media and information group based in the UK. Its three divisions are:
- business services
- consumer publishing
- broadcasting and entertainment, including the Meridian, Anglia and HTV ITV companies and a 29% share in Channel 5 in the UK.

Main subsidiaries include: Blenheim Exhibitions & Conferences Ltd; Miller Freeman PlC; Visual Communications Group Ltd; NOP Research Group Ltd; Express Newspapers PLC; United Provincial Newspapers Ltd; Yorkshire Post Newspapers Ltd; Sheffield Newspapers Ltd; United Advertising Publication PLC; Anglia Television Ltd; HTV Group Ltd; Meridian Broadcasting Ltd; Survival Anglia Ltd; TSMS Group Ltd.

UK employees: 18,150

Charitable donations

1997: £487,000
1996: £387,000
1995: £430,000
1994: £424,000
1993: £230,322

Community support policy

United News & Media is a corporate partner to The Prince's Youth Business Trust. The company also operates the Give As You Earn payroll giving scheme and supports employees fundraising and giving by matching these.

Local companies support local/regional appeals in their own area and trade/professional charities.

In addition to direct donations totalling £487,000 in 1997, the group also helps raise large sums for many charities through appeals launched by its national and regional newspapers (mainly in the north of England, Wales and south east England), and its magazines.

Exclusions

No support is given to circular appeals, fundraising events, purely denominational (religious) appeals, local appeals not in areas of company presence or overseas projects.

Applications

In writing to the correspondent.

United Utilities PLC

Birchwood Point Business Park, Birchwood Boulevard, Birchwood, Warrington WA3 7WB
01925-285000; Fax: 01925-285199

Correspondent: Helen Norris, Acting Communications Manager

Chief officers: *Chairman:* Sir Christopher Harding; *Chief Executive:* Derek Green

Year end	Turnover	Pre-tax profit
31/3/98	£2,150,000,000	£467,000,000

Nature of company business
A multi-utility supplying water/wastewater, electricity, gas and telecommunications worldwide.

Main subsidiaries include: North West Water Ltd; NORWEB PLC; Vertex Data Science Ltd; North West Water Scotland Ltd; Carefree Insurance Ltd; Talbot Insurance Ltd.

UK employees: 10,000

Charitable donations

1998: £576,163
1997: £814,986
1996: £257,537

Total community contributions: £3,000,000

Membership: *ABSA BitC*

Community support policy

Charitable donations in 1997/98 totalled £576,163, down from £814,986 the previous year. Community investment totalled almost £3 million, just over 1% of pre-tax profit.

The company gave a brief report on its community involvement in its annual report, including the following: 'This year we adopted a formal community policy: to work in partnership with the community for mutual benefit in a way which involves our employees, helps us achieve our business objectives and reflects the priorities of our stakeholders.'

A Community Forum (chaired by the company chairman) has been set up to coordinate the policy across all the group's businesses. 'Through a wide range of community partnerships, employee volunteers are involved in education, the environment, working with young people and people with extra needs, and promoting regional enterprise.' The company implements its policy in a way which:

- aims to make a visible difference for the business, employees and the community
- involves employees and the community in creating partnerships for mutual benefit
- ensures our actions are open and accountable. Support is given for the following:
- to protect and improve the environment
- to provide educational resources relevant to our services
- to promote the economic health and regeneration of the community
- to support organisations and community groups to help people with extra needs
- to help to protect public health and safety
- to support the arts.

The company's website gave the following examples of recent major projects supported.

Hospital appeal: £1 million has been pledged to two major hospital appeals – Alder Hey Children's Hospital and Christie Hospital, Manchester.

Royal National Institute for the Blind: The partnership has involved the company producing the first National Curriculum materials on the water cycle for visually impaired children, and company employees received training from RNIB on how to communicate better with blind and partially-sighted customers. The company has an ongoing commitment to the RNIB Sunshine House School in Southport. It has supported their hydrotherapy pool appeal, employee volunteers have decorated rooms, and one of the company's managers is a governor.

Van

Universities in Manchester: Part of the company's five-year £1 million commitment to higher education includes: sponsorship of a chair in quality management at UMIST; a new chair in water resources at the University of Salford; a three-year research programme at Telford Institute of Cybernetics.

Wigan Education Business Partnership: One of the company's partners involved in running a free environmental education centre, situated in Leigh.

United Utilities Venture Fund: This fund was launched to provide small, high-tech businesses with capital to grow. The company has committed £4 million, creating with other partners a total fund of £10 million. The fund will have a ten-year life and could provide between £100,000 and £600,000 for up to 30 businesses.

Mersey Basin Campaign: The company is a major contributor to this campaign. It supports campaign projects including conferences, publications and community action.

Hallé & Royal Liverpool Philharmonic Orchestra: The company has made a three-year £125,000 commitment, which has attracted matching funding through ABSA. The outcome is 'Classics in Parallel', a series of concerts by these two orchestras, with the Manchester Camerata. The funding enables the orchestras to perform outside Liverpool and Manchester, in towns with no regular access to such music.

Exclusions
No support for appeals from individuals, religious appeals or political appeals.

Applications
In writing to the correspondent.

Van Leer (UK) Holdings Ltd

Merseyside Works, Ellesmere Port, South Wirral L65 4EZ
0151-355 3644; Fax: 0151-355 8187

Correspondent: D J Tillotson, Financial Director

Chief officers: *Chairman:* W de Vlugt; *Managing Director:* P L Butler

Year end	Turnover	Pre-tax profit
31/12/97	n/a	(£238,000)

Nature of company business
The company is a manufacturer of packaging, and is owned by the Dutch-based Royal Packaging Industries Van Leer BV.

Main subsidiaries include: Lurgan Fibre; C R Bailey.

Main locations: Burton-on-Trent; Deeside; Ellesmere Port; Hull; Poole; Caerphilly; Blaenavon; Lurgan; Belfast; Leeds.

UK employees: n/a

Charitable donations
1997: £3,649,000
1996: £3,431,000
1995: £311,000
1994: £1,100,000
1993: £931,000

Community support policy
The major shareholder of Royal Packaging Industries Van Leer NV is the Van Leer Group Foundation which uses its funds to support the Bernard Van Leer Foundation. Both are philanthropic foundations, established under Dutch law. The company gave £3,649,000 to the Bernard Van Leer Foundation (UK) Trust. The foundation carries out projects for the benefit of socially and culturally disadvantaged children, primarily those living in areas where a Van Leer company has a presence. Details can be found in *A Guide to the Major Trusts Volume 1*. Other donations by the company are very minor and mainly to local appeals in areas of company presence.

Charitable donations: The UK donations budget is limited, but small grants are given to local appeals in areas of company presence. Charities within the fields of medical, health and welfare are supported.

Exclusions
No grants for appeals from individuals, purely denominational (religious) appeals, local appeals not in areas of company presence, overseas projects, advertising in charity brochures, animal welfare, enterprise/training, environment/heritage, fundraising events, medical research, political appeals, science/technology, sport or the arts.

Applications
Appeals to the company should be addressed to the correspondent. Appeals to the Bernard Van Leer Foundation should be sent to PO Box 85905, 2508 The Hague, Netherlands.

Reg Vardy plc

Houghton House, Wessington Way, Sunderland SR5 3RJ
0191-549 4949; Fax: 0191-516 3622

Correspondent: D Williams, Group Public Relations Manager

Chief officers: *Chairman:* P Vardy; *Chief Executive:* G J Potts

Year end	Turnover	Pre-tax profit
30/4/98	£773,557,000	£19,503,000

Nature of company business
The main activity is motor vehicle distribution.

Main subsidiaries include: Tyne Tees Properties Ltd; Trustee Co Ltd; Victoria Ltd.

UK employees: 2,619

Charitable donations
1998: £38,046
1997: £44,103
1996: £32,735
1995: £20,733
1994: £21,330

Community support policy
The company has been a major sponsor of Emmanuel College CTC on Tyneside. In general the company aims to assist education and make a positive contribution to the

communities where it operates. The company also operates the BEN payroll giving scheme.

Exclusions
No support for circular appeals, local appeals not in areas of company presence or political appeals.

Applications
In writing to the correspondent.

Other information: The Vardy Foundation, set up in 1989, is also administered from the company's head office. Its assets comprise mainly of shares in the company and it supports education in the North East, especially the CTC mentioned above.

Vaux Group plc

The Brewery, Sunderland SR1 3AN
0191-567 6277; Fax: 0191-567 3753
Website: www.vaux-group.co.uk

Correspondent: Mrs Hilary Florek, Secretary, Vaux Foundation

Chief officers: *Chairman:* Sir Paul Nicholson; *Chief Executive:* M Grant; *Managing Directors:* F Nicholson, W P Catesby

Year end	Turnover	Pre-tax profit
30/9/97	£282,515,000	£34,834,000

Nature of company business
Principal activities: brewing, bottling and canning of ales and lager; wholesaling and retailing of beers, wines, spirits and soft drinks; the ownership and operation of hotels, public houses and property development.

Main subsidiaries include: Swallow Hotels Ltd; Percheron Properties Ltd; Vaux Breweries; Wards Brewery.

Main brands include: Samson; Lambtons; Scorpion.

UK employees: n/a

Charitable donations
1997: £167,000
1996: £157,000
1995: £139,000
1994: £144,000
1993: £101,000

Total community contributions: £200,000

Membership: ABSA BitC %Club

Community support policy
The 1997 annual report states: 'The group recognises that it has a major role to play in community affairs and provides financial assistance and other resources to support a number of local institutions and initiatives such as Manchester Metropolitan University, The Northern Development Company, County Durham Foundation and Cleveland Community Foundation. During the year the group, together with the Vaux Group Foundation, contributed to these organisations and other charities a total of £167,000 of which the group donated £40,000'.

The company is a member of the PerCent Club and Business in the Community. Most of the donations are made through the Vaux Foundation, which meets every three months. The foundation was set up in 1990, with an initial donation of £1,075,000 from the company. The foundation has a preference for groups operating in Wearside, the North West and Yorkshire. Areas local to the company's Swallow hotels may also be supported. Preferred areas of support include advertising in charity brochures, animal welfare charities, the arts, educational projects, elderly people, enterprise/training, environment/heritage, political appeals, religious appeals, social welfare and sport.

Major grants given by the foundation went to County Durham Foundation (£15,000), Diana, Princess of Wales Memorial Fund (£10,000), Charities Aid Foundation (£9,037 to match employee contributions through Give As You Earn), Midland Enterprise Fund for the North East (£7,500), Manchester Metropolitan University (£7,000), Hospitality Training Foundation and Hotel & Catering Benevolent Association (£5,000 each), Prince's Youth Business Trust, Manor Training & Resource Centre and South Yorkshire Foundation (£4,500 each), North East Civic Trust and Weston Spirit (£2,000 each) and Business in the Community (£1,500).

There were a further 19 grants of £1,000 to City of Durham CCTV, RNLI Harrogate, North East Civic Trust, Academy of Food & Wine Service, South Tyneside MBC, Motor Neurone Disease Association, Byers Green Methodist Church, Hexham Community Initiative, Berwick Family Centre, Reserve Forces Ulysees Trust, National Museums & Galleries on Merseyside, Pride in Pennywell, Transplant Sports Association, Durham Univesity Student Community Action, Manor Residents Association, Sheffield New Year's Honours Awards, County Durham Common Purpose, North of England Cadet Forces Trust Fund and Cutlers Hall Preservation Trust Ltd.

The company prefers to make grants to specific projects rather than to fundraising events or to large national appeals.

The main areas of non-cash support are good-cause sponsorship, gifts in kind and enterprise agencies. The company is a member of ABSA. The company matches employee fundraising.

Exclusions
No support for appeals from individuals or overseas projects.

Applications
In writing to the correspondent. Trustees meet quarterly to consider applications.

Vauxhall Motors Ltd

Public Affairs–B5, Griffin House, Osborne Road, Luton LU1 3YT
0181-658 1819; Fax: 0181-658 3292
Website: www.vauxhall.co.uk

Correspondent: Paul Patten, Charities Coordinator

Chief officer: *Chairman:* D N Reilly

Year end	Turnover	Pre-tax profit
31/12/96	£4,115,900,000	£10,100,000

Vendôme

Nature of company business
The company manufactures, markets and services passenger cars, recreational vehicles and light vans. Vehicle and component manufacturing activities are located at Ellesmere Port, Cheshire and Luton, Bedfordshire. The V6 engine plant located at Ellesmere Port produces engines for GM's European and worldwide operations. Parts and accessories for the UK market are supplied from the Aftersales warehouse situated at Luton Road, Chalton, Bedfordshire.

UK employees: 9,651

Charitable donations
1996: £335,345
1995: n/a
1994: £116,545
Membership: BitC

Community support policy

Charitable donations: The company states that each request for support, be it an appeal for a financial contribution, sponsorship, a product, personnel, secondment or promotional support, receives appropriate consideration. Every request received is replied to. The company concentrates its support on activities directly associated with the industry and its employees' interests, and in areas covered by its plants (ie. Luton and Ellesmere Port). A wide range of organisations are supported including sickness/disability, education, elderly people, family support, social welfare, sport and children/youth. It takes a proactive role in supporting a small number of national organisations such as BEN (The Motor Allied Trades Benevolent Fund) and Crime Concern. Other major beneficiaries have included NSPCC, Scout Association, Special Olympics UK and Mencap (Blue Sky Appeal).

Enterprise: Vauxhall is a member of Business in the Community and supports enterprise agencies.

The arts: The company is not a member of ABSA but it does undertake arts sponsorship.

Exclusions
No grants for circular appeals, appeals from individuals, local appeals not in areas of company presence, overseas projects, political, religious or sectarian organisations. The company does not give raffle prizes or company products.

Applications
Enquiries regarding charitable sponsorships and donations should be addressed to the correspondent. Enquiries about educational matters and secondment should be sent to R B Lindop, Manager, Educational Affairs, Personnel Department. Commercial sponsorship to Alan Denton, Manager, Promotions/Sponsorship.

Vendôme Luxury Group Ltd

27 Knightsbridge, London SW1X 7YB
0171-838 8500; Fax: 0171-838 8555

Correspondent: Lord Douro, Deputy Chairman

Chief officers: n/a

Year end	Turnover	Pre-tax profit
31/3/98	£177,762,000	(£31,558,000)

Nature of company business
Principal activity: the marketing of luxury consumer products including fashion clothing and accessories, watches, pens, leather goods, jewellery and fragrances, under the Alfred Dunhill, Hackett and Purdey brand names.

UK employees: n/a

Charitable donations
1998: £96,000
1997: £91,000
1996: £95,000
1995: £89,000

Community support policy

Preferred areas of support are the arts, children and youth, education, elderly people, sickness/disability, social welfare and people with disabilities. National charities are supported, but there is a preference for London and Westminster. Beneficiaries have included charities such as Queen Elizabeth Foundation for the Disabled, Samaritans, St John Ambulance, Birkbeck College and the Royal British Legion.

The group gives support to the Royal College of Art where Alfred Dunhill supports design students.

Exclusions
No support for circular appeals, animal welfare charities, appeals from individuals, enterprise/training, environment/heritage, medical research, political appeals, science/technology, sport or purely denominational (religious) appeals.

Medical research is not supported. This is because the Dunhill Medical Trust was once a significant shareholder in the company and distributes its dividend to medical research. This trust gave grants totalling nearly £3.5 million in 1995/96, further details in *A Guide to the Major Trusts Volume 1*.

Applications
In writing to the correspondent.

Vickers plc

Vickers House, 2 Bessborough Gardens, London SW1V 2JG
0171-828 7777; Fax: 0171-828 6585
Website: www.vickers.co.uk

Correspondent: Paul Forster, Deputy Secretary

Chief officers: *Chairman:* Sir Colin Chandler;
Chief Executive: Baron Buysse

Year end	Turnover	Pre-tax profit
31/12/97	£1,196,900,000	£19,400,000

Nature of company business
Principal activities are the production and sale of marine propulsion systems, superalloys for the aerospace and automotive industries and armoured fighting vehicles.
Main subsidiaries include: Brown Brothers & Co; Michell Bearings; Ross & Catherall Group; Ross Catherall Ceramics; Trucast.
Main locations: Leeds; Newcastle upon Tyne; Edinburgh; Sheffield; Derby; Isle of Wight; Shrewsbury; Crewe; London.

UK employees: n/a

Charitable donations

1997: £165,000
1996: £175,000
1995: £175,000
1994: £160,000
1993: £139,834

Total community contributions: £265,000

Membership: *BitC*

Community support policy

The company is a member of Business in the Community. Charitable donations are distributed by head office and local operating units. The main area of non-cash support is good-cause sponsorship.

Head office support

Head office makes major donations to the British Heart Foundation, Understanding Industry and SSAFA. A small residual pool of money caters for ad hoc donations to a wide range of causes. Head office spending falls into the categories of:

Medical and social welfare	34%
International relations	21%
Education and training (including enterprise schemes)	7%
Youth and sports	3%
Service charities	2%
Miscellaneous	33%

Head office welcomes appeals from national charities and community organisations, particularly those having a presence in areas where the company has an operating unit; approaches are also welcome when made direct to such units as each of them has its own discretionary fund. Priority is not necessarily restricted to projects where members of staff have an involvement. Grants to national organisations range from £25 to £15,000 and local grants range from £10 to £3,000. Examples of the company's involvement are mentioned in the latest annual report.

Local support

Local operating units have a high-level of autonomy and are largely decentralised. The donations policy involves more than 50% of the charitable budget allocation being devolved to these units. In addition to cash donations, donations in kind and other contributions are made. Operating companies support local activities, for example Vickers Defence Division participates in the City Challenge, Newcastle Education Business Partnership and the Engineering Education Scheme.

Other community support: In addition to cash donations the company provides in kind support in the form of equipment or materials, free or subsidised accommodation and the use of in-house facilities, either free of charge, at cost price or with a discount.

Exclusions

No response to appeals from individuals, purely denominational (religious) appeals, local appeals not in areas of company presence, circular appeals, advertising in brochures, circulars, matching funds schemes, sponsorship of students for overseas expeditions, secondments to social welfare projects. Fundraising events are supported infrequently as are sponsorship appeals from the arts.

Applications

Depending on amount donations at head office are decided upon by a specialist staff member (smaller amounts), the donations committee (chaired by the chief executive) or the main board. The annual budget meeting is held in March/April each year. Other meetings are held on an ad hoc basis. Occasionally appeals are circulated to committee members with a proforma requesting their comments. The company secretariat manager is responsible for the administration of charitable spending and requests should be directed to her. Bernard LeBargy, Director of Corporate Personnel, is responsible for youth training, job sponsorship schemes, etc. The chief executive is the main board director who is ultimately responsible for public affairs.

Appeals which have been turned down year after year should be directed elsewhere as a well established pattern of refusal simply indicates that a positive response is unlikely. Local appeals should be directed to the chief executive of the local operating unit.

Viridian Group PLC

PO Box 2, Danesfort, 120 Malone Road, Belfast BT9 5HT
01232-661100
Website: www.viridiangroup.co.uk

Correspondent: Dermot Davey, Northern Ireland Electricity Charities Committee

Chief officers: *Chairman:* David Jefferies;
Chief Executive: Patrick Haren

Year end	Turnover	Pre-tax profit
31/3/98	£500,400,000	£76,70,000

Nature of company business
The main activities are electricity transmission, distribution and supply.
Main subsidiaries include: Northern Ireland Electricity.

UK employees: 2,350

Vodafone

Charitable donations
1998: £190,000
1997: £175,000
1996: £134,000
1995: £54,000
1994: £36,000
Membership: *BitC*

Community support policy
The charities committee considers any registered charity, but has a preference for local charities in Northern Ireland. UK charities may, however, be supported. The community affairs committee prefers sponsorship opportunities in the fields of the arts, children/youth, education, elderly people, enterprise/training, environment/heritage, fundraising events, medical research, science/technology, sickness/disability charities and social welfare. In 1997/98, Marie Curie Cancer Care received £57,000, with the remainder allocated to around 70 to 80 charities with a maximum of about £1,500 per charity.

The company operates employee volunteering and payroll giving (Give As You Earn) schemes. Financial support and company time-off is given to employee volunteering/charitable activities. Money raised by employees is matched by the company.

The company is a member of Business in the Community. Non-cash support is given via gifts in kind, enterprise agencies and secondments.

Exclusions
No support for circular appeals, advertising in charity brochures, appeals from individuals, purely denominational (religious) appeals, local appeals not in areas of company presence, large national appeals, overseas projects or sport (unless heavily associated with education or disability).

Applications
In writing to the correspondent.

Vodafone Group plc

Courtyard, 2–4 London Road, Newbury, Berkshire RG14 1JX
01635-33251; Fax: 01635-45713
Website: www.vodafone.co.uk

Correspondent: P R Williams, Group Personnel Director

Chief officers: *Chairman:* Sir Ernest Harrison; *Chief Executive:* C Gent

Year end	Turnover	Pre-tax profit
31/3/98	£2,471,000,000	£650,000,000

Nature of company business
Mobile telecommunications.

UK employees: n/a

Charitable donations
1998: £373,000
1997: £391,000
1996: £261,000
1995: £239,000
1994: £157,000

Community support policy
The Vodafone Group Charitable Trust (Charity Commission number 1013850), was established in August 1992. The company was giving 0.05% of its pre-tax profits to the trust, rising to 0.075% from 1996/97. The general policy of the trust is to give approximately 20% of the budget to each of medical research, social welfare, education and disability, with about 10% given to each of arts/environment and miscellaneous.

In 1997/98, major grant beneficiaries included: Meridian Broadcasting Charitable Trust Spotlight Week, Variety Club Children's Charity, Newbury College, Stroke Association and Cystic Fibrosis Trust. Only registered charities (national and local) are supported, with a preference for those in areas where the company has a presence.

The company operates the South West Charitable Giving payroll scheme.

Exclusions
No support for: advertising in charity brochures; appeals from individuals; fundraising events; overseas projects; political appeals; religious appeals; local appeals not in areas of company presence or bodies which are not registered charities.

Applications
In writing to the correspondent. The trustees meet once a quarter to consider appeals.

Vosper Thornycroft Holdings plc

Victoria Road, Woolston, Southampton SO19 9RR
01703-426000; Fax: 01703-426040

Correspondent: P G Dawes, Company Secretary

Chief officers: *Chairman:* Lord Wakeham; *Chief Executive:* M Jay

Year end	Turnover	Pre-tax profit
31/3/98	£214,079,000	£32,809,000

Nature of company business
Principal activities: shipbuilding, support services and marine products.

UK employees: n/a

Charitable donations
1998: £60,415
1997: £61,317
1996: £54,064
1995: £41,105
1994: £23,405

Community support policy

The company has a preference for charities local to main areas of company presence (Southampton and Portsmouth) and appeals relevant to company business. Preferred areas of support are social welfare, sickness/disability charities, children/youth, education, elderly people, medical research science/technology and advertising in charity brochures.

Exclusions

No response to circular appeals. No grants for the arts, environment/heritage, overseas projects, political or religious appeals, local appeals not in areas of company presence, or large national appeals.

Applications

In writing to the correspondent.

Waddington plc

Wakefield Road, Leeds LS10 1DU
0113-277 0202; Fax: 0113-271 3503
Email: sue.shaw@waddington.plc.uk
Website: www.waddington.plc.uk

Correspondent: Sue Shaw, Corporate Services Manager

Chief officers: *Chairman:* J C Orr; *Chief Executive:* M H Buckley

Year end	Turnover	Pre-tax profit
4/4/98	£330,529,000	£39,563,000

Nature of company business
The main activities are divided between the following divisions: food services, pharmaceutical packaging, and specialist printing.
Main subsidiaries include: PFB Creative Marketing Solutions.

UK employees: 1,457

Charitable donations

1998: £44,466
1997: £25,442
1996: £38,067

Community support policy

The company supports local and trade charities. It prefers to support charities concerned with elderly people, disadvantaged people, children and education. Main beneficiaries included Whizz-Kidz, Macmillan Cancer Relief, Leeds City Council – 1998 Youth Games, Education 2000 and Lineham Farm, Leeds.

Exclusions

Sports sponsorship for individuals.

Applications

In writing to the correspondent.

Wagon plc

3100 Solihull Parkway, Birmingham Business Park, Birmingham B37 7YE
0121-717 2000

Correspondent: N Brayshaw, Chief Executive

Chief officers: *Chairman:* P D Taylor; *Chief Executive:* N Brayshaw

Year end	Turnover	Pre-tax profit
31/3/96	£410,300,000	£19,900,000

Nature of company business
A broadly based engineering group with four operating divisions: storage products; retail systems; precision engineering; automotive components.
Main subsidiaries include: Link 51; Polypal; Radford Retail Systems; Westward Refrigeration; Oleo International; Forkardt; Edward Rose; Avenell Engineering; Barrett Engineers; Eric N Baylis; Ashlight S S & P; Wm Tyers; Wilmid; Formex.
Main locations: Telford; Brierley Hill; Bolton; Bristol; Gloucester; Newcastle upon Tyne; Milton Keynes; Newbury; Coventry; Redditch; Brownhills; Oxford; Wantage; Birmingham; Alcester; Solihull.

UK employees: n/a

Charitable donations

1996: £46,000
1995: £37,000
1994: £26,000
1993: £24,000

Community support policy

The company stated that giving has been frozen for the time being. Previously, the company supplied the following information about its community support policy.

Most donations are by Charities Aid Foundation vouchers, unless the cause is not a registered charity. The company prefers to make direct donations rather than undertake sponsorship, to charities local to the company's area of presence. Preference for animal welfare, children and youth, elderly, enterprise and training, environment and heritage, medical research, overseas projects, sickness and disability and social welfare charities. Grants to national and local organisations range from £25 to £250.

Exclusions

No grants for advertising in charity brochures, purely denominational appeals or circular appeals.

Applications

In writing to the correspondent.

Warburtons Ltd

Blackburn Road, Bolton, Lancashire BL1 8HJ
01204-523551; Fax: 01204-528883

Correspondent: Jill Kippax, Corporate Affairs Manager

Chief officers: *Chairman:* W R Warburton; *Joint Managing Directors:* J & W B Warburton

Year end	Turnover	Pre-tax profit
30/9/97	£147,871,000	£18,563,000

Nature of company business
Bakers.

UK employees: 2,000

Charitable donations
1997: £113,000
1996: £100,000
1995: £100,000
1994: £19,769
1993: £53,000
Membership: *BitC   %Club*

Community support policy

The company is a member of the PerCent Club and Business in the Community. It prefers to support appeals from local charities in areas of company presence (from the Midlands, through the north of England, to southern Scotland), especially projects concerned with children and youth, education, elderly people, fundraising events, sickness/disability charities, and social welfare. Grants to local organisations can be for up to £10,000.

The company reported on its community involvement in the 1998 PerCent Club annual report from where the following information is taken.

In 1997, substantial donations were made to a variety of causes including the Children's Ward at the Royal Victoria Infirmary in Newcastle upon Tyne, Kids in Need and Distress (KIND) in Liverpool, RNIBH – Sunshine House in Southport, Books for Babies Project in Edinburgh, Bolton Lads and Girls Club (after school club) and a four-year covenant (total £50,000) to the Christies Against Cancer Appeal.

In addition to these donations administered from the central office, the company's eight production units control their own charity budgets for donations at a local level of both cash and kind. A matched funding scheme is operated for employees fundraising.

Exclusions
No support for advertising in charity brochures; animal welfare charities; appeals from individuals; the arts; enterprise/training; environment/heritage; medical research; overseas projects; political appeals; religious appeals or science/technology.

Applications
In writing to the correspondent.

Warner Lambert UK Ltd

Lambert Court, Chestnut Avenue, Eastleigh, Hampshire SO5 3ZQ
01703-620500; Fax: 01703-628010

Correspondent: Lyn Applin, Public Affairs Executive

Chief officer: *Managing Director:* Alan K I Walker

Year end	Turnover	Pre-tax profit
31/12/97	£241,589,000	£11,004,000

Nature of company business
The principal activities of the company are the manufacture and sale of pharmaceuticals, over-the-counter medicines, proprietary and confectionery products, razors, razor blades and swords and the distribution of toiletries and manicure products.

Main subsidiaries include: Parke Davis & Co Ltd; Wilkinson Sword Ltd; Lambert Chemical Co Ltd.

UK employees: 2,011

Charitable donations
1997: £82,037
1996: £117,710
1995: £176,017
1994: £33,269

Community support policy

The company gives preference to charities associated with children/youth, elderly people, fundraising events, medical research and science/technology in Hampshire. The company operates a payroll giving scheme and will match employee giving and fundraising.

Exclusions
Donations are not made to religious or political organisations, or in the form of fundraising dinners, journal advertising, membership fees, symposia, etc.

Applications
In writing to the correspondent.

Wassall plc

39 Victoria Street, London SW1H 0EE
0171-333 0303; Fax: 0171-333 0304

Correspondent: Simon Pearce, Company Secretary

Chief officers: *Chairman:* J D Miller; *Chief Executive:* J C Miller

Year end	Turnover	Pre-tax profit
31/12/97	£542,000,000	£332,000,000

Nature of company business
Principal activity: manufacture and distribution of copper wire and cable, adhesives and sealants, bottle closures, office furniture and travel goods.

Main subsidiaries include: MCG Closures Ltd; IDEM Furniture Ltd; Antler Ltd.

UK employees: n/a

Charitable donations
1997: £90,000
1996: £92,000
1995: £74,000
1994: £38,000
1993: £38,000

Community support policy
The company prefers to support local charities in areas of company presence and charities in which a member of company staff is involved, particularly in the fields of children/youth and medical causes. Grants are usually for £250 to £500.

Exclusions
No support for fundraising events, advertising in charity brochures or overseas aid/development.

Applications
In writing to the correspondent.

Waterford Wedgwood UK plc

Barlaston, Stoke-on-Trent, Staffordshire ST12 9ES
01782-204141; Fax: 01782-204402

Correspondent: Angela Beard, Communications Administrator

Chief officer: *Chairman:* R H Niehaus

Year end	Turnover	Pre-tax profit
31/12/97	£339,000,000	(£8,000,000)

Nature of company business
Manufacture of fine bone china and earthenware.

Main subsidiaries include: Statum Ltd.

UK employees: n/a

Charitable donations
1997: £103,000
1996: £59,000
1995: £74,000
1994: £61,000
1993: £42,000

Community support policy
The company has a preference for local charities in areas of company presence. Preferred areas of support are environment/heritage and the arts. Recent recipients of support include: Common Purpose, New Victoria Theatre, Staffordshire Wildlife Trust and Young Enterprise.

Gifts in kind may be donated to local or industry-related charities.

Exclusions
No support for advertising in charity brochures or circular appeals. Unsolicited appeals may not be considered.

Applications
In writing to the correspondent.

Weetabix Ltd

Weetabix Mills, Burton Latimer, Kettering NN15 5JR
01536-722181; Fax: 01536-726148

Correspondent: P Davidson, Media & Public Relations Manager

Chief officer: *Chairman:* R W George

Year end	Turnover	Pre-tax profit
3/8/96	£271,411,000	£36,635,000

Nature of company business
Manufacture of cereal foods.

Main subsidiaries include: B L Marketing Ltd; Vibixa Ltd.

UK employees: n/a

Charitable donations
1996: £756,000
1995: £722,000
1994: £756,000
1993: £380,000

Community support policy
The company supports all kinds of appeals within the Northamptonshire area.

The only information on the company's support is that it appears to make its contributions through the Weetabix Charitable Trust (Charity Commission number 1044949). In 1997, this trust had an income of £674,000 and gave grants totalling £603,000. No further information was available on the size of grants given or types of causes supported.

Applications
In writing to the correspondent.

The Weir Group PLC

149 Newlands Road, Cathcart, Glasgow G44 4EX
0141-637 7111; Fax: 0141-637 2221
Email: investor-relations@wg.weir.co.uk
Website: www.weir.co.uk

Correspondent: Emrys Inker, Public Relations Manager

Chief officers: *Chairman:* Viscount Weir;
Chief Executive: Sir Ronald Garrick

Year end	Turnover	Pre-tax profit
26/12/97	£636,829,000	£60,135,000

Nature of company business
Engineering services and specialist engineering products.

Main subsidiaries include: Darchem Engineering; Hopkinsons; Liquid Gas Equipment; Strachan & Henshaw.

Main locations: Cathcart, Glasgow; Newton Heath; Huddersfield; South Gyle; Aylestone; Petersfield; Bristol; Stockton on Tees; Altens.

UK employees: c. 5,000

Wessex

Charitable donations
1997: £68,313
1996: £77,248
1995: £79,816
1994: £76,375
1993: £80,617

Community support policy
Of the total donations figure, £45,000 was given to the Weir Group Educational Trust and £23,313 for general charitable purposes.

Charitable donations: The company tends to support sea charities such as King George's Fund for Sailors, and general charities such as cancer charities and hospices. Donations are usually made to charities the company chooses to support year after year. Preference is given to charities located in areas of company presence but not necessarily to charities in which a member of staff is involved. Grants range from £100 to £5,000.

Advertising in charity brochures, fundraising events, circular appeals, larger national appeals and overseas projects (where related to the commercial interests of the company) are all supported. Subsidiaries outside London have their own donations budget.

Exclusions
Individuals are rarely supported, nor are appeals from non-charities, requests for secondments or arts sponsorships.

Applications
In writing to the correspondent. The main decisions are made by the board once a year but a less formal decision process exists where smaller amounts are involved.

Wessex Water plc

Wessex House, Passage Street, Bristol BS2 0JQ
0117-929 0611; Fax: 0117-929 3137

Correspondent: Marilyn Smith, Head of Corporate Community Relations

Chief officers: *Chairman:* Nicholas Hood;
Chief Executive: Colin Skellett

Year end	Turnover	Pre-tax profit
31/3/98	£266,000,000	£139,000,000

Nature of company business
Principal activity: water and sewerage services.

UK employees: 1,414

Charitable donations
1998: £122,000
1997: £109,000
1996: £102,300
1995: £100,217
1994: £60,000

Total community contributions: £304,693

Membership: *BitC %Club*

Community support policy
The company is a member of the PerCent Club and in the latters 1998 annual report gives a community investment figure over £500,000 equivalent to 1.1% of dividends. The company is also a member of Business in the Community.

Grants are given to registered charities operating in the area administered by Wessex Water ie. South Gloucestershire, Wiltshire, Dorset, and Somerset.

In addition, the company supports a wide variety of causes by way of sponsorship to local, environmental and water-related activities and gifts in kind. This includes support for nature conservation trusts, education, swimming clubs, overseas projects, social welfare, water sports for disabled people and a variety of charities providing benefits for the local community.

Wessex Watermark was launched in 1993 in association with the company. 40 awards ranging from £150 to £1,000 were made in 1996/97 to environmental projects which have links with water in the counties mentioned above. Many of the organisations supported were schools, with awards also given to a canal amenity group, parish council, Dorset Wildlife Trust, a scout association and a playgroup.

The company also supports employee volunteering through giving time-off to volunteers and by matching employee fundraising through the Community Plus Fund. Thanks to the efforts of staff, some £248,000 was raised for WaterAid. It also operates the Give As You Earn payroll giving scheme.

Exclusions
National charities and political appeals.

Applications
In writing to the correspondent. The Community Involvement Committee meets monthly.

Whitbread PLC

Chiswell Street, London EC1Y 4SD
0171-606 4455; Fax: 0171-615 1172
Website: www.whitbread.co.uk

Correspondent: I S Anderson, Community Investment Director

Chief officers: *Chairman:* Sir Michael Angus;
Chief Executive: D M Thomas

Year end	Turnover	Pre-tax profit
28/2/98	£3,198,000,000	£381,000,000

Nature of company business
The company is a major food, drinks and leisure company.

Main subsidiaries include: Bright Reasons Group Ltd; David Lloyd Leisure PLC; The Pelican Group PLC.

Main locations: Beefeater Restaurants; Brewers Fayre; TGI Fridays; Pizza Hut; Cafe Rouge; Bella Pasta; Costa Coffee Shops; Boddingtons; Heineken; Murphy's; Stella Artois; Marriott Hotels; David Lloyd Leisure; Travel Inn.

UK employees: 80,000

Charitable donations

1998: £836,707
1997: £721,233
1996: £529,456
1995: £482,963
1994: £564,525

Total community contributions: £2,200,000

Membership: ABSA BitC %Club

Community support policy

The company is a member of the PerCent Club, Business in the Community and the Corporate Responsibility Group. It was the first company to receive three Dragon Awards for business involvement in the community and in 1998 was named company of the year in the first Business in the Community Awards for Excellence in corporate community investment.

Charitable donations: The company supports a wide range of charities, through its charitable trust, under six broad headings: medical and health, welfare, education, humanities, environmental resources, and the arts. Each year the company highlights a number of priority areas to support, which may vary slightly from year to year.

A priority is also given to local appeals in areas where the company has a strong trading and employment presence (donations of around £200 are given to charities when staff members or pensioners are involved). The typical level of support for local appeals is £50 to £500. Appeals should be initially directed to the Company's Charity Co-ordinator who will consult with a Regional Community Affairs Director or Regional Education Manager on the merit of each application.

Grants made through the Whitbread 1988 Charitable Trust to national organisations usually range from £250 to £5,000. Priority is given to charities working in the fields of education, social welfare and medical care. Grants totalling about 50% of the company's donations budget are made through this trust.

The company also promotes and administers a payroll giving scheme, and matches employee giving and fundraising.

Sponsorship: Whitbread's main commercial sponsorship covers national sport and literary awards. Community sponsorship is generally of a local nature covering a wide range of issues.

Volunteering: The company provides various types of resource to organisations such as the National Centre for Volunteering, NAVB and REACH. It is an acknowledged leader in the encouragement, support and recognition of employee volunteers, and has 46 operational site volunteering committees across its various businesses.

For the past 15 years it has run the Whitbread Volunteer Action Awards to promote volunteering and raise public awareness of volunteering generally. Awards of £1,000 are made to winners from Wales, Scotland, Northern Ireland and seven English regions, as well as the Young Volunteer Award and the Senior Award. In partnership with the Home Office these awards have been extended to recognise organisations supporting volunteers.

Education: Whitbread established the first Business-Education Compact in East London in 1987. The compact provided a bridge between schools in areas of under achievement or high unemployment, with the guarantee of a job for any school leavers reaching specified achievement levels. The success led to government funding for a further 60 compacts.

Facilitated by a team of six full-time education managers, the various Whitbread businesses identify educational projects to support which are incorporated into their annual business plans. The main activities are work experience, teacher placement and curriculum development across the primary, secondary and tertiary sectors. Whitbread has received two Dragon Awards specifically for their education involvement.

Social and economic regeneration: The company has 10 Regional Community Affairs Directors who are responsible for promoting and implementing the company's involvement with local communities. Whitbread is a supporter of small business, and currently assists 21 enterprise agencies. The company is also involved in many local partnerships and, recognising the value of different types of support, has an active programme to identify resources no longer needed in its various businesses and making them available to the community.

Exclusions

The following are not usually supported: advertising in charity brochures, ticket purchases for charity events, appeals from religious bodies (unless for the benefit of the community as a whole), political organisations, medical research, charitable organisations operating overseas and individuals.

Applications

All appeals must be made in writing accompanied by a copy of the organisations current annual report and accounts and should be sent to: Paul Patten, Charities Co-ordinator at the above address.

The Board Director responsible for community affairs is D M Thomas (Group Chief Executive). The Community Investment Director is I S Anderson.

Wickes plc

Wickes House, 120-138 Station Road, Harrow, Essex HA1 2QB
0181-901 2000; Fax: 0181-424 9937

Correspondent: K Stokes-Smith, Company Secretary

Chief officers: *Chairman:* M von Brentano; *Chief Executive:* W Grimsey

Year end	Turnover	Pre-tax profit
31/12/97	£553,998,000	(£6,466,000)

Nature of company business

The group trades as a retailer, merchant and distributor of timber, building materials, home improvement products and associated services, and through its Hunter subsidiaries as an importer, processor and distributor of timber and timber products.

Wilkinson

Main subsidiaries include: HTJ Ltd; Hunter Estates Ltd.

UK employees: n/a

Charitable donations
1997: £32,000
1996: £69,000
1995: £129,000
1994: n/a
1993: £136,000
Membership: %Club

Community support policy
The company is a member of the PerCent Club, although with the company making a pre-tax loss in 1997, donations fell to only £32,000.

It prefers to support projects by awarding gifts in kind rather than cash donations and only supports local charities in areas of company presence. Typical grants to range from £100 to £2,500. Fundraising activities are also supported locally.

Enterprise: Support continues to be given to the Wickes Task Undertakings Employment Training Centre in Coventry which provides training in home improvement skills for long-term unemployed people. The scheme was set up by the company and Task Undertakings, a charitable organisation originally established as part of the Prince's Trust.

Environment: The company remains the principal sponsor of Project Barito Ulu in the Kalimantan province of Indonesia. The project is supported by the Indonesian Ministry of Forestry, the Smithsonian Institute and Cambridge University, and is investigating the regeneration of tropical forests and related issues. It has supported the project for several years.

Exclusions
The company will not give to sports-related charities or to individuals.

Applications
In writing to the correspondent.

Wilkinson Hardware Stores Ltd

PO Box 20, Roebuck Way, Manton Wood, Worksop, Northants S80 3YY
01909-505505

Correspondent: Adele Jenkinson, Charity Administrator

Chief officers: *Chairman:* A H Wilkinson;
Managing Director: B K Fairhurst

Year end	Turnover	Pre-tax profit
2/2/96	£274,597,000	£10,949,000

Nature of company business
Principal activity: sale of domestic hardware and other related goods.

UK employees: n/a

Charitable donations
1996: £44,407
1995: n/a
1994: £41,925
1993: £22,697

Community support policy
The company now has 150 stores throughout the UK and tends to support charities local to those stores.

Applications
In writing to the correspondent.

Williams PLC

Pentagon House, Sir Frank Whittle Road, Derby D21 4AX
01332-202020; Fax: 01332-387066
Email: marie.dixon@williams-plc.com
Website: www.williams-plc.com

Correspondent: J B Cunningham, Company Secretary

Chief officers: *Chairman:* Sir Nigel Rudd;
Chief Executive: R M Carr

Year end	Turnover	Pre-tax profit
31/12/97	£1,492,700,000	£254,000,000

Nature of company business
The activities of the group fall into three major divisions: fire protection (covering aerospace and defence, hazard sensing, industrial, and portable extinguishers); security (covering CCTV and access control, alarms, monitoring and service, security hardware); home improvement (coatings and fillers).

Main subsidiaries include: Angus; Kidde-Graviner; Kidde Thorn Fire Protection; Yale Security Products Ltd; Chubb Alarms Ltd; Chubb Fire Ltd; Chubb Union Locks Ltd; Chubb Wardens Ltd; Cuprinol Ltd; Hammerite Products Ltd; Polycell Products Ltd.

Main brands include: Chubb; Cuprinol; Hammerite; Kidde; Polycell; Yale.

UK employees: n/a

Charitable donations
1997: £217,000
1996: £184,000
1995: £209,000
1994: £55,000
1993: £151,000

Community support policy
The group's policy is to fulfil a responsibility, for the benefit of the community as a whole, to young people in the development of their talents. In 1997, support was given to programmes dedicated to the training of young people in music, sport and education.

The group continues to be an active sponsor of music with a long-standing commitment to the National Youth Orchestra, which reached its 50th year celebration in 1998. The Williams Fairey Brass Band enjoyed a successful year and are current All England Masters, as well as being the North West Champions.

Williams has maintained its commitment to Derby Boys' Grammar School and Landau Forte City Technology College.

In the area of sport, the group has maintained its level of sponsorship, particularly in the East Midlands, with lawn tennis, cricket and soccer benefiting from this active support.

In the arts, the company was the main sponsor for a recent Royal Shakespeare Company Gala performance of Hamlet performed before the Lord Mayor of London at the Barbican.

Promoting fire safety amongst the young is also an important part of Kidde's role in the community. Kidde International is sponsoring the Scouts' Fire Safety Badge, which means that half a million scouts throughout the UK will become aware of the dangers of fire. The badge's requirements include implementing various fire precautions and knowing what actions to take, and why, if faced with an outbreak of fire.

Applications
In writing to the correspondent, but note the above.

Willis Corroon Group plc

10 Trinity Square, London EC3P 3AX
0171-488 8111; Fax: 0171-488 8223
Website: www.williscorroon.com

Correspondent: Mrs Janice Ashby, Charities and Events Manager

Chief officer: *Chairman:* J Reeve

Year end	Turnover	Pre-tax profit
31/12/97	£652,000,000	£96,000,000

Nature of company business
The group is one of the largest international insurance and reinsurance intermediary, risk management and financial consultancy groups. The company's main UK locations are London and Ipswich.

Main subsidiaries include: Willis Faber and Dumas Ltd.

UK employees: n/a

Charitable donations
1997: £296,862
1996: £250,000
1995: £230,000
1994: £238,000
1993: £308,000

Total community contributions: £1,000,000 (worldwide)
Membership: *BitC %Club*

Community support policy
The company is a member of the PerCent Club and of Business in the Community. It supports a wide range of local charities in areas of company presence (ie. Birmingham, Cardiff, Ipswich, London and Maidstone) and charities in which a member of company staff is involved, as well as national charities. In 1997, many of the donations were to organisations supporting education, youth and general welfare programmes. Support is also given to the arts, medicine and armed services.

Main commitments in 1997 continued to be to Fairbridge in London, which received £65,000, and the Ipswich Education Initiative. Other major beneficiaries included: East London Partnership, Research into Ageing, Crisis and Disability Care Enterprise. Total community contributions worldwide in 1997 were £1,000,000. The main areas of non-cash support are arts sponsorship, good-cause sponsorship and gifts in kind. The company supports employee volunteering financially and assists employee fundraising, as well as operating the Give As You Earn payroll giving scheme.

Support is sometimes given to major overseas emergencies eg. the Polish flooding emergency appeal was given £5,000 in 1997. The company's subsidiaries give limited support to causes in their areas of operation. During the year £750,000 was given to organisations in the USA.

Exclusions
No response to circular appeals. No support for advertising in charity brochures; animal welfare charities; appeals from individuals; enterprise/training; environment/heritage; fundraising events; overseas projects; political appeals; science/technology; sport; or local appeals not in areas of company presence.

Applications
In writing to the correspondent. All donations are made through a Charities and Community Support Committee which considers requests received from staff, subsidiary companies and direct from charities. The response is positive in about 10% of cases, with emphasis on requests supported by staff members who are themselves working for community projects.

Willmott Dixon Ltd

34 Upper Brook Street, London W1Y 2NA
0171-409 2716; Fax: 0171-629 0013

Correspondent: John Bayliff, Company Secretary

Chief officers: *Chairman:* I Dixon; *Chief Executive:* C Enticknap

Year end	Turnover	Pre-tax profit
31/12/95	£143,630,000	£159,000

Nature of company business
A holding company for a group engaged in all sectors of the building industry.

UK employees: 1,048

Charitable donations
1995: £55,000
Membership: *BitC %Club*

Community support policy
The company stated in the 1996 PerCent annual report that it had continued to extend its level of contribution to charitable concerns. It did not give details of its support in the 1998 annual report, although it continues to be a member.

Wilson

Strong emphasis is placed on involvement by staff with their favoured charities, coupled with a commitment to support clients' preferred causes wherever possible.

Grants range upwards from £25, to an exceptional £10,000.

Exclusions
General and unsolicited appeals are not considered. No grants for local appeals not in areas of company presence or for overseas projects.

Applications
In writing to the correspondent.

Wilson Bowden plc

Wilson Bowden House, 207 Leicester Road, Ibstock, Leicester LE67 6WB
01530-260777; Fax: 01530-262805

Correspondent: Pauline Turnbull, Group Marketing Director

Chief officer: *Chairman:* D W Wilson

Year end	Turnover	Pre-tax profit
31/12/97	£459,600,000	£67,000,000

Nature of company business
The main activities are housebuilding, and property development and investment.
Main subsidiaries include: David Wilson Homes Ltd; Trenchwood Commercial Ltd; David Wilson Estates Ltd.

UK employees: 1,312

Charitable donations
1997: £35,000
1996: £58,200
1995: £39,000
1994: £18,000
1993: £18,000

Community support policy
Despite an increase in the pre-tax profits of the company of £26 million in 1997 compared to 1996, charitable donations decreased to £35,000.

The company has stated that it has no set policy, and both national and local appeals are considered. However, all the following were marked as being areas of support: advertising in charity brochures, appeals from individuals, the arts, children/youth, education, enterprise/training, environment/heritage, fundraising events, medical research, overseas projects, science/technology, sickness/disability charities, social welfare and sport.

Exclusions
The only areas not supported are animal welfare charities, elderly people, political appeals or religious appeals.

Applications
In writing to the correspondent.

Wogen Group Ltd

4 The Sanctuary, Westminster, London SW1P 3JS
0171-222 2171; Fax: 0171-222 5862

Correspondent: Ms Liz O'Dwyer, Personal Assistant to the Chairman

Chief officers: n/a

Year end	Turnover	Pre-tax profit
30/9/95	£253,429,000	£6,673,000

Nature of company business
The main activity of the company is metal trading.

UK employees: 56

Charitable donations
1995: £150,000
1994: £76,000

Community support policy
The company usually has a preference for local charities in Westminster and charities with which a member of company staff is involved. Causes supported fall into the following categories: the arts; children/youth; education; environment/heritage; medical research; sickness/disability charities, social welfare and homelessness. Grants range from £100 to £1,000 and may be for up to £2,000.

The company will provide financial support for employee volunteering and will match employee giving.

The company's subsidiaries in China support causes in their local areas.

Exclusions
No support for promotional work.

Applications
In writing to the correspondent.

Rudolf Wolff & Co Ltd

80 Cheapside, London EC2V 6EE
0171-836 1536; Fax: 0171-579 1234
Website: www.rwolff.com

Correspondent: Brian Barr, Chief Executive

Chief officer: *Chief Executive:* Brian Barr

Year end	Turnover	Pre-tax profit
31/12/98	£22,000,000	£3,600,000

Nature of company business
Commodity brokers.

UK employees: 120

Charitable donations
1998: £58,074
1997: £83,646
1996: £64,385
1995: £135,579
1994: £72,097
Membership: %Club

Community support policy

The company is a member of the PerCent Club and gives a full 1% of pre-tax profits to charitable causes. Grants are given through the Rudolf Wolff Charitable Trust and the charities committee is made up of all levels of company staff.

It prefers to support children/youth, elderly people, medical research, overseas projects, and sickness/disability charities. The company has a preference for charities relevant to company business and charities in which a member of company staff is involved. Grants to national organisations range from £250 to £5,000, and to local charities from £25 to £1,000.

In 1997, main grant beneficiaries included: Rainbow Trust Children's Charity, Tommy's Campaign, Winged Fellowship, Diana, Princess of Wales Memorial Fund and DEMAND.

The company supports employee volunteering by matching employee giving and fundraising.

Exclusions

No grants for political appeals, advertising in charity brochures, animal welfare charities, appeals from individuals, education, environment/heritage or religious appeals. Telephone requests are not encouraged.

Applications

In writing to the correspondent. All written requests received by the trust (with accompanying financial information) are considered by a staff committee. This committee meets about twice a year to consider all applications received in the previous six months.

Wolstenholme Rink PLC

Springfield House, Lower Eccleshill Road,
Darwen, Lancashire BB3 0RP
01254-873888; Fax: 01254-703430

Correspondent: Miss S J Banks, Company Secretary

Chief officers: *Chairmen:* P J E Rink and A A Rink

Year end	Turnover	Pre-tax profit
31/12/97	£83,952,000	£7,570,000

Nature of company business
Manufacture and merchandising of materials used in the international print industry.

Main subsidiaries include: Openshaw Ltd; Faust Thermographic Supply Ltd; Graphic Printing Chemicals Ltd.

UK employees: n/a

Charitable donations
1997: £62,568
1996: £47,124
1995: £55,600
1994: £44,057
1993: £74,287
Membership: %Club

Community support policy

The company is a member of the PerCent Club with charitable donations totalling over £62,000 in 1997. In addition to donations to charities, support is given to local enterprise agencies, schools and training schemes.

Charitable donations: Support is usually given to causes concerned with children/youth, elderly people, enterprise/training, environment/heritage, fundraising events, medical research, and sickness/disability charities. There is a preference for local appeals in areas of company presence (Bolton, Blackburn, Todmorden area). The company summarises its policy as follows:

- support our own employees
- support people in our own locality
- support local causes/charities.

The group's community involvement includes environmental regeneration and the education and training of young people. Divisional support of the local Groundwork Trust and its own internal Green Group continues. Employees work in their own time with the local communities on projects using Groundwork environmental expertise.

In 1997, main grant beneficiaries included: Guide Association – Bolton Divisions, the Bolton Lads and Girls Club, Darwen Masters Swimming Club, Blackburn and District Children's Homes and Blackamoor School PTA.

Exclusions

No response to circular appeals or national charities. No support for advertising in charity brochures, animal welfare charities, appeals from individuals, the arts, overseas projects, political appeals, religious appeals, science/technology, social welfare or sport.

Applications

In writing to the correspondent.

John Wood Group plc

John Wood House, Greenwell Road,
East Tullos, Aberdeen AB12 3AX
01224-851000; Fax: 01224-871997

Correspondent: Shirley Muir, Head of Corporate Communications

Chief officer: *Chairman:* Sir I C Wood

Year end	Turnover	Pre-tax profit
31/12/97	£467,000,000	£24,300,000

Nature of company business
Engineering services to the oil and gas, petrochemical and power-related industries.

UK employees: 3,500

Charitable donations
1997: £50,000
1996: £48,000
1995: £100,499
1994: n/a
1993: £81,300

Woolwich

Total community contributions: £100,000
Membership: *BitC %Club*

Community support policy

The company is a member of the PerCent Club and Scottish Business in the Community. In addition to cash donations, support is given through good-cause sponsorship, secondments and training schemes.

Charitable donations: Wood Group's objectives in making charitable donations are:

- to demonstrate that Wood Group is a good corporate citizen
- to provide benefit at an appropriate level to selected worthy causes
- to generate local or national publicity for the charity and Wood Group, when appropriate
- to ensure that Wood Group has good relationships in the communities where it does business
- to assist worthy causes that Wood Group employees already support.

In general the company will consider supporting charities which fall into the following categories:

- charitable causes in the categories of: arts, community, sports, education and environment
- charities that are already supported by a Wood Group employee
- charities that are local to Wood Group offices or bases.

The company only supports local community projects in areas of company presence (Grampian/Aberdeen) and projects in which employees are directly involved. National charities are generally not supported except in special circumstances, in which case the donation must receive approval from Sir Ian Wood.

Most grants range from £50 to £250, except for a few covenants and Gift Aid agreements which are larger. Main grant beneficiaries in 1997 included: Scotland Against Drugs, Haddo Choral & Operatic Society, Aberdeen University Quincentenary Appeal, Aberdeen International Youth Festival and Student Charity Appeal.

Employee involvement: The company encourages employee volunteering through financial support and matches employee fundraising. It has established an Employee Community Fund to support charities with which company employees are involved. Employees also participate in business–education partnerships, such as training young people in job interview skills.

Sponsorship: When sponsoring the arts, the company favours arts programmes with an educational bias, particularly involving youth groups. Education projects receiving long-term sponsorship include a Wood Group newsletter competition for primary school children, Livewire – a touring environmental theatre group, and Techfest – a festival of science and technology.

Exclusions

The following causes, are not likely to receive support: specific religious groups, political organisations, sports organisations with no Wood Group employee involvement, organisations without charitable status.

Applications

In writing to the correspondent. All requests for donations are reviewed monthly by the charity and community relations committee.

Woolwich plc

Watling Street, Bexleyheath, Kent DA6 7RR
0181-298 5000; Fax: 0171-298 4737
Website: www.woolwich.co.uk

Correspondent: Gail Johnson, Public Relations Coordinator

Chief officers: *Chairman:* Sir Brian Jenkins; *Chief Executive:* John Stewart

Year end	Turnover	Pre-tax profit
31/12/97	n/a	£455,700,000

Nature of company business
A leading provider of personal financial services and products, including mortgages, personal loans, insurance, unit trusts, and financial advice in the UK, and residential mortgage businesses in France and Italy. The Woolwich has around four million customers, more than 400 branches in the UK and nearly 150 Woolwich Property services estate agency branches.

UK employees: 7,149

Charitable donations
1997: £452,000
1996: £449,000
1995: £208,000
1994: £241,000
1993: £294,000
Membership: *ABSA*

Community support policy

The Woolwich's Community Involvement Programme provides support for national charities and organisations within the areas of the head offices in south east London and north Kent. The Woolwich will consider appeals for funding and resources for projects submitted by (a) charities, (b) voluntary organisations, and (c) educational organisations, situated within the above areas.

The major community affairs programme covers enterprise and the built environment, education and the national curriculum, and training for unemployed people.

The Woolwich provides help in the form of financial assistance, practical resources, advice, information and secondment for projects connected with enterprise and the environment, as well as training and education partnerships for young unemployed people.

The main area of non-cash support is arts sponsorship; in kind support is not quantified.

In 1998, the company supported over 150 community, arts, environmental and charitable organisations. The community involvement programme concentrates on work experience, teacher placement and curriculum projects, particularly in south east London and north Kent.

Donations are given to medical charities, and those supporting conservation and the arts and people who are disadvantaged. Main beneficiaries included Bexley and Greenwich Education Business Partnerships, Prince's Youth Business Trust, National Asthma Society, Crimestoppers and the Weston Spirit.

Charitable donations: The Woolwich will consider appeals for funding and support from organisations within the UK primarily directed towards:
- help for disadvantaged people, providing relief for human suffering and disabled people, with special heed being paid to appeals from south east London
- appeals of national importance
- building, housing and conservation causes. It prefers to support specified projects rather than core funding.

Grants to national organisations up to £20,000, and to local organisations up to £5,000.

In kind support: The Woolwich donates surplus equipment and furniture and gives professional advice for the production of annual reports and newsletters and computer hardware.

Employee involvement: A payroll giving scheme is operated. Staff are allowed company time off to volunteer, which may be backed up with financial support. The Woolwich also match employee fundraising and encourage staff to become school governors. A staff charitable fund, Reliefline, raises and distributes funds to charitable organisations and individuals. For further details contact Alan White, Reliefline, Woolwich plc, Watling Street, Bexleyheath, Kent DA7 6RR.

Education: The core purpose of the education programme is to help prepare young people to contribute effectively both to the life of the community and eventually to business and economic activity. Much of its support is linked to the National Curriculum Project. The Woolwich is involved in providing work experience to fifth and sixth formers, mainly in and around south east London, as well as an expanding curriculum-based programme for schools. It has sponsored industrial conferences, educational projects and school management training.

Environment: Support has been given to Kent Thames-side Groundwork Trust and Young Environmentalist of the Year.

Sponsorship: The Woolwich sponsors a range of regional events and organisations, with sponsorship ranging from £500 to £5,000. The company is a member of ABSA. The Woolwich was the principal sponsor of the Greenwich and Docklands International Festival, and the Woolwich Young Radio Playwrights' competition. It has also supported the National Children's Orchestra, the Mayor of Dartford's Art Bursaries, Bexley Arts Bursaries, Woolwich Junior Table Tennis League and Woolwich Ramsgate Week.

Exclusions
No support is given for fundraising events, advertising in charity brochures, individuals, purely denominational (religious) appeals, overseas projects, political groups or animal charities.

Applications
In writing to the correspondent. Applicants should specify the project for support and give full information on the funding required. Sponsorship proposals should be addressed to Charity Community & Arts: Gail Johnson, Public Relations Coordinator; Sports: Jane Adams, Advertising Services Controller.

WPP Group plc

27 Farm Street, London W1X 6RD
0171-408 2204; Fax: 0171-493 6819
Email: fmcewan@wpp.com
Website: www.wpp.com

Correspondent: Feona McEwan, Communications Director

Chief officers: *Chairman:* Hamish Maxwell; *Chief Executive:* Martin Sorrell

Year end	Turnover	Pre-tax profit
31/12/97	£7,287,300,000	£177,400,000

Nature of company business
Principal activity: the provision of communications services worldwide.

Main subsidiaries include: Ogilvy & Mather; J Walter Thompson; Conquest; Cole & Weber; MindShare; Research International; Millward Brown International; Kantar Media Research; BMRB International; IMRB International; Winona Group; Goldfarb Consultants; Hill and Knowlton; Timmons and Company; The Wexler Group; Carl Byoir & Associates; Buchanan Communications; Addison; Banner MacBride; BDG McColl; Coley Porter Bell; EWA; Henley Centre; Mando Marketing; Metro Group; Oakley Young; Primary Contact; Promotional Campaigns Group; Scott Stern Associates.

UK employees: 3,625

Charitable donations
1997: £200,000
1996: £300,000
1995: £300,000
1994: £253,000
1993: £200,000
Membership: *BitC*

Community support policy
The following policy relates to donations and support provided by the UK parent company. Support is also provided by the operating companies, particularly from the UK advertising agencies, J Walter Thompson and Ogilvy & Mather (see the addresses below).

WPP Group has a preference for appeals relevant to company business and charities in the areas of children and youth, medical, enterprise, sickness/disability and education. Other areas of support are advertising in charity brochures, appeals from individuals, the arts, elderly people, overseas projects, social welfare and sport. Grants to national organisations range from £100 to £40,000, and to local organisations from £100 to £5,000. No geographical area is given preference; each application will be considered on merit.

Main areas of non-cash support include gifts in kind (eg. donations of office equipment/office supplies to charities and children's hospitals), arts sponsorship and training schemes.

Wyevale

Applications

In writing to the correspondent.

J Walter Thompson: 40 Berkeley Square, London W1X 6RD. *Charity Co-ordinator:* Amanda Fisher.

Ogilvy & Mather: 10 Cabot Square, Canary Wharf, London E14 4QB. *Charity Co-ordinator:* Peter Walker.

Wyevale Garden Centres plc

Kings Acre Road, Hereford HR4 0SE
01432-276568; Fax: 01432-263289

Correspondent: Rosemary Stephens, Contracts Secretary

Chief officers: *Chairman:* B A Evans; *Managing Director:* R Hewitt

Year end	Turnover	Pre-tax profit
31/12/97	£63,008,000	£9,118,000

Nature of company business
Garden centres.

Main subsidiaries include: Great Gardens of England Investments Ltd.

UK employees: n/a

Charitable donations

1997: £64,000
1996: £52,000
1995: £54,000
1994: £37,000
1993: £32,000

Community support policy

The company prefers to support causes local to its garden centres (which appear to be throughout England and Wales), such as schools, gardening-related organisations and sports associations. In addition to direct donations the company undertakes good-cause sponsorship and joint promtions.

Applications

In writing to the correspondent.

Xerox (UK) Ltd

Bridge House, Oxford Road, Uxbridge UB8 1HS
01895-251133; Fax: 01895-254095

Correspondent: Tracy Anderson, Communications Department

Chief officer: *Managing Director:* V A Zelmer

Year end	Turnover	Pre-tax profit
31/10/95	£4,139,000,000	£570,000,000

Nature of company business
Principal activity: the marketing of Xerox products and services in the UK. Products range from small desktop plain paper copiers, printers and fax, to large volume document production and publishing systems. It also has a Supplies Business (Xerox Office Supplies) and a Facilities Management and Copy Centre Business (Xerox Business Services).

Xerox (UK) Ltd is the UK operating company for Xerox Ltd, which has its international HQ in Marlow, Buckinghamshire, and factories in Welwyn Garden City and Mitcheldean, Gloucestershire. There is also a research centre (EUROPARC) in Cambridge.

UK employees: 4,300

Charitable donations

1995: £300,000
1994: £90,000
1993: £79,000

Community support policy

The company makes major donations through the Xerox (UK) Trust (donations of £5,000 to £10,000), and smaller grants through the Community Relations Team (up to £500).

The Xerox (UK) Trust (Charity Commission number 284698) operates to provide several 'meaningful' donations to qualifying charities each year. The selection criteria are charities concerned with equality of opportunity especially for:

- disability
- education
- terminally-ill or disadvantaged youth.

All selected charities are local to areas where the company operates. The trust only makes donations in the region of £5,000 to £10,000 for specific projects.

In 1997, the trust's income was £69,000 with grants totalling only £29,000. Only seven grants were given, four of £5,000 to: Drugsline Chabad, REACT, Royal Academy of Music and St Basil's Centre for Homeless People. The recipients of smaller grants were Jubilee Sailing Trust, National Information Forum and Watford Peace Memorial Hospice.

The company is a member of the PerCent Club, it is also currently supporting the following: National Education Unit of Understanding British Industry, Employers Forum on Disability, Opportunity 2000, Jubilee Sailing Trust and King's Concert Symphonia.

The employee double up scheme provides 'like for like' donations for employee fundraising for registered charities.

Appeals outside the UK should be addressed to the local facility in the country of operation.

Exclusions

No support for purely denominational (religious) appeals, appeals from individuals or teams, sponsorship of individuals, teams or other fundraising events, advertising in charity brochures or purely denominational appeals. No support for charities concerned with 'non UK' activities or causes. Applications for overseas projects *must* be addressed to the local Rank Xerox operation in the country concerned.

Applications

Applications must be received, in writing, *between* 1 February and 1 March. They will not be acknowledged and those received outside the above dates will not be processed, nor will any correspondence be entered into. The trustees meet in March/April to consider applications. Those successful will be notified soon after a decision has been made. Unsuccessful applications will receive a pre-printed standard reply, and should not re-apply again for a minimum of three years. Telephone enquiries are not welcome – only written applications will be considered.

Yattendon Investment Trust plc

Barn Close, Yattendon, Newbury, Berkshire RG16 0UX
01635-202909; Fax: 01635-202564

Correspondent: See below

Chief officer: *Chairman:* R P R Iliffe

Year end	Turnover	Pre-tax profit
29/6/97	£59,857,000	£8,350,000

Nature of company business
The main activities are newspaper publishing, marina management and development, property management and development, and health care.

Main subsidiaries include: Burton Daily Mail Ltd; Staffordshire Newspapers Ltd; Staffordshire Newsletter Ltd; Cambridge Newspapers Ltd; Herts & Essex Newspapers Ltd; MDL Management PLC; Marina Developments Ltd; Dean & Dyball Ltd; Hartridge Investments Ltd.

UK employees: 1,989

Charitable donations
1997: £85,000
1996: £79,000
1995: £77,000
1994: £78,000
1993: £78,000

Community support policy

The company is linked with the Iliffe Family Charitable Trust by reason of funding. Applications to the company will merely duplicate one to the trust, and result in unnecessary expenditure.

The trust has an income of around £150,000 a year. Further details can be found in *A Guide to Major Trusts Volume 2*.

Applications

The trust is administered from the same address as the company. Applications should be addressed to J R Antipoff, one of the trustees. Only successful applications are acknowleged.

Yorkshire Bank plc

20 Merrion Way, Leeds LS2 8NZ
0113-247 2000; Fax: 0113-242 0733

Correspondent: The Secretary, Yorkshire Bank Charitable Trust

Chief officers: *Chairman:* Lord Clitheroe;
Chief Executive: D T Gallagher

Year end	Turnover	Pre-tax profit
30/9/97	£609,823,000	£154,938,000

Nature of company business
The group provides a comprehensive banking system in the North and Midlands. The bank is a member of the National Australia Bank Group.

Main subsidiaries include: Yorlease Ltd; Northern and General Finance Ltd; Sorecard Ltd; Allerton House Investment Co Ltd; Eden Vehicle Rentals Ltd.

UK employees: 6,482

Charitable donations
1997: £114,000
1996: £148,000
1995: £114,000
1994: £119,000
1993: £114,541

Community support policy

Charitable donations: The donations of £114,000 include those made directly by the bank and those made through the Yorkshire Bank Charitable Trust. Recipients must be registered charities and within the area covered by branches of the bank ie. in England from north of the Thames Valley to Newcastle upon Tyne. The trust's guidelines state that it supports:

- charities engaged in youth work
- facilities for less able-bodied and mentally disabled people
- counselling and community work in depressed areas
- the arts and education, occasionally.

The trustees are unlikely to make more than one donation to a charity within any 12-month period. Grants are usually one-off for a specific project or part of a project, ranging from £100 to £1,000.

In 1997, the trust had assets of £861,000 and an income of £138,000. Grants totalled £82,000 and were categorised as follows:

Arts £1,500
Buildings £50
Conservation/environment £2,600
Youth/job creation £1,250
Physical/mental health £9,000
Aged/disabled £3,000
Social/general £13,000
Education/research £6,150
Covenant/special £45,000

The most recent grants list available was that for 1993 when grants totalled £115,000. About 200 grants were made with most for under £500. The largest was £20,000 to the University of Leeds Foundation. 14 other grants were for £1,000 or more, most in Yorkshire, including Yorkshire Youth & Music (£8,000), Wheatfields Hospice and Selby Abbey Trust (both £2,500), Sheffield Common Purpose (£2,000) and Age Concern Leeds (£1,000).

36 grants were to churches and nearly half of the remaining grants were to charities based in Yorkshire.

Education: The bank sponsors a BA Hons Financial Course and Professor of Financial Services at Sheffield Hallam University.

The bank runs a School Bank Savings Scheme which aims to introduce schoolchildren to financial management, through manual or computer-based systems, and can also be used for National Curriculum project work in secondary schools. The bank also helps schools to stimulate interest in extracurricula activities through a conservation grants award scheme administered by the British Trust for Conservation Volunteers. This scheme is available to all schools operating a Yorkshire Bank Savings Scheme. Schools involved in environmental or conservation projects undertaken on school premises may apply for grants of up to £100 and additional special cash awards are made for projects of particular merit.

The arts: The bank sponsors organisations and events throughout the UK. It has sponsored the Leeds International Festival, Harrogate International Festival, Oldham Girls Choir and the Faure Festival and York Singing Day.

Exclusions

Applications from individuals, including students, are ineligible, as are appeals for advertising in charity brochures, animal welfare charities, environment/heritage, medical research, overseas projects, political appeals, religious appeals and science/tehnology. No grants for general appeals from national organisations.

Applications

In writing to the correspondent, including relevant details of the need the intended project is designed to meet. Grants decisions are made by a donations committee which meets twice a month; responses may take three or four weeks to process. Requests for community involvement should be addressed to the Secretary to the Yorkshire Bank Charitable Trust and for arts sponsorship to the Corporate Communications Manager.

Yorkshire Building Society

Yorkshire House, Yorkshire Drive, Bradford BD5 8LJ
01274-740740
Website: www.ybs.co.uk

Correspondent: Joanne Howarth, Community Involvement Officer

Chief officers: *Chairman:* D F Roberts; *Chief Executive:* D Anderson

Year end	Turnover	Pre-tax profit
31/12/96	n/a	£45,225,000

Nature of company business
Building society.

UK employees: n/a

Charitable donations
1996: £60,000
1995: £60,000

Community support policy

The Yorkshire Building Society Foundation was set up in April 1998. All requests made to the society will be referred to the foundation. There are five trustees, three of which are independent.

The foundation's priorities are to support registered charities or good causes operating in local communities and involving the elderly, anyone who is vulnerable (particularly children or people with special needs) and people suffering hardship. Other local charities and organisations that the society's staff wish to support will be considered. The maximum amount given is £500, as the foundation wants 'to help as many people in as many areas as possible'.

The foundation's geographical area of operation is limited to the UK, principally to areas where the society's members live and work and where the branches or subsidiaries are located. The foundation works through the society's branches and head office departments to support local charities and good causes in the areas they think are most important. It prefers to assist with specific items rather than a general fund.

The following (non-exhaustive) list provides examples of projects or activities which the foundation would consider as likely to fall within its main areas of focus:

- Anything specifically to help priority cases of vulnerable people, people who are in need such as children, the elderly, or anyone with special needs, or people who are suffering hardship.
- People who are in genuine financial need – to be genuine a person does not have to be classed as destitute.
- Activities relating to the relief of hardship. 'Hardship' does not have to be permanent or long-term. It may be possible to consider grants where temporary hardship has been caused by job loss or long-term sickness.
- Help to be given to those who are sick, or with special needs, or learning difficulties and/or who are physically disabled.
- Provision towards the welfare of sick and neglected animals and the prevention of cruelty to animals.
- the provision of land, buildings or machinery for public use, eg. community centres, specially adapted buses, other vehicles or equipment. This may extend to provision of equipment for youth clubs.
- The resettlement and rehabilitation of offenders and drug abusers.
- The provision of relief for victims of natural and civil disasters.
- Help to be given to an individual beneficiary eg. special equipment for a disabled person or for a child in need.
- Help given to particular geographic or social areas of benefit, or groups of people where it can be shown that such areas or groups are in need. Examples would be groups of people suffering hardship, pupils at a special school, residents of a particular community or an individual within a community.

The foundation received an initial £200,000 from the society in 1998.

Exclusions

The following fall outside the foundation's priority areas:
- Fundraising for the purposes of pursuing political or propagandist activities
- The support of religious activities or the advancement of religion (although this would not prevent consideration for support to members of a group or community that was otherwise in need)

- Any fundraising or activity under which those organising the fundraising activity would or could have a personal benefit
- Provision of support for a person or people who do not come within the priority of the foundation or are not in genuine need
- Provision of support for an activity where assistance is otherwise available from national or local organisations or authorities, ie. from local social services, local housing authorities, Department of Social Services, or other authorities
- Any organisation considered to be illegal or which may act illegally, or where funds are raised from, or for immoral purposes
- Provision of sport generally or seeking to achieve excellence or professionalism in sport. For example this would exclude any sponsorship activities, or the provision of equipment for sports teams. The only exception to this would be, for example, some sporting activity for children who are in need, or disabled people, or other people suffering hardship
- Support for individuals or groups engaged in expeditions or projects requiring them to raise funds to enable them to particpate
- Proposals which are purely concerned with raising funds for other organisations or charities and/or where such funds are likely to go to the administration expenses of such organisations eg. provision of sponsorship to an individual or individuals participating in another charitable event
- Carnivals or shows which are concerned with mainly entertaining the public and where there is no control over the eventual destination of funds raised
- Any purposes concerned with the promotion of friendship or international friendship eg. town twining associations
- Projects or activities outside the foundations geographic area.

Applications
In writing to the correspondent. Initially applications will be assessed by the branches or head office departments then forwarded to the foundation. Decisions are made continuously by the trustees.

Yorkshire Electricity Group plc

Wetherby Road, Scarcroft, Leeds LS14 3HS
0113-289 2123; Fax: 0113-289 5466
Website: www.yeg.co.uk

Correspondent: Regan Cooper, Community Affairs Manager

Chief officers: *Chairman:* E L Draper;
Chief Executive: J M Chatwin

Year end	Turnover	Pre-tax profit
31/3/96	£1,332,000,000	£219,000,000

Nature of company business
Principal activities: generation, distribution and supply of electricity in the UK, together with the supply of gas.

Main subsidiaries include: Scarcroft Insurance Ltd; Regional Power Generators Ltd; Yorkshire Energy Ltd; Cyril Exelby Ltd; Scarcroft Leasing Ltd; Scarcroft Investments Ltd; Scarcroft Holdings Yorkshire Cogen Ltd.

UK employees: n/a

Charitable donations
1996: £77,400
1995: £160,353
1994: £179,533
1993: £205,539

Total community contributions: £228,000

Membership: *BitC*

Community support policy
Total community contributions in 1995/96 were £228,000, of which a third was given in charitable donations. The main area of non-cash support is in the form of secondments. It also operates a payroll deduction scheme for employee giving, and while not matching this, it does operate a £ for £ matching scheme for employee fundraising (up to a maximum of £1,000).

Charitable donations: The company has a preference for local charities in areas of company presence and appeals relevant to company business. Preferred areas of support: children and youth, social welfare, education, recreation, elderly people, fundraising events, sport, sickness/disability, economic regeneration, environment and heritage and the arts.

Some of the projects supported recently have included the following.

A Sporting Chance for Disabled People – sponsorship of a scheme to encourage the region's governing bodies of sport to make more activities available for people with disabilities. The programme is backed by a government Sportsmatch award and is part of the company's Building on Ability Programme to provide opportunities for disabled people to take part in sporting, cultural and leisure events.

South Yorkshire & Humberside Police Lifestyle Project – to provide meaningful activities for young people during the summer holidays, with a beneficial effect on the community eg. reduced vandalism.

Poles & Trees Campaign – a partnership with the British Trust for Conservation Volunteers to plant over 2,000 trees at a number of sites across Yorkshire & Humberside.

National Playing Fields Association – a regional competition in association with the Sports Council aiming to reward schools which are developing their involvement with sport.

Yorkshire Electricity Cup – a pre-season tournament organised through West Riding FA involving some of the region's professional football clubs. The competition raises money for the Sports Aid Foundation and the development of junior football at grass roots level.

Live Music Now – for a programme of concerts in special needs schools and adult training centres.

Education: Regular contact is maintained with schools and colleges through visits, work shadowing, help with projects, teacher placements and the promotion of electrical safety awareness.

The arts: The company is a member of ABSA and sponsors local events in its operating area. Organisations/projects supported include Northern Ballet Theatre Schools Dance Programme, West Yorkshire Playhouse, Remould Theatre, Yorkshire Sculpture Park, Yorkshire Mining Museum, Live Music Now and Opera North.

Exclusions

No response to circular appeals, individual schools, joint fundraising projects with other commercial organisations, project running costs, appeals from individuals, purely denominational appeals, enterprise/training, advertising in charity brochures, science/technology, local appeals not in areas of company presence, large national appeals, overseas projects, medical research, animals or political campaigning or pressure groups. No donations of company equipment, including office furniture and vehicles.

Applications

On a form available from the correspondent. Applications should be made in September/October for the following financial year budgets (April – March).

Information available: The company has published a brochure titled: *Community Matters,* which gives examples of its current community relations programmes. A copy of its policy of sponsorship and donations is available.

Yorkshire – Tyne Tees Television Ltd

The Television Centre, Leeds LS3 1JS
0113-243 8283

Correspondent: Ms Chris Hirst, Press and Regional Affairs Manager

Chief officer: *Chairman:* Ward Thomas

Year end	Turnover	Pre-tax profit
31/12/96	n/a	£30,223,000

Nature of company business
Principal activities: the production and broadcasting of television programmes and the sale of television advertising.

Main subsidiaries include: Yorkshire Television Ltd; Tyne Tees Television Ltd.

Main locations: Leeds; Grimsby; Hull; Lincoln; London; Sheffield; York.

UK employees: 1,092

Charitable donations

1996: £341,000
1995: £312,000
1994: n/a
1993: £311,000
Membership: *BitC*

Community support policy

The company is now owned by Granada Group which has a separate entry in this guide. However, it has its own budget for appeals from groups which have charitable status and are based in the company's operating area. Most of the budget for supporting education goes to the Northern School for Film and Television in Leeds, and other education-related appeals are unlikely to be successful.

We do not know the current size of the company's charitable budget, but it is substantially lower than the £341,000 of 1996.

Exclusions

No grants to individuals.

Applications

In writing to the correspondent. There is a regional affairs committee which considers appeals.

Yorkshire Water plc

2 The Embankment, Sovereign Street, Leeds LS1 4BG
0113-234 3234; Fax: 0113-234 2322

Correspondent: Cheryl Wright, Community and Education Manager

Chief officers: *Chairman:* Brandon Gough; *Managing Director:* Johnson Cox

Year end	Turnover	Pre-tax profit
31/3/98	£635,400,000	£205,600,000

Nature of company business
Water and sewerage services.

Main subsidiaries include: Yorkshire Environmental Solutions Ltd; BDR Waste Disposal Ltd; Derbyshire Waste Ltd; WasteNotts Ltd; Arbre Energy Ltd; Ridings Insurance Co Ltd; 3C Waste.

UK employees: 4,333

Charitable donations

1998: £250,000
1997: £100,000
1996: £100,000
1995: £97,000
1994: £125,500

Total community contributions: £315,000

Membership: *BitC %Club*

Community support policy

The company is a member of the PerCent Club and gives a detailed report on its community involvement in their report, from which the following information is taken.

The company has for several years focused support on young people, economic regeneration and the environment. It is now developing a programme with greatly strengthened focus on employee volunteering and the response to the community interests of its own staff.

Programmes recently run, some of which are continuing, include skills development for young people on the estates of Hull, consultancy and other support for deprived youngsters in Leeds, working with the *Hull Daily Mail* on its Reading Passport Scheme, working with the Sheffield Lifestyles Project and People United Against Crime as routes to creating partnerships with the local police and other organisations actively supporting them. In Bradford and Leeds, two major Barnardo's projects have received financial support from a fund established with the charity in 1996 and 1997. A donation was also given to the National Coal Mining Museum in Wakefield to help them launch a fundraising appeal. Other main beneficiaries have included Calderdale Community Foundation, South Yorkshire Foundation, QED Ethnic Minorities, Coalfields Learning Campaign and National Park Annual Conference.

The company aims to support the economic development of the region through membership of Rotherham Economic Partnership, Sheffield City Liaison Group and several education and business partnerships.

It has supported education in partnership with the local authority, by sponsoring a water efficiency programme in Calderdale schools which are receiving free audits and being fitted with water-efficient devices in a pilot programme to help them reduce costs and protect the environment. In Kirklees, the company sponsored the Kirklees Riverside Project and provided accommodation for the Prince's Youth Business Trust.

Other initiatives supported include the Leeds-based Swimsave scheme which improves swimming skills for people of all ages; the Bradford Centenary Festival through its creation of a community fund; and the launch of the Business in the Environment Programme in Yorkshire.

Yorkshire Water Community Trust

This is a trust set up in 1995 by the company to help those in financial need meet the payments of their water bills. In other words, the company is giving money via a trust to individuals in need who then pay the company back the money they owe. In other words the tax benefits of the charitable trust are helping the company recover the cost of unpaid bills. The trustees report for 1996/97 stated that grants may also be made to other charities, although this does not appear to have happened yet.

In 1997/98, the company paid £199,500 to the trust. As the total donations reported by the company were £250,000, this would imply that only £50,000 was available for other causes. The trust received 1,421 applications and made 670 grants.

Exclusions

No grants for purely denominational appeals, local appeals not in areas of company presence, appeals from individuals, political appeals, medical research, overseas projects, religious appeals, science/technology, social welfare or animal welfare.

Applications

In writing to the correspondent.

Young & Rubicam Holdings UK plc

Greater London House, Hampstead Road, London NW1 7QP
0171-387 9366; Fax: 0171-388 6570

Correspondent: John Kelaff, Finance Director

Chief officers: n/a

Year end	Turnover	Pre-tax profit
31/12/95	£283,188,000	£1,317,000

Nature of company business
Principal activities: advertising, public relations, design and marketing practitioners.

Main subsidiaries include: Mornington Productions Ltd; Prima Europe Ltd; Sudler & Hennessey Ltd; Cohn & Wolfe Ltd; Landor Associates/Europe PLC; Burson-Marsteller Ltd; Marsteller Advertising Ltd; Wunderman Cato Johnson Ltd; City and Corporate Counsel Ltd; Corporate Vision Ltd; MML Field Marketing Ltd; Marketing Dynamic International Ltd; Burmarst UK Ltd; Allan Burrows Ltd; Phoenix Travel Ltd.

UK employees: 1,358

Charitable donations
1995: £51,997
1994: £37,206
1993: £32,947
Membership: %Club

Community support policy

The company is a member of the PerCent Club, although the latest figures available were for 1995. It prefers to support charities in the areas of children and youth, medical care, the elderly and the arts.

Exclusions

No support for circular appeals, appeals from individuals, purely denominational (religious) appeals, local appeals not in areas of company presence, the arts, sport or overseas projects.

Applications

In writing to the correspondent. The company decides in January on the charities to be supported that year.

Yule Catto & Co plc

Temple Fields, Harlow, Essex CM20 2BH
01279-442791; Fax: 01279-641360

Correspondent: Richard Atkinson, Company Secretary

Chief officers: *Chairman:* Lord Catto; *Chief Executive:* A Walker

Year end	Turnover	Pre-tax profit
31/12/97	£268,574,000	£38,050,000

Nature of company business
Principal activities: speciality chemicals and building products. Holliday Chemical Holdings PLC were acquired in January 1998.

ZENECA

Main subsidiaries include: Arrow Chemicals; Autoclenz; Brencliffe; Dimex; Greenhill Chemical Products; Nielson Chemicals; Revertex Chemicals; Techsol; Synthomer; Harlow Chemical Co; Viking Polymers; Coxdome; Screenbase; Unilock; Williaam Cox Plastics Stockholding.

UK employees: 2,474

Charitable donations

1997: £40,000
1996: £30,000
1995: £35,000

Community support policy

The company supports an established list of charities, mainly in the fields of children and youth, education, sickness/disability, social welfare and medical. Both local and national charities are supported.

Exclusions

No support for animal welfare, circular appeals, fundraising events, advertising in charity brochures, political appeals, purely denominational (religious) appeals, local appeals not in areas of company presence, the arts, sport or overseas projects.

Applications

In writing to the correspondent, but please note that as the company has charities which it supports regularly, unsolicited applications are unlikely to be successful.

ZENECA Group PLC

15 Stanhope Gate, London W1Y 6LN
0171-304 5000; Fax: 0171-304 5188/5196
Website: www.zeneca.com

Correspondent: Jane Juniper, Appeals Committee

Chief officers: *Chairman:* Sir Sydney Lipworth; *Chief Executive:* Sir David Barnes

Year end	Turnover	Pre-tax profit
31/12/97	£5,194,000,000	£1,081,000,000

Nature of company business
Research, manufacture and sale of pharmaceuticals, agrochemicals, seeds and specialty chemicals and allied products.

UK employees: 12,300

Charitable donations

1997: £5,700,000
1996: £700,000
1995: £700,000
1994: £500,000
1993: £300,000

Total community contributions: £7,800,000 (worldwide)

Membership: *BitC*

Community support policy

The company's declared donations figure of £5.7 million includes the first donation of £5 million to the Zeneca Science Teaching Trust (see below). £700,000 was given to other charities, to which the following policy applies.

A committee meets quarterly and prefers to support health, nutrition, young people and social welfare. Other areas of support include animal welfare charities, the arts, education, enterprise/training, environment/heritage, medical research, science/technology and sickness/disability charities. Support from the Corporate Office in London is only given to UK-based charities and charities local to the office or to manufacturing sites around the UK. Overseas aid is given by the overseas branches/companies.

Donations can be approved and sent out between meetings of the Appeals Committee. Main beneficiaries during the year included Marie Curie Cancer Care, Roy Castle Lung Foundation, Florence Nightingale Foundation, Help the Hospices and Shelter.

Zeneca operates the Give As You Earn payroll giving scheme.

The Zeneca Science Teaching Trust

Zeneca established this trust to provide financial assistance to help improve the teaching of science in the UK – with particular emphasis for the first two or three years on the primary school level. The company is going to provide £20 million by the year 2000 to the trust.

The trust is currently working on the development of a portfolio of teacher training models which may be adopted by educational providers in conjunction with groups of up to 20 local schools. Once the model most suited to the particular training needs of a particular group of schools and the relevant provider has been selected, a bid for funding can be made to the trust. Four pilot projects are currently being assessed, and two more started in January 1999. Following this development work, models for achieving improvements in science in primary schools will be widely disseminated in the year 2000, and further opportunities for schools and providers to work together will be available then.

Further enquiries about the trust should be addressed to the Trust Administrator, Mrs Jean Smith, Yeo Vale, Spreyton, Nr Crediton, Devon EX17 5AX.

Zeneca Schools Life Science Programme

The programme was launched in 1994 aimed at promoting science among secondary school pupils. It consists of a series of competitions, based on project work. The schools of the winning students receive a financial contribution towards science-related teaching equipment.

Exclusions

No support for circulars, individuals, political/discriminationary groups, religious appeals, sport, anything contrary to company business or, with very limited exceptions, capital projects.

Applications

In writing to the correspondent. Circular letters, whether or not addressed to an individual and not signed personally, will not be supported unless accompanied by a personal letter. National appeals should be addressed to the head office above, local appeals should be sent to the appropriate local office.

PerCent Club Members

The PerCent Club is a group of companies who commit themselves to contribute at least 0.5% of pre-tax profits or 1.0% of dividends in contributions to the community. This will include cash donations as well as other forms of support. The aim is to promote increased levels of support by the private sector both for charities generally but also for social issues which most concern businesses and the communities in which they operate. Many of the main company donors are members.

It should not be assumed that these companies are necessarily the best to approach when seeking support. They should already be giving the required amount for membership, and will not necessarily have extra resources to give away. This list is over a year old and although we were informed that there have been several changes, a complete list was not available.

Abbott Mead Vickers
Acatos & Hutcheson
Action Planning
AEA Technology
Alexander Russell
Allied Domecq
Allied Dunbar Assurance
Allied Irish Banks
Allied Partnership Group
AMEC
Anglia Television Group
Arcadia
Armour Trust
Arthur Andersen
Associated Newspapers
Avon Cosmetics

Bain United Kingdom
Barclays Bank
Bayer UK
Beale
Bentalls
Bernard Matthews
Bernstein Group
Bestway Cash & Carry
Betterware
A F Blakemore & Son
Blue Circle Industries
BMP DDB Needham Worldwide
BNFL
BOC Group
Bodycote International
Bombardier Aerospace Short Brothers
The Boots Company
Brintons
British Aerospace
British Airways
The British Land Company
BT
Bucknall Austin
Bunzl
BUPA

Burmah Castrol
Burnson-Marsteller

Cadbury Schweppes
Calor Gas
Campbells (UK)
Canon (UK)
Cargill UK
Centrica
Charnos
Charter
Christie's International
Citibank
Claremont Garments
Close Invoice Finance
The Co-operative Bank
Coats Viyella
Coca-Cola GB & Ireland
Cooper-Parry
Coopers & Lybrand
Crone Corkill Group

De La Rue
Deloitte & Touche
Deutsche Morgan Grenfell
DHL International UK
Diageo
Dixons Group
DMB & B Holdings
Donaldsons
Dow Chemical Co
Dresdner Kleinwort Benson

Eastern Group
Economist Group
J A Elliott (Holdings)
EMI
Enterprise
Ernst & Young
Espree Leisure
Eurotherm

F I Group
Forbes Trust
Foster Wheeler Energy

Geest Holdings
Gerrard & National
Michael Gerson
Girobank
GKN
GlaxoWellcome
Grant Thornton
Greycoat Group
The Grosvenor Estate
Guinness Mahon Holdings

Harris Ventures
Healey & Baker
Hewden Stuart
Highland Distilleries Co
Hillier Parker May & Rowden
HSBC Investment Bank
Hunting
Hyder

IBM United Kingdom
Indespension

Johnson Matthey
S C Johnson Wax
Jones Lang Wootton
Just Rentals

Kellogg's
KPMG

Ladbroke Group
John Laing
Lamont Holdings
Legal & General Group
Linklaters & Paines
Littlewoods

PerCent Club members

Lloyds TSB Group
Louis Newmark
Low & Bonar
LucasVarity
MacFarlane Group (Clansman)
E D & F Man
Manchester Airport
Manweb
Marc Rich & Co
Marks & Spencer
J & H Marsh & McLennan
Martini & Rossi
McCarthy & Stone
McDonald's Restaurants
MCL Group
Medical & Media Communications
John Menzies
Merck Sharp & Dohme
Meridian Broadcasting
Meyer International
Midland Bank
Miller Group
Mitsubishi Corporation UK

National Power
National Westminster Bank
Nestlé Holdings (UK)
Neville Russell
The Newcastle Breweries
NFC
Northern Electic
Northern Foods
Northern Ireland Electricity
Northumbrian Water Group
NORWEB
Norwich Union Insurance Group
Nuclear Electric
Nycomed Amersham

Ocean Group
Oxford Instruments Group

Pacific Investments
Pannell Kerr Forster
Peabody Trust

Pearl Assurance Company
Pearson
Pentland Group
Pentos
Persimmon
Peugeot Motor Co
Pifco Holdings
Pilkington
Portsmouth & Sunderland News
Powell Duffryn
PowerGen
Price Waterhouse
Procter & Gamble
Prudential Corporation
Psion

Reckitt & Colman
Reed Executive
Reuters Holdings
Richard Ellis
Richer Sounds
Rio Tinto
J Rothschild Group
Royal Bank of Scotland

J Sainsbury
Save & Prosper Group
Savills
Schroders
Sedgwick Group
Severn Trent
Sharpe & Fisher
Simmons & Simmons
Slough Estates
W H Smith
Smith & Nephew
Smiths Industries
Sony United Kingdom
Spencer Stuart
Stanley Leisure Organisation
Stephenson Harwood
Sun Life & Provincial
Sunley Holdings
SWEB

Tarmac
Tate & Lyle
The Telegraph Group
Tesco
Texaco
Thorn Group
Thorntons
3i
3M UK
T I Group
TNT (UK)
Top Technology
Toyota Motor Manufacturing (UK)
Tullis Russell & Co
Tyne Tees Television

Unilever (UK) Holdings
Unipart Group of Companies
United Biscuits (Holdings)

Vaux Group
Virgin Group of Companies

Warburtons
Wembley
Wessex Water
Whatman
Whitbread
Wickes
Wiggins Group
Willis Corroon Group
Willmott Dixon
Wostenholme International
John Wood Group
Woolwich Building Society

Xerox (UK)

Yorkshire Water
Young & Rubicam

Zetters Group

Professional Firms Group

What is a Professional Firms Group?

A Professional Firms Group (PFG) is made up of a group of professional practices each of which have offered to provide their professional services free of charge to voluntary and community groups in the local community.

The guiding principle of the group is that members approach this sort of work in just the same way as they would for any other fee-paying customer. The only difference is that the community client is not charged for the work which is done.

Members of a group include surveyors, architects, accountants, solicitors, public relations specialists, property consultants and engineers.

What help can they provide?

The professional firms undertake short assignments which include feasibility studies, structural surveys, marketing and business plans, legal and accountancy advice and property valuations.

Will my project be eligible?

You must be a community-based not-for-profit organisation working for the social and economic regeneration of your local area and should fit within the following criteria:

- you must have a track record of working successfully with the local community
- you must not have the funding for the specific piece of work to be done nor be retaining paid advisors to do the work
- if you are a branch of a national organisation, you must be locally constituted and prove that neither the expertise nor the funding to pay for the work is available centrally
- your project must be realistic and viable; and
- your governing body must authorise the involvement of the PFG.

When will a project not qualify?

- applications for assistance with litigation will not be considered;
- help is generally not given to animal welfare organisations whose primary focus is overseas aid; and
- assistance to religious groups will only be offered if the project benefits the wider community.

What do I do now?

If you have a project in mind which could benefit from help from the Professional Firms Group, please get in touch. Local group contacts are listed below.

What will happen then?

If your project is appropriate, you will be asked to fill in a standard questionnaire. It may also be necessary for you to meet with a representative from the PFG to develop a fuller brief for the assignment. A summary of your project will then be taken to the group who will decide whether or not your project meets the eligibility criteria and if there is a firm available to do the work. A meeting will then be arranged between yourself and the interested professional firm.

Local group contacts

Belfast
Jenny Allen
Business in the Community
c/o European components Ltd
770 Upper Newtownards Road
Dundonald
Belfast BT16 0UL
Tel: 01232-410410

Birmingham
Denise Snipe
Business in the Community
c/o Cadbury Ltd
83 Bournville Lane
Birmingham B30 2LU
Tel: 0121-451 2227

Bolton & Bury
Lois Patel
CSDC Mere Hall
Thomasson Park
Mere Hall Street
Bolton BL1 2QT
Tel: 01204-396979

Brighton
Lynne Richards
Business in the Community
15 West Street
Brighton BN1 2RE
Tel: 01273-770075

Bristol
Alan Davies
Business in the Community
165 Whiteladies Road
Bristol BS8 2RN
Tel: 0117-923 8750

Cambridge
Ann Scott
DHL International Ltd
The Links Industrial Park
Trafalgar Way
Bar Hill
Cambridge CB3 8UD
Tel: 01954-789970

Cardiff
Roger Green
Business in the Community
6th Floor
Empire House
Mount Stuart Square
Cardiff CF1 6ND
Tel: 01222-483348

Professional Firms Group

Edinburgh
Jennifer McCulloch
Scottish Business in the Community
Romano House
43 Station Road
Corstorphine
Edinburgh EH12 7AF
Tel: 0131-334 9876

Gloucester
Norman Pickering
Business in the Community
Chargrove House
Shurdington
Cheltenham GL51 5GA
Tel: 01452-509541

Hull and East Riding
Elaine Spencer
Business in the Community
Room 234, Queens House
Paragon Street
Hull HU1 3ND
Tel: 01482-225416

London
Mandy Jones & Claire Bourne
Business in the Community
44 Baker Street
London W1M 1DH
Tel: 0171-224 1600

Manchester
John Tolley
Business in the Community
c/o Chamber of Commerce
56 Oxford Street
Manchester M60 7HU
Tel: 0161-228 3363

Merseyside
Deryk Martindale
Business in the Community
26 Hope Street
Liverpool L1 9BX
Tel: 0151-709 2774

Norfolk
Gary Towers
Partnership House
25 Avenue Road
Wymonham
Norfolk NR18 0QG
Tel: 01953-601975

North Staffordshire
Elizabeth Cornforth
Stoke-on-Trent Community Partnership
3 Counties House
Festival Way
Stoke-on-Trent ST1 5PX
Tel: 01782-281666

North Wales
Business in the Community
11A Vaughan Street
Llandudno
North Wales LL30 1AB
Tel: 01492-870924

North West Ireland
See Belfast

North Yorkshire
Pam Lee/Julie Palfreeman
Business in the Community
Progress House (1st Floor)
99 Bradford Road
Pudsey
Leeds LS28 6AT
Tel: 0113-236 1888

Nottingham
Margaret Blount
Business in the Community
2nd Floor
12 Pilcher Gate
The Lace Market
Nottingham NG1 1QE
Tel: 0115-911 6666

Oxfordshire
Peter Mudie
Business in the Community
44 Baker Street
London W1M 1DH
Tel: 0171-224 1600

Plymouth
Chris Carter
County House Office Centre
12/13 Sussex Street
Plymouth PL1 2HR
Tel: 01752-221552

Portsmouth
Marion Dawson
Portsmouth & South East Hampshire Partnership
Regional Business Centre
4th Floor, Baltic House
Kingston Crescent
Portsmouth PO2 8QL
Tel: 01705-666622

South Derbyshire
Jane Stretton
Business in the Community
7th Floor, St Peter's House
Gower Street
Derby DE1 1SB
Tel: 01332-364784

South Yorkshire
Jackie Bird
Business in the Community
The Management Suite
1 The Oasis
Meadowhall Centre
Sheffield S9 1EP
Tel: 0114-261 0846

Stafford
Andrew Gough, Community Officer
Stafford Borough Council
Civic Offices
Riverside
Stafford ST16 3AQ
Tel: 01785-233181

Sutton
Ian Beever
Sutton CVS
Unilink House
21 Lewis Road
Sutton SM1 4BR
Tel: 0181-770 4861

Swansea
See Cardiff

Teeside
Brent Godfrey
Tees Valley Tomorrow
Unit 20
Manor Way
Belasis Hall Technology Park
Billingham
Cleveland TS23 4HN
Tel: 01642-330102

Thanet
Jane DeRose
Business in the Community
The Business Centre
NatWest Bank
13 Cecil Square
Margate
Kent CT9 1QY
Tel: 01843-291222

Tyneside
Avril Gibson
Business in the Community
Design Works
William Street
Felling
Tyne & Wear NE10 0LP
Tel: 0191-469 5333

West London
Jane Hickie
West London Leadership
Elliott House
Victoria Road
Park Royal
London NW10 6NY
Tel: 0181-453 0910

West Yorkshire
Tie Doepel
Business in the Community
Progress House (First Floor)
99 Bradford Road
Pudsey
Leeds LS28 6AT
Tel: 0113-236 1888

Wirral
Pat & Paul Wilson
21 Magazine Brow
Wallasey
Merseyside L45 1HP
Tel: 0151-630 2225

Business in the Community Members

Business in the Community aims to make *community involvement a natural part of successful business practice, and to increase the quality and extent of business activity in the community.* It exists to work with companies to mobilise resources (skills, expertise, influence, products and profits) to promote social and economic regeneration. There are several main programmes including: Employees in the Community; Regeneration; Education; Race for Opportunity; Business in the Environment; Opportunity 2000. The Per Cent Club and Professional Firms Group (see separate listings in this Guide) are also initiatives of Business in the Community.

The head office is : 44 Baker Street, London WIM 1DH (0171-224 1600). There are also ten regional offices:

Northern Ireland (01232-739639); Wales (01222-483348); North East (0191-469 5333); Yorkshire & Humberside (0113-236 1888); North West (01925-239625); West Midlands (0121-451 2227); East Midlands (01332-258331); South West (0117-923 8750); South East (0171-224 1600).

There is an independent, but associated organisation in Scotland (see list on page 372). Scottish Business in the Community, Romano House, 43 Station Road, Corstorphine, Edinburgh EH12 7AF (0131-334 9876).

Member companies

Abbey National
Abbott Mead Vickers BBDO
ABN AMRO Hoare Govett
ABSA
ADTRANZ
AEA Technology
Allen & Overy
Alliance & Leicester
AMEC
American Express Europe
Arthur Andersen & Co
Anglia Railways
Anglian Water
Aquascutum
Arcadia
ARCO British
ARRIVA
Asda Stores
Ashurst Morris Crisp
Association of British Chambers of
    Commerce
WS Atkins
The Automobile Association
Avon Cosmetics
Axa Sun Life

BAA plc
B&Q Plc
Bain United Kingdom Inc
Baker & McKenzie
Bamford Hall Holdings

Bank of England
Bankers Trust International
Barclays Bank
BASF
Bass
BAXI Partnership
Bell Pottinger
The Benefits Agency
BG
BICC
Blue Circle Industries
BOC Group
Bombardier Aerospace Shorts
Booker
Boots Company
Bradford & Bingley Building Society
Brand Leonard
Bristol & West Building Society
Bristol Port Company
Bristol Water
British Aerospace
British Airways
British American Tobacco
British Energy
The British Land Company
British Nuclear Fuels
British Petroleum Company
British Steel (Industry)
BT
BTR
Leo Burnett
Bunzl

BUPA
Burmah Castrol
Burson-Marsteller

C & A
Cable & Wireless Communications
Cadbury Ltd
Cadbury Schweppes
Calor Gas
Camelot Group
Cameron McKenna
Canadian Imperial Bank of Commerce
Candover Investments
Canon (UK)
Cap Gemini UK
Capital Action
Caradon
Cazenove & Co
Central Broadcasting
Centrica
CGU
Charter
Charterhouse
Child Support Agency
Church Commissioners
CIMA
Citibank NA
Clifford Chance
Cluttons Daniel Smith
Co-operative Bank
Coats Viyella
Coca-Cola GB & Ireland

Business in the Community members

Compass Group
Confederation of British Industry
Cookson Group
Corporation of the City of London
Coutts & Company
Credit Suisse First Boston
The Crown Estate
Cummins Engine

Daily Mail & General Trust Plc
Dean Clough Industrial Park Ltd
Debenhams
Deloitte & Touche
Department for Education & Employment
Department of the Environment, Transport & the Regions
Department of Trade & Industry
DHL International (UK)
Diageo
Dixons Group
Donaldsons Chartered Surveyors
Dresdner Kleinwort Benson
Duchy of Cornwall
Dun & Bradstreet

East Midlands Electricity
Eastern Group
ECC International Europe
EDS
Electra Fleming
EMI
Enterprise
Ernst & Young
Esso UK

FI Group
Financial Times
FirstGroup
Fishburn Hedges
Albert Fisher Group
Fishmongers' Company
Forbes Trust
Ford Motor Company
Forte
FPD Savills
Freshfields
Friends Provident

Gallaher Group
Gardiner & Theobald
GE Capital Europe
GE Lighting
General Electric Company
General Utilities
Gestetner Holdings
GlaxoWellcome
Goldman Sachs International
Granada Group
Granada Television

Grant Thornton
Greenalls Group
Grey Communications
R Griggs Group
Grimley
Groundwork Foundation
GTECH UK Corporation
Guardian Royal Exchange
GWR Group

Hans Haenlein Architects
Halifax plc
Halliburton Brown & Root
SG Hambros
Hasbro UK
Healey & Baker
Hewlett-Packard
HFC Bank
Hillier Parker May & Rowden
Historical Royal Palaces
The Home Office
Honda UK Manufacturing
Honeywell Control Systems
Hyder

IBM United Kingdon
ICI
ICL
IMI
The Industrial Society
Institute of Directors
Invesco Europe

Jaguar Cars
Johnson Controls
Johnson Matthey
S C Johnson Wax
Jones Lang Wootton

Kellogg Marketing and Sales Co
Kimberly-Clark
Kingfisher
KPMG

Ladbroke Group
John Laing
Land Securities
The Law Society
Legal & General Group
Lehman Brothers International
LIFFE
Linklaters & Alliance
Littlewoods Organisation
Liverpool Daily Post & Echo
Lloyd's Commuity Programme
Lloyds TSB Group
Local Government Association
London Electricity
Lorien
Lovell White Durrant

LucasVarity
LWT (Holdings)

Mailcom
E D & F Man
Manchester Airport
Mansfield Brewery
Manweb
Marks & Spencer
Mars Confectionery
J & H Marsh & McLennan
Mazars Neville Russell
McBride
McDonald's Restaurants
McKinsey & Co Inc UK
Merck Sharp & Dohme
Merrill Lynch Mercury Asset Management
Midland Bank
Midlands Electricity
Thomas Miller & Co
Mitsubishi Corporation UK
MORI

Nabarro Nathanson
National Centre for Volunteering
National Council Voluntary Organisations
National Grid Company
National Power
National Westminster Bank
A Nelson & Co
Nestle Holdings (UK)
The Newcastle Breweries
Newmond
Next
NFC
Nortel
Northcliffe Newspapers
Northern Electric
Northern Foods
Northern Ireland Electricity
Northern Ireland Office
Northumbrian Water Group
Norwich Union
Novartis
Nycomed Amersham

Ocean Group
Olayan Europe
Oracle Corporation UK
Orange
Oxford Instruments Group

Panasonic UK
Pannell Kerr Forster
Peabody Trust
Pearl Assurance
Pearson
Pentland Group

Business in the Community members

Perot Systems (Europe)
Perpetual
Peugeot Motor Company
Pfizer
Philips Electronics
Phillips & Drew
Pilkington
Pinsent Curtis
Port of London Authority
The Post Office
Post Office Counters
PowerGen
PricewaterhouseCoopers
Procter & Gamble UK
Prudential Corporation
Psion
Publicis

Racal Electronics Group
Railtrack Group
Random House UK
Ranger Oil (UK)
The Rank Group
Reckitt & Colman
Redrow Group
Reuters Holdings
Rio Tinto
RJB Mining
RMC
Rolls-Royce
N M Rothschild & Sons
Rover Group
Royal Bank of Scotland
Royal Institution Chartered Surveyors
Royal London Insurance
Royal Mail
Royal & Sun Alliance
Rural Development Commission

Safeway
J Sainsbury
Salomon Smith Barney

Save & Prosper Group
Saxton Bampfylde Hever
Schroders
Charles Schwab Europe
Scottish & Newcastle
Scottish Office
Seagram Distillers
Sears
Sedgwick Group
Severn Trent
Shell UK
Simmons & Simmons
SKF (UK)
Slaughter & May
Slough Estates
David S Smith (Holdings)
Smith & Nephew
SmithKline Beecham
Smiths Industries
Sony United Kingdom
South Western Electricity
Southern Electric
Southern Water
Spencer Stuart
St George
St James's Investments
St James's Place Capital
Standard Chartered Bank
Sumitomo Bank

Tarmac
Tate & Lyle
Telewest Communications
Tesco
Texaco
Thames Water
Thorn
Thorntons
3i
3M United Kingdon
TI Group
TNT (UK)

Top Technology
Toshiba Corporation
Toyota Motor Manufacturing (UK)
Trades Union Congress
TRW Systems Integration Group

Unigate
Unilever (UK) Holdings
Union Railways
Unipart Group of Companies
United Biscuits (Holdings)
United Utilities
Unity Trust Bank

VAG (United Kingdon)
Reg Vardy
Vaux Group
Vauxhall Motors
Video Arts (Distribution)

W H Smith Group
Walker Snackfoods
J Walter Thompson Co
SBC Warburg Dillon Read
Warburtons
Wella
Welsh Office
Wessex Water
Whitbread
Willis Corroon Group
Willmott Dixon
Wilson (Connolly) Holdngs
WPP Group
Workspace Group

Yorkshire Bank
Yorkshire Electricity Group
Yorkshire-Tyne Tees Television
Yorkshire Water
Young & Rubicam

Zeneca Group
Zurich Financial Services

Business in the Community members

Members of Scottish Business in the Community

Adam & Company plc
Alcan Smelting & Power UK
Arthur Andersen & Co
Arcadia Group plc
Arjo Wiggins Fine Papers Ltd
Bank of England
Bank of Scotland
Barr Holdings Ltd
The Boots Company plc
BP Exploring Operating Co Ltd
British Airports Authority
British Airways Scotland
Brodies WS
Canon (Scotland) Business
   Machines Ltd
Capital Copiers (Edinburgh) Ltd
CBI Scotland
CGU Insurance
Child Support Agency
Clydesdale Bank plc
Coats Viyella plc
COSLA
D B Projects
Daily Record & Sunday Mail
DX Communications
The Edrington Group Ltd

Ethicon Ltd
James Finlay plc
Forward Scotland
Highlands and Islands Enterprise
Johnson & Johnson
Johnston Press plc
Kidsons Impey
KPMG
Kwik-Fit Holdings plc
John Laing Construction Ltd
Marks & Spencer plc
John Menzies Ltd
Midland Bank plc
Morrison Construction Group plc
Motherwell Football Club
PRM Marketing Ltd
Prudential Corporation plc
Quality Scotland Foundation
Right Track
Royal Bank of Scotland plc
Royal Mail Scotland & NI
Rural Forum
Alexander Russell plc
J Sainsbury plc
The Scotsman Publications Ltd

Scottish Amicable Life Assurance
   Society
Scottish Brewers Ltd
Scottish Chambers of Commerce
Scottish Enterprise
Scottish Gas
Scottish Homes
Scottish Life Assurance Co
The Scottish Office
ScottishPower
Scottish Widow's Fund & Life
   Assurance Society
SCVO
Shaw Marketing & Design Ltd
Shell UK Limited
Simmers of Edinburgh
CR Smith Glaziers (Dunfermline) Ltd
Standard Life Assurance Co
D C Thomson
Trainer Outdoor Advertising
TSB Bank Scotland plc
United Biscuits
United Distillers and Vintners
The Weir Group plc
Whitbread in the Community
John Wood Group plc

Arts & Business

Arts & Business (formerly ABSA – Association for Business Sponsorship of the Arts) exists to *promote and encourage partnerships between the private sector and the arts, to their mutual benefit and to that of the community at large.* Its priority is to provide a service for its members but a number of its services are of value to arts organisations as well. Among its activities are: annual award ceremonies; the Business Sponsorship Incentive Scheme (a government-funded incentive to businesses to sponsor the arts for the first time or increase their commitment); Business in the Arts (aiming to improve the quality of management in the arts through business involvement). ABSA produces a quarterly bulletin and an annual report.

Contacts

ABSA: Nutmeg House, 60 Gainsford Street, Butlers Wharf, London SE1 2NY (0171-378 8143).

Scotland: Room 204, West Port House, 102 West Port, Edinburgh EH3 9HS (0131-228 4262).

Northern Ireland: 185 Stramillis Road, Belfast BT9 5DU (01232-664736).

Wales: c/o Welsh Arts Council, 9 Museum Place, Cardiff CF1 3NX (01222-221382).

North: Dean Clough Office Park, Dean Clough, Halifax, West Yorkshire HX3 5AX (01422-345631).

Midlands: Central House, Broad Street, Birmingham B1 2JP (0121-634 4104).

Members *(including members of Creative Forum for Culture and the Economy* *)*

A1 Design
Abbey National plc
Admiral
AEA Ltd
AEA Technology
Alliance & Leicester (NI)
Allied Domecq PLC *
Amerada Hess Ltd
American Airlines
Amoco (UK) Exploration Co
AM-PM Errington
Arthur Andersen *
Andersen Consulting
Arts & Industry Ltd
Arts Council of England
Arts Council of Wales
Ashquay Group Plc
AT & T Ltd

BAT Industries Plc
Baillie Gifford & Co
Bank of Ireland
Bank of Scotland
Banque Internationale a Luxembourg
Barclays Bank PLC
Bass Brewers Ltd
Bass Ireland Ltd
Bayer plc
Belfast Telegraph Newspapers Ltd
Birmingham City Council
Birmingham International Airport Ltd
Bloomberg LP
BMW (GB) Ltd
BMW Finance (GB) Ltd
BOC Group
Booker Plc
The Boots Company PLC
BP in Scotland
Bradford & Bingley Building Society
Bristol & West plc
British Aerospace Military Aircraft Division
British Council
British Energy plc
British Film Institute
BG plc
British Land Company PLC
British Petroleum Company Plc
British Petroleum Oil UK Ltd (NI)
Britsh Steel Plc
British Telecommunications plc *
Bruce Naughton Wade
Brunswick Group *
BT Northern Ireland
Burnside Citygate Communications Ltd
Business in the Community

C T Bowring (Charities Fund) Ltd
Cable & Wireless
Cable Tel Northern Ireland Ltd
Caledonian Brewery Ltd
Capital & Regional Properties Ltd
Cardiff Marketing Limited
Carlton Communications plc
Central Broadcasting
Channel 4 Television Corporation
Chevron UK Ltd
Christopher Jonas
City Acre Property Investment Trust Ltd
City of Bradford Metropolitan Council
Clydesdale Bank
Co-operative Union Ltd
Coats Viyella Plc
Coca-Cola Bottlers (Ulster) Ltd
Collyer-Bristow
Commercial Union plc
Confederation of British Industry
Coolkeeragh Power Ltd
Coopers & Lybrand
Coopers & Lybrand (NI)
Crafts Council
Credit Suisse
Crowcroft & Partners
Crown Buckley Ltd

David Patton & Sons NI
Dean Clough Limited
De Beers Centenary
Debenhams Plc
Deloitte & Touche
Dentsu Europe Ltd
Deutsche Morgan Grenfell
Dillon Bass Limited
Downtown Radio/Cool FM
Drambuie Liquer Co Ltd
Du Pont De Nemours International
Dunadry Inn & Country Club
Dunfermline Building Society

Eastern Group plc *
Edinburgh Solicitors Property Centre
Elf Exploration UK plc
EMI Group plc
The Energy Group plc
English Heritage
Ernst & Young
Eversheds Phillips & Buck
Experian Ltd

Faloon Construction
Faulds Advertising Ltd
Anthony Fawcett Consultants
Fiat UK Limited
Fina plc
Financial Times
First National Building Society
First Trust Bank

Arts & Business

Forward Publishing
Friends Provident

Gallaher Limited (NI)
Gallaher Limited
Gartmore Investment Management
General Accident plc
General Electric Company plc
Gilbeys of Northern Ireland Ltd
Girobank plc
Glaxo Wellcome plc
Gotch Saunders & Surridge
Great North Eastern Railway
Grey Abbey Estates
R Griggs Group Ltd
Grimmit Holdings Ltd
Groupe Chez Gerard plc
Guinness plc
Arthur Guinness Son & Co (NI) Ltd

Habitat UK Ltd
Halifax plc *
Hammond Suddards Solicitors
Hastings Hotels Group
Headland Food Ltd
Helix Associates Ltd
Honeywell Limited
Horton's Estate Ltd
HSBC Holdings plc

IBM UK Ltd (NI)
IBM United Kingdom Limited
ICI
The Irish News Ltd

J Sainsbury plc
Jaguar Cars Ltd
JBA International Ltd
J & H Marsh & McLennon (UK) Ltd
John Laing Plc
Johnson Matthey Plc
Kahn Thomas Shankland
Kallaway (Consultants & Management) Ltd
Karen Earl Limited
Kimberly-Clark Ltd
Konica Peter Llewellyn Ltd
KPMG

Laganside Corporation
Legal & General Group Plc
Lehman Brothers
Lehmann Communications
Lisney Estate Agents
Lloyds Bank (Wales)
Lloyds TSB Group Plc
London Docklands Development Corpn
London Electricity Plc
London Weekend Television
Loot Ltd

Mactaggart Scott & Co Ltd
Maersk Air Ltd
Manchester Airport plc
Manweb Plc
Marks & Spencer *
Marks & Spencer Northern Ireland
Mars UK Limited
Marsh Christian Trust
Maskreys Ltd
McCain Foods (GB) Ltd
McCoubrey & McClelland
Merrill Lynch Europe Plc

Midland Bank Plc
Midland Bank Plc (Wales)
Midlands Electricity plc
Milton Keynes Borough Council
Mishcon de Reya
Mobil Oil Co Ltd (NI)
Mobil Services Company Ltd
Mont Blanc
Montupet (UK) Ltd
Moore Stephens
Morgan Stanley & Co International ltd
Museums & Galleries Commission

N M Rothschild & Sons Ltd
National Grid Co Plc
National Heritage Memorial Fund
NatWest Group plc *
NatWest Life
NatWest Retail Banking Services
Nestlé UK Ltd
Newton Investment Management
Next Retail Ltd
Nicholson & Bass Ltd
North West Water
Northern Bank Limited
Northern Electric plc
Northern Foods plc
Northern Ireland Electricity plc
Northern Rock
Nortel
Northumbrian Water Group Plc
Nottingham City Council

Orange plc *

P & O Properties Ltd
Panasonic UK Ltd
Paul Monaghan Chartered Architect
Pearl Assurance plc
Pearson plc
Perfecseal Ltd
Perrier Vittel (UK) Limited
Peugeot Motor Company plc
Phillips, Fine Art Auctioneers
PowerGen plc
Premier Waters Limited
Price Waterhouse
Principality Building Society
Project Planning International
Prudential Corporation plc *

Railtrack plc
REL Consultancy Group
Reuters Ltd
Rio Tinto plc
Rodney Miller Associates
Rover Group Ltd
Royal & Sun Alliance Insurance Group plc
Royal & Sun Alliance (NI)
The Royal Bank of Scotland plc
Royal Insurance Holdings plc
Royal Mail North East
Royal Mail North Wales & North West
Royal Mail Northern Ireland
Royal Mail of Scotland & Northern Ireland

S C Johnson Wax
S4C
Saga Group Ltd
Schroders Ltd
Scottish & Newcastle Breweries
Scottish Hydro-Electric plc

Scottish Power plc
Scottish Media Group
Scotwork Management Consultants
Sea Containers Ferries Scotland
Seagram Europe & Africa *
Sedgwick Noble Lowndes
SEEBOARD plc
Severn Trent plc
Shandwick NI
Shanghai Tang *
Sheffield City Council
Shell UK Limited
Shiseido Co Ltd
Siemens plc
Silent Night Holdings plc
S J Berwin & Co
Sotheby's
SWALEC
Spero Communications
St David's Hotels Ltd
St Regis Paper Company Ltd
Standard Chartered plc
Stewarts Supermarkets plc

3M United Kingdom Plc
TACK International
Tarmac PLC
Telewest Communications Scotland
Tennants Auctioneers
Tesco Stores Ltd
TEXACO Ltd
The Times Supplements Limited
TI Group plc
Toshiba Info. Systems (UK) Ltd
TOTAL
Translink
TSW Consultancy Ltd

Ulster Bank Limited
Ulster Carpet Mills (Holdings) Ltd
Ulster Television plc
Unilever plc
Union Bank of Switzerland
UNISON
United Distillers plc
United Utilities plc

Vendome Luxury Group
Vertex Data Science Ltd
Victorian Arts Centre Trust
VISA
Vision Information Consulting Ltd
Walker Morris
Warehouse Systems Ltd
Warwick International Group Ltd
WCRS
Welbeck Golin/Harris Communications Ltd
Welsh Development Agency
West Merchant Bank Limited
Whitbread Beer Co, Magor
Whitbread PLC
Wm Morrison Supermarkets plc
Wolff Olins
Woolwich plc
Workplace Systems plc
WPP Group plc

Yorkshire Cable Communications
Yorkshire Electricity Group plc
Yorkshire Tyne Tees Television

Zeneca Limited

Omitted companies

About 60 companies which were included in the last edition do not appear in this guide, at least not under the same name. We have categorised them as follows:

1. Name changes
Amedo Crown UK plc (now Asprey Holdings)
Northern Ireland Electricity PLC (now Viridian Group)
Rank Xerox (UK) Ltd (now Xerox UK)
SWEB Holdings Ltd (now South West Electricity plc)
Watson & Philip plc (now Alldays)

2. Takeovers, mergers, demergers
Amersham International plc (now Nycomed Amersham)
BAT Industries plc (now British American Tobacco)
Beneficial Bank plc (now part of Household International)
Commercial Union plc (now CGU)
Courtaulds plc (now Akzo Nobel)
Dalgety plc (now PIC International)
East Midlands Electricity plc (now part of PowerGen)
Energy Group plc (Within Eastern Group)
General Accident plc (now CGU)
Grand Metropolitan PLC (now Diageo)
Guinness PLC (now Diageo)
Kwik Save Group plc (now part of Somerfield)
London & Manchester Group plc (now part of Friends' Provident)
Magnox Electric plc (now British Energy)
Marshall Food Group Ltd (now Grampian Foods)
Midland Bank plc (now trading under HSBC)
PPP Healthcare Group plc (now part of Guardian Royal Exchange / AXA Sun Life)
Short Brothers plc (now Bombardier Aerospace – Short Brothers)
Sun Life Assurance Society plc (now AXA Sun Life)
VSEL PLC (now Marconi Marine)

3. Companies which now give under £40,000 or for which no recent information was available
Abbott Laboratories Ltd
ANZ Banking Group Ltd
AXA Equity & Law plc (now AXA Sun Life)
Babcock International Group PLC
Blackwell Science Ltd
Bluebird Toys PLC
Cape plc
CIA Group plc
Citibank
DAKS Simpson plc
Duchy of Cornwall
Felixstowe Dock & Railway Co
First Choice Holidays plc
Fyffes Group Ltd
Gestetner Holdings PLC
Grey Communications Group Ltd
Guinness Peat Group plc
John Henderson Ltd
Hitachi Europe Ltd
Kuoni Travel Ltd
London International Group plc
Lonrho plc
Mayne Nickless Europe plc
Merril Lynch Europe plc
Millennium & Copthorne Hotels plc
Miller Group Ltd
Mott Macdonald Group Ltd
National Car Parks Ltd
Reed International
T & N plc
Twil Ltd
Reg Vardy plc
Waste Management International plc

Useful contacts

In this section we list national agencies which may be helpful in the context of company giving, under the general headings employees, sponsorship, enterprise and training, education, donations, promoting good practice, media, general and informal contacts.

Employees/professional advice

Business in the Community
44 Baker Street, London W1M 1DH (0171-224 1600)

Chartered Surveyors Voluntary Service
12 Great George Street, Parliament Square, London SW1 3AD (0171-3343788)

Community Service Volunteers
237 Pentonville Road, London N1 9NJ (0171-278 6601)

National Association of Volunteer Bureaux (NAVB)
New Oxford House, 16 Waterloo Street, Birmingham B2 5UG (0121-633 4555)

National Centre for Volunteering
Regents Wharf, 8 All Saints Street, London N1 9AL (0171-520 8900)

Pre-Retirement Association of Great Britain & Northern Ireland
9 Chesham Road, Guildford, Surrey GU1 3LS (01483-301170)

Professional Firms Group
c/o Business in the Community, 44 Baker Street, London W1M 1DH (0171-224 1600)

REACH (Retired Executives Action Clearing House)
Bear Wharf, 27 Bankside, London SE1 9ET (0171-928 0452)

Retirement Trust
19 Borough High Street, London SE1 9SL (0171-378 9708)

Sponsorship

Community Links
105 Barking Row, London E16 4HQ (0171-473 2270)

Arts & Business
Nutmeg House, 60 Gainsford Street, Butlers Wharf, London SE1 2NY (0171-378 8143)

For regional contacts see section on Arts & Business members.

Groundwork Foundation
85–87 Cornwall Street, Birmingham B3 3BY (0121-236 8565)

Enterprise & training

Common Purpose
Companies House, 55–71 City Road, London EC1Y 1BB
There are also 44 regional offices.

Community Development Foundation (CDF)
60 Highbury Grove, London N5 2AG (0171-226 5375)

Local Enterprise Agencies
There are over 300 local enterprise agencies all over the country which provide advice and training to small businesses and to people setting up in business.

Education

Confederation of British Industry
Centre Point, 103 New Oxford Street, London WC1A 1DU (0171-379 7400)

Council for Industry and Higher Education (CIHE)
100 Park Village East, London NW1 3SR (0171-468 2211)

Industrial Society
Robert Hyde House, 48 Bryanston Square, London W1H 7LN (0171-479 2000)

Useful contacts

Donations

Charities Aid Foundation
Kings Hill, West Malling, Kent ME19 4TA (01732-520000)

Charities Trust
c/o John Moores Building, 100 Old Hall Street, Liverpool L70 1AB (0151-235 2222)

Charity Commission
London: Harmsworth House, 13–15 Bouverie Street, London EC4Y 8DP (0870-333 0123)
Liverpool: 2nd Floor, 20 Kings Parade, Queen's Dock, Liverpool L3 4DQ (0151-703 1500)
Taunton: Woodfield House, Tangier, Taunton, Somerset TA1 4BL (01823-345000)

Gifts in Kind UK
PO Box 140, 4 St Dunstan's Hill, London EC3R 5HB (0171-204 5003)

Promoting good practice

Business in the Community
44 Baker Street, London W1M 1DH (0171-224 1600)

Scottish Business in the Community
Romano House, 43 Station Road, Corstorphine, Edinburgh EH1 7AF (0131-334 9876)

Charities Tax Reform Group
12 Little College Street, London SW1P 3SH (0171-222 1265)

The Corporate Responsibility Group
31 Great Peter Street, Westminster, London SW1P 3LR (0171-222 2112)

Directory of Social Change
London – Stephenson Way, London NW1 2DP (0171-209 5151)
Liverpool – Federation House, Hope Street, Liverpool L1 9BW (0151-708 0136)

EIRIS Services
80–84 Bondway, London SW8 1SF (0171-735 1351)

Out of This World
52 Elswick Road, Newcastle-upon-Tyne NE4 6JH (0191-272 1601)

The Per Cent Club
c/o Business in the Community, 44 Baker Street, London W1M 1DH (0171-224 1600)

The Prince of Wales Business Leaders Forum (PWBLF)
15–16 Cornwall Terrace, Regent's Park, London NW1 4QP (0171-467 3600)

Media

BBC Appeals Unit
PO Box 7, London W12 8UD (0181-735 5057)

Campaign for Press & Broadcasting Freedom
8 Cynthia Street, London N1 9JF (0171-278 4430)

Channel Four Television Co
124 Horseferry Road, London SW1P 2TX (0171-396 4444)

CSV Media
237 Pentonville Road, London N1 9NJ (0171-278 6601)

ITV Network Centre
200 Gray's Inn Road, London WC1X 8YZ (0171-843 8000)

Media Trust
3–6 Alfred Place, London WC1E 7EB (0171-637 4747)

General company information

Companies House
Crown Way, Cardiff CF4 3UZ (01222-380801)

Trades Union Congress (TUC)
Congress House, 23–28 Great Russell Street, London WC1B 3LS (0171-636 4030)

Industrial Common Ownership Finance Ltd
115 Hampstead Road, Handsworth, Birmingham B20 2BT (0121-523 6886)

Industrial Common Ownership Movement Ltd
Vassalli House, 20 Central Road, Leeds LS1 6DE (0113-246 1737)

British Urban Regeneration Association
33 Great Sutton Street, London EC1V 0DX (0171-253 5054)

Urban & Economic Development Group
19 Store Street, London WC1E 7DH (0171-436 8050)

Young Enterprise
Ewart Place, Summertown, Oxford OX2 7BZ (01865-311180)

Informal contacts

Association of Inner Wheel Clubs in Great Britain & Northern Ireland
51 Warwick Square, London SW1V 2AT (0171-834 4600)

Rotary International in Great Britain & Ireland
Kinwarton Road, Alcester, Warwicks B49 6BP (01789-765411)

Index

Abbey:
    Abbey National plc 48
Abbott:
    Abbott Mead Vickers plc 49
Acatos:
    Acatos & Hutcheson plc 49
AEA:
    AEA Technology plc 50
Aggregate:
    Aggregate Industries plc 50
Air:
    Air Products plc 51
Airtours:
    Airtours plc 51
Akzo:
    Akzo Nobel UK plc 52
Albright:
    Albright & Wilson plc 52
Alldays:
    Alldays plc 53
Allders:
    Allders plc 53
Alliance:
    Alliance & Leicester plc 53
Allied:
    Allied Domecq PLC 54
    Allied Dunbar Assurance plc 55
    Allied London Properties plc 56
AMEC:
    AMEC plc 57
Amerada:
    Amerada Hess Limited 57
Andersen:
    Arthur Andersen 58
    Andersen Consulting 59
Anglian:
    Anglian Water plc 59
Antofagasta:
    Antofagasta Holdings plc 60
Aon:
    Aon UK Ltd 60
Arcadia:
    Arcadia Group plc 61
Argos:
    Argos plc 61
Arjo:
    Arjo Wiggins Appleton plc 62
Arriva:
    Arriva plc 62
ASDA:
    ASDA Group plc 63
Asprey:
    Asprey Holdings UK Ltd 64
Associated:
    Associated British Foods plc 64
    Associated British Ports Holdings PLC 65
Astra:
    Astra Pharmaceuticals Ltd 65
Avon:
    Avon Cosmetics Ltd 66
    Avon Rubber plc 66
AXA:
    AXA Provincial Insurance plc 67
    AXA Sun Life Assurance plc 67
BAA:
    BAA plc 68

Bader:
    Scott Bader Company Ltd 69
Baird:
    William Baird plc 71
Bamford:
    J C Bamford Excavators Ltd 71
Bank:
    Bank of England 72
    Bank of Scotland 72
Barclays:
    Barclays PLC 73
Barlow:
    Barlow International PLC 74
BASF:
    BASF plc 75
Bass:
    Bass plc 76
Batley:
    L Batley (Holdings) Ltd 77
Bayer:
    Bayer plc 77
BBA:
    BBA Group plc 77
BCH:
    BCH Group plc 78
Bellway:
    Bellway plc 78
Bentalls:
    Bentalls plc 78
Berkeley:
    Berkeley Group plc 79
Bestway:
    Bestway (Holdings) Ltd 79
Betterware:
    Betterware plc 80
BG:
    BG plc 80
BHP:
    BHP Petroleum Ltd 82
BICC:
    BICC plc 82
Birmingham:
    Birmingham International Airport plc 83
    Birmingham Midshires Building Society 83
Biwater:
    Biwater PLC 84
Black:
    Peter Black Holdings plc 84
Blue:
    Blue Circle Industries PLC 85
BMP:
    BMP DDB Ltd 86
BMW:
    BMW GB Ltd 86
BOC:
    BOC Group plc 87
Body:
    Body Shop International Plc 88
Bombardier:
    Bombardier Aerospace – Short Brothers plc 89
Booker:
    Booker plc 90
Boots:
    The Boots Company PLC 91

BPB:
    BPB plc 92
Bradford:
    Bradford & Bingley Building Society 93
Bristol:
    Bristol & West plc 93
Bristol-Myers:
    Bristol-Myers Squibb Holdings Ltd 94
Britannia:
    Britannia Building Society 94
Britannic:
    Britannic Assurance plc 95
British:
    British Aerospace plc 96
    British Airways plc 97
    British Alcan Aluminium plc 97
    British American Tobacco plc 98
    British Energy plc 98
    British Land Company plc 99
    British Nuclear Fuels plc 99
    British Petroleum Company plc 100
    British Sky Broadcasting Group plc 101
    British Steel plc 102
    British Sugar plc 103
    British Telecommunications plc 103
    British Vita PLC 105
Brixton:
    Brixton Estate plc 106
BTP:
    BTP plc 106
BTR:
    BTR plc 107
Bulmer:
    H P Bulmer Holdings plc 107
Bunzl:
    Bunzl plc 108
BUPA:
    BUPA Ltd 108
Burmah:
    Burmah Castrol plc 109
C & A:
    C & A Stores 110
Cable:
    Cable & Wireless plc 111
Cadbury:
    Cadbury Schweppes plc 112
Cadogan:
    Cadogan Estates Ltd 112
Caledonia:
    Caledonia Group Services Ltd 113
Camellia:
    Camellia plc 113
Camelot:
    Camelot Group plc 114
Canon:
    Canon (UK) Ltd 115
Caparo:
    Caparo Group Ltd 116
Caradon:
    Caradon plc 116
Cargill:
    Cargill plc 117
Carlton:
    Carlton Communications plc 117
CEF:
    CEF Holdings Ltd 120

Index

Celtic:
　Celtic Group Holdings Ltd 120
　Celtic PLC 120
Centrica:
　Centrica plc 121
CGU:
　CGU plc 122
Charnos:
　Charnos plc 122
Charter:
　Charter plc 123
Charterhouse:
　Charterhouse plc 123
Chelsfield:
　Chelsfield plc 124
Chevron:
　Chevron UK Ltd 124
Christie's:
　Christie's International plc 125
Ciba:
　Ciba Specialty Chemicals PLC 126
Citroen:
　Citroen UK Ltd 126
Claremont:
　Claremont Garment Holdings plc 127
Clerical:
　Clerical Medical Investment
　　Group Ltd 127
Clinton:
　Clinton Cards Plc 127
Clydesdale:
　Clydesdale Bank PLC 128
Co-operative:
　Co-operative Bank plc 128
　Co-operative Insurance
　　Society Ltd 129
　Co-operative Retail Services Ltd 130
Coats:
　Coats Viyella plc 130
Cobham:
　Cobham plc 131
Coca-Cola:
　Coca-Cola Great Britain 131
Colgate-Palmolive:
　Colgate-Palmolive Ltd 132
Compaq:
　Compaq Computer Group Ltd 132
Compass:
　Compass Group plc 132
Congregational:
　Congregational & General
　　Insurance plc 133
Conoco:
　Conoco Ltd 133
Cookson:
　Cookson Group plc 134
Cooper:
　Cooper Gay (Holdings) Ltd 135
Cordiant:
　Cordiant Communications
　　Group plc 135
Cornhill:
　Cornhill Insurance plc 136
Courtaulds:
　Courtaulds Textiles plc 136
Coutts:
　Coutts & Co 137
Cummins:
　Cummins Engine Co Ltd 138
Cussons:
　Cussons International Ltd 138

Daejan:
　Daejan Holdings plc 139
Daily:
　Daily Mail and General Trust plc 139
Danka:
　Danka UK PLC 140
De:
　De La Rue plc 140
Debenhams:
　Debenhams plc 141
Deloitte:
　Deloitte & Touche 141
Delta:
　Delta plc 142
Deutsche:
　Deutsche Morgan Grenfell Group 142
Devro:
　Devro plc 143
Dewhirst:
　Dewhirst Group plc 143
Dhamecha:
　Dhamecha Foods Ltd 143
Diageo:
　Diageo plc 144
Diamond:
　Diamond Trading Company 145
Dixons:
　Dixons Group plc 145
Dow:
　Dow Chemical Company Ltd 146
Dresdner:
　Dresdner Kleinwort Benson 147
Eastern:
　Eastern Group plc 148
Ecclesiastical:
　Ecclesiastical Insurance Group plc 148
Economist:
　Economist Newspaper Ltd 149
EDS:
　EDS International Ltd 150
Eidos:
　Eidos plc 150
Electrocomponents:
　Electrocomponents plc 150
Elementis:
　Elementis plc 151
Elf:
　Elf Petroleum UK PLC 151
Ellis:
　Ellis & Everard plc 152
EMAP:
　EMAP plc 152
EMI:
　EMI Group plc 153
Empire:
　Empire Stores Group plc 154
English:
　English China Clays plc 154
Enterprise:
　Enterprise Oil plc 155
Essex:
　Essex & Suffolk Water plc 155
Esso:
　Esso UK plc 155
Eurotunnel:
　Eurotunnel plc 156
Evans:
　Evans of Leeds plc 156
Express:
　Express Dairies plc 157
　Express Newspapers plc 157

Exxon:
　Exxon Chemical Ltd 158
Favermead:
　Favermead Ltd 158
Fenwick:
　Fenwick Ltd 158
FI:
　FI Group plc 159
Fiat:
　Fiat Auto (UK) Ltd 159
Field:
　Field Group plc 159
Filtronic:
　Filtronic plc 160
Fine:
　Fine Art Developments plc 160
FirstGroup:
　FirstGroup plc 161
Fisher:
　The Albert Fisher Group plc 161
FKI:
　FKI plc 161
Fleming:
　Robert Fleming Holdings Ltd 162
Flextech:
　Flextech plc 162
Ford:
　Ford Motor Company Ltd 163
Foster:
　Foster Wheeler Ltd 164
Friends:
　Friends' Provident Life Office 164
Gallaher:
　Gallaher Group Plc 165
Gardner:
　Gardner Merchant Services
　　Group Ltd 165
General:
　General Electric Company plc 166
Gent:
　S R Gent plc 167
Gerrard:
　Gerrard Group plc 167
GGT:
　GGT Group plc 167
Gillette:
　Gillette Industries plc 168
GKN:
　GKN plc 168
GlaxoWellcome:
　GlaxoWellcome plc 169
Glencore:
　Glencore UK Ltd 170
Glynwed:
　Glynwed International plc 171
Go:
　Go Ahead Group PLC 171
Grampian:
　Grampian Holdings plc 172
Granada:
　Granada Group PLC 172
Grant:
　William Grant & Sons Distillers Ltd 173
Great:
　Great Portland Estates plc 173
Greenalls:
　Greenalls Group plc 174
Greggs:
　Greggs plc 174
Griggs:
　R Griggs Group Ltd 176

Index

GTECH:
  GTECH UK Corporation 177
Guardian:
  Guardian Media Group plc 177
  Guardian Royal Exchange plc 178
Halifax:
  Halifax plc 179
Hallmark:
  Hallmark Cards (Holdings) Ltd 180
Hambros:
  Hambros PLC 181
Hammerson:
  Hammerson plc 181
Hanover:
  Hanover Acceptances Ltd 182
Hanson:
  Hanson plc 182
Hays:
  Hays plc 183
Hazlewood:
  Hazlewood Foods plc 183
Heath:
  Heath Group plc 183
Heinz:
  H J Heinz Company Ltd 184
Henderson:
  Henderson plc 185
Hewlett-Packard:
  Hewlett-Packard Ltd 185
Highland:
  Highland Distillers plc 186
Hillsdown:
  Hillsdown Holdings plc 186
Honda:
  Honda Motor Europe Ltd 187
House:
  House of Fraser PLC 187
Household:
  Household International UK Ltd 187
HSBC:
  HSBC Holdings plc 188
Hunting:
  Hunting plc 188
Huntleigh:
  Huntleigh Technology plc 189
Hyder:
  Hyder plc 189
IBM:
  IBM United Kingdom Holdings Ltd 190
Iceland:
  Iceland Group plc 191
ICL:
  ICL plc 191
IMI:
  IMI plc 192
Imperial:
  Imperial Chemical Industries plc 193
  Imperial Tobacco Group PLC 194
Inchcape:
  Inchcape plc 194
Independent:
  Independent Insurance Group plc 195
Intel:
  Intel Corporation UK Ltd 195
Interpublic:
  Interpublic Ltd 195
Jaguar:
  Jaguar Cars Ltd 196
Jardine:
  Jardine Lloyd Thompson Group Services 196

Johnson:
  Johnson Matthey plc 197
  Johnson Wax Ltd 198
Jupiter:
  Jupiter Asset Management 198
Kalon:
  Kalon Group plc 198
Kellogg's:
  Kellogg's 199
Kimberly:
  Kimberly Clark Ltd 200
Kingfisher:
  Kingfisher plc 200
Kodak:
  Kodak Ltd 202
KPMG:
  KPMG 202
Kraft:
  Kraft Jacobs Suchard Ltd 203
Kwik-Fit:
  Kwik-Fit Holdings plc 203
Ladbroke:
  Ladbroke Group PLC 204
Laird:
  Laird Group plc 204
Lambert:
  Lambert Fenchurch Group plc 205
Land:
  Land Securities PLC 205
Laporte:
  Laporte plc 205
LASMO:
  LASMO plc 206
Lazard:
  Lazard Brothers & Co Ltd 207
Legal:
  Legal & General plc 207
Levi:
  Levi Strauss (UK) Ltd 208
Lewis:
  John Lewis Partnership plc 209
Lex:
  Lex Service PLC 210
Liberty:
  Liberty International Holdings PLC 211
Lilly:
  Eli Lilly Group Ltd 211
Limit:
  Limit plc 212
Linpac:
  Linpac Group Ltd 212
Littlewoods:
  Littlewoods Organisation PLC 212
Liverpool:
  Liverpool Victoria Friendly Society 213
Lloyd's:
  Lloyd's of London 213
Lloyds:
  Lloyds TSB Group plc 214
Lofthouse:
  Lofthouse of Fleetwood Ltd 216
London:
  London Electricity plc 216
  London Forfaiting Company PLC 217
  London Stock Exchange 217
Low:
  Low & Bonar PLC 218
Lowe:
  Lowe Group 219
LucasVarity:
  LucasVarity plc 219

M:
  M & G Group plc 220
Makro:
  Makro Self-Service Wholesalers Ltd 220
Man:
  E D & F Man Plc 220
Manchester:
  Manchester Airport plc 221
Manweb:
  Manweb plc 222
Marconi:
  Marconi Marine 223
Marks:
  Marks and Spencer plc 223
Marley:
  Marley plc 226
Marlowe:
  Marlowe Holdings Ltd 227
Mars:
  Mars UK Ltd 227
Marsh:
  J & H Marsh & McLennan Ltd 228
Matsushita:
  Matsushita Electric (UK) Ltd 229
Matthews:
  Bernard Matthews plc 229
Mayflower:
  Mayflower Corporation plc 230
McBride:
  McBride plc 230
McCain:
  McCain Foods (GB) Ltd 230
McDonald's:
  McDonald's UK 231
MCL:
  MCL Group Ltd 231
Medeva:
  Medeva plc 232
Medical:
  Medical Insurance Agency Ltd 232
Menzies:
  John Menzies plc 233
MEPC:
  MEPC plc 233
Merck:
  Merck Sharp & Dohme Ltd 234
Mercury:
  Mercury Asset Management Group Ltd 234
Mersey:
  Mersey Docks & Harbour Company 234
Meyer:
  Meyer International plc 235
MFI:
  MFI Furniture Group plc 236
Michelin:
  Michelin Tyre plc 236
Midlands:
  Midlands Electricity plc 237
Mirror:
  Mirror Group plc 237
Mobil:
  Mobil Holdings Ltd 238
Monsanto:
  Monsanto plc 238
Morgan:
  Morgan Crucible Company plc 239
  Morgan Stanley & Co International Ltd 239

Index

Morrison:
    Morrison Construction Group Ltd 240
    Wm Morrison Supermarkets plc 241
Napier:
    Napier Brown Holdings Ltd 241
National:
    National Express Group plc 241
    National Grid Group plc 242
    National Magazine Co Ltd 243
    National Power PLC 243
Nationwide:
    Nationwide Building Society 244
NatWest:
    NatWest Group 244
Nestlé:
    Nestlé UK Ltd 246
Neville:
    Neville Russell 247
Newarthill:
    Newarthill plc 247
Newcastle:
    Newcastle Building Society 248
News:
    News International plc 248
Next:
    Next plc 249
NFC:
    NFC plc 250
Norcros:
    Norcros plc 251
Nortel:
    Nortel plc 251
North:
    North West Water Ltd 252
Northern:
    Northern Electric plc 253
    Northern Foods plc 254
    Northern Rock plc 254
    Northern & Shell Group Ltd 257
Northumbrian:
    Northumbrian Water Group plc 257
Norwich:
    Norwich Union plc 258
Nycomed:
    Nycomed Amersham plc 258
Oakhill:
    Oakhill Group Ltd 259
Ocean:
    Ocean Group plc 259
Orange:
    Orange plc 260
Osborne:
    Osborne & Little plc 260
Oxford:
    Oxford Instruments PLC 260
P & O:
    P & O Steam Navigation Company 261
Pall:
    Pall Europe Ltd 261
Palmer:
    Palmer & Harvey McLane Ltd 261
Panasonic:
    Panasonic UK Ltd 262
Pannell:
    Pannell Kerr Forster 262
Pearl:
    Pearl Assurance plc 263
Pearson:
    Pearson plc 263
Pennon:
    Pennon Group plc 264

Pentland:
    Pentland Group plc 264
Perkins:
    Perkins Foods plc 265
Perpetual:
    Perpetual plc 265
Persimmon:
    Persimmon plc 265
Peugeot:
    Peugeot Motor Company PLC 266
Pfizer:
    Pfizer Group Ltd 267
Philips:
    Philips Electronics UK Ltd 267
PIC:
    PIC International Group PLC 267
Pilkington:
    Pilkington plc 268
Polypipe:
    Polypipe plc 269
Post:
    The Post Office 269
Powell:
    Powell Duffryn plc 270
PowerGen:
    PowerGen plc 271
PricewaterhouseCoopers:
    PricewaterhouseCoopers 271
Procter:
    Procter & Gamble UK 272
Provident:
    Provident Financial plc 272
Prudential:
    Prudential Corporation plc 273
Psion:
    Psion plc 274
Racal:
    Racal Electronics plc 274
Railtrack:
    Railtrack Group PLC 275
Raine's:
    Raine's Dairy Foods Ltd 275
Ramco:
    Ramco Energy plc 276
Rank:
    The Rank Group Plc 276
Raychem:
    Raychem UK Ltd 276
Reader:
    Reader's Digest Association Ltd 277
Reckitt:
    Reckitt & Colman plc 278
Redrow:
    Redrow Group plc 278
Reed:
    Reed Executive plc 279
Renishaw:
    Renishaw plc 279
Rentokil:
    Rentokil Initial plc 280
Reuters:
    Reuters Holdings PLC 280
Rexam:
    Rexam PLC 281
Richer:
    Richer Sounds plc 281
Rio:
    Rio Tinto plc 282
RJB:
    RJB Mining plc 283

RM:
    RM plc 284
RMC:
    RMC Group plc 284
Roche:
    Roche Products Ltd 285
Rockwell:
    Rockwell International Ltd 285
Rolls-Royce:
    Rolls-Royce plc 285
Rothmans:
    Rothmans International Tobacco (UK) Ltd 286
Rothschild:
    N M Rothschild & Sons Ltd 286
Royal:
    Royal Automobile Club Limited 287
    Royal Bank of Scotland Group plc 287
    Royal London Mutual Insurance Society Ltd 288
    Royal & Sun Alliance Insurance Group plc 288
Rugby:
    Rugby Group plc 289
Safeway:
    Safeway plc 290
Saga:
    Saga Leisure Ltd 291
Sainsbury:
    J Sainsbury plc 292
Saint:
    St James Place Capital plc 293
Salomon:
    Salomon Smith Barney Europe Ltd 293
Salvesen:
    Christian Salvesen PLC 293
Samsung:
    Samsung Electronics UK Ltd 294
Sanofi:
    Sanofi Winthrop Ltd 294
Sapalux:
    Sapalux Ltd 294
Save:
    Save & Prosper Group Ltd 295
Savills:
    Savills plc 295
Scapa:
    Scapa Group plc 296
Schroders:
    Schroders plc 296
Scotia:
    Scotia Holdings PLC 297
Scottish:
    Scottish Amicable Life plc 297
    Scottish Equitable plc 298
    Scottish Hydro-Electric plc 298
    Scottish Media Group plc 299
    Scottish & Newcastle plc 299
    Scottish Widows' Fund & Life Assurance Society 300
ScottishPower:
    ScottishPower plc 301
Seagram:
    Seagram Distillers PLC 302
Sears:
    Sears plc 302
Securicor:
    Securicor plc 303
Sedgwick:
    Sedgwick Group plc 303

Index

SEEBOARD:
SEEBOARD plc 305
Serco:
Serco Group plc 306
Seton:
Seton Scholl Healthcare plc 306
Severn:
Severn Trent Plc 306
Shell:
Shell UK Limited 307
Shepherd:
Shepherd Building Group Ltd 309
Siebe:
Siebe plc 309
Silentnight:
Silentnight Holdings Plc 309
Singer:
Singer & Friedlander Group plc 310
Slough:
Slough Estates plc 310
Smith:
David S Smith Holdings plc 312
Smith & Nephew plc 312
W H Smith Group plc 311
SmithKline:
SmithKline Beecham plc 313
Smiths:
Smiths Industries plc 314
Somerfield:
Somerfield Stores plc 315
Sony:
Sony United Kingdom Limited 315
South:
South Western Electricity plc 316
Southern:
Southern Electric plc 316
Spandex:
Spandex plc 317
Specialist:
Specialist Computer Holdings Ltd 318
Spirax:
Spirax Sarco Engineering plc 318
Stagecoach:
Stagecoach Holdings plc 318
Standard:
Standard Chartered plc 319
Stanley:
Stanley Leisure plc 320
Stobart:
Stobart Investments Ltd 320
Storehouse:
Storehouse plc 320
Swire:
J Swire & Sons Ltd 321
Tarmac:
Tarmac plc 321
Tate:
Tate & Lyle plc 322
Taylor:
Taylor Woodrow Plc 323
TBI:
TBI plc 323
Telegraph:
Telegraph Group Ltd 324
Tempus:
Tempus Group plc 324
Tesco:
Tesco plc 325
Tetra:
Tetra Pak Ltd 326

Texaco:
Texaco Ltd 326
Thames:
Thames Water plc 327
Thistle:
Thistle Hotels plc 327
Thomson:
Thomson Corporation 328
Thorn:
Thorn UK 328
Thorntons:
Thorntons PLC 329
3:
3i Group plc 329
3M UK Holdings plc 330
TI:
TI Group plc 331
Tibbett:
Tibbett & Britten Group plc 331
Tioxide:
Tioxide Group Ltd 331
TNT:
TNT UK Ltd 332
Tomkins:
Tomkins PLC 332
Toshiba:
Toshiba Information Systems (UK) Ltd 333
Total:
Total Oil Marine plc 333
Toyota:
Toyota Motor Manufacturing (UK) Ltd 334
Transport:
Transport Development Group PLC 334
Travis:
Travis Perkins plc 334
Trinity:
Trinity International Holdings plc 335
TT:
TT Group plc 335
Tullis:
Tullis Russell Group Ltd 335
UGC:
UGC Ltd Unipart Group of Companies 336
Unigate:
Unigate plc 336
Unilever:
Unilever 337
Unisys:
Unisys Ltd 338
United:
United Assurance Group plc 339
United Biscuits (UK) Ltd 339
United News & Media plc 340
United Utilities PLC 341
Van:
Van Leer (UK) Holdings Ltd 342
Vardy:
Reg Vardy plc 342
Vaux:
Vaux Group plc 343
Vauxhall:
Vauxhall Motors Ltd 343
Vendôme:
Vendôme Luxury Group Ltd 344
Vickers:
Vickers plc 345

Viridian:
Viridian Group PLC 345
Vodafone:
Vodafone Group plc 346
Vosper:
Vosper Thornycroft Holdings plc 346
Waddington:
Waddington plc 347
Wagon:
Wagon plc 347
Warburtons:
Warburtons Ltd 348
Warner:
Warner Lambert UK Ltd 348
Wassall:
Wassall plc 348
Waterford:
Waterford Wedgwood UK plc 349
Weetabix:
Weetabix Ltd 349
Weir:
Weir Group PLC 349
Wessex:
Wessex Water plc 350
Whitbread:
Whitbread PLC 350
Wickes:
Wickes plc 351
Wilkinson:
Wilkinson Hardware Stores Ltd 352
Williams:
Williams PLC 352
Willis:
Willis Corroon Group plc 353
Willmott:
Willmott Dixon Ltd 353
Wilson:
Wilson Bowden plc 354
Wogen:
Wogen Group Ltd 354
Wolff:
Rudolf Wolff & Co Ltd 354
Wolstenholme:
Wolstenholme Rink PLC 355
Wood:
John Wood Group plc 355
Woolwich:
Woolwich plc 356
WPP:
WPP Group plc 357
Wyevale:
Wyevale Garden Centres plc 358
Xerox:
Xerox (UK) Ltd 358
Yattendon:
Yattendon Investment Trust plc 359
Yorkshire:
Yorkshire Bank plc 359
Yorkshire Building Society 360
Yorkshire Electricity Group plc 361
Yorkshire – Tyne Tees Television 362
Yorkshire Water plc 362
Young:
Young & Rubicam Holdings UK plc 363
Yule:
Yule Catto & Co plc 363
ZENECA:
ZENECA Group PLC 364

VOLUNTARY ACTION CAMDEN

INSTRUMENT HOUSE
207/215 KINGS CROSS ROAD
LONDON WC1X 9DB

REG. CHARITY NO 802186